Readings in Christian Theology

Readings in Christian Theology

Volume 3

The New Life

Millard J. Erickson, Editor

BAKER BOOK HOUSE

Grand Rapids, Michigan 49506

Copyright 1979 by
Baker Book House Company

ISBN: 0-8010-3340-3

Fourth printing, April 1992

Printed in the United States of America

To my daughter
Shari

Preface

This volume of readings in systematic theology is a companion to two earlier anthologies, *The Living God* and *Man's Need and God's Gift*. Together, they cover the doctrines of the Christian faith. The reception accorded the other two works has confirmed my estimation of the value of introducing students to a variety of perspectives on theological issues.

I appreciate the fine working relationship with the editorial staff of Baker Book House, on this as on earlier projects. Mrs. Allie Jo Lano, Miss Sheila Ledin, and Miss Carla Dahl faithfully typed the manuscript; and my teaching assistants, Mrs. Ines Bowers, Mr. Philip Humbert, and Mr. Paul Widen, did important research work and proofreading. My students at Bethel Seminary during the spring quarters of 1977 and 1978 helped me evaluate selections for inclusion.

I wish to acknowledge the cooperation of the following publishers, who granted permission to reprint copyrighted materials: Westminster Press, *The Case for Orthodox Theology* and *The Case for a New Reformation Theology;* Concordia Publishing House, *Christian Dogmatics* and *Luther's Works;* T. and T. Clark, *The Christian Doctrine of Justification and Reconciliation;* Westminster Theological Seminary, "Toward a Biblical Doctrine of the Church"; Charles Scribner's Sons, *Jesus Christ and Mythology; Christianity Today*, "Perils of Independency," "Perils of Ecumenism," "Christian Hope and a Millennium," "Christian Hope and the Millennium," "The Revelation of Christ's Glory," and "Dispensational Premillennialism"; Macmillan Publishing Company, *The Modern Use of the Bible* and *The Problem of Pain;* The Society for Promoting Christian Knowledge, *Paul and Rabbinic Judaism;* Harper and Row, *How the Church Can Minister to the World Without Losing Itself* and *A Theology of the Living Church;* Zondervan Publishing House, *A Systematic Theology of the Christian Religion;* Wm. B. Eerdmans Publishing Company, *The Reformed Doctrine of Predestination; Introductory Lectures in Systematic Theology; Redemption, Accomplished and Applied; International Standard Bible Encyclopedia; Our Reasonable Faith; Them He Glorified; Faith and Perseverance; Systematic Theology;* and *Doctrines of the Christian Religion;* Dallas Theological Seminary, "The Meaning of Conversion"; Collins Publishers, *The Problem of Pain;* and American Baptist Board of Education and Publication, *The Christian Religion in Its Doctrinal Expression*.

The Authors

Herman Bavinck was professor of theology at the University of Amsterdam. He wrote *Our Reasonable Faith* in Dutch (1895–1901).

Louis Berkhof was president and professor of systematic theology at Calvin Theological Seminary. He authored *Systematic Theology* in 1938.

G. C. Berkouwer, a leading continental conservative theologian, is professor of systematic theology at the Free University of Amsterdam. *Faith and Perseverance* appeared in 1958.

Loraine Boettner, a spokesman for postmillennialism, was professor of Bible at Pikeville College, Kentucky. He published *The Reformed Doctrine of Predestination* in 1932 and "Christian Hope and a Millennium" in 1958.

Geoffrey W. Bromiley, formerly an Episcopal priest in England and Scotland, is professor of church history and history of theology at Fuller Seminary. "The Holy Spirit" was published in 1975.

Rudolf Bultmann has proven to be one of the most influential voices in the twentieth century in New Testament studies. He taught New Testament at Marburg for thirty years. *Jesus Christ and Mythology* was published in 1958.

James O. Buswell, dean of the graduate faculty of Covenant College and Seminary, St. Louis, Missouri, published his *Systematic Theology of the Christian Religion* in 1963.

Edward Carnell was a leader in the intellectual awakening of conservative evangelicalism in the wake of World War II. He served Fuller Seminary for nineteen years, five years as its president, and was teaching ethics and the philosophy of religion at his death in 1967. *The Case for Orthodox Theology* was published in 1959.

An Orthodox Presbyterian minister, **Edmund Clowney** is now serving as president of Westminster Theological Seminary. "Toward a Biblical Doctrine of the Church" was published in 1968.

W. D. Davies has taught New Testament at Princeton University, religion at Duke University Divinity School, and biblical theology at Union Theological Seminary. His *Paul and Rabbinic Judaism* was originally published in 1948.

L. Harold DeWolf, after many years at Boston University School of Theology, became professor of systematic theology and dean of Wesley Theological Seminary, Washington, D.C. He authored *A Theology of the Living Church* in 1953.

C. H. Dodd, the eloquent proponent of realized eschatology, held many professorships in New Testament, including the Norris-Hulse professorship in divinity at Cambridge, England. *The Apostolic Preaching and Its Developments* was initially published in 1937.

Y. Feenstra, a contemporary Reformed scholar, contributed "Baptism (Reformed View)" to the *Encyclopedia of Christianity* in 1964.

Harry Emerson Fosdick, the great liberal preacher at Riverside Church of New York, taught practical theology at Union Theological Seminary. *The Modern Use of the Bible* appeared in 1924.

Formerly professor of theology at the Divinity School of Vanderbilt University, **Langdon Gilkey** currently teaches theology at the University of Chicago. *How the Church Can Minister to the World Without Losing Itself* came forth in 1964.

W. J. Grier, an amillennialist, was pastor of Botanic Avenue Irish Evangelical Church in Belfast, Ireland. "Christian Hope and the Millennium" was published in 1958.

Carl Henry has taught at Northern Baptist Theological Seminary and Fuller Theological Seminary. He was editor of *Christianity Today* for twelve years and currently serves as editor-at-large. Henry is presently lecturer-at-large for World Vision. He wrote "The Perils of Independency" and "The Perils of Ecumenicity" as editorials.

Edward Hiscox was an American Baptist pastor who wrote many short, concise books on Baptist polity and practice in the latter part of the nineteenth century. He wrote *The New Directory for Baptist Churches* in 1894.

William Hordern is president of Lutheran Theological Seminary, Saskatoon, Canada. He formerly taught at Garrett Theological Seminary. His *Case for a New Reformation Theology* along with Edward Carnell's *Case for Orthodox Theology* formed two parts of a trilogy published by Westminster Press in 1959.

Formerly professor of systematic theology at Gordon Divinity School, Hamilton, New York, **Paul Jewett** now teaches at Fuller Theological Seminary. "Baptism (Baptist View)" was published in the *Encyclopedia of Christianity* in 1964.

George Eldon Ladd, former professor of New Testament at Gordon Divinity School, Boston, is professor of New Testament theology at Fuller Theological Seminary. "The Revelation of Christ's Glory" appeared in 1958.

C. S. Lewis, the novelist, poet, and apologist, taught medieval and Renaissance literature at Oxford and Cambridge. He wrote prolifically in many areas and is responsible for such works as *The Screwtape Letters, Mere Christianity,* and the *Chronicles of Narnia* series. *The Problem of Pain* appeared in 1944.

When **Martin Luther,** the great German theologian, nailed his Ninety-five Theses to the Wittenberg door, he began a religious revolution that still affects us deeply today. "Galatians" was written in the sixteenth century.

Leon Morris is vice-principal of Ridley College in Melbourne, Australia. "Nature and Government of the Church (Episcopalian View)" was published in 1968.

E. Y. Mullins was president and professor of theology at Southern Baptist Theological Seminary, Louisville, Kentucky, during the first quarter of this century. *The Christian Religion in Its Doctrinal Expression* came from his pen in 1917.

John Murray, professor of systematic theology at Westminster Theological Seminary, published *Redemption: Accomplished and Applied* in 1955.

John L. Nuelson was a Methodist bishop. He wrote widely on Methodism and biblical criticism and edited a number of major theological works. His article "Regeneration" was published in 1929.

George W. Peters, former president of Pacific Bible Institute in Fresno, California, is professor of world missions at Dallas Theological Seminary. He authored "The Meaning of Conversion" in 1961.

Franz Pieper, a Lutheran theologian, taught at Concordia Seminary, St. Louis, Missouri. His *Christian Dogmatics* was first published in 1917.

Joseph Pohle was a Catholic theologian who taught philosophy, theology, and apologetics at several European schools and the Catholic University in Washington. His article "Eucharist" was published in *The Catholic Encyclopedia* in 1909.

Bernard Ramm is professor of systematic theology at the American Baptist Seminary of the West, Covina, California. *Them He Glorified* was published in 1963.

Albrecht Ritschl, the liberal German Protestant theologian, was one of the early movers in the nineteenth-century search for the historical Jesus. *The Christian Doctrine of Justification and Reconciliation* was published in 1874.

William G. T. Shedd was a Calvinist theologian who taught at the University of Vermont and at Andover, Auburn, and Union seminaries in the latter part of the nineteenth century. His *Dogmatic Theology* was published in 1888.

William Stevens is professor of Bible and New Testament Greek at Mississippi College. *Doctrines of the Christian Religion* first appeared in 1967.

Thomas Summers was professor of systematic theology at Vanderbilt University. His *Systematic Theology* was published in 1888.

Henry Thiessen was the dean of the graduate school, Wheaton College, Wheaton, Illinois. His *Introductory Lectures in Systematic Theology* was published in 1949.

John F. Walvoord is president and professor of systematic theology at Dallas Theological Seminary. "Dispensational Premillennialism" appeared in 1958.

John Wesley formed the Methodist Church from the fruits of his evangelistic crusades in England. He wrote *A Plain Account of Christian Perfection* in 1777.

Contents

14

PART THREE: THE NEW LIFE IN FUTURE EXTENSION

PART ONE

The New Life in Individual Experience

Editor's Introduction

There is a sense in which, in the doctrine of God, each member of the Trinity plays a role unique to him. Thus, the Father is pictured as the creator of all, the originator and sustainer of life, and the giver of moral truth. The second person of the Trinity, Jesus Christ, God the Son, has accomplished salvation for humankind by living a life of complete and perfect obedience, dying upon the cross, taking upon himself the sins of men. This salvation, however, is of no value to humans unless it is actually applied to their lives. According to the Scripture, this application of salvation is the particular work of the Holy Spirit. He gives new life, progressively makes the believer more holy, and brings this process of salvation to completion.

Consequently, we begin our discussion of the doctrine of salvation with an examination of the person and the work of the Holy Spirit. In his selection, **Geoffrey W. Bromiley** discusses the status of the Holy Spirit as a personal member of the Trinity. Bromiley describes the relationship of the Holy Spirit to creation, Christ, the Scripture, the church, and the Christian, the last of these being most significant for our purposes here.

Salvation is a rich, involved, and complex occurrence in the life of a person. Consequently, many terms denoting and many aspects of salvation are to be found in Scripture. The traditional term for this complex of the doctrine of salvation is *ordo salutis* (the order of salvation). The use of this term is a bit misleading, for it suggests a sequential treatment of the action of the Holy Spirit. While some aspects of the doctrine of salvation logically precede others, some at least are virtually simultaneous in their occurrence. The treatment of salvation under several terms and concepts should, however, not be thought of as a dissection of the Spirit's working or separate discrete actions, but as an organizing and analyzing principle by which the whole meaning can be grasped and expressed. We find in the Scripture no full-fledged outline of the doctrine of salvation. One text, however, would seem to give at least the roots of the order of salvation. It is found in Romans 8:29, 30—"For those whom he foreknew he also predestined to be conformed to the image of his Son, in order that he might be the firstborn among many brethren. And those whom he predestined he also called; and those whom he called he also justified; and those whom he justified he also glorified" (RSV).

Even before discussing the actual fact of the salvation of the individual, we must first face the question of who becomes a Christian and why this comes to pass. This is the question of the doctrine of election, or more broadly, predestination. Traditionally there have been two basic viewpoints on this subject. One, dating back to the thought of Augustine and more fully developed by Calvin, is generally referred to as Calvinism, or the Reformed view. In this volume, the Calvinist position is presented by **Loraine Boettner:** before time began, before any creation took place, God, in planning to create, selected certain individuals to believe. This decision was with full realization that all would sin and be lost and be incapable of believing or accepting the offer of salvation. Not because of any particular merit of the individuals involved, but simply out of his own free choice God designated certain men to believe and thus to receive salvation. Others were permitted to remain in their fallen condition, and, without the special enablement of God, were unable to believe. The other position has taken its name from James Arminius. This position is represented here by the selection from **Henry Thiessen.** Basically its says that all people are given an opportunity to respond, all are capable of accepting the gospel. Usually this position states that general or prevenient grace is granted to all, sufficiently freeing them from the effects of original sin so that they are able to believe. Those who believe do so not because God has chosen them out from among others, but simply because they exercise their free will in the light of the offer of salvation. God indeed does designate some for salvation, but he does so on the basis of foreknowledge. That is to say, God in his omniscience knows in advance who will believe, and who will not. And those who he knows will believe are included in his plan as receiving salvation. None, however, is lost because God failed to give him the opportunity. He is lost only because he chooses not to accept salvation. Both sides in this dispute cite both specific and general Scripture references in support of their position.

We come, then, to the first of the aspects of salvation itself, conversion, treated in the article by **George W. Peters.** Conversion means, literally, a turning. Man in his natural condition is not oriented toward God in trust, love, commitment, and discipleship. Rather, man in his sin displays rebellion and rejection and indifference. Peters' article points out the large number of references in the Scripture that insist it is necessary to return to the Lord and turn away from sin, to change the whole direction of one's life. He emphasizes that conversion is not simply human reformation, because God initiates man's conversion, by calling him, warning him, inviting him. Rather, conversion is man's response to this calling of God. It is a conscious radical decision to turn from his sin toward God. As such it has two points of reference, the old life of sin and the new life of relatedness to God. It therefore may be thought of under two aspects or subcomponents: repentance, which is the turning away from sin, and faith, which is the turning towards God. These two aspects, which will be considered separately in Murray's article, are not two separate steps, but two sides of one occurrence. While there is a tendency in some recent extremes of theology to neglect or to minimize the necessity of conversion, Peters insists that it is biblically described as an essential for salvation.

John Murray, in the writing which we have here, examines in greater detail this doctrine of repentance. He poses the question: "Which is prior, faith or repentance?" and notes that there is no priority, that each presupposes the other. They are so entangled with one another that we cannot separate them. Repentance is a change of heart and mind and will with respect to sin. Throughout the preaching of Jesus, Peter, and Paul, repentance was emphasized. Real faith assumes that there will be a contrition for sin and an abhorrence of that sin. Not only at the beginning of the Christian life but throughout it, there will be this continued turning from sin.

But what of the other side of conversion, faith? Here we have two somewhat contrasting viewpoints presented. Faith, at times, particularly in medieval Catholicism and in post-Reformation Protestant orthodoxy, often was pictured as primarily intellectual belief or assent to the truth of certain doctrines. Against this particular position, **William Hordern** reacts rather vigorously in his discussion of faith. Hordern writes from the standpoint of what has often been called neo-orthodox theology. Faith, he insists, is not primarily intellectual assent to truths. Faith is primarily commitment to a person. In Hordern's treatment, faith is also a form of knowledge. Note that there is a relationship between Hordern's view of faith and his view of revelation. If revelation, as the orthodox maintain, primarily conveys propositional information, then faith, as the appropriate response to it, is believing those propositions to be true. If, on the other hand, revelation is primarily the self-presentation of a personal God, then faith, as the appropriate response, is a personal trust in him.

Edward Carnell, representing the post-World War II evangelical orthodoxy, sees the contrast between faith and trust as a false distinction. He speaks of two aspects of faith. General faith is believing something to be true. This is the kind of faith we have about persons, institutions, statements. Vital faith goes beyond this. It is believing in the person, committing oneself to the person. Both dimensions of faith must be present, says Carnell. Without general faith, vital faith might be blind or superstitious. Without vital faith, general faith would simply be a form of intellectual assent.

If faith is man's response to God's initial reaching out to him, or God's calling of him, then regeneration or the new birth is what God effects because man has believed. The article by **John L. Nuelsen** points out that both in the Old Testament, and in the teaching of Jesus and the apostles, there is the emphasis that man must be transformed or made a new creature or given a new birth. This is not merely a self-produced alteration. It is a divine work of God in the life of the person. "Without this," said Jesus, "it is impossible to please God, or to enter into his presence." While this supernatural work of God is not something within our conscious observation or our psychological awareness, it is nonetheless manifested in some results which are subsequently discernible. Hence, there will be a dramatic change of life of the person. Generally, regeneration is considered a result of a direct personal relationship of trust, and Nuelsen would so regard it. A somewhat different view is presented by **Franz Pieper.** He argues for the instrumental role of the sacraments in mediating the grace of regeneration. One commonly found version of this is the doctrine of baptismal regeneration. According to this teaching, the new birth takes place at the time of, and because of, baptism.

Salvation necessarily requires an alteration of the legal or forensic status of the person. Sin, as a violation of God's law, is punishable by the penalty of death. This condemnation must be removed. The person must be placed in a right standing in relationship to God. This right standing has been achieved by the death of Christ on the cross. To possess the righteousness of Christ is to be just. In the selection from **Martin Luther** we find an expression of the discovery which this tortured man made, after realizing his own unworthiness and attempting every possible means of pleasing God. He through the course of his studies of Scripture came to the realization that right standing is not something earned or achieved or attained. It is something received. It is God's declarative act, not of infusing righteousness into man, but of giving him right standing because of his identification with Christ. It is like the act of a judge. A judge does not make a person good or evil. The judge is not the cause of the individual's having committed or not having committed the crime in question. What the judge does is to discern and declare that this person is righteous or unrighteous in the sight of the law.

A different view of justification is propounded by **Albrecht Ritschl.**

Observing that the traditional view of justification is based upon the idea of God as Lawgiver and Judge, Ritschl relates justification rather to the idea of God as Father.

If regeneration is a supernatural act in which God changes the position and the direction or tendency of human life, then it is important to notice that at this time the Holy Spirit enters the life of the individual and continues the work begun in regeneration. This activity of the Spirit is called sanctification. Whereas justification is a matter of declaring a person righteous, sanctification is God's actually constituting that person righteous or good by progressively making him a better or holier person so his actions increasingly conform to his status. Where justification is complete in all of the justified, sanctification is progressive. It makes no sense to speak of one as partially justified. He is either justified entirely or not at all. Sanctification, however, is a matter of degree so that a person may logically be thought of as more fully sanctified as he progresses through life. This should be seen as the work of God in the life of the believer, not as the accomplishment of the efforts of the believer.

One of the points of difference among theologians on the doctrine of sanctification is the question of perfection. Is it possible for a Christian to reach a state of complete sanctification within his lifetime? That is to say, Can the Christian expect that sometime between his new birth and his death he will reach the point where he does not sin? One group, known as the perfectionists, have maintained that not only is it possible, but that it does occur. **John Wesley,** the founder of Methodism, was one of the primary advocates of this position. And it is from him that many perfectionist groups have taken their direction and inspiration. In "A Plain Account of Christian Perfection" Wesley outlines his position. This does not mean that the Christian ever reaches a state where he is not tempted, or where it would not be possible to sin, or where he does not need to depend upon the means of grace which God has provided. Quite to the contrary. It is essential that the dynamic relationship to God be constantly maintained. What Christian perfection does mean, however, is that by God's grace the Christian can reach the point where sin does not actually occur.

Taking the opposite position is **Herman Bavinck.** Bavinck represents the traditional Reformed, Calvinistic position. According to this view, there is the necessity of continued striving against sin throughout one's life. While complete sanctification is the goal towards which we press, we will not reach that goal in this lifetime. He suggests that when sin is seen not merely as external acts, but as thoughts, intentions, and motivations, it is very difficult indeed to conceive of arriving at perfection within this life.

One further aspect of salvation which tends to be somewhat neglected is the doctrine of glorification treated in the selection by **Bernard Ramm.** He points out that there are constant contrasts between the imperfection of this life and this world and the perfection which is to be. There will be a time, Scripture notes, when the believer will be made complete, when the imperfect will pass away, when the perfect will come. This will involve the full participation of the soul of the believer in eternal life and in the freedom of the sons of God. In particular, this means complete deliverance from the force and effect of Satan.

A final issue of the doctrine of salvation is the permanence of salvation. Virtually all theologians would agree that once a believer dies his condition is permanently fixed and salvation can never be lost. The question on which there is difference, however, is whether the genuine believer, having once obtained salvation, can ever lose it within this life, or whether he will always persist in his faith. This is known either as the perseverance of the saints (when thought of from the perspective of the believer's own endurance) or as eternal security (from the perspective of God's sustaining work). Arminians (represented here by **Thomas Summers**) generally hold that even genuine believers can and do lose their salvation in some cases. Calvinists such as **G. C. Berkouwer,** on the other hand, teach that no believer, truly regenerated, ever loses his salvation, but successfully endures to the end.

The Giver

1

Geoffrey W. Bromiley

The Holy Spirit

One of the greatest failures in Christian thought and practice has to do with the Holy Spirit. Far too often Christians have assumed that the Spirit and His operation are easier to understand than, say, the person and work of Christ. In almost every age, too little attention has been paid to pneumatology (the doctrine of the Holy Spirit), and this has resulted in a distortion of Christian doctrine and an impoverishment of Christian life and work.

Now, it is true that the economy of God's saving work of reconciliation and revelation does not lead to a concentration of interest on the Holy Spirit. In the objective fulfillment of the divine purpose, the leading role is played by the divine Son. Thus Jesus Christ is the primary content of the Gospel, object of faith, and theme of the Spirit's witness. In evangelism, theology, worship, devotion, and work, He rightly has the preeminence (Col. 1:18). The Spirit is self-effacing: "He shall take of mine, and shall show it unto you" (John 16:15).

Yet this does not mean that the Spirit can be taken for granted, or that He can be neglected with impunity. In fact, failure to see the proper relation between the Spirit and Christ is responsible for many of the worst

From *Fundamentals of the Faith*, ed. Carl Henry (Grand Rapids: Baker Book House, 1975), pp. 145–165. Used by permission.

shortcomings in this field. For one, the Spirit may be given a false prominence, as in the Montanist-enthusiast view that direct filling or inspiring by the Spirit is a higher stage of spiritual life, or in the rationalistic view (cf. Lessing's *Education of the Human Race*, §72ff.) that the age of the Son will yield to the supreme age of the Spirit. Again, separation of the Spirit and the incarnation can give rise to a false dichotomy between spirit and body, so that salvation becomes a purely "spiritual" matter and the wholeness of God's saving work is lost. This is the peculiar error of Gnosticism, with a parallel in the liberal denial of the resurrection of the body. Thirdly, the Spirit may be set in a wrong antithesis to the letter (cf. Harnack's distinction between husk and kernel, *What Is Christianity?*, New York, 1903, p. 160), with grave consequences for the proper understanding and interpretation of Holy Scripture. Finally, belief in Christ and a correct regard for Scripture can be lifeless and ineffective if divorced from the sovereign and dynamic activity of the Spirit. This results in the sorry phenomenon of ossified orthodoxy.

An ancient principle holds that God's outward acts are undivided acts of the whole Trinity *(opera trinitatis ad extra sunt indivisa)* (cf. Bucan, *Institutiones Theologicae*, III, 14—cited in H. Heppe, *Reformed Dogmatics* [first German ed. 1861], trans. by G. T. Thomson, London, 1950, p. 116). If this is true, then depreciation of the Spirit's role implies defective understanding, and distortion at one point leads to distortion at all points. In the doctrine of the Spirit, as in that of Father and Son, everything is at stake. This principle does not mean, of course, that there is not a special office of Father, Son, and Holy Spirit. The particular work of the Spirit, generally speaking, lies in the intimate area of subjective application. But this is a sensitive sphere, for, as modern existentialism shows, subjective application can easily be construed as subjectivization, which begins by swallowing up the objectivity of the Spirit and finally ends up, possibly in the name of the Spirit, with an anthropocentricity (self-centeredness) that is the mark of sinful man and the negation of all true knowledge of God (cf. Barth's trenchant criticism of Bultmann in his essay, *Rudolf Bultmann*).

The proper antidote to this, as to other errors on the right or the left, is to see the Holy Spirit in firm relation to God and His works according to the revelation of the Bible. Only in this light is it possible both to appreciate the reality of His person and to gain a true and balanced understanding of His ministry.

The Holy Spirit and the Trinity

When we speak of the Holy Spirit, we refer, not to a vague essence, a world soul, a nebulous power, or a divine emanation, but specifically and distinctly to the third person of the triune Godhead.

It is true that the word "spirit" has a more general connotation in both secular and biblical usage. Thus the Hebrew *ruah* can be used for "wind," and it also denotes the spirit of man. The Greek *pneuma* is also a term for "wind," though rarely used in this sense in the New Testament (cf. John

3:8). As the breath of life in man, it can easily assume the sense of the human spirit. Indeed, one reads also of evil spirits.

It is also true that in the Bible the simple "Spirit" can be used instead of "Spirit of the Lord" or "Holy Spirit." Thus in Galatians 5 Paul can speak of walking in the Spirit, of the conflict between the flesh and the Spirit, of leading by the Spirit, and of the fruit of the Spirit. Here the content and context leave no doubt that the reference is to the Holy Spirit. In other passages, however, there can be a certain ambivalence. For instance, in Romans 8 one cannot always be sure whether Paul is speaking of our spirit or of the Holy Spirit.

But this does not mean that the two are ultimately one and the same. The very fact of ambiguity implies a fundamental distinction. This distinction is brought out in the many passages, both Old Testament and New, in which the Spirit is "my Spirit," "the Spirit of the Lord," "the Spirit of Christ," or, more commonly in the New Testament, "the Holy Spirit." The latter term seems to be based on Isaiah 63:10f. and Psalm 51:11 (cf. *Theologisches Wörterbuch zum Neuen Testament* [*TWNT*], ed. by G. Kittel and G. Friedrich, I, 104ff.; in English, *Theological Dictionary of the New Testament* [*TDNT*], trans. by G. Bromiley, Eerdmans, I, 103ff.).

The phrase "Holy Spirit" is particularly well suited to bring out the deity of the Spirit, for already in the Old Testament the word "holy" is referred to the person of God. Indeed, it contains the "innermost description of God's nature" [*TWNT*, I, 101; *TDNT*, I, 100). God Himself is the Holy Father in John 17:11, and Jesus is the Holy One of God (cf. John 6:69; Mark 1:24). In view of the distinctiveness imparted by this predicate, spirit in the absolute "is, in context, fully adequate to express the matter, especially on Hebrew soil" (*TWNT*, I, 105; *TDNT*, I, 104).

The deity of the Spirit is also expressed by the manner of His coming at Pentecost. As Jesus puts it, "I will pray the Father, and he shall give you another Comforter" (John 14:16). The Father sends this Paraclete, the Holy Spirit, in the name of Jesus to teach the disciples all things (v. 26). The Paraclete is sent by Jesus from the Father, and proceeds from the Father (15:26). His dwelling with and in the disciples is parallel to the fact that the Father and Jesus make their abode in them (14:23). In this whole complex, the Father, Son, and Spirit are presented in a unique relation that leaves us in no doubt that to have dealings with the Spirit, no less than with the Father and the Son, is to have dealings with God.

What is implied in these statements is brought out explicitly in the trinitarian formulas of the New Testament. In Matthew 28:19, the disciples are to baptize in the name of the Father, the Son, and the Holy Spirit. In II Corinthians 13:14, Paul prays that "the grace of the Lord Jesus Christ, and the love of God, and the communion of the Holy Ghost" will be with his readers. A little more loosely, Paul in I Thessalonians 1:1ff. speaks of "hope in our Lord Jesus Christ, in the sight of God and our Father," and of the coming of the Gospel in the Holy Spirit (cf. Col. 1:1ff.). Similarly, Peter in I Peter 1:2 refers to election by "God the Father, through sanctification of the Spirit, unto obedience and sprinkling of the blood of Jesus

Christ." Jude, too, has a trinitarian formulation when (vv. 20ff.) he speaks of "praying in the Holy Ghost, keep[ing] yourselves in the love of God, looking for the mercy of our Lord Jesus Christ unto eternal life." In I John 3, verses 21–24 link confidence toward God, belief in His Son, and the witness of the Spirit. In view of the development of this thought in I John 4 and 5, the inauthentic saying in 5:7 is not at variance with, nor a fanciful advance upon, the immediate context.

Three points that emerge from this survey of the New Testament data are: (1) The Holy Spirit is everywhere regarded as God; (2) He is God in distinction from the Father and the Son; (3) His deity does not infringe upon the divine unity. In other words, the Holy Spirit is the third person of the triune Godhead. This finds expression in three articles of the creed: I believe in God the Father... and in Jesus Christ... and in the Holy Ghost. It is also illustrated in the early practice of threefold immersion at baptism in the name of the Father, Son, and Holy Ghost (*Didache*, 7, 1; *Apostolic Tradition*, 21, 22).

The early Church did not find it easy to maintain balance among the three theses. Rather surprisingly, in view of the widespread polytheism of the pagan world, perhaps the least danger was tritheism. There are, it is true, loose phrases in some of the earliest writers. We also read that Dionysius of Alexandria was thought by his namesake of Rome to preach three gods, "dividing the sacred Monad into three substances foreign to each other" (cf. J. Stevenson, *A New Eusebius*, pp. 268ff.). But even if this were true—and Dionysius strenuously denied it—it was only an implication ("a pelting from afar with those two poor ill-fitting phrases of mine"), not a deliberate doctrine.

Denial of theses (1) and (2) has always been a more serious problem, corresponding as it does to the even more pressing Christological denial. Thus the failure to recognize the true deity of the Spirit is found in the various forms of subordinationism from Gnosticism to the so-called Tropici and Macedonianism (*Ibid.*, p. 216; for a good summary see J. N. D. Kelly, *Early Christian Doctrines*, London, 1958, pp. 128ff., where Kelly rightly points out that the implication is a hierarchical polytheism). In the Gnostic schemes the Spirit seems to be an emanation, so that true deity is ruled out at once. In rather a different way, Origen reaches a similar conclusion in his speculations on the Trinity, for while he recognizes the unity of the three persons he does not accept their equal deity. "God the Father is superior to every being, the Son, being less than the Father, is superior to rational creatures alone, the Holy Spirit is still less" (*Ibid.*). Arianism had a similar implication that was worked out by Aetius and Eunomius and came to fruition in Eustathius of Sebaste, the true leader of the so-called Macedonians, who did "not choose to call the Spirit God, nor presume to call him a creature" (see Kelly, *op. cit.*, pp. 255ff., on this whole question). Obviously if Jesus is not of one substance with the Father, no more is the Holy Spirit. As Basil of Caesarea points out in his work *On the Holy Spirit*, an attempt was made to show that the distinctions are biblical, especially through the use of different prepositions. But this sophistry was effectively dispelled in the writings of Cyril of Jerusalem, Athanasius, and Basil himself, who all contended for the true and necessary deity of the Spirit. Denial of the deity, which finds a new form in the modern evaporation of the Spirit into an impersonal force of influence, is a rejection of the biblical teaching that entails misunderstanding of the Spirit's person and misconception of His work.

Nevertheless, the modalistic overemphasis on unity at the expense of true trinity is an equal danger. How confusing this teaching can be is evident in the supposed view of Callistus of Rome, that the Father and Son are one and the same and that all things are full of the divine Spirit, who, incarnate in the Son, is not different from the Father (Stevenson, *op. cit.,* p. 164). Here is a mixture of the express patripassianism of Noetus (and Praxeas) and the more general Sabellian thesis that there is only one person of God manifested in the different modes of Father, Son, and Spirit. The point here is a rejection of the essential distinction of persons, which is no less integral a part of the biblical testimony than the deity of Son and Spirit, and which thus corresponds alone to the being of God as He has revealed Himself to be. It is true that, according to John 4:24, God is Spirit. This does not mean, however, that God is simply the Holy Spirit, or the Holy Spirit God. What it does mean is that the whole being of the triune Godhead is Spirit as distinct from created matter. The whole Godhead, and each person, is Spirit in this sense. But modalistic equation, or obliteration of the persons, is not implied.

The interrelation of the Holy Spirit to the Trinity finds restatement along with the definition of the deity of Christ. Against all forms of subordination it is asserted that Son and Spirit are of one substance with the Father (Athanasius, Cyril of Jerusalem). Nevertheless, this is no vindication of modalism, for, as Basil pointed out, the divine unity cannot be subjected to mathematical ideas of unity. The fourth century learned to speak of three hypostases or persons within the deity, not in the tritheistic sense of three centers of consciousness, but also not in the weaker sense of three purely economic manifestations. From Nicaea and Constantinople on, the creeds sought to do justice to the essential biblical data along these lines, and a Reformation confession like the Anglican gives an excellent summary of the true teaching: "And in unity of this Godhead there be three persons of one substance, power, and eternity, the Father, the Son, and the Holy Ghost" (Art. I; for longer expositions see the Belgic, Arts. VIII–IX, and Second Helvetic, Art. III). The Holy Spirit, the third person in the triune Godhead, is Himself God.

What difference does this confession make? There are six main answers: (1) Any other account is a distortion of the normative biblical teaching. (2) On this confession alone we know God as He truly is, as He has shown Himself to be. (3) Only in terms of this definition is the Spirit's work known as a distinctive and yet also a divine work. (4) This understanding preserves us from transforming God's actions into cosmic or creaturely action, which involves the dissolution of theology in psychology and cosmology. (5) Appreciation of the inner wealth of the Godhead is safeguarded, in contrast to the sterility that results when God is seen only as a solitary monad. (6) The way is thus open for the true knowledge of the Spirit in His work.

The Holy Spirit and Creation

As noted already, all the outward operations of God are indivisible works of the whole Trinity. In Scripture, God the Father is presented primarily as the Creator of heaven and earth. This is why dogmatics usually present the Father as the fount of all things. It is also said, however, that by Jesus Christ, the Logos, all things were made (John 1:3), and there is a similar line of scriptural teaching that speaks of the Holy Spirit, the Lord and Giver of life, as the Creator. As the *Leiden Synopsis* puts it: "The Father of himself created the world through the Son and the Holy Spirit; the Son of the Father through the Holy Spirit; and the latter of the Father and the Son" (X, 9 [in Heppe, *op. cit.,* p. 191]).

The first passage relating the Spirit to creation is Genesis 1:2, where it is said that the Spirit of God moved over the waters. This enigmatic verse has been variously interpreted. In view of 1:1 (unless this is treated as a general heading), it can hardly refer to original but formless matter that was given shape by the Spirit. Nor is there much to commend the odd suggestion of Karl Barth in his exposition in *Church Dogmatics* (III, 1, pp. 102ff.) that the verse represents quasi-mythologically the dismissal of what God rejects to make way for creation by divine *fiat*. Perhaps the elements of truth behind these views are (1) that creation implies selection, and (2) that creation is also the impressing of order and purpose, not just the calling into being of formless matter. This leads us to the positive significance of the verse. The whole work, which has the wonderful universe as its end, stands under the sign not only of the will of the Father and the word of the Son but also of the moving of the Spirit. Creation is the work of the Spirit.

What is true of the cosmos in general is specifically true of man. For we read also in Genesis 2:7: "And the LORD God formed man of the dust of the ground, and breathed into his nostrils the breath of life." Now there is, of course, no express mention here of the Holy Spirit. But the reference to breathing and breath is a convincing indication of the Holy Spirit, in view of the fact that this is God's inbreathing. With this verse might be linked the well-known saying in Psalms 104:29, 30: "Thou takest away their breath, they die. . . . Thou sendest forth thy spirit, they are created." Also relevant is the fact that man's own "spirit" comes from God and finally returns to the God who gave it (Eccles. 12:7; Luke 23:46; cf. John 19:30). To be sure, Genesis 1:20 refers generally to moving creatures that have life, and there can be no doubt that the Spirit is active in all things as Creator. Nevertheless, the inbreathing of the breath of life would seem, along with the divine image and likeness of Genesis 1:26, 27, to constitute the distinctiveness of man within creation. This is why, to Ecclesiastes 3:19, 20, with its reference to physical death, there is rightly added the qualification of 3:21, the distinction between the spirit of man and the spirit of beasts. The Holy Spirit is at work in man in a distinctive way.

The first specific truth that emerges from the creative activity of the Holy Spirit is that of the sovereignty of God as the author of life. What Jesus said of the Spirit's work in regeneration, "the wind bloweth where it listeth . . .; so is every one that is born of the Spirit" (John 3:8), is no less true of ordinary generation. Creation could not and cannot emerge of itself. It had and has no ultimate control over the non-existent. It is certainly not self-existent. With every creature within it, it owes its being and its continuation in being, not only to the purpose of the Father and the authoritative *fiat* of the Son, but also to the transcendent breathing of the Spirit.

The participation of the Spirit in creation, however, is also an expression of the immanence of God in His works. As noted, animals as well as men are moving creatures that have life. They, too, have breath, "spirit." The physical life and breath are a pointer to the life and breath of God, without which they could not be. The intimacy is a reminder of the intimacy of the divine indwelling. Nevertheless, there is a clear safeguard against the identification of creature and Creator. Life can be withdrawn, and breath finally expelled. Creatures do not hold them in definitive possession. Similarly, God is in His works, but He is not identical with His works. Distinction remains between God Himself as life and breath, and the creature to which life and breath are imparted.

This is no less true of man. Inasmuch as God breathed into his nostrils the breath of life, one might say that God made him a participant in the Spirit. One cannot say, however, that man became an emanation or a part of the Spirit. Indeed, there is good reason to say, with Barth in *Church Dogmatics* (III, 2, pp. 344ff.; cf. "Spirit" in *Baker's Dictionary of Theology*), that while man *is* body and soul, he *has* spirit. The only difficulty is that this way of putting it perhaps runs the very risk it seeks to avoid, namely, suggesting that there is a bit of God that comes into man and then returns to Him. The Spirit who gives life and breath is the transcendent Spirit who is also immanent, the immanent Spirit who is also transcendent. God dwells in His works but is also distinct from them. Just because they could not be without God, they are not God, and yet they stand in the most intimate relation to Him.

The more specific relation of the Spirit to man, by virtue of which one may not incorrectly speak of man's spirit, is a reminder that all that is good and noble in man and his works, all that is in accordance with God's nature and purpose, is owed to the Holy Spirit. This is the truth that finds expression in the doctrine of what is sometimes called common grace. Notwithstanding man's fall and sin, creation and the new creation are not so distinct that the former is wholly the realm of the devil and the latter alone the sphere of the Spirit. To say this is not to engage in natural theology, for without the special work of the Word and Spirit, man is now excluded from the knowledge and salvation of God. It is to engage rather in a theology of creation. Even sinful man is still the creature of God. He is still the creature into whose nostrils God breathed the breath of life. Even sinful man can still do many things proper to his humanity. He can think high thoughts, write fine poems and music, make discoveries, establish law and order, cultivate the mind, stay the ravages of disease. To be sure, he will not do these things without the blight and curse of sin. But the fact that he can do them at all he owes to the Creator Spirit who has made him man.

At this point there are, of course, two special dangers. The first is Gnosticism, which identifies the Spirit's operation, not with the whole life of man, but solely with the intellectual or "spiritual" side. Now, it is true that man's special relation to God is linked with his being or having "spirit" in a way that other creatures are or have not. Nevertheless, to say this is not to disenfranchise other living creatures or even the inorganic world. By the Spirit, God is immanent in all His works, each after its kind. Man himself is both body and soul, and God's common grace is to man in his totality, not just to a special part of man that is exclusively or specifically from God. Indeed, the tendency of Reformed theology is to find the greatest distance from God, the most severe effect of the fall, "in spiritual and inward things" (*Leiden Synopsis,* XVII, 24 [Heppe, *op. cit.,* p. 365]).

The second danger is different, yet related. It is that of a natural theology, that, minimizing the fall, draws a straight line from the spiritual aspiration and achievement of natural man to the new life and knowledge in the Spirit that is the work of special grace. It is true that the breath of God is not immediately and definitely withdrawn from the sinner. It is true that the sinner, too, can think, speak, and do many things that bear the mark of the Spirit, that are even a distorted reflection of what may be known of God by His self-revelation in nature and conscience. But to know God in truth, to enjoy salvation, to be heir of eternity, to do that which abides, the sinner must receive new life and breath from above in a new creative work of the Spirit (cf. the dictum of Keckermann [*Systema,* 263; Heppe, p. 364]: "Man cannot either know or love God savingly without the special grace of the Holy Spirit"). God has not abandoned fallen creation in the sense that there is nothing within it that is of the Spirit. But God's definitive purpose for creation, the perfection of His transcendent immanence, is not achieved without the new creation, the new breathing of the Creator Spirit.

The Holy Spirit and Christ

The new man in whom the Holy Spirit puts forth His power afresh is the second man, the quickening spirit, the Lord from heaven (I Cor. 15:47f.). Unlike Adam, the first-begotten of the new creation is Himself Spirit (cf. II Cor. 3:17). He is in fact the second person of the Godhead, the Son of God, Himself God.

The fact that the new work of the Spirit is accomplished first in Jesus Christ, and that Jesus Christ is Himself God, is a reminder that prior to the relation of Son and Spirit on earth there is an eternal relation within the triune deity. Of this relation we hardly have the data to speak, and speculation avails little. The most that can be said is that it involves both richness of fellowship and intimacy of unity. Beyond that, the Church has been emboldened to say that, as the Son is eternally begotten of the Father, so there is an eternal possession of the Spirit from the Father (John 15:26). The western churches have added that this procession is also from the Son *(filioque)*. There are weighty considerations in favor of this. John tells us that the Spirit was sent by the Father in the name of the Son (14:26), and also that He was sent by the Son (16:7). The threefold order in the Trinity suggests that there should not be a direct jump to the Spirit that bypasses the Son. The triunity implies that in inward being as well as outward work, no person of the Trinity is without the other two. A necessary safeguard against such overemphases as Christomonism, Montanism, frozen or-thodoxy, or uncontrolled inwardness is also afforded by the grounding of the strong soteriological link between Son and Spirit in an ultimate trini-tarian relation. On the other hand, there is no need to be overdogmatic here, for, as the *Leiden Synopsis* puts it, "some said, not unsuitably, that the Father breathes the Holy Spirit through the Son, and the Holy Spirit pro-ceeds from the Father through the Son" (IX, 19 [Heppe, p. 131]). The main point is the link itself, not the precise mode of stating it.

The final trinitarian relation sheds a light, perhaps, on the Son's concep-tion by the Spirit at the incarnation. This does not mean that the Holy Spirit is the Father of the incarnate Word, for the Spirit is the efficient, not the material, cause of the conception. But why does not the earthly birth of Jesus correspond to His eternal begetting? If the holy thing born of Mary is the Son of God, why does not God the Father come upon her? One simple reason is, of course, that the Son does not become such (again) at the incarnation. But there is also, perhaps, a reminder that even within the triune relationship there is no dispensability of persons. As Father and Spirit are not without the Son, so Father and Son are not without the Spirit.

There are, of course, other considerations. It is by the Spirit that the Godhead operates in the world. More specifically, the role of the Spirit is that of life-giver. It is thus supremely congruent that in the work of new creation God should act by the Holy Spirit. Nor is that just the ordinary work of the Spirit, as in all generation. Conception by the Spirit marks a break in the normal process of procreation. If Christ's human nature origi-nates from the seed of Abraham and David, the man who is now born, though truly man, is the one who bears the image of the heavenly. His conception by the Spirit signifies that the new race will be filled with and directed by the Spirit. It is a sign that He is come from above, from God, in order that those who are from below might be raised up to God in Him. Although the Virgin Birth may not be a very prominent part of the apostolic preaching, in the light of the conception of the Spirit it is indispensable to Christ's person and saving work.

As Jesus Christ was conceived of the Spirit, so His whole life, work, and ministry was in the power of the Spirit. (For a fuller treatment see "The Spirit of Christ," *Essays in Christology for Karl Barth,* ed. T. H. L. Parker, pp. 135ff.) The Spirit alighted on Him at His baptism. He was led by the Spirit into the wilderness. He taught by the Spirit, and spoke the words of God, for God gave not the Spirit by measure to Him. He claimed the Spirit's authority for His ministry. He healed in the Spirit. Finally, He offered Himself through the eternal Spirit without spot to God. Rather oddly, it is not explicitly stated that He was raised by the Spirit, but in the resurrection He was declared to be the Son of God with power according to the Spirit of holiness. Prior to His crucifixion He promised that the Spirit would come to be the Paraclete, and after His resurrection He breathed on His disciples and said, "Receive ye the Holy Ghost" (John 20:22). He also told the disciples to wait for the baptism and power of the Spirit (Acts 1:8). Begun in the Spirit, His ministry was accomplished in the Spirit, and then in its new form continued in the Spirit.

If Christ Himself sends the Spirit, and the Spirit comes in connection with His work, this means that the interrelation between Word and Spirit does not end with the ascension. The incarnation of the Son took place to effect the objective work of revelation and reconciliation. But as the Spirit is active in and with this work, so Christ is active in and with the subjective work of the Spirit. Christ is, of course, at the right hand of the Father between the ascension and return. But He is also present now, and the Spirit is the intervening mode of this presence. Light is hereby shed on the vexed question of Christ's presence in word and sacrament. As the French Confession puts it in relation to the Lord's Supper (Art. XXXVI): "Although he be in heaven . . . by the secret and incomprehensible power of his Spirit he feeds and strengthens us with the substance of his body and of his blood."

The relation between Son and Spirit is also a reminder of the Spirit's role in revelation and reconciliation. The first aspect of this is that the incarnate life of Jesus is life in and by the Spirit. It is this in the old sense that all life is from the Spirit. The Son's solidarity with the race is thus assured by the conception of the Spirit no less than by the Virgin Birth, for in a general way all men are conceived of the Spirit. Nevertheless, the Son's life is in and by the Spirit in a new sense. Jesus is not just one man among others. He is the new man, the Lord from heaven, the first of a new race, which, in distinction from the fallen posterity of Adam, may enjoy the fullness of the Spirit. Conception by the Spirit does, of course, mean more than this. It implies the true and proper deity of Christ, which is no less essential to salvation than His humanity. In terms of humanity, however, it also signifies new humanity, though without severance from the old.

This humanity of Jesus is humanity for us. By identifying Himself with fallen man (Rom. 8:3), and also with the new spiritual body of resurrection, Jesus accomplishes in His person the death of the old man and the coming of the new. He does this in the incarnation, with its coming together of Son of God and seed of David. He does it supremely, however, in His death and resurrection, where the old man is brought to his end and the new man established as the true man. In Jesus, the Man who takes the place of other men, the work of the Spirit is also in a sense representative and substitutionary. Jesus effects in the Spirit for us that which, by virtue of this work, may be brought to fulfillment by the Spirit in us.

This work is not vicarious in the sense that it rules out the fulfillment by the Spirit in us. Already in Christ the old is indeed abolished and the new present. But we, who are of the old, are to have a place in the new. That we may do so is also the work of the Holy Spirit, whose present ministry is to cause us, too, to be born from above, to die to the old man, to be raised again in newness of life, not in addition to or in imitation of Jesus but in, with, and under His vicarious birth, death, and resurrection.

In sum, Christology is no less ineffectual than inconceivable without pneumatology, whether at the level of the "for us" or that of the "in us." Both are equally unthinkable, of course, without "Patrology," if we may so use the word. One cannot abstract Son from Spirit, or Spirit from Son, or both from Father. The work of revelation and reconciliation is the work of the triune Godhead therein reconciling and revealed.

The Holy Spirit and Scripture

The relation of the Holy Spirit to Jesus Christ carries with it a relation to Holy Scripture, the divinely inspired record and interpretation of God in His saving word and work. This is stated in part in the third article of the Nicene Creed: "Who spake by the prophets."

The saving word and work of God covered many centuries and the most varied events. Men and women from the patriarchs to the apostles lived, spoke, and acted in fulfillment of the divine purpose. For the word and work of God to be known, believed, and understood in objective reality, it was necessary that there should be an authentic and authoritative account and exposition, and that this, being itself part of the word and work, bear the same divine endorsement. Holy Scripture is this record; its inspiration implies the endorsement.

It must be emphasized that Holy Scripture is itself part of the word and work, the revelation and reconciliation. This is why the word "witness" can be misleading when applied too exclusively or narrowly to the Bible. To be sure, Scripture is witness. Yet it is so in an internal, not an external, sense. The record is part of the work, the interpretation part of the word. Thus the prophets, moved by the Spirit, play an active role in events by the word embodied in their writings. Paul's writing of the epistles in exposition of the saving work of Christ is itself part of the divine work and word. Scripture does not stand apart as an additional, external factor that has only an instrumental role. *Mutatis mutandis,* it is evoked, guided, and empowered by the Spirit no less than the word or person of an Elijah, Isaiah, or John the Baptist. Thus, while the Scriptures are, in Calvin's phrase, "public records," God Himself "commanded his servants . . . to commit his revealed Word to writing" (Belgic Confession, Art. III).

The Bible does not greatly emphasize its own inspiration, but what is said is plain and definite. The Spirit's activity is particularly displayed at three levels. First, there is the word or act later recorded; for example, the spoken statements of the prophets with their "Thus saith the LORD." Then there is the recording or interpreting of the word or act, or a direct utterance in written form. This, too, is attributed to the breathing of the Spirit (II Tim. 3:16). Finally, there is the moving of the Spirit in the hearer or reader to give certainty of the truth of Scripture, illumination in saving understanding, and the principle of true interpretation: "The Holy Spirit is the only interpreter of Scripture." In the broad sense in which it covers all operations of the Spirit, inspiration may justly be used at all these levels so long as there is no one-sided concentration, but theologically it has been customary to apply the word more narrowly to the second level in terms of II Timothy 3:16.

Scripture itself is silent about the nature of the Spirit's operation, so that what can be said is mostly negative. It is not possession or frenzy. The personalities of the authors are not overthrown. Inspiration is not divine dictation in the sense of a mechanical transmission of thoughts and words in which the writer's role is purely passive. On the other hand, this is not just the kind of inspiration that, on the basis of common grace, any author or scholar might enjoy. Analogically, the relation of Holy Spirit and human author is perhaps best understood in terms of Holy Spirit and incarnated Son, or of the divine and human natures in the one person of Christ. The Holy Spirit, from whom life comes, is the master of personal relations; we may confidently affirm that, as His work, the inspiring of Scripture is effected without either violence to the writers or prejudice to the finished work.

The fact that Holy Scripture is an inspired record implies the factual truth of the statements. God has spoken and acted, and His objective speech and action find authentication in Holy Scripture. But if this is true authentication, it must itself be authentic. If an absence of record would cast a haze over the finished words and deeds, so, too, would an untrustworthy record. A first implication of inspiration is genuine authentication (cf. Luke 1:1ff.). Without this (i.e., on the assumption that the factual biblical material is in part erroneous or even mythological), it is idle to speak of "inspiration" and "existential encounter" in the reader.

The fact that Holy Scripture is interpretation and speech implies the truth of the doctrine. There are many opinions about God and many interpretations of events, such as the birth and death of Jesus. If Scripture were not an inspired work, then it would be no more than an account of the interesting and perhaps admirable opinions and interpretations of great religious teachers. But the God who acts gives also His own speech and interpretation, and what He says about Himself and His work is authoritatively embodied in Holy Scripture. Inspiration implies not merely the authenticity of the facts but also the truth of the doctrine (cf. the twofold *authentia* of Turretinus, *Institutio*, II, 4, 2: the *authentia historiae* and *authentia normae*).

Because the Bible is inspired speech as well as recorded, we may correctly refer to biblical propositions. These are not, of course, abstract propositions in the sense of theoretical statements constituting, quasi-Euclidian demonstration. They have a point of reference in God. But they are still statements (propositions) about God, who He is, what He has done, the meaning and purpose of His work. As God is truth, so what is said under the Spirit about Him is also truth. The truth of the propositions is backed by the God who is both their object, for the truths are about Him, and their subject, for in the person of the Holy Spirit He is their author.

The inspiration of Holy Scripture is the ground of its infallibility and authority (cf. Westminster Confession, I, v). The former has two aspects: certainty in terms of truth and certainty in terms of efficacy. The Holy Spirit, both Spirit of truth and Spirit of power, invests Scripture with this twofold certainty. Authority is also twofold. It is normativeness for right belief about God and normativeness for the right response in human conduct. The Holy Spirit, Himself God, knows the deep things of God with a fullness and immediacy that alone can give a valid and definite norm both for knowledge of God and also for knowledge of His will for us. For this reason, on the basis of its inspiration, Scripture is rightly called the supreme rule of faith and practice.

Two final points must be made. First, the letter should not be divorced from the Spirit. This is the particular danger that threatens dogmatic orthodoxy or moral legalism. Rightly affirming an objective inspiration, literalism easily forgets (1) that Scripture's authority is truly that of the Spirit, (2) that the Spirit is the living Lord, (3) that Scripture is not normative truth and command by some quasi-magical quality imparted to it, and (4) that it cannot be equated directly with an ecclesiastical or academic system of belief or conduct. Scripture itself rightly has a warning against the disjunction that makes the letter a letter that kills. Evangelical theology makes the same point by pressing the inner testimony of the Spirit (cf. Belgic Confession, Art. V: "Especially because the Holy Ghost witnesseth in our hearts") and by making the final reservation that, for all the clarity of the letter, "without the Holy Spirit's aid a man cannot either rightly perceive Holy Scripture or be subject to it" (Riissen, *Compendium Theologiae,* I, 10 [Heppe, p. 41]; cf. Heidegger, *Corpus Theologiae,* XXI, 21 [Heppe, p. 517]).

On the other hand, we are also not to separate the Spirit from the letter. This is the error of much modern theology. In the name of the Spirit, Scripture has been revised or discarded as hampering and outmoded letter. The result has been a confusion of the Holy Spirit and the individual spirit, or the spirit of the age. Each man thinks and acts as the "spirit" moves. This spirit is, however, purely subjective. It is without objective reference. Now the Holy Spirit is indeed dynamic and sovereign, but He is not variable and capricious. He stands by the written Word He Himself has given. He may be recognized as the Holy Spirit, not merely by His freedom, but also by His committal to the letter. This does not mean that He is the letter's slave. It means that He takes the letter He has inspired and gives it life and power in illumination and application. The Holy Spirit is the Spirit of Holy Scripture.

The Holy Spirit and the Church

The ministry of the Holy Spirit is in and through the Church. This is true by reason of the work in the members. But it is true collectively as well as individually. When Jesus promised endowment with power, it was a promise to a group. When power came on the infant Church, it was as they were all together in one place. If power lighted on each in particular, the descent was upon the whole body.

The Epistles as well as the Gospels and Acts connect this interrelation of the Spirit and the Church with the promises and gifts of the ascended Lord (cf. John 14–16; Eph. 4:8ff.; Acts 2:33). Because Jesus Christ Himself is so closely bound to His people, so is the Spirit of Christ. Corporate life in the body of Christ, to which believers are called, is life in the common Spirit. The Spirit means Christ Himself present in life-giving power and sovereignty. With one Father and one Christ, it is natural that there is reference also to one Spirit (Eph. 4:4ff.).

Since Christ is the head of the body, one may justly say that this headship is discharged through the Spirit. In this connection the links between the Spirit and Christ and the Spirit and Scripture are of supreme importance. No error can be more disastrous than to try to ascribe to the Spirit a false autonomy, for this will give scope only to the individual spirit or the spirit of the group, whether in the form of *esprit de corps* or of clerical or intellectual domination. Neither pope, nor presbytery, nor individual conscience is the vicar of Christ. This office is fulfilled by the Spirit ruling in living power by the Word.

As members of the Church are one in Christ, the Spirit is the bond of this fellowship. Love is shed abroad in the hearts of God's people by the Spirit (Rom. 5:5). They love one another in the Spirit (Col. 1:8). The graces of Christian life are the fruit of the Spirit (Gal. 5:22). The many members have different gifts, but all are gifts of one and the same Spirit (I Cor. 12:4ff.). The fellowship for which Paul prays, along with the grace of Christ and the love of God, is the fellowship of the Spirit (II Cor. 13:14). The Church is a dwelling place for God, and God dwells there through the Spirit (Eph. 2:22).

The common life in the Church is a life in growth and edification. The great passages in Corinthians and Ephesians in which the Church is described as Christ's body make it clear that, while there is obviously individual edification, the great concern of the Epistles is with the edification of the community. The Church is to be edified, or to receive edification (I Cor. 14:4, 5). The body is to be integrated and to grow to the edifying of itself in love (Eph. 4:16). The gifts of the ascended Lord are given for the edifying of the body of Christ (Eph. 4:12). This work of edification, which consists both in extension and also in progress in Christian life, is accomplished (1) through men separated and called by the Spirit, and (2) through spiritual gifts.

Ministers are, of course, called and sent forth by Christ. But this calling is in and through the Holy Spirit. Even the disciples are not finally sent out until Jesus breathes on them and says: "Receive the Holy Spirit." They are to stay in Jerusalem until the outpouring of Pentecost. Paul, too, is commissioned by Christ (Acts 26:16), but his specific work is by the ordination (Acts 13:2, 4) and under the direction (Acts 16:6, 7) of the Holy Spirit.

Hence Bucan rightly concludes that inward calling "takes place through the Holy Spirit" (*Institutiones Theologicae,* XLII, 35 [Heppe, p. 674]). The gift of individual ministries is ultimately comprehended in the supreme gift of the ministry of the Spirit by which believers are added and the community is strengthened.

The endowments that are given for the edifying of the Church are directly linked with the Spirit both in Acts 2 and in I Corinthians 12–14, where there is an enumeration and discussion. Paul states plainly here that all gifts are from one and the same Spirit, and he describes the gifts as spiritual in this sense. The reference is not so much to native talents, though these may be dedicated to God and used by the Spirit to edification. What Paul has in view are special gifts of miracles, particularly healing, and utterance, particularly tongues, interpretation, and prophecy.

It is often asked whether these gifts were conferred only on the apostolic Church or whether they may be expected in any age. Three points may be made in this regard: (1) There are certainly expressed promises to the apostles that cannot necessarily be claimed by all Christians. (2) There is no way to bring the immediate gifts of the Spirit under ecclesiastical control—by ordination, for example. (3) Scripture does not explicitly restrict these gifts to the apostles or their day, and hence we have no ground on which to limit the sovereign disposing of the Spirit. A difficult problem of interpretation is involved here, namely, the use of New Testament precedents. It is a safe conclusion, however, that though we may not command or claim the *charismata,* or any specific *charisma,* the Spirit's donation may still be looked for as and when He Himself decides.

A second question is whether charismatic endowment is a second Christian blessing (often, and probably erroneously, associated with sanctification) without which one is not a complete Christian. Ought everyone to undergo an outpouring of the Spirit subsequent to initial repentance and faith? Several points may be noted: (1) There is a singularity to Pentecost as the first coming of the Spirit upon the Church. (2) Charismatic endowment may, as in the case of Cornelius and Paul, accompany conversion. (3) There may be repeated filling with the Spirit (Acts 4:31), which does not have to be equated with charismatic endowment. (4) The total witness of the New Testament hardly supports a twofold-blessing schema, such as that represented by sacramentalists in baptism-confirmation, monastics in baptismal-monastic consecration, and certain evangelicals in conversion-sanctification or conversion-charismatic endowment (especially, in some cases, tongues). No one will resist prayer for the Spirit, or dismiss the possibility of His sovereign filling or endowment. But to impose a fixed pattern of operation at this point is surely to carry zeal to the excess where it brings only confusion, disruption, and disappointment.

The most valuable endowment is not necessarily the most spectacular. From Corinthian times, speaking with tongues has had a strange fascination for some, but Paul in his discussion of the hierarchy of gifts does not rate it very highly. Love is the greatest *charisma* of all. Without it, other gifts are futile, and love without other gifts can still be all-conquering. This gives us the clue to the criterion for assessing gifts. This criterion is edification. By this standard the most important of other gifts is prophecy—here surely, in the main, and forthtelling of God's Word. The reason is that God's work is done in and by the Word. The whole man is claimed for God, but understanding is of supreme importance. Neither visual perception nor emotional impress nor mere activity is adequate alone. If God's people are to grow, whether inwardly or outwardly, the ministry of the Word must be central. But this has to be the Spirit-filled Word, delivered by Spirit-filled men. In other words, the gift of prophecy is demanded.

Mention of the Word reminds us that there is another criterion—namely, Holy Scripture. No message, admonition, or revelation is genuinely of the Spirit unless it conforms to the primary record. Examples of supposedly spiritual utterances that are exposed by this rule may be found in the *Didache* (11, 7ff.) and also in the sayings attributed to the Montanists (Epiphanius, *Haer,* 48f.). In the *Didache,* the rule of edification is also broken. But even where it might appear to us that a message or action will edify the congregation, no spiritual gift is exercised, nor will there be authentic edification, if what is said or done is not according to Scripture. In this way spiritual gifts are safeguarded against arbitrary subjectivism or ecclesiasticism.

As noted, the upbuilding of the Church implies expansion as well as inner development. Both ministers and *charismata* serve to summon new believers as well as to strengthen the old. This means, however, that the Holy Spirit is active in, with, and by the Church in its fulfillment of the Great Commission. Indeed, the calling of men to faith in Jesus Christ, and their refashioning in the obedience of faith, is the supreme office and work of the Holy Spirit. Calling is the act of the Holy Spirit.

Thus in the parting discourses in John, the promises of the Spirit relate to the work of the Church as well as its life. Again, Pentecost is set wholly in the framework of evangelism, and leads at once to the first sermon and the first conversions. The story is the same in the rest of Acts and the Epistles. The first missionary journey (cf. also Philip) is ordained by the Spirit. Genuine success in Christ's work is impossible without the Spirit, by whom alone the deep things of God may be known. As John puts it in the third chapter of his Gospel, entry into the Kingdom is by the new birth from above, by the Spirit. The only effectual calling to the Church is calling in the Spirit.

This means that the community must be a community of the Spirit. It is this as it gives itself to the work of the Spirit in the power of the Spirit, not searching for relevance or adaptation but relying on the Word and Spirit. Prayer in the Spirit is also demanded. As Paul says in Romans 8:26, only the Spirit can enable us to pray as we ought, and the Spirit is Himself the Spirit of intercession. Working, preaching, and praying in the Spirit, the Church can say with confidence: "We are his witnesses of these things; and so is also the Holy Ghost" (Acts 5:32).

There are three important implications: (1) To enjoy the Spirit's presence and power, the Church must give itself to the task commanded. (2) It must not doubt the Spirit's adequacy. (3) It must not try—intellectually, ecclesiastically, financially, or in any other way—to substitute itself and its resources for the Spirit. Zechariah 4:6*b*—"Not by might, nor by power, but by my Spirit, saith the Lord of hosts"—might well serve as the Church's motto. This verse expresses its apparent weakness but also its real confidence, after the pattern of its Lord who lived, died, and rose again in the Spirit.

The Holy Spirit and the Christian

What has been said thus far makes it apparent that the Holy Spirit stands related to the Christian in every aspect of life. The Holy Spirit is God; hence relation to God is relation to the Spirit. The Holy Spirit is Creator; hence natural life, the presupposition of salvation, is from the Spirit. The Holy Spirit is the Spirit of Christ; hence the work of salvation effected in Christ is the work of the Spirit. The Holy Spirit is the Spirit of Scripture; hence the word of truth and redemption derives from and is applied by the Spirit. The Holy Spirit is the Spirit of the Church; hence membership in the body of God's people, without which there is no Christian, implies an ineluctable relation to the Spirit. The Christian is the man for whom and in whom the work of the Spirit is accomplished.

The Spirit's work in the Christian is so vast and comprehensive that there can be no hope of covering every aspect. Perhaps it may best be summarized in terms of the new life-giving, the giving of eternal life in Jesus Christ. This yields three main divisions—the commencement, course, and consummation—in terms of the three aspects of the Spirit's operation: the evangelistic, ethical, and eschatological. To put it in another way, the Spirit is the Spirit of regeneration, renewal, and resurrection.

As natural life commences with a creative act, so too does the Christian life. This is the new birth of John 3. Beginning the Christian life can, of course, be described in other ways, such as conversion, new perception, response to the ministry of the Word, committal to discipleship. Taken alone, these might be understood as human possibilities for which there are parallels in other areas of life. But the Christian is convinced that beginning the Christian life has no parallels. It is unique and miraculous. This is implied in the fact that it is also and supremely the new birth, the new giving of life by the Spirit.

This truth has many ramifications in Scripture. There is a real sense in which the new birth is a fulfillment of the first birth. But it is a fulfillment in close relation to Jesus Christ in His Virgin Birth (see especially John 1:12,13). The meaning of baptism is also apparent here, for while sacramentalist error should be avoided, the linking of water and Spirit cannot be ignored. Again, the centrality of the Word calls for attention. Those born of the Spirit are begotten of the Word, which is the Word of life (James 1:18). This does not mean competition, for Spirit and Word are complementary. Regeneration takes place as the Word is faithfully presented in the power of the Spirit. In this sense, regeneration and effectual calling are, in practice, one and the same, at least in the initial aspect of calling: "The first effect of calling is regeneration" (Burmann, *Synopsis Theologiae,* VI, iii, 1 [Heppe, p. 518]).

The fact that Christian life begins with this sovereign act of the Spirit also has important implications: (1) It destroys comparative religion at the root. (2) It rules out the Pelagian heresy that believes self-salvation is possible. "This beginning does not depend on the natural strength of the will, but is the beginning of grace alone" (Keckermann, *Systema Sacrosanctae Theologiae,* 263, 264 [Heppe, p. 521]). It also rules out the degenerate Arminianism that grants man the power of autonomous response to the Gospel. Although man is born, he does not bear himself. Even ministers of the Word can discharge only the function of midwife in this new birth. And they cannot discharge even this function if they do not present the given message.

Regeneration thus carries with it a certain abasement, but it also gives a strong assurance. It cannot be explained away or relativized. The deepest experiences, divorced from the Spirit, can be broken down, codified, compared, possibly evaporated. Failure to see this is the great error of the apparently promising apologetic of Schleiermacher, with his offer of a pragmatic inward citadel to cultured despisers. Now Christianity is undoubtedly empirical. But it cannot find authenticity at this anthropological level. Only when the Christian sees that he is grounded in God's work by Word and Spirit can he be sure that he is a Christian, that Christianity is authentic, and that it is exclusive and unique. For only then does he truly believe in the Holy Spirit, who in anthropological religion is taken for granted or reduced to the level of an explicable force. Right at the outset, this regenerating operation of the Spirit is a *sine qua non* that dethrones arrogance and establishes assurance.

The Spirit is also the Spirit of renewal. This is the process whereby the life of the regenerate is made new in conformity with Jesus Christ. It is the lifelong renovation that is the growing up of the Christian, the outworking in thought, word, and practice of the life received from the Spirit. It is the sanctification that is the product and consequence and also the goal and end of justification. The New Testament makes is abundantly clear that in every aspect, this work, too, is the work of the Holy Spirit.

Romans 8 is perhaps the classic passage here. It draws an antithesis between walking after the flesh and walking after the Spirit. The note of joy and triumph that rings through this whole section derives from the fact that the Spirit is life and power. The Christian has not just been given a fresh start and then left to work it out with a little assistance. He is given a new life, and his task is to live this life in the strength of the Spirit and in orientation to Jesus Christ crucified and risen. Since this is genuine renewal, there has to be a negative side, the putting off of the works of the man who was put to death in Christ, the denial of self, the mortification of sinful members and affections. But the accent is not on the dying with Christ. If the death is indispensable, the end is life. The Lord who died is now risen in Him. Hence mortification is with a view to renewal. The old man is put off in order that the new man in Christ may live and grow—vibrant and positive, filled and impelled by the Spirit.

The antithesis between old and new means that there is conflict in the work of renewal. The carnal man, though crucified with Christ, is, in Luther's graphic phrase, unwilling to die. His death throes are dangerous and even violent. Galatians 5 expresses this as a mortal struggle between flesh and Spirit. Romans 8 should not mislead us here. Its assurance is justified, for the Spirit will not be defeated. But the conflict is real enough, and we are poor allies (or subjects) in the conflict. The fullness of victory is not yet. What we see is only the provisional fruit of the Spirit in His work of moral transformation. But this fruit is an installment, a down payment, a guarantee. We are sealed by the Spirit to the day of redemption. The Spirit's presence and work authenticate our regeneration, effect our progress in sanctification, and pledge the infallibility of final consummation.

Because God works in us by the Spirit, there are warnings in Scripture not to contend against the Spirit but to open the heart and life to Him. Ephesians 5:18 has the exhortation, "Be filled with the Spirit." Negatively, care must be taken not to grieve the Spirit (Eph. 4:30) and, even more seriously, not to quench the Spirit (I Thess. 5:19). Above all, one must not lie to the Spirit, pretending to obey His promptings but in fact circumventing them (Acts 5:1ff.). Since the reference, in the Epistles at least, is to true Christians, one can hardly assume that a complete crushing of the Spirit out of life is at issue. But failure to work with the Spirit in renewal is serious all the same. It involves controversy with God, stultification of Christian life and service, and a harmful repression of the good, which is surely even more dangerous than the commonly censured repression of the bad!

Since renewal is a refashioning on the basis of Christ's vicarious death and resurrection, it is naturally a transforming into the likeness of Christ. This carries with it a fulfillment of the purpose of creation (the image of God), and the way is opened for a fruitful theology of creation within that of reconciliation, though the fall and sin of man rule out a straight line from the one to the other. The orientation of Christ, however, provides us also with the foundation, theme, and goal of Christian ethics. Indeed, it points us to the eschatological fulfillment as well, for we "are changed into the same image from glory to glory" (II Cor. 3:18; cf. v. 17).

This leads us to the third point: the Spirit is the Spirit of resurrection. Rather surprisingly, this thought is not greatly developed in Holy Scripture. God (the Father) raised up Jesus, and Jesus Himself is the quickening Spirit through whom we are to bear the image of the heavenly. Nevertheless, there are indications that the Spirit has also His function in the final life-giving. Thus even in I Corinthians 15, Christ defined resurrection in terms of Spirit, and the new bodies are to be spiritual. Again, in Romans 8:11 God quickens our mortal bodies by His Spirit. The testimony of Ezekiel 37, in its broader connotation, is to the same effect.

Two important truths are implied in the fact that resurrection is the Spirit's work. The first is that the consummation of God's work, like its commencement, is a miracle of divine grace and power. The second is that at the end, as at the beginning, we have to do with the whole Trinity. Although the divine persons have distinctive functions and offices, the totality and unity of God's work comes out with particular clarity here. As God the Father creates us by the Word and through the Spirit, so God the Father raises us again by the Word and through the Spirit. As the *Leiden Synopsis* puts it, "The resurrection of the dead [which cannot be accomplished by the virtue of any natural cause, LI, 22] is the action of God, Father, Son and Holy Spirit" (LI, 16). The triune God is one God from whom all men come, to whom all go, and in whom all believers find fulfillment.

Conclusion

The work of God by the Holy Spirit is His subjective, personal and intimate work in man. We may conclude briefly with three important warnings and three equally important assurances.

On the negative side, it is vital (1) not to forget the objectivity of the Spirit because of the subjectivity of His work; (2) not to think it possible to lie to the Spirit successfully; (3) not to give the lie to the Spirit by finally resisting-or rejecting His testimony.

The third of these dangers is the most serious, for many theologians believe that this is the blaspheming of the Spirit for which there is no forgiveness: "This sin . . . is committed against the proper office of the Holy Spirit, which is to illumine our mind, engender faith, and sanctify us wholly to God" (Walaeus, *Loci Communes,* p. 285; cf. Heidegger, X, 73; Cocceius, *Aphorism,* VI, 11, 21 [Heppe, pp. 352ff.]). There can be no forgiveness for this, because definitive rejection of the Spirit's work is self-exclusion from the divine salvation.

Three other things need to be said, however, on the positive side: (1) If it is God who brings His work to fulfillment, there is no need to depend on self in its weakness and uncertainty. (2) We can also be sure that the work is done at the most inward and intimate level, with the guarantee of thoroughness and totality. (3) Finally, while the work of God is objective and comprehensive, it is also intensely personal: the Creator God is Abba, Father; and the Saviour of the world is the Son of God who loved me and gave Himself for me.

If it is the office of the Spirit to be subjective executor of the divine salvation, it is obviously not enough merely to talk or write or read about the Spirit. His testimony is to be heeded, and the mind and heart and will should be opened to His gracious illuminating, regenerating, and sanctifying work. Therefore it is fitting for our study to close with the ancient prayer:

Come, Holy Ghost, our souls inspire,
And lighten with celestial fire.

Veni, Creator Spiritus.

A Select Bibliography

The Holy Spirit

W. Barclay, *The Promise of the Spirit*. London, 1960.

K. Barth, *Church Dogmatics*. Edited and/or translated by G. W. Bromiley *et al*. Edinburgh, 1936–. I, 1; I, 2; IV, 3.

H. Berkhof, *The Doctrine of the Holy Spirit*. Richmond, 1964.

E. F. Harrison (ed.), *Baker's Dictionary of Theology*. Baker, 1960. "Spirit"; "Holy Spirit."

G. S. Hendry, *The Holy Spirit and Christian Theology*. London, 1957.

H. Heppe, *Reformed Dogmatics*. London, 1950.

J. N. D. Kelly, *Early Christian Doctrines*. London, 1958.

G. Kittel and G. Friedrich (eds.), *Theological Dictionary of the New Testament*. Translated by G. W. Bromiley. Grand Rapids, 1964—. I, "Hagios"; V, *"Pneuma."*

A. Kuyper, The Work of the Holy Spirit. Grand Rapids, 1946.

B. Ramm, *The Witness of the Spirit*. Grand Rapids, 1959.

G. Smeaton, *The Doctrine of the Holy Spirit*. Edinburgh, 1882.

H. B. Swete, *The Holy Spirit in the New Testament*. London, 1910.

———, *The Holy Spirit in the Ancient Church*. London, 1912.

The Plan

Loraine Boettner

Unconditional Election

Statement of the Doctrine

The doctrine of Election is to be looked upon as only a particular application of the general doctrine of Predestination or Foreordination as it relates to the salvation of sinners; and since the Scriptures are concerned mainly with the redemption of sinners, this part of the doctrine is naturally thrown up into a place of special prominence. It partakes of all the elements of the general doctrine; and since it is the act of an infinite moral Person, it is represented as being the eternal, absolute, immutable, effective determination by His will of the objects of His saving operations. And no aspect of this elective choice is more constantly emphasized than that of its absolute sovereignty.

The Reformed Faith has held to the existence of an eternal, divine decree which, antecedently to any difference or desert in men themselves, separates the human race into two portions and ordains one to everlasting life and the other to everlasting death. So far as this decree relates to men it designates the counsel of God concerning those who had a supremely favorable chance in Adam to earn salvation, but who lost that chance. As a

From *The Reformed Doctrine of Predestination* (Nutley, New Jersey: Presbyterian and Reformed Pub. Co., 1948), pp. 83–94. Used by permission.

result of the fall they are guilty and corrupted; their motives are wrong and they cannot work out their own salvation. They have forfeited all claim upon God's mercy, and might justly have been left to suffer the penalty of their disobedience as all of the fallen angels were left. But instead the elect members of this race are rescued from this state of guilt and sin and are brought into a state of blessedness and holiness. The non-elect are simply left in their previous state of ruin, and are condemned for their sins. They suffer no unmerited punishment, for God is dealing with them not merely as men but as sinners.

The Westminster Confession states the doctrine thus:

> By the decree of God, for the manifestation of His glory, some men and angels are predestinated to everlasting life, and others are foreordained to everlasting death.
>
> These angels and men, thus predestinated and foreordained, are particularly and unchangeably designed; and their number is so certain and definite that it cannot be either increased or diminished.
>
> Those of mankind that are predestinated unto life, God, before the foundation of the world was laid, according to His eternal and immutable purpose, and the secret counsel and good pleasure of His will, hath chosen in Christ, unto everlasting glory, out of His mere grace and love, without any foresight of faith or good works, or perseverance in either of them, or any other thing in the creature, as conditions, or causes moving Him thereunto; and all to the praise of His glorious grace.
>
> As God hath appointed the elect unto glory, so hath He, by the eternal and most free purpose of His will, foreordained all the means thereunto. Whereby they who are elected, being fallen in Adam, are redeemed by Christ, are effectually called unto faith in Christ by His Spirit working in due season; are justified, adopted, sanctified, and kept by His power through faith unto salvation. Neither are any other redeemed by Christ, effectually called, justified, adopted, sanctified, and saved, but the elect only.
>
> The rest of mankind, God was pleased, according to the unsearchable counsel of His will, whereby He extendeth or withholdeth mercy as He pleaseth, for the glory of His sovereign power over His creatures, to pass by, and to ordain them to dishonor and wrath for their sin, to the praise of His glorious justice.[1]

It is important that we shall have a clear understanding of this doctrine of divine Election, for our views in regard to it determine our views of God, man, the world, and redemption. As Calvin rightly says, "We shall never be clearly convinced as we ought to be that our salvation flows from the fountain of God's free mercy, till we are acquainted with this eternal election, which illustrates the grace of God by this comparison, that He adopts not all promiscuously to the hope of salvation but gives to some what he refuses to others. Ignorance of this principle evidently detracts from the divine glory, and diminishes real humility."[2] Calvin admits that this doctrine arouses very perplexing questions in the minds of some, for, says he, "they consider nothing more unreasonable than that of the common mass of mankind, some should be predestinated to salvation; and others to destruction."

The Reformed theologians consistently applied this principle to the actual experience of spiritual phenomena which they themselves felt and saw in others about them. The divine purpose, or Predestination, alone could explain the distinction between good and evil, between the saint and the sinner.

Proof from Scripture

The first question which we need to ask ourselves then, is, Do we find this doctrine taught in the Scriptures? Let us turn to Paul's letter to the Ephesians. There we read: "He chose us in Him before the foundation of the world, that we should be holy and without blemish before Him in love; having foreordained us unto adoption as sons through Jesus Christ unto Himself, according to the good pleasure of His will" (1:4, 5). In Romans 8:29, 30 we read of that golden chain of redemption which stretches from the eternity that is past to the eternity that is to come, "For whom He foreknew, He also foreordained to be conformed to the image of His Son, that He might be the first-born among many brethren; and whom He foreordained, them He also called: and whom He called, them He also justified: and whom He justified, them He also glorified." Foreknown, foreordained, called, justified, glorified, with always the same people included in each group; and where one of these factors is present, all the others are in principle present with it. Paul has cast the verse in the past tense because with God the purpose is in principle executed when formed, so certain is it of fulfillment. "These five golden links," says Dr. Warfield, "are welded together in one unbreakable chain, so that all who are set upon in God's gracious distinguishing view are carried on by His grace, step by step, up to the great consummation of that glorification which realizes the promised conformity to the image of God's own Son. It is 'election,' you see, that does all this; for 'whom He foreknew, . . . them He also glorified.' "[3]

The Scriptures represent election as occurring in past time, irrespective of personal merit, and altogether sovereign, "The children being not yet born, neither having done anything good or bad, that the purpose of God according to election might stand, not of works, but of Him that calleth, it was said to her, The elder shall serve the younger. Even as it is written, Jacob I loved, but Esau I hated" (Rom. 9:11–13). Now if the doctrine of Election is not true, we may safely challenge any man to tell us what the apostle means by such language.

> We are pointed illustratively to the sovereign acceptance of Isaac and rejection of Ishmael, and to the choice of Jacob and not of Esau before their birth and therefore before either had done good or bad; we are explicitly told that in the matter of salvation it is not of him that wills, or of him that runs, but of God that shows mercy, and that He has mercy on

whom He will, and whom He will He hardens; we are pointedly directed
to behold in God the potter who makes the vessels which proceed from
His hand each for an end of His appointment, that He may work out His
will upon them. It is safe to say that language cannot be chosen better
adapted to teach Predestination at its height.[4]

Even if we were without any inspired utterances other than those quoted
from Paul, so clear and unambiguous are those that we should be constrained to admit that the doctrine of Election finds a place in Scripture. By
looking at the Scripture references in the Confession of Faith, we find that
it is abundantly sustained in the Bible. If we admit the inspiration of the
Bible; if we admit that the writings of the prophets and apostles were
breathed by the Spirit of God, and are thus infallible, then what we find
there will be sufficient; and thus on the irrefutable testimony of the Scriptures we must acknowledge Election, or Predestination, to be an established truth, and one which we must receive if we are to possess the whole
counsel of God. Every Christian must believe in some kind of election; for
while the Scriptures leave unexplained many things about the doctrine of
Election, they make very plain the FACT that there has been an election.

Christ explicitly declared to His disciples, "Ye did not choose me, but I
chose you, and appointed you, that ye should go and bear fruit" (John
15:16), by which He made God's choice primary and man's choice only
secondary and a result of the former. The Arminian, however, in making
salvation depend upon man's choice to use or abuse proffered grace reverses this order and makes man's choice the primary and decisive one.
There is no place in the Scriptures for an election which is carefully
adjusted to the foreseen actions of the creature. The divine will is never
made dependent on the creaturely will for its determinations.

Again the sovereignty of this choice is clearly taught when Paul declares
that God commended His love toward us in that while we were yet sinners
Christ died for us (Rom. 5:8), and that Christ died for the ungodly (Rom.
5:6). Here we see that His love was not extended toward us because we
were good, but in spite of the fact that we were bad. It is God who chooses
the person and causes him to approach unto Him (Ps. 65:4). Arminianism
takes this choice out of the hands of God and places it in the hands of man.
Any system which substitutes a man-made election falls below the Scripture teaching on this subject.

In the darkest days of Israel's apostasy, as in every other age, it was this
principle of election which made a difference between mankind and kept a
remnant secure. "Yet will I leave me seven thousand in Israel, all the
knees which have not bowed unto Baal, and every mouth which hath not
kissed him" (I Kings 19:18). These seven thousand did not stand by their
own strength; it is expressly said that God reserved them to Himself, that
they might be a remnant.

It is for the sake of the elect that God governs the course of all history
(Mark 13:20). They are "the salt of the earth," and "the light of the

world''; and so far at least in the world's history they are the few through whom the many are blessed—God blessed the household of Potiphar for Joseph's sake, and ten righteous people would have saved the city of Sodom. Their election, of course, includes the opportunity of hearing the Gospel and receiving the gifts of grace, for without these means the great end of election would not be attained. The elect are, in fact, elected to all that is included in the idea of eternal life.

Apart from this election of individuals to life, there has been what we may call a national election, or a divine predestination of nations and communities to a knowledge of true religion and to the external privileges of the Gospel. God undoubtedly does choose some nations to receive much greater spiritual and temporal blessings than others. This form of election has been well illustrated in the Jewish nation, in certain European nations and communities, and in America. The contrast is very striking when we compare these with other nations such as China, Japan, and India.

Throughout the Old Testament it is repeatedly stated that the Jews were a chosen people. ''You only have I known of all the families of the earth'' (Amos 3:2). ''He hath not dealt so with any [other] nation; And as for His ordinances, they have not known them'' (Ps. 147:20). ''For thou art a holy people unto Jehovah thy God: Jehovah thy God hath chosen thee to be a people for His own possession, above all the peoples that are upon the face of the earth'' (Deut. 7:6). It is made equally plain that God found no merit or dignity in the Jews themselves which moved Him to choose them above others. ''Jehovah did not set His love upon you, nor choose you, because ye were more in number than any other people; for ye were the fewest of all peoples: but because Jehovah loveth you, and because He would keep the oath which He swore unto your fathers, hath Jehovah brought you out with a mighty hand, and redeemed you out of the house of bondage from the hand of Pharaoh king of Egypt'' (Deut. 7:7, 8). And again, ''Only Jehovah had a delight in thy fathers to love them, and He chose their seed after them, even above all peoples'' (Deut. 10:15). Here it is carefully explained that Israel was honored with the divine choice in contrast with the treatment accorded all the other peoples of the earth, that the choice rested solely on the unmerited love of God, and that it had no foundation in Israel itself.

When Paul was forbidden by the Holy Spirit to preach the Gospel in the province of Asia, and was given the vision of a man in Europe calling across the waters, ''Come over into Macedonia, and help us,'' one section of the world was sovereignly excluded from, and another section was sovereignly given, the privileges of the Gospel. Had the divinely directed call been rather from the shores of India, Europe and America might today have been less civilized than the natives of Tibet. It was the sovereign choice of God which brought the Gospel to the people of Europe and later to America, while the people of the east, and north, and south were left in darkness. We can assign no reason, for instance, why it should have been Abraham's seed, and not the Egyptians or the Assyrians, who were chosen; or why Great Britain and America, which at the time of Christ's appearance on earth were in a state of such complete ignorance, should today possess so largely for themselves, and be disseminating so widely to others, these most important spiritual privileges. The diversities in regard to religious privileges in the different nations are to be ascribed to nothing else than the good pleasure of God.

A third form of election taught in Scripture is that of individuals to the external means of grace, such as hearing and reading the Gospel, association with the people of God, and sharing the benefits of the civilization which has arisen where the Gospel has gone. No one ever had the chance to say at what particular time in the world's history, or in what country, he would be born, whether or not he would be a member of the white race, or of some other. One child is born with health, wealth, and honor, in a favored land, in a Christian home, and grows up with all the blessings which attend the full light of the Gospel. Another is born in poverty and dishonor, of sinful and dissipated parents, and destitute of Christian influences. All of these things are sovereignly decided for them. Surely no one would insist that the favored child has any personal merit which could be the ground for this difference. Furthermore, was it not of God's own choosing that He created us human beings, in His own image, when He might have created us cattle or horses or dogs? Or who would allow the dumb brutes to revile God for their condition in life as though the distinction was unjust? All of these things are due to God's overruling providence, and not to human choice.

> Arminians have labored to reconcile all this, as a matter of fact, with their defective and erroneous views of the Divine sovereignty, and with their unscriptural doctrines of universal grace and universal redemption; but they have not usually been satisfied themselves with their own attempts at explanation, and have commonly at last admitted, that there were mysteries in this matter which could not be explained, and which must just be resolved into the sovereignty of God and the unsearchableness of His counsels.[5]

We may perhaps mention a fourth kind of election, that of individuals to certain vocations—the gifts of special talents which fit one to be a statesman, another to be a doctor, or lawyer, or farmer, or musician, or artisan, gifts of personal beauty, intelligence, disposition, etc. These four kinds of election are in principle the same. Arminians escape no real difficulty in admitting the second, third, and fourth, while denying the first. In each instance God gives to some what He withholds from others. Conditions in the world at large and our own experiences in everyday life show us that the blessings bestowed are sovereign and unconditional, irrespective of any previous merit or action on the part of those so chosen. If we are highly favored, we can only be thankful for His blessings; if not highly favored, we have no grounds for complaint. Why precisely this or that one is placed in circumstances which lead to saving faith, while others are not so placed, is indeed a mystery. We cannot explain the workings of Providence; but we do know that the Judge of all the earth shall do right, and that when we attain to perfect knowledge we shall see that He has sufficient reasons for all His acts.

Furthermore, it may be said that in general the outward conditions with which the individual is surrounded do determine his destiny—at least to this extent, that those from whom the Gospel is withheld have no chance for salvation. Cunningham has stated this very well in the following paragraph:

> There is an invariable connection established in God's government of the world, between the enjoyment of outward privileges, or the means of grace, on the one hand, and faith and salvation on the other; in this sense, and to this extent, that the negation of the first implies the negation of the second. We are warranted by the whole tenor of Scripture, in maintaining that where God, in His sovereignty, withholds from men the enjoyment of the means of grace—an opportunity of becoming acquainted with the only way of salvation—He at the same time, and by the same means, or ordination, withholds from them the opportunity and power of believing and being saved.[6]

Calvinists maintain that God deals not only with mankind in the mass but with the individuals who are actually saved, that He has elected particular persons to eternal life and to all the means necessary for attaining that life. They admit that some of the passages in which election is mentioned teach only an election of nations, or an election to outward privileges; but they maintain that many other passages teach exclusively and only an election of individuals to eternal life.

There are some, of course, who deny that there has been any such thing as an election at all. They start at the very word as though it were a spectre just come from the shades and never seen before. And yet, in the New Testament alone, the words *eklektos, ekloge,* and *eklego* (elect, election, choose), are found some forty-seven or forty-eight times (see Young's *Analytical Concordance* for complete lists). Others accept the word *election,* but attempt to explain it away. They profess to believe in a "conditional election," based, as they suppose, upon foreseen faith and evangelical obedience in its objects. This, of course, destroys election in any intelligible sense of the term, and reduces it to a mere recognition or prophecy that at some future time certain persons will be possessed of those qualities. If election is based on faith and evangelical obedience, then, as it has been cynically phrased, God is careful to elect only those whom He foresees will elect themselves. In the Arminian system election is reduced to a mere word or name, the use of which only tends to involve the subject in greater obscurity and confusion. A mere recognition that those qualities will be present at some future time is, of course, an election falsely so-called, or simply no election at all. And some Arminians, consistently carrying out their own doctrine that the person may or may not accept, and that if he does accept he may fall away again, identify the time of this decree of election with the death of the believer, as if only then his salvation becomes certain.

Election extends not only to men but also and equally to the angels since they also are a part of God's creation and are under His government. Some of these are holy and happy, others are sinful and miserable. The same reasons which lead us to believe in a predestination of men also lead us to believe in a predestination of angels. The Scriptures confirm this view by references to "elect angels" (I Tim. 5:21) and "holy angels" (Mark 8:38), which are contrasted with wicked angels or demons. We read that God "spared not angels when they sinned, but cast them down to hell, and committed them to pits of darkness to be reserved unto judgment" (II Peter 2:4); of the "eternal fire which is prepared for the devil and his angels" (Matt. 25:41); that "angels that kept not their own principality, but left their former habitation, He hath kept in everlasting bonds under darkness unto the Judgment of the great day" (Jude 6); and of "Michael and his angels going forth to war with the dragon; and the dragon warred and his angels" (Rev. 12:7). A study of these passages shows us that, as Dabney says:

> There are two kinds of spirits of that order; holy and sinful angels, servants of Christ and servants of Satan; that they were created in an estate of holiness and happiness, and abode in the region called Heaven (God's holiness and goodness are sufficient proof that He would never have created them otherwise); that the evil angels voluntarily forfeited their estate by sinning, and were excluded forever from heaven and holiness; that those who maintained their estate were elected thereto by God, and that their estate of holiness and blessedness is now forever assured.[7]

Paul makes no attempt to explain how God can be just in showing mercy to whom He will and in passing by whom He will. In answer to the objector's question, "Why doth He still find fault?" (with those to whom He has not extended saving mercy), he (Paul) simply resolves the whole thing into the sovereignty of God, by replying, "Nay but, O man, who art thou that repliest against God? Shall the thing formed say to him that formed it, Why hast thou made me thus? Or hath not the potter a right over the clay, from the same lump to make one part a vessel unto honor, and another unto dishonor?" (Rom. 9:19-21). (And let it be noticed here that Paul says that it is not from different kinds of clay, but "from the same lump," that God, as the potter, makes one vessel unto honor and another unto dishonor.) Paul does not drag God from His throne and set Him before our human reason to be questioned and examined. These secret counsels of His, which even the angels adore with trembling and desire to look into, are left unexplained, except that they are said to be according to His own good pleasure. And after Paul has stated this, he puts forth his hand, as it were, to forbid us from going any further. Had the Arminian assumption been true, namely, that all men are given sufficient grace and that each one is rewarded or punished according to his own use or abuse of this grace, there would have been no difficulty for which to account.

Notes

[1]Ch. III, sections III–VII.

[2]*Institutes,* Book III, Ch. XXI, section I.

[3]Pamphlet, "Election," p. 10.

[4]Warfield, *Biblical Doctrines,* p. 50.

[5]Cunningham, *Historical Theology,* II, p. 398.

[6]*Historical Theology,* II, p. 467.

[7]*Theology,* p. 230.

Further Scripture Proof

Ps. 105:6: Ye children of Jacob, His chosen ones.

Matt. 24:24: There shall arise false Christs, and false prophets, and shall show great signs and wonders; so as to lead astray, if possible, even the elect.

Matt. 24:31: And they [the angels] shall gather together His elect from the four winds, from one end of heaven to the other.

Mark 13:20: For the elect's sake, whom He chose, He shortened those days [at the destruction of Jerusalem].

John 6:37: All that the Father giveth me shall come unto me.

John 6:65: No man can come unto me, except it be given unto him of the Father.

John 13:18: I speak not of you all; I know whom I have chosen.

John 15:16: Ye did not choose me, but I chose you.

John 17:9: I [Jesus] pray not for the world, but for those whom thou hast given me; for they are thine.

Acts 13:48: And as the Gentiles heard this, they were glad, and glorified the word of God; and as many as were ordained to eternal life believed.

Rom. 8:33: Who shall lay anything to the charge of God's elect?

Rom. 9:23: Vessels of mercy, which He afore prepared unto glory.

Rom. 11:5: Even so at the present time also [in comparison with Elijah's time] there is a remnant according to the election of grace.

Rom. 11:7: The election obtained it, and the rest were hardened.

I Thess. 1:4: Knowing, brethren, beloved of God, your election.

I Thess. 5:9: For God appointed us not unto wrath, but unto the obtaining of salvation through our Lord Jesus Christ.

II Thes. 2:13: God chose you from the beginning unto salvation in sanctification of the Spirit and belief of the truth.

I Tim. 5:21: I charge thee in the sight of God, and Jesus Christ, and the elect angels.

II Tim. 2:10: I endure all things for the elect's sake.

Titus 1:1: Paul, a servant of God, and an apostle of Jesus Christ, according to the faith of God's elect.

I Peter 1:1: Peter, an apostle of Jesus Christ, to the elect.

I Peter 2:9: But ye are an elect race.

I Peter 5:13: She that is in Babylon, elect together with you.

(See also references already quoted in this chapter—Rom. 8:29, 30; 9:11–13; Eph. 1:4, 5, 11; etc.)

3

Henry Thiessen

Election and Vocation

In treating election and calling as the application of Christ's redemption, we imply that they are, in God's decree, logically subsequent to the decree of redemption. But even so, several views of the order of the decrees are possible. Sublapsarianism holds that the decrees of God are in this order: (1) the decree to create; (2) the decree to permit the fall; (3) the decree to provide salvation sufficient for all; (4) the decree to secure the acceptance of this salvation by some, or the decree of election. This view holds to an unlimited atonement and to irresistible grace. The Infralapsarian view agrees in the first two points, but makes (3) the decree to provide salvation for the elect. It is evident that this view holds both to a limited atonement and to irresistible grace. Hyper-Calvinism holds what is known as Supra-lapsarianism. According to this view the order of the decrees is as follows: (1) the decree to save some, and to reprobate the rest; (2) the decree to create both those who are to be saved and those who are to be reprobated; (3) the decree to permit (some would say, effectually to secure) the fall of both groups; and (4) the decree to provide salvation only for the former, that is, the elect. It may be said that Calvin gives some ground for

From *Introductory Lectures in Systematic Theology* (Grand Rapids: Wm. B. Eerdmans Pub. Co., 1949), pp. 343–351. Used by permission.

this view (*Institutes,* III, 23, 5). But compare this with another statement where he says: "Man therefore falls, divine providence so ordering, but by his own fault" (III, 23, 8). In later life Calvin accepted the theory of unlimited atonement. How else, for instance, could we explain his comment on I John 2:2, which is as follows:

> Christ suffered for the sins of the whole world, and in the goodness of God is offered unto all men without distinction, His blood being shed not for a part of the world only, but for the whole human race; for although in the world nothing is found worthy of the favor of God, yet He holds out the propitiation to the whole world, since without exception He summons all to the faith of Christ, which is nothing else than the door unto hope.

I. The Doctrine of Election

Our own view is a modification of the Sublapsarian conception. We believe that the decrees are in this order: (1) the decree to create; (2) the decree to permit the fall; (3) the decree to provide salvation for all; and (4) the decree to apply that salvation to some, to those who believe. This view naturally affects our definition of election, to which we now turn.

1. The Definition of Election

By election we mean that sovereign act of God in grace whereby He chose in Christ Jesus for salvation all those whom He foreknew would accept Him. This is election in its redemptive aspect. The Scriptures also speak of an election to outward privileges (Luke 6:13, 16, Judas; Acts 13:17; Rom. 9:4; 11:28, Israel), to sonship (Rom. 8:29, 33, Eph. 1:4, 5); and to a particular office (Moses and Aaron, Ps. 105:26; David, I Sam. 16:12; Solomon, I Chron. 28:5; and the Apostles, Luke 6:13–16; John 6:70; Acts 1:2, 24; 9:15; 22:14). But we are here concerned with election as related to salvation, and so we analyze the above definition more fully.

(1) Election and Foreknowledge. Election is a sovereign act of God; He was under no obligation to elect any one, since all had lost their standing before God. Even after Christ had died, God was not obligated to apply that salvation, except as He owed it to Christ to keep the agreement with Him as to man's salvation. Election is a sovereign act, because it was not due to any constraint laid upon God. It was an act in grace, in that He chose those who were utterly unworthy of salvation. Man deserved the exact opposite, but in His grace God chose to save some. He chose them "in Christ." He could not choose them in themselves because of their ill-desert; so He chose them in the merits of another. Furthermore, He chose those who He foreknew would accept Christ. The Scriptures definitely base God's election on His foreknowledge: "Whom He foreknew, He also foreordained, . . . and whom He foreordained, them He also called" (Rom. 8:29, 30); "to the elect . . . according to the foreknowledge of God the Father" (I Peter 1:1, 2). Although we are nowhere told what it is in the foreknowledge of God that determines His choice, the repeated teaching of

Scripture that man is responsible for accepting or rejecting salvation necessitates our postulating that it is man's reaction to the revelation God has
made of Himself that is the basis of His election. May we repeat: Since
mankind is hopelessly dead in trespasses and sins and can do nothing to
obtain salvation, God graciously restores to all men sufficient ability to
make a choice in the matter of submission to Him. This is the salvation-
bringing grace of God that has appeared to all men. In His foreknowledge
He perceives what each one will do with this restored ability, and elects
men to salvation in harmony with His knowledge of their choice of Him.
There is no merit in this transaction, as J. O. Buswell has clearly shown in
his allegory of the captain who is beaten into unconsciousness by the crew
on deck of his vessel, if that captain is revived by restoratives and then
accepts the proffered leadership of a captain from another vessel who has
come to his rescue (*Sin and Atonement* [Grand Rapids: Zondervan
Brothers, 1937], pp. 112–114).

(2) Election and Predestination. Something should here be said about
the terms "predestination" and "foreordination." "Predestinate" occurs
in the Authorized Version only at Romans 8:29, 30, and "predestinated"
only at Ephesians 1:5, 11. The American Standard Version translates all
four of these by "foreordained." The A.V. has the term "foreordained" in
I Peter 1:20, but the A.S.V. correctly changes this to "foreknown." Fortunately, the words "foreordained" and "predestinated" mean the same
thing. Scofield's definition of predestination is, therefore, also the definition of foreordination. He defines the former as "that effective exercise of
the will of God by which things before determined by Him are brought to
pass." As applied to redemption this would mean that in election God has
decided to save those who accept His Son and the proffered salvation, and
in foreordination He has determined effectively to accomplish that purpose.

2. The Proof of This View of Election

In the minds of some people, election is a choice that God makes for
which we can see no reason and which we can hardly harmonize with His
justice. We are asked to accept the theory of "unconditional election" as
true but unexplainable in spite of the fact that the persistent demand of the
heart is for a theory of election that does commend itself to our sense of
justice and that harmonizes the teaching of Scripture concerning the sovereignty of God and the responsibility of man. Let us submit the following in
proof of the definition of election we have suggested.

(1) Election Is Based on Foreknowledge. This is in accord with Scripture (Rom. 8:28–30; I Peter 1:1, 2). To say that God foreknew all things
because He had arbitrarily determined all things is to ignore the distinction
between God's efficient and His permissive decrees. Certainly only few
who hold the view of "unconditional election" would teach that God is the
efficient cause of sin: practically all would agree that God merely permitted
sin to enter the universe, and all would admit that He foresaw that it would
enter, before He ever created anything. If, then, God could foresee that sin

would enter the universe without efficiently decreeing that it should enter, then He can also foresee how men will act, without efficiently decreeing how they shall act. God is not limited in the carrying out of His plans, except as He has limited Himself by the choices of man. He knew before He created how far man would depart from holiness, and who would thus depart; and in the light of this knowledge He thought it well to create man and to permit such a departure from the right way. God's plan with regard to sin will be fully realized, in the sense that He has foreseen what would happen and has decided to let it happen. There is here no contradiction between the terms "decrees," "foreknowledge," and "election."

(2) Christ Died for All Men. . . . Our Lord died in a real sense for all. See I Timothy 2:6, Hebrews 2:9; I John 2:2. In harmony with this is His expressed desire that none should perish, but that all should come to repentance (II Peter 3:9). "For I have no pleasure in the death of him that dieth, saith the Lord Jehovah: wherefore turn yourselves, and live" (Ezek. 18:32). With this agree also the many invitations to all. Surely, these are not mere mockery—invitations that will in the case of some be backed up by God's efficient work of regeneration, and in the case of others be held out as glorious opportunities that can neither be appreciated nor appropriated for lack of God's efficient assistance.

(3) God Is Just. It is admitted that God is under no obligation to provide salvation for anyone, since all are responsible for their present lost condition. It is also admitted that God is not obliged actually to save anyone even though Christ has provided salvation for men. But it is difficult to see how God can choose some from the mass of guilty and condemned men, provide salvation for them and efficiently secure their salvation, and do nothing about all the others, if, as we read, righteousness is the foundation of His throne. God would not be partial if He permitted all men to go to their deserved doom; but how can He be other than partial if He selects some from this multitude of men and does things for them and in them that He refuses to do for the others, if there is not something about the two classes that makes the difference? We hold that common grace is extended to all, and that everyone has the ability restored to him to "will to do His will." The salvation-bearing grace of God has appeared to all men, but some receive the grace of God in vain. It seems to us that only if God makes the same provisions for all and makes the same offers to all, is He truly just. Someone may object that Jesus speaks of the unequal opportunities of Chorazin, Bethsaida, and Capernaum, as compared with those of Tyre and Sidon (Matt. 11:21–23); but to this we reply that God is under no obligation to perform supernatural works among men to induce them to repent, but He did this during the earthly life of Christ for the proof of His Deity, which proof was intended for all generations to come, and the privilege afforded the generation then living was incidental and not an act of partiality. We may also say that the responsibility for the opportunities presented to a people must rest, in part at least, upon the people of God, who have been commissioned to carry the Gospel to every creature (Ezek. 3:17–19).

(4) This View of Election Inspires Missionary Activity. Acceptance of this view tends logically to great missionary endeavor. Christ sent His

disciples into all the world, and He instructed them to preach the Gospel to every creature. If, then, election means that all those whom God has arbitrarily chosen will certainly get to heaven, and that all those whom He has not chosen will certainly not get there, no matter how faithfully and frequently the Gospel may be preached to them, then why be greatly agitated about it? True, we have the command to take the Gospel into all the world; but if only some are thus "elected," why be greatly disturbed about it? Furthermore, how shall the servant of Christ keep up his courage in a difficult field, if men are thus "elected" or not chosen? Perhaps there is no one in the hard field who belongs to the favored few! It is easiest to conclude that further effort is in vain and that one might just as well stop and go elsewhere. But both Scripture and experience testify, that often fruit appears only after many years of prayer and effort. Amos R. Wells says that Morrison had to labor for seven years before the first Chinese convert, Tsai-A-Ko, was baptized (*Into All the World* [Boston: United Society of Christian Endeavor, 1903], p. 70).

3. Objections to This View of Election

It is perhaps impossible so to state the doctrine of election as to do away with all possible objections. The view we have here expounded has fewer objections than any other, and best commends itself in the light of what we know of the righteousness and holiness of God on the one hand, and of human responsibility on the other. We note, however, briefly such objections as have been brought against it.

(1) The Simpler Objections. The simpler ones are mentioned first. (a) There is the recurring declaration that certain men have been *given* to Christ (John 6:37; 17:2, 6, 9), and it is assumed that this was an arbitrary act of God by which the rest were left to perish. But we reply that it is nowhere indicated what caused God to give certain men and not others to Christ. In the light of God's revealed character, it is more probable that He did this because of what He foresaw they would do, than merely to exercise sovereign authority. (b) There is further the statement that no man can come to Christ, "except the Father . . . draw him" (John 6:44). But in John 12:32 Jesus says that when He is lifted up from the earth, *He will* "draw all men" to Himself. It is interesting to note that in both references we have the same Greek word (*helkuo*). It is used of drawing a net (John 21:6, 11) and a sword (John 18:10), and of dragging a person forcibly, against his will (Acts 16:19; 21:30; James 2:6). We conclude that from the Cross of Christ there issues a power that goes out to all men, though many continue to resist that power.

There are other objections of the same kind. (c) There is the declaration that God works in us both to will and to do of His good pleasure (Phil. 2:13). It is assumed that there is nothing a sinner can do until God does these things in him. But the mistake is in applying this text to the unsaved. Paul had been telling the Philippians to work out their salvation with fear and trembling, and he encourages them to attempt it by the assurance that God will work all these things in them. Jesus plainly said to some of the Jews: "Ye will not come to me, that ye may have life" (John 5:40), clearly implying that they could if they would. (d) Then in Romans 9:11–16 God is said to have chosen Jacob rather than Esau, even before they were born and before they had done either good or bad. But two things should be noted here. Though it is said that they had not yet done either good or bad, it is not said that God did not know who would do the good and who would do the bad. Esau consistently chose the "profane" things of life, and Jacob, though far from constant in the things of God in his early life, chose the more spiritual things. And further, the choice of Jacob rather than Esau was at most a choice to outward and national privilege: it was not a choice to salvation directly. No doubt God, in foreseeing that Jacob and his descendants would much more fully than Esau and his descendants choose the things of spiritual value, chose Jacob for the covenant relationship which he and his descendants later came to enjoy. That this is the meaning of God's choice of Jacob is evident from the fact that Scripture itself declares that not all the descendants of Israel (Jacob) are Israel, and not all the children of Abraham are children of promise. A descendant of Esau could, no doubt, be saved as readily as a descendant of Jacob.

(2) The More Difficult Objections. Several other objections are more difficult to meet. (a) Thus we read in Acts 13:48: "And as many as were ordained to eternal life believed." Knowling shows that this cannot refer to an absolute decree, for in v. 46 Paul had already declared that the Jews by their own choice rejected the message, and he cannot mean anything other than that individual choice decided the question of appointment (*esan tetagmenoi*). . . (b) Again, Ephesians 1:5–8 and 2:8–10 represent salvation as originating in the choice of God and as being all of grace. But that is not in contradiction to the view we are setting forth. God must take the initiative, and He does take it. If it were not for the operation of His grace upon the heart of the sinner, no man could be saved. It is hardly necessary to repeat that prevenient grace does not save a man—it merely enables him to choose whom he will serve. (c) In the third place we are reminded that repentance and faith are the gift of God (Acts 5:31; 11:18; II Tim. 2:25; Rom. 12:3; Eph. 2:8–10). To this we reply that it would seem very strange if God should call upon all men everywhere to repent (Acts 17:30; II Peter 3:9) and believe (Mark 1:14, 15), when only some men may receive the gift of repentance and faith. (d) And finally, some claim that if predestination is not unconditional and absolute, then God's whole plan is uncertain and liable to miscarriage. But this could be true only if God had not foreknown the outcome and had not adopted it as His plan. Since God has foreseen all that will happen, and has accepted these eventualities in going ahead with the plan of the ages, we dare not say that His plan is uncertain and liable to miscarriage. His plan is certain though not all the events in it are necessitated.

II. The Doctrine of Vocation

This is the doctrine of God's call. The grace of God is magnified, not only in the provision of salvation, but also in the offer of salvation to the undeserving. We may define God's call as that act of grace by which He invites men to accept by faith the salvation provided by Christ. Strong distinguishes between God's general or external call to all men, and His special, efficacious call to the elect. But if our conception of election is correct, there is no just ground for such a distinction. We, therefore, follow a simple Biblical outline of the subject.

1. The Persons Called

The Scriptures indicate that salvation is offered to all. It is offered to the "predestinated" (Rom. 8:30), all that "labor and are heavy laden" (Matt. 11:28), to "whosoever believes," etc. (John 3:15, 16; 4:14; 11:26; Rev. 22:17), to "all the ends of the earth" (Isa. 45:22; Ezek. 33:11; Matt. 28:19; Mark 16:15; John 12:32; I Tim. 2:4; II Peter 3:9), and to "as many as ye shall find" (Matt. 22:9). In the light of these passages we dare not distinguish between a general call to all and a special call to the elect. Nor need we decide whether God's general call is sincere and His special call is irresistible. God does not mock men. If He offers salvation to all, then He also desires to save all, and to extend the same help to all who choose Him. Man's will is the only obstacle to the salvation of anyone. God does not give one man the will to do good and leave the other without all help in this respect.

2. The Object of the Call

Briefly stated, God does not call men to reformation of life, to good works, to baptism, to church membership, etc. These are all proper things in themselves, but they are merely the sure fruit of that to which He does call men. The things to which He calls men are repentance (Matt. 3:2; 4:17; Mark 1:14, 15; Acts 2:38; 17:30; II Peter 3:9) and faith (Mark 1:15; John 6:29; 20:30, 31; Acts 16:31; 19:4; Rom. 19:9; I John 3:23). May we repeat: God does not call upon anyone to do anything he cannot do or which He is not anxious to give man help in doing.

3. The Means of the Call

God has a variety of means by which to call men. There is first of all His Word. (a) He calls men through the Word of God directly (Rom. 10:16, 17; II Thess. 2:14). That is why it is necessary to get the Bible into all parts of the world. (b) Then He also calls men by His Spirit (Gen. 6:3; John 16:8; Heb. 3:7, 8). The Holy Spirit urges the sinner to come and accept Christ. (c) Further, He calls men through His servants (II Chron. 36:15; Jer. 25:4; Matt. 22:2-4, 9; Rom. 10:14, 15). Jonah is a good example of His use of human messengers to bring a city to repentance. The Word of God must be brought to the unsaved by regenerated persons, persons who can testify to the power of that Word in their own lives. (d) And finally, He calls by His providential dealings with men. His goodness is intended to bring men to repentance (Jer. 31:3; Rom. 2:4), but if that does not succeed, then His judgments are to do it (Ps. 107:6, 13; Isa. 26:9).

The Beginning

George W. Peters

The Meaning of Conversion

The salvation of God has an objective as well as a subjective aspect, which is eternal as well as in-time.

The eternal and objective aspect refers to God's gracious purpose and plan of salvation when His saving entrance into history in and through Christ Jesus, who was born of the virgin Mary, took on true humanity and thus was the true God-man. According to the Scriptures: "He was made sin for us who knew no sin" (II Cor. 5:21) and "was made of God unto us wisdom, and righteousness, and sanctification, and redemption" (I Cor. 1:30). In obedience "He emptied Himself . . . and became obedient unto death, even the death of the cross" (Phil. 2:7, 8). His sinless, yea perfect life, vicarious death, victorious bodily resurrection and glorious exaltation procured salvation for all mankind. Thus stands the eternal salvation of God in Christ, having neither been foreseen nor pleaded for by man. It is of God alone as it is also in Christ alone that our glorying be in God and not in man.

The salvation of God, however, has very definitely a subjective and an in-time aspect. Eternity with its spiritual glory, fullness, and blessings is invading time. Salvation is now and here. God in Christ Jesus and through

From *Bibliotheca Sacra,* July 1961, pp. 235–242. Used by permission.

the Holy Spirit is entering the human life; salvation is entering me. Thus salvation is not merely an objective reality to be wondered at, a theological dictum to be debated about, a philosophical theory to be speculated about, not even merely a marvelous subject to be preached about. It is a divine reality entering the human being to transform his fundamental disposition, clean him from sin and unrighteousness, redeem him from bondage and corruption, impart unto him the nature of God, recreate him into the image of Christ, make him a child of God, a member of the household of God, and qualify him in the gift of the Holy Spirit to live for God in a life of true discipleship in the midst of a world almost destitute of the consciousness of God and eternity.

Our study concerns itself with the subjective and in-time aspect of salvation under the subject "The Meaning of Conversion." After a brief general statement we shall consider the subject in the following order: the historical-exegetical unfolding of the doctrine: the exegetical-theological presentation of conversion; essential elements of Biblical conversion; the theological interpretation of conversion.

A brief general statement. The doctrine of conversion is written in bold letters across the pages of the Bible. It is set forth with great emphasis in the Old Testament, is strongly reiterated in the Gospels and boldly preached by the apostles. It is a concept deeply rooted in divine revelation. As such it has been recognized by Biblical theology and as such it was emphatically preached by our fathers in the faith.

The Historical-exegetical Unfolding of the Doctrine

The Hebrew Old Testament. The word *conversion* and its related terms are a translation of the Hebrew verb *schub* which is found approximately 1056 times in the Old Testament. The word *schub* is used in a variety of ways and in general carries the meaning of: turning, returning, turning away, restoring, converting, turning unto, etc. It is a most general term and appears in many different relationships and is used both of things and of persons.

Approximately 118 times it is used in a moral and religious sense in the Old Testament and definitely expresses the idea of religious conversion in the sense of returning to the Lord, turning from sin, with the consequent restoration of fellowship, restoration into a position of blessing and usefulness.

The following references in the Old Testament are listed for comparison: *Unto the Lord*—Deuteronomy 4:30; 30:2, 10; I Samuel 7:3; I Kings 8:33; II Chronicles 6:38; 30:9; Nehemiah 9:26; Job 22:23; Psalm 22:27; 51:13; Isaiah 19:22; 55:7; 60:5; Jeremiah 3:7; 4:1; 24:7; Lamentations 3:40; Hosea 12:6; 14:2, 3; Joel 2:12, 13; Malachi 3:7. *From sins*—I Kings 8:35, II Chronicles 6:26; Nehemiah 9:35; Isaiah 59:20; Jeremiah 25:5; Ezekiel 18:28; 33:11, 14; Jonah 3:10. *God's work*—I Kings 18:37; Psalm 23:3; Isaiah 10:22; 52:8; Jeremiah 31:18, 19; Lamentations 5:21; Malachi 4:6.

The Greek Old Testament. In the Septuagint, the Greek translation of the Old Testament, the Hebrew verb *schub* is translated by *epistrephein, apostrephein,* and *anastrephein,* words which express the same general idea as *schub.*

The New Testament. The New Testament follows the Septuagint and employs the same words to convey the Christian idea of conversion. Thus the word *epistrephein* is used 36 times (according to some manuscripts 39 times), of which 18 times have a religious meaning (Matt. 13:15; Mark 4:12; Luke 1:16, 17; 22:32; Acts 3:19; 9:35; 11:21; 14:15; 15:19; 26:18; 26:20; 28:27; II Cor. 3:16; I Thess. 1:9; James 5:19, 20; I Peter 2:25); *strephein* is employed only in Matthew 18:3 and John 12:40; *apostrephein* is found only in Acts 3:26, and the noun *epistrophe* only in Acts 15:3.

The above list of references from the Old and New Testaments establishes the following facts regarding the basic meanings of conversion in the historical-exegetical unfolding:

1. Conversion in its concept and experience originates in God. It is neither a human invention nor the product of the human mind, will, or emotions. It originated in the mind and will of God. As in Genesis 1:1 so also here we write, "In the beginning God."

2. God Himself is the initiator of the conversion of man by: (a) commanding man to be converted; (b) calling man to return unto Him; (c) calling man to forsake sin; (d) upholding before man the promise of the forgiveness of sins, restoration and a life of rich blessings; and (e) warning man of judgment if he fails to heed God's call and command.

In order to save the Biblical concept of conversion from all religious humanism, it is well to realize that the Word of God is not only self-authoritative, it is also dynamic, quickening, motivating, and causative. The command, call, promise, and warning of God carry in them the power of God to motivate and to enable man to respond positively to the Word of God. In faith man opens himself to the power of God in the Word and is thereby enabled to follow the command of God and to respond to the call for conversion (cf. Ps. 19:7, 8; John 6:63; Heb. 4:12).

3. God Himself is operative in conversion and thus in the final end, the ultimate cause of man's conversion rests in God and not in man himself. Without the gracious operation of the Holy Spirit spoken of at times as prevenient grace, known as the convicting (John 16:8), drawing (John 12:32), and illuminating ministry of the Holy Spirit, no man would ever turn to God and be converted (John 1:7-9).

4. Conversion as seen from the above data is a conscious, radical, principal turning of man with all his heart to God and from sin and ungodliness, a turning which affects the whole of man's life in all its relationships.

5. There is a possibility of false "conversions," conversions which are merely psychological, an escape from judgments rather than sin, or half-heartedness, or to false gods. Thus they are inadequate in the dynamic, motivation, or purpose.

The Exegetical-theological Meaning of Conversion

The word *conversion* seems to have a threefold meaning in the Bible: (1) It refers to any kind of turning, whether physical, mental or otherwise. This is the *general* usage and is not of special interest in this study. (2) It may refer to a change of attitude, relationship, or life due to clearer insight, changed circumstances, changed motivations, changed purposes, or repentance. In this sense the Christian life is a life of conversion. (3) In a moral, religious sense it means that vital experience which in an inclusive manner expresses the totality of man's initial experience of salvation and thus in its idea includes regeneration, justification, adoption, initial sanctification, and union with Christ.

Basically the exegetical-theological meaning may be stated in the following definition: Conversion is that principal act of faith in which the soul by the initiative and the enablement of the Holy Spirit on the basis of the finished work of Christ on Calvary and in response to the Word of God voluntarily turns to God from sin and ungodliness and enters into an abiding relationship with the Lord which vitally and permanently affects life in its various aspects and relationships and leads to its eventual and complete restoration.

Our definition establishes the following principles: (1) Conversion is a principal act of faith; (2) Conversion is an act of the soul by the initiative and the enablement of the Holy Spirit; (3) Conversion is based upon the finished work of Christ on Calvary; (4) Conversion is an act of the soul in response to the Word of God; (5) Conversion is a voluntary act; (6) Conversion is an act of turning to God from sin and ungodliness; (7) Conversion is an act which results in a relationship with the Lord; (8) Conversion is an act which vitally affects life in its various aspects and relationships; (9) Conversion is an act which leads to a process in the restoration of life. These principles are illustrated by the various Biblical records on conversion.

Essential Elements of Conversion

Conversion is essentially a turning to God and a turning away from sin. The two elements are usually expressed by the two Biblical terms of *faith* and *repentance*.

It is very important to realize that the Bible emphasizes both aspects, although the emphasis upon the positive definitely outweighs the negative, far more passages speaking of turning to God than turning away from sin. It must be understood, however, that both aspects are always present, the one expressed, the other implied. They form an indissoluble unit in a Biblical conversion.

It is dangerous to read chronological order into the experience of conversion as though faith precedes and conditions repentance or vice versa. To grasp the real meaning of these vital elements of conversion is of greater significance. We, therefore, turn our attention to them.

Repentance. The word *repentance* and its various derivatives are a translation of the Hebrew word *nocham* and the Greek words *metamelomai* and *metanoia*. The root meaning of *nocham* and *metanoia* in the religious usage indicates a principal change of mind and moral purpose, while *metamelomai* is used to express a state of sensibility as regret, remorse, and sorrow. Thus we are dealing with a deeply moral, religious concept that expresses man's relationship to sin and ungodliness, a concept full of spiritual significance which in its deepest meaning expresses man's practical sharing in Christ's view and attitude toward sin. Repentance thus becomes a holy abhorrence, a righteous condemnation, a conscious repudiation and renunciation of sin, a voluntary turning away from a life of sin, a determinate breaking with evil. If repentance were only a hard and painful duty, it would be negative and discouraging to the individual, but repentance is positive when it is seen in its relation to Christ, as a sharing in Christ's view and attitude toward sin.

> The change may be comparatively a calm and quiet one, or it may be accompanied by sharp mental pain. The man may abhor himself, and be in an agony of sorrow before God in view of his sins. A man who knows himself a sinner may well find penitence painful. But the sharpness of sorrow is not what constitutes the repentance; the repentance consists in the change of mind, resulting in change of life, and the sorrow for sin is its accompaniment. A man repents when at last he begins to feel as Christ feels about evil in himself, and to act accordingly.[1]

Faith. Repentance looks back and forsakes. Faith looks forward and appropriates. Repentance expresses man's attitude toward sin and ungodliness. Faith manifests man's relationship towards Christ and His promises. In conversion experience "saving faith never outruns repentance."

The significance of the doctrine of faith is difficult to overstate. It is most prominent in the Bible. It is basic, central, fundamental, and consistent throughout the whole Bible. Its footprints can be discovered on every page of the divine record and it is the one universal distinctive mark of all great Bible characters. It begins where divine grace begins to manifest itself in relation to man. In Christian experience it is the human complement to divine grace, being the response of the human soul to God's gracious manifestations and operations.

Basic to all faith is God and His gracious relation to man, making Himself known to man. "For whoever would draw near to God must believe that he exists and that he is a rewarder of them that diligently seek him" (Heb. 11:6).

A careful study of the word *faith* in the Old and New Testaments and the numerous Biblical illustrations will justify the statement that faith is made up of spiritual illumination, conviction and acknowledgment, personal surrender, commital, dependence, trust, rest, appropriation, interaction, and obedience. All of this is most certainly substantial and beautifully illustrated by a careful study of John's use of the verb *to believe* and its synonyms, and the noun *faith* in Hebrews 11 and in the writings of Paul.

As we further penetrate the Scriptures we discover that saving faith never stands by itself. It is always solidly anchored in an object, which object is God, predominantly Jesus Christ, the eternal Son of God (cf. John 1:12; 3:16, 18, 36; 6:35, 40; 7:37–39; 11:25, 26; 12:36).

It should be noted that in most of these verses the verb *to believe* is dominated by the preposition *eis* governing the accusative case and indicating movement towards or relationship with.

We believe that in the light of the above stated data we are within Scriptural truth when we say that saving or conversion-faith is a personal, living, interactive relationship between Christ and the sinner, a psychological compound which includes the illumination of our spiritual perception, a readiness of receptivity, the persuasion of trust, the exercise of appropriation, the dynamic of expression or obedience and the assurance to the degree of rest and confidence.

No Bible student will dispute that such faith is not human in origin. It is the gracious work of God wrought in the heart of man by the Holy Spirit and through the Word of God to which man must yield and which man must exercise. This is the will of God for every sinner.

Converting faith thus has as its origin the will of God; as its basis the Word of God; as its initiative the Spirit of God; as its object the Son of God; as its responsibility the exercise of man; as its result the transformation of the personality of man; as its end the eternal glory of God and the welfare of man.

The Theological Interpretation of Conversion

As we turn to the theological usage of the term *conversion,* we find that in the main conversion is considered the human aspect of the salvation experience. Thus the salvation experienced is described as consisting of: regeneration (the divine aspect); justification (the legal aspect); reunion with Christ (the mystic-realistic aspect); adoption (the filial aspect); and conversion (the human-moral aspect).

In keeping with this view several authorities will be quoted:

"Conversion refers specifically to the voluntary act of the individual in turning from sin and seeking forgiveness and the new life. . . . Conversion, from the Latin *com, together, and vertere, to turn,* means primarily a turning forward. Theologically conversion is the changing of purpose, direction and spirit of life from one of self-seeking and enmity toward God to one of love toward God and man."[2]

"By conversion is meant the response of a sinner under the conviction of the Holy Spirit, in which the sinner repents, renouncing his sin, and exercises faith in Christ as Savior and Lord."[3]

"Conversion is the word employed in theology to designate the turning of a sinner from his sins unto Christ for his salvation. This includes both the forsaking of sin which we have defined as repentance, and the trust in Christ which we have defined as faith. The term *conversion* usually refers to the outward act of the changed man which is the manifestation of the inner change in his soul. A converted man is one in whom the grace of God has wrought a spiritual change. That change has found inward expression in his turning from the old life of disobedience to the new life of service."[4]

"Conversion is the human side or aspect of the fundamental spiritual change, which, as viewed from the divine side, we call regeneration. It is simply man's turning. . . . By conversion is meant that voluntary change in the mind of the sinner, in which he turns, on the one hand, from sin, and on the other hand, to Christ."[5]

"In its more restricted meaning the word denotes the action of man in the initial process of salvation as distinguished from the action of God. Justification and regeneration are purely divine acts, repentance, faith, conversion are human acts, although under the influence and by the power of the divine agency. Thus conversion denotes the human volition and act by which man in obedience to the Divine summons determines to change the course of his life and turns to God. Arrested by God's call man stops to think, turns about, and heads the opposite way."[6]

From these theological presentations certain principles evolve: (1) Conversion presupposes a gracious operation of God. (2) Conversion separates man in his will and practice from guilt, servitude, and love of sin. (3) Conversion converges upon Christ as Savior and Lord, receiving from Him forgiveness of sin, a new content, meaning, and direction of life, a submission to obedience and the dynamic to serve Him. (4) Conversion is an outer manifestation of an inwrought work of grace from which it cannot be dissociated essentially. Nor can the two be classified chronologically.

Conclusion

In the light of the historical-exegetical unfolding and the exegetical-theological analysis and definition it seems that the theological usage of the word has suffered serious limitations. Adding to this the psychological studies in "conversion" the word has been thoroughly "humanized." Thus it has disappeared to a great extent from evangelical preaching and teaching. Theology needs to rediscover the Biblical significance of conversion and the proper usage of the word. Its disappearance from the theological vocabulary cannot be justified on Biblical grounds. Indeed, it is tragic. The concept, however, must be guarded lest it mean no more than a "human turning" or the exercise of the will in human strength and thus become an act of self-redemption or reformation.

Conversion is a Biblical concept, expressing a great Biblical truth and describing an experience which is of God, by God, and unto God.

Notes

[1] W. N. Clarke, *Christian Theology*, p. 402.

[2] *Mennonite Encyclopedia*, I, 704.

[3] John C. Wenger, *Introduction to Theology*, p. 272.

[4] E. Y. Mullins, *The Christian Religion in Its Doctrinal Expression*, p. 377.

[5] E. H. Bancroft, *Christian Theology*, p. 173.

[6] J. L. Nuelsen, *The International Standard Bible Encyclopedia*, II, 706.

John Murray

Faith and Repentance

Regeneration is inseparable from its effects and one of the effects is faith. Without regeneration it is morally and spiritually impossible for a person to believe in Christ, but when a person is regenerated it is morally and spiritually impossible for that person not to believe. Jesus said, "All that the Father giveth me shall come to me" (John 6:37), and he was referring in this case surely to the giving of the Father in the efficacious drawing of the Father mentioned in the same context (John 6:44, 65). Regeneration is the renewing of the heart and mind, and the renewed heart and mind must act according to their nature.

Faith

Regeneration is the act of God and of God alone. But faith is not the act of God; it is not God who believes in Christ for salvation, it is the sinner. It is by God's grace that a person is able to believe but faith is an activity on the part of the person and of him alone. In faith we receive and rest upon Christ alone for salvation.

From *Redemption, Accomplished and Applied* (Grand Rapids: Wm. B. Eerdmans Pub. Co., 1955), pp. 106–116. Used by permission.

It might be said: this is a strange mixture. God alone regenerates. We alone believe. And we believe in Christ alone for salvation. But this is precisely the way it is. It is well for us to appreciate all that is implied in the combination, for it is God's way of salvation and it expresses his supreme wisdom and grace. In salvation God does not deal with us as machines; he deals with us as persons and therefore salvation brings the whole range of our activity within its scope. By grace we are saved through faith (cf. Eph. 2:8).

If we are to have a better understanding of what faith is we must examine it as to its *warrant* and as to its *nature*.

The Warrant. Faith, as we shall see later, is a whole-souled movement of self-commitment to Christ for salvation from sin and its consequences. It is not unnecessary to ask the question: what warrant does a lost sinner have to commit himself to Christ? How may he know that he will be accepted? How does he know that Christ is able to save? How does he know that this confidence is not misplaced? How does he know that Christ is willing to save him? These are urgent questions, perhaps not urgent for the person who has no true conception of the issues at stake or of the gravity of his lost condition, but exceedingly urgent and pertinent for the person convicted of sin and in whose heart burns the reality and realization of the wrath of God against sin. There are the following facts which constitute the warrant of faith.

I. The Universal Offer of the Gospel

This offer may be regarded from several viewpoints. It may be regarded as invitation, as demand, as promise, and as overture. But from whatever angle we may view it, it is full, free, and unrestricted. The appeals of the gospel cover the whole range of divine prerogative and of human interest. God entreats, he invites, he commands, he calls, he presents the overture of mercy and grace, and he does this to all without distinction or discrimination.

It may surprise us that this universal offer should receive such prominence in the Old Testament. Under the Old Testament the revelation of God's saving grace was given to a chosen people and to them were committed the oracles of God. The psalmist could sing, "In Judah is God known: his name is great in Israel. In Salem also is his tabernacle, and his dwelling place in Zion" (Ps. 76:1, 2). And Jesus could say of this Old Testament period, "Salvation is of the Jews" (John 4:22). There was a middle wall of partition between Jew and Gentile. But it is in the Old Testament we find such an appeal as this: "There is no God else beside me; a just God and a Saviour; there is none beside me. Look unto me, and be ye saved, all the ends of the earth; for I am God and there is none else" (Isa. 45:21, 22). Again we read: "As I live, saith the Lord God, I have no pleasure in the death of the wicked; but that the wicked turn from his way and live; turn ye, turn ye from your evil ways; for why will ye die, O house of Israel?" (Ezek. 33:11; cf. 18:23, 32). Here is the most emphatic negation—"I have no pleasure in the death of the wicked," affirmation—"but that the wicked turn from his way and live," asseveration—"as I live, saith the Lord God," exhortation—"turn ye, turn ye from your evil ways," protestation—"why will ye die?"

If there is universality of exhortation and appeal when God's covenant grace was concentrated in Israel, how much more apparent must this be when there is now no longer Jew nor Gentile and the middle wall of partition is broken down, when the gospel is proclaimed in terms of Jesus' commission, "Go ye therefore and disciple all the nations" (Matt. 28:19)? The words of Jesus are redolent of this indiscriminate invitation, "Come unto me, all ye that labour and are heavy laden, and I will give you rest" (Matt. 11:28); "him that cometh unto me I will in no wise cast out" (John 6:37). And the words of the apostle are unmistakably clear: "And the times of this ignorance God winked at, but now he commandeth men that they should all everywhere repent, inasmuch as he hath appointed a day in which he will judge the world in righteousness, by the man whom he hath ordained, having given assurance unto all men in that he hath raised him from the dead" (Acts 17:30, 31). It is not simply that God entreats men everywhere that they should turn and repent; he commands them to do so. It is a charge invested with the authority and majesty of his sovereignty as Lord of all. The sovereign imperative of God is brought to bear upon the overture of grace. And that is the end of all contention. From his command to all no one is excluded.

2. *The All-Sufficiency and Suitability of the Saviour Presented*

Christ presented himself in the glory of his person and in the sufficiency of his saviourhood when he said, "Come unto me, all ye that labour and are heavy laden, and I will give you rest" (Matt. 11:28), and again, "Him that cometh unto me I will in no wise cast out" (John 6:37). It is this truth that is enunciated when it is written, "Wherefore he is able to save them to the uttermost that come unto God by him, seeing he ever liveth to make intercession for them" (Heb. 7:25). The sufficiency of his saviourhood rests upon the work he accomplished once for all when he died upon the cross and rose again in triumphant power. But it resides in the efficacy and perfection of his continued activity at the right hand of God. It is because he continues ever and has an unchangeable priesthood that he is able to save them that come unto him and to give them eternal life. When Christ is presented to lost men in the proclamation of the gospel, it is as Saviour he is presented, as one who ever continues to be the embodiment of the salvation he has once for all accomplished. It is not the possibility of salvation that is offered to lost men but the Saviour himself and therefore salvation full and perfect. There is no imperfection in the salvation offered and there is no restriction to its overture—it is full, free, and unrestricted. And this is the warrant of faith.

The faith of which we are now speaking is not the belief that we have been saved but trust in Christ in order that we may be saved. And it is of paramount concern to know that Christ is presented to all without distinction to the end that they may entrust themselves to him for salvation. The gospel offer is not restricted to the elect or even to those for whom Christ died. And the warrant of faith is not the conviction that we are elect or that we are among those for whom, strictly speaking, Christ died but the fact that Christ, in the glory of his person, in the perfection of his finished work, and in the efficacy of his exalted activity as King and Saviour, is presented to us in the full, free, and unrestricted overture of the gospel. It is not as persons convinced of our election nor as persons convinced that we are the special objects of God's love that we commit ourselves to him but as lost sinners. We entrust ourselves to him not because we believe we have been saved but as lost sinners in order that we may be saved. It is to us in our lost condition that the warrant of faith is given and the warrant is not restricted or circumscribed in any way. In the warrant of faith the rich mercy of God is proffered to the lost and the promise of grace is certified by the veracity and faithfulness of God. This is the ground upon which a lost sinner may commit himself to Christ in full confidence that he will be saved. And no sinner to whom the gospel comes is excluded from the divine warrant for such confidence.

The Nature. There are three things that need to be said about the nature of faith. Faith is *knowledge, conviction,* and *trust.*

1. *Knowledge.* It might seem very confusing to say that faith is knowledge. For is it not one thing to know, another thing to believe? This is partly true. Sometimes we must distinguish between faith and knowledge and place them in contrast to each other. But there is a knowledge that is indispensable to faith. In our ordinary human relations do we trust a person of whom we know nothing? Especially when that for which we trust him is of grave importance for us we must know a good deal regarding his identity and his character. How much more must this be the case with that faith which is directed to Christ; for it is faith against all the issues of life and death, of time and eternity. We must know who Christ is, what he has done, and what he is able to do. Otherwise faith would be blind conjecture at the best and foolish mockery at the worst. There must be apprehension of the truth respecting Christ.

Sometimes, indeed, the measure of truth apprehended by the believing person is very small, and we have to appreciate the fact that the faith of some in its initial stages is very elementary. But faith cannot begin in a vacuum of knowledge. Paul reminds us of this very simply when he says, "Faith is of hearing, and hearing of the word of Christ" (Rom. 10:17).

2. *Conviction.* Faith is assent. We must not only know the truth respecting Christ but we must also believe it to be true. It is possible, of course, for us to understand the import of certain propositions of truth and yet not believe these propositions. All disbelief is of this character, and the more intelligently the import of the truths concerned is understood the more violent may be the disbelief. A person who rejects the virgin birth may understand well what the doctrine of the virgin birth is and for that very reason reject it. But we are now dealing not with disbelief or unbelief but with faith and this obviously implies that the truths known are also accepted as true.

The conviction which enters into faith is not only an assent to the truth respecting Christ but also a recognition of the exact correspondence that there is between the truth of Christ and our deeds as lost sinners. What Christ is as Saviour perfectly dovetails our deepest and most ultimate need. This is just saying that Christ's sufficiency as Saviour meets the desperateness and hopelessness of our sin and misery. It is conviction which engages, therefore, our greatest interest and which registers the verdict: Christ is exactly suited to all that I am in my sin and misery and to all that I should aspire to be by God's grace. Christ fits in perfectly to the totality of our situation in its sin, guilt, misery, and ill-desert.

3. *Trust.* Faith is knowledge passing into conviction, and it is conviction passing into confidence. Faith cannot stop short of self-commitment to Christ, a transference of reliance upon ourselves and all human resources to reliance upon Christ alone for salvation. It is a receiving and resting upon him. It is here that the most characteristic act of faith appears; it is engagement of person to person, the engagement of the sinner as lost to the person of the Saviour able and willing to save. Faith, after all, is not belief of propositions of truth respecting the Saviour, however essential an ingredient of faith such belief is. Faith is trust in a person, the person of Christ, the Son of God and Saviour of the lost. It is entrustment of ourselves to him. It is not simply believing him; it is believing in him and on him.

The Reformers laid special emphasis upon this element of faith. They were opposing the Romish view that faith is assent. It is quite consistent with Romish religion to say that faith is assent. It is the genius of the Romish conception of salvation to intrude mediators between the soul and the Saviour—the Church, the virgin, the sacraments. On the contrary, it is the glory of the gospel of God's grace that there is one mediator between God and man, the man Christ Jesus. And it was the glory of our Protestant Reformation to discover again the purity of the evangel. The Reformers recognized that the essence of saving faith is to bring the sinner lost and dead in trespasses and sins into direct personal contact with the Saviour himself, contact which is nothing less than that of self-commitment to him in all the glory of his person and perfection of his work as he is freely and fully offered in the gospel.

It is to be remembered that the efficacy of faith does not reside in itself. Faith is not something that merits the favour of God. All the efficacy unto salvation resides in the Saviour. As one has aptly and truly stated the case, it is not faith that saves but faith in Jesus Christ; strictly speaking, it is not even faith in Christ that saves but Christ that saves through faith. Faith unites us to Christ in the bonds of abiding attachment and entrustment and it is this union which insures that the saving power, grace, and virtue of the Saviour become operative in the believer. The specific character of faith is that it looks away from itself and finds its whole interest and object in Christ. He is the absorbing preoccupation of faith.

It is at the point of faith in Christ that our responsibility is engaged to the fullest extent, just as it is in the exercise of faith that our hearts and minds and wills are active to the highest degree. It is not our responsibility to regenerate ourselves. Regeneration is the action of God and God alone. It is our responsibility to be what regeneration effects. It is our responsibility to be holy. But the act of regeneration does not come within the sphere of our responsible action. Faith does. And we are never relieved of the obligation to believe in Christ to the saving of our souls. The fact that regeneration is the prerequisite of faith in no way relieves us of the responsibility to believe nor does it eliminate the priceless privilege that is ours as Christ and his claims are pressed upon us in full and free overtures of his grace. Our inability is no excuse for our unbelief nor does it provide us with any reason for not believing. As we are presented with Christ in the gospel there is no reason for the rejection of unbelief and all reason demands the entrustment of faith.

Repentance

The question has been discussed: which is prior, faith or repentance? It is an unnecessary question and the insistence that one is prior to the other futile. There is no priority. The faith that is unto salvation is a penitent faith and the repentance that is unto life is a believing repentance. Repentance is admirably defined in the Shorter Catechism. "Repentance unto life is a saving grace, whereby a sinner out of a true sense of his sin, and apprehension of the mercy of God in Christ, doth, with grief and hatred of his sin, turn from it unto God, with full purpose of, and endeavour after new obedience." The interdependence of faith and repentance can be readily seen when we remember that faith is faith in Christ for salvation from sin. But if faith is directed to salvation from sin, there must be hatred of sin and the desire to be saved from it. Such hatred of sin involves repentance which essentially consists in turning from sin unto God. Again, if we remember that repentance is turning from sin unto God, the turning to God implies faith in the mercy of God as revealed in Christ. It is impossible to disentangle faith and repentance. Saving faith is permeated with repentance and repentance is permeated with faith. Regeneration becomes vocal in our minds in the exercises of faith and repentance.

Repentance consists essentially in change of heart and mind and will. The change of heart and mind and will principally respects four things: it is a change of mind respecting God, respecting ourselves, respecting sin, and respecting righteousness. Apart from regeneration our thought of God, of ourselves, of sin, and of righteousness is radically perverted. Regeneration changes our hearts and minds; it radically renews them. Hence there is a radical change in our thinking and feeling. Old things have passed away and all things have become new. It is very important to observe that the faith which is unto salvation is the faith which is accompanied by that change of thought and attitude. Too frequently in evangelical circles and particularly in popular evangelism the momentousness of the change which faith signalizes is not understood or appreciated. There are two fallacies. The one is to put faith out of the context which alone gives it significance and the other is to think of faith in terms simply of decision and rather cheap decision at that. These fallacies are closely related and condition each other. The emphasis upon repentance and upon the deep-seated change of thought and feeling which it involves is precisely what is necessary to correct this impoverished and soul-destroying conception of faith. The nature of repentance serves to accentuate the urgency of the issues at stake in the demand of the gospel, the cleavage with sin which the acceptance of the gospel entails, and the totally new outlook which the faith of the gospel imparts.

Repentance we must not think of as consisting merely in a change of mind in general; it is very particular and concrete. And since it is a change of mind with reference to sin, it is a change of mind with reference to particular sins, sins in all the particularity and individuality which belong to our sins. It is very easy for us to speak of sin, to be very denunciatory respecting sin, and denunciatory respecting the particular sins of other people and yet not be penitent regarding our own particular sins. The test of repentance is the genuiness and resoluteness of our repentance in respect of our own sins, sins characterized by the aggravations which are peculiar to our own selves. Repentance in the case of the Thessalonians manifested itself in the fact that they turned from idols to serve the living God. It was their idolatry which peculiarly evidenced their alienation from God and it was repentance regarding that that proved the genuineness of their faith and of their hope (I Thess. 1:9, 10).

The gospel is not only that by grace are we saved through faith, but it is also the gospel of repentance. When Jesus, after his resurrection, opened the understanding of the disciples that they might understand the Scriptures, he said unto them, "Thus it is written, and thus it behooved Christ to suffer, and to rise from the dead the third day: and that repentance unto the remission of sins should be preached in his name unto all the nations" (Luke 24:46, 47). When Peter had preached to the multitude on the occasion of Pentecost and they were constrained to say, "Men and brethren, what shall we do?" Peter replied, "Repent, and be baptized every one of you in the name of Jesus Christ unto the remission of your sins" (Acts 2:37, 38). Later on, in like manner, Peter interpreted the exaltation of Christ as exaltation in the capacity of "Prince and Saviour to give repentance to Israel and forgiveness of sins" (Acts 5:31). Could anything certify more clearly that the gospel is the gospel of repentance than the fact that Jesus' heavenly ministry as Saviour is one of dispensing repentance unto the forgiveness of sins? Hence Paul, when he gave an account of his own ministry to the elders from Ephesus, said that he testified "both to the Jews and also to the Greeks repentance toward God and faith toward our Lord Jesus" (Acts 20:21). And the writer of the Epistle to the Hebrews indicates that "repentance from dead works" is one of the first principles of the doctrine of Christ (Heb. 6:1). It could not be otherwise. The new life in Christ Jesus means that the bands which bind us to the dominion of sin are broken. The believer is dead to sin by the body of Christ, the old man has been crucified that the body of sin might be destroyed, and henceforth he does not serve sin (Rom. 6:2, 6). This breach with the past registers itself in his consciousness in turning from sin unto God "with full purpose of, and endeavour after new obedience."

We see, therefore, that the emphasis which the Scripture places upon faith as the condition of salvation is not to be construed as if faith were the only condition. The various exercises or responses of our spirits have their own peculiar function. Repentance is that which describes the response of turning from sin unto God. This is its specific character just as the specific character of faith is to receive and rest upon Christ alone for salvation. Repentance reminds us that if the faith we profess is a faith that allows us to walk in the ways of this present evil world, in the lust of the flesh, the lust of the eyes, and the pride of life, in the fellowship of the works of darkness, then our faith is but mockery and deception. True faith is suffused with penitence. And just as faith is not only a momentary act but an abiding attitude of trust and confidence directed to the Saviour, so repentance results in constant contrition. The broken spirit and the contrite heart are abiding marks of the believing soul. As long as sin remains there must be the consciousness of it and this conviction of our own sinfulness will constrain self-abhorrence, confession, and the plea of forgiveness and cleansing. Christ's blood is the laver of initial cleansing but it is also the fountain to which the believer must continuously repair. It is at the cross of Christ that repentance has its beginning; it is at the cross of Christ that it must continue to pour out its heart in the tears of confession and contrition. The way of sanctification is the way of contrition for the sin of the past and of the present. The Lord forgives our sins and forgiveness is sealed by the light of his countenance; we do not forgive ourselves.

William Hordern

Faith and Reason

Twentieth-century theology has been preoccupied with the problems of theological method expressed particularly in the form of a debate about reason and faith. Liberal theologians have seen ominous dangers of irrationalism in neo-orthodoxy while the neo-orthodox have argued that the rationalism of the liberals destroys the Christian faith. Barth and Brunner, long theological allies, came to the parting of the ways over the question of what part, if any, a rational system, or natural theology, could play in Christian thought. This is no new debate in Christian history, but the modern age has given it a new urgency.

Liberalism generally has insisted that reason is vital and necessary to theology. Without reason, it is argued, we cannot judge between various claims to revelation; we are at the mercy of the first fanatic who comes along claiming to have a revelation. It is superstitious and immoral to hold a faith that does not have a rational basis. Every advance made by man has been made by the application of reason to his problems. If theology does not use reason, it can only lead to a new dark age. And so neo-orthodoxy is charged with having brought about a "religious revolt against reason."[1]

From *The Case for a New Reformation Theology,* pp. 31–52, by William Hordern. The Westminster Press. Copyright 1959, W. L. Jenkins. Used by permission.

Over against the liberals are those, often called "fideist," who have insisted that faith must be primary. Man is in no position to judge God; he is judged by God. If liberals have a rational criterion to judge revelation, they do not need revelation; the criterion is higher than revelation. A vital relationship to God demands a decision, a commitment, but reason does not end with a commitment; it ends with a conclusion. A man may rationally prove something to be true and good and still make no commitment to it. When sinful man makes reason his primary source of knowing God, he idolatrously creates God in his own image, he creates the God that he wants to worship. Reason forms its systems, sets its standards, and then demands that God fit the standards that it has erected. Instead of accepting God on God's terms, it insists upon God meeting our terms.

One reads the conflicting claims and is impressed with the convincing case that each side can make. And then it becomes clear that the two sides seldom come to grips with each other. What one side condemns as reason or faith is not what the other side extols. Therefore, if there is to be more light than heat, we must analyze carefully the meaning of the terms in order to isolate the real issues.

Reason, like many aspects of life that we deal with daily, is difficult to define precisely. Reason is the activity whereby man tries to organize, interpret, and understand his environment. It includes the use of logic, argumentation, inference, deduction, induction and so on. By reason we analyze and synthesize the elements of our experience to understand and comprehend the world.

There are many paths by which reason may arrive at understanding. There are, for example, scientific experimentation, pragmatism, the rule of logical coherence, and so on. But central to all types of reason is the drawing of conclusions by some method of logic from some set of given propositions and/or facts. It is thus the essence of reason that it implies universalism. If an argument is truly rational, it will persuade all qualified persons. Furthermore, reason in the nature of the case aims to be objective; the emotions and desires of the reasoning man must not change the conclusions to which rational thought leads.

With reason so defined, I think that it is evident that any person who thinks or who tries to communicate his thoughts must use reason. Furthermore, I know of no responsible theologian who would deny that reason is an indispensable tool of theology. Often those theologians who, like Kierkegaard, use paradox are called "irrational." But, as Martin Heinecken shows, paradox in Kierkegaard's thought depends upon reason. Paradox is the point where reason humbly confesses that God is beyond our comprehension. "It is really quite amazing why anyone should seriously object to the admission of such a possibility and should condemn it as a cult of irrationalism. . . . All that is meant is that a man should admit he is confronted with something the intellect cannot handle, and how else could he be persuaded more convincingly than by means of the absolute paradox?"[2] We may or may not accept Kierkegaard's point, but we cannot call it irrational. On the contrary, Kierkegaard has as much of a stake in reason as any liberal. If irrationalism is accepted, there is no significance in a paradox. But Kierkegaard is convinced that there is great significance in the paradoxical; so he has to take the claims of reason seriously. In short, Kierkegaard's use of paradox is a highly rational procedure; it is reason's way of pointing to the mystery of God.

I find little evidence that there is a religious revolt against reason. Barth is often charged with being a foe of reason, but Barth has never suggested that reason is not to be used as a tool in theology. Actually, one of the strongest defenses of reason in modern theology is found in Barth, who deplores the de-emphasis upon the intellect in religion.[3] And thus he argues that whatever it is, Rudolf Otto's "numinous" is not the Word of God because it is the "irrational."[4]

The question is not, Will theology use reason? but, Is a natural theology possible? Natural theology seeks a knowledge of God found without any appeal to revelation or faith. It would be a knowledge of God arrived at through appeals to evidence and logic that are available to all rational men. It is natural theology in this sense that Barth denies. But, as we shall try to show, it does not follow that because a man denies natural theology he is irrational.

Faith is more difficult to define than reason. We live in a culture that uses the term *faith* in ways that distort the Christian meaning. We commonly say that we have knowledge where we have complete evidence for something. Where we have good but not complete or irrefutable evidence, we say that we believe. And where we have little or no evidence for something, we say that we "have faith" in it. Faith thus becomes associated with the lowest grade of evidence. It is close to superstition, "woman's intuition," emotionalism, and wishful thinking.

Wherever there is this popular view of faith, a theology that builds upon faith will naturally be held in suspicion. L. H. DeWolf has defined faith as "a commitment of the will to an object not indisputably proved worthy of such commitment," or support of a judgment or belief "not indisputably proved to be true."[5] With this definition of faith, it is natural that he finds fideists to be revolting against reason, for he sees a lack of evidence as a defining principle of faith. But it is difficult to find any theologian who is building on faith in this sense.

There are actually at least three meanings of religious faith, and we should have three words to distinguish them. We might call them *credentia, fiducia, and fides.*[6] By *credentia* I mean the acceptance of propositions, information, conclusions, directions, etc., without demanding normal evidence or proof. *Credentia* is the "faith" that accepts an authoritarian rule. Protestantism has little place for *credentia*. Luther protested against the authoritarianism of the Roman church, but it was, I believe, a betrayal of the Reformation when Protestants insisted upon *credentia* in the writings of the Bible. To accept any statement because "the Bible says so" is *credentia*.

Protestantism, from Luther on, has asserted that faith is not the acceptance of unproved dogmas, but that it is *fiducia,* trust. To have faith in God is to trust God, to take him at his word. But when we trust someone, we commit ourselves. To have *fiducia* is to make a decision. This means that faith is never simply belief. Of course, faith normally includes some belief, but it cannot be identified with belief. When Paul is speaking about faith, it is quite evident that he is not preaching salvation through belief. For example, he can say, "I am crucified with Christ: nevertheless I live; yet not I, but Christ liveth in me: and the life which I now live in the flesh I live by the faith of the Son of God, who loved me, and gave himself for me" (Gal. 2:20). Paul is not speaking about belief intellectually held; he is pointing to a radical reorientation of the whole direction of life. The commitment of faith is one so radical that Paul can speak of his old self as crucified. No matter what a man may believe or know, he does not have faith until he has taken the "leap of faith" and committed his life to what is believed or known. As John Wesley put it, faith "is not barely a speculative, rational thing, a cold, lifeless assent, a train of ideas in the head; but also a disposition of the heart."[7]

But there is a further element to faith as it is used by fideist theologians. Faith also contains a cognitive element; it is not only *fiducia,* it is also *fides.* For example, Gustaf Aulén says, "Whatever else faith may say about itself, it does not say that it is some sort of subordinate knowledge, a kind of uncertain opinion about God and his work."[8] On the contrary, as Luther put it, God and faith belong together, for faith implies a relationship to God. We cannot speak about faith without being conscious of man's relationship to God. What is signified by faith is therefore a "personal fellowship between God and man."[9] When the new reformation writers speak about the primacy of faith, they do not mean the primacy of uncertain beliefs; they mean the primacy of a particular cognitive claim. Faith is a way of knowing.

Karl Barth's name usually leads all the rest when liberals are denouncing the men who have made theology irrational But this interpretation comes from reading "faith" in Barth's writings as *credentia.* An analysis of what Barth means will reveal that this is not what he is saying. For Barth the Word of God, spoken to man through the Bible, is not something to be accepted because the Bible has authority or because the church says so. On the contrary, it is accepted only because it comes with its own cognitive; claim upon us. "It comes to us as a datum."[10] That is, it is analogous to our statements about the physical world. As sensory data are cognitive raw material, so is faith. Faith is a cognitive relationship to a reality beyond ourselves. This is why, although the Reformers emphasized faith as trust or decision, they also affirmed that faith is a gift. In faith man makes his decision, but he does it in the light of something given to him; he is confronted; he is gripped by that to which he commits himself.

It is significant that Barth insists that this knowledge which comes through faith must immediately be examined by reason. "It would not be a serious awareness of this reality were it not immediately to turn to understanding also."[11] Barth further clarifies his concept of reason and faith when he says, "If we would or could merely be aware without wanting to understand, merely let ourselves be told without also telling ourselves what had been told, merely have faith without knowledge, it certainly would not be God's revelation with which we had to do.'"[12] In short, Barth does not call us to swallow some set of doctrines or conclusions. He witnesses to the fact that God is made known to man through faith. And this faith immediately moves man to seek understanding. Reason does not produce the faith, but reason is necessary to comprehend what has been disclosed. This is no more irrational than is the scientist who begins with his sensory perceptions, accepts them as objective, and then seeks to understand them.

There is a reason for the misunderstanding of those called fideist. From Luther to Barth we find such men often making sharp attacks upon "reason." Reason is referred to as a "whore," and faith is extolled because it takes reason by the throat and strangles the beast. Such language often leaves the impression that these men are calling us to the deathbed of all rational thought. If our aim is simply to get rid of them by branding them as irrational, we can find plenty of quotes for our ammunition. But if we really desire to come to grips with what they are saying, we must see their words in context. None of them has argued for a theology without reason.

What those called fideist have been denying is that man has, within himself and his material world, the means whereby he can build a ladder from earth to heaven and gain some knowledge of God. They claim that our knowledge of God must come from God himself. This is why faith must have its cognitive element. Knowledge of God has to be given to us, for we never possess this within ourselves. We do not find God as a thing within the physical world, because God is not a thing. God is the Lord and he is the Creator; he is not, therefore, to be found as a part of this world, nor is he to be inferred from it. In other words, if God is not found at the beginning of our process of reasoning, he cannot be dragged in at the conclusion as an inference from something less than himself.

The natural theologian, whether Thomist or Protestant, usually believes that the finite world can give us some clue to God. There is an analogy between the cause and the effect. By examining the world (i.e., the effect) we can reason analogously to the cause (God). This method, often referred to as the *analogia entis* (analogy of being), runs into difficulties. Logic tells us that we can prove nothing by analogy.[13] To be persuasive an analogy must be based on considerable knowledge of both sides of the analogy. We cannot say that because every event in the universe has a cause, so the universe must have a cause, for we do not know whether the universe is an "effect." If we had several universes and each of them had a cause, we could argue by analogy that this universe also has a cause. But when we have only one universe, we have no way of knowing whether or not it needs a cause. Similarly, we cannot say that all designs have designers, the universe is a design, therefore it has a designer; for, as Hume showed in his *Dialogues Concerning Natural Religion,* we can explain the universe as well if we assume that it is a vegetable or an animal as we can by assuming that it is a design. In short, if we have no knowledge of God when we begin, analogy cannot give us any knowledge about him.

Therefore, Barth has suggested that we need to use the analogy of faith. That is, only after God reveals himself can man speak analogously about God because only then does he know what kind of analogy will fit. This is an attack upon reason only in the sense that it recognizes the limits of reason. Reason can deal only with that which is given to it, and therefore it cannot speak about God until he has given himself to it. Unless reason is illuminated from God's side, it cannot get to God.

The natural theologian is disposed to boast that he lays a rational foundation under his religion; he is not like the fideist who superstitiously begins with faith. But this claim must be taken with a grain of salt. If the analytic philosopher is right, it is the natural theologian who commits the greatest crime against reason. Any rational arguments that he uses to establish belief in God are found to be not only illogical but also nonsensical.[14] This may not be a final disproof of natural theology, but it is strange, to say the least, that the philosophical theologian's arguments are declared unphilosophical by capable philosophers. This is not analogous to two scientists disagreeing about the effects to be expected from atomic radiation. This is as if one of the scientists in the dispute were denying the ability of science to deal with the question. In this situation it seems dubious that the philosophical theologian can claim to be more rational than the fideist.

We do not escape this dilemma by doing as Tillich does. He grants the philosopher that we cannot prove God's existence, but he tries to restore a natural theology through an "ontological analysis." But renaming metaphysics and calling it ontology does not satisfy the philosopher. He still finds Tillich guilty of logical confusion.

What do we make of this situation? We can try to outargue the analytic philosopher, although personally I find the natural theologian's replies unconvincing. Or we can, as most natural theologians are doing, ignore analytic philosophy, but that is the very obscurantism that the natural theologian condemns in others. Or we may say that the analytic philosopher works with presuppositions that we do not accept. But what does this mean? It means that the faith from which one begins to reason predetermines the outcome. The natural theologian must then admit that he begins with a faith, and only if you accept his faith, can you come to his conclusions. He is not so different from the fideist as he has pretended to be.

Even if one does not accept the arguments of the analytic philosopher, his very existence proves an important point. The natural theologian's reason is incapable of persuading all rational men. In fact, he fails to make them see that there is even a sensible argument to be discussed. What can we conclude but that something more than reason is involved in this? As I shall try to show, the problem is not that we all can reason to some point and then some may go on in faith and some may not. The situation is that every act of reason is an act performed in the light of a faith. The natural theologian, no less than Barth or the analytic philosopher, begins with faith.

The position that I wish to defend is that reason and faith cannot be separated any more than the modern physicist can separate space and time. Of course, for the purpose of analysis, we can distinguish between them, but in a living situation they are never to be found apart. Every act of faith is an act that only a rational creature could make, and hence involves reason. But every act of reasoning involves an act of faith. Reason and faith are not exclusive principles between which we must choose; they are aspects of life that go hand in hand.

This position, often called Augustinian, is expressed by the slogans, "Faith seeking understanding" and "I have faith in order that I may know." These slogans show the intimate relation of reason and faith. They recognize the presence of faith in every act of knowing, and they see that it is of the nature of faith to seek understanding.

To say, "I have faith in order that I may know," is to argue that every act of reasoning is preceded or accompanied by an act of faith. In our context this is to say that reason presupposes a cognitive experience which leads to an act of trustful decision. Since the days of Thomas Aquinas it has been widely held that we can start thinking with reason alone. The religious rationalist has argued, therefore, that we ought to go as far as reason can take us in gaining knowledge about God. After we have done this, it is then rational to go on with faith and accept what has not been proved by reason, although even here one should aim to keep his faith in harmony with the findings of reason. Thus Aquinas believed that reason alone can prove God exists but it is only by faith, accepting revelation, that we can know that God exists as a Trinity. Liberal theology generally has taken the attitude that reason comes first and that we are justified in having faith only after reason reaches its limits. It is our thesis that this is a mistaken conception.

If faith comes after reason, then it inevitably has an element of *credentia,* and is distinguished from the findings of reason by the fact that it lacks the degree of verification that reason gives. But it is our thesis that faith as cognition, trust, and commitment comes not after but before and with reason. It is the prerational framework within which reason operates. It is not a conclusion lacking verification; it is the frame of reference which decides what the criteria are that will verify. It is the presupposition of all verification. So considered, it is not true, as often claimed, that the Christian operates on faith and the atheist does not. Before discussing the nature of Christian faith, therefore, I shall try to indicate how a faith element operates in all reasoning.

A mathematician, Frank De Sua, writes:

> Suppose we loosely define a *religion* as any discipline whose foundations rest on an element of faith, irrespective of any element of reason which may be present. Quantum mechanics, for example, would be a religion under this definition. But mathematics would hold the unique position of being the only branch of theology possessing a rigorous demonstration of the fact that it should be so classified.[15]

And it is a philosopher, Victor Kraft, who says:

> If we regard a proposition about a repeatedly tested state of affairs as indubitable, this is because we presuppose that things have not changed in the meantime, that there is uniformity in the world, i.e., that there are laws in the world. But this presupposition itself cannot be known to be true with certainty. . . . That the unexpected will not happen, we cannot know for certain. It is an article of faith, so firm that we even risk our life on it, but it is not a proposition that could be proved.[16]

In other words, even the most rigorously rational enterprises—mathematics, science, and philosophy—begin their reasoning in the light of a faith. All of their proofs rest finally in a frame of reference that cannot be proved.

It might be objected that while no doubt science and mathematics make presuppositions, they hardly need "faith" in the way in which we have defined it. But I think that we can argue that this is at least analogous to the operation of Christian faith, viewed from its human side. The scientist begins with a basic trustful commitment of the self. The scientist is committed to the premise that it is possible and that it is good to treat the world rationally. If someone objects to the whole scientific enterprise by saying, "Where ignorance is bliss, 'tis folly to be wise." there is no scientific answer. The objector has denied the relevance of anything that science could say. And in an age of hydrogen bombs and the displacement of men and honored occupations by mechanisms, in the hustle, rush, and anxiety of modern life with its increase of mental disturbance over that of primitive societies, it can hardly be claimed to be self-evident that science is valuable. The scientist must work with a faith-commitment to the value of science whether the faith be explicit or implicit. But the commitment does not end here. A philosopher, Richard Von Mises reminds us that every act of induction, so central to the reasoning of the scientist, involves an act of personal decision.[17]

Central to Augustine's concept of reason was his conviction that the will is prior to knowledge. "Before I can know, I must will to know." The terminology is somewhat dated, but, as John Hutchison has suggested, what philosophers traditionally have called the "will" might be called "the active or functioning unity of the human self."[18] That is, the self does make decisions, and whatever this decision-making power is, that is what Augustine meant by the "will." Today we are inclined to believe that the whole of a human person is involved in his decisions—his reason, emotions, and all other aspects of his being. Reasoning is always the act of a self, and it is, therefore, dependent upon the decision of the thinker.

The function of the "will" is evident to anyone who has been in a classroom. The correlation between achievement and native intelligence is far from complete, because motivation plays an important part in any process of learning or thinking. If a man has no will to know something, he will not bother to think about it.

The modern world has made a great deal of "objectivity," the position of detachment from which the learner must approach knowledge. The objective man is one who has no prior commitments, who does not allow his wishes to affect his conclusions; he simply "lets the facts speak for themselves." This is seen as the ideal of the scientist, and it is argued that it should be the ideal for all scholarship. Because of this, one often hears college students arguing that an atheist would be a more objective professor of religion than a Christian because the Christian already has committed himself to a religion while the atheist is "unbiased." But if Augustine is right, and experience seems to prove that he is, this is a naïve view.

In any subject matter a man must be committed in the sense that he is sufficiently attracted by the subject matter to commit himself to studying it; he wills to know. Thus we hear the scientist praised in one breath as the great example of objectivity, and in the next breath he is hailed for his noble dedication (i.e., commitment) to science. If an atheist were really uncommitted in religion, he could not have enough interest in the subject to know it. To say that such a man should teach religion is like saying that a witch doctor should teach physics because he has made no commitment to any of the theories of modern physicists. On the other hand, if the atheist is committed to religion, so that he has willed to know it, then he cannot be judged a priori to have any less "bias" than the Christian. One man is committed to atheism, the other man to Christianity. Either or neither may be a good teacher of religion.

In the light of what has been said, it is well to take a further look at the popular cry of "let the facts speak for themselves." It is obvious that the one thing facts cannot do is speak for themselves. Facts have to be interpreted and understood, for knowledge is never a simple snapshot of reality; it is always an interpretation. But an interpretation implies that one has a frame of reference, a basic perspective, within which he interprets the facts. I once heard a scientist say that science has countless facts to which it pays no attention because it has no frame of reference in which they can be interpreted. It is interesting to note that he said this during a discussion of the many facts claimed by various forms of psychic research. Because such facts do not fit into the frame of reference with which the scientist operates, he ignores them.

G. K. Chesterton, in his vivid manner of speaking, insists that it is quite wrong to say that the madman has lost his reason; he has lost everything but his reason. This recalls the classic story of the psychiatrist's patient who thought that he was dead. The psychiatrist told him, "You know that dead men do not bleed, don't you?" The man agreed, so the psychiatrist triumphantly pricked the man's finger, and as the man watched the blood come, he shook his head in bewilderment and said: "What do you know? Dead men do bleed!" The man's reason was perfect; it was his frame of reference that was defective. Hume demonstrated that our thinking about the world always operates within the framework of certain basic perspectives about the nature of causality, the external world, the unity of the self, and so on. Reason does not establish these; they are the basic framework within which reason works; if a man denies them, there are no arguments by which they can be established. In other words, when the facts speak for themselves, what they say depends upon the frame of reference within which they "speak" as well as what the facts actually are.[19]

Another annoying aspect of facts is that, as E. T. Ramsdell has made so clear, they do not come before us with marks to denote their relative significance.[20] One set of facts points to conclusion A and another set to conclusion B, but which is the more significant? The facts cannot decide that; we must make a decision and we make it in the light of our frame of reference. This judgment of relative significance plays a crucial part in all thinking. We tend to perceive and to remember only those things which we deem significant (a fact that causes much trouble between men and their wives). And consequently, the varying interpretations of the same set of facts is most often the result of differing estimates of their relative significance.

This is why the cult of objectivity in education can be dangerous. When a teacher prides himself upon objectivity, he hides both from himself and others the frame of reference within which he approaches the facts and by which he selects the facts that seem to be significant. As a result, he gives his findings an aura of finality that they do not deserve. The danger is that the student will accept his teacher's prejudices because they seem to be the necessary result of rational thought. This is why I believe that the most truly objective teaching can occur only where the professor honestly confesses the frame of reference to which he is committed. Having done this, he should try to present as sympathetically as possible all opposing positions. But because his students know his frame of reference, they can guard against the inevitable bias that will appear.

In short, instead of being impossible where there is a faith-commitment, objectivity is possible only where a faith-commitment is made to objectivity. Objectivity is never a matter of reason alone; it requires a moral decision on the part of the self. It is the good man rather than the brilliant thinker who can achieve it in the highest degree. But the man who claims that his thinking is purely objective, that he has no frame of reference, or who claims that he has the only possible frame of reference—this man is simply demanding that his frame of reference and evaluation of relative significance must be adopted by all men who are to think. This is why the most prejudiced thinking is quite frequently dressed up in the robes of objectivity. This is also why the self-styled "rationalist" often holds his religious beliefs in the most dogmatic fashion.

If so much depends upon a man's will and his frame of reference, what do they depend upon in their turn? Obviously they are grounded upon the whole experience of a man's life. Ramsdell says, "Reasoning never occurs in the abstract. It is always the activity of an individual mind. It can never be separated from the crucial experience of a particular living person. . . . What we evaluate as meaningful is inextricably bound up with our total life as persons."[21] We all have had the experience of disliking some subject although we had heard many arguments why it was important for us. Then one day we were fortunate enough to have a teacher who made the subject live for us. Suddenly our wills were motivated; we longed to know.

It was not that the facts of the subject matter were changed. We still needed to sit down as a little child before the facts, but the perspective from which we viewed them was changed and their significance for us was completely new. We looked at the old subject matter in a new light because we had been confronted by something that we had missed before. It was not the result of a logical argument; it was, rather that the facts "gripped" us in a new manner. This experience, common to most men, provides an analogy to what I have called the *fides* element in religious faith. The religious man witnesses that certain facts, overlooked as insignificant by the irreligious, have gripped him; he has been confronted by a new significance in them.

In other words, reason is never productive by itself, for experience in some sense must precede reason. We cannot reason about the Christian faith, for example, until the Christian faith has been given to us to reason about. This may sound so obvious that it appears to be trivial, but precisely because it is so obvious it is often overlooked. Reason does not start from scratch and work out its systems by pure logic. Every line of reasoning presupposes the total experience of the person who is reasoning; it works in direct correlation with what life has presented to us and with what has impressed us as being significant.

What we have been saying about the reasoning process is true, I believe, for all types of thought. But it is obviously more important for thinking in some fields than in others. In some areas the frame of reference is of minimum importance, since there may be no serious alternatives. This is most likely to be the case in mathematics and the natural sciences, where man is not so crucially involved in the subject matter. But certainly as we move into the social sciences and the humanities, a man's frame of reference becomes more and more crucial, and his abstract arguments will have less and less persuasive power. It is an obvious fact that a man's environment, profession, and personal experience play a large role in his political decisions. When, however, we come to the religious questions of life, we are dealing with a man's ultimate frame of reference, his ultimate criteria of what makes life significant and meaningful. At this level the role played by the frame of reference is most crucial.

In forming a religion, or one's ultimate relationship to life, no facts can be eliminated, for all are potentially relevant. But obviously all cannot be dealt with equally; a decision must be made as to their relative significance. The philosophy or religion by which a man lives can never be the simple result of letting facts speak for themselves; it is, on the contrary, the principle by which he chooses and selects the facts that are considered significant.

The attempts to prove God's existence illustrate our point. The various "proofs" have been argued from both sides *ad infinitum* but they seldom persuade anyone. It is not difficult to see why this is the case. We must look to the whole of reality to decide our question. But within the totality of reality we find many facts. The theist accepts the teleological argument because he finds that the facts showing order in the universe are the most significant. But the skeptic points to the facts of disorder and they seem more significant to him. No appeal to the facts can solve this dilemma, for both sets of facts are equally real. The question is, Which are the more significant? The theist may turn to religious experience to prove God because he finds such experience the most important and significant fact in his life. But the skeptic rejects the argument because the appeal is to "subjective" experience and the unbeliever's frame of reference is such that he believes that only facts that are open to public observation are significant. Again no facts can decide, for what is at stake is not the facts. The unbeliever will concede that the believer has probably had some deep personal experience. What is at stake is the frame of reference that decides which facts are significant. If the unbeliever were to have the believer's experience, he might change his opinion, but no argument alone can change it.

In short, the very idea of proving God presupposes that there is some common neutral arena into which believer and unbeliever alike can come to settle the question rationally. But each man comes wearing his particular set of spectacles that colors everything that he sees. This is why increasingly those philosophers of religion who still consider the proofs of God as important see their importance not as arguments, but as analyzing what we mean when we speak about God. They cannot establish faith in God; they explicate what it involves.

J. C. Smart says that if someone asks, "Do electrons exist?" the question is meaningless by itself. In order to answer it you need a lot of experience with physics, experiments, cathode-ray tubes, and so on. When we get this experience, we find that the concept of electrons is a useful and indispensable item in physical theory. At this stage the question of whether electrons exist no longer rises. Before this, it is a meaningless question. From this Smart concludes:

> Similarly, I suggest the question "Does God exist?" has no clear meaning for the unconverted. But for the converted the question no longer arises. . . . Within religion the question "Does God exist?" does not arise any more than the question "Do electrons exist?" arises within physics. Outside religion the question "Does God exist?" has as little meaning as the question "Do electrons exist?" as asked by the scientifically ignorant.[22]

In other words, a man can raise the question of God's existence only from out of the context of his whole life and experience. The man who has been confronted by God in the context of the Christian church and its revelation cannot pretend that he does not bring this experience with him to any discussion of God, for it is precisely this experience which has formed his view of what is ultimately significant in life. On the other hand, the unbeliever cannot pretend that he comes to the debate apart from the context of his life in which he has made his ultimate faith commitment to an other than God.

There is further implication in Smart's point. Because of the different experience from which men come, the "God" discussed in a philosophical debate is not necessarily the God of faith. In many a philosophical discussion of God, the Christian feels like Mary before the tomb: "They have taken away my Lord, and I know not where they have laid him." What does the First Cause, the Absolute, the abstract God of speculation, have to do with him "who so loved the world, that he gave his only begotten Son"? This is why Pascal called upon the God of Abraham, Isaac, and Jacob, the God who revealed himself in the life of a historical community, not the God of the philosophers. Paul Tillich has argued that the God of the philosophers is the same as the God of the prophets, but Will Herberg counters very effectively by simply asking, "Which philosophers?"[23] It may be that philosophers who have the Judaeo-Christian God in their experience are speaking about Abraham's God, but to say that all philosophers are doing so is to ignore the realities.

An analogy may help to make our point. I recall a picture that appears to be a black-and-white landscape, but you are told that, when rightly seen, it is a portrait of Christ. So you sit looking at the picture and feeling sillier and sillier as someone says, "Look, here are his eyes and his mouth," but still you cannot see it. Then suddenly something comes into focus and the portrait of Jesus stands out clearly, and you wonder at your stupidity in not seeing it before. You see the lines as before, but the whole perspective and the significance of the lines have changed. The *Gestalt* is completely different.

This illustration is symbolic of what Christianity itself is like. The first disciples knew Jesus the man; they met in him a new and moving experience. Then suddenly their eyes were opened and they saw, with Peter, "Thou art the Christ, the Son of the living God." The facts were not materially different for Peter than they were for Caiaphas, but Peter's perspective enabled him to see what Caiaphas' perspective forced him to miss. This was the point that the Reformers made. We do not become Christians because our reason has been persuaded by a brilliant argument. Rather, we are "converted"; in the experience of life a light breaks and we see what we did not see; we are no longer blind. And just as I was not aware of doing anything when the portrait of Christ came into focus, so Luther and Calvin affirmed that faith is a gift. That is, something happens to us in the light of which faith is born.

Man finds himself in a universe that bombards him with experience. At an early date he begins to find significance in these experiences; they are saying something to him. He begins the mysterious process of coming to know. No one does, or can, pay attention to everything that comes to him as experiential raw material; he begins to interpret and select his experience in terms of relative significance. We can see this by comparing the sensitivities of a primitive man and a civilized man. Their potentialities are so developed that in the face of the same experiential raw material they will see, hear, smell, and think about different things.

In the process of coming to know his world, man begins to develop his frame of reference, his judgments of relative significance. Certain things grip him; to him they seem ultimately significant, and so he trusts them, he commits his life to them, he has a faith. Reason does not establish this faith; on the contrary, this is what gives a light to his reason. This faith may be implicit or it may be explicitly developed. But life has to be lived and this means that the faith must enable one to live meaningfully, and so it has to seek understanding.

When a faith seeks understanding, it may fail. It may be unable to incorporate a man's experience meaningfully within its framework. When this occurs it becomes increasingly difficult to live by the faith, and two things may happen. A man may close his eyes to more and more of the facts of his life and live by just those facts which his faith can comprehend. Or he may undergo the costly and difficult decision to change his faith. He is converted.

Many theological rationalists argue that we must test all beliefs in terms of whether they fit together coherently with each other and with experience. That system is most likely to be true which is the most comprehensively coherent. Of course, in one sense the test of coherence is a tautology; to think means to think coherently; there is no other way of thinking. But as an ultimate test of truth, coherence runs into a practical difficulty. When a man faces a fact that does not fit coherently into his preconceptions, he can do one of two things: he can deny the significance of the new fact and ignore it as the scientist ignores the findings of psychic research, or he can change his preconceptions so that the new fact will be contained coherently. But which he does cannot be decided by the claims of coherence, for both alternatives result in a coherent system. Which he does will depend upon his will, his decision, and his *fides* experience.

The point, of course, is that a man's faith succeeds or fails, not in the forming of a coherent system of thought, but in the living of life. Our position is existential in that it sees that man's faith is something that must be lived and that comes out of life. Religion is never worked out like a syllogism of logic; it is hammered out in the experiences of life; it is a matter of life and death. It is the perspective from which we view life, in the light of which we make our decisions, and by which we live. It is when a faith fails at this level that it is abandoned. Several former communists wrote a book with the suggestive title *The God That Failed*. The "God" in this case was the communist faith. Here we get case studies in what happens when a man changes his ultimate philosophy of life; he finds that in the task of living his god has failed him. Instead of illuminating his life, his ultimate faith becomes itself a major problem.

There are many ways in which a "god" may fail a man, but generally speaking it occurs when experience causes a man to see a new significance in certain facts. We sometimes sneer at the way in which people turn to religion when death or disaster strikes. We called it "foxhole" religion a few years ago. Of course it may be shallow, but it is not necessarily so. Many persons can live with their faith until they experience tragedy for themselves. At that point their faith is revealed to be inadequate. We have always known that tragedy is a part of life, but now it is *my* tragedy, and the perspective by which one lives is put to a crucial test. And there is no simple logic here—the tragedy that brings one man to God will drive another man away.

But it is not only tragedy, for the joys of life can also bring a man to see that his faith cannot find understanding. Sometimes it is falling in love, having a child, meeting a new appreciation of beauty and joy, which changes our faith. In short, there are many experiences of life that can disrupt a man's frame of reference, but it is doubtful that any ultimate frame of reference can be undermined except by life itself.

It is not unusual, however, for a man's "god" to fail without the man's recognizing that this has happened. He goes on living his life and hiding his eyes from realities that face him. It is here that a negative apologetic can be useful. Many twentieth-century men were living by the faith that society was continually progressing. This was their basic frame of reference in the light of which they saw the significance of all facts. The twentieth century's history made this faith more and more difficult to square with the facts. But many continued living by the faith until Reinhold Niebuhr's apologetic drove home to them the incongruity between their faith and their life. Of course, even here, the rational argument has its limits; the man may still argue that the twentieth century's ills are but the birth pangs of the new era of utopia. But the facts of life along with the critique may lead a man to adopt a new perspective.

This explains why we "witness" to our faith. We do not have iron-clad proof and we cannot assure a man of the truth of a religious faith, but we witness to it. We try to show him how life looks and is lived from the perspective of our faith, and then we invite him to take his "leap of faith" and to stand where we stand. We have to have enough confidence in our faith to believe that if a man does that, he too will come to see its truth.

One of the main reasons that we cannot prove the truth of the Christian faith to the man outside is, of course, that his criteria of judgment have to be changed. Accepting Christianity brings a radical change in a man's set of values. Things that were formerly thought to be valuable and significant are now seen as worthless (Phil. 3:7, 8). But until this change has occurred, it is difficult to persuade the man that Christianity is superior to his present frame of reference. To the man whose first allegiance is to economic success, the acid question is, Will it make me more wealthy? To the man who worships pleasure, the acid test is, Will I have more fun? The man who worships science will want to know what scientific problems a Christian faith can help to solve. And so each man from his particular perspective scans the Christian faith and asks if it can meet his present wishes, desires, and evaluations of significance. This creates a serious temptation to the Christian, and today there are many who are ready to give a glib "yes" to such questions. Become a Christian, we are told, you will be happy, healthy, wealthy, popular; you will have peace of mind and serene security. In short, man is promised that Christianity will give him everything that he has wanted most as an unbeliever. But it is impossible to verify one frame of reference by the criteria of an alien frame of reference, and the attempt to do so can only lead to disillusionment.

In summary, we have argued that faith implies both *fides,* a cognitive relationship, and *fiducia,* a trustful decision to commit oneself. Faith, so defined, naturally seeks understanding, and so it reasons. The Christian faith is not something that goes beyond what reason attains; it is a perspective within which reason works. All reasoning operates on the basis of a cognitive relationship to reality out of which is formed a perspective, a frame of reference, by which the relative significance of facts is judged. On the basis of this perspective a man makes his trustful commitment; he wills to know. As Ramsdell has put it:

> It is not a matter of rationality but of the perspective of rationality. It is never, at bottom, a matter of the opposition between faith and reason but rather between the faiths which define the divergent perspectives of reason. The natural man is no less certainly a man of faith than the spiritual, but his faith is in the ultimacy of something other than the Word of God. The spiritual man is no less certainly a man of reason than the natural, but his reason, like that of every man, functions within the perspective of his faith.[24]

Notes

[1]See L. Harold DeWolf, *The Religious Revolt Against Reason.* Harper & Brothers, 1949.

[2]M. J. Heinecken, *The Moment Before God,* pp. 41–42. Muhlenberg Press, 1956.

[3]K. Barth, *Church Dogmatics,* Vol. I, Pt. 1, pp. 231ff.

[4]*Ibid.,* p. 153.

[5]L. Harold DeWolf, *A Theology of the Living Church,* p. 37. Harper & Brothers, 1953.

[6]There is an obvious similarity between my terms and the scholastic distinction of *notitia, fiducia,* and *assensus.* But the differences are so significant that I prefer to use somewhat different terms.

[7]E. H. Sugden, editor, *Standard Sermons of John Wesley,* Vol. I, p. 40. Epworth Press, London, n.d.

[8]Gustaf Aulén, *The Faith of the Christian Church,* p. 23. Muhlenberg Press, 1948.

[9]*Ibid.,* p. 24.

[10]K. Barth, *Church Dogmatics,* Vol. I, Pt. 2, tr. by G. T. Thomson and H. Knight, p. 172. Charles Scribner's Sons, 1956.

[11]*Ibid.,* p. 26.

[12]*Ibid.*

[13]E.g., see M. C. Beardsley, *Practical Logic,* pp. 105–112. Prentice-Hall, Inc., 1950.

[14]E.g., see J. Hospers, *An Introduction to Philosophical Analysis,* pp. 359–365. Prentice-Hall, Inc., 1953.

[15]F. De Sua, "Consistency and Completeness," *The American Mathematical Monthly,* Vol. 63, No. 15, p. 305. May, 1956.

[16]Victor Kraft, *The Vienna Circle,* pp. 143–144. Philosophical Library, Inc., 1953.

[17]Richard Von Mises, *Positivism: A Study in Human Understanding,* p. 142. George Braziller, Inc., 1956.

[18]John Hutchison, *Faith, Reason, and Existence,* p. 106. Oxford University Press, 1956.

[19]R. M. Hare has argued this point half humorously in terms of what he calls a man's "blik." See Flew and MacIntyre, editors, *New Essays in Philosophical Theology,* pp. 99–103. The Macmillan Company, 1955.

[20]Edward T. Ramsdell, *The Christian Perspective,* pp. 23ff. Abingdon Press, 1950.

[21]*Ibid.,* p. 31.

[22]Flew and MacIntyre, *op. cit.,* p. 41.

[23]Will Herberg, "Can Faith and Reason Be Reconciled?" *New Republic,* Vol. 133, No. 17, p. 19. October 24, 1955.

[24]E. T. Ramsdell, *op. cit.,* p. 42.

Edward Carnell

Faith

Faith is the capacity of belief or trust. This capacity relieves the mind of a critical desire to reassess the grounds of settled judgment. Samuel Johnson observes that of an opinion that is no longer doubted, the evidences cease to be examined. When we believe in a product, we buy it with confidence. When we trust a person, we yield ourselves in fellowship.

Orderly conduct traces to a settled judgment. For example, a businessman gets off a commuter train and walks home. His conduct is orderly because his mind rests in the sufficiency of the evidences. He does not continually inquire: "Am I dreaming? Is sense perception reliable? Can I prove that I exist?" Hardly. He opens the door and greets his wife and family without demanding fresh proof that they *are* his wife and family. A wise man is critical about many things but not all things. He does not believe contradictions, and he does not trust a fool. But he forthrightly believes whenever he confronts sufficient evidences. He is wise because he knows when to believe and when not to believe. He has faith.

From *The Case for Orthodox Theology,* pp. 23–32, by Edward John Carnell. The Westminster Press. Copyright 1959, W. L. Jenkins. Used by permission.

The Psychological Basis of Faith

The capacity of belief or trust belongs to man as man. It is not necessarily a religious virtue. Suppose we are walking along a beach when suddenly we observe movement on the horizon. Another person is coming. We discover that this person is our friend Paul. A state of confidence is born. This state continues as long as the mind is satisfied with the sufficiency of the evidences. And by "mind" I do not mean bare rational assent. I mean the whole man in a responsible act of judgment.

Zealots often contend that faith requires a leap of the will or a risk of the intellect. Orthodoxy repudiates this in the name of both common sense and revelation. To believe on insufficient evidence—what is this but to believe what may not be true?

People make mistakes when they believe. They may even want something so badly that passion creates its own evidences. Reprehensible though these habits are, they nonetheless fall within the pale of man's general effort to conform the self to things as they are. But when a person *acknowledges* the deficiency of evidences and yet goes right on believing, he defends a position that is large with the elements of its own destruction. Any brand of inanity can be justified on such a principle.

Theologians speak a great deal about faith, but they do not always speak accurately. For example, Thomas Aquinas drew a sharp line between faith and knowledge. "Now, as was stated above, it is impossible that one and the same thing should be believed and seen by the same person. Hence it is equally impossible for one and the same thing to be an object of science and of belief for the same person."[1] This distinction overlooks the fact that all belief rests on authority. The authority can be direct or indirect. I may say, "I believe there is an ocean because I am standing in it" or "I believe the law of relativity because I have reviewed its mathematics." These illustrate *direct* authority—direct because the object, in each case, is immediately confronted. On another occasion I may say, "My doctor tells me I have a tumor" or "I see by this schedule that the train leaves at four." These illustrate *indirect* authority—indirect because a mediator stands between the object and my judgment. But this mediation in no way alters the axiom that all belief rests on authority. And what else is authority if not the power of sufficient evidences to elicit assent?

Protestant theologians frequently echo the Thomistic error. For example, Abraham Kuyper says, "By faith you are sure of all those things of which you have a *firm conviction,* but which conviction is *not* the outcome of observation or demonstration."[2] Kuyper forgets that the ground of belief is the sufficiency, not the kind or source, of evidence. Sometimes this sufficiency rises to demonstration—as in logic, mathematics, and geometry. In other cases it does not. A man of faith will not accept Euclid's propositions unless he confronts perfect demonstration. But he will accept the reality of pain on the testimony of a crushed finger.

Aristotle observed that an ability to decide what degree of precision may fairly be expected in any inquiry is the mark of an educated man. An educated man consults a physician, not a plumber, when he is ill; and when he consults a physician, he knows on what balance of evidence to believe. He expects sufficient evidence, but not mathematical demonstration.

The Moral Quality in Faith

Although faith traces to a satisfied judgment, a state of faith is not induced by the sheer display of sufficient evidences; for personal interest may build a protective wall around the intellect. Don Quixote is the literary symbol of this eventuality. When Sancho chided him for thinking that river mills were castles, Quixote was incensed at the effrontery of his squire. "Hold thy peace, Sancho," said Don Quixote; "though they look like mills they are not so; I have already told thee that enchantments transform things and change their proper shapes; I do not mean to say they really change them from one form to another, but that it seems as though they did, as experience proved in the transformation of Dulcinea, sole refuge of my hopes."

Every man has some sort of faith, for faith is the ground of orderly conduct. Even Quixote could distinguish between bread and sand at lunch time. Sancho often admired the sagacity of his master. Quixote's difficulty was that he failed to take this sagacity into the wider, and more critical, areas of life. He passed trivial tests, while failing the important.

As we move from formal truth (Two and two are four) to material truth (Is gambling wrong?), the threat of prejudice intensifies and the likelihood of dispassionate judgment abates. We often see what we prefer to see. Christian Science is an instructive example of this. A very precise objectivity goes into *The Christian Science Monitor*. The excellence of this paper is acclaimed by men of the fourth estate everywhere. But Christian Scientists cannot impartially judge evil, for they have surrendered their judgment to Mary Baker Eddy. When confronted with the most frightful cases of suffering, they reply, "Pain and death have no reality; they are errors of the material sense." It may be pleasant to believe that pain and death are errors of the material sense, but the cruel lines of reality are in no way changed by religious presuppositions.

Prejudice creeps in when we least suspect it. Samuel Johnson observed this with unusual candor. In his celebrated essay on Richard Savage he notes, "But this is only an instance of that partiality which almost every man indulges with regard to himself; the liberty of the press is a blessing when we are inclined to write against others, and a calamity when we find ourselves overborne by the multitude of our assailants; as the power of the crown is always thought too great by those who suffer by its influence, and too little by those in whose favor it is exerted; and a standing army is generally accounted necessary by those who command, and dangerous and oppressive by those who support it." No one can defeat the threat of prejudice unless he comes to himself and acknowledges the threat, and especially the manner in which the threat tinctures his own judgments. A man of faith is a man of character, and character implies a spiritual willingness to be honest before the facts. Pride says, "Believe what is congenial with personal interest." Honesty says, "Believe things as they are." Faithless men play fast and loose with evidences; their testimony is inadmissible. The rational life cannot get on with it unless the moral life is firm.

Jesus illustrated this by the native innocence of a child. "And calling to him a child, he put him in the midst of them, and said, 'Truly, I say to you, unless you turn and become like children, you will never enter the kingdom of heaven'" (Matt. 18:2, 3). Prejudice does not corrupt the child's judgment; the true voice of reality is heard. The symbol of childhood is imperfect, of course, for the powers of prejudice are inchoate. But the symbol is useful, for we can become *like* a child. We can be honest in our approach to reality, and honest in conforming ourselves to it.

A child is a friend of common sense. He expects evidence, but not unreasonable evidence. He believes that the road to the park is uphill, but not uphill on the way back too. He believes in fairies, but not in *foolish* fairies. Even the preternatural world must conform to the limits of common sense.

Since a child stays in tune with life, he grasps things that often elude the wise of this world. (*a*) A child knows what truth is. Truth represents things as they are. If a child has taken cookies, but says he has not, he lies. And he knows it. His word does not conform to reality. (*b*) A child knows what goodness is. A good man is kind and thoughtful; a bad man is not. A child knows that love is the law of life, for he has experienced both the joys and the duty of love. (*c*) A child knows what beauty is. He can tell when his mother looks especially pretty. Excessive analysis does not corrupt his aesthetic intuitions. A cat is nice; so is a leaf.

Adults have more exacting standards than children; and between adults, according to the capacity of the mind, standards will differ. Boswell said that Johnson required more evidences because of his increased capacity. "He was only *willing* to believe; I *do* believe. The evidence is enough for me, though not for his great mind. What will not fill a quart bottle will fill a pint bottle."

But this observation in no way depresses the force of Christ's counsel that we must become like little children. Great minds and little children have important things in common. They are friends of general wisdom; they proportion their expectations to the nature of reality before them; they stay with the true order of things.

Culture is purest when the tribe interacts with reality in a free and natural manner. The wisdom of folklore is timeless because childlike values are raised to philosophic status. The common man distrusts sophistication; he is a friend of the straightforward.

The opposite of childlike trust is hardness of heart. While Quixote was *blinded,* hardness of heart is *perverse.* This is proved by the manner in which refractory evidences are resisted. And there is no more graphic illustration of this than the crucifixion of Jesus Christ. Whereas the common man came to Jesus gladly, the hardened heart took up stones to stone him. "It is to fulfill the word that is written in their law, 'They hated me without a cause' '' (John 15:25). To hate without a cause means to hate without a *justifiable* cause. Resentment is a desperate expedient. It seeks to nullify distasteful evidences. Carlyle wisely observes that there are some attitudes like jealousy, which, though causeless, yet cannot be removed by reasons as apparent as demonstration can make any truth.

Hardness of heart invalidates common sense. Pharaoh illustrates this pathos. Though given abundant proof that the Lord was God, he was so opinionated that no amount of evidence could unlearn him. In the end Pharaoh destroyed himself. Any child could have told him he was playing the fool.

Prejudice curtailed the effectiveness of Jesus' ministry. "And *he* did not do many mighty works there, because of their unbelief" (Matt. 13:58). Jesus was *able* to do many mighty works, but a display of Messianic credentials before resentment would have been pointless pedagogy. *All* learning is based on humility before the facts.

The Two Kinds of Faith

Faith is the capacity of belief or trust. This capacity is expressed in two separate, though mutually supporting, ways. *To believe a thing* is general faith; *to trust a person* is vital faith. Let us examine these in this order.

General faith is a resting of the mind in the sufficiency of the evidences. Two rules govern general faith: *first,* withhold judgment until the evidences are sufficient; *secondly,* act consistently on all warranted belief. A life of faith is a life of wisdom. Foolishness either believes when it should doubt (the cultic mind), or it doubts when it should believe (hardness of heart). The cultic mind courts credulity; hardness of heart courts incredulity. Credulity believes too soon; incredulity, not soon enough.

Orthodoxy has little patience with the cliché that religious people have faith while men of science and philosophy have knowledge. General faith spans the entire human enterprise. To believe on insufficient evidence is folly, not faith. Faith may stress *commitment,* whereas knowledge stresses *apprehension,* but both make an equal draft on facts "out there." Whether we believe the word of man or the Word of God, we believe because we are satisfied with the sufficiency of the evidences. And we deem the evidences to be no less objective in the one case than we do in the other.

Vital faith is richer than general faith because the act of trusting a person calls for a greater measure of commitment than the act of believing a thing. The meaning of geometry can be understood by the intellect alone, but the meaning of a person remains veiled until the intellect is joined by the intuitions of the heart. If we seek access to another person, we must come by way of revelation—the revelation that he makes when we show spontaneous signs of receiving the dignity of his life. In other words, we must proportion our methods of knowing to the kind of reality under consideration. Philosophy is thought; pudding is tasted; and a person is encountered in fellowship.

Whenever genuine fellowship is enjoyed, the distinction between faith

and knowledge disappears, for to *know* another person is to *trust* him.
"Now Adam knew Eve his wife, and she conceived and bore Cain" (Gen.
4:1). The marital due requires such a total act of personal surrender that it is
equated with knowledge. Again, "I never knew you," says the Lord;
"depart from me, you evildoers" (Matt. 7:23). While the Lord *ap-
prehends* evildoers, he does not know them in the only way that counts,
namely, fellowship. Sin issues in autonomy, not surrender.

Vital faith is not unique to the religious life, let alone to Christianity.
Like general faith, it belongs to the order of man as man. When a little boy
sees his friend with a sack of candy he says, "*You know me!*" And he
certainly does not mean that his friend can give an intellectual account of
his person. He means, "We are on speaking terms; we like each other; so,
share your jelly beans!" He appeals to the moral obligation in fellowship—the obligation to surrender benefits as well as the self.

General faith is the foundation of vital faith. This is true on every level
of life. Before a husband can embrace his wife, he must be convinced that
it is his wife, and not a stranger, before him. The same is true in our
approach to God. We must be convinced that we are confronting *God,* not
a counterfeit.

General faith is a resting of the mind in the sufficiency of the evidences;
vital faith is cordial trust. General faith is censured only when it pretends to
do the work of vital faith. For example, the demons are credited with
general faith. They address Jesus Christ with language that is strikingly
similar to that used by the angels. "You believe that God is one; you do
well. Even the demons believe—and shudder" (James 2:19). The faith of
demons profits nothing because it is general faith and nothing more. It is
not "a vital faith, such as is required in the gospel; a living and active
principle, serving at once to connect us with Christ, and to constrain us to
live no longer to ourselves, but to him that died for us, and that rose again.
In a word, it must be 'the faith which worketh by love.' LOVE is the sum
of God's law, and the spring of all acceptable obedience."[3]

The difference between general and vital faith ought to be clear by now.
When a person assents to truth, or when he believes in an object, he
commits *part* of himself. This is general faith. But when he trusts another
person, he commits the *whole* of himself. This is vital faith. Fellowship is
a union of life with life. The essence of one person passes into that of
another.

The Trial of Faith

Faith is often put to trial. For example, Cinderella believed in the ultimate triumph of goodness. She rested in the sufficiency of the evidences.
But when her wicked stepmother gained the upper hand and Cinderella
could not go to the ball, faith was on trial. Cinderella ran to the garden and
wept. But to the relief of children—and all who are children in heart—a
fairy godmother appeared and renewed the evidences. Faith revived.

A Christian believes that God is sovereign over the affairs of men. Yet the Christian lives in a "world with devils filled." The righteous suffer and the unrighteous prosper. The heroes of the faith "were stoned, they were sawn in two, they were killed with the sword; they went about in skins of sheep and goats, destitute, afflicted, ill-treated" (Heb. 11:37). The heroes of the faith passed the trial of faith. The present evil world prompted them to look for a better world—a world with foundations, whose builder and maker is God.

The trial of faith does not mean that a Christian rallies courage to act on insufficient evidence. To say it is Saturday, when it is Sunday; or that one possesses gold, when he is sifting sand; or that the stomach is sated, when one is starving—these are signs of foolishness, not faith. Faith is the subjective element in *warranted* belief, and warranted belief rests in the sufficiency of the evidences.

A Christian is like a physicist at a magic show. Each successful trick is a threat to the physicist's faith in the law of uniformity. Large rabbits are drawn from small hats, and a lady floats through the air. The physicist is admittedly baffled. But his faith is not overturned, for the law of uniformity is settled on scientific, not private, grounds. In a similar way, a Christian keeps the promises of God before him. "The true way to have faith strengthened is not to consider the difficulties in the way of the thing promised, but the character and resources of God, who has made the promise."[4] Conflicting evidences may *baffle* the Christian, but they do not cast him down; for the promises of God are decided on Biblical, nor empirical grounds.

Christians often pray, "I believe; help my unbelief!" (Mark 9:24). And they pray thus because they are suspended between voluntary belief and involuntary unbelief. Ambivalence of this sort is *normal* to Christian faith. "When we inculcate, that faith ought to be certain and secure, we conceive not of a certainty attended with no doubt, or of a security interrupted by no anxiety; but we rather affirm, that believers have a perpetual conflict with their own diffidence, and are far from placing their consciences in a placid calm, never disturbed by any storms. Yet, on the other hand, we deny, however they may be afflicted, that they ever fall and depart from that certain confidence which they have conceived in the divine mercy."[5]

The difference between voluntary belief and involuntary unbelief can easily be illustrated. Suppose we reach our favorite picnic spot, only to worry whether we locked the front door. To settle our minds, we think back on the events of the morning. We decide that the door is, in fact, locked. But this deliberation does not eradicate the threat of involuntary unbelief. Anxiety may linger on the edge of our dominant affections. About all we can do is see that anxiety does not ruin our picnic. "The door *is* locked!" we remind ourselves. And having labeled the source of our problem, we let the matter go.

Deliverance from involuntary unbelief will not be enjoyed until we walk by sight in the Kingdom of Heaven. When we receive our resurrection bodies, the discord in our hearts will end. But until then, the Christian must deliberately superintend his own affections. "Keep your heart with all vigilance; for from it flow the springs of life" (Prov. 4:23).

Since God can no more fail in his covenantal promises than he can cease to be God, involuntary unbelief is never a decisive threat to the Christian.

> Though the fig tree do not blossom,
>   nor fruit be on the vines,
> the produce of the olive fail
>   and the field yield no food,
> the flock be cut off from the fold
>   and there be no herd in the stalls,
> yet I will rejoice in the Lord,
>   I will joy in the God of my salvation.
>
> (Hab. 3:17, 18)

Collateral Reading

[1]The theology of faith: Calvin, *Institutes*, III. ii.

[2]The psychology of faith: Warfield, B. B., "On Faith in Its Psychological Aspects," in *Biblical and Theological Studies*, pp. 375–403 (The Presbyterian and Reformed Publishing Company, 1952).

Notes

[1]Thomas Aquinas, *Summa Theologica*, Second Part of the Second Part, Q. I, Art. 5.

[2]Abraham Kuyper, *Principles of Sacred Theology*, p. 131. Wm. B. Eerdmans Publishing Company, 1954.

[3]James Buchanan, *The Office and Work of the Holy Spirit*, p. 194. John Johnstone, Edinburgh, 1842.

[4]Charles Hodge, *Commentary on the Epistle to the Romans*, p. 130. Wm. B. Eerdmans Publishing Company, 1950.

[5]John Calvin, *Institutes*, III.ii.17.

John L. Nuelsen

Regeneration

I. The Term Explained

The theological term "regeneration" is the Lat tr of the Gr expression παλινγενεσία, *palingenesía*, occurring twice in the NT (Mt. 19:28; Tit. 3:5). The word is usually written παλιγγενεσία, *paliggenesía*, in classical Gr. Its meaning is different in the two passages, though an easy transition of thought is evident.

1. First Biblical Sense (Eschatological)

In Mt. 19:28 the word refers to the restoration of the world, in which sense it is synonymical to the expressions ἀποχατάστασις πάντων, *apolkatástasis pántōn*, "restoration of all things" (Acts 3:21; the vb. is found in Mt. 17:11, ἀποκαταστήσει πάντα, *apokatastései pánta*, "shall restore all things"), and ἀνάψυχις, *anápsuxis*, "refreshing" (Acts 3:19), which signifies a gradual transition of meaning to the second sense of the word under consideration. It is supposed that regeneration in this sense denotes the final stage of development of all creation, by which God's purposes regarding the same are fully realized, when "all things [are

From *The International Standard Bible Encyclopedia* (Grand Rapids: Wm. B. Eerdmans Pub. Co., 1952), Vol. IV, pp. 2546–2550. Used by permission.

put] in subjection under his feet'' (I Cor. 15:27). This is a "regeneration in the proper meaning of the word, for it signifies a renovation of all visible things when the old is passed away, and heaven and earth are become new'' (cf. Rev. 21:1). To the Jew the regeneration thus prophesied was inseparably connected with the reign of the Messiah.

> We find this word in the same or very similar senses in profane literature. It is used of the renewal of the world in Stoical philosophy. Jos (*Ant.* XI, iii, 9) speaks of the anáktēsis kai paliggnesia tés patridos, "a new foundation and regeneration of the fatherland," after the return from the Bab captivity. Philo (ed. Mangey, ii. 144) uses the word, speaking of the post-diluvial epoch of the earth, as of a new world, and Marcus Aurelius Antoninus (xi. 1), of a periodical restoration of all things, laying stress upon the constant recurrence and uniformity of all happenings, which thought the Preacher expressed by "There is no new thing under the sun" (Eccl. 1:9). In most places, however, where the word occurs in philosophical writings, it is used of the "reincarnation" or "subsequent birth" of the individual, as in the Buddhistic and Pythagorean doctrine of the transmigration of souls (Plut., ed. Xylander, ii. 998c; Clem. Alex., ed. Potter, 539), or else of a revival of life (Philo i. 159). Cicero uses the word in his letters to Atticus (vi. 6) metaphorically of his return from exile, as a new lease of life granted to him. See *Eschatology of the NT, IX* [in *International Standard Bible Encyclopaedia*].

2. Second Biblical Sense (Spiritual)

This sense is undoubtedly included in the full Bib. conception of the former meaning, for it is unthinkable that a regeneration in the eschatological sense can exist without a spiritual regeneration of humanity or the individual. It is, however, quite evident that this latter conception has arisen rather late, from an analysis of the former meaning. It is found in Tit. 3:5 which, without absolute certainty as to its meaning, is generally interpreted in agreement with the numerous nouns and vbs. which have given the dogmatical setting to the doctrine of regeneration in Christian theology. Clem. Alex. is the first to differentiate this meaning from the former by the addition of the adj. πνευματική, *pneumatikoe*, "spiritual" (cf. *anapsuxis,* Acts 3:19; see REFRESHING[*ISBE*]). In this latter sense the word is typically Christian, though the OT contains many adumbrations of the spiritual process expressed thereby.

II. The Biblical Doctrine of Regeneration

1. In the OT

It is well known that in the earlier portions of the OT, and to a certain degree all through the OT, religion is looked at and spoken of more as a national possession, the benefits of which are largely visible and tangible blessings. The idea of regeneration here occurs therefore—though no technical expression has as yet been coined for the process—in the first meaning of the word elucidated above. Whether the Divine promises refer to the

Messianic end of times, or are to be realized at an earlier date, they all refer to the nation of Israel as such, and to individuals only as far as they are partakers in the benefits bestowed upon the commonwealth. This is even true where the blessings prophesied are only spiritual, as in Isa. 60:21–22. The mass of the people of Israel are therefore as yet scarcely aware of the fact that the conditions on which these Divine promises are to be attained are more than ceremonial and ritual ones. Soon, however, great disasters, threatening to overthrow the national entity, and finally the captivity and dispersion which caused national functions to be almost, if not altogether, discontinued, assisted in the growth of a sense of individual or personal responsibility before God. The sin of Israel is recognized as the sin of the individual, which can be removed only by individual repentance and cleansing. This is best seen from the stirring appeals of the prophets of the exile, where frequently the necessity of a change of attitude toward Jeh is preached as a means to such regeneration. This cannot be understood otherwise than as a turning of the individual to the Lord. Here, too, no ceremony or sacrifice is sufficient, but an interposition of Divine grace, which is represented under the figure of a washing and sprinkling from all iniquity and sin (Isa. 1:18; Jer. 13:23). It is not possible now to follow in full the development of this idea of cleansing, but already in Isa. 52:15 the sprinkling of many nations is mentioned and is soon understood in the sense of the "baptism" which proselytes had to undergo before their reception into the covenant of Israel. It was the symbol of a radical cleansing like that of a "new-born babe," which was one of the designations of the proselyte (cf. Ps. 87:5; see also the tractate *Y^e bhāmōth* 62a). Would it be surprising that Israel, which had been guilty of many sins of the Gentiles, needed a similar baptism and sprinkling? This is what Ezk. 36:25 suggests: "I will sprinkle clean water upon you, and ye shall be clean: from all your filthiness, and from all your idols, will I cleanse you." In other passages the cleansing and refining power of fire is alluded to (e.g., Mal. 3:2), and there is no doubt that John the Baptist found in such passages the ground for his practice of baptizing the Jews who came to him (Jn. 1:25–28 and ‖ 's).

The turning of Israel to God was necessarily meant to be an inward change of attitude toward Him, in other words, the sprinkling with clean water, as an outward sign, was the emblem of a pure heart. It was Isaiah and Jeremiah who drew attention to this (Isa. 57:15; Jer. 24:7; 31: 33–35; 32:38–40, *et passim*). Here again reference is made to individuals, not only to the people in general (Jer. 31:34). This promised regeneration, so lovingly offered by Jeh, is to be the token of a new covenant between God and His people (Jer. 31:31; Ezk. 11:19–21; 18:31–32; 37:23–24).

The renewing and cleansing here spoken of is in reality nothing else than what Dt. 30:6 had promised, a circumcision of the heart in contradistinction to the flesh, the token of the former (Abrahamic) covenant (of circumcision, Jer. 4:4). As God takes the initiative in making the covenant, the conviction takes root that human sin and depravity can be effectually eliminated only by the act of God Himself renewing and transforming the heart of man (Hos. 14:4). This we see from the testimony of some of Israel's best sons and daughters, who also knew that this grace was found in the way of repentance and humiliation before God. The classical expression of this conviction is found in the prayer of David: "Create in me a clean heart, O God; and renew a right [m "stedfast"] spirit within me. Cast me not away from thy presence; and take not thy holy Spirit from me. Restore unto me the joy of thy salvation; and uphold me with a willing spirit" (Ps. 51:10–12). Jeremiah puts the following words into the mouth of Ephraim: "Turn thou me, and I shall be turned" (Jer. 31:18). Clearer than any passages of the OT, John the Baptist, forerunner of Christ and last flaming torch of the time of the earlier covenant, spoke of the baptism, not of water, but of the Holy Spirit and of fire (Mt. 3:11; Lk. 3:16; Jn. 1:33), leading thus to the realization of OT foreshadowings which became possible by faith in Christ.

2. In the Teaching of Jesus

In the teaching of Jesus the need of regeneration has a prominent place, though nowhere are the reasons given. The OT had succeeded—and even the gentile conscience agreed with it—in convincing the people of this need. The clearest assertion of it and the explanation of the doctrine of regeneration is found in the conversation of Jesus with Nicodemus (Jn. 3). It is based upon (1) the observation that man, even the most punctilious in the observance of the Law, is dead and therefore unable to "live up" to the demands of God. Only He who gave life at the beginning can give the (spiritual) life necessary to do God's will. (2) Man has fallen from his virginal and Divinely appointed sphere, the realm of the spirit, the Kingdom of God, living now the perishing earthly life. Only by having a new spiritual nature imparted to him, by being "born anew" (Jn. 3:3, RVm "from above," Gr ἄνωθεν, *anothen*), by being "born of the Spirit" (3: 6–8), can he live the spiritual life which God requires of man.

These words are a NT exegesis of Ezekiel's vision of the dead bones (37:1–10). It is the "breath from Jeh," the Spirit of God, who alone can give life to the spiritually dead.

But regeneration according to Jesus, is more than life, it is also *purity*. As God is pure and sinless, none but the pure in heart can see God (Mt. 5:8). This was always recognized as impossible to mere human endeavor. Bildad the Shuhite declared, and his friends, each in his turn, expressed very similar thoughts (Job 4:17; 14:4): "How then can man be just with God? Or how can he be clean that is born of a woman? Behold, even the moon hath no brightness, and the stars are not pure in his sight: how much less man, that is a worm! and the son of man, that is a worm!" (25:4–6).

To change this lost condition, to impart this new life, Jesus claims as His God-appointed task: "The Son of man came to seek and to save that which was lost" (Lk. 19:10); "I came that they may have life, and may have it abundantly" (Jn. 10:10). This life is eternal, imperishable: "I give unto them eternal life; and they shall never perish, and no one shall snatch them out of my hand" (Jn. 10:28). This life is imparted by Jesus Himself: "It is the spirit that giveth life; the flesh profiteth nothing: the words that I have spoken unto you are spirit, and are life" (Jn. 6:63). This life can be received on the condition of faith in Christ or by coming to Him (Jn. 14:6). By faith power is received which enables the sinner to overcome sin, to "sin no more" (Jn. 8:11).

The parables of Jesus further illustrate this doctrine. The prodigal is declared to have been "dead" and to be "alive again" (Lk. 15:24). The new life from God is compared to a wedding garment in the parable of the Marriage of the King's Son (Mt. 22:11). The garment, the gift of the inviting king, had been refused by the unhappy guest, who, in consequence, was "cast out into the outer darkness" (Mt. 22:13).

Finally, this regeneration, this new life, is explained as the knowledge of God and His Christ: "And this is life eternal, that they should know thee the only true God, and him whom thou didst send, even Jesus Christ" (Jn. 17:3). This seems to be an allusion to the passage in Hos. (4:6): "My people are destroyed for lack of knowledge: because thou hast rejected knowledge, I will also reject thee, that thou shalt be no priest to me."

3. In Apostolic Teaching

It may be said in general that the teaching of the apostles on the subject of regeneration is a development of the teaching of Jesus on the lines of the adumbrations of the OT. Considering the differences in the personal character of these writers, it is remarkable that such concord of views should exist among them. St. Paul, indeed, lays more stress on the specific facts of justification and sanctification by faith than on the more comprehensive head of regeneration. Still the need of it is plainly stated by St. Paul. It is necessary to salvation for all men. "The body is dead because of sin" (Rom. 8:3–11; Eph. 2:1). The flesh is at enmity with God (Eph. 2:15); all mankind is "darkened in their understanding, alienated from the life of God" (4:18). Similar passages might be multiplied. Paul then distinctly teaches that thus is a new life in store for those who have been spiritually dead. To the Ephesians he writes: "And you did he make alive, when ye were dead through your trespasses and sins" (2:1), and later on: "God, being rich in mercy, . . . made us alive together with Christ" (2:4–5). A spiritual resurrection has taken place. This regeneration causes a complete revolution in man. He has thereby passed from under the law of sin and death and has come under "the law of the Spirit of life in Christ Jesus" (Rom. 8:2). The change is so radical that it is possible now to speak of a "new creature" (II Cor. 5:17; Gal. 6:15, m "new creation"), of a "new man, that after God hath been created in righteousness and holiness of truth" (Eph. 4:24), and of "the new man, that is being renewed unto knowledge after the image of him that created him" (Col. 3:10). All "old things are passed away; behold, they are become new" (II Cor. 5:17).

St. Paul is equally explicit regarding the author of this change. The "Spirit of God," the "Spirit of Christ," has been given from above to be the source of all new life (Rom. 8); by Him we are proved to be the "sons" of God (Gal. 4:6); we have been adopted into the family of God (υἱοθεσία, *huiothesia*, Rom. 8:15; Gal. 4:5). Thus St. Paul speaks of the "second Adam," by whom the life of righteousness is initiated in us; just as the "first Adam" became the leader in transgression, He is "a life-giving spirit" (I Cor. 15:45). St. Paul himself experienced this change, and henceforth exhibited the powers of the unseen world in his life of service. "It is no longer I that live," he exclaims, "but Christ liveth in me: and that life which I now live in the flesh I live in faith, the faith which is in the Son of God, who loved me, and gave himself up for me" (Gal. 2:20).

Regeneration is to St. Paul, no less than to Jesus, connected with the conception of purity and knowledge. We have already noted the second NT passage in which the word "regeneration" occurs (Tit. 3:5-6): "According to his mercy he saved us, through the washing [m "laver"] of regeneration and renewing of the Holy Spirit, which he poured out upon us richly, through Jesus Christ our Saviour." In I Cor. 12:13 such cleansing is called the baptism of the Spirit in agreement with the oft-repeated promise (Joel 2:28 [in the Heb. text 3:1]; Mt. 3:11; Mk. 1:8; Lk. 3:16; Acts 1:5; 11:16). There is, of course, in these passages no reference to mere water-baptism, any more than in Ezk. 36:25. Water is but the *tertium comparationis*. As water cleanseth the outer body, so the spirit purifies the inner man (cf. I Cor. 6:11; I Pet. 3:21).

The doctrine that regeneration redounds in true knowledge of Christ is seen from Eph. 3:15-19 and 4:17-24, where the darkened understanding and ignorance of natural man are placed in contradistinction to the enlightenment of the new life (see also Col. 3:10). The church redeemed and regenerated is to be a special "possession," an "heritage" of the Lord (Eph. 1:11, 14), and the whole creation is to participate in the final redemption and adoption (Rom. 8:21-23).

St. James finds less occasion to touch this subject than the other writers of the NT. His Ep. is rather ethical than dogmatical in tone, still his ethics are based on the dogmatical presuppositions which fully agree with the teaching of other apostles. Faith to him is the human response to God's desire to impart His nature to mankind, and therefore the indispensable means to be employed in securing the full benefits of the new life, i.e. the sin-conquering power (1:2-4), the spiritual enlightenment (1:5) and purity (1:27). There seems, however, to be little doubt that St. James directly refers to regeneration in the words: "Of his own will he brought us forth by the word of truth, that we should be a kind of firstfruits of his creatures" (1:18). It is supposed by some that these words, being addressed "to the twelve tribes which are of the Dispersion" (1:1), do not refer to individual regeneration, but to an election of Israel as a nation and so to a *Christian* Israel. In this case the aftermath would be the redemption of the Gentiles. I understand the expression "firstfruits" in the sense in which we have noticed St. Paul's final hope in Rom. 8:21-32, where the regeneration of the believing people of God (regardless of nationality) is the first stage in the regeneration or restoration of all creation. The "implanted [RVm "inborn''] word'' (Jas. 1:21; cf. I Pet. 1:23) stands parallel to the Pauline expression, ''law of the Spirit'' (Rom. 8:2).

St. Peter uses, in his sermon on the day of Pentecost, the words ''refreshing'' (Acts 3:19) and ''restoration of all things'' (3:21) of the final completion of God's plans concerning the whole creation, and accordingly looks here at God's people as a whole. In a similar sense he says in his Second Ep., after mentioning ''the day of God'': ''We look for new heavens and a new earth, wherein dwelleth righteousness'' (II Pet. 3:13). Still he alludes very plainly to the regeneration of individuals (I Pet. 1:3, 23). The idea of a second birth of the believers is clearly suggested in the expression, ''newborn babes'' (I Pet. 2:2), and in the explicit statement of I Pet. 1:23: ''having been begotten again, not of corruptible seed, but of incorruptible, through the word of God, which liveth and abideth.'' It is in this sense that the apostle calls God ''Father'' (1:17) and the believers ''children of obedience'' (1:14), i.e. obedient children, or children who ought to obey. We have seen above that the agent by which regeneration is wrought, the incorruptible seed of the word of God, finds a parallel in St. Paul's and St. James's theology. All these expressions go back probably to a word of the Master in Jn. 15:3. We are made partakers of the word by having received the spirit. This spirit (cf. the Pauline ''life-giving spirit,'' I Cor. 15:45), the ''mind'' of Christ (I Pet. 4:1), is the power of the resurrected Christ active in the life of the believer. St. Peter refers to the same thought in I Pet. 3:15, 21. By regeneration we become ''an elect race, a royal priesthood, a holy nation, a people for God's own possession,'' in whom Divine virtues, ''the excellencies of him who called you'' (I Pet. 2:9), are manifested. Here the apostle uses well-known OT expressions foreshadowing NT graces (Isa. 61:6; 66:21; Ex. 19:6; Dt. 7:6), but he individualizes the process of regeneration in full agreement with the increased light which the teaching of Jesus has brought. The theology of St. Peter also points out the contact of regeneration with purity and holiness (I Pet. 1:15–16) and true knowledge (1:14) or obedience (1:14; 3:16). It is not surprising that the idea of purity should invite the OT parallel of ''cleansing by water.'' The flood washed away the iniquity of the world ''in the days of Noah,'' when ''eight souls were saved through water: which also after a true likeness [RVm ''in the antitype''] doth now save you, even baptism, not the putting away of the filth of the flesh, but the interrogation [RVm ''inquiry,'' ''appeal''] of a good conscience toward God, through the resurrection [-life] of Jesus Christ'' (I Pet. 3:20–21).

The teaching of St. John is very closely allied with that of Jesus, as we have already seen from the multitude of quotations we had to select from St. John's Gospel to illustrate the teaching of the Master. It is esp. interesting to note the cases where the apostle didactically elucidates certain of these pronouncements of Jesus. The most remarkable apostolic gloss or commentary on the subject is found in Jn. 7:39. Jesus had spoken of the change which faith in Him (''coming to him'') would cause in the lives of His disciples; how Divine energies like ''rivers of water'' should issue forth from them; and the evangelist continues in explanation: ''But this spake he of the Spirit, which they that believed on him were to receive: for the Spirit was not yet given; because Jesus was not yet glorified.'' This recognition of a special manifestation of Divine power, transcending the experience of OT believers, was based on the declaration of Christ, that He would send ''another Comforter [RV ''advocate,'' ''helper,'' Gr *Paraclete*], that he may be with you for ever, even the Spirit of truth'' (Jn. 14:16–17).

In his Epp. St. John shows that this Spirit bestows the elements of a Godlike character which makes us to be ''sons of God,'' who before were ''children of the devil'' (I Jn. 3:10: 24; 4:13, etc.). This regeneration is ''eternal life'' (I Jn. 5:13) and moral similarity with God, the very character of God in man. As ''God is love,'' the children of God will love (I Jn. 5:2). At the same time it is the life of God in man, also called fellowship with Christ, victorious life which overcomes the world (I Jn. 5:4); it is purity (I Jn. 3:3–6) and knowledge (I Jn. 2:20).

The subject of regeneration lies outside of the scope of the Ep. to the He, so that we look in vain for a clear dogmatical statement of it. Still the ep. does in no place contradict the dogma, which, on the other hand, underlies many of the statements made. Christ, ''the mediator of a better covenant, which hath been enacted upon better promises'' (8:6), has made ''purification of sins'' (1:3). In contradistinction to the first covenant, in which the people approached God by means of outward forms and ordinances, the ''new covenant'' (8:13) brought an ''eternal redemption'' (9:12) by means of a Divine cleansing (9:14). Christ brings ''many sons unto glory'' and is ''author of their salvation'' (2:10). Immature Christians are spoken of (as were the proselytes of the OT) as babes, who were to grow to the stature, character and knowledge of ''fullgrown men'' (5:13–14).

III. Later Development of the Doctrine

Very soon the high spiritual meaning of regeneration was obscured by the development of priestcraft within the Christian church. When the initiation into the church was thought of as accomplished by the mediation of ministers thereto appointed, the ceremonies hereby employed became means to which magic powers were of necessity ascribed. This we see plainly in the view of baptismal regeneration, which, based upon half-understood passages of Scripture quoted above, was taught at an early date. While in the post-apostolic days we frequently find traces of a proper appreciation of an underlying spiritual value in baptism (cf. *Didache*, vii) many of the expressions used are highly misleading. Thus Gregory Nazianzen (*Orations*, xi. 2) calls baptism the second of the three births a child of God must experience (the first is the natural birth, the third the resurrection). This birth is ''of the day, free, delivering from passions, taking away every veil of our nature or birth, i.e. everything hiding the Divine image in which we are created, and leading up to the life above'' (Ullmann, *Gregor v. Nazienz*, 323). Cyril of Jerus (*Cat.*, xvii, c. 37) ascribes to baptism the power of absolution from sin and the power of endowment with heavenly virtues. According to Augustine baptism is essential to salvation, though the baptism of blood (martyrdom) may take the place of water-baptism, as in the case of the thief at the cross (Aug., *De Anima et Eius Origine*, i.11, c. 9; ii.14, c. 10; ii.16, c. 12). Leo the Great compares the spirit-filled water of baptism with the spirit-filled womb of the Virgin, in which the Holy Spirit engenders a sinless child of God (Serm. xxiv. 3; xxv. 5; see Hagenbach, *Dogmengeschichte*, §137).

In general this is still the opinion of pronounced sacramentarians, while evangelical Christianity has gone back to the teaching of the NT.

IV. Present Significance

Although a clear distinction is not always maintained between regeneration and other experiences of the spiritual life, we may summarize our belief in the following theses:

(1) Regeneration implies not merely an addition of certain gifts or graces, a strengthening of certain innate good qualities, but a radical change, which revolutionizes our whole being, contradicts and overcomes our old fallen nature, and places our spiritual center of gravity wholly outside of our own powers in the realm of God's causation.

(2) It is the will of God that all men be made partakers of this new life (I Tim. 2:4) and, as it is clearly stated that some fall short of it (Jn. 5:40), it is plain that the fault thereof lies with man. God requires all men to repent and turn unto Him (Acts 17:30) before He will or can effect regeneration. Conversion, consisting in repentance and faith in Christ, is therefore the human response to the offer of salvation which God makes. This response gives occasion to and is synchronous with the Divine act of renewal (regeneration). The Spirit of God enters into union with the believing, accepting spirit of man. This is fellowship with Christ (Rom. 8:10; I Cor. 6:17; II Cor. 5:17; Col. 3:3).

(3) The process of regeneration is outside of our observation and beyond the scope of psychological analysis. It takes place in the sphere of subconsciousness. Recent psychological investigations have thrown a flood of light on the psychic states which precede, accompany and follow the work of the Holy Spirit. "He handles psychical powers; He works upon psychical energies and states; and this work of regeneration lies somewhere within the psychical field." The study of religious psychology is of highest value and greatest importance. The facts of Christian experience cannot be changed, nor do they lose in value by the most searching psychological scrutiny.

Psychological analysis does not eliminate the direct working of the Holy Spirit. Nor can it disclose its process; the "underlying laboratory where are wrought radical remedial processes and structural changes in the psychical being as portrayed in explicit scriptural utterances: 'Create in me a clean heart' (Ps. 51:10); 'Ye must be born again' (Jn. 3:7 AV); 'If any man be in Christ, he is a new creature: old things are passed away; behold all things are become new' (II Cor. 5:17 AV), is in the region of subconsciousness. To look in the region of consciousness for this Person or for His work is fruitless and an effort fraught with endless confusion. Christian psychology thus traces to its deep-lying retreat the Divine elaboration of the regenerated life. Here God works in the depths of the soul as silently and securely as if on the remotest world of the stellar universe'' (H. E. Warner, *Psychology of the Christian Life,* 117).

(4) Regeneration manifests itself in the conscious soul by its effects on the will, the intelligence and the affections. At the same time regeneration supplies a new life-power of Divine origin, which enables the component parts of human nature to fulfil the law of God, to strive for the coming of God's kingdom, and to accept the teachings of God's spirit. Thus regenerate man is made conscious of the facts of justification and adoption. The former is a judicial act of God, which frees man from the law of sin and absolves him from the state of enmity against God; the latter an enduement with the Spirit, which is an earnest of his inheritance (Eph. 1:14). The Spirit of God, dwelling in man, witnesses to the state of sonship (Rom. 8:2, 15–16; Gal. 4:6).

(5) Regeneration, being a new birth, is the starting-point of spiritual growth. The regenerated man needs nurture and training. He receives it not merely from outside experiences, but from an immanent power in himself, which is recognized as the power of the life of the indwelling Christ (Col. 1:26–27). Apart from the mediate dealings of God with man through word and sacraments, there is therefore an immediate communication of life from God to the regenerate.

(6) The truth which is mentioned as the agent by whom regeneration is made possible (Jn. 8:32; Jas. 1:18; I Pet. 1:23), is nothing else than the Divine Spirit, not only the spoken or written word of God, which may convince people of right or wrong, but which cannot enable the will of man to forsake the wrong and to do the right, but He who calls Himself the Truth (Jn. 14:6) and who has become the motive power of regenerated life (Gal. 2:20).

(7) Recent philosophy expressive of the reaction from the mechanical view of bare materialism, and also from the depreciation of personality as seen in socialism, has again brought into prominence the reality and need of personal life. Johannes Müller and Rudolf Eucken among others emphasize that a new life of the spirit, independent of outward conditions, is not only possible, but necessary for the attainment of the highest development. This new life is not a fruit of the free play of the tendencies and powers of natural life, but is in sharp conflict with them. Man as he is by nature stands in direct contrast to the demands of the spiritual life. Spiritual life, as Professor Eucken says, can be implanted in man by some superior power only and must constantly be sustained by superior life. It breaks through the order of causes and effects; it severs the continuity of the outer world; it makes impossible a rational joining together of realities; it prohibits a monistic view of the immediate condition of the world. This new life derives its power not from mere Nature; it is a manifestation of Divine life

within us (*Hauptprobleme der Religionsphilosophie,* Leipzig, 1912, 17ff; *Der Kampf um einen geistigen Lebensinhalt,* Leipzig, 1907; *Grundlinien einer neuen Lebensanschauung,* Leipzig, 1907; Johannes Müller, *Bausteine für persönliche Kultur,* 3 vols., München, 1908). Thus the latest development of idealistic philosophy corroborates in a remarkable way the Christian truth of regeneration. See also CONVERSION[ISBE].

Franz Pieper

The Means of Grace

In reconciling the world unto Himself by Christ's substitutionary satisfaction, God asked no one's advice concerning His singular method of reconciliation. In like manner, without asking any man's advice, He ordained the means by which He gives men the infallible assurance of His gracious will toward them; in other words, He both confers on men the remission of sins merited by Christ and works faith in the proffered remission or, where faith already exists, strengthens it. The Church has appropriately called these divine ordinances the means of grace, *media gratiae, instrumenta gratiae*—Formula of Concord: *"Instrumenta sive media Spiritus Sancti" (Trigl.* 903, Sol. Decl., II, 58). They are the Word of the Gospel, Baptism, and the Lord's Supper, as will be shown more fully on the following pages.

According to Scripture, a twofold power inheres in these means: first, an exhibiting and conferring, or imparting, power *(vis exhibitiva, dativa, collativa)*, and, secondly, as a result of this, an efficacious, or operative, power *(vis effectiva sive operativa)*. The conferring, or imparting, power consists in this, that these means offer men the forgiveness of sins,

From *Christian Dogmatics,* by Franz Pieper. Vol. II, 1953 by Concordia Publishing House. Used by permission. pp. 103–114.

supplied through Christ's work of reconciliation, hence God's grace *(favor Dei)*.[1] In other words, through the means of grace God reveals and declares to men that He is fully reconciled through Christ, that because of Christ's work He loves them and would have them believe it. The efficacious, or operative, power of the means of grace consists in this, that through them the Holy Spirit works and strengthens faith, faith in the very forgiveness, God's love and grace, which these means declare and reveal.[2]

One would think that men would not take exception to the means of grace, ordained by God Himself. But history reports the opposite. As critics have declared God's method of reconciling the world unworthy of God and man, so they have also taken exception to the means of grace ordained by God. Some, for instance Zwingli, have argued strongly that it does not befit God to bind His revelation and operation to such external means as the Word and the Sacraments, that for His work the Holy Ghost does not need a vehicle.[3] In other words, Zwingli and his numerous adherents declare that the means God has ordained are unnecessary and hinder true piety. Others, particularly the Papists, create their own means of grace and "improve" those which God has ordained. On this account a manual of Christian dogmatics must devote considerable space to a presentation of the Christian doctrine of the means of grace. The study will also show that the rejection and every alteration of the divinely appointed means of grace impair the core and center of the Christian faith, the article of justification by faith without the deeds of the Law. When the means of grace are rejected or impaired, human works regularly take the place of Christ's substitutionary satisfaction as the basis of salvation.

The Means of Grace in General

Seeberg correctly writes: "The doctrinal understanding of the means of grace begins with the relation of these means to the work of Christ."[4] Unfortunately the term "work of Christ" has, in both the past and the present, been given widely different connotations, and this ambiguity lessens the value of the statement. Some do not regard the work of Christ as perfect in extent, for they let it count only for a part of mankind. This is done by the Calvinists. Others refer Christ's work of reconciliation to all men, but deny its perfection in value by asserting that His work is insufficient for man's actual salvation and must be supplemented by *aliquid in homine*—some achievement of man, an innate goodness in man, faith as a moral achievement, the free choice of man, faith as the germ of good works, the new life and the good works themselves, etc. Without this complement the work of Christ or the grace earned by Christ could not secure man's salvation. Where such warped conceptions of the "work" of Christ prevail, almost anything except the Scriptural concept of the means of grace can be the outcome. The means of grace do not remain means dispensing grace, but become means of prodding man to virtuous endeavors, variously named and of various grades.

The starting point in presenting the doctrine of the means of grace must be the universal objective reconciliation or justification. This is the procedure of Scripture. What it says of the divine transmission of the grace which Christ has gained for all men it joins immediately to the objective reconciliation or justification of sinful mankind.... The reconciliation which Christ brought about is history, a finished event lying in the past θεὸς ἦν ἐν Χριστῷ κόσμον καταλλάσσων ἑαυτῷ), that pertains to all mankind and is of an entirely objective character. For it does not consist in a change of mind or "moral transformation" on the part of man, but in a change in God; God in His heart is not imputing their trespasses unto men, but forgiving them (μὴ λογιζόμενος αὐτοῖς τὰ παραπτώματα αὐτῶν, II Cor. 5:19). To the report of the finished universal objective reconciliation the Apostle immediately adds that God has committed unto us the Word or news of this complete reconciliation (καὶ θέμενος ἐν ἡμῖν τὸν λόγον τῆς καταλλαγῆς) in order that men may share in the finished reconciliation.

Hence the first means of grace is "the Word of Reconciliation," the Word of the Gospel. The Law of God, which is also contained in Scripture, must be excluded from the concept "means of grace," because the Law does not assure those who have transgressed it—and all men have transgressed it—of the remission of their sins, or God's grace, but on the contrary proclaims God's wrath and damnation. For this reason the Law is expressly called ἡ διακονία τῆς κατακρίσεως, "the ministration of condemnation,"[5] whereas the Gospel is ἡ διακονία τῆς δικαιοσύνης, "the ministration of righteousness" (II Cor. 3:9).[6]

Two things must here be kept in mind. The Gospel is means of grace not only in the sense that it tells of a readiness on the part of God to forgive, but in the sense that whenever we hear the Gospel, we hear God pronouncing absolution upon us, forgiving our sins. Luther: "The Gospel is in itself a general absolution, for it is a promise which all and everyone in particular should appropriate on God's command" (St. L. XXIb:1849).

Furthermore, the Gospel is such a means of grace in every form in which it reaches men, whether it be preached (Mark 16:15, 16; Luke 24:47),[7] or printed (John 20:31; I John 1:3, 4),[8] or expressed as a formal absolution (John 20:23),[9] or pictured in symbols or types (John 3:14, 15),[10] or pondered in the heart (Rom. 10:8),[11] and so forth. Some recent Lutheran theologians, too, have assailed the inspiration of Scripture with the strange contention that not the read, but only the preached Word is a means of grace.[12] But Scripture equates the read and the preached Word of God as it pertains to the conferring of grace and the working of faith. This fact is evident from the passages cited above. To the appeal to Romans 10:17 Gerhard has given the sufficient answer:

The statement (Rom. 10:17) that "faith cometh by hearing" is not to be understood as excluding the written Word, but as including it, as meaning that God works faith and salvation not only through the oral Word but also through the written Word, since it is and remains one and the same Word whether it is preached and heard or written and read. On this account John significantly states of the written Gospels, and hence of the entire Scriptures of the Old and the New Testament: "These things write we unto you that your joy may be full," I John 1:4. Accordingly, faith and spiritual joy, and consequently also salvation, can be obtained from the written Word of God, too, when it is put to use by reading and pondering it. (*Loci,* "De Scriptura," §365)

To the opinion that "the Word of Scripture, when multiplied by printing, takes on the character in the case of ever so many thousands of people of a remote or weak action *(actio in distans)* as to space and time,"[13] we reply: That is not occasioned by Scripture, but is the fault of the readers who do not recognize the Word of Scripture as the Word of God, and particularly the fault of those theological professors who spread such erroneous thoughts about Scripture among the people. He, however, who considers Scripture to be the very Word of God, as Scripture itself demands (I Cor. 14:37; II Tim. 3:16; II Peter 1:21[14]), does not think of a "remote action as to space and time," but as he reads his Bible, he is aware that God Himself is speaking to him, that through the Word of the Law He is convincing him of his sin and just condemnation and that through the Word of the Gospel He is assuring him of the forgiveness of his sins and salvation and inviting him to believe this Word of the Gospel. So Christ instructs us to recognize the demands of the Law from the written Law: "What is written in the Law? How readest thou?" (Luke 10:26–28; Matt. 22:35–40). And so Christ teaches us to know Him as our Savior from the written Gospel: "Search the Scriptures; for in them ye think ye have eternal life; and they are they which testify of Me" (John 5:39), and: "Had ye believed Moses, ye would have believed Me; for he wrote of Me" (John 5:46). Just so the Formula of Concord equates the heard and the read Gospel: "And by this means, and in no other way, namely, through the His holy Word, when men hear it preached, or read it, and the holy Sacraments, when they are used according to His Word, God desires to call men to eternal salvation, draw them to Himself, and convert, regenerate, and sanctify them" (*Trigl.* 901, Sol. Decl., II, 50, 53).

Furthermore God has attached the promise of the forgiveness of sins to certain external acts which He has ordained *(actiones circa elementum quoddam externum et visibile occupatae),* namely, Baptism and the Lord's Supper. Scripture says expressly that Baptism takes place "for the remission of sin," or "to wash away sins" (Acts 2:38; 22:16).[15] In the Lord's Supper Christ likewise bestows His body as given (διδόμενον) and His blood as shed (ἐκχυννόμενον) "for the remission of sins" (Matt. 26:26–28; Luke 22:19, 20). For this reason also Baptism and the Lord's Supper are means of grace. Because the actions with which the forgiveness of sins is connected are visible, these rites, in distinction from the mere Word of the Gospel, have been called *"verbum visibile"* and "Sacraments."[16]

All Means of Grace Have the Same Purpose and the Same Effect

According to Scripture, all means of grace have the same purpose and the same effect, namely, the conferring of the forgiveness of sins and the resultant engendering and strengthening of faith. We are not to imagine that each one of the three means transmits one third of the forgiveness. We saw before that Scripture ascribes the forgiveness of sins without reservation to the Word of the Gospel, to Baptism, and to the Lord's Supper. Therefore all means of grace have also the *vis effectiva,* the power to work and to strengthen faith.[17] And where there is forgiveness of sins, there is also life and salvation, with the full measure of divine gifts.

Modern theologians in particular have the idea that a different effect must be attributed to each means of grace. Baptism, they say, differs from the Word of the Gospel in working regeneration, and the Lord's Supper differs from both Word and Baptism by a special physical effect, for example, the implanting of the resurrection body.[18] But this is taught without Scripture basis. As surely as Baptism is a means of regeneration (λουτρὸν παλιγγενεσίας καὶ ἀνακαινώσεως πνεύματος ἁγίου, Titus 3:5), so surely the Word of the Gospel works regeneration (ἀναγεγεν-νημένοι... διά λόγου ζῶντος θεοῦ, I Peter 1:23). And as certainly as Christ gives His true body and blood, and not mere symbols of His body and blood, in the Lord's Supper, so sure it is also that He names as purpose of this wonderful gift not a special physical effect, but merely the assurance and attestation that God is graciously disposed toward those who eat and drink, because of the body given and the blood shed by Christ. That is the only possible meaning of the words: "This is My body, which is given for you; this do in remembrance of Me" (Luke 22:19)[19] and: "This is My blood of the new testament, which is shed for many for the remission of sins" (Matt. 26:28).[20]

We find the same teaching in our Lutheran Symbols. They stress emphatically that the Sacraments have no other purpose than the Word of the Gospel, namely, the attestation and conferring of the forgiveness of sins and the engendering and strengthening of faith in this forgiveness. Listen to the Apology:

> Therefore Baptism, the Lord's Supper, and Absolution, which is the sacrament of Repentance, are truly Sacraments. For these rites have God's command and the promise of grace, which is peculiar to the New Testament. For when we are baptized, when we eat the Lord's body, when we are absolved, our hearts must be firmly assured that God truly forgives us for Christ's sake. And God, at the same time, by the Word and by the rite, moves hearts to believe and conceive faith, just as Paul says, Rom. 10:17: "Faith cometh by hearing." But just as the Word enters the ear in order to strike our heart, so the rite itself strikes the eye, in order to move the heart. The effect of the Word and of the rite is the same, as has been well said by Augustine that a Sacrament is a visible Word, because the rite is received by the eye and is, as it were, a picture of the Word, signifying the same things as the Word. Therefore the effect of both is the same. (*Trigl.* 309, XIII, 4f.)

Just so the Augsburg Confession declares that the purpose of the Sacraments is "to be signs and testimonies of the will of God toward us, instituted to awaken and confirm faith in those who use them" (*Trigl.* 49,

XIII). This terminology of the Augsburg Confession, that the Sacraments are "signs and testimonies of the [scil., gracious] will of God toward us" and therefore awaken and strengthen faith, rests on the universal objective reconciliation and deserves to be called classic.

The objection of modern theologians that the Sacraments are diminished in value if the conferring and confirming of the forgiveness of sins is taught as their one purpose is out of place entirely. For one thing, determining the purpose of the Sacraments is God's business, who instituted them, and it is decidedly improper for men to presume to improve on the divinely determined purpose. Moreover, is not the forgiveness of sins the real and chief good *(Hauptgut),* "the new testament," so that he who has remission of sins forfeits nothing? Scripture presents all other spiritual gifts and activities as resulting from the forgiveness of sins: the state of grace, the indwelling of the Holy Spirit, the *unio mystica,* sanctification, the love of God and the neighbor, membership in the Christian Church and all privileges which this includes.[21] If, therefore, we content ourselves with the purpose of the Sacraments as God determined it, namely, that they are means of creating and strengthening faith, the reception of all remaining goods and gifts is guaranteed us. Specifically, the resurrection of the body on the Last Day is then also provided for. The notion that the resurrection body is implanted through the receiving of Christ's body and blood in the Lord's Supper is superfluous. The divine promise guarantees the resurrection of the body to all who believe that they have the forgiveness of their sins in Christ,[22] even if, due to certain circumstances, they have not eaten and drunk Christ's body and blood in the Sacrament, as, for instance, in the case of believing children in the Lutheran Church and of believers in Christ in the Reformed bodies.

Some theologians who teach a physical bestowal of the resurrection body on the communicants claim Luther as their champion. Luther does indeed teach that the hope of the resurrection of the body is strengthened by partaking of the Lord's Supper. But he does not teach it as a physical result in the body of Christians because of their bodily eating, but as the effect of the spiritual eating which a Christian combines with the bodily eating, of his faith in the word of absolution, "Given and shed for you for the remission of sins." The Reformer writes (St. L. XX:831): "Of course, nobody can force the words down his throat into his stomach, but through his ears he must take them to heart. But what is it that he takes to heart through these words? Nothing else than what the words say: 'the body given for us.' This is the spiritual eating. And we have added that he who receives the Sacrament orally without these words or without this spiritual eating not only has no benefit from his eating, but even experiences harm, as St. Paul says in I Cor. 11:27: 'Whosoever shall eat this bread unworthily shall be guilty of the body of the Lord.' Hence there was no reason for you to instruct us that bodily eating does not profit." To these words Luther then adds the comment that a Christian may entertain the hope that Christ on the Last Day will raise the body which He deigned to honor here on earth by a union with His body through the oral eating in the Lord's

Supper. "The mouth, which eats Christ's flesh bodily, does of course not know what it is eating or what the heart is eating; nor would it have any benefit from it because it cannot grasp or perceive what the words say. But the heart is well aware of what the mouth is eating. For it understands the words and eats spiritually what the mouth eats bodily. Since, however, the mouth is a member belonging to the heart, it [the mouth and accordingly the whole body] must in the end live eternally by reason of the heart which receives eternal life through the Word, because the mouth in a bodily manner eats the same eternal food which its heart eats spiritually."

Moreover, ascribing a physical effect to the Sacraments is by no means a harmless speculation. Thereby we fall into the Romanist error of an operation of the Sacraments *ex opere operato sine bono motu utentis,* by the mere performance of the act without participation of the heart, an imparting of grace without faith as the receiving hand of man. Saving grace is then no longer conceived of as the forgiveness of sins, or the *favor Dei propter Christum,* but as the infusion of a grace substance. The remission of sins and faith, or, in other words, justification by faith, is thereby set aside and the foundation of Christianity impaired.

For this reason our Lutheran Confessions so stress the *idem effectus* of the Word and the Sacraments, emphasizing that the offer of the favor of God and the engendering and strengthening of faith must be maintained. The Confessions add the following critical remarks:

> Here we condemn the whole crowd of scholastic doctors, who teach that the Sacraments confer grace *ex opere operato* (through the act performed), without a good disposition on the part of the one using them, provided he does not place a hindrance *(obicem)* in the way. This is absolutely a Jewish opinion, to hold that we are justified by a ceremony, without a good disposition of the heart, i.e., without faith. And yet this impious and pernicious opinion is taught with great authority throughout the entire realm of the Pope. Paul contradicts this and denies, in Romans 4:9, that Abraham was justified by circumcision, but asserts that circumcision was a sign presented for exercising faith. Thus we teach that in the use of the Sacraments faith ought to be added, which should believe these promises, and receive the promised things, there offered in the Sacraments. . . . The promise is useless unless it is received by faith. . . . And here we speak of special faith which believes the present promise, not only that which in general believes [*fides generalis*] that God exists, but which believes that the remission of sins is offered. This use of the Sacrament consoles godly and alarmed minds. Moreover, no one can express in words what abuses in the Church this fanatical opinion concerning the *opus operatum,* without a good disposition on the part of the one using the Sacraments, has produced. Hence the infinite profanation of the Masses. . . . Yea, Augustine says the contrary, that the faith of the Sacrament, and not the Sacrament, justifies." (*Trigl.* 313, Apol., XIII, 18ff.)

Also the objection that there is no need of offering and confirming to Christians one and the same forgiveness of sins in several ways betrays an astonishing ignorance. Both Scripture and experience teach that men who feel the weight of their sins find nothing harder to believe than the forgiveness of their sins. Hence repetition of the assurance of the forgiveness of sins in various ways through the means of grace meets a practical need of Christians. This need Luther, too, pointed out in the Smalcald Articles: "The Gospel not merely in one way gives us counsel and aid against sin; for God is superabundantly rich [and liberal] in His grace [and goodness]. First, through the spoken Word by which the forgiveness of sins is preached in the whole world; which is the peculiar office of the Gospel. Secondly, through Baptism. Thirdly, through the holy Sacrament of the Altar. Fourthly, through the power of the keys, and also through the mutual conversation and consolation of brethren, Matt. 18:20: 'Where two or three are gathered together,' etc." (*Trigl.* 491, Part III, Art. IV)

Notes

[1]Formula of Concord: "Christ . . . offers to all men His grace [*clementiam*] in the Word and holy Sacraments" (*Trigl.* 903, Sol. Decl., II, 57).

[2]Formula of Concord: "The Word of God preached and heard is [truly] an office and work of the Holy Ghost, by which He is certainly efficacious and works in our hearts" (*Trigl.* 903, Sol. Decl., II, 56). Augustana: "That we may obtain this faith, the ministry of teaching the Gospel and administering the Sacraments was instituted. For through the Word and Sacraments, as through instruments, the Holy Ghost is given, who works faith, where and when it pleases God, in them that hear the Gospel" (*Trigl.* 45, V, 1, 2).

[3]*Fidei Ratio,* ed. Niemeyer, p. 24; Jacobs, *Book of Concord,* II, 168.

[4]R. E., 3d ed., VI, p. 726.

[5]Luther: *"das Amt, das die Verdammnis predigt"*; Meyer: "the office transmitting condemnation."

[6]Luther: *"das Amt, das die Gerechtigkeit predigt"*; Meyer: "the office transmitting righteousness." That "righteousness" must here be understood juridically as acquittal or justification is evident from its antithesis to "condemnation." Meyer: "Observe the antithesis of κατάκρισις and δικαιοσύνη. The former is an *actus forensis,* hence the latter, too, is founded on imputation. This against Hofmann, *Schriftbeweis,* I, 627f."

[7]Mark 16:15, 16: Κηρύξατε τὸ εὐαγγέλιον . . . ὁ πιστεύσας . . . σωθήσεται Luke 24:47: ἔδει κηρυχθῆναι . . . ἄφεσιν ἁμαρτιῶν.

[8]John 20:31: Ταῦτα δὲ γέγραπτει, ἵνα πιστεύητε ὅτι Ἰησοῦς ἐστιν ὁ Χριστός. I John 1:3, 4: "That which we have seen and heard declare we unto you . . . and these things write we unto you, that your joy may be full."

[9]John 20:23: Ἄν τινων ἀφῆτε τὰς ἁμαρτίας ἀφέωνται αὐτοῖς. The term "whosoever" indicates that Christ here has in mind the application of the Gospel to definite persons; hence the absolution pronounced on an individual.

[10]E.g., by a crucifix or some picture. Luther often recalls that in the Papacy many, when in the throes of death, were reminded of Christ's substitutionary satisfaction

by means of a crucifix held before their eyes and thus died a blessed death. St. L. XIII:2575: "Thus I believe that our dear Lord preserved many of our forefathers in the gross darkness of the Papacy. In that blindness and darkness so much still remained that a crucifix was held before the eyes of the dying and that some laymen would urge them: 'Behold Jesus, who died for you on the Cross!' This induced many a dying man to turn again to Christ, though previously he, too, believed the lying wonders and was given to idolatry." Similar statements: St. L. VIII:183; XI:528; XXII:471.

[11]Here the Word of the Gospel is meant, in contrast to the Word of the Law (vv. 5–7). He who ponders a Gospel statement in his heart has in that word the divine absolution from all his sins, and no more is necessary than that he appropriate the absolution by faith. That the Word of God, when pondered in the heart, is a means of grace, the Formula of Concord, too, teaches in the words: "Through the preaching and consideration [*meditatione*] of the holy Gospel concerning the gracious forgiveness of sins in Christ a spark of faith is kindled in him, which accepts the forgiveness of sins for Christ's sake, and comforts itself with the promise of the Gospel, and thus the Holy Ghost *(who works all this)* is sent into the heart, Gal. 4:6" (*Trigl.* 903, Sol. Decl., II, 54).

[12]Thus particularly the theologians of Dorpat in the early eighties of the last century. Volck of Dorpat, for example, says in *Die Bibel als Kanon,* p. 14: "What is it that brings the individual to faith in Christ and thus makes him a Christian? Is it perhaps his reading of the Bible? No, it is rather the Church's testimony of Christ that approaches him in this or that form. 'Faith cometh by hearing,' says Paul. If it were engendered by the reading of the Bible, the task of missions would be a simple one. They would then merely have to send Bibles to the various peoples in their native tongue, provided, of course, that they were literate." A number of Baltic pastors wrote against these Dorpat professors, e.g., F. Neerling, *Die Bibel als Heilsoffenbarung,* 1886.

[13]A. v. Oettingen, *Luth. Dogmatik,* II, 2d ed., 335.

[14]The προφητεία γραφῆς is spoken of.

[15]Meyer on Acts 22:16: "Here, too, Baptism is the means through which the sins which were committed before conversion are forgiven. See Acts 2:38; Eph. 5:26; I Cor. 6:11. Calvin employs restrictions in order to sever grace from the Sacraments."

[16]Apology: "But just as the Word enters the ear in order to strike our heart, so the rite itself strikes our eye in order to move the heart. The effect of the Word and of the rite is the same, as it has been well said by Augustine that a Sacrament is a *visible Word,* because the rite is received by the eye and is, as it were, a picture of the Word, signifying the same thing as the Word. Therefore the effect of both is the same" (*Trigl.* 309, XIII, 5).

[17]Augsb. Conf., Art. V, XIII.

[18]R. E., 2d ed., XIII, 298f. Luthardt reviews briefly the recent attempts to find a different purpose for Baptism and for the Lord's Supper (*Dogmatik,* 11th ed., pp. 373, 386f.; cp. Nitzsch-Stephan, *Ev. Dogmatik,* p. 646ff.). In his edition of Baier's *Compendium* (III, 526f.) Walther adduces a longer quotation from Georg Koenig (d. 1654) which shows that also the old Lutheran theologians gave considerable thought to the question whether a physical effect is to be ascribed to the

Lord's Supper. Koenig denies this and thereby opposes not only men like Weigel, but also a few *"ex nostratibus"* (of our own men). Koenig writes in *Casus consc.*, p. 484ff., 494ff.: "May one correctly hold that the reception of Communion effects an essential union of Christ with us? We here do not desire to contend with anyone but Weigel, who believes that from Communion, that is, from the use of the Lord's Supper, in which with the bread the body of Christ and with the chalice His blood is distributed, there follows an essential union of our body and blood with Christ's body and blood. Be pleased to hear his very words. . . . Most clearly he sets forth his meaning in Part I of his postil, p. 214: 'Christ,' he says, 'gives us the bread from heaven not only in faith, spiritually, without bread and wine, but also in the Supper with bread and wine; not that the visible bread and wine is Christ's body and blood perceptibly, but in it He is given to us. For the bread from heaven is His Word, and He is the Word, and the Word is in the bread, and this invisible Bread from heaven, or the Word, becomes flesh and blood in us and is joined to our flesh and blood. On this account we are, when we receive this memorial food, united with Christ's crucified body and are bodily united with Him.' . . . This assertion of Weigel is of such a nature that we cannot assent to it with a good conscience for the following reasons: 1. It has no foundation at all in Scripture. . . . For where did Christ say: 'Take and drink so that My body and blood may be transformed into a common substance with you'? Where did He say: 'Take, eat and drink; this, when it is eaten and swallowed, works in you a common essence with Me'? Where did He say: 'Eat; this is the invisible Bread from heaven which becomes flesh and blood in you and is closely united with your flesh and blood'? Where did He say: 'Eat, in order to be made one in substance with My crucified body'? . . . 2. The Sacrament confers upon us what is promised in the Word. For the Sacraments are seals of the Word; but seals do not confirm more than the writing to which they are appended contains. But nowhere is it promised to us in the words of Scripture that either in Communion or outside it Christ should be essentially united with us. . . . 3. If the communicants are united essentially with Christ by the mere [*nudo*] use of the Supper of our Lord, also the unbelieving should be acknowledged participants in this union, because they, too, use the Lord's Supper, and this uncorrupted. For what he who receives the Sacrament believes, or with what sort of faith he is imbued, makes no difference when we deal with the integrity and sanctity of the Sacrament. Of course, it makes a great difference in regard to the way of salvation, but as to the nature of the Sacrament it makes no difference. For it can happen that a man has the Sacrament uncorrupted, but has a perverted faith, says Augustine 1, 3, *contra Donat.*, c. 14; see him 1, 4, c.24. But the aforementioned conclusion is absurd. For in this manner would be united the purest and the most impure essence, the Son of God and the child of the devil, Christ and Belial, contrary to the manifest Scriptures, 2 Cor. 6:15 . . . You say: 'Then, beside the spiritual, there is not to be placed a certain sacramental union between Christ and the believers, flowing from participation in the body and blood of Christ? Are there not such among us, too, who believe that there is such a sacramental union which flows from the power and efficacy of the Communion and is equally common to both the worthy and the unworthy?' . . . I judge that this cannot be asserted or defended without injury to the truth: I. Because in this manner the term 'union' is plainly misused. Now the *unio sacramentalis*, simply spoken of so far, is that which takes place between the earthly and the heavenly element; from this then are to be deduced the sacramental propositions, as the personal from the personal union. Now, however, a new sacramental union is added. But of it Scripture is entirely unaware; nor does it furnish any foundation for it. Paul in 1 Cor. 10:16–17 indeed mentions an at least twofold communion which occurs by virtue of the Eucharist: 1. the sacramental, pertaining to the Eucharist symbols united with the heavenly element; 2. the mystical, which pertains to the mystical body of Christ and its members. Since, however, hypocrites are not members of that mystical body, except by sham, it is not to be believed that any union, properly so called and derived from the Eucharist, pertains to them or occurs between them and Christ, whether through the one usually called sacramental or otherwise. II. This other sacramental union, if it can trace its origin to anything, occurs only through the eating of the body and drinking of the blood. But it is one thing that the godless eat Christ's body and drink Christ's blood, and another that they are mystically united with Christ by virtue of the Sacrament. The former we necessarily grant because of the true sacramental union, which takes place between the earthly and the heavenly element and results from the authority of the Institutor, not from the condition of the eater. The latter, on the contrary, we necessarily reject because of the absence of the condition required of him who eats and drinks, namely, faith. He, therefore, who has no faith can by no means experience the salutary effect of the Sacrament, the circle of which must also include union with Christ. Unless this is conceded, any salutory effect attributed to the Sacrament would have to be *ex opere operato sine bono motu utentis.* But this sentence of the old Scholastics is for the most part given up also by the modern Jesuits. III. A comparison made with the Baptism of adults also opposes the alleged sacramental union. What spiritual effect, pray, has Baptism that is common to believers and hypocrites? None evidently as regards salvation; merely external communion with the Church because both by Baptism were received into the periphery [*pomoeria*] of the Church. The same reasoning applies here, and no other. We must indeed admit that the fathers at times have spoken a trifle strongly regarding the effect of the Sacrament . . . for many statements have been furnished which can easily be twisted in favor of those hypocrites, but such utterances should be read *cum grano salis.* "

[19]Luther: "I hope it is not necessary to say much as to what the remembrance of Christ might be. In other places we have often and amply explained this term. It is not such a contemplation of the suffering as some practice, hoping by such a good work to render service to God and to obtain grace by occupying themselves in sorrowing over the bitter sufferings of Christ, etc. The remembrance of Christ rather consists in teaching and believing the power and fruit of His suffering; accordingly, that our works and merit are worthless, that the free will is dead and lost, that, on the contrary, we are absolved from our sin and become righteous solely through Christ's suffering and death; hence that the remembrance consists in teaching or recalling the grace of God in Christ and not in a work done by us" (St. L. X:2188).

[20]Luther: "Therefore this Luther has correctly taught that he who has an evil conscience because of sin should receive the Sacrament and get consolation, not from the bread and wine, not from the body and blood of Christ, but from the Word which in the Sacrament offers, presents, and gives to me Christ's body and blood as given and shed for me" (St. L. XX:275).

[21]See the Survey of Soteriology, Vol. II, 406ff.

[22]See Luther, St. L. XVII:2212.

10

Martin Luther

Galatians 3:13

Christ redeemed us from the curse of the Law, having become a curse for us—for it is written: Cursed be everyone who hangs on a tree.

Here again Jerome and the sophists who followed him are distressed.[1] They most miserably lacerate this passage, which is filled to overflowing with comfort; and they strive anxiously with what they think is godly zeal not to permit the insult of being called a curse or an execration to come to Christ. Therefore they evade this statement this way. "Paul was not speaking in earnest here." Thus they said, in a way that was as reprehensible as it was wicked, that Scripture, whose passages do not contradict themselves, does contradict itself in Paul. They show this as follows: "The statement from Moses that Paul cites here does not speak about Christ. In addition, the universal expression 'everyone' that Paul has is not added in Moses. Furthermore, Paul omits the phrase 'by God,' which occurs in Moses. In short, it is obvious enough that Moses is speaking about a criminal or a thief who has deserved the cross by his wicked deeds, as Scripture testifies clearly in Deut. 21: 22, 23." Therefore, they ask how

From *Luther's Works,* ed. Jaroslav Pelikan (St. Louis: Concordia Publishing House, 1963), Vol. 26, pp. 276–291. Used by permission.

this sentence can be applied to Christ, that He is accursed by God and hanged on a tree, since He is not a criminal or a thief but righteous and holy. Perhaps this may impress the inexperienced; for they suppose that the sophists are speaking in a way that is not only subtle but also very pious, and that they are defending the honor of Christ and are religiously admonishing all Christians not to suppose wickedly that Christ was a curse. Therefore it must be determined what Paul's intent and meaning are.

Paul guarded his words carefully and spoke precisely. And here again a distinction must be made; Paul's words clearly show this. For he does not say that Christ became a curse on His own account, but that He became a curse "for us." Thus the whole emphasis is on the phrase "for us." For Christ is innocent so far as His own Person is concerned; therefore He should not have been hanged from the tree. But because, according to the Law, every thief should have been hanged, therefore, according to the Law of Moses, Christ Himself should have been hanged; for He bore the person of a sinner and a thief—and not of one but of all sinners and thieves. For we are sinners and thieves, and therefore we are worthy of death and eternal damnation. But Christ took all our sins upon Himself, and for them He died on the cross. Therefore it was appropriate for Him to become a thief and, as Isaiah says (53:12), to be "numbered among the thieves."

And all the prophets saw this, that Christ was to become the greatest thief, murderer, adulterer, robber, desecrator, blasphemer, etc., there has ever been anywhere in the world. He is not acting in His own Person now. Now He is not the Son of God, born of the Virgin. But He is a sinner, who has and bears the sin of Paul, the former blasphemer, persecutor, and assaulter; of Peter, who denied Christ; of David, who was an adulterer and a murderer. . . . In short, He has and bears all the sins of all men in His body—not in the sense that He has committed them but in the sense that He took these sins, committed by us, upon His own body, in order to make satisfaction for them with His own blood. Therefore this general Law of Moses included Him, although He was innocent so far as His own Person was concerned; for it found Him among sinners and thieves. Thus a magistrate regards someone as a criminal and punishes him if he catches him among thieves, even though the man has never committed anything evil or worthy of death. Christ was not only found among sinners; but of His own free will and by the will of the Father He wanted to be an associate of sinners, having assumed the flesh and blood of those who were sinners and thieves and who were immersed in all sorts of sin. Therefore when the Law found Him among thieves, it condemned and executed Him as a thief.

This knowledge of Christ and most delightful comfort, that Christ became a curse for us to set us free from the curse of the Law—of this the sophists deprive us when they segregate Christ from sins and from sinners and set Him forth to us only as an example to be imitated. In this way they make Christ not only useless to us but also a judge and a tyrant who is angry because of our sins and who damns sinners. But just as Christ is wrapped up in our flesh and blood, so we must wrap Him and know Him to be wrapped up in our sins, our curse, our death, and everything evil.

"But it is highly absurd and insulting to call the Son of God a sinner and a curse!" If you want to deny that He is a sinner and a curse, then deny also that He suffered, was crucified, and died. For it is no less absurd to say, as our Creed confesses and prays, that the Son of God was crucified and underwent the torments of sin and death than it is to say that He is a sinner or a curse. But if it is not absurd to confess and believe that Christ was crucified among thieves, then it is not absurd to say as well that He was a curse and a sinner of sinners. Surely these words of Paul are not without purpose: "Christ became a curse for us" and "For our sake God made Christ to be sin, who knew no sin, so that in Him we might become the righteousness of God" (II Cor. 5:21).

In the same way John the Baptist called Christ "the Lamb of God" (John 1:29). He is, of course, innocent, because He is the Lamb of God without spot or blemish. But because He bears the sins of the world, His innocence is pressed down with the sins and the guilt of the entire world. Whatever sins I, you, and all of us have committed or may commit in the future, they are as much Christ's own as if He Himself had committed them. In short, our sin must be Christ's own sin, or we shall perish eternally. The wicked sophists have obscured this true knowledge of Christ which Paul and the prophets have handed down to us.

Isaiah 53:6 speaks the same way about Christ. It says: "God has laid on Him the iniquity of us all." These words must not be diluted but must be left in their precise and serious sense. For God is not joking in the words of the prophet; He is speaking seriously and out of great love, namely, that this Lamb of God, Christ, should bear the iniquity of us all. But what does it mean to "bear"? The sophists reply: "To be punished." Good. But why is Christ punished? Is it not because He has sin and bears sin? That Christ has sin is the testimony of the Holy Spirit in the Psalms. Thus in Psalm 40:12 we read: "My iniquities have overtaken me"; in Psalm 41:4: "I said: 'O Lord, be gracious to Me; heal Me, for I have sinned against Thee!' "; and in Psalm 69:5: "O God, Thou knowest My folly; the wrongs I have done are not hidden from Thee." In these psalms the Holy Spirit is speaking in the Person of Christ and testifying in clear words that He has sinned or has sins. These testimonies of the psalms are not the words of an innocent one; they are the words of the suffering Christ, who undertook to bear the person of all sinners and therefore was made guilty of the sins of the entire world.

Therefore Christ not only was crucified and died, but by divine love sin was laid upon Him. When sin was laid upon Him, the Law came and said: "Let every sinner die! And therefore, Christ, if You want to reply that You are guilty and that You bear the punishment, You must bear the sin and the curse as well." Therefore Paul correctly applies to Christ this general Law from Moses: "Cursed be everyone who hangs on a tree." Christ hung on a tree; therefore Christ is a curse of God.

And this is our highest comfort, to clothe and wrap Christ this way in my sins, your sins, and the sins of the entire world, and in this way to behold Him bearing all our sins. When He is beheld this way, He easily removes all the fanatical opinions of our opponents about justification by works. For the papists dream about a kind of faith "formed by love." Through this they want to remove sins and be justified. This is clearly to unwrap Christ and to unclothe Him from our sins, to make Him innocent, to burden and overwhelm ourselves with our own sins, and to behold them, not in Christ but in ourselves. This is to abolish Christ and make Him useless. For if it is true that we abolish sins by the works of the Law and by love, then Christ does not take them away, but we do. But if He is truly the Lamb of God who takes away the sins of the world, who became a curse for us, and who was wrapped in our sins, it necessarily follows that we cannot be justified and take away sins through love. For God has laid our sins, not upon us but upon Christ, His Son. If they are taken away by Him, then they cannot be taken away by us. All Scripture says this, and we confess and pray the same thing in the Creed when we say: "I believe in Jesus Christ, the Son of God, who suffered, was crucified, and died for us."

This is the most joyous of all doctrines and the one that contains the most comfort. It teaches that we have the indescribable and inestimable mercy and love of God. When the merciful Father saw that we were being oppressed through the Law, that we were being held under a curse, and that we could not be liberated from it by anything, He sent His Son into the world, heaped all the sins of all men upon Him, and said to Him: "Be Peter the denier; Paul the persecutor, blasphemer, and assaulter; David the adulterer; the sinner who ate the apple in Paradise; the thief on the cross. In short, be the person of all men, the one who has committed the sins of all men. And see to it that You pay and make satisfaction for them." Now the Law comes and says: "I find Him a sinner, who takes upon Himself the sins of all men. I do not see any other sins than those in Him. Therefore let Him die on the cross!" And so it attacks Him and kills Him. By this deed the whole world is purged and expiated from all sins, and thus it is set free from death and from every evil. But when sin and death have been abolished by this one man, God does not want to see anything else in the whole world, especially if it were to believe, except sheer cleansing and righteousness. And if any remnants of sin were to remain, still for the sake of Christ, the shining Sun, God would not notice them.

This is how we must magnify the doctrine of Christian righteousness in opposition to the righteousness of the Law and of works, even though there is no voice or eloquence that can properly understand, much less express, its greatness. Therefore the argument that Paul presents here is the most powerful and the highest of all against all the righteousness of the flesh; for it contains this invincible and irrefutable antithesis: If the sins of the entire world are on that one man, Jesus Christ, then they are not on the world. But if they are not on Him, then they are still on the world. Again, if Christ Himself is made guilty of all the sins that we have all committed, then we are absolved from all sins, not through ourselves or through our own works or merits but through Him. But if He is innocent and does not carry our sins, then we carry them and shall die and be damned in them. "But thanks be to God, who gives us the victory through our Lord Jesus Christ! Amen" (I Cor. 15:57).

Now let us see how two such extremely contrary things come together in this Person. Not only my sins and yours, but the sins of the entire world, past, present, and future, attack Him, try to damn Him, and do in fact damn Him. But because in the same Person, who is the highest, the greatest, and the only sinner, there is also eternal and invincible righteousness, therefore these two converge: the highest, the greatest, and the only sin; and the highest, the greatest, and the only righteousness. Here one of them must yield and be conquered, since they come together and collide with such a powerful impact. Thus the sin of the entire world attacks righteousness with the greatest possible impact and fury. What happens? Righteousness is eternal, immortal, and invincible. Sin, too, is a very powerful and cruel tyrant, dominating and ruling over the whole world, capturing and enslaving all men. In short, sin is a great and powerful god who devours the whole human race, all the learned, holy, powerful, wise, and unlearned men. He, I say, attacks Christ and wants to devour Him as he has devoured all the rest. But he does not see that He is a Person of invincible and eternal righteousness. In this duel, therefore, it is necessary for sin to be conquered and killed, and for righteousness to prevail and live. Thus in Christ all sin is conquered, killed, and buried; and righteousness remains the victor and the ruler eternally.

Thus also death, which is the almighty empress of the entire world, killing kings, princes, and all men in general, clashes against life with full force and is about to conquer it and swallow it; and what it attempts, it accomplishes. But because life was immortal, it emerged victorious when it had been conquered, conquering and killing death in turn. About this wondrous duel the church beautifully sings: "It was a great and dreadful strife when death with life contended."[2] The Prince of life, who died, is alive and reigns. Through Christ, therefore, death is conquered and abolished in the whole world, so that now it is nothing but a picture of death. Now that its sting is lost, it can no longer harm believers in Christ, who has become the death of death, as Hosea sings (13:14): "O death, I shall be your death!"

Thus the curse, which is divine wrath against the whole world, has the same conflict with the blessing, that is, with the eternal grace and mercy of God in Christ. Therefore the curse clashes with the blessing and wants to damn it and annihilate it. But it cannot. For the blessing is divine and eternal, and therefore the curse must yield to it. For if the blessing in Christ could be conquered, then God Himself would be conquered. But this is impossible. Therefore Christ, who is the divine Power, Righteousness, Blessing, Grace, and Life, conquers and destroys these monsters—sin, death, and the curse—without weapons or battle, in His own body and in Himself, as Paul enjoys saying (Col. 2:15): "He disarmed the principalities and powers, triumphing over them in Him." Therefore they can no longer harm the believers.

This circumstance, "in Himself," makes the duel more amazing and outstanding; for it shows that such great things were to be achieved in the one and only Person of Christ—namely, that the curse, sin, and death were to be destroyed; that the blessing, righteousness, and life were to replace them; and that through Him the whole creation was to be renewed. If you look at this Person, therefore, you see sin, death, the wrath of God, hell, the devil, and all evils conquered and put to death. To the extent that Christ rules by His grace in the hearts of the faithful, there is no sin or death or curse. But where Christ is not known, there these things remain. And so all who do not believe lack this blessing and this victory. "For this," as John says, "is our victory, faith" (I John 5:4).

This is the chief doctrine of the Christian faith. The sophists have completely obliterated it, and today the fanatics are obscuring it once more. Here you see how necessary it is to believe and confess the doctrine of the divinity of Christ. When Arius denied this, it was necessary also for him to deny the doctrine of redemption. For to conquer the sin of the world, death, the curse, and the wrath of God in Himself—this is the work, not of any creature but of the divine power. Therefore it was necessary that He who was to conquer these in Himself should be true God by nature. For in opposition to this mighty power—sin, death, and the curse—which of itself reigns in the whole world and in the entire creation, it is necessary to set an even higher power, which cannot be found and does not exist apart from the divine power. Therefore to abolish sin, to destroy death, to remove the curse in Himself, to grant righteousness, to bring life to light (II Tim. 1:10), and to bring the blessing in Himself . . . all these are works solely of the divine power. Since Scripture attributes all these to Christ, therefore He Himself is Life, Righteousness, and Blessing, that is, God by nature and in essence. Hence those who deny the divinity of Christ lose all Christianity and become Gentiles and Turks through and through.

As I often warn, therefore, the doctrine of justification must be learned diligently. For in it are included all the other doctrines of our faith; and if it is sound, all the others are sound as well. Therefore when we teach that men are justified through Christ and that Christ is the Victor over sin, death, and the eternal curse, we are testifying at the same time that He is God by nature.

From this it is evident enough how horribly blind and wicked the papists were when they taught that these fierce and mighty tyrants—sin, death, and the curse—who swallow up the whole human race, are to be conquered, not by the righteousness of the divine Law (which, even though it is just, good, and holy, cannot do anything but subject one to a curse) but by the righteousness of human works, such as fasts, pilgrimages, rosaries, vows, etc. But, I ask you, who has ever been found who conquered sin, death, etc., if he was equipped with this armor? In Ephesians 6:13ff. Paul describes a far different armor to be used against these savage beasts. By putting us, naked and without the armor of God, up against these invincible and almighty tyrants, these blind men and leaders of the blind (Matt. 15:14) have not only handed us over to them to be devoured but have also made us ten times greater and worse sinners than murderers or harlots. For it belongs exclusively to the divine power to destroy sin and abolish death, to create righteousness and grant life. This divine power they have attributed to our own works, saying: "If you do this or that work, you will conquer sin, death, and the wrath of God.'' In this way they have made us true God by nature! Here the papists, under the Christian name, have shown themselves to be seven times greater idolaters than the Gentiles. What happens to them is what happens to the sow, which "is washed only to wallow in the mire" (II Peter 2:22). And, as Christ says (Luke 11:24–26), after a man has fallen from faith, the evil spirit returns to the house from which he was expelled and brings along seven other spirits more evil than himself and dwells there; and the last state of that man becomes worse than the first.

With gratitude and with a sure confidence, therefore, let us accept this doctrine, so sweet and so filled with comfort, which teaches that Christ became a curse for us, that is, a sinner worthy of the wrath of God; that He clothed Himself in our person, laid our sins upon His own shoulders, and said: "I have committed the sins that all men have committed." Therefore He truly became accursed according to the Law, not for Himself but, as Paul says, ὑπὲρ ἡμῶν. For unless He had taken upon Himself my sins, your sins, and the sins of the entire world, the Law would have had no right over him, since it condemns only sinners and holds only them under a curse. Therefore He could neither have become a curse nor have died, since the cause of the curse and of death is sin, of which He was innocent. But because He took upon Himself our sins, not by compulsion but of His own free will, it was right for Him to bear the punishment and the wrath of God—not for His own Person, which was righteous and invincible and therefore could not become guilty, but for our person.

By this fortunate exchange with us He took upon Himself our sinful person and granted us His innocent and victorious Person. Clothed and dressed in this, we are freed from the curse of the Law, because Christ Himself voluntarily became a curse for us, saying: "For My own Person of humanity and divinity I am blessed, and I am in need of nothing whatever. But I shall empty Myself (cf. Phil. 2:7); I shall assume your clothing and mask; and in this I shall walk about and suffer death, in order to set you free from death." Therefore when, inside our mask, He was carrying the sin of the whole world, He was captured, He suffered, He was crucified, He died; and for us He became a curse. But because He was a divine and eternal Person, it was impossible for death to hold Him. Therefore He arose from death on the third day, and now He lives eternally; nor can sin, death, and our mask be found in Him any longer, but there is sheer righteousness, life, and eternal blessing.

We must look at this image and take hold of it with a firm faith. He who does this has the innocence and the victory of Christ, no matter how great a sinner he is. But this cannot be grasped by loving will; it can be grasped only by reason illumined by faith. Therefore we are justified by faith alone, because faith alone grasps this victory of Christ. To the extent that you believe this, to that extent you have it. If you believe that sin, death, and the curse have been abolished, they have been abolished, because Christ conquered and overcame them in Himself; and He wants us to believe that just as in His Person there is no longer the mask of the sinner or any vestige of death, so this is no longer in our person, since He has done everything for us.

Therefore if sin makes you anxious, and if death terrifies you, just think that this is an empty specter and an illusion of the devil—which is what it surely is. For in fact there is no sin any longer, no curse, no death, and no devil, because Christ has conquered and abolished all these. Accordingly, the victory of Christ is utterly certain; the defects lie not in the fact itself, which is completely true, but in our incredulity. It is difficult for reason to believe such inestimable blessings. In addition, the devil and the sectarians—the former with his flaming darts (Eph. 6:16), the latter with their perverse and wicked doctrine—are bent on this one thing: to obscure this doctrine and take it away from us. It is above all for this doctrine, on which we insist so diligently, that we bear the hate and persecution of Satan and of the world. For Satan feels the power and the results of this doctrine.

Now that Christ reigns, there is in fact no more sin, death, or curse—this we confess every day in the Apostles' Creed when we say: "I believe in the holy church." This is plainly nothing else than if we were to say: "I believe that there is no sin and no death in the church. For believers in Christ are not sinners and are not sentenced to death but are altogether holy and righteous, lords over sin and death who live eternally." But it is faith alone that discerns this, because we say: "I believe in the holy church." If you consult your reason and your eyes, you will judge differently. For in devout people you will see many things that offend you; you will see them fall now and again, see them sin, or be weak in faith, or be troubled by a bad temper, envy, or other evil emotions. "Therefore the church is not holy." I deny the conclusion that you draw. If I look at my own person or at that of my neighbor, the church will never be holy. But if I look at Christ, who is the Propitiator and Cleanser of the church, then it is completely holy; for He bore the sins of the entire world.

Therefore where sins are noticed and felt, there they really are not present. For, according to the theology of Paul, there is no more sin, no more death, and no more curse in the world, but only in Christ, who is the Lamb of God that takes away the sins of the world, and who became a curse in order to set us free from the curse. On the other hand, according to philosophy and reason, sin, death, etc., are not present anywhere except in the world, in the flesh, and in sinners. For the theology of the sophists is unable to consider sin any other way except metaphysically, that is: "A quality clings to a substance or a subject. Therefore just as color clings to a wall, so sin clings to the world, to the flesh, or to the conscience. Therefore it must be washed away by some opposing motivations, namely, by love." But the true theology teaches that there is no more sin in the world, because Christ, on whom, according to Isaiah 53:6, the Father has laid the sins of the entire world, has conquered, destroyed, and killed it in His own body. Having died to sin once, He has truly been raised from the dead and will not die any more (Rom. 6:9). Therefore wherever there is faith in Christ, there sin has in fact been abolished, put to death, and buried. But where there is no faith in Christ, there sin remains. And although there are still remnants of sin in the saints because they do not believe perfectly, nevertheless these remnants are dead; for on account of faith in Christ they are not imputed.

Therefore this is an important and powerful argument that Paul is presenting here against the righteousness of works: "Neither the Law nor works redeem from the curse, but only Christ." Therefore I implore you for God's sake to distinguish Christ from the Law and to pay diligent attention to how Paul is speaking and to what he is saying. "It is necessary," he says, "that all who do not keep the Law be under a curse." But no one keeps the Law. Therefore the first proposition is true, namely, that all men are under a curse. Then he adds a second proposition: "Christ has redeemed us from the curse of the Law, having become a curse for us." Therefore the Law and works do not redeem from the curse. On the contrary, they drag us down and subject us to the curse. Therefore love, which, according to the sophists, "informs" faith, not only does not redeem from the curse but forces and wraps us into it even more.

But just as Christ is something different from the Law and from the works of the Law, so the redemption of Christ is altogether different from our merit based on works of the Law; for it had to be Christ Himself who redeemed us from the curse of the Law. Therefore whoever does not take hold of Christ by faith remains under the curse. Not even the sophists are so stupid as to say that Christ is our work or our love, for Christ is something altogether different from a work that we do. No papist, no matter how insane he is, will have the audacity to say that the alms he grants to someone in need or the obedience that a monk yields is a Christ. For Christ is God and man, "conceived by the Holy Spirit, born of the Virgin Mary," etc. Now about Him Paul says that He became a curse for us to redeem us from the curse of the Law. Therefore the Law, works, love, vows, etc., do not redeem; they only wrap one in the curse and make it even heavier. Therefore the more we have performed works, the less able we are to know and to grasp Christ.

But Christ is grasped, not by the Law or by works, but by a reason or an intellect that has been illumined by faith. And this grasping of Christ through faith is truly the "speculative life," about which the sophists chatter a great deal without knowing what they are saying.[3] The speculation by which Christ is grasped is not the foolish imagination of the sophists and monks about marvelous things beyond them; it is a theological, faithful, and divine consideration of the serpent hanging from the pole, that is, of Christ hanging on the cross for my sins, for your sins, and for the sins of the entire world (John 3:14, 15). Hence it is evident that faith alone justifies. But once we have been justified by faith, we enter the active life. In this way the sophists could have made a correct distinction between the contemplative and the active life, if they had called the former Gospel and the latter Law; that is, if they had taught that the speculative life should be included and directed by the Word of God and that in it nothing else is to be looked at except the Word of the Gospel, but that the active life should be sought from the Law, which does not grasp Christ but exercises itself in works of love toward one's neighbor.

And so this text is clear, that all men, even the apostles or prophets or patriarchs, would have remained under the curse if Christ had not put Himself in opposition to sin, death, the curse of the Law, and the wrath and judgment of God, and if He had not overcome them in His own body; for those savage monsters could not be overcome by any human power. Now Christ is not the Law, He is not a work of the Law, He is not an "elicited act"; but He is a divine and human Person who took sin, the condemnation of the Law, and death upon Himself, not for Himself but for us. Therefore the whole emphasis is on the phrase ὑπὲϱ ἡμῶν.

Therefore we should not imagine Christ as an innocent and private person who is holy and righteous only for Himself; this is what the sophists and nearly all the fathers, Jerome and others, have done.[4] It is, of course, true that Christ is the purest of persons; but this is not the place to stop. For you do not yet have Christ, even though you know that He is God and man. You truly have Him only when you believe that this altogether pure and innocent Person has been granted to you by the Father as your High Priest and Redeemer, yes, as your Slave. Putting off His innocence and holiness and putting on your sinful person, He bore your sin, death, and curse: He became a sacrifice and a curse for you, in order thus to set you free from the curse of the Law.

You see, then, with what a completely apostolic spirit Paul treats this serious argument about the blessing and the curse, when he not only subjects Christ to the curse but even says that He became a curse. Thus he calls Him "sin" in II Corinthians 5:21 when he says: "For our sake God made Him to be sin who knew no sin." Although these statements could be correctly expounded by saying that Christ became a "curse," that is, a sacrifice for the curse, or "sin," that is, a sacrifice for sin; nevertheless, it is more pleasing if the precise meaning of the terms is preserved for the sake of greater emphasis. For when a sinner really comes to a knowledge of himself, he feels himself to be a sinner not only concretely or adjectively but abstractly and substantively. That is, he seems to himself to be not only miserable but misery itself; not only a sinner, and an accursed one, but sin and the curse itself. Thus in Latin, when we want a strong way to say that someone is a criminal, we call him a "crime."[5] It is something awful to bear sin, the wrath of God, the curse, and death. Therefore a man who feels these things in earnest really becomes sin, death, and the curse itself.

Thus Paul treats this topic in a truly apostolic way, because no sophist or legalist or Jew or fanatic or anyone else speaks this way. Who would dare quote this passage from Moses, "Cursed be everyone who hangs on a tree," and apply it to Christ Himself? By the same principle by which Paul applied this sentence, "Cursed be everyone," etc., to Christ, we can apply not only all of Deuteronomy 27 but all collected curses of the Mosaic Law to Christ. For just as Christ for His own Person is innocent of this general Law, so He is of all others. And just as for us He violated this general Law and was hanged on the tree as a criminal, a blasphemer, a parricide, and a traitor, so He violated all other laws as well. For all the curses of the Law were gathered together in Him, and therefore He bore and sustained them in His own body for us. Consequently, He was not only accursed; but He became a curse for us.

This is really the apostolic way to interpret the Scriptures. For without the Holy Spirit a man cannot speak this way; that is, he cannot include the entire Law in one word and gather it all at once in Christ, and, on the other hand, include all the promises of Scripture and say that these are fulfilled in Christ once and for all. Therefore this argument is apostolic and very powerful, based as it is, not on one passage in the Law but on all the laws; and Paul relies heavily on it.

You see here with what diligence Paul read the Scriptures and how carefully he weighed and considered the individual words of this passage (Gen. 22:18): "In you shall all the nations be blessed." First he argues as follows from the term "bless": "If the blessing is to come upon all nations, then all nations are under the curse—even the Jews, who have the Law of Moses." And he quotes evidence from Scripture by which he proves that the Jews, who are under the Law, are under the curse: "Cursed be everyone who does not abide," etc.

Next Paul diligently weighs the words "all nations," on the basis of which he argues as follows: "The blessing pertains not only to the Jews but also to all the nations of the entire world. But if it pertains to all nations, it is impossible for it to come through the Law of Moses, since no nations except the Jews had this. Moreover, although the Jews had the Law, still the blessing did not come to them through it; on the contrary, the more they tried to keep it, the more subject they became to the curse of the Law. Therefore there has to be another righteousness, one that far surpasses the righteousness of the Law; through it the blessing comes not only to the Jews but also to all nations in the whole world."

Finally Paul explains the phrase "in your offspring" as follows: "A certain man was to be born of the offspring of Abraham. I mean Christ, through whom the blessing was to come upon all nations. Since Christ was to bless all nations, whom He found to be accursed, He Himself had to remove the curse from them. But He could not remove it through the Law, because the curse is only increased by this. So what did He do? He attached Himself to those who were accursed, assuming their flesh and blood; and thus He interposed Himself as the Mediator between God and men. He said: 'Although I am flesh and blood and live among those who are accursed, nevertheless I am the blessed One through whom all men are to be blessed.' Thus He joined God and man in one Person. And being joined with us who were accursed, He became a curse for us; and He concealed His blessing in our sin, death, and curse, which condemned and killed Him. But because He was the Son of God, He could not be held by them. He conquered them and triumphed over them. He took along with Him whatever clung to the flesh that He had assumed for our sake. Therefore all who cling to this flesh are blessed and are delivered from the curse."

Undoubtedly Paul treated these things at great length in the presence of the Galatians. For this is the proper task of the apostles: to illuminate the work and the glory of Christ and to strengthen and comfort troubled consciences. For the rest, when those who know no other righteousness than that of the Law fail to hear what one ought to do or ought not to do, but hear only that Christ, the Son of God, has assumed our flesh and joined Himself to the accursed in order to bless all nations this way—they either understand none of this or understand it in a purely physical way. They are preoccupied with other thoughts and with fantastic imaginings. Therefore these things are nothing but riddles to them. Even for us, who have the first fruits of the Spirit (Rom. 8:23), it is impossible to understand and to believe fully, because all this is so contradictory to human reason.

In short, all evils were to flood over us, as they will flood over the wicked eternally. But Christ, who became guilty of all laws, curses, sins, and evils for us, stepped in between; He took upon Himself and abolished all our evils, which were supposed to oppress and torment us eternally. They overwhelmed Him once, for a brief time, and flooded in over His head, as in Psalm 88:7 and 16 the prophet laments in Christ's name when he says: "Thy wrath lies heavy upon Me, and Thou dost overwhelm Me with all Thy waves" and: "Thy wrath has swept over Me; Thy dread assaults destroy Me." Being delivered in this way from these eternal terrors and torments by Christ, we shall enjoy eternal and indescribable peace and joy, provided that we believe this.

These are the adorable mysteries of Scripture, the true cabala,[6] which even Moses disclosed rather obscurely in a few places; which the prophets and apostles knew and handed down from hand to hand to their posterity; and in which, though it was still in the future, the prophets rejoiced more than we do, even though it has now been revealed.

Notes

[1]Jerome, *Commentarius in Epistolam S. Pauli and Galatas,* II, *Patrologia Series Latina,* XXVI, 387–388.

[2]On this *mirabile duellum* cf. *Luther the Expositor,* pp. 185–186.

[3]Cf - the discussion in *Luther's Works,* 3, pp. 275–276.

[4]See p. 138, note 1.

[5]The term *scelus* was a vulgar word for "scoundrel."

[6]The renewal of contacts between Christians and Jews in the time of humanism had aroused interest in the cabala; Johannes Reuchlin had written a book about it in 1517, *De arte cabbalistica.* Here Luther sets "the true cabala" against this speculative doctrine.

Albrecht Ritschl

The General Relations of Justification

[It is] impossible to define justification without taking into account its relation to the subjective consciousness of guilt. In order, however, to determine with complete accuracy the place of this thought within the Christian religion, it is necessary both to know the Subject or Author of justification under the corresponding predicate, and to estimate the characteristic note of faith which is to be found in the objects of justification along with, and apart from, their consciousness of guilt. Then we shall be able to consider the scope and the definite sphere within which the Divine judgment of justification must be conceived as operative, in order to hold good as the special basis of the religious quality in the Christian subject.

The attribute of God through which the older theology seeks to understand justification is that of *Lawgiver and Judge*. It is precisely in ascetic representations of the doctrine that this preconceived idea of God receives special and intentionally strong emphasis.[1] The conception of God as Lawgiver and Judge, it is true, has no direct bearing on the general idea of pardon, or the forgiveness of sins: it belongs rather to the special means by which the older school attempted to solve the contradiction between the

From *The Christian Doctrine of Justification and Reconciliation* (Edinburgh: T. and T. Clark, 1900), pp. 86–115. Used by permission.

grace and the justice of God, in order to explain the forgiveness of sins which is received in Christianity. But we meet the same preconceived idea of God also in Tieftrunk, although his idea of the way in which Christ mediates the forgiveness of sins departs from orthodox lines. The special influence which works on Tieftrunk is the Kantian estimate of the moral law. Recognising the facts of the transgressor's consciousness of guilt before the law, and his feelings of awe and shame in presence of the Lawgiver—feelings which are not removed by moral reformation—he explains the bestowal of pardon by the Judge as the chief need of the guilty person. Here, therefore, we find a ground for the common assumption in a quite different motive from that assigned by the orthodox theology.

This assumption, however, when compared with the ideas with which it stands connected, is, to say the least, incomplete. We may at the outset concede to the orthodox theology that the imputation of the double obedience of Christ to the law, for the purpose of judging sinners as righteous, may be represented as a special instance of the application of law by the Judge. We cannot, however, represent this act as isolated from the antecedent gracious purpose of God, His purpose namely, to bless sinners; nor must we lose sight of the fact that God has Himself brought into court the Righteous One, whose obedience to the law, according to the presupposition, He judicially imputes to sinners. On these two accounts, God, in executing the judicial act of imputing the righteousness of Christ to sinners, cannot be conceived as Lawgiver and Judge, but as the Dispenser of grace and love to men. The act of imputation, moreover, when placed in its true connection with the whole, is only the means to an end. The judicial quality in God, therefore, can be admitted only as a co-operating element in the act of justification, or as a subordinate trait in the conception of His character as the Author of justification. Even the above-quoted writers are compelled either to supplement their own representations by saying that "in this work" God reveals Himself in the character of love, or, by actually designating justification as an "act of grace," to indicate the real principle of the matter. One may, of course, insist upon the fact that, in ascetic representations, paradoxes are used as means of stimulating the attention. But the above-quoted expressions are not to be regarded as mere harmless exaggerations. Their effect is really the dislocation of one member of an organism, the isolation of one proposition, which, we maintain, can be rightly represented only in connection with quite different propositions.

But if we fix our attention more closely on this analogy of the power of the State, which has been applied to explain God's method in bringing about the remission of guilt and punishment, we find that justification cannot possibly be represented as a judicial act. For the right of bestowing pardon, which is vested in the head of the State, is no prerogative of his power as lawgiver and supreme judge; it is a right altogether independent of these attributes, explicable from an entirely different aspect of the idea of the State. As lawgiver, the head of the State unites the various members thereof for the purpose of common organised action; and as holder of the

power of punishment, he defends the legal order of the community, preserving it against the violations to which it is exposed. The right of pardon,
on the other hand, follows from the fact that the legal order is only a means
to the moral ends of the people, and that consequences of legal action are
conceivable, which are incongruous with the respect that is due to public
morality, as well as to the moral position of guilty persons. In order to
prevent such incongruous results of judicial condemnation, the right of
pardon is exercised by the authority to which the case of the moral well-
being of the community is officially entrusted. The bestowal of pardon thus
appears, it is true, always in the form of a judgment of the head of the
State—not, however, a judicial, but an extra-judicial judgment. This relation of different functions has remained for the most part hidden from the
older theologians,[2] partly because they were not accustomed to determine
accurately the meaning of the symbols they used, and partly because they
combined two different ideas in the act of justification, namely, the vicarious satisfaction of the law, and the pardon of sins through imputation of the
righteousness of Christ. A conception of justification was thus formed,
which should correspond, not with the simple idea of pardon, but also with
the judicial act of the execution of punishment. By means of this conception, therefore, it appears as though justification could be represented as at
least as much a judicial as an extra-judicial judgment. The apparent contradiction was explained through the peculiarly Divine character of the
judgment, which transcends the analogies derived from the notion of the
State. But these two ideas which have thus been brought into relation in the
judgment of justification are not co-ordinate. The extra-judicial bestowal of
pardon can alone be regarded as the specific form of the judgment of
justification, the judicial acceptance of the satisfaction of the law through a
substitute being but the presupposition of that judgment. In this way,
therefore, we cannot arrive at the conclusion that justification is judicial in
character. We should then have to decide, with the Reformed theologians,
that the imputation of Christ's obedience to those for whom, as their Head,
He rendered that obedience, is an act of Divine justice. But this view of the
matter would be least of all able to escape the force of the argument which
Faustus Socinus urges in refutation of the orthodox doctrine, namely, that
the ideas of satisfaction and forgiveness are absolutely self-contradictory.
If, as is assumed, justification be held to be an act of Divine justice, then it
cannot conceivably be regarded as an act of grace. But the scope of this
argument extends even further; for it raises the question whether the judicial recognition of the satisfaction and the merit of Christ can possibly be
the ground of their extra-judicial imputation in the act of pardon. For in the
penal law absolutely no provision is made for the transference of punishment and personal obligation to persons other than those under such obligations. If such a procedure on the part of God be admitted in the mediation
of justification, then the recognition of vicarious satisfaction as such would
have of necessity to be understood, not as the act of the Judge, or the
Executor of the law, but as an antecedent act of grace. And, finally, the
formula directed against the Catholic doctrine, namely, that Divine justifi-

cation is to be understood *sensu forensi,* is anything but complete and accurate. Justification, it is true, has the form of a judgment, not of a material operation; but the judgment in this case is the synthetic judgment of a resolution of the will. On the other hand, every judicial judgment is an analytic judgment of knowledge. The consequent decree of punishment or acquittal is equally an analytic judgment, being a conclusion from the prohibitive or permissive law involved and the knowledge of the guilt or innocence of the person accused. Therefore in whatever way we view the matter, the attitude of God in the act of justification cannot be conceived as that of Judge.

The justification of sinners by God, when explained by the analogy of the bestowal of pardon by the head of the State, can just as little be deduced from the attribute of *Lawgiver.* It could rather be shown that the bestowal of pardon is in direct contradiction to the attribute of Lawgiver. For the lawgiver as such is interested in the absolute validity and universal observance of the law, whereas through the bestowal of pardon exceptions are admitted. Nevertheless the combination of these two attributes in the full power of the State is perfectly rational. No real contradiction exists between them, because, as we have said, they are differently related ideas, and because they do not come into collision with one another at the same moment. For the legislative power, which insists upon the absolute validity of the law, is satisfied when the bestowal of pardon does not in any instance interfere with legal procedure, but only follows after a verdict of guilt has been legally passed. Seeing, however, that legal right is not itself the highest good, but in all cases only a means to secure the moral goods which further the true life of the people, the full power of bestowing pardon is, in order to attain this end, united with the right of legislation in the person of one supreme authority, so that, in individual instances of legal procedure, due regard should be paid to the question, whether or not the complete execution of the demands of the law and of the judicial sentence would be more detrimental to the public moral interests than their non-execution.

It is from this side also that Tieftrunk has explained the possibility of Divine forgiveness of sins, notwithstanding the strictly obligatory character of the moral law, of which he is convinced. God is recognised by Tieftrunk as the correlate of the final end of practical reason. This end is the commonwealth in which the moral laws alone are authoritative, the Kingdom of God. In order to make this end conceivable as the standard of one's own action, practical reason postulates the existence of God as Creator, Lawgiver, Judge, and Ruler. If, now, the moral end of the world is to be maintained in spite of the sinfulness of men, God must be thought as the Author of forgiveness, through which act compensation is made for the transgressions of the moral law. In this argument the point has been duly recognised, the validity of which we have been maintained, namely, that the attribute of lawgiver in the character of the head of the State is not the highest, inasmuch as the judicial legislation is only a means subserving the moral ends of the people. But the attribute in the character of the head of the State which corresponds to the moral destiny of the people, namely, the right of bestowing pardon, has a narrower sphere of operation, and, so to speak, only accidental validity, because the head of the State cannot actually bring about the fulfilment of the moral destiny of the people, inasmuch as he cannot play the part of moral Providence for the people. On this point, therefore, the idea of God and His Kingdom transcends the analogy of State processes. The moral legislation of God is, under all circumstances, the means toward the moral commonwealth, the Kingdom of God. The attribute of God as Founder and Ruler of His Kingdom is therefore absolutely superior to His attribute as Lawgiver. If He recognises pardon as the fitting means for the maintenance of His Kingdom, no general objection can be brought against the possibility of such pardon from His attribute as Lawgiver. It follows then that pardon, or the forgiveness of sins, is connected, not with God's special attribute as Lawgiver, but with His general attribute as King and Lord of His Kingdom among men.

This result, which we have reached under the direction of Tieftrunk, is free from the contradictions involved in the thesis of the older school, that God carries out the act of justification as Judge, and therefore as Executor of the law given by Himself. The principle of the advance beyond the older position consists in this, that use has been made of the idea of the Kingdom of God as the common moral end for God and men, an idea altogether foreign to the representatives of the older school. And yet the idea of the all-comprehensive Divinely-instituted moral law, which formed for those theologians the inseparable correlate of their idea of God, can hold good only as a deduction from the notion of that moral commonwealth, as certainly as every moral and judicial law is deduced from the nature of the corresponding community. If, therefore, the thought of forgiveness of sins, or justification, is to have vital significance in the Christian view of the world, and if it is to be understood through comparison with the right of pardon which is enjoyed by the head of the State, it must be conceived only as standing in relation to the universal sovereignty of God over the completed moral commonwealth which is to be formed of men. Tieftrunk has, however, at the same time taken into consideration the fact that the Divine forgiveness of sins, as a deduction from the final end of the Kingdom of God conditioned by the continual transgression of the law, yet cannot be indifferent to the unconditional authority of the law. He demands therefore, that the Divine forgiveness be conceived, not merely as a result of the law, but also as an act in harmony with the law. He finds the first prerequisite fulfilled, when forgiveness leads men to love the law; the second, when reconciliability becomes a commandment of outstanding importance in the law, and when irreconciliability, conceived as the law of a moral kingdom, would be self-contradictory. Tieftrunk has here, it is true, raised an important problem, but his solution is sophistical. Reconciliability is certainly a principle which claims paramount importance as between those who are equal in every respect, but which has no unconditioned validity as between those of whom the one is superior in authority to the other. Else the result would be, that through unlimited application of this particular principle, the universal legal order of common life would be destroyed. The solution of the question, how the Christian truth of the Divine forgiveness of sins can be reconciled with the unconditioned validity of the moral law, must therefore be reserved for future consideration.

In the meantime our task is to ascertain in general the attribute of God through which the positively Christian conception of the forgiveness of sins is to be understood. Now it is almost inconceivable that the orthodox theologians, in spite of their endeavours to reproduce the ideas of Holy Scripture, have been entirely oblivious of the fact that Jesus explicitly connected this operation of God with *His attribute as Father*. He directed His disciples to invoke God as Father when they prayed to Him for forgiveness of their sins; and, to bring home to them the necessity of their forgiving their fellow-men, He promised them that their Father in heaven would also forgive them their sins (Matt. 6:9–15; Mark 11:25; Luke 11:2–4). In so far, too, as the forgiveness of sins is mediated through the expiatory death of Christ, the apostles recognise the love, or the grace, or the righteousness, that is, the self-consistent saving purpose, of God as the ground of that scheme (Rom. 3:25, 26; 5:8; Heb. 2:9). Moreover, the Old Testament idea of sacrifice, through which this whole circle of conceptions must be understood, contains nothing analogous to the judicial procedure of vicarious punishment; the sacrifices of the law are rather the symbols of a Divinely-ordered scheme for the appropriation of the Covenant-grace. It is true that the God whom we invoke as Father, has also inherent in His nature the attribute of impartial Judge (I Peter 1:7); but He acts as Judge only in vindicating the rights of His people. The title of Judge as applied to God has therefore for Christians no real place alongside of, or over, the relation in which He stands to them as Father. It is only, therefore, when the love of God, regarded as Father, is conceived as the will which works toward the destined end, that the real equivalence of forgiveness and justification, which is represented in the religious conception of things can be made good. If, however, God be preconceived as Judge in the forensic sense, the two ideas come into direct antagonism with one another, as was indeed explicitly maintained by the leading representatives of the older theology. The man who has gone through the punishment he has merited can, of course, be no more looked upon as a criminal, but he cannot by any means yet be regarded as an active and successful member of the moral community; in order to attain this place, the discharged culprit must give special evidence of his fitness for membership in the community. If, therefore, a judicial procedure on the part of God is recognised in this, that He regards sinners as free from punishment and guilt on account of the satisfaction which Christ has made, He must also, in order to judge them as positively righteous, impute to them the merit of Christ. It has been shown (p. 141) that this train of thought carries us beyond the limits of the conceptions derived from the analogy of the human judge. But the forgiveness extended by a father to his child combines in one act the judgment that a fault committed by the child ought to bring about no alienation between father and child, and the expression of the purpose to admit the child, as a right and gracious action, to the unfettered intercourse of love.

The attribute of father stands in relation to the peculiar moral and legal fellowship of the family. Therefore all the preceding arguments regarding the attitude of God to the forgiveness of sins, which have been derived from the analogy of the head of the State, that is, the legal and only relatively moral society of the people, are found to be incongruous with the Christian idea of God. The representation of God under the attribute of Father corresponds exactly to the transference to the whole of mankind of His relative moral and legal Lordship over the people of Israel for the bringing about of the highest moral end. Now, not only does this universal destination of the Kingdom of God exclude comparison with the form of government of any definite people, but the designation of God as our Father shows expressly that the real analogy for the Kingdom of God should be sought, not in the national State, but in the family. The consequences which this principle involves for the representation of the Christian view of the world cannot yet be brought out. One result, however, is the confirmation of [the position] that the forgiveness of sins by God as Father finds no real standard of comparison in the right of pardon which belongs to the head of the State. The difference between the two is seen in this, that the right of pardon is exercised only in individual instances of legal condemnation, which as such stand in no connection with one another and always form exceptions to the recognised legal order, while the forgiveness of sins by God as Father is a universal, though not unconditioned, fundamental law, established in the interest of the community of the Kingdom of God.

If, then, justification in the Christian sense is related to God under the attribute—to use a human analogy—of Father, not of Judge, the ground on which Heidegger distinguished justification and adoption becomes untenable. The only valid distinction between the two ideas is that forgiveness, or justification, or reconciliation, refers generally to the admission of sinners to fellowship with God in spite of sin, whereas in adoption the confidential relation to God which is thereby established is specially described in terms of the normal relation of children to a father. The connection being such, the idea of reconciliation is shown to be of equal constitutive significance for Christianity with the name of God as the Father of our Lord Jesus Christ. But the ideas of *reconciliation* and *adoption* agree with one another also in a formal respect. For adoption must also be conceived as a resolution of will in the form of a synthetic judgment. The Reformed theologians, who alone give the idea of adoption an independent place in the Christian system, occupy themselves with describing the distinctions between the notions of Divine and human adoption. But we ought rather to seek to ascertain the harmony between the two. Now such harmony cannot be found in the idea of the establishment of a right of inheritance for a person of alien descent. For those persons who have in the Christian sense been adopted by God as His children, attain that rank only under the presupposition that in a certain real sense they derive their being from God, that is, that they have been created in His image. In harmony therewith, and in contrast to the alienation which sin causes between God and men, the adoption of the believing signifies their reception into that peculiar fellowship with God which is represented under the analogy of the family. Now, the moral fellowship of the human family rests not only on national descent but on a judgment of the value of this fellowship by the husband and wife, and on the purpose of the father to educate his children to become spiritual and moral persons. The father's moral relation to his children therefore rests in every case on an act of υἱοθεσία, so that this idea is not exclusively applicable to children of alien descent. The certainty of blood-relationship is not the sufficient ground of the father's care, for there are fathers who shirk their responsibilities. Therefore the resolution to bring up one's children does not follow from the analytic judgment that one is the author of the children's life. On the contrary, this resolution, like every other resolution, is a synthetic judgment, even though it usually appears as a logical conclusion from the recognition of blood-relationship. The latter, however, is the case only when the resolution to give moral education to the children is included in the resolution to form the marriage union. On the other hand, the resolution to assume charge of a natural child for the purpose of moral education is usually absent, unless the purpose or resolution to enter upon the marriage state be combined with the sexual connection. If, therefore, the Divine υἱοθεσία in the Christian sense is understood in reference to the closest conceivable spiritual fellowship between man and God, then the form of the resolution, which is a synthetic judgment, is in exact harmony with that of the analogous resolution in the relationship of the human family, which we have taken as our standard of comparison. Seeing, however, that the resolution to admit children to moral fellowship applies not only, as a general rule, to children of the blood, but also, in extraordinary cases, to alien children, and that the resolution can extend in these cases only to the transmission of property rights, the idea of the Divine υἱοθεσία cannot be held to be completely harmonious in these essential respects with its human analogue. For those who are admitted to the rank of children of God are all, by virtue of their innate moral destiny, "of Divine race," but all in reality, because of sin, "as alien children" to God. Through the paramount influence of this fact, therefore, the Divine υἱοθεσία appears as most closely analogous to the human legal form of adoption. If, now, justification is an operation in which God appears under the attribute of Father, then the adoption of men as God's children is a substantially equivalent idea. The latter modifies the former only in this respect, that the fellowship with God to which sinners are admitted is conceived to be as close as that which exists between the head and the members of a family. Therefore the functions in which the believing make manifest their justification and reconciliation must also be conceived as the functions of sonship to God.

The union (*Gleichheit*) with God, which must be included among the privileges which the justified enjoy as the children of God, finds expression in the formula, that justification brings the believing into possession of *eternal life.* In Luther's proposition (in chap. v), "Where the forgiveness of sins is, there is life and blessedness," this attribute is conceived as a present possession. It will be sufficient to recall propositions of similar import in the *Apology of the Augsburg Confession*.[3] Calvin holds precisely the same views.[4] To take a final example, in the Formula of Concord, Art. 4, the connection between justification and eternal life is made so close, that good works are regarded as equally invalid as the condition for eternal life as they are for justification. In these propositions, as contrasted with the Catholic view, the possession of eternal life is brought from the sphere of the future and the world-to-come into the present state of the earthly life of the believing. By this interpretation of justification we also rise beyond the mystical standpoint. The mystics claim to enjoy the blessedness of the future in moments of ecstasy in the present life. They have, however, to suffer for their elevation of spirit at such moments through subsequent lassitude, aridity and barrenness of the feelings, and the sense of desertion by God. The Reformers, on the other hand, live in the faith that eternal life, and the joy which attaches to it, namely, blessedness, are present gifts, continually enjoyed as the result of the forgiveness of sins. But yet this thought, although presented in a series of proof-passages, has not been made quite clear by them. From the Catholic use of the formula, which was familiar to the Reformers, we must conclude that "eternal life," in their view, denotes a peculiar union and fellowship with God. In the Greek Church, indeed, "deification" is used as an expression equivalent to "eternal life." This usage has extended also to the Western Church. Bernard, for example, started from this idea in his exposition of the doctrine. The mediaeval mystics, although they strove to attain blessedness in the ecstatic knowledge of God, or the annihilation of their own wills, were yet led through their Neoplatonic conception of God as the only Reality beyond the idea of blessedness as consisting in union with God, to that of blessedness as consisting in the losing of self in the Divine essence. But Luther had no such idea in mind. This is evident from the fact that ever since 1518 he set himself in deliberate antagonism to all mysticism.[5] Moreover, the re-acceptance of the mystical view is out of harmony with the doctrine of justification. Therefore the original Lutheran sense of eternal life cannot be ascertained through the notion of the *unio mystica*. To determine the precise method in which we must conceive this relation of justification will, however, require a special investigation.

As an operation of God upon men, justification is correlative to *faith*. This is the condition which prevents justification, or the forgiveness of sins, being represented as a contradiction to the presupposed estimate of sin. Up to this point, in our definition of justification, man has been treated in his peculiar characteristic as sinner, and the subject of the consciousness of guilt. It was presupposed that with sin a state of alienation between God and men was brought about through the existence of real moral opposition between them. Justification, then, signifies the bringing back of the sinner into nearness with God, the removal of the alienating effect of the existent opposition to God and the accompanying consciousness of guilt. If, however, man in his relation to justification were to be represented only as sinner, his alienation from God, both in the objective and in the subjective respect, would continue, and the opposite status, that, namely, of justification, could not even be conceived. The sinner must therefore be thought of likewise as the subject of faith. Here, it is true, a new difficulty may be found. For if the condition must be fulfilled before the result can be reached, the faith of the sinner really appears to precede his justification. The question then will be whether and how the sinner can fulfil this condition. This difficulty may, however, be waived in the meantime, if we take into account the opposite fact that the idea of reconciliation, in which justification is represented inclusive of its result, makes the faith of the sinner to appear precisely as the result of justification. Justification effects a change in the consciousness of guilt in this respect, that the feeling of mistrust towards God which is bound up with that consciousness, and the shrinking from Him which results therefrom, are replaced by a consenting movement of the will towards God. This new direction of the will to God which is evoked by reconciliation is, in the Evangelical view, faith; and, in so far as it expects to be determined solely by God, it belongs as a special class to the general idea of obedience.

The meaning of the idea of faith, and the relation in which it stands to justification, have indeed been accurately determined in Evangelical theology. From various passages in Melanchthon[6] we ascertain that faith means neither the acknowledgment of the correctness of traditional facts, nor the acceptance of orthodox propositions, but trust in God's grace. Calvin has elucidated the idea of faith with still greater care than Melanchthon.[7] He emphasizes the fact that the knowledge which is included in faith, having for its object the goodness of God, is of quite a different nature from our knowledge of the world, which consists in the explanation of phenomena and perceptions. Faith is emotional conviction of the harmony between the Divine purposes and the most intimate interests of man. A certain interest, it is true, attaches to our ordinary knowledge of the world, as is shown in the act of attention. But the interest which expresses itself in emotion—that is, interest not in the discovery of truth for itself, but in the feeling of moral pleasure and in the satisfaction of our own spirit—is of quite a different nature, inasmuch as it connects the maintenance of our whole personality with the highest standard of our life, the Divine goodwill and our own blessedness. In this analysis of Calvin's main theses it will be seen that the strong emphasis which Melanchthon laid on the will has disappeared. Calvin does, however, also recognise the place of the will in the act of faith, when, in treating of the emotional character of faith, he brings out the significance of faith as obedience. But his treatment of the matter is not quite clear. Emotion is a modification of feeling; and many emotions, especially those with which we are here concerned, have a peculiar resemblance to the will. But in acts of will we recognise a clear purpose, and this characteristic mark is just what is wanting in movements of emotion. Here, then, a difference comes to light between Melanchthon and Calvin. This difference is clearly expressed in Calvin's statement that the apostles *de-*

rive trust from faith. Luther and Melanchthon, on the contrary, define the idea of faith accurately, making it precisely equivalent to the idea of trust in God. We may understand Calvin's statement in the same sense if we conceive him to have meant "derivation" analytically. But Calvin's further explanations do not make this clear. In Calvin's school, as, for example, in the Heidelberg Catechism, §21, the original Protestant interpretation of faith as trust continues, but by the high Reformed Orthodoxy Calvin was understood to maintain that *fiducia* stands in a synthetic relation to *fides,* and therefore does not in all cases accompany the latter.[8] But trust is a function of the will, and therefore also, in the case under discussion, conceived as trust in the saving will of God, bound up with the characteristic mark of a clear purpose. We trust in God, who, through the promise of forgiveness, shows our blessedness to be His aim. This connection of ideas governs the self-consciousness of the believer, as well as all the characteristic marks of emotion, conviction, certainty, obedience, and pleasure, as Calvin has rightly shown.

That the will plays a part in the act of faith is recognised also by Thomas Aquinas, even when he attributes faith specifically to the *intellectus,* and defines it as assent to the truths revealed by God. For, in order to distinguish faith from knowledge, he lays down the principle that in knowledge one is moved to assent to the truth through the object itself, but in faith and opinion not through the object of knowledge alone, but therewith also through the cooperation of the will. If these be the common distinguishing marks, then knowledge is opinion, if it be accompanied by doubt, or fear of the opposite possibility; and the knowledge of revealed truth supported by the will is faith, if it be accompanied by certainty regarding what is known.[9] In the Tridentine Decree, Session vi, it is recognised that faith in this sense is *fundamentum et radix justificationis;* it is acknowledged, however, that something else must accompany this initial act of faith, in order to attain justification. Here then it is admitted that a rational knowledge of Revelation, comprehended in a formal resolution of the will, is not a sufficient ground for justification. It is therefore further maintained that, in order to attain justification, love must accompany faith and that in a relation so close that love becomes the very essence of faith. Now the argument which Thomas advances in support of his thesis goes directly to prove that love to God as the highest good gives its essential character to faith.[10] If the Catholic idea of *fides caritate formata* were here accurately and exhaustively described, I should see nothing therein to contradict the Evangelical idea of faith. For faith, regarded as trust, is no other than the direction of the will towards God as the highest end and the highest good. When, therefore, Möhler[11] represents to us that trust in the love of God is begotten from a corresponding movement of the human soul, namely, love to God, he tells us nothing new or startling. But the above-mentioned conclusion of Thomas is not the whole Catholic doctrine. In the elaboration of the thema in the third article of the Tridentine Creed—*quod unumquodque operatur per suam formam: fides autem per dilectionem operatur, ergo dilectio caritatis est fidei forma*—"love" is indeed used strictly in the sense of "love to God"; but it is undoubtedly the fact, in spite of Möhler's fine colouring, that in the Catholic doctrine this Pauline principle is used as the correlate of *justificatio* in the sense of "active love to men."[12] For this is intentionally not distinguished from "love to God" as the unrelated expression *caritas* shows.

Thomas, indeed, proceeds to argue that love to God and love to men are not different acts, but one and the same act, only with different extensions.[13] The principle on which he bases this argument is, that the specific character of an act is determined by the essential ground of the object to which the act relates. According to this principle, the act which relates to a given object, and that which extends directly to the essential ground of the object, are specifically identical. For example, the seeing of light and the seeing of colours on the ground of light, are specifically one act. In the same way, love to God and love to men are represented as one act, because God is the ground of love to one's fellow-men, and because the aim of such love is that every man should be in God, that is, should find his blessedness in God. But in my opinion the essential ground of an object is related to the object as the universal to the particular. Therefore the act which is directed to the particular on the ground of the universal will always have its relation also to the universal—but not *vice versa*. Therefore, if God is the ground of genuine love to one's fellow-men, that is, love which desires for one's fellow-men that perfection and blessedness which they will find in God, every act of love to one's fellow-men will also be an act of love to God; but not *vice versa,* every act of love to God will not also extend to one's fellow-men. It may be urged as an argument for the latter thesis, that the seeing of light is always also the seeing of colours. But the analogy is not valid. For light appears only in its colours, but God does not exist only in men. The passage I John 4:21, too, the meaning of which Thomas attempts to turn to fit in with his own conclusion, contains only the commandment that he who loves God shall love his brother also. That is, love to God is not in itself bound up with love to one's fellow-men; but the latter is a special resolution of the will, quite distinct from love to God.

We must accordingly, it is true, concede to the Roman Catholic theologians that love to God constitutes the essence of faith, if in that idea the thought is expressed that the will is directed to God as its highest end. The determination of the specific character of faith will then depend on such conditions as the attributes under which God is conceived, the idea entertained regarding man's own power of will, and the estimate of the present capacity of the will for faith, compared with its former incapacity. Through these conditions, and others yet to be considered, therefore through the necessary modes of representing faith, it will be shown that faith is *in intellectu tanquam in subjecto.* That is, faith has for its material content the ideas which mediate the movement of the will which is expressed in it. This material element of faith, however, is not really faith in its specific character, apart from the essential form of the love to God which is related to it. The error in the Thomist theology consists only in this, that *fides informis* is treated, contrary to the above principle, as a real stage of faith, and that the qualifying phrase *formatio per caritatem* is introduced as merely the complement of the hitherto imperfect faith. This method of procedure, of course, involves a contradiction in itself. For either *caritas* is *forma fidei,* in which case *fides informis,* regarded as *actus intellectus,* is formless matter, and therefore the possibility, not the reality, of faith; or *caritas* is real *fides,* in which case the act of will in faith is merely accidental, not the essential element. If, then, *caritas Dei,* as Thomas has really shown, is to be conceived as the essence of faith, one is unable to see how this thought can be made to appear contradictory to the Evangelical idea of faith as *fiducia Dei.* The latter is only a specialised mode of conceiving the same idea. But the notorious Catholic interpretation of *caritas* as "the active exercise of love to men"—the identity of which with "love to God" has not been demonstrated by Thomas—stands in direct contradiction to the Evangelical idea.

The general ground on which this Catholic assumption must be rejected is that the characteristic marks which distinguish Christianity as a religion, and those which denote its ethical purpose, are therein confused with one another; whereas, if Christianity is not to be distorted and falsified in both respects, they ought to be clearly distinguished. Justification depends solely on faith, that is, trust in God, as its direct correlate, because, in the Christian sense, it denotes the definite relation of men to God as their Father, which is necessary under the presupposition of sin, and possible in view of the consciousness of guilt. Now the active exercise of love to men does not enter as an element into this definite relation to God. The recognised Evangelical doctrine, it is true, maintains that the impulse to love one's fellow-men, which is the fundamental principle of active human life, is essentially bound up with the very idea of justification. For Christianity is the ethical religion; and wherever entrance into the specifically Christian status before God is realised, Christianity brings into exercise also the corresponding moral impulse. But for the very reason that the religious character of Christianity and its ethical purpose are different, active love to men, which is directed towards the ethical end of Christianity, cannot hold good also as the direct condition for the religious relation to God which justification denotes. The Christian designation of God as our Father, it is true, comprises also the notion of His Lordship over the Kingdom of God. For under that title we pray to God that His Kingdom may come. Now, love to one's fellow-men is a deduction from the highest principle which dominates all moral action, namely, regard to the Kingdom of God. Therefore the impulse to such love stands also in relation to the idea of God as Father. But the mutual relation which exists between God as Father and believers means one thing when represented as the peculiar status before the Father into which Christianity brings believers, and quite another when represented as their cooperation with the Father in advancing the common end of the Kingdom of God. The peculiar status before God into which Christianity brings believers, therefore, consists in this, that God receives believers, in spite of their sin and their consciousness of guilt, into that fellowship with Himself which guarantees their salvation or eternal life.

This relationship extends to all Christians as such. In so far, therefore, as we are dealing with the entrance of each individual through faith, that is, trust, into fellowship with God, the question of the moral relationship between the believers, the impulse to which is given therewith, does not come directly into consideration: nor is it possible to see how this question should come into consideration.

Where the faith which is related to justification comes into exercise, it is related also to God. And as it is called forth by reconciliation on God's part, it must be considered, in its relation to justification, not as a work of man possessed of independent value, but rather as the act through which the new relation of men to God, realised in justification, is religiously recognised and actually established.[14] Therefore the Pietistic wrestling of the idea of justification to mean an analytic judgment on the value of faith is an approach to the Catholic view. We must not, however, fail to observe, as a difference between the two, that in the Pietistic view the idea of love to men is not included as an element in faith. Rather, in that view, only the manifold strivings of love to God, the aspirations after full faith, that is, the desire for the knowledge of saving truth, the hungering and thirsting after righteousness, and, finally, the acceptance of Christ, through which the knowledge of and assent to the saving doctrine are raised from the sphere of intellect to that of personal conviction—only these, regarded as worthy effects of union with Christ, are brought under the special judgment of justification. This view is in perfect harmony with the first application of the Thomist notion of *fides caritate formata,* namely, the proposition that love to God gives reality and value to merely intellectual faith. The Pietists, however, distinctly avoid the further step which Thomas takes, the attempt to pass off love to men as identical with love to God. The language they use, moreover, does not warrant our bringing any one of them into harmony with the Tridentine Creed.

The ground of justification, or the forgiveness of sins, is the benevolent, gracious, merciful purpose of God to vouchsafe to sinful men the privilege of access to Himself. The form in which sinners appropriate this gift is faith, that is, the emotional trust in God, accompanied by the conviction of the value of this gift for one's blessedness, which, called forth by God's grace, takes the place of the former mistrust which was bound up with the feeling of guilt. Through trust in God's grace the alienation of sinners from God, which was essentially connected with the unrelieved feeling of guilt, is removed. This is evidence that the guilt, so far as it prevents access to God, is forgiven by God. The purpose of God to forgive sinners is represented by the Reformers, under the notions of *promissio* and *evangelium,* not only as an openly revealed volition, but also as one which lays the foundation of a *fellowship* among men. In the gradation of the bearers of this Revelation, Christ, as the Mediator of the Gospel, is reckoned first. The next place after Him is accorded to the community which He founded, every member of which has authority to proclaim the justifying grace of God, especially the official representatives of the Church, whose function is to transmit the *promissio remissionis peccatorum propter Christum*. Besides these human organs, who by their word make the Revelation of God in Christ efficacious for the community which He founded, the sacraments are channels of the same sin-forgiving grace, inasmuch as they contain the Word or Gospel of God as their essence, and apply the Gospel in a peculiar way to the members of the community. Therefore the unity of the church is essentially bound up with the pure preaching of the Gospel and the proper administration of the two sacraments, and in the same degree with nothing else. Now the pure Gospel is defined in the Augsburg Confession (chap. vii) as the preaching of justification in the above-represented sense, namely, as depending on the merit of Christ, and thus excluding the idea of human merits.[15] This preaching of the Gospel is the distinctive mark of the existence of a community of believers; for, according to the same Confession (chap. v), it is only through the Word of God, in preaching and sacraments, that faith is called into existence. It follows, then, that, through the operation of the Holy Spirit, faith is identical in each individual case, and common to all the members of the community. Against this representation, however, the objection has been made that faith may be awakened in men through their own efforts, without the regular instrumentality of the publicly preached Word.

But these fundamental views of the Reformation are not disproved by the fact that very many hear the preaching of the Word without being led through any mechanical compulsion to the point of faith, and the contrary fact that very many attain to faith without being directly led thereto through the hearing of a preached sermon. The principle was not arrived at from the consideration of such instances. Therefore it ought not to stand in the way of a full investigation of the manifold experiences of life. The recognition of the principle, in reality, involves only the proviso that one cannot arrive at and maintain individual conviction of faith in isolation from the already existing community of faith, and that that community is coextensive with the spread of the Gospel, that is, the public preaching of the forgiveness of sins. And even if a man's conversion were as far as possible from being occasioned by the hearing of such preaching, yet the thesis in the 5th Article of the Augsburg Confession would be proved true by the fact that all the spiritual ideas which are effective in bringing about a conversion are derived from the Gospel, and become known to the converted person only through the Gospel; that, therefore, his conversion is entirely dependent on the purpose of God revealed in the Gospel. The maintenance of this principle is necessary for the welfare of the Church, in order that the individual's own struggle for faith may not be esteemed as independent of, or opposed to, the public preaching of the Word. The effect of such individualistic ideas would be, as seen, for example, in the history of the Anabaptists, that the Church would be given over to the conflicts of sectarianism, and that the faith itself would be falsified. The connection of faith with the revelation of grace through the Word was also plainly recognised by Calvin.[16] If, therefore, the community of believers is coextensive with the influence of the Gospel, and if the Gospel has no other sphere for the proclamation of its glad tidings of God's readiness to forgive sins, then those striking statements of Luther are intelligible, namely, that "the Church is full of the forgiveness of sins"; that "within the fold of the Christian Church God daily and richly forgives me, the individual, all my sin"; and that "the Church, as a mother, bears and nurtures every individual through the Word." Calvin repeats the latter statement (*Inst.*, iv. 1. 4). Finally, Luther pursues the same thought in a characteristic way. He loves, namely, to represent the Church as the Bride of Christ, with whom, in accordance with marriage right, Christ joins in a mutual exchange of benefits, He taking upon Himself the sins of the believing, and Himself imparting His righteousness to them.[17] In this representation of the process of justification by faith, however, Luther insists on the fact that the blessings which accrue to the individual are imparted to him only in common with all the others with whom he is bound up, through the same salvation, in the unity of the Church.

This idea, that the benefit of justification accrues to individuals as constituting the community of believers, corresponds to the significant expressions used in the New Testament regarding the sacrifice of Christ. For the conception of Christ's sacrifice through the types of the covenant sacrifice and the yearly sin-offering of the Israelites brings the forgiveness of sins which results from Christ's sacrifice into direct relation to the community founded by Him. The individual can therefore appropriate the forgiveness of sins by faith only when he unites in his faith at once trust in God and Christ, and the intention to connect himself with the community of believers. For the individual who is led to faith always finds the domain of human life which is determined and governed by the forgiveness of sins already marked out for him; and, moreover, he has to attach himself to the community of believers all the more decisively since he is indebted to that community for the knowledge of salvation and for stimuli of incalculable strength urging him to appropriate salvation. The relation of justification to the community of believers has been recognised not only by Brenz, who followed strictly in Luther's footsteps, but also by successive ascetics and theologians from Spener to Jer. Friedr. Reuss.[18] The idea has disappeared, however, in the orthodox Lutheran Dogmatics, because Melanchthon, the founder of that Dogmatics, rejected the above-quoted statements of Luther. The first edition of his *Loci theologici* contains no article at all on the Church. Here, therefore, he explains justification as exclusively an experience of the individual. In the following editions he has appended a chapter on the doctrine of the Church. He has, however, preserved unaltered his former scheme of justification. Melanchthon has indeed kept in view the factor of the Gospel, or the Word of God, or the Divine promise. But he has nowhere made it clear that the community, to which the ministry of the Gospel is committed, thereby comprehends within its scope the process which he analyses as the experience of the individual. He testifies on several occasions that the community is the bearer of the Gospel;[19] but he nowhere brings this idea into connection with the explanation of justification as mediated through the promises, or the Gospel, of God. The Reformed theology, on the other hand following Calvin's example, has rightly understood and maintained Luther's view, and has accordingly represented the justification of the individual as conditioned by the existence of the community. In spite of this representation, however, the mystical conception of the scheme of salvation, which completely isolates the individual from connection with the Church, has gained a place within the sphere of the Reformed Church as well as the Lutheran.

Mysticism, which claims to lead men to the attainment of essential union with God, is quite different from the Evangelical doctrine of justification by faith; and its sentimental communion with Christ as the Bridegroom is quite different from trust in Christ as the Bearer of the Divine promise. The mystical communion of love with Christ, it is claimed, transcends trust in the merits of Christ. The true believers, says Wilhelm Brakel, receive the Lord Jesus into their hearts; they do not remain content with the benefits guaranteed by Him, but turn for full satisfaction to the Source Himself. Union with God, says Johann Arndt, in agreement with Tauler, is found in one's own heart; for "the Kingdom of God is within you." "In our heart is the real school of the Holy Ghost, the real workplace of the Holy Ghost, the real house of prayer in spirit and in truth." In this statement, so little account is taken by Arndt of the authoritative instrument of grace, the preached Word of God, that he expressly maintains the Revelation of the eternal Word within the pious soul, the communication of God's mind within the loving heart.[20] The *doctrine* of justification in the usual orthodox representation is indeed recognised by the mystics as the presupposition of these inner experiences, but has no influence on their circle of thought. If that doctrine had been still rightly understood, they would not have returned to the mediaeval types of religious life which had been condemned by Luther. Wherever Mysticism is found, the thought of justification no longer retains its true significance as the key to the whole domain of Christian life, but is so depreciated as to become a mere formal precondition of the immediate union with God, or the immediate communion with Christ, which Mysticism strives to attain.[21] One of the chief marks of distinction between the two opposite views, however, is that, wherever men give way to mystical states or aspirations, they imagine that the sphere of the preached Word and the promises of grace, therefore the necessary subordination to the public Revelation in the Church, is transcended and may be forgotten. The falsehood of this pretended immediate communion with, or immediate relation to, Christ, in which men endeavour to enjoy all possible forms of blessedness apart from and beyond the forgiveness of sins, has also been shown by Calvin in the passage: "*Haec vera est Christi cognitio, si eum qualis offertur a patre, suscipimus, nempe evangelio suo vestitum*" (*Inst.*, iii. 2. 6). Now the Song of Songs, from the allegorical exposition of which all those plays of fancy are derived, does not belong to the Gospel with which Christ is invested (*vestitus*). The whole mystical scheme, in fine, lies outside the spiritual horizon of the Reformers; it has no point of agreement with their doctrinal standards; it stands in contradiction to both the direct and the indirect estimate of the value of the community of believers and the public preaching of the Word of grace, which the standards attest; and, judged in its own special character, it is no improvement on the Reformed type of religious life, as certainly as it is derived from the practice of Monasticism. . . .

Notes

[1]Cf. Joh. Friedr. Fresenius, *Abhandlung über die Rechtfertigung eines armen Sünders vor Gott* (1747. New edition by A. F. C. Vilmar, 1857), p. 8: "As regards the Author of justification, He can be no other than the Supreme Lawgiver. For justification is a judicial act, which proceeds according to Divine law." F. A. Lampe, *Geheimnis des Gnadenbundes*, part i (1726), p. 429: "Seeing that the expression 'to justify' refers to a judicial act, it will be most fitting to represent the whole scheme of justifying grace under the form of a judicial process."

[2]Compare, however, Amesius, *Medullá*, i. 27. 10: "Iustificatio est gratiosa sententia, quia non fertur proprie a iustitia dei, sed a gratia. Eadem enim gratia, qua Christum vocavit ad mediatoris munus et electos ad unionem cum Christo attraxit, censet etiam cos iam attractos et credentes ex illa unione iustos."

[3]iii. 176: "Iustificamur ex promissione, in qua propter Christum promissa est reconciliatio, iustitia et vita aeterna." 233: "Sicut iustificatio ad fidem pertinet, ita pertinet ad fidem vita aeterna . . . Fatentur enim adversarii, quod iustificati sint filii dei et cohaeredes Christi."

[4]*Inst.* iii. 14. 17: "Efficientem vitae aeternae nobis comparandae causam scriptura praedicat patris coelestis misericordiam et gratuitam erga nos dilectionem, materialem vero Christum cum sua obedientia, qua nobis iustitiam acquisivit; formalem quoque vel instrumentalem quam esse dicemus nisi fidem?"

[5]See the corresponding expressions on this subject in his *Operat. in Ps.v (Opp. exeg. lat.* xiv, p. 239), and *De captiv. Babylon ecclesiae (Opp. lat. var. arg.* v, p. 104). Cf. also the fragment which Löscher, *Vollständ. Timotheus Verinus,* i, p. 31, communicates from a manuscript in his own possession: "Ad speculationes de maiestate dei nuda dederunt occasionem Dionysius cum sua mystica theologia et alii eum secuti, qui multa scripserunt de spiritualibus nuptiis, ubi deum ipsum sponsum, animam sponsam finxerunt. Atque ita docuerunt, homines posse conversari et agere in vita mortali et corrupta natura et carne cum maiestate dei inscrutabili et aeterna sine medio. Et haec certe doctrina recepta est pro summa et divina, *in qua et ego aliquamdiu versatus sum, non tamen sine magno meo damno.* Ut istam Dionysii mysticam theologiam et alios similes libros, quibus tales nugae continentur, detestemini tanquam pestem aliquam, hortor. Metuo enim, *fanaticos homines futuros, qui talia portenta rursum in ecclesiam invehant* et per hoc sanam doctrinam obscurent et prorsus obruant." Cf. *Gesch, der Pietismus*, vol. ii, p. 32.

[6]*Apologia C. A.,* ii. 48: "Fides quae iustificat, non est tantum notitia historiae, sed est assentiri promissioni dei,—est velle et accipere promissionem remissionis peccatorum et iustificationis." 77: "Sola fide in Christum, non per dilectionem, non propter dilectionem aut opera consequimur remissionem peccatorum etsi dilectio sequitur fidem." *Loci theol. C. R.,* xxi, p. 744: "Fides est assentiri universo verbo dei nobis proposito, adeoque et promissioni gratuitae reconciliationis, estque fiducia misericordiae dei promissae propter mediatorem Christum. Nam fiducia est

motus in voluntate, necessario repondens assensioni, sen quo voluntas in Christo acquiescit.''

[7]*Inst. chr. rel.*, iii. 2. 7: ''Nunc iusta fidei definitio nobis constabit, si dicamus esse divinae erga nos *benevolentiae firmam certamque cognitionem*, quae gratuitae in Christo promissionis veritate fundata per spiritum sanctum et revelatur mentibus nostris et *cordibus* obsignatur.'' 8: ''Assensionem ipsam iterum repetam cordis esse magis quam cerebri, et *affectus* magis quan intelligentiae. Qua ratione *obedientia* vocatur fidei.'' 14: ''Cognitionem non intelligimus comprehensionem, qualis esse solet earum rerum, quae sub humanum sensum cadunt . . . Sed dum *persuasum* habet, quod non capit, plus ipsa *persuasionis certitudine* intelligit, quam si humanum aliquid sua capacitate perciperet . . . Unde statuimus, fidei notitiam *certitudine* magis quam apprehensione contineri.'' 15: ''Sensus plerophoriae, quae fidei tribuitur, est nempe qui dei bonitatem perspicue nobis propositam extra dubium ponat. Id autem lieri nequit, quin eius *suavitatem* vere *sentiamus et experiamur* in nobis ipsis. Quare apostolus ex fide deducit *fiduciam* . . . Ostendit, non esse rectam fidem, nisi cum *tranquillis animis* audemus nos in conspectum dei sistere.''

[8]Gomarus, *Loci communes*, p. 425, maintains that *fiducia* is *effectus fidei*, and denies that it is *forma fidei*. Cf. *Geschichte des Pietismus*, vol. i, p. 323.

[9]See *Summa theol.*, ii. 2, qu. 1, art. 4.

[10]Qu. 4, art. 3: ''Actus voluntarii speciem recipiunt a fine, qui est voluntatis objectum. Id autem, a quo aliquid speciem sortitur, se habet ad modum formae in rebus naturalibus. Et ideo cuiuslibet actus voluntarii forma quodammodo est finis ad quem ordinatur . . . Actus fidei ordinatur ad obiectum voluntatis, quod est bonum, sicut ad finem. Hoc autem bonum, quod est finis fidei, scilicet bonum divinum est proprium obiectum caritatis, et ideo caritas dicitur forma fidei, in quantum per caritatem actus fidei perficitur et formatur.''

[11]*Symbolik* (6th ed. 1843), §17, pp. 169, 170.

[12]*Conc. Trid.*, Sess. vi, cap. 7.

[13]Qu. 25, art. 1: ''Habitus non diversificantur, nisi ex hoc, quod variant speciem actus. Omnis enim actus unius speciei ad eundem habitum pertinet. Cum autem species actus ex obiecto sumatur secundum formalem rationem ipsius, necesse est, quod idem specie sit actus, qui fertur in rationem obiecti et qui fertur in obiectum sub tali ratione, sicut eadem est specie visio, qua videtur lumen et qua videtur color secundum luminis rationem. Ratio autem diligendi proximum deus est. Hoe enim debemus in proximo diligere, ut in deo sit. Unde idem specie actus est, quo diligitur deus et quo diligitur proximus. Et propter hoc habitus caritatis non solum se extendit ad dilectionem dei sed etiam ad dilectionem proximi.''

[14]*Apol. Conf. Aug.*, ii. 56: ''Fides non ideo iustificat aut salvat, quia ipsa sit opus per sese dignum, sed tantum quia accipit misericordiam promissam.''

[15]*Apol. C. A.*, iv. 20, 21; ii. 101; viii. 42, 43, 58–60.

[16]*Inst. chr. rel.*, iii. 2. 6: ''Principio admonendi sumus, perpetuam esse fidei relationem cum verbo, nec magis ab eo posse divelli, quam radios a sole, unde oriuntur.''

[17]Cf. *Geschichte des Pictismus*, vol. iii, p. 122.

[18]Cf. *Ibid.*, vol. ii, p. 26ff.

[19]*Apol. C. A.*, iv: "Ecclesia proprie est columna veritatis; retinet enim purum evangelium." *Tractatus de potestate papae*, 24: "Tribuit Christus principaliter claves (i.e. evangelium) ecclesiae et immediate."

[20]*Geschichte des Pictismus*, vol. i, p. 296; vol. ii, p. 50.

[21]*Ibid.*, vol. ii, p. 23.

The Continuation and Completion

12

John Wesley

A Plain Account of Christian Perfection

[In the following discourse] I endeavoured to show—(1) In what sense Christians are not, (2) in what sense they are, perfect.

1. In what sense they are not. They are not perfect in knowledge. They are not free from ignorance; no, nor from mistake. We are no more to expect any living man to be infallible, than to be omniscient. They are not free from infirmities, such as weakness or slowness of understanding, irregular quickness or heaviness of imagination. Such, in another kind, are, impropriety of language, ungracefulness of pronunciation, to which one might add a thousand nameless defects, either in conversation or behaviour. From such infirmities as these none are perfectly freed till their spirits return to God. Neither can we expect, till then, to be wholly freed from temptation: "For the servant is not above his Master." But neither in this sense is there any absolute perfection on earth. There is no perfection of degrees, none which does not admit of a continual increase.

2. In what sense, then, are they perfect? Observe, we are not now speaking of babes in Christ, but adult Christians. But even babes in Christ

From *A Plain Account of Christian Perfection* (Nashville: Methodist Church Division of Higher Education, 1910), pp. 16–29.

are so far perfect as not to commit sin. This St. John affirms expressly, and it cannot be disproved by the examples of the Old Testament. For what if the holiest of the ancient Jews did sometimes commit sin? We cannot infer from hence, that "all Christians do and must commit sin as long as they live."

But does not the Scripture say, "A just man sinneth seven times a day"? It does not. Indeed it says, "A just man falleth seven times." But this is quite another thing. For, first, the words, *a day,* are not in the text. Secondly, here is no mention of falling into sin at all. What is here mentioned is falling into temporal affliction.

But elsewhere Solomon says, "There is no man that sinneth not." Doubtless thus it was in the days of Solomon; yea, and from Solomon to Christ there was then no man that sinned not. But whatever was the case of those under the law, we may safely affirm, with St. John, that since the Gospel was given, "he that is born of God sinneth not."

The privileges of Christians are in no wise to be measured by what the Old Testament records concerning those who were under the Jewish dispensation; seeing the fulness of time is now come; the Holy Ghost is now given; the great salvation of God is now brought to men by the revelation of Jesus Christ. The kingdom of heaven is now set up on earth, concerning which the Spirit of God declared of old time (so far is David from being the pattern or standard of Christian perfection), "He that is feeble among them at that day shall be as David; and the house of David shall be as the angel of the Lord before them" (Zech. 12:8).

But the apostles themselves committed sin: Peter by dissembling, Paul by his sharp contention with Barnabas. Suppose they did, will you argue thus: "If two of the apostles once committed sin, then all other Christians, in all ages, do and must commit sin as long as they live"? Nay, God forbid we should thus speak. No necessity of sin was laid upon them: the grace of God was surely sufficient for them; and it is sufficient for us at this day.

But St. James says, "In many things we offend all" [3:2]. True: but who are the persons here spoken of? Why, those *many masters* or teachers whom God had not sent. Not the apostle himself, nor any real Christian. That in the word *we* (used by a figure of speech, common in all other as well as the inspired writings) the apostle could not possibly include himself, or any other true believer, appears, first, from the ninth verse: "Therewith bless *we* God, and therewith curse *we* men." Surely not *we apostles!* not *we believers!* Secondly, from the words preceding the text: "My brethren, be not many masters," or teachers, "knowing that we shall receive the greater condemnation: for in many things we offend all." *We!* Who? Not the apostles, nor true believers, but they who were to "receive the greater condemnation," because of those many offences. Nay, thirdly, the verse itself proves that *"we offend all"* cannot be spoken either of all men, or all Christians. For in it immediately follows the mention of a man *who offends not,* as the *we* first mentioned did; from whom, therefore, he is professedly contradistinguished, and pronounced a *perfect man.*

But St. John himself says, "If we say that we have no sin, we deceive ourselves''; and, "if we say we have not sinned, we make Him a liar, and His word is not in us" [I John 1:8, 10].

I answer—(1) The tenth verse fixes the sense of the eighth. "If we say we have no sin," in the former, is explained by, "If we say we have not sinned," in the latter verse. (2) The point of consideration is not whether we have or have not sinned heretofore; and neither of these verses asserts that we do sin, or commit sin now. (3) The ninth verse explains both the eighth and tenth: "If we confess our sins, He is faithful and just to forgive us our sins, and to cleanse us from all unrighteousness." As if we had said, I have before affirmed, "The blood of Christ cleanseth from all sin." And no man can say, "I need it not; I have no sin to be cleansed from." "If we say we have no sin," that we have not sinned, "we deceive ourselves," and make God a liar. But "if we confess our sins, He is faithful and just," not only "to forgive us our sins," but also "to cleanse us from all unrighteousness," that we may "go and sin no more." In conformity, therefore, both to the doctrine of St. John, and the whole tenor of the New Testament, we fix this conclusion: A Christian is so far perfect as not to commit sin.

This is the glorious privilege of every Christian, yea, though he be but a babe in Christ. But it is only of grown Christians it can be affirmed they are in such a sense perfect, as to be freed from evil thoughts and, secondly, evil tempers. First, from evil or sinful thoughts. Indeed, whence should they spring? "Out of the heart of man," if at all, "proceed evil thoughts." If, therefore, the heart be no longer evil, then evil thoughts no longer proceed out of it. For, "a good tree cannot bring forth evil fruit."

And as they are freed from evil thoughts, so likewise from evil tempers. Every one of these can say, with St. Paul, "I am crucified with Christ: nevertheless I live; yet not I, but Christ liveth in me"—words that manifestly describe a deliverance from inward as well as from outward sin. This is expressed both negatively, "I live not"—my evil nature, the body of sin, is destroyed; and positively, "Christ liveth in me"—and, therefore, all that is holy and just and good. Indeed, both these, "Christ liveth in me," and "I live not," are inseparably connected. For what communion hath light with darkness, or Christ with Belial?

He, therefore, who liveth in these Christians, hath purified their hearts by faith, insomuch that every one that has Christ in him, "the hope of glory, purifieth himself even as He is pure." He is purified from pride, for Christ was lowly in heart. He is pure from desire and self-will, for Christ desired only to do the will of His Father. And he is pure from anger, in the common sense of the word, for Christ was meek and gentle. I say, "in the common sense of the word," for He is angry at sin while He is grieved for the sinner. He feels a displacency at every offence against God, but only tender compassion to the offender.

Thus doth Jesus save His people from their sins—not only from outward sins, but from the sins of their hearts. "True," say some, "but not till death; not in this world." Nay, St. John says, "Herein is our love made perfect, that we may have boldness in the day of judgment; because, as He is, so are we in this world." The apostle here, beyond all contradiction, speaks of himself and other living Christians, of whom he flatly affirms, that not only at or after death, but "in this world," they are as their Master.

Exactly agreeable to this are his words in the first chapter [I John]: "God is light, and in Him is no darkness at all. If we walk in the light, as He is in the light, we have fellowship one with another, and the blood of Jesus Christ His Son cleanseth us from all sin." And again: "If we confess our sins, He is faithful and just to forgive us our sins, and to cleanse us from all unrighteousness." Now, it is evident the apostle here speaks of a deliverance wrought in this world. For he saith not, The blood of Christ *will* cleanse (at the hour of death, or in the day of judgment), but it "cleanseth," at the present time, us living Christians "from all sin." And it is equally evident, that if any sin remain, we are not cleansed from all sin. If *any* unrighteousness remain in the soul, it is not cleansed from all unrighteousness. Neither let any say that this relates to justification only, or the cleansing us from the guilt of sin—First, because this is confounding together what the apostle clearly distinguishes; who mentions first, "to forgive us our sins," and then, "to cleanse us from all unrighteousness." Secondly, because this is asserting justification by works in the strongest sense possible. It is making all inward, as well as all outward holiness, necessarily previous to justification. For if the cleansing here spoken of is no other than the cleansing us from the guilt of sin, then we are not cleansed from guilt, that is, not justified, unless on condition of walking "in the light as He is in the light." It remains, then, that Christians are saved in this world from all sin, from all unrighteousness; that they are now in such a sense perfect, as not to commit sin, and to be freed from evil thoughts and evil tempers.

It could not be but that a discourse of this kind, which directly contradicted the favourite opinion of many, who were esteemed by others, and possibly esteemed themselves, some of the best Christians (whereas, if these things were so, they were not Christians at all), should give no small offence. Many answers or animadversions, therefore, were expected; but I was agreeably disappointed. I do not know that any appeared: so I went quietly on my way.

Not long after, I think in the spring, 1741, we published a second volume of hymns. As the doctrine was still much misunderstood, and consequently misrepresented, I judged it needful to explain yet farther upon the head; and this was done in the preface to it as follows:

This great gift of God, the salvation of our souls, is no other than the image of God fresh stamped on our hearts. It is a "renewal of believers in the spirit of their minds, after the likeness of Him that created them." God hath now laid "the axe unto the root of the tree," "purifying their hearts by faith," and "cleansing all the thoughts of their hearts by the inspiration of His Holy Spirit." Having this hope that they shall see God as He is, they "purify themselves even as He is pure"; and they are "holy, as He that hath called them is holy, in all manner of conversation." Not that they have already attained all that they shall attain, either are already (in this sense) perfect. But they daily "go on from strength to strength"; "beholding" now, "as in a glass, the glory of the Lord, they are changed into the same image, from glory to glory, by the Spirit of the Lord."

And "where the Spirit of the Lord is, there is liberty"—such liberty "from the law of sin and death" as the children of this world will not believe, though a man declare it unto them. "The Son hath made them free," who are thus "born of God," from that great root of sin and bitterness, pride. They feel that all their "sufficiency is of God"; that it is He alone who "is in all their thoughts," and "worketh in them both to will and to do of His good pleasure." They feel that "it is not they" that "speak, but the Spirit of" their "Father who speaketh in them"; and that whatsoever is done by their hands, "the Father, who is in them, He doeth the works." So that God is to them all in all, and they are nothing in His sight. They are freed from self-will, as desiring nothing but the holy and perfect will of God: not supplies in want, not ease in pain,[1] nor life, or death, or any creature; but continually crying in their inmost soul, "Father, Thy will be done." They are freed from evil thoughts, so that they cannot enter into them; no, not for a moment. Aforetime, when an evil thought came in, they looked up, and it vanished away. But now it does not come in, there being no room for this in a soul which is full of God. They are free from wanderings in prayer. Whensoever they pour out their hearts in a more immediate manner before God, they have no thought[2] of anything past, or absent, or to come, but of God alone. In times past wandering thoughts darted in, which yet fled away like smoke; but now that smoke does not rise at all. They have no fear or doubt, either as to their state in general, or as to any particular action.[3] The "unction from the Holy One" teacheth them every hour what they shall do, and what they shall speak.[4] Nor, therefore, have they any need to reason concerning it.[5] They are, in one sense, freed from temptation: for though numberless temptations fly about them, yet they trouble them not.[6] At all times their souls are even and calm, their hearts are steadfast and unmovable. Their peace, flowing as a river, "passeth all understanding," and they "rejoice with joy unspeakable and full of glory." For "they are sealed by the Spirit unto the day of redemption," having the witness in themselves, that "there is laid up for them a crown of righteousness, which the Lord will give" them "in that day."[7]

Not that every one is a child of the devil till he is thus renewed in love. On the contrary, whoever has a sure "confidence in God, that, through the merits of Christ his sins are forgiven," he is a child of God, and, if he abide in Him, an heir of all the promises. Neither ought he in any wise to cast away his confidence, or to deny the faith he has received, because it is weak, or because it is "tried with fire," so that his soul is "in heaviness through manifold temptations."

Neither dare we affirm, as some have done, that all this salvation is given at once. There is indeed an instantaneous, as well as a gradual, work of God in His children; and there wants not, we know, a cloud of witnesses who have received, in one moment, either a clear sense of the forgiveness of their sins, or the abiding witness of the Holy Spirit. But we do not know a single instance, in any place, of a person's receiving, in one and the same moment, remission of sins, the abiding witness of the Spirit, and a new, a clean heart.

Indeed, how God may work, we cannot tell; but the general manner wherein He does work is this: Those who once trusted in themselves that they were righteous, that they were rich, and increased in goods, and had need of nothing, are, by the Spirit of God applying His word, convinced that they are poor and naked. All the things that they have done are brought to their remembrance, and set in array before them; so that they see the wrath of God hanging over their heads, and feel that they deserve the damnation of hell. In their trouble they cry unto the Lord, and He shows them that He hath taken away their sins, and opens the kingdom of heaven in their hearts, "righteousness, and peace, and joy in the Holy Ghost." Sorrow and pain are fled away, and sin has no more dominion over them. Knowing they are justified freely, through faith in His blood, they "have peace with God through Jesus Christ"; they "rejoice in hope of the glory of God," and "the love of God is shed abroad in their hearts."

In this peace they remain for days, or weeks, or months, and commonly suppose that they shall not know war any more; till some of their old enemies, their bosom sins, or the sin which did most easily beset them (perhaps anger or desire), assault them again, and thrust sore at them that they may fall. Then arises fear that they should not endure to the end, and often doubt whether God has not forgotten them, or whether they did not deceive themselves in thinking their sins were forgiven. Under these clouds, especially if they reason with the devil, they go mourning all the day long. But it is seldom long before their Lord answers for Himself, sending them the Holy Ghost to comfort them, to bear witness continually with their spirits that they are the children of God. Then they are indeed meek, and gentle, and teachable, even as a little child. And now first do they see the ground of their heart,[8] which God before would not disclose unto them, lest the soul should fail before Him, and the spirit which He had made. Now they see all the hidden abominations there, the depths of pride, self-will, and hell; yet they have the witness in themselves, "Thou art an heir of God, a joint-heir with Christ," even in the midst of this fiery trial; which continually heightens both the strong sense they then have of their inability to help themselves, and the inexpressible hunger they feel after a full renewal in His image, in "righteousness and true holiness." Then God is mindful of the desire of them that fear Him, and gives them a single eye and a pure heart; He stamps upon them His own image and superscription; He createth them anew in Christ Jesus; He cometh unto them with His Son and blessed Spirit; and, fixing His abode in their souls, bringeth them into the "rest which remaineth for the people of God."

Here I cannot but remark—(1) That this is the strongest account we ever gave of Christian perfection; indeed, too strong in more than one particular, as is observed in the notes annexed; (2) that there is nothing which we have since advanced upon the subject, either in verse or prose, which is not either directly or indirectly contained in this preface. So that, whether our present doctrine be right or wrong, it is, however, the same which we taught from the beginning.

I need not give additional proofs of this, by multiplying quotations from the volume itself. It may suffice to cite part of one hymn only, the last in that volume:

Lord, I believe a rest remains
　To all Thy people known;
A rest where pure enjoyment reigns,
　And Thou art loved alone.

A rest where all our soul's desire
　Is fixed on things above;
Where doubt, and pain, and fear expire,
　Cast out by perfect love.

From every evil motion freed
　(The Son hath made us free),
On all the powers of hell we tread,
　In glorious liberty.

Safe in the way of life, above
　Death, earth, and hell we rise;
We find, when perfected in love,
　Our long-sought paradise.

O that I now the rest might know,
　Believe, and enter in!
Now, Saviour, now the power bestow,
　And let me cease from sin!

Remove this hardness from my heart,
　This unbelief remove;
To me the rest of faith impart,
　The Sabbath of Thy love.

Come, O my Saviour, come away!
　Into my soul descend;
No longer from Thy creature stay,
　My Author and my End.

The bliss Thou hast for me prepared
　No longer be delay'd;

Come, my exceeding great reward,
For whom I first was made.

Come, Father, Son, and Holy Ghost,
And seal me Thine abode!
Let all I am in Thee be lost;
Let all be lost in God.

Can anything be more clear than—(1) That here also is as full and high a salvation as we have ever spoken of? (2) That this is spoken of as receivable by mere faith, and as hindered only by unbelief? (3) That this faith, and consequently the salvation which it brings, is spoken of as given in an instant? (4) That it is supposed that instant may be now; that we need not stay another moment; that "now," the very "now, is the accepted time; now is the day of" this full "salvation"? And, lastly, that if any speak otherwise, he is the person that brings new doctrine among us?

About a year after, namely, in the year 1742, we published another volume of hymns. The dispute being now at the height, we spoke upon the head more largely than ever before. Accordingly, abundance of the hymns in this volume treat expressly on this subject. And so does the preface, which, as it is short, it may not be amiss to insert entire:

(1) Perhaps the general prejudice against Christian perfection may chiefly arise from a misapprehension of the nature of it. We willingly allow, and continually declare, there is no such perfection in this life as implies either a dispensation from doing good, and attending all the ordinances of God; or a freedom from ignorance, mistake, temptation, and a thousand infirmities necessarily connected with flesh and blood.

(2) First, we not only allow, but earnestly contend, that there is no perfection in this life which implies any dispensation from attending all the ordinances of God; or from doing good unto all men while we have time, though "especially unto the household of faith." We believe that not only the babes in Christ, who have newly found redemption in His blood, but those also who are "grown up into perfect men," are indispensably obliged, as often as they have opportunity, to "eat bread and drink wine in remembrance of Him," and to "search the Scriptures," by fasting, as well as temperance, "to keep their bodies under, and bring them into subjection"; and, above all, to pour out their souls in prayer, both secretly, and in the great congregation.

(3) We, secondly, believe that there is no such perfection in this life as implies an entire deliverance, either from ignorance or mistake, in things not essential to salvation, or from manifold temptations, or from numberless infirmities, wherewith the corruptible body more or less presses down the soul. We cannot find any ground in Scripture to suppose that any inhabitant of a house of clay is wholly exempt either from bodily infir-

mities, or from ignorance of many things; or to imagine any is incapable of mistake, or falling into divers temptations.

(4) But whom then do you mean by "one that is *perfect*"? We mean one in "whom is the mind which was in Christ," and who so "walketh as Christ also walked"; a man "that hath clean hands and a pure heart," or that is "cleansed from all filthiness of flesh and spirit": one in whom is "no occasion of stumbling," and who accordingly "does not commit sin." To declare this a little more particularly: We understand by that scriptural expression, "a perfect man," one in whom God hath fulfilled His faithful word, "From all your filthiness and from all your idols I will cleanse you: I will also save you from all your uncleannesses." We understand hereby, one whom God hath "sanctified throughout, in body, soul, and spirit"; one who "walketh in the light as He is in the light; in whom is no darkness at all: the blood of Jesus Christ His Son having cleansed him from all sin."

(5) This man can now testify to all mankind, "I am crucified with Christ: nevertheless I live; yet not I, but Christ liveth in me." He is "holy as God who called him is holy," both in heart and "in all manner of conversation." He "loveth the Lord his God with all his heart," and serveth Him with "all his strength." He "loveth his neighbour," every man, "as himself"; "yea," as Christ "loveth us"; them in particular that "despitefully use him, and persecute him, because they know not the Son, neither the Father." Indeed his soul is all love, filled with "bowels of mercies, kindness, meekness, gentleness, long-suffering." And his life agreeth thereto, full of "the work of faith, the patience of hope, the labour of love." "And whatsoever he doeth, either in word or deed, he doeth it all in the name," in the love and power, "of the Lord Jesus." In a word, he doeth "the will of God on earth, as it is done in heaven."

Notes

[1]This is too strong. Our Lord Himself desired ease in pain. He asked for it, only with resignation: *Not as I will,* I desire, *but as Thou wilt.*

[2]This is far too strong. See the Sermon on *Wandering Thoughts.*

[3]Frequently this is the case, but only *for a time.*

[4]For a time it may be so, but not always.

[5]Sometimes they have no need; at other times they have.

[6]Sometimes they do not; at other times they do, and that grievously.

[7]Not all who are saved from sin; many of them have not attained it yet.

[8]Is it not astonishing that, while this book is extant, which was published four-and-twenty years ago, anyone should face me down that this is a new doctrine, and what I never taught before? [This note was first published in the year 1765.]

13

Herman Bavinck

Sanctification

Inasmuch as the image of God consisted not only of knowledge and righteousness, but also of holiness, the restoration of man must not only restore him to a right relationship with God, but must also renew him internally according to the demand of His holy law. Sin is guilt, but it is also pollution. Justification delivers him from the pollution of sin. By the former his consciousness is changed, and by the latter his being is changed. By means of the first, man comes to stand in a right relationship again; by means of the second, man becomes good again and able to do good.

The word *holy* occurs on virtually every page of the Holy Scriptures. Just what the original, natural meaning of the Hebrew word translated *holy* in our version meant is not to be made out with certainty; in Scripture the word is never used in that original, natural sense, but always has a religious significance. Nevertheless the word as used in Scripture very probably came from a root which meant *to be cut off*, or *to be separated*. Nor is it possible to say definitely in what sense the world was first introduced into religious discussion. According to some, persons and things were first called holy because they were set apart from other persons and things, and

From *Our Reasonable Faith* (Grand Rapids: Wm. B. Eerdmans Pub. Co., 1956), pp. 469–513. Used by permission.

were, so to speak, removed from common use. The opposite of the word *holy* is, according, unholy, unconsecrated, mean, profane.[1] According to others the word first meant, in reference to religious things, that persons and objects stood in a particular relationship to God, and were in that sense different from others. So much can be said for this view, namely, that people and things are never by nature themselves holy, but can become this only through a definite action which accrues to them. Nor can they sanctify themselves, for all holiness and sanctification proceeds from God. Jehovah is holy, and therefore He wants a holy people, a holy priesthood, a holy temple.[2] It is He who designates those who are His own and who are holy (Num. 16:5).

Again and again, accordingly, God is in the Old Testament called the Holy One. It is only in Daniel 4:8, 9, 18, that Nebuchadnezzar too speaks of his holy gods (cf. 5:11). This word *holy* when used in reference to the Divine Being does not intend to designate a particular attribute which He possesses alongside of others, but is used, rather, to give expression to His Divine greatness, sublimity, majesty, and unapproachableness. There is none holy as the Lord, for there is none beside Thee: neither is there any rock like our God (I Sam. 2:2). He is God, and not man (Hos. 11:9). No one is able to stand before this holy God (I Sam. 6:20). He is exalted high above the gods, glorious in holiness, fearful in praises, doing wonders (Exod. 15:11). He is terrible out of His holy places (Ps. 68:35); His name is great and terrible (Ps. 99:2, 3); to swear by His holiness is to swear by Himself (Amos 4:2; 6:8). In short, holiness points to God in His distinction from and elevation above all creatures. He is the Holy One because He is God. Isaiah especially likes to make use of this word for God.[3]

The holiness of God manifests itself in all the relationships in which He has placed Himself over against His people. The whole of the lawgiving in Israel has its first principle in the holiness of Jehovah and has its end in the sanctification of the people. He is holy in all His revelation, in all that proceeds from Him: His name is holy (Lev. 20:3); His arm is holy (Ps. 98:1); His covenant is holy (Dan. 11:28); His word is holy (Ps. 105:42); and His Spirit is holy (Ps. 51:11; Isa. 63:10, 11). Hence He wants His people to be holy also.[4] And among that people He particularly wants the priests and Levites, who minister in the holy things and who are consecrated by particular ceremonies for their office, to be holy (Exod. 29). In fact, everything that stands in some relationship to the service of God, whether places, times, offerings, the garments of the priests, or the temple, and the like, must be dedicated to the Lord and be holy. The whole meaning of the giving of the law is that Israel must be a priestly nation and a holy people unto the Lord (Exod. 19:6). And the people of Israel actually is holy if in everything it answers to the law which the Lord has given it.

We must remember that this law in Israel comprised not merely moral, but also many civic and ceremonial, commandments. Holiness, therefore, consisted of perfection, in total correspondence to the law, but this perfection was not merely of a moral but also of a civic and ceremonial nature. The people, however, frequently fell into one-sidedness and sought the essence of religion in external, Levitical purity. The prophets, consequently, had to protest against this and had to proclaim that obedience was better than sacrifice and to hearken than the fat of rams (I Sam. 15:22); and they had to say that God desired mercy and not sacrifice, and the knowledge of God more than burnt offerings (Hos. 6:6). The prophets had to preach that the Lord required nothing of the people but to do justly, and to love mercy, and to walk humbly with God (Mic. 6:8). They pointed out that the holiness of God consisted especially in His moral perfection, in His exaltedness above and His contrast to the sinfulness of the creature (Isa. 6:3–7). When people profane His name and His covenant, then God sanctifies Himself in righteousness (Isa. 5:16; Ezek. 28:22). As the Holy One He most certainly punishes the enemy in order that they may know that He is the Lord (Jer. 50:29; Ezek. 36:23; 39:7), but He will deliver His people by purging it of all unrighteousness, establishing a new covenant with it, and causing it to walk in His ways with a new heart (Jer. 31:31–34; Ezek. 36:25–29). And He will do this not for Israel's sake, but for the sake of His own great name (Isa. 43:25; Ezek. 36:22).

In the same way in which God in the New Testament has in Christ given His people righteousness so in the Son of His love He has given them holiness. Christ is our holiness, our sanctification, in the same way and in the same sense as He is our wisdom, our redemption. We must know that He was first of all one who shared in a personal holiness, for otherwise He could not have achieved a holiness for us. That which was conceived in Mary by the Holy Spirit and was born of her was the Holy Thing and was given the name of the Son of God (Luke 1:35). Later, at His baptism, He received the Holy Spirit without measure and was full of the Holy Spirit (Luke 3:22; 4:1). Those who were possessed of devils acknowledged Him as the Holy One of God (Mark 1:24; Luke 4:34), and the disciples by the mouth of Peter made the confession: "Lord, to whom shall we go? Thou hast the words of eternal life, and we have believed and known that Thou art the Holy One of God" (John 6:68, 69). In Acts 4:27 (compare 3:14), the same apostle speaks of Him as the Holy Child of God (or the holy servant of God), and in Revelation 3:7 He calls Himself the Holy and the True One. Just as Christ was conscious of His sinlessness,[5] so also all His apostles testify that He has done no wrong and that there is no deceit in His mouth.[6]

We must, however, make a distinction in Christ between the holiness which He possessed by nature and that which He accomplished by His perfect obedience. His being conceived and born holy had this benefit, first of all, that He could be our Mediator (Heidelberg Catechism, Answer 16), but it also had the further benefit that He, being our Mediator from the very moment of His conception, covers the sin in which we are conceived and born with His innocence and perfect holiness before the face of God (Heidelberg Catechism, Answer 36). The holiness in which He was born He immediately made a part of the holiness which He throughout His life, even up to His death, had to achieve for His church. We know, for exam-

ple, that the Father already sanctified Him before His incarnation, conse-
crating Him to the office of Mediator, and precisely to that end sent Him
into the world (John 10:36). And Christ sanctified Himself and gave Himself up to the will of His Father before He was conceived in Mary and born
of her; His incarnation was already a fulfillment of the Father's will, a deed
of sanctification (Heb. 10:5–9). It was not enough that Christ was holy: He
had to sanctify Himself from the moment of His conception up to the hour
of His death.

As Mediator, after all, He was subjected to the severest trials and temptations, especially after He had received baptism, had been anointed by the
Holy Spirit, and had begun to carry out His public ministry. The temptation
of which we read in the Gospels, was the beginning of a life full of
struggle; when this temptation was finished, the devil departed from Him
for only a period (Luke 4:13). We cannot picture to ourselves what these
temptations were, but we are expressly told that He became like the brethren *in all things,* and that He was in all points tempted like as we are, yet
without sin (Heb. 2:17; 4:15); we have no weakness but He knows of it,
and no temptation but He can help us. But whereas we succumb every
moment, He remains faithful to the end; He was tempted in all things, but
without sin; He was obedient unto death, even the death of the cross (Phil.
2:8). He did not pray that He be spared death, but He did offer up prayers
and supplications with strong crying and tears to Him that was able to save
Him from death, that He might remain steadfast in His suffering and might
by His death accomplish life. And He was answered in this prayer (Heb.
5:7).

But, although He was the Son, He nevertheless had to learn obedience
by the things which He suffered (Heb. 5:8). He was obedient from the
beginning and He *wanted to be* obedient: His meat was to do the Father's
will (John 4:34). But in His passion He received the opportunity to prove
that obedience; in and through His suffering He had to translate into deed
and action His disposition and will to obey. Thus He was sanctified by the
things which He suffered (Heb. 2:11; 5:9), sanctified, that is, not in the
moral sense but finished, brought to the conclusion He had envisioned all
along and so, by reason of the passion of His death, crowned with glory
and honor (Heb. 2:9; 12:2). Thus He was made the Captain of the salvation
of the children of God and the Finisher of their faith (Heb. 2:10; 12:2). By
bearing the cross and despising the shame with a view to the joy that would
await Him after His humiliation, He became the initiator, the pioneer, and
the workman of the salvation of His own, and, at the same time, the One
who begins that faith in them and finishes it. By perfecting Himself in the
way of obedience, by seeking the glory at the right hand of the Father in no
other way than through the deepest humiliation, He became the author of
the eternal salvation of all those who obey Him (Heb. 5:9). He sanctified
Himself, gave Himself up as a sacrifice unto death, in order that His
disciples might be sanctified in truth (John 17:19). And so He was given us
of God unto our sanctification (I Cor. 1:30).

In order to understand the sanctification of the believers properly, one must see clearly that Christ is our sanctification in the same sense that He is our righteousness. He is a perfect and adequate Savior; He does not accomplish His work in part only, but actually and perfectly saves us; and He does not leave off His work until He has caused us to share fully in eternal life and the heavenly blessedness. By His righteousness, therefore, He not only restores us to the state of the righteous, of those who stand free in the judgment of God, in order for the rest to leave the matter in our own hands, so that, so to speak, we ourselves now proceed to earn eternal life by doing good works and conforming ourselves to the image of God; no, Christ also finishes all this work for us. He bore the guilt and penalty of sin for us, and He also kept the law for us and earned eternal life. His obedience was both *passive* and *active,* and it was both at the same time.

His resurrection was the evidence of this. By it we know that God did not leave His soul in hell (thought of in this connection, of course, not as the place of the damned, for the soul of Christ after His death was in Paradise, but as the grave, the realm of the dead, to which Christ also belonged so long as He remained in the state of death) and did not suffer His Holy One to see corruption, but made known to Him the ways of life, and filled Him full of joy with His countenance (Acts 2:27, 28; 13:35–37). In accordance with the Spirit of holiness which dwelt in Him, He was after the resurrection from the dead designated and appointed by God as His Son with power (Rom. 1:4), to be a Prince and a Savior, in order to give repentance to Israel, and forgiveness of sins (Acts 5:31), to be a Prince of life who has achieved eternal life and now gives it to His own (Acts 3:15).

But this sanctification which Christ has achieved for His church is not something which remains outside of us but something, rather, which is really shared with us. In justification we are declared free of guilt and punishment on the basis of a righteousness which is outside of us in Christ Jesus, and which through God's grace is reckoned to us and on our own part is received in faith. In sanctification, however, the holiness of Christ is most certainly poured out in us through the Holy Spirit. When Roman Catholicism therefore speaks of a grace which is poured into us, we have no objection to that in itself; we object only to the fact that this grace is regarded as a part of the righteousness on the basis of which we are declared free before God. For, if that were so, then justification and sanctification, the deliverance from guilt and the removal of the pollution, would be confused with each other; and then Christ would be robbed of the perfection of His achieved righteousness and the believing soul of its comfort and assurance. But there is actually such a thing as a grace that is poured in; there is such a thing as a Christ in us as well as a Christ for us; there is such a thing as a renewal after the image of God as well as a transmission to the state of the righteous; there is such a thing as a change in our moral condition as well as in our status before God.

As a matter of fact this sanctification must be maintained with no less resoluteness and power than justification. There have always been those

who have regarded the forgiveness of sins as the one great benefit of
Christ, and who denied the inner renewal of men after the image of God or,
at least, neglected it and left it unexplored. These hold that if a person is
justified and is conscious of this in faith, nothing further needs to happen to
him. They maintain that the consciousness of the forgiveness of sins already makes him a different person. In short, for such observers, justification and regeneration are two names for one and the same thing.

Now it is altogether true that the Christian who with a true faith believes
that all his sins, out of pure grace, and solely because of the merits of
Christ, have been forgiven does most certainly by his awareness become a
different person. He feels himself acquitted of all guilt; he has, being
justified by faith, found peace with God; he stands in the freedom with
which Christ has made him free; and, together with David, he can rejoice
and say: Blessed is he whose trespass has been forgiven, whose sin is
wholly covered; blessed is the man to whom the Lord has not reckoned his
unrighteousness! Such a change can even in a certain sense be called a
regeneration, a renewal of consciousness.

But if one goes on to infer from this that justification and regeneration
are altogether the same thing, he is in error and is going absolutely counter
to the testimony of Holy Scripture. After all, the true, saving faith which
accepts the righteousness of Christ and becomes aware of the forgiveness
of sins does not come up out of the natural man but is a fruit of regeneration, and therefore already assumes a spiritual change which has taken
place through the Holy Spirit. And the hearty joy and peace which the
believer enjoys by reason of the assurance of the forgiveness of his sins are
attributes of the spiritual man who in communion with Christ has been
raised from death in sin.

Moreover, a distinction must be made between the status in which a
person stands and the condition in which he finds himself. These two are so
far apart that an innocent person is sometimes accused and condemned and
a guilty person is sometimes acquitted by the judge. A person's status,
therefore, does not yet change his condition, nor vice versa. This holds true
in the natural but also in the spiritual sphere. Sin is not merely guilt, but
also pollution; we are delivered from the first by justification, from the
second by sanctification. Perfect salvation consists not alone of knowledge
and righteousness, but also of sanctification and redemption. And therefore
Christ gave out both of them: the forgiveness of sins and eternal life.

And, what is conclusive in this regard, Scripture distinguishes justification and regeneration very clearly. The promise of the Old Testament
contained the idea that in the new covenant the Lord would forgive the
unrighteousness of His people, but it contained the idea also that He would
give a new heart upon which He would write His law.[7] He would put His
Spirit in them, and cause them to walk in His statutes, and to keep His
judgments, to do them (Ezek. 36:27). In order to fulfill that promise Christ
not only gave His soul as a ransom for many, but after His exaltation to the
right hand of the Father He also sent the Holy Spirit, in order that this Spirit
should dwell and work in the church. What His Spirit accomplishes in the

church we have previously noted: in and through the Spirit Christ shares Himself and all His benefits with His people.

Accordingly, after Paul in his letter to the Romans has first dealt with the subject of justification he proceeds in chapter 6 to the subject of sanctification. Just as there were later on, so there were in the days of the apostles certain people who thought that the doctrine of free justification would affect the moral life unfavorably. They feared that people, prompted by such a confession, would proceed to sin in order that good might issue from it and grace be made to abound (Rom. 3:8; 6:1). Paul refutes this charge and says that it is impossible for those who have died to sin to live in it any longer (Rom. 6:2).

He proves this by pointing out that the believers who by their faith have received the forgiveness of sins and peace with God have also by witness of their baptism been buried with Christ in His death and been raised with Him to a new life (Rom. 6:3–11). For Paul believers are always persons who have not only accepted the righteousness of God in Christ unto the forgiveness of their sins, but also have personally died and been raised in the communion with Christ, and therefore are dead to sin and alive in God.[8] In other words, the death of Christ has not only justifying power but also sanctifying power (II Cor. 5:5ff). And the faith which has the true stamp upon it accepts Christ not only as a justification but also as a sanctification: in fact, the one is impossible without the other. For Christ is not to be divided and His benefits are inseparable from His person. He is at the same time our wisdom and our righteousness, our sanctification and our redemption (I Cor. 1:30). Such He became for us of God and as such He was given us by God.

The sanctification which we must share, therefore, lies perfectly achieved in Christ. There are many Christians who, at least in their practical life, think very differently about this. They acknowledge that they are justified through the righteousness which Christ has accomplished, but they maintain or at least act as though they hold that they must be sanctified by a holiness that they must themselves achieve. If this were true, then we, in flat contradiction of the apostolic testimony,[9] would not be living under grace in freedom but under the bondage of the law. However, the evangelical sanctification is distinguished just as well from the legal one as the righteousness of God revealed in the gospel is distinguished, not in its content but in the mode of sharing it, from that which was demanded by the law. It consists of this: that in Christ God gives us the perfect sanctification along with the justification, and that He gives us this as an internal possession through the regenerating and renewing operation of the Holy Spirit.

Sanctification is therefore God's work, a work of His righteousness and of His grace at the same time. First He reckons Christ and all His benefits to our account, and thereupon He shares Him with us in all the fulness that is in Him. For it is He who circumcises the hearts (Deut. 30:6), who takes away the heart of stone and supplants it with a heart of flesh (Ezek. 12:19), who pours out His Spirit upon them (Joel 2:28), who creates a new spirit within them (Ezek. 11:19; 36:26), who writes His law in their hearts, causes them to walk in His ways and makes them His people.[10] The matter is, if possible, put even more strongly in the New Testament where we read that the believers are God's workmanship, created in Christ Jesus (Eph. 2:10), a new creature (II Cor. 5:17; Gal. 6:15), and the work of God (Rom. 14:20). There the believers are also called God's husbandry and God's building,[11] and there we are told that all things are of God (II Cor. 5:18). When they were buried with Christ and raised with Him, they were also washed and sanctified;[12] and they continue to be sanctified in the future,[13] until they have been wholly conformed to the image of the Son.[14] The chain of salvation cannot be broken because from beginning to end it is the work of God. Whom He has known, called, and justified, him He has also glorified (Rom. 8:30).

On the basis of this work of sanctification which God brings about through the Spirit of Christ in the church the believers are frequently designated *saints* in Holy Scripture. Israel was already so called in the old day (Exod. 19:6). Israel was separated from the nations in order to be the Lord's (Lev. 20:26), and in order that it should walk in His ways (Exod. 19:5). And in the future, when God established His new covenant, He with even more right and with a profounder sense called His holy people the redeemed of the Lord.[15] When in the days of the New Testament the High Priest sanctified Himself for His people, in order that they too should be sanctified in truth (John 17:19), the believers also immediately received the name of holy ones or saints.[16] This name does not imply that in a moral sense they are free of all sin and above all sin, but rather that the New Testament church has now supplanted the ancient Israel and become the property of the Lord,[17] inasmuch as it has been sanctified in Christ and become a temple of the Holy Spirit.[18]

But this sanctification which Christ has given the church and which at the first was given it by the Holy Spirit places a heavy obligation upon the believers. Sanctification is a work of God, but it is intended to be a work in which the believers themselves are also active in the power of God. In the Old Testament we read at one time that the Lord Himself sanctifies His people,[19] and at another time that the people must sanctify themselves.[20] Sometimes we read that the Lord circumcises the heart (Deut. 30:6), and another time that Israel is called upon to circumcise the foreskin of their hearts (Deut. 10:16; Jer. 4:4). At one point regeneration is called the work of God (Jer. 31:18; Lam. 5:21), and at another time it is called the responsibility of the person himself (Jer. 3:12, 13, and elsewhere). Just so in the New Testament sanctification is also presented as a gift of God in Christ and as a work of the Holy Spirit by which the believers are sanctified.[21] And yet these believers are repeatedly admonished to be perfect even as their Father in Heaven is perfect (Matt. 5:48), to do good works which glorify the Father who is in Heaven (Matt. 5:16; John 15:8), to yield their members as servants to righteousness unto holiness (Rom. 6:19), to be holy in all their walk and conduct (I Peter 1:15; II Peter 3:11), to pursue sanctification and to fulfill it in the fear of God,[22] and to do this because without holiness no man shall see the Lord (Heb. 12:14).

The first is by no means incompatible with the second. It were truer to say that the effort of the believers in working towards their own sanctification is made possible only by the fact that it is a work of God which He fulfills in them. Certainly, grace, so far from obliterating nature, restores it. Inasmuch as man because of sin lacked the desire and the ability to walk in the ways of the Lord, he by virtue of the re-creation is again inclined and equipped, at least in principle, to live uprightly not merely in some but in all the commandments of God. When God penetrates the inward parts of the human being with the powerful operation of the regenerating Spirit, He opens the heart that is closed, mellows what is hard, and circumcises what is uncircumcised. He implants new potentialities in the will, and causes the will that was dead to become alive again, the will that was evil to become good, and the will that did not want to obey to choose His ways, and the will that was rebellious to be obedient. He moves and strengthens that will in such a way that as a good tree brings forth fruits so it can also bring forth good works.

Consequently, when the Reformed Churches express themselves in this way in their confession (Canons of Dort) they thereby place themselves on the basis of Holy Scripture, and find definite support in the profound statement of the apostle Paul: Work out your own salvation with fear and trembling, *for* it is God who works in you both to will and to do of His good pleasure (Phil. 2:12, 13). Just as in justification the forgiveness of sins, completely prepared in Christ, can on our part be received and enjoyed only through a living and active faith, so God effects the sanctification in us only by means of us ourselves. He does not annihilate our personality, but lifts it up; He does not kill our reason and our will and our desires, but rather quickens them inasmuch as they were dead, and puts them to work. He makes us His allies and co-laborers.

But this sanctification of the believers must then be properly understood. It must not become a legal sanctification, but is and must remain an evangelical sanctification. It does not consist of the fact that the believers proceed to sanctify themselves by means of a holiness which they themselves newly and for the first time bring into being, or of one which exists already but which they by means of their exertion and good works must appropriate. The holiness revealed by God in the gospel is not only completely prepared by Christ but by His Spirit is also applied to our hearts and worked out there. Paul says it so beautifully in Ephesians 2:10: We are His workmanship, created in Christ Jesus unto good works, which God has before ordained that we should walk in them. Just as the first creation was brought into being by the Word, so the re-creation gets its being in the communion with Christ. The believers are crucified, die, are buried, and they are also raised and reborn to a new life in the fellowship with Christ.

And that re-creation has a specific purpose. It has its end in the good works which the believers do. God does not care about the tree but about the fruits, and in those fruits about His own glorification. But those good works are not independently and newly brought into being by the believers themselves. They lie completely prepared for them all and for each one of

them individually in the decision of God's counsel; they were fulfilled
and were earned for believers by Christ who in their stead fulfilled all
righteousness and the whole law; and they are worked out in them by the
Holy Spirit who takes everything from Christ and distributes it to each and all
according to Christ's will. So we can say of sanctification in its entirety and
of all the good works of the church, that is, of all the believers together and
of each one individually, that they do not come into existence first of all
through the believers, but that they exist long before in the good pleasure of
the Father, in the work of the Son, and in the application of the Holy Spirit.
Hence all glorying on man's part is also ruled out in this matter of sanctification. We must know that God in no way becomes indebted to us, and that
He therefore never has to be grateful to us, when we do good works; on the
contrary, we are beholden to God for them, and have to be grateful to Him
for the good works that we do.

From this there follows also the significance of faith in the work of
sanctification. It is by no means in justification only, but quite as much in
sanctification, that by faith exclusively we are saved. For we on our part
can accept Christ and His benefits and make them our own only through
faith. If righteousness and holiness were products of the law we should
have to bring both of them about by the doing of good works. But in the
gospel they are a gift of God granted us in the person of Christ; in Him
there is a fulness of grace and truth (John 1:17), of wisdom and knowledge
(Col. 2:3), of righteousness and holiness (I Cor. 1:30). In Him all spiritual
blessings are contained (Eph. 1:3), and the fulness of the Godhead dwells
bodily (Col. 2:9). This Christ gives Himself to us through the Holy Spirit,
and joins Himself with us so intimately as does the vine with the branches
(John 15:2ff.), as the head with the body (Eph. 1:22, 23), as the husband
with the wife (Eph. 5:31, 32), and as He Himself as Mediator is conjoined
with the Father (John 14:20; 17:21–23). The believers are one spirit with
Him (I Cor. 6:17), and one flesh (Eph. 5:30, 31). Christ lives in them and
they in Christ (Gal. 2:20). Christ is all in them all (Col. 3:11).

If Christ is in this way the workman of our sanctification, then on our
own part the work of sanctification can be fulfilled only by faith. For
sanctification is, like all the other benefits of Christ, so inseparably related
to the person of Christ that we cannot receive it except in communion with
Christ Himself; and this is, viewed from our side, to be obtained and
enjoyed only through a true faith. After all, it is only through faith that
Christ dwells in our hearts (Eph. 3:17), and that we live in Christ (Gal.
2:20). It is only through faith that we become children of God (Gal. 3:26),
that we receive the promise of the Spirit (Gal. 3:14), and that we receive
the forgiveness of sins (Rom. 4:6) and eternal life (John 3:16). To live by
faith: that is simply the opposite side of saying that Christ dwells in us (II
Cor. 13:5; Gal. 2:20). The whole life of Christ is thus a life of faith just as
the Bible saints are presented to us in Hebrews 11 as the heroes of faith; so
we too are admonished to live by faith (II Cor. 5:7), to let faith work by
love (Gal. 5:6), with the shield of faith to quench the fiery darts of the

wicked (Eph. 6:16), and to overcome the world (I John 5:4). And all these admonishments correspond fully with those others which make it obligatory for the believers not to walk according to the flesh but according to the Spirit (Rom. 8:4ff.), to put aside the old man and to put on the new man,[23] to accept the Lord Jesus Christ and to walk in Him (Col. 2:6; I Peter 3:16), to put on the Lord Jesus Christ and to fulfill all things in His name (Rom. 13:14; Col. 3:17), to become mighty in the Lord and in the strength of His might (Eph. 6:10; II Tim. 2:1), and to grow in the grace and knowledge of our Lord and Savior (II Peter 3:18). In short, sanctification in an evangelical sense is a continuous activity and exercise of faith.

Many people have objections to this teaching of Scripture. They regard it as one-sided and as being dangerous for the moral life. Sometimes they are willing to concede that in justification the law is out of the question and faith alone is determinative. But when they discuss sanctification, they maintain that faith alone is inadequate, and that the law with all that it commands and all that it forbids, with all its rewards and penalties, must also come into play if a holy walk is to be fruitfully pursued and if there is to be an incentive to good works. And even though it is altogether true that the law remains the rule of life for the Christian, still the gospel never derives the exhortations to a holy war from the terrors of the law, but derives them rather from the high calling to which the believers in Christ are called. Be perfect even as your Father in Heaven is perfect (Matt. 5:48). Jesus is the vine, the disciples are His branches; they who remain in Him bear much fruit, for without Him they can do nothing (John 15:5). Together with Christ the believers have died to sin, but in Him they have become alive unto God (Rom. 6:11). They are not under the law, but under grace, and therefore sin may not reign over them (Rom. 6:14). They have through the law died to the law and belong to Christ, in order that they may live unto God (Rom. 7:4; Gal. 2:19). They are not in the flesh but in the Spirit, and must therefore walk after the Spirit (Rom. 8:5). The night has passed by, the day has come; the works of darkness must therefore be cast off and the armor of light must be put on (Rom. 13:12). The bodies of the believers are members of Christ and temples of the Holy Spirit; hence they must flee the sin of adultery (I Cor. 6:15ff.). They are bought with a price, and therefore they must glorify God in their body and in their spirit, for these are God's (I Cor. 6:20). They stand in freedom, the freedom with which Christ has made them free; and in Christ nothing avails anything but faith working by love (Gal. 5:1, 6). From that Christ they have heard and from Him they have learned that they must cast off the old man and put on the new man created after God in true righteousness and holiness (Eph. 4:21ff.). As dear children they must be followers of God (Eph. 5:1). They must walk in love even as Christ has loved them (Eph. 5:2). They are light in the Lord, and accordingly must walk as the children of light (Eph. 5:8).

In short, we should have to record all the moral exhortations in the New Testament if we were fully to summarize all the imperatives set forth to encourage the believers to a holy walk. But the passages cited are sufficient to indicate that they are all derived from the gospel and not from the law.

Irrespective of whether the apostles are addressing themselves to men or to women, to parents or to children, to masters or to servants, to women or to maids, to rulers or to subjects, they exhort them all *in the Lord*.[24] The sure foundation of God stands firm and bears this seal: Let every one who names the name of Christ depart from iniquity (II Tim. 2:19).

Faith, then, is the one great work which the Christian must fulfill in his sanctification according to the principles of the gospel (John 6:29). Although this faith presents itself in a different way and is viewed from a different vantage point in sanctification than it is in justification, it is in both of these benefits the only and sufficient means by which we come to share in them. The gospel demands nothing other from us than faith, than the reliance of the heart upon God's grace in Christ. That faith not only justifies us, but also sanctifies and saves us. And the sanctifying power of the faith comes into fine clarity in the following considerations.

In the first place, it must be remarked that the true, unfeigned faith breaks off our false self-confidence, knocks our pride off its pedestal, and makes an end of all self-righteousness. If we leave those out of consideration who do not trouble themselves about God or His commandments, and who consume sin as they do water, and if we leave out of consideration also all those who do the good only externally out of fear of punishment, of loss, or of shame, there still remain those who earnestly strive to fulfill the demands of the moral law in their own strength. But in doing this they can never find the right vantage point to take over against the moral law, nor the genuine principle by which they are to fulfill it. They take position either above or below the law and make themselves serviceable to it or it serviceable to them. In the first instance they say that the good must be done for the benefit and profit that accrues to the individual or to the group because of it. In the second instance they put the moral law high above man, and so make its fulfillment, inasmuch as it is regarded the more seriously, so much more impossible. Thus the natural man vacillates between Saducceeism and Pharisaism, between freedom and authority. He cannot find the balance between the demand of the moral law and the will of man.

But faith puts an end to this vacillation. It enables us to see that the moral law stands high above us and that it demands unconditional obedience, and that it nevertheless cannot actually be fulfilled and cannot give us eternal life. And in this apparently irreconcilable opposition it surrenders itself to the grace of God, trusts His mercy, and glories in the righteousness which He Himself has brought. The true believer gives up all pretension of being able to do according to the demands of the moral law. He lets that moral ideal stand in all its sublime requirement, but at the same time gives up the hope that he can ever by his own exertion do justice to it. And thus he fixes his hope on God who in the law, but afterwards also in the gospel, has revealed His righteousness. Such a faith is, consequently, immediately the mother of many virtues: it fosters humility in man, and it fosters dependence and trust, attributes, all of them, of the greatest significance for the moral life. And thus the doing of the good gets from religion a sure foundation and an unconquerable strength.

Still other virtues go combined with these. According to the order which God Himself has appointed in the church, the promises of the gospel precede the commandments of the law. First He assures us of His favor, of the forgiveness of our sins and of our inheritance with the saints, and thereupon He leads us in the way of His testimonies and ordinances. The good tree comes before the good fruits. We do not live through good works but for them; we fulfill the law not for eternal life but out of it, for this life has been planted in our hearts through faith. It is according to this order alone that a true moral life is possible. Whoever wants to change this order about, and wants to draw his comfort, certainty, and salvation from his works, will never achieve his purpose, will be constantly torn by doubts, and will live in fear all the days of his life. God takes another way. In the gospel He gives us everything for nothing: the forgiveness of sins; the reconciliation; the annihilation of punishment; the salvation and the blessedness. He tells us that through faith in His grace we can altogether lean upon Him, and He gives us the certainty of this through the testimony of the Holy Spirit. Faith, accordingly, by virtue of its own nature, brings us comfort, peace, joy, and happiness, and these are in turn of invaluable worth for the moral life. They are all together principles and motives of a holy conduct. The purging of the conscience of all dead works has as its end and goal the services of the living God (Heb. 9:14). Those who are comforted of God are thereupon strengthened by Him in every good word and work (II Thess. 2:17). The joy of the Lord is the strength of His people (Neh. 8:10).

In the next place, it should be pointed out that a severing as well as an appropriating activity, a destructive as well as a constructive effort, is common to the saving faith which leans entirely upon God's grace in Christ. It causes the prodigal son to return from his sinful life to the father's house. It puts us into the fellowship of Christ's death and of His resurrection; it crucifies us and raises us up to a new life. Whoever truly believes in Christ dies to sin; he feels heartily sorry for it, because he has drawn down the wrath of God by it, and therefore he begins to hate and to flee it. He brings about a separation between it and himself so that he can say uprightly: I want to do the good although I do not do it and I do not want to do the evil, although I do do it (Rom. 7:19). And on the other hand faith appropriates Christ and His righteousness; it causes Christ Himself to dwell in the heart and constantly lives more fully in His communion. It causes Christ to take form in us and transforms us more and more according to His image. In short, the believer can repeat Paul's statement: I can do all things through Christ who strengthens me (Phil. 4:13).

Finally, to mention nothing further, faith is often compared, and properly so, with a hand. But a hand is not only the organ with which to take something and to make it our own: it is also the instrument by which we objectify our thought and our will. Thus faith is not only a receiving organ, but also an active force. The faith which justifies and saves is not a dead faith, but a living one. In its own nature it brings forth fruits of good works; it works by love (Gal. 5:6). Man is not justified by love, but the faith which justifies him proves his living active power in love. Without love faith is not the true saving faith (I Cor. 13:2); and the work of love is always associated with the true faith (I Thess. 1:3), for the end of the law (that is, of the whole apostolical preaching) is love, out of a pure heart and of a good conscience, and of faith unfeigned (I Tim. 1:5). And this love, as the fruit of faith, is a perfect love which casts out fear (I John 4:18), and it is at the same time the perfect fulfillment of the law.[25]

Accordingly, the gospel does not make the law of no effect, but restores and establishes it. It is true that an end has been made of the demand and curse of the law, because Christ has placed Himself under the law, satisfied its demand, and borne its curse.[26] Hence we are no longer a servant but walk in liberty and in the spirit.[27] And where the Spirit of the Lord is, there is freedom (II Cor. 3:17; Gal. 5:18). But this freedom of faith does not remove the law, but rather brings it to fulfillment; the righteousness of the law, that which the law asks in its commandments, is fulfilled precisely in those who do not walk according to the flesh but according to the Spirit (Rom. 8:4). While the flesh makes the law of no effect because it does not want to and cannot subject itself to the law (Rom. 8:3, 7), it is precisely the Spirit of Christ which gives men life (II Cor. 3:6), and it is the Spirit which gives light in order to prove what is the good and acceptable will of God.[28]

And for Jesus and for the apostles that will of God, despite the fact that the law has in the sense designated above been discarded, continues to be known from the Old Testament. Jesus did not come to destroy the law and the prophets, but to fulfill them (Matt. 5:17). He never so much as mentions the abandonment of the law except in so far as He prophesies the fall of the city and the temple, and the whole of the civic regime and the public worship (Matt. 24; John 4:21–24), but He does purge it of the human doctrines which have been added to it by the Jewish schools (Matt. 5:20ff.). In His conception of the law He returns from the Pharisees back to the prophets, penetrates through to the inner character of that law, and places the internal high above the external characteristics (Mark 7:15), mercy above sacrifice (Matt. 9; 12:7), and joins prophets and law together in love over against God and the neighbor.[29] The moral laws retain their force.

All the apostles take the same attitude towards the law and the prophets. The Old Testament retains for them the divine authority. It has been given by God (II Tim. 3:15), has been written by holy men under the leading of the Spirit of God (II Peter 1:21), and has been given for our instruction and comfort.[30] Hence again and again that Old Testament is quoted in order to cause the Christian church to know the will of God: Paul, for example, appeals in I Corinthians 14:34, to indicate the subordination of the wife to the husband, to Genesis 3:16; in II Corinthians 9:9, in order to urge liberality to the poor, to Psalm 112:9; and in I Corinthians 1:31, for the admonition to glory only in the Lord, to Jeremiah 9:23, 24. In other words, the moral law is, so far as its content is concerned, quite the same in the Old and the New Testament. It is contained in the one law of love.[31] True, Christ speaks of the love which the disciples must exercise among one another as of a new commandment.[32] But by this He does not mean that the commandment to love one another as believers was quite unknown before, for Leviticus 19:18 plainly teaches the opposite and Psalm 133 speaks of the loveliness of the living together in community of the brethren.

But this love which must bind the believers mutually together took on a new character in the New Testament. Because in the days of the Old Testament the church and the nation coincided, the difference between the love of the brethren and the love of the neighbor could not yet clearly be distinguished. But in the New Testament this changed: the church was severed from the national history of Israel and became an independent community. In the Holy Spirit it received its own principle of life. Now a distinction began to be made between the love of the brother and the love of all.[33] To this extent brotherly love can be called a new commandment; it binds the believers together in their difference from the world. But, for the rest, there is a single religion and a single moral law in the Old and the New Testament. There is some clarification, it is true, and there is also a different development and application, but no external addition or mechanical amplification takes place. Christ was not a new law-giver alongside of and above Moses, but He Himself in His own life and death fulfilled the law and by His Spirit He brings it to fulfillment in all those who are His disciples.

Although Christ and His apostles regularly relate the moral law of the Old Testament to the love of God and the neighbor, there gradually grew up in the Christian moral teaching the habit of explaining the virtues and the duties of man in explication of the Ten Commandments. This was done especially by the Reformers, because they saw one of the earmarks of good works to be this, namely, that they take place according to the will of God. In so doing they took position against the Roman Catholic Church which reckoned among the good works also those actions which are based on human ordinances and laws (compare the Heidelberg Catechism, Answer 91).

Rome makes a distinction between commandments and advices, and holds that these advices were added to the law of Moses by Christ as a new and higher law-giver. In its earliest period the Christian church did not yet know this distinction; but when the period of persecution passed for the church and all kinds of people joined themselves to her, people who joined the church solely for prestige and distinction, then the moral level fell off and many seriously disposed persons withdrew into solitude. The monasticism which thus put in its appearance tried to cling to the moral idea, but it did this in a way which could not be followed by the ordinary Christians, living as they were in family and vocation. Thus there gradually came to be a distinction between the religious or clerical and the lay people, and so a higher and a lower morality came to be discriminated, a difference between commandments and advices. In other words, the commandments contained in the ten statements were binding for all Christians, but the advices were left to the optional choice of people. Among these additions there were soon reckoned the so-called chastity, or the celebate state, on the basis of Matthew 19:11, 12 and I Corinthians 7:7ff.; poverty, or the disposition of all earthly possessions, in appeal to Matthew 19:21 and I Corinthians 9:14; and the absolute obedience to the superior under whose directions one places himself, in reference to Matthew 16:24 and Luke 14:26, 27. But in the monastic orders these are often supplemented by all kinds of abstinences, mortifications, chastisements, all in appeal to Matthew 5:29, 39, and 42. It is true that in doing this, Rome wants to maintain that the ideal of moral perfection is the same for all believers and must be pursued by them all in the way of obedience to the commandments. But whoever adds the advices to the commandments follows a faster and a safer way to the achievement of the purpose, and also attains a greater worth and a richer reward. While the ordinary believer, who fulfills the law, remains an unprofitable servant, who has done only what was demanded of him (Luke 17:10), the other Christian, who has also followed up the advices, hears himself addressed as the good and faithful servant who has been faithful over little and is being appointed ruler over many things (Matt. 25:21).

It is natural enough that the Reformation could not endorse this distinction. Deeply convinced of the depravity of human nature, it taught that the regenerate too could not keep the law perfectly, that their best works were still tainted with sin, and that even the most saintly could achieve nothing more than a small beginning of the perfect obedience (Heidelberg Catechism, Answers 62 and 114). The believer, in other words, could never arrive at the point of achieving the advices, simply because he had more than enough to do in fulfilling the commandments themselves. Anyhow, God requires in the moral law that we love Him with all our mind, and with all our strength, and our neighbor as ourselves (Matt. 22:37; Luke 10:27). How, then, can anything further be added to such a commandment? If God demands us in our entirety in all times and in all places for His service, then nothing remains which represents an option that we can either take or ignore, and which we can according to our free choice either give Him or withhold.

There is consequently no basis for the claim that Christ added anything as a sort of law of freedom to the required commandments of the Mosaic law. For although there are instances in which a person must refrain from marrying, must dispose of his property, must withdraw from his ordinary environment and vocation, no special option comes to him which he can follow up or neglect. Rather, the one and the same law demands in terms of the nature of the circumstances a particular application and constitutes this application a duty. The rich young man did not receive an option from Christ which he could reject as well as accept, but he received, as a touchstone of the integrity and resoluteness of his heart, the commandment to sell all that he had and to give it to the poor. From this it would be manifest whether or not he was totally committed to Christ and His kingdom. We must distinguish therefore between law and duty: the law is one and the same for all, but duty is the particular way in which the general moral law must be applied by each individual in accordance with his nature and circumstances.

The Reformers accordingly rejected all works which depended upon the determinations of men or upon the prescriptions of the church, and returned to the will of God as the norm of good works. That will, they found briefly and substantially expressed in the Ten Commandments. But the law of the Ten Commandments does not stand loosely and independently by itself; it finds itself, rather, in the middle of a rich environment. In its material content it originally was written on the heart of man created as he was by God Himself. It is partially still preserved there inasmuch as people continue to do naturally the things of the law, and so prove that the works of the law are written in their hearts (Rom. 2:14, 15). Every human being has the awareness that in his existence and in his conduct he is bound to certain definite moral laws, and he feels that when he transgresses these his conscience accuses him. In Israel that law was restored by way of a particular revelation to its original purity, was made serviceable to the covenant of grace which, according to its introductory words, God had set up with His people, and was taken up in a body of rights and ordinances which had to govern the whole life of the people. Besides, this law was explained, developed, and applied throughout the history of Israel by the psalmists, proverb writers, and prophets, so that Jesus could say that the whole law and the prophets hung on the two commandments of love towards God and the neighbor (Matt. 22:40).

Accordingly, when Christ brings on the fulfillment of the Old Testament promises of salvation, He does not discard the law, but fulfills all its righteousness; by His perfect obedience He paves the way and in the Holy Spirit grants the power by which His disciples can and will walk, in principle, according to the commandments of the law. In fact, we can say that the whole bearing of the gospel is that the righteousness of the law is fulfilled in those who do not walk according to the flesh but according to the Spirit. The spiritual life of regeneration is made serviceable to the restoration of the moral life. The long series of admonishments with which the apostles as a general rule conclude their epistles are an amplification and application of the holy law of the Lord, and they are intended to help the believers to live in all their relationships and circumstances according to the will of God and the glorification of His name. The law of the Ten Commandments may not be separated from this rich context of affairs. Indeed, the Decalogue must be viewed and explained in the light of the whole revelation of God in nature and in Scripture.

Understood in this way, the Ten Commandments are a brief summary of the Christian ethic and an unsurpassed rule for our life. There are also many other laws to which we are bound. God also laid down the laws for our thinking, for our appreciation of the beautiful, for our social life, for our study and use of nature. He laid down laws for all His creatures, for heaven and earth, for sun and moon and stars, for day and night, for summer and winter, for seed time and harvest.[34] But the moral law far outrivals these ordinances, for in distinction from them all, the moral law directs itself to the will of man, or rather to man himself as a willing being, and thus to the innermost essence of his existence, to the core of his personality. And the moral law lays down the demand that it be kept not merely in words and deeds but quite as well in thoughts and desires; the law is spiritual (Rom. 7:14); we must be perfect even as our Father who is in Heaven is perfect (Matt. 5:48); and in the tenth commandment the law burrows through to the root of sin, to covetousness or desire, and constitutes this also guilty and impure before the face of God.

Besides, this law governs all the relationships in which man finds himself, whether to God, whether to his fellow man, to himself, or to the whole of nature. It governs his relationship to his fellow human beings in their various ranks and gradations, in their life, their vocations, and their property. It governs his relationship to the truth of his reason and to the integrity of his heart. And in all this it governs his relationship to the whole nature which is his environment, to his office and his calling, to his work and recreation, to the whole of animate and inanimate nature. And in this innermost core of his being as well as in these rich relationships the moral law requires of man that in everything he does he shall do it to the glory of God (I Cor. 10:31; Col. 3:17).

When we first sense the law in this deep, spiritual sense, we are appalled and despair of fulfilling it. If we knew of no other righteousness than that which the law requires of us, we should not be in a position to fulfill it and would not even have the desire to do so. We should then be trying always to rob the law of its spiritual content, to externalize it, to suit it to our fallen condition, and would deceive ourselves into believing that we could by a respectable civic life satisfy its high demands. The natural man is offended by the spiritual significance of the law, that is, by its perfection; internally he resists the absolute righteousness and holiness which it demands. But the moment we have learned to know that other righteousness and holiness which God has given in Christ and which through faith He makes our own, our attitude towards the law and our sense of its significance changes entirely. True, we may still complain as Paul does that we are still carnally sold under sin. but even so we let the law stand in its exalted sublimity, and make no effort to pull it down off its high pedestal. We continue to honor it as holy and righteous and good, for it is the law of God. We love it precisely because it is so spiritual in character. We delight in it according to the inner man. And we thank God not for the gospel only but also for His law, for His holy, righteous, perfect law. That law too becomes to us a revelation and a gift of His grace. How love I Thy law; it is my meditation all the day!

Although the believers receive immediately in regeneration an inner desire and love, and thus want to live according to the will of God in all good works, they are not immediately perfect and, as a matter of fact, do not achieve this perfection in this life. Sanctification is to be distinguished from justification. Justification consists of a divine acquittal which is at once completed. True, it is repeatedly applied to the conscience, but it is not developed and increased. But the life of sanctification is, like all the life of the creature, bound to the law of development. It has its point of origin in regeneration, it requires nourishment in order to grow strong, and it reaches its apex only when it will be fully revealed with Christ.

In the Old Testament it was already said of the Messiah that He would feed His flock like a shepherd; He would gather the lambs with His arm and carry them in His bosom, and would gently lead those that are with young (Isa. 40:11). And elsewhere we are told even more fully concerning Him that the Lord has anointed Him to preach good tidings to the meek, to bind up the brokenhearted, to proclaim liberty to the captives, to comfort those that mourn in Zion, to give them the garment of praise for the spirit of heaviness, beauty for ashes, in order that they be called trees of righteousness, the planting of the Lord, in order that He may be glorified (Isa. 61:1–3; compare Ezek. 34:16).

Hence Christ during the period of His ministry on earth does not direct Himself only to the mature in Israel, but He comes also to the children and ascribes the Kingdom of Heaven to them (Matt. 18:1–6; 19:13, 14). He calls not only the inhabitants of Chorazin and Bethsaida, of Capernaum and Jerusalem, to repentance but also the publicans and sinners, and He invites all those who labor and are heavy laden in order to give them rest. He calls the heirs of the kingdom by various names, speaking of them as those who are poor and those who mourn, as those who hunger and those who thirst, as those who are meek and those who are peaceful (Matt. 5:3–9), and He distinguishes between those who are lesser and those who are greater, those who are first and those who are last in the kingdom (Matt. 11:11; 20:16). He often complains about the smallness of the faith, the timidity and the obtuseness of His disciples.[35] He rejoices when He finds great faith in some (Matt. 8:10; 15:28). And over against all He proves Himself to be the good Shepherd who gathers all His sheep together into one flock, who gives them all life and abundance, who preserves them all and sees to it that none of them is lost (John 10:1–30).

Similar distinctions are made among the believers of the apostolic churches. The believers of the Old Testament were still minors who were placed under wards and guardians and to this extent did not yet differ from servants (Gal. 4:1, 2). Compared with these, the believers of the New Testament are free sons and daughters, accepted by God as His children and heirs, and standing in the freedom with which Christ has made them free (Gal. 4:4–7). Nevertheless all kinds of differences still distinguish them. True, the faith which is given to the members of the church is the same in all, but it is nevertheless given to each in accordance with his nature and in a particular measure (Rom. 12:3); the gifts which the Holy Spirit distributes in the church are differing gifts (Rom. 12:6–8; I Cor. 12:4–11); the place which each member of the church occupies is as different from that of other members as is true of the members of the body (Rom. 12:4, 5; I Cor. 12:12ff.). But, quite apart from this difference of gift and function, there is among the believers also a difference between the strong and the weak,[36] between children who still require milk (I Cor. 3:2; 5:12) and the perfect, the mature, who can tolerate meat and who by the exercise of discrimination have the ability to distinguish between good and evil.[37] Further, there is a difference among the believers between the young men, who have indeed overcome the wicked one but must nevertheless be careful lest they lose this victory, and the fathers who have had long experience in the struggle and have received a deeper insight into the knowledge of Him, namely, Christ, who was from the beginning (I John 2:12–14). In addition to this, a distinction was made in the apostolic period between churches or believers who were steadfast in the faith, abundant in love, patient in suffering, and those others who allowed themselves to be misled by all kinds of error and succumbed to all kinds of sins. The letters of the apostles and particularly that of Christ to the seven churches in Asia Minor (Rev. 1–3) give us detailed descriptions of these varying circumstances.

All this teaches that man is in his spiritual as well as his natural life born as a small and weak and needy creature, and that he must gradually grow in the grace and knowledge of our Lord and Savior Jesus Christ (II Peter 3:18). If the spiritual life develops healthily and normally, if it feeds on spiritual nourishment and drinks of the spiritual drink which is Christ (John 6:48ff.; I Cor. 10:3, 4) a continuous growing in grace, an establishment in it, and a progressive renewal according to the image of Christ take place.[38] But all kinds of obstacles interpose themselves on the way of this normal development. The life of the Christian is not a quiet growth, but a continuous struggle, a struggle against enemies without, and no less a struggle against the enemy who dwells within our own bosoms.

In order to understand the nature of this struggle properly, we ought first to note that in the unregenerate also there is often a struggle present. But this is not a spiritual struggle. It is a rational struggle, a conflict between the human reason and conscience, on the one hand, and his will and desire on the other. By his reason and conscience man still remains bound to the moral law, to the world of invisible and eternal things. In his heart he still hears the imperative: Thou shalt. The moment he wants to do the evil, his better judgment offers resistance, warns him and tries to impede him. There is not a single human being who has strayed off so far or sunk so deep that he does not know something of the duality of this tension in his being. And man can under favorable circumstances sometimes be the victor in this struggle. He can counter his appetites and desires by this reason, can suppress them, and silence them; if he does, he becomes a brave, virtuous human being and he lives an honorable life. But that is not yet the true morality; it is not the Christian sanctification. For the struggle in the natural man is constantly the struggle between reason and passion, duty and desire, conscience and appetite. The battle is not waged against all of the sins, but only against some of them, and for the most part only against certain external and publicly offensive sins. The struggle is not waged against sin as sin because it elicits the wrath of God, but against certain particular sins which stand high in the world's estimate of evils, and which go accompanied by loss or shame. And the human being may on a favorable occasion restrain the evil inclination and harness it, but he cannot root it out and he can bring no internal change to pass inside his heart.

The spiritual struggle which the believers must conduct inside their souls has a very different character. It is not a struggle between reason and passion, but between the flesh and the spirit, between the old and the new man, between the sin which continues to dwell in the believers and the spiritual principle of life which has been planted in their hearts.[39] These two forces are not spatially separated, as though one part of the man—the reason, for example—were regenerated, and another part of him—the heart, for example—were not. Rather, these two forces spread themselves out over the whole man and over all his powers and abilities, so that either one of them can be called a man—the one the old, and the other the new.

It is thus that Paul usually gives expression to the distinction, but in Romans 7 he makes use of other names. There he designates the new, spiritual man as the will that loves the good and wants to do it, as the inward man who delights in the law of God. And he calls the old man the flesh, the sin that dwells in him, the law in his members which wars against the law of his spirit and takes him captive under the law of sin which is in his members. This constitutes a difference in statement, but it is the same matter. In Paul the flesh is often the name used to designate the sinful which continues in the believer and which very certainly continues to dwell in the inner man, in his soul and heart and spirit. The works of the flesh, after all, are not only adultery, fornication, and the like, but also idolatry, hatred, variance, wrath, and the like (Gal. 5:19, 20). And when he thinks of the inward man, the apostle is not thinking only of something which lies deep inside the human being, which continues hidden there and which never in any way comes to external expression, for he plainly states that the believers walk after the spirit and constitute their members weapons of righteousness. But he calls the new man the inward man in this connection because in the fearful struggle against the flesh this man so often lies deeply imbedded and so rarely reveals himself.

The struggle between the two forces consists of this, that the Spirit of Christ who dwells in the believers tries to arouse all kinds of good thoughts, deliberations, inclinations and drives (such as love, joy, peace, and the like: Gal. 5:22) in their mind, heart, and will, and that the flesh on the contrary thereupon raises its voice and tries to defile the whole man with its evil lusts and desires (Gal. 5:19, 20). And in this struggle the flesh appears so mighty again and again that the believers do not do, in the way and in the measure they intended, the thing they wanted to do (Gal. 5:17). When they want to do the good, evil is present with them (Rom. 7:21). The spirit, indeed, is willing, but the flesh is weak (Matt. 26:41).

The conflict, in other words, is not between reason and will, between duty and desire, but is quite differently between willing and doing, between the inner disposition and the sinful act which interposes itself and stands in its way, between the inward man of the heart recreated to God in true righteousness and holiness, and the old man who, though having lost the position of centrality, nevertheless wants to maintain himself, and who fights the harder in proportion to the extent that he loses more and more ground. This is not a battle between two faculties or two parts of man as it would be if it were conducted by the head against the heart, the reason against the passions, or the soul against the body. Rather, these two forces stand, armed and militant, over against each other battling for the whole of the human person. In one and the same reason of one and the same person there is a battle going on between faith and unbelief, between truth and falsehood; in one and the same heart there is an opposition between pure drives and desires and impure ones; in one and the same will an evil lust opposes a good one and an evil disposition takes issue with a pure one. The struggle is in very fact a struggle between two beings in one and the same being.

Psychologically this can be explained in such a way that in the field of consciousness two groups of ideas have taken position over against each other, and in the field of the heart and desires two series of passions oppose each other. True, we speak of an old and a new man in the believer, and so we give expression to the fact that in the new life the whole man has in principle been changed, and that nevertheless the power of sin continues to dwell in all his faculties and members. But actually what it is is that there are two groups of interests, ideas, inclinations, and the like, which do battle against each other and of which neither the one nor the other has been able to gain the full control of any single human faculty. If the truth of God had completely taken over and conquered the consciousness of the believer, there would naturally be no room left for error and falsehood; and if the love of God had wholly filled the heart, there would be no room for hatred, envy, wrath and the like. But that, as every one knows from his experience, is not the case; and Scripture testifies that we cannot look forward to such a perfect condition in this life. The struggle will remain until the end because faith, hope, love, and all the Christian virtues will never be perfected in this life and therefore room remains in our soul for unbelief, doubt, discouragement, fear, and the like.

In every deliberation and deed of the believer, consequently, the good and the evil lie, as it were, mingled through each other. The measure and the degree to which both are present in any particular thought or deed differ greatly, of course, but nevertheless there is something of the old and something of the new man in all our actions and thoughts. All our ideas, words, and deeds are consequently tainted by sin; they require reconciliation and purging. All the same, they may be called good works to the extent that they are mingled with faith. For all these reasons we must be on guard against Antinomianism, for this heresy separates the old from the new man and sets them over against each other in spatial distinction in a way somewhat like that which distinguishes the spirit from matter, and the soul from the body.

The result of this kind of erroneous thinking is the harmful doctrine that the sinful thoughts and deeds are to be reckoned to the account of the old man and have nothing to do with the new man. Scripture and experience both, on the contrary, teach that the believer is not an external combination of two beings, but that he remains one being, a single self, a single consciousness, heart, and will, and that no two independent beings but rather two groups of desires and dispositions are conflicting inside one and the same person.

The seriousness of this struggle already intimates that it will be a long time before the new man achieves the victory. Nevertheless many Christians have the idea that believers achieve perfection already upon the earth, and can here and now subdue every sinful deed and inclination. The Pelagians had taught this long ago. In the Council of Trent, Rome took a similar position, and many a Protestant group assumes it also. People tend to appeal to the fact that Holy Scriptures frequently use such glorious words to describe the Christian's condition, for example, I Peter 2:9, 10; II Peter 1:4; and I John 2:20. They point out that Paul, after his conversion, is fully assured of his salvation, and that he remembers the sinful past only as a memory and nothing else, and that the admonishments to the saints to be blameless in their conduct are absolute in their demands (Matt. 5:48), that these admonishments assume the possibility of achieving perfection,[40] and that the grace of God which can be obtained by prayer can avail all things.[41] Accordingly, these people argue that it were doing injustice to the riches of God's love if one regarded the moral perfection of the believer in this life unattainable, and one would at the same time be removing from the believers a strong incentive by the exertion of all their power to strive after such perfection.

Now there is in very fact no doubt about it that the Holy Scriptures speak of the privilege and the status of the people of God in the most arresting way. They refer to the Israel of the Old Testament as a priestly kingdom which God has chosen out of all the nations of the earth as His own, as an object of His love, as His portion and His honor, His son and His servant, His bride whom He adorned and perfected by the glory which He laid upon her.[42] And the believers in the New Testament are called the salt of the earth (Matt. 5:13), the light of the world (Matt. 5:14), the children of God who are born of God and accepted by Him (John 1:13; Gal. 4:5), elect, called, holy, and sanctified (I Cor. 1:2), a chosen generation and royal priesthood (I Peter 2:9, 10), partakers of the divine nature (II Peter 1:4), anointed with the Holy Spirit (I John 2:20), made to be kings and priests by Christ Himself (Rev. 1:6), and heirs of God and joint heirs with Christ (Rom. 8:17). That which eye hath not seen, nor ear heard, neither have entered into the heart of man, the things which God hath prepared for them that love Him, *that* God has prepared for His own now in the days of the New Testament (I Cor. 2:9). Whoever rejects the teaching of Scripture concerning sin and grace can see only gross exaggeration in all this. A radical change, such as takes place in justification and regeneration, is then neither necessary nor possible. But for Scripture, the change which the human being undergoes in faith and conversion is a change from darkness to light, from death to life, from bondage to liberty, from falsehood to truth, from sin to righteousness, from the expectation of the wrath of God to the hope of glory. And the believers who loom up before us in the Old and New Testament, and who are aware of this enormous change, can only glory in the God of their salvation, and rejoice in His fellowship. How far we stand behind them in the joy of this faith!

Further, Scripture holds up the highest of moral ideals before the believers. The tendency is to ride roughshod over this fact. It is said that the moral life which Christendom wants is one-sided, over-spiritual, exclusively directed to the life in heaven, quite averse to the embrace of earthly concerns, antagonistic to culture, the sort of thing which throws the poor and the oppressed the sop of eternal life hereafter but is altogether indifferent to the improvement of their condition here on earth, something which may be perhaps rich in passive virtues and full of prescriptions about subjection, long-suffering, and patience, but poor in the active virtues which can lead to a conquest and reform of the world. Hence there were many who aspired to a different, better, and higher morality, to an ethical teaching which laid down a dedication to the service of humanity as the highest duty, and which limited its point of view to that of the life on earth.

A concern for earthly interests is in itself, however, in such little conflict with Christian morality that it can in fact be said to be based and founded on the creation of man according to God's image. Man was and in a certain sense still is the image bearer of God, and he is therefore called to subdue the earth and to have dominion over the fish of the sea, the fowl of the air, and all the animals that creep upon the earth (Gen. 1:26–28; Psalm 8). There is no book that does so much justice to the whole of nature as the Holy Scripture. Paganism is always vacillating between an arrogant abuse of the world and a slavish, superstitious fear of its mysterious power. But Moses and the prophets, Christ and the apostles, stand perfectly free over against the world, because they are raised above it by the fellowship with God. And, although it is true that Scripture enjoins it upon us to seek the Kingdom of Heaven first, and although it is further true that the Christians of that early period, tiny group as they were, had to withdraw from numerous circles of life and had to abstain from many things because in the world of that time virtually everything was permeated by the pagan spirit, Christianity in principle included within itself all of the elements which not only gave the freedom to subdue the world and have dominion over the earth but also made these accomplishments the duty and the calling of man.

After all, the Christian ethic is none other than the one briefly and pointedly comprised in the Ten Commandments and which, for the rest, is illuminated and interpreted throughout the whole of Scriptures. In those commandments the love of God stands in the foreground, but the love of the neighbor is the second law, like unto the first. In this love of the neighbor there lies contained, provided it be properly understood, not in a Buddhistic, passive sense but in its Christian, active character, the duty of mission, of reformation, and of culture. By missions the religious and moral possessions of Christianity accrue to all peoples and nations; by reformation, which is not limited to one period in the church of Christ, nor to one moment in the life of the Christian but must always go on, there takes place the progressive renewal of heart and life, of family and society, according to the demand of the Lord's will; and by culture the subduing of the earth to the control of man, the dominion of matter by spirit, and of nature by the reason, takes place.

The Kingdom of Heaven, which must be sought first, brings all the other things in its wake (Matt. 6:33). Godliness is profitable to all things, having promise of the life that now is, and of that which is to come (I Tim. 4:8). Nothing is unclean of itself, for every creature of God is good, and nothing is to be refused if it is received with thanksgiving, for it is sanctified through the word of God and through prayer (Rom. 14:14; I Tim. 4:4, 5). Christianity, which finds the basis of all culture in the creation of man according to the image of God and its restoration in the resurrection of Christ, calls its faithful confessors to the deliberation of whatsoever things are true, honest, just, pure, lovely, of good report, and if there be any other virtue or other praise, of that also (Phil. 4:8).

No higher morality, nor any higher religion is thinkable than the one which is preached to us in the gospel. True, one can go in pursuit of another, but if he does he soon strays off into by-paths. The time in which we are living offers us the strongest evidence for this. The morality of the Scriptures is rejected, but the thing that takes its place is continually coming into conflict with the simplest laws of the ethical life.

The first thing that happens is that all the commandments which are related to the love of God are taken out of the moral teaching. There is then no longer any concern for the love of God, of His name, His truth, and His service; indeed, how should people be able to love God when as a matter of fact they doubt or deny that He can be known, that He reveals Himself, or even that He exists? But in doing this, those who deny the relevancy of the first law undermine the commandments of the second table, for if there is no God who makes it obligatory for man to love his neighbor, what ground for such love can there exist? Consequently, the proponents of a moral teaching independent of religion are hopelessly divided on the question of what principle lies behind the love of man for his fellow man. Some try to base this love on self-interest, some on the happiness it brings about, a third group on the virtue of pity, of compassion, a fourth group on the conscience, but they all together prove that without divine authority for the duty which binds the conscience there can be no such imperative.

As a consequence the proponents of such a morality get into difficulty with each of the particular commandments in which the love of the neighbor is more specifically worked out and circumscribed. It is generally said that people, although they differ greatly in religion, nevertheless remain close together in the sphere of morality. There may be some truth in this, for nature fortunately is stronger than theory, and because the work of the law stands written on the heart of every man, but for the rest reality teaches us something very different. There is not a single commandment of the second table of the law which remains unchallenged in our time. The authority of father and mother and of all those appointed over us is openly attacked and rejected. Murder is being taken less seriously as time goes on: in the case of suicide it is often smoothed over, and in the case of abortion it is not seldom defended. Marriage is regarded as a contract which is assumed for an arbitrary length of time, and adultery has its defenders and supporters. Property is, in the estimate of many, another name for theft. Truth is made serviceable to utility, is made dependent upon evolutional development, and is distinguished from falsehood only in time and place, or in form and degree. And as for covetousness, it celebrates its triumph in the mammonistic spirit of our age.

Over against all these bastardizations of morality Scripture maintains the moral ideal in uncurtailed and unadulterated form. It never does violence to the holiness of God and the sanctity of His law, but again and again places these in all their majesty sharply before the consciences of men. The thing that Jesus said to His disciples, Be ye perfect even as your Father in Heaven is perfect, is repeated in different words by all the apostles in their admonishments to the believers. Sin has no right at all to existence, least of all in those who are named by the name of Christ. Nothing may ever be subtracted from the demand of the moral law, least of all by those who have died with Christ and with Him been raised to a new life. And if then, in the providence of God, the old man only gradually dies out in the believer, and the new man only gradually grows up and only hereafter accomplishes perfection, all this points to the great long-suffering and forbearance of God. This is a forbearance which He can exercise because Christ covers the sin of the church with His righteousness and holiness and guarantees the perfecting of His people.

Although the moral law, which is the rule of life for the believers, can be satisfied with nothing other than a perfect love of God and of the neighbor, it is nevertheless quite as evident that according to Scripture no single believer has ever reached such perfection or ever can reach it in this life. The saints of the Bible were all people who often faltered or stumbled, and some of them, such as a David or a Peter, fell into grave sins, although they also in the deepest remorse made confession of it afterwards. No matter whom we may choose to overhear, we never hear the affirmation which can sometimes be spoken by Christians: I do and I have no more sin. On the contrary, Abraham, Isaac, Jacob, Moses, David (Ps. 51), Solomon (I Kings 8:46), Isaiah (Isa. 6:5), Daniel (Dan. 9:4), these, and others like them, all confess to transgression and acknowledge their sins and errors.

The same holds true of the apostle Paul. He was crucified with Christ and he then walked in newness of the Spirit. He stands justified before God and is fully assured of his salvation. He gets glory, humanly speaking, for his apostolic work and is conscious of the faithfulness with which he has fulfilled his calling.[43] But besides ascribing all this to the grace of God,[44] he confesses that no good dwells in his flesh (Rom. 7:18), that the flesh lusts against the Spirit (Gal. 5:17), that to will and to do are in continual conflict in him (Rom. 7:7–25), and that he follows after perfection, but has not yet attained it (Phil. 3:12).

Moses and the prophets make a similar testimony concerning the people of Israel, Christ makes it of His disciples, the apostles of the churches entrusted to their care. Jesus calls His disciples to perfection (Matt. 5:48), and nevertheless teaches them to pray for the forgiveness of their guilt (Matt. 6:12). The Christians in Rome have been raised with Christ to dwell in newness of life (Rom. 6:3ff.), and are nevertheless admonished to make their members serviceable to righteousness unto holiness (Rom. 6:19). The Corinthians were washed, sanctified, justified in the name of the Lord Jesus, and by the Spirit of God (I Cor. 6:11), and were nevertheless carnal (I Cor. 3:1-4). The Galatians had received the Spirit by the preaching of the faith (Gal. 3:2), and nevertheless permitted themselves to be tempted into disobedience to the truth (Gal. 3:1). The good work was begun in the Philippians, but it was not completed (Phil. 1:6). In all the churches there are conditions, errors, and defections which are not in harmony with the Christian life. And the apostles are themselves all convinced that sin will continue to cling to the believers so long as they live. We all offend in many things (James 3:2). If we say that we have no sin, we deceive ourselves, and the truth is not in us (I John 1:8).

Still, although perfection is not attainable in this life, the admonishments and appeals nevertheless continue useful and serious. Those who hold to the perfectibility of the believers in this life do, of course, raise this objection, and say that admonishments which cannot or at least cannot *fully* be carried out must necessarily lose their force and in time sap the energy of the believers. This is however a false piece of argumentation. From the fact that a person must do something it does not follow that he can do it. A man may have to pay a sum of money and yet not be able to pay it; in that event he nevertheless remains obligated to pay. And in this same way the moral law can never stop laying down its demand, even though human beings because of sin cannot satisfy it. And, on the contrary, it can be argued with more justice that the person who teaches the perfectibility of the believers always comes out at a lowering of the moral ideal and at a less serious sense of sin.

Certainly, whoever in thinking of sin does not think merely of external, sinful deeds, but also includes within it sinful thoughts and inclinations, can hardly seriously maintain that in this life the believers can be wholly delivered from it. One can hold to the perfectibility of the saints only if one does not take seriously the sinful nature of man, if one does not regard his sinful thoughts and inclinations as sin, and if one does violence to the absolute holiness of the law. In the form for the administration of the Holy Supper in the Reformed churches it is said that we rest assured that no sin or infirmity which still remains in us *against our will* can hinder us from being received of God in grace. There has been much dispute about whether or not the regenerate can still fall into such sins as do not take place from infirmity but are deliberate in character and must therefore be called sins of evil aforethought. Two things however are certain: the one is that in those who are really born again not only the conscience but also the new life, the disposition and the will, in a lesser or greater degree come into opposition against those sins; and the other is that even the sins of infirmity which we do against our will are sins and are in conflict with the holiness of the law.

Moreover, the admonishments to a holy walk, so far from being useless and unbeneficial, are precisely the means by which Christ applies the righteousness and holiness given to the believers in Christ and works them out. Christ in His highpriestly prayer prays that the Father may sanctify His disciples in the truth, that is, by means of His word, which is truth (John 17:17; compare 15:3). The word which God gave us is in very fact the chief means for our sanctification; the blessing which has accrued, not only to the public preaching, but also to the reading, study, and meditation of that word in the solitude of the family circle, has simply been immeasurable for the nurture of a Christian life. To this word as the means of sanctification there is added the prayer in Jesus' name (John 14:13, 14; 16:23, 24) which gives us access to the divine majesty and fills us with confidence, since there is no one in Heaven nor on earth who loves us more than does Jesus Christ. To these are added further the singing of psalms and hymns and spiritual songs (Eph. 5:19; Col. 3:16), for these exercise a deep influence on the attitude of the heart and the readiness of the will. And finally there are the watchings and fastings,[45] practices which have unjustly fallen into virtually complete disuse. All these means of sanctification prove that in this work also He does not despise the use of means.

Naturally, God is the Almighty One, and He could, had He wanted to, have perfectly sanctified all His children in the moment of regeneration. But that apparently was not His will; in the re-creation He does not deny Himself as Creator. All the life of the creature is born, grows up, and only gradually reaches its maturity. Because the spiritual life is actually life it comes to be and it develops in this same way. God does not inject the righteousness and holiness of Christ into us mechanically, or pour it out as one does water into a vessel, but He works it out in us in an organic way. Hence the one detail does not conflict with the other when the Scripture constantly presents the matter as though the believers must *become* that which they *are*. The Kingdom of Heaven is a gift of God (Luke 12:32) and yet it is a treasure of great worth which must be sought after (Matt. 6:33; 13:45, 46). The believers are the branches of the vine, and they can, accordingly, do nothing without Christ, and yet they are told in His word to remain in Him, in His word, and in His love (John 15). They were elected in Christ from before the foundation of the world, and yet they must be diligent to make their calling and their election sure (Eph. 1:4; II Peter 1:10). They have been sanctified by the one sacrifice of Christ, and must nevertheless follow after sanctification, without which no man shall see the Lord (Heb. 10:10; 12:14). They are complete, and nevertheless require constant perfecting and establishment (Col. 2:10; I Peter 5:10). They have put on the new man, and must nevertheless constantly put him on (Eph. 4:24; Col. 3:10). They have crucified the flesh with the affections and lusts, and must nevertheless still mortify their members which are upon the earth (Gal. 5:24; Col. 3:5). It is God who works in them both to will and to do according to His good pleasure, and yet they must work out their salvation with fear and trembling (Phil. 2:12, 13).

These data do not conflict with each other. The one is simply the ground and guarantee of the other. Because sanctification, like the whole of salvation, is the work of God, we are admonished, obliged, to a new obedience, and we are also qualified for it. He grants abundant grace not that we should instantly or suddenly be holy and continue to rest in this holiness, but that we should persevere in the struggle and remain standing. He hears our prayers but does it in accordance with the law and order which He has fixed for the spiritual life. Hence we are always of good courage, for He who has begun a good work in us will finish it until the day of Jesus Christ. The believers can and they will *become* holy because in Christ they *are* holy.

Notes

[1]Lev. 10:10; I Sam. 21:5; Ezek. 22:26.

[2]Exod. 19:6; 29:43; Lev. 11:45ff.; 19:2.

[3]Isa. 5:16; 6:3; 29:23; 30:11, 12; compare Ezek. 37:28; 39:7; Hab. 1:12; 3:3.

[4]Exod. 19:6; 29:43–46; Lev. 11:44; 19:2.

[5]Matt. 12:50; John 4:34; 8:46.

[6]II Cor. 5:21; Heb. 4:15; 7:26; I Peter 1:19; 2:22; 3:18; I John 2:1; 3:5.

[7]Jer. 31:33, 34; Ezek. 36:25, 26.

[8]Gal. 2:20; 3:27; Col. 2:12.

[9]Rom. 6:14; Gal. 4:31; 5:1, 13.

[10]Jer. 31:33; 32:38; Ezek. 36:27, 28.

[11]I Cor. 3:9; Eph. 2:20; Col. 2:7; I Peter 2:5.

[12]I Cor. 1:2; 6:11; Titus 3:5.

[13]John 17:17; II Cor. 3:18; Eph. 5:26; I Thess. 5:23; Titus 2:14; Heb. 13:20, 21.

[14]Rom. 8:29; I Cor. 15:49; Phil. 3:21.

[15]Isa. 62:12; Joel 3:17; Obad. 17: Zech. 8:3; 14:20.

[16]Acts 9:13, 32, 41; 26:10; Rom. 1:7; I Cor. 1:2 and elsewhere.

[17]II Cor. 6:16; Gal. 6:16; I Peter 2:5.

[18]John 17:19; I Cor. 1:30; 3:16; 6:11, 19.

[19]Exod. 31:13; Lev. 20:8; 21:8.

[20]Lev. 11:44; 20:7; Num. 11:18.

[21]John 17:17–19; I Cor. 1:2; I Thess. 5:23.

[22]II Cor. 7:1; I Thess. 3:13; 4:3.

[23]Rom. 6:4ff.; Eph. 4:22–24; Col. 3:10.

[24]Eph. 5:22ff.; 6:1ff.; Col. 3:18ff.; I Peter 2:13ff.; 3:1ff.

[25]Matt. 22:37–40; Rom. 13:8–10; Gal. 5:14; James 2:8.

[26]Matt. 3:15; Gal. 3:13; 4:4.

[27]Rom. 7:1–6; Gal. 4:5; 26ff.; 5:1.

[28]Rom. 12:2; Eph. 5:10; Phil. 1:10.

[29]Mark 12:28–34; compare Matt. 7:12.

[30]Rom. 15:4; I Cor. 10:11; II Tim. 3:15; I Peter 1:12.

[31]Rom. 13:8–10; Gal. 5:14; II James 2:8.

[32]John 13:34; compare 15:12; I Thess. 4:9; I Peter 4:8; I John 3:23; 4:21; II John 5.

[33]Gal. 6:10; I Thess. 3:12; II Peter 1:7.

[34]Gen. 8:22; Jer. 31:35; 33:25.

[35]Matt. 6:30; 8:26; 14:31; 16:8; Luke 24:25.

[36]Rom. 14:1ff.; 15:1; I Cor. 8:7ff.; 9:22; 10:25.

[37]I Cor. 2:6; 3:2; 14:20; Phil. 3:15; Heb. 5:14.

[38]Rom. 12:2; II Cor. 3:18; 4:16; Eph. 3:16; I Peter 5:10.

[39]Rom. 6:6; 7:14–25; 8:4–9; Gal. 5:17–26; Eph. 4:22–24; Col. 3:9, 10.

[40]Phil. 2:5; I Thess. 2:10; 3:13.

[41]John 14:13, 14; II Cor. 12:10; Eph. 3:20.

[42]Exod. 19:5, 6; 29:43; Deut. 7:6ff.; 32:6ff.; Isa. 41:8ff.; Ezek. 16:14.

[43]Rom. 15:17ff.; I Cor. 4:3; 9:15; 15:31; II Cor. 1:12; 6:3ff; 11:5ff; Phil. 2:16ff.; 3:4ff.; I Thess. 2:10ff.

[44]I Cor. 15:10; II Cor. 12:9; Phil. 4:13.

[45]Matt. 17:21; 26:41; Eph. 6:18.

14

Bernard Ramm

The Glorification of the Soul

The Glorification of the Soul Involves Its Perfection

The Old and New Testament teach (1) that God is a God of glory; (2) that Jesus Christ is the Lord of Glory; (3) that God intends to share his glory with his children in the form of their glorification; and (4) that our present salvation, already begun, is a process which shall terminate in end-time, eschatological glory. [Our topic is] the details of this final glorification.

Salvation can be studied in the New Testament according to several themes. One of the more neglected ones is the concept of perfection. This involves a number of similar words in the Greek language (*telos, teleiōtēs, teleiōsis, teleō, teleios*). One of the reasons that there is so little constructive material on perfection is that the literature on the subject bogs itself down in debates over the degree of sanctification attainable in this life. Accordingly, the theme of perfection as a motif for salvation and as a strong eschatological concept is neglected.[1]

The perfection motif can be briefly sketched as follows. God intends a goal (*telos*) for his people. This goal involves the perfection (*teleion*) of

From *Them He Glorified* (Grand Rapids: Wm. B. Eerdmans Pub. Co., 1963), pp. 62–91. Used by permission.

the individual believer. But this calls for a Perfecter (*teleiōtēs*) who himself must undergo perfecting and so become perfect (*teleiōtheis*). Thereby he can perfect (*teleioō*) those who come unto God with a perfection (*teleion*). In this life perfection means spiritual, moral, and doctrinal maturity, but in the life to come it means perfection in the sense of the completion of salvation. The divinely intended purpose (*telos*) comes thereby to its consummation.[2]

The doctrine of perfection can accordingly be summed up in three theses: (1) Christ, having been perfected in virtue of his own experience, is the Perfecter of believers and also their perfection. (2) In this life Christ formally gives us his perfection but calls us to Christian maturity. (3) In the age to come maturity gives way to full-orbed perfection. This is part of the structure of glorification and in this sense perfection and glorification coincide.

(1) Looking to the first of these theses we note the perfection of Jesus Christ. This is the theme uniquely developed in Hebrews. Spicq writes: "The entire epistle to the Hebrews attempts to prove the perfection of the New Covenant by the perfection of its high priest who procures perfection for his believers."[3]

Thus Christ is the Leader (*arxēgos*) of believers for he first attains perfection. Hebrews 2:10 calls him the Perfected Leader. He attained this perfection by submitting to the conditions of our existence (Heb. 2:14–18), suffering the deepest lessons of obedience (Heb. 5:7–10) and finally suffering death itself. Risen from the dead he appears as the perfect fulfillment of all that the Old Testament promised. He is the perfect Moses, the perfect Aaron, the perfect minister in the perfect temple, the perfect sacrifice for sin, and the perfect Saviour for all who come unto God by him.

(2) The second thesis asserts that Christ bestows his perfection upon those who believe. Hence in this life his bestowed perfection is equivalent to salvation (*sōtēria*, Heb. 2:10; 5:9). In this sense Christ is the perfection of believers. As Frerichs emphasizes, Christ, the perfect One, is secretly present in the believer and in the Church as their hidden perfection.[4]

In leading us to glory Christ invites us to maturity in our own Christian experience. This is the burden of several New Testament passages. But it must be kept in mind that in each of these passages there is an eschatological arrow, for the present maturing anticipates the future perfecting. For this reason such passages suggest something of the character of final glorification.

"I in them and thou in me, that they may become perfectly one" (John 17:23). This is a plea for the perfection of unity. That this should be the effort of the Church now cannot be denied. Paul exhorts the Ephesians to maintain the unity of the Spirit (Eph. 4:3). But the fragmentized nature of the Church indicates how far the Church has remained from perfect unity. Only in the end-time, in the glorification of the Church, will this unity emerge as perfected.[5]

"But when the perfect comes the imperfect will pass away" (I Cor. 13:10). The perfect (*teleion*) is contrasted with the partial (*meros*). The passage speaks of the mature gifts succeeding the childish (*nēpios*) gifts, but also of the perfection of the world to come succeeding the partial and limited character of our present experience. This is evident in verse 12, which speaks of our knowing with a fullness which corresponds to the fullness of God's knowledge of us. Du Plessis says that the emphasis is not on the mere partial character of our knowledge but upon the fragile character of our organs of perception compared to what they shall be in the future world.[6] Glorification in this connection means, then, proceeding from faculties and gifts which are partial to those which are perfect.[7]

"Having begun in the Spirit, are you now ending with the flesh?" (Gal. 3:3). In this verse to begin something is opposed to completing (*epiteleō*) something. If the latter verb is taken in the middle voice it means—as the Revised Standard Version translates it—to end up with an attempt at sanctification in the flesh. If it is taken in the passive it means to be perfected in the flesh. Du Plessis[8] believes that the sense of the verb is passive. The verse speaks of a beginning and a completion. He thus translates the verse, "You were put under way by the Spirit, must the flesh now complete it?" Suffice it to say that the beginning of salvation in the Spirit is perfected by the same Spirit in the glorification of the end-time.

"And his gifts were that some should be apostles, some prophets, some evangelists, some pastors and teachers, for the equipment of the saints, for the work of ministry, for building up the body of Christ, until we all attain to the unity of the faith and of the knowledge of the Son of God, to mature manhood, to the measure of the stature of the fulness of Christ" (Eph. 4:11–13). This is a most remarkable passage in that it sets forth the goals of the divers ministries in the Church. These goals are the perfecting of the saints, the work of the ministry, and the edification of the body of Christ. But these goals in turn have goals! These goals are the attainment by all of the unity of the faith, the profound knowledge (*epignōsis*) of the Son of God, the complete (*teleios*) man, and the mature stature measured by the fullness of Christ.

Several features stand out in this passage. The first is the forward motion in salvation. Faith must move steadily towards perfection and fullness. The second is the predominant physical imagery. Salvation proceeds, like the human body, from infancy (*nēpios*) to manhood (*anēr*). Hence the momentum of faith is not kinetic as in a rolling ball but as in a growing body. The third is the richness of this growth-imagery. It is the attainment of a goal; it is the acquiring of intimate knowledge; it is the perfection of manhood; and it is a fullness measured by the perfection of Christ. This fourfold standard will come into absolute fullness (as far as human nature is concerned) in the end-time glorification of the believer. The goal will be perfectly attained, the knowledge will be face-to-face knowledge, the manhood will be unqualified perfection, and the fullness will be fullness in its totality.

"Not that I have already obtained this or am already perfect; but I press on to make it my own, because Christ Jesus has made me his own. . . . Let those of us who are mature be thus minded" (Phil. 3:12, 15). Here again we note a momentum. The first movement of the chapter is an account of Paul's moral and spiritual excellence as a Jew. The second movement is the great transition to faith in Christ and his righteousness. The third movement is the tremendous drive to come to the full realization of that which the gospel contains and offers. This third movement is intensely a *now* and *then* movement, or a *present-life* and an *eschatological* realization. It is a profound present knowing of Christ which anticipates the resurrection (vv. 10, 11). It is an attempt to grasp Christ with the same intention with which Christ grasped us. It is a driving at the fastest pace to reach the finish line and receive the prize (vv. 13, 14). The spiritual intensity of the passage is overpowering.

Those who are so intensely minded are the mature (*teleios*), and what they strive for is a perfection which is denied them in this life. The eschatological realization of the goals of this passage coincides with the glorification of the believer at the end-time.

"That we may present every man mature in Christ" (Col. 1:28). As Du Plessis indicates, the character of redemption is a dynamic moving from a beginning (*arxē*) of faith in Christ to the goal (*telos*) which is the final eschatological perfection (*teleion*).[9] This goal, we would add, is included in the more comprehensive Christ.

(3) Third, we see perfection as an act of God in the age to come. Spicq says that to perfect somebody is to render that person perfect (*teleiōsis*), and the perfection is the achievement of the goal (*telos*) of the person. Thus God perfects the Christian with the perfection which corresponds to God's *telos* in salvation.[10] Du Plessis affirms that the goal of perfection is the soteriological and eschatological work of Jesus Christ, the Messiah.[11]

Two references in Hebrews use perfection in this sense: "Since God had foreseen something better for us, that apart from us they should not be made perfect" (11:40); ". . . to the spirits of just men made perfect" (12:23). It must be admitted that Hebrews 11:40 could mean the perfection which Christ brought. In this sense it would mean that the benefits of Christ were withheld from the believers during the Old Testament until the coming of Christ. Or, it could refer to the end-time when the perfection of all things occurs. Hebrews 12:23 refers to the transformation undergone by the believers of the Old Covenant as they entered the glorious world described in Hebrews 12:22–24.

The intention of all these verses is obvious. The newborn Christian in this life is to press on to maturity. But the maturity of this life will always be partial. In the end-time glorification the imperfect maturity of this life will give way to the fullness of perfection.

The Glorification of the Soul Involves
Its Final Vindication and Moral Perfection

(1) Paul has written that those whom God justifies he glorifies. This suggests strongly that glorification is the final realization of justification. Thus justification is at root eschatological, namely, the present justification

of the believer will be consummated in end-time glorification.[12] The present vindication of the believer in Jesus Christ will then receive a final, perfect, and eternal vindication.

There are two passages in particular which discuss this end-time vindication, namely, Romans 5:9, 10 and Romans 8:31–39. In Romans 5 we have a powerful treatment of the atonement in its fullest reaches. Christ died for the helpless, the ungodly, the sinners, and the enemies of God. This was a *vicarious* death, as is seen in the repeated use of the preposition *for* (*huper*).[13] The total impress of the passage is that Christ does something for sinners which they cannot do for themselves. His death manifests the love of God (v. 8), provides justification (v. 9), and effects reconciliation (vv. 10, 11). This justification and reconciliation is the present blessing of the believer. But Paul extends the virtue of the death of Christ and the justification to the end-time. The vicarious atoning death represented here by the word *blood* (v. 9)[14] which *now* justifies us will *then* save us from the wrath of God. The wrath of God is the holiness of God excited by the sinfulness of man. The death of Christ before the righteousness of God (Rom. 3:25) enables God to be just in the justification of the ungodly (Rom 3:26). This *present* justification results in *present* freedom from condemnation (Rom. 8:1). But in the end-time when the wrath of God must make a final and eternal reckoning with mankind's sins the believers shall not be counted in. Paul argues from the greater to the lesser. If the death of Christ could vindicate us in the present age from the absolutely wretched condition we were in, it shall have no trouble with our final vindication before the wrath of God.

Paul continues. The death of Christ is also our present reconciliation (Rom. 5:10). Again Paul moves from the greater to the lesser. If the death of Christ could reconcile us to God in our present wicked condition of enmity, the intercessory life of Christ at God's right hand shall thoroughly and completely save us from the wrath of God.

In Romans 8:31–39 the same theme of final vindication is discussed from a different perspective. The great affirmation of Paul is that God is for us. God has made our cause his cause. God seeks not first our condemnation but our justification. If God is for us nothing can be against us (v. 31). Then Paul again employs a logical principle. If God did such an enormous thing as to spare not his Son but deliver him up to death for us, then he will grace us with all things. Here the eschatological overtone enters. This promise does not refer so much to our earthly lives as to the matchless benevolence of God towards us in the end-time.

Speaking again of the present vindication of believers, Paul says that no man can successfully bring a charge against God's elect (v. 33). No man can dare condemn whom God has justified. Our vindication rests not in us as such, but in the past death of Christ for us and in the present intercession of Christ for us (v. 34). Our past justification and our present exoneration are secure for us by the love of Christ. But this love is so great that it shall be our guard for all the future, including the end-time. This is seen in such expressions as "neither death nor life" and "nor things to come" (v. 38).

Therefore the believer stands completely secure in the love of Christ and his glorification as complete vindication at the end-time.[15]

(2) The New Testament represents our glorification not only as a complete juridical exoneration but also as a moral perfection. This is revealed by the naming of certain moral qualities which will be bestowed upon believers at the return of Christ or at the end-time. Some of the more important moral qualities are:

Amōmos.[16] A *mōmos* was a fault, or a cause for blame, or a reason for censure. To be *amōmos* means to be free from such fault or blame. *Mōmos* was used also to indicate a spot or a blemish in a sacrificial animal. An animal without blemish was called *amōmos*. For example, the writer to the Hebrews calls Christ a perfect sacrifice (Heb. 9:14; see also I Peter 1:19). The sense of spotting is seen in II Peter 2:13, where evil men are moral blemishes in the Christian fellowship whereas the Church when perfected and glorified (*endoxos*) by God will be without a moral blemish or spot (*amōmos*, Eph. 5:27).

The complete moral faultlessness[17] of the believer and the Church at the end-time is seen in the use of the verb "to present" with *amōmos* (Col. 1:22; Jude 24). We are so morally perfected that we may be presented to God completely faultless, spotless, and free from all censure. The same thought is present in Ephesians 1:4. Thus to be glorified is to be rendered *amōmos*. This is brought out in Jude 24, where in our faultlessness we can be "presented before the presence of his glory with rejoicing." If we are blameworthy it could be a presentation only with lament.

Hagios. Paul represents the believers as both blameless (*amōmos*) and holy (*hagios*) before God (Eph. 1:4; Col. 1:22). The concept of the holy is certainly one of the most complex and important in Scripture.[18] The God of both the Old and New Testaments is holy in that he is morally perfect. Negatively speaking, there is no darkness in him (I John 1:5, *oudemia*—"not at all, by no means"). To attribute anything morally imperfect to God is unthinkable, inconceivable and blasphemous. God is holy, his Son is holy, and his Spirit is holy. In the final assessment of all things only the holy can endure and be with God in eternity. The unclean or unholy is forever banished from his presence (Rev. 21:27; 22:15). No unholy person may take one small step into the New Jerusalem.

Our glorification in Christ involves, then, our being rendered holy to the degree that we perfectly satisfy the holiness of God; then our presence in the New Jerusalem will be completely free from all offense.

Aproskopos.[19] This word is derived from *proskoptō*, the literal meaning of which is "to strike against something, to beat against, to stumble"; its figurative meaning is "to take offense at, feel repugnance for." From this verb two nouns are derived. *Proskopē* means an occasion for taking offense (II Cor. 6:3), and *proskomma* means a stumbling or occasion for stumbling. *Aproskopos* thus describes an absence of offensiveness. It means to be free from cause of stumbling. In Philippians 1:10 Paul prays that Christians will be *aproskopos* in the day of Christ. The end-time reference here is unmistakable. Stählin[20] discusses three possibilities here.

The word either means blamelessness, or without offense to God, or having reached the goal. Stählin prefers the latter, although the possibilities mentioned are not starkly opposed to each other. In the day of the believer's glorification he shall be completely without offense before God and his entry into the heavenly kingdom shall cause none to take offense for all such causes will have been removed from him.

Eilikrinēs. In Philippians 1:10 Paul associates *eilikrinēs* with *aproskopos.* This word has an interesting derivation.[21] It means to be tested by the sun; thence it means to be completely clear or pure or spotless and immaculate. In the day of Christ believers shall be tested by the sunlight and not be found wanting. Their glorification shall bestow upon them an immaculate purity which shall stand up under the eyes of him whose eyes burn like a flame of fire (cf. Rev. 1:14; 2:18; 19:12).

Anegklētos. This word, like so many words in this context, is formed by negating a word with a bad ethical meaning. *Egkaleō* means to bring a charge against somebody. The legal character of the word is seen in the remarks made by the town clerk in Ephesus (Acts 19:38, 40), in the letter of Claudius Lysias to Felix (Acts 23:28, 29), and in Paul's speech before Agrippa (Acts 26:2, 7). The verb also occurs in Romans 8:33 where Paul asks if anybody can bring a charge against God's elect.

To be *anegklētos* means, then, to be free from an incriminating charge.[22] In the Pastorals it means that the servants of Jesus Christ are to be free from any civil charge, but in I Corinthians 1:8 it refers to the end-time status of Christians.[23] They stand before God completely free from any charge. According to Romans 8:31–34, when God justifies no man dare accuse. When Christ dies for sinners and intercedes for them there is no ground left for condemnation. In this realization of our salvation through glorification the Christian is rendered completely free from all moral objections.

Amemptos. This word is similar to *amōmos,* but it is not as strong a juridical word as *anegklētos.* It is derived from *memphomai* which means "to find fault with, blame, censure," etc. *Amemptos* means to be without fault, blame or censure. It is used of the excellent moral and religious behavior of men in this life (Zechariah and Elizabeth in Luke 1:6; Christians in Phil. 2:15; Paul's life prior to his conversion in Phil. 3:6; and his life as an apostle in I Thess. 2:10).

In I Thessalonians 3:13 and 5:23 the word has a eschatological meaning. These passages set forth ethical blamelessness as the chief characteristic of our sanctification. According to the first, our hearts are to be found free from all fault before the Father at the return of Jesus Christ. In the second, Paul sets out the completeness of our sanctification by using two Greek words which express totality and thoroughness. This through-and-through sanctification involves the entire man—spirit, soul, and body. The product of this thorough sanctification is end-time blamelessness. The surety of this blamelessness is immediately attributed to God—"He who calls you is faithful, and he will do it" (v. 24). Thus our glorification involves our perfect faultlessness before God in the end-time appearing of Jesus Christ.

Freedom from *Spilos* and *rhutis.* In Ephesians 5:25–27 Paul discusses how Christ shall perfect the Church. His sacrificial death enables him to sanctify and cleanse the Church, so that finally he might present the Church to himself gloriously (*endoxos*). This *endoxos* is elaborated by four other words, two of which we have already examined (*hagios and amōmos*). The other two words specify what the Church is free from in her glory, namely, *spilos* (spot, stain, blemish) and *rhutis* (wrinkle, a wrinkle from old age). There is the subtle overtone here of the groom inspecting the bride for faults which destroy the physical perfection of the bride. But Christ shall morally perfect his Church so that it shall be free from all moral spots and wrinkles. This is part of the glorification of Christians in the end-time.

The Glorification of the Soul Involves Its Full Participation in Eternal Life

The Old and New Testaments represent God as a living God (Deut. 5:26; Ps. 42:2; Matt. 16:16; Acts 14:15). The concept of God as the living God stems from two biblical motifs. The first is that as Creator God is also the Author of life; the second is that the God of Israel is the true God in contrast to the idols and gods of the pagans. The God of Israel is a living God whereas gods and idols are lifeless and powerless.

In the remarkable phrase of John 5:26 we are told that God has life in himself. He has uncreated life, life which has no beginning nor ending, and needing no sustenance. Barth says that to define God we must begin by saying that he is life. "Only the voice of the Living is God's voice. Only the work of the Living is God's work, only the worship and fellowship of the Living is God's worship and fellowship. So, too, only the knowledge of the Living is knowledge of God."[24]

Paralleling the statement of John 5:26 is I Timothy 6:16, which tells us that God is the only one possessing immortality (*athanasia*). Only God has this everlasting, uncreated life. This refers not only to the immutability and the eternity of the divine life, but also to its fullness and perfection.

It is in virtue of this divine life that created reality has life.[25] The living Elohim speaks in Genesis 1 and the earth *responds* with living forms. Life in the land, in the sea, and in the air stems from this living God. Whether it be vegetable or tree, creeping thing or cattle, it lives in virtue of the living God. The climax is the representation of man coming to life by the special spiration of God (Gen. 2:7). To this we may compare John's words when he wrote, "In him was life, and the life was the light of men" (John 1:4).

Man, in common with all living things, shares in life because the living God has given such life. But man is in the image and likeness of God and thereby shares a special, spiritual life. This is a gift to man above that of the other creatures. It is life as communion, as fellowship, as worship, as covenantal partnership with God. But as Scripture says repeatedly, this special life was forfeited by sin and turned into death. The breath of God in the nostrils of man makes him a living creature (Gen. 2:7), but disobedience is threatened with death just a few verses later (2:17). That the just end of sin is death (Rom. 6:23) is the common presupposition of both

Testaments. Thus, as Bultmann points out, death for man in Scripture is never a "natural" event but is always viewed as a judgment of God upon sin.[26] The clearest passage on the unnatural character of death in its connection with sin is Romans 5:12–21.

The restoration of man's spiritual and divine life is represented as "life" or "eternal life."[27] There is no Platonism in the Scriptures, as if man's life were itself an immutable part of the eternal order.[28] Man's life finds its origin in God's gift, its forfeiture in man's sin, and its restoration through redemption, especially redemption seen as a new creation. This restoration is *in Christ*. In the great fifth chapter of John it is not only asserted that God has life in himself but also that the Son has life in himself (v. 26). Therefore the Son can execute two of God's absolute prerogatives: he can bestow upon the soul regenerate life in the present time (v. 24), and he can raise the dead at the last hour (vv. 21, 25, 28, 29).

Eternal life finds its first recovery in Christ as the living Son of God; it finds its second basis for recovery in Christ's resurrection from the dead.[29] Here again we note the absence of customary philosophical arguments. The entire future of man's body and soul, their end-time destiny, rests upon the person and work of Jesus Christ.[30]

The eternal life in Christ has three elements. It is first of all a new relationship. It is a knowing of the Father and the Son (John 17:3). It is therefore the restoration of the sinner to such a relationship with God that life is possible and truly does occur. But it is a restoration inseparable from Jesus Christ who is called the Author (*arxēgos*) of life[31] (Acts 3:15).

Secondly, eternal life is a new quality of life. It is a fellowship. The connection of eternal life and fellowship is seen in I John 1:1–3. It is the recovery of and participation in man's real life. Barth has described it as follows:

> The purpose of God in His judgment is the sanctification of man, i.e., his direction, preparation and exercise for the eternal life ordained and promised. Eternal life is a life which, ascribed to man in his creatureliness, is invested with God's own glory, i.e., as an object of the openly revealed love of God in which God has turned to him and in possession of the openly revealed freedom which He has granted him in fellowship with Himself. It is man's indissoluble, indestructible, unceasing and unlimited life with God, his life in the clarity which is proper to God, in which God sees Himself, in which He has always seen man, too, and still sees him but in which here and now man is so far unable to see either God or himself.... Eternal life is man's life in harmony with the life of God.[32]

Thirdly, eternal life is life into eternity. It is endless life. This is especially seen in the contrasts which are drawn. In II Timothy 1:10 it is contrasted with death; in Matthew 25:46 with eternal punishment; in John 3:16 with destruction; in John 5:24 with judgment and death.[33]

The firm teaching of the New Testament is that eternal life is a present possession. The following verbs show how eternal life is now received: enter (Matt. 18:8); have (Matt. 19:16); inherit (Mark 10:17); receive (Mark

10:30); see (John 3:36). Therefore in this life eternal life as a relationship and as a quality of life is already begun and as such it is an earnest of eternity.[34] Althaus describes it as follows:

> So eternal life is for the Christian transcendent and at the same time his own possession, future and present, a secret of faith which will reveal itself in the future and faith yet already knows it at work here and now.[35]

This introduces us to the central issue: our glorification involves the full bestowal of eternal life upon the soul—a perfect relationship, a sublime quality, and an eternal duration. Thus the concept is through and through eschatological and redemptive.[36] For this reason Althaus says very emphatically that eternal life is not built on any doctrine of the continuity or durability of the soul. Such a concept is neutral with regard to salvation or damnation. The biblical doctrine of eternal life is grounded in salvation[37] and is thoroughly eschatological.[38]

The Glorification of the Soul Involves Its Full Participation in the Freedom of the Sons of God

The concept of freedom[39] in Scripture is rooted in the concept of the freedom of God. The traditional theological term which expresses the freedom of God is the sovereignty of God. To be sovereign is to be free to do what one wills. To be free in a real and final sense is to be sovereign. Although theologians have differed regarding the degree to which God expresses his sovereignty or the manner in which God expresses it, nevertheless they are uniform in ascribing freedom and sovereignty to God.

The concept of the freedom of God is one of the basic axioms of Barth's theology. No theologian in the history of theology has treated the topic so extensively and in so many divisions of systematic theology.[40] The freedom of God is the root and foundation for all freedom for the creature. God's freedom is, first, negative: it is complete freedom from limits, restrictions, and conditions.[41] But second and more important is the positive element in God's freedom. In speaking of the positive side of freedom Barth writes:

> But freedom in its positive and proper qualities means to be grounded in one's own being, to be determined and moved by one's self. This is the freedom of the divine life and love. In this positive freedom of His, God is also unlimited, unrestricted and unconditioned from without. He is the free Creator, the free Reconciler, the free Redeemer . . . . He in Himself is power, truth and right. Within the sphere of His own being He can love and love in absolute plenitude of power, as we see Him in love in His revelation.[42]

It is out of God's own freedom that he wills to create a universe, that he wills to bring life into existence, and that he wills to form man as his supreme creature. It is out of this selfsame freedom that God wills to be the

Lord and Partner of this man, that he wills to enter into communion with this man, and that he grants out of his own freedom a freedom for man to be the man before God. Thus man's freedom grows out of God's freedom, it is a gift of God's freedom, and he can exist as man within this special form of freedom.

Deep in the history of theology is the conviction that man's freedom is not an abstract concept. It is not merely freedom to will or to choose, freedom to hew out one's own destiny, freedom to do one's own pleasure. When Augustine opened the *Confessions* by saying that man was made for God and could not rest until he rested in God, he was affirming that man's freedom is a freedom to be realized in God. When Thomas said that God is man's beatitude he was asserting that the being of man is a being which can come to its fulfillment only in God. And if this is true of man's being as such it is also of man's freedom.

We therefore come to the conclusion that freedom is a fundamental characteristic of man. To be free is to be the true man before the living God, to display the divine image. Freedom for man is therefore also to be the lord of creation (Gen. 1:28). Man is free to be the mate of woman, as she is free to be the helpmeet of man. Freedom means man's freedom to originate and order a society, and to live within the terms of grace and love in the divine covenant.

That day in which man attempted to live in any other terms than the terms of his freedom would be the day man would die (Gen. 2:17). Sin terminates the fullness of this freedom. The presupposition of Scripture is that man is in bondage—a thesis expressed in a thousand different ways. Therefore the great emphasis in the New Testament is not about freedom as such or even the original freedom of man but upon the freeing of man.[43]

Man, as a sinner, is in bondage. If freedom is the sign of sinlessness under the perfect law of Edenic existence, then bondage (*douleia*) is the sign of his sinnerhood. Thus man is a slave (*doulos*) enslaved (*douleuō*) in slavery (*douleia*).

The wonderful witness of the New Testament is that Christ redeems man from his slavery. When our Lord commenced his ministry and gave his famous address to the synagogue in Nazareth he said in citing Isaiah that he would "proclaim release to the captives" (Luke 4:18). This is certainly a great theme of the Christian gospel.

The great bondage-freedom section of Scripture is Romans 6. Man is represented as enslaved to sin (v. 6), under the dominion of death (v. 9), under the reign of sin (v. 12), under the law (v. 14), a slave of sin (vv. 16, 17, 20), and free from righteousness (v. 20). That which smites the chains of sin, the law, and death, providing release and freedom, is the death and resurrection of Jesus Christ. As Schlier[44] points out, it is the complete self-surrender of Christ to a vicarious death which is the basis for our freedom.

Romans 6 also illustrates the character of the biblical doctrine of freedom. Man's freedom is not fulfilled in the complete freedom from restraint to act as he pleases. It is the freedom of the new life in Christ (v. 4); it is to live free from sin (v. 7); it is to be alive to God in Jesus Christ (v. 11); it is yielding one's self as risen men are yielded (v. 13); it is to be under grace (v. 14); it is to be the slave of righteousness (v. 18); it is to be rewarded with sanctification in this life and eternal life in the end-time (v. 22). Thus Thornton-Duesberry is correct when he writes that "Christian freedom is part and parcel of the new order of things inaugurated by God in Jesus Christ."[45]

The book of Galatians is in complete harmony with Romans 6. The bondage of man due to his sinfulness is overcome in the life, death, and resurrection of Jesus Christ. By taking the curse of the law upon himself (Gal. 3:13) Christ ends our bondage and secures our liberty (5:1).

The freedom lost in sin, rescued again by the redemption of Jesus Christ, is now, in this age, bestowed upon the believer. Freedom in Christ is one of the greatest blessings of our present salvation in Christ.[46] If the death and resurrection of Christ is the historical foundation of our freedom (as Rom. 8:3 indicates), the present in-this-life foundation is the Holy Spirit of God.[47] The important passages which speak directly of the Holy Spirit as the immediate source of Christian freedom are: Romans 8:3–27; II Corinthians 3:17; Galatians 3:3, 14; 4:5–7; 5:5, 16, 18, 22, 25; 6:8. It is the Spirit who accomplishes directly and concretely in Christian experience the freedom we have in Christ.[48] These freedoms are:

(1) Freedom from sin. Our Lord, speaking of the Christians, said, "The sons are free" (Matt. 17:26). The mark of the Christian is that Christ the Son sets the sons free from the dominion of sin (John 8:33–36). The truth does set free! But it is the truth about Jesus Christ the Son of God, not truth in general. Few biblical texts are more abused than John 8:36. The Son does not basically set free from superstition or ignorance but from sin. Christ the Redeemer calls us to freedom (Gal. 5:1, 13).

Freedom from sin (Rom. 6, 7, 8) does not mean freedom from temptation nor from ever sinning again, but freedom from the compulsion to sin.[49] Thus John writes that the person who thinks that he does not sin is deceived (I John 1:8), yet Christians born of God do not sin (I John 3:4–9), i.e., do not live under the compulsive power of sin. They live under the law of the Spirit of life in Christ Jesus which frees them from the compulsion of the law of sin and death (Rom. 8:2). Paul contrasts spirit and flesh at this point. To walk in the Spirit is to walk in freedom from the compulsion of sin; to walk in the flesh is to live under the compulsion of sin (Rom. 8:1–8). Bultmann defines the relationship of spirit and flesh as follows:

> The Spirit is the opposite of "flesh.". . . As "flesh" is the quintessence of the worldly, visible, controllable, and transitory sphere which becomes the controlling power over man who lives "according to the flesh," so "Spirit" is the quintessence of the non-worldly, invisible, uncontrollable, eternal sphere which becomes the controlling power for and in him who orients his life "according to the Spirit."[50]

(2) Freedom from the deception of sin. Life in sin is a life of deception. This much is clear from John 9:39–41. That it is also life as a *lie* is the

implication of John 8:39–47.[51] To exist in deception and in a lie is a most vicious form of bondage.

When Jesus Christ redeems he enables the sinner to recover himself from the deception and the lie of sin. He discovers himself as he *was* in virtue of what he now *is* in Christ. Christian freedom includes freedom from deception:[52] this is brought out in Paul's personal remarks in Philippians 3. Paul's life before conversion was really the life of Paul deceived. It was Paul in sin but deceived into thinking he was in righteousness. It was Paul full of fault before God but deceived into thinking that he was faultless. It was Paul in terrible disservice to God deceived into thinking that he served God with a holy zeal. But when Paul found Christ he also found himself, for in finding Christ he found freedom from deception. The whole bent of his life changed, for now the impetus in Paul's life was not to justify Paul but to know Christ.

(3) Freedom from the law. Paul represents the bondage of the law in a twofold manner. First, it is bondage to a false method of salvation. It presumes that man can establish his own righteousness (Rom. 10:3; Phil. 3:1–6). Second, it is bondage to a false method of sanctification. It presumes that in the keeping of the law there is growth in sanctification (Gal. 3:1–5). The great theme of freedom from the law is discussed in Romans, Galatians, and II Corinthians 3.

The details of this great antithesis of bondage under the law and freedom in Christ are too many for a thorough treatment here. The law is holy, just, and good (Rom. 7:12). But it is commandment and not gospel. Its broken statutes bring a curse (Gal. 3:13) and guilt (James 2:10). It is written on the slate of stone and not upon the human heart. It rests its heavy demands upon a sinful heart. The sinful heart responds adversely to the law and thus the law excites dormant sinful propensities (Rom. 7:7–12). It was given to direct life (Rom. 7:10) but it cannot bestow life for it is commandment and not promise (Gal. 3:21). Therefore for wicked sinners it turns out to be a ministration of death and damnation (II Cor. 3:7–9).

Christ died to redeem us from the curse of the law (Gal. 3:13), nailing its charges against us on the cross (Col. 2:14). We are then dead to the law (Rom. 7:4) and discharged from the law (Rom. 7:6). We now live in the freedom of the Holy Spirit, for where the Spirit of the Lord is, there is liberty (II Cor. 3:17). We are free from the whole sacrificial system of the Old Testament, for it is shadow and Christ is reality (Col. 2:17). We are free from attempting to justify or sanctify ourselves by the law. We are free from the seal and sign of the law—circumcision. We are free from all the rules, regulations, and institutions of the law. We are free to live under the perfect law of freedom (James 1:25). We are free to be "inlawed" to Christ (I Cor. 9:21). We are free to live as free men (I Peter 2:16). We are free from all the veiled and disguised forms of legalism.[53] We are free from all the standards and conventions of men so that we might be our true selves in Jesus Christ.[54]

(4) Freedom from idolatry and world systems. In Galatians Paul goes beyond freedom from the law. We are children of the free woman (Gal.

4:31) and in this freedom from the bondage of the law we are to stand firmly (Gal. 2:4; 5:1, 13). But Paul makes it clear that idolatry is a form of bondage (Gal. 4:8). The true knowledge of God frees the believer from this bondage (Gal. 4:9).

Paul also sees the whole pagan religious life as a form of bondage (Gal. 4:9, 10; Eph. 2:2). To be in Christ is to be free from the fear, the superstition and the regulations of pagan religion in all its forms. Thus in Colossians 2:8 he warns the Christians against being taken prey by powerless philosophy, human tradition, and the elemental spirits of the universe. In Colossians 2:18 he warns against self-abasement and worship of angels. In Colossians 2:16 he sounds a clear note of Christian freedom from all pagan religion—"let no man pass judgment on you!"

Again, in Colossians 2:20–3:4 Paul maintains the liberty we have in Christ against "the elemental spirits of the universe" (v. 20), against "regulations" (v. 20), against "human precepts and doctrines" (v. 22). The Christian's life is free from all of this in order that it might be free for the life in Christ.

(5) Freedom from death. Because the Christian is free from sin's compulsion and free from the bondage of the law he is free from the sting of death. Paul puts all three together in I Corinthians 15:56. The power of sin is the law; and death is the sting (*kentron*, the poisonous, deadly sting of the insect) of the law. The Christian is not exempt from the experience of dying but he is exempt from its sting. Having been united with the crucified and risen Lord he is passed beyond all the threat and terror of death.

Hebrews 2:14–18 is beautifully clear on this point. In our fear of death before we knew Christ we became willing prey to the religious systems of Satan and thus entered into his bondage. Christ comes, however, in our human nature, suffers our death, expiates our sins, and delivers us into the freedom of his great salvation.

The climax, fulfillment, and complete realization of our freedom in Christ is part of our glorification. This is the great theme of Romans 8:18–25 and II Corinthians 4:16–18. In Romans 8:18 Paul speaks of the present sufferings (*pathēma*, suffering, misfortune, of the redemptive sufferings of Christ);[55] and in II Corinthians 4:16 of the wasting away of the outer nature, which he calls in verse 17 "slight momentary afflictions" (*thlipsis*, oppression, afflication, tribulation, distress). Added to these sufferings and these tribulations is the curse imposed on creation due to man's sin which Paul calls a frustration (*mataiotēs*) in Romans 8:20. The frustration inhibits the goal (*telos*) of creation from reaching its realization. This is compounded with the effects of the curse upon our bodies, for they too suffer from the frustration imposed upon the creation (Rom. 8:23). Therefore Christians groan inwardly, longing for the release from the frustrations of their spiritual life arising from hindrances from their bodies. This is again compounded with a fourth factor, namely, human weakness (*astheneia*) or frailty (Rom. 8:26). Insofar as our sufferings, our tribulations, our existence under frustration, and our weakness prevent our full and unhindered life as God's redeemed children, our present life is a life of bondage. *Therefore our glorification represents a total removal of all these restrictions, permitting the children of God to live in glorious freedom, to be fully conformed to what they truly are.*

Thus our eschatological freedom is freedom from sin, freedom from the law, freedom from death. It is freedom from suffering, frustration, and tribulation. But it is more than this; it is freedom to be true to our natures as God's children. Release from this bondage is entry into complete freedom and glory. Thus our glorification and our full freedom coincide. The former produces the latter. In Romans 8:21 Paul uses the unique expression "glorious freedom," i.e., freedom which is glorious. In II Corinthians 4:17 he speaks of the "eternal weight of glory" which shall be ours when we enter into those things which are eternal.

The Glorification of the Soul Is Bestowed upon the Soul When It Enters into Its Full Inheritance in Jesus Christ

The biblical doctrine of inheritance[56] is founded in the promise made to Abraham, namely, that having left his fatherland he would be granted another country for the possession of his offspring. It received a more extensive development in the promises to Moses that those redeemed out of Egypt should enter into a land flowing with milk and honey, and was partially fulfilled in the conquest of Joshua. Milk and honey were luxury items with the ancients and a land *flowing* with such luxurious fare was certainly a land blessed of the Lord.

The Israelites were continually reminded, however, that they did not receive this inheritance because they deserved it.[57] It was not originally their rightful property, nor was it bequeathed to them in reward for national excellence. Furthermore, they did not conquer it by their own power even though they fought for it. It is everywhere regarded as a bestowal of the Lord, a grant of his grace and a continued possession in virtue of his grace, power, and will.

The more legally flavored concept of inheritance grows out of the need to partition the land through lot and thus to transmit it from father to son. But the concept of inheritance as gracious bestowal is more fundamental than and prior to the concept of inheritance as a rightful bequest.[58]

The concept of inheritance takes on a spiritual overtone in the Old Testament which foreshadows what will happen to it in the New Testament. The first overtone is suggested where we read that the Levites shall not have a lot of the land, for the Lord is their lot. The second overtone is seen in those passages where Israel is set forth as God's possession in the same sense as the land is God's possession or Israel's.[59] The third is to be found in Psalm 16:5, 6, "The Lord is my chosen portion and my cup; thou holdest my lot. The lines have fallen for me in pleasant places." The Psalmist contrasts his portion in the Lord with the portion of those who have chosen idols (v. 4). He boldly applies terms used literally of the partition of the land into lots for his spiritual heritage in the Lord. The surveyor's lines which marked out the assigned lot[60] mark out the Lord as the pleasant place of the Psalmist.

The New Testament transposes the Old Testament concept of inheritance in certain significant ways. First, the heir is designated to be Jesus Christ.[61] This means that all inheritance will hereafter be mediated through this Heir. There is no inheriting apart from Christ (Gal. 3:29). Foerster thinks it is decisive that the Son of the parable of Mark 12:1–10 is also the Heir.[62] Equally decisive is Hebrews 1:2, which affirms that Christ is the Heir of all things.[63] Spicq comments as follows on Hebrews 1:2:

> It is remarkable that Jesus as only a man having belonged to one of the smallest nations of the world, which rejected and crucified him, has been established as heir not only of Palestine or the Orient, but of the universe, of all the riches of earth and heaven. He is the Lord and Master of all that exists.[64]

The inheritance was hidden during the earthly life of Christ. Only as the Risen Lord does he come into the full exercise of this lordship implied in being heir of all things.[65] As Gerhard Koch spells it out in such great detail and emphasis in his work, *Die Auferstehung Jesu Christi,* the Risen Christ appears to his disciples as THE LORD.[66]

The second transformation comes in the reinterpretation of the heirs of God. According to Foerster's account of Jewish theory, Abraham's heirs were his descendants and proselytes who kept the law.[67] But Paul, according to Foerster, modifies this concept in the light of four theses:[68] (1) The promise given to Abraham was given before the law and was received as a promise and not by fulfilling the law. (2) Therefore the true sons of Abraham are those who have faith. (3) The real seed of Abraham is one person, Jesus Christ. Therefore to be a seed of Abraham one must belong to Christ. This further displaces the keeping of the law as the ground for heirship. (4) Paul reinterprets Abraham in the light of Christ and holy history. The real heir of Abraham, then, is the person who participates in holy history.

The third transformation comes in the addition of an eschatological note to the concept of inheritance.[69] What was promise in the Old Covenant becomes eschatological anticipation in the New Testament. There is eschatological anticipation in the Old Testament insofar as both Israel and the land are called God's heritage, which heritage is not based upon Israel's industry and business but upon God's gift.[70] But in the New Testament it clearly emerges that the concept of inheritance belongs not only to the present but also to the end-time (Acts 26:18; Col. 1:12).

The fourth transformation is seen in what is inherited (according to the New Testament). No longer is the object of inheritance the land[71] or Israel or the temple or the Torah, but the kingdom or eternal life or salvation. According to Foerster the true perspective of the New Testament doctrine of inheritance is to be gained from Revelation 21:2–7. Here is the final realization of the end-time of the kingdom of God, of life, of salvation and of blessing.[7] The land-promise to Abraham has now gone through a complete transformation.[73]

Our inheritance in Christ is both present and future and therefore its fullness is part of our glorification. Christians are heirs because they are sons. Paul uses a strong word, adoption (*huiothesia*), to indicate how believers are brought into the divine family (Gal. 4:5; Eph. 1:5; Rom. 8:15).[74] In Romans 8:17 Paul deduces the Christians' status as that of heirs from their status as sons, and from the status of heirship he deduces co-heirship with Christ. Virtually the same thing is affirmed in Galatians 3:6, 7.

In analogy with Israel, believers are in turn called God's heritage. Peter thus calls the Christians God's possession (I Peter 5:3, *hoi klēroi*).[75] Ephesians 1:14 may mean either that Christians are given an inheritance or that they have been made God's heritage. Salmond prefers the latter.[76] Ephesians 1:18 is more emphatic: "Having the eyes of our hearts enlightened, that you may know what is the hope to which he has called you, what are the riches of his glorious inheritance in the saints." Here is the clear union of eschatological hope and Christian inheritance.

Christians are represented as inheriting. They inherit (*klēronomeō*) as their lot (*klēros*) salvation or the kingdom of God or eternal life (Acts 26:18; Col. 1:12). They are thus said to have an inheritance (*klēronomia*). The *heir* who is given his *lot* and so *inherits* his *inheritance* comes into its fullness in the end-time, and thus his inheritance corresponds to the believer's glorification. That our full inheritance is yet future and corresponds with our glorification is expressed absolutely in Romans 8:17, 18, 23. Insofar as the inheritance is itself eschatological (the kingdom, I Cor. 6:9; eternal life, Matt. 19:29; eternal sonship, Rev. 21:7), the time of the inheriting must be the end-time. Peter clearly affirms that the living hope of the Christian is an imperishable, undefiled and unfading inheritance which is reserved in heaven by God for us and shall be revealed in that last day (I Peter 1:3–5).[77]

In Titus 3:7 Paul connects justification, inheritance. and eternal life. In our justification we become heirs of an end-time bestowal of eternal life in its fullness. And this coincides with the Christian's glorification. By way of summary, then, the Christian's inheriting of his inheritance is an end-time event and an integral part of the glorification of the saints.

The Glorification of the Soul Is
Its Conformity to the Spiritual Image of Jesus Christ

Jesus Christ is everywhere in the New Testament assumed to be the moral and spiritual ideal of the Christian. In his purity of life, perfect obedience to the Father, composure in the hour of persecution, steadfastness in suffering, and resistance to sin he is the model for the Christian when he enters into similar situations. In this life we strive to be like the Saviour; in our end-time glorification our souls shall be perfectly conformed to his image.

This conformity to Christ is the announced purpose of God as recorded in Romans 8:28, 29. Christ is the first-born among the Christians. He is the elder Brother who is the pattern to which all the other brothers shall conform. But the hope here is eschatological and awaits the end-time fulfillment.[78] The image of the Son is not attained until the brothers have gone through the resurrection as has the elder Brother.[79]

This being our goal, we move in this life towards that goal, a goal which is on the other side of the resurrection. In Colossians 1:28 Paul speaks of his desire to present every man to Christ as mature in Christ. Christian maturity in this life finds it realization in conformity to Christ's perfect human nature in the world to come. This is taught more explicitly in Ephesians 4:13, a passage we discussed under the topic of perfection, but it is relevant simply to restate here that maturity and perfection have as their standard Christ-likeness. Just as the unity of faith yields to end-time perfect unity, the knowledge of the Son of God yields to end-time complete knowledge, the manhood of the believer yields to the perfect image of the manhood of Christ at the end-time. Glorification is then the perfecting of our manhood into the image of the perfect human nature of Jesus Christ.

This is also the theme of Philippians 3:10–13, which was also discussed under the concept of perfection. But here, as in the Ephesians passage, the concept of perfection and the concept of conformity to the image of Christ overlap. In the Philippians passage Paul desires to *know* Christ in his suffering and in his resurrection, and certainly this *knowing* implies a *becoming like* Christ. Paul admits that he has not achieved the end of this knowing in this life (v. 12) but presses on towards it even though he knows it can be fully achieved only at the resurrection. Thus the goal is an eschatological goal since it can be fully realized only at the time of the resurrection, and it is a Christological goal because Paul wishes to grasp Christ so that he may become like him.

The most striking of those passages which refer to our becoming like Christ is II Corinthians 3:18. Just as Moses gazed on the glory of the Lord and his face shone with the glory of the Lord, so we look upon the Lord of glory and his glory radiates upon us. In this exposure to the glory of Christ we are transposed into the image or likeness (*eikōn*) of the Lord. But this is not a sudden change: it is from glory to glory, i.e., from degree to degree. Ultimately, when the transformation is complete, Christians will possess the complete image of Christ. And this amazing chemistry of personality transformation is effected by the Lord, the powerful Holy Spirit. We need only add that the final transformation into the image and glory of Christ corresponds with our glorification.

That this final transformation is eschatological and therefore belongs to the end-time is clear from I John 3:2. Although we undergo change in this life from glory to glory, the final change is at the appearing of Christ. We are now (*nun*) God's children, but there is no visible sign that distinguishes us from those who are not Christians. One cannot surmise the future state from the present condition. But in some future date it will be revealed. What we secretly are now shall become apparent. As God's children we are destined to become like God's Son. When he is revealed in his glory at his return, then we shall see him in his radiant glory and become as he is. Thus conformation to the perfect human nature of Jesus Christ coincides with glorification.

Notes

[1]A survey of encyclopedia articles will reveal that most of them do not discuss perfection as a motif of salvation nor as an eschatological concept. However, in P. J. Du Plessis, *Teleios, The Idea of Perfection in the New Testament,* we have an adequate treatment of perfection. Fr. Frerichs recognizes the eschatological element in perfection in his article, "Vollkommenheit," *Evangelisches Kirchenlexikon,* III, 1700.

[2]The book of Hebrews is the only book of the New Testament in which this is developed. Cf. Du Plessis, *op. cit.,* pp. 206–232, and C. Spicq, *L'Épître aux Hébreux,* I, 64, and II, 214.

[3]*Op. cit.,* I, 64.

[4]*Op. cit.,* III, 1700. Cf. Du Plessis, *op. cit.,* pp. 167–168.

[5]Du Plessis, *op. cit.,* p. 174.

[6]*Ibid.,* p. 185.

[7]"This [perfection] is brought about at the *parousia*—it 'comes' with the Lord from heaven." *EGT,* II, 900. So also *TWNT,* IV, 600.

[8]*Op. cit.,* pp. 130–131.

[9]*Op. cit.,* p. 200.

[10]*Op. cit.,* II, 214.

[11]*Op. cit.,* p. 167.

[12]For the eschatological intensity of justification see Richardson, *An Introduction to the Theology of the New Testament,* p. 237; R. Bultmann, *Theology of the New Testament,* I, 273f.; G. Quell and G. Schrenk, "Righteousness," in *Kittel's Bible Key Words* (translated and edited by J. R. Coates).

[13]Although *huper* fundamentally means "for the benefit of," it also means, "in the place of." There are some things which can be done for another person's benefit only by doing it in his place, hence vicariously. Therefore in many instances *huper* is equivalent to *anti.* There are many instances of this in the papyri. Cf. Arndt and Gingrich, *A Greek-English Lexicon of the New Testament,* p. 846.

[14]"Blood and life as in expiatory sacrifice . . . as the means of freeing from guilt." Arndt and Gingrich, *op. cit.,* p. 22.

[15]Cf. I Thess. 1:10, "Jesus who delivers us from the wrath to come," and references to white robes in Revelation (6:11; 7:9, 13, 14), and to white linen (15:6; 19:8, 14) or raiment (3:5; 4:4). White is the eschatological color and signifies glory, the radiance, and the righteousness of the wearers of the white garments.

[16]*TWNT,* IV, 835–836.

[17]In the LXX *amōmos* stands for the complete blamelessness of Yahweh. Cf. *TWNT*, IV, 836.

[18]Cf. *TWNT*, I, 87–116, especially "6. Die Ecclesia triumphans," pp. 111–112.

[19]*TWNT*, VI, 745–759.

[20]*Ibid.*, p. 757.

[21]*TWNT*, II, 396.

[22]*TWNT*, I, 358.

[23]Grundmann is strongly against Haupt at this point, for Haupt wishes to make these verses refer to the present life. *TWNT*, I, 358.

[24]*Church Dogmatics,* II/1, p. 263.

[25]"Life is represented [in the Old Testament] as a direct gift of God, and dependent absolutely upon Him for its continuance." J. J. Reeve, "Life," *ISBE,* p. 1888.

[26]*TWNT,* III, pp. 14, 15. Cf. also Conzelmann, "Ewiges Leben," *RGG* (3), II, 804.

[27]Cf. the excellent summary of M. S. Terry, "Eternal Life," *Dictionary of Christ and the Gospels,* I, 538–540. Terry has a real appreciation for the eschatological elements of the expression and its connection with glorification.

[28]Conzelmann, *op. cit.,* p. 805.

[29]So Bultmann emphatically in *TWNT*, II, 866.

[30]This is seen in II Tim. 1:10 where it is attributed to the gospel of Christ that it lightens up, i.e., reveals, life and immortality. E. F. Scott's very able article on "Life" (*Dictionary of Christ and the Gospels,* II, 30–32) nevertheless fails to grasp the radical theological, Christological, and eschatological character of eternal life. The interpretation is too moralistic and Ritschlian to do justice to the New Testament.

[31]It could also be translated "Prince of Life," or "Leader of Life."

[32]*Op. cit.,* II/2, pp. 772–773.

[33]Althaus says that the opposite of eternal life is existence unto death (*Totsein*). RGG (3), II, 805.

[34]The fullness of the New Testament teaching about life is too great to reproduce here; e.g., there is a gate and a way which lead to life; there is the light of life; the inner spring of life; the abundance of life; the food of life; the words of life, etc. Cf. *"Zaō," TWNT,* II, 831–877.

[35]*Op. cit.,* p. 808.

[36]Negatively speaking, eternal life is to be saved; put positively, it is entering into glory. So Bultmann, *TWNT,* II, 871.

[37]Althaus calls it a *Heils-Begriff. Op. cit.,* p. 806.

[38]*Ibid.,* p. 808.

[39]J. P. Thornton-Duesbery, "Free, freedom, etc.." *A Theological Word Book of the Bible,* p. 87. E. Fahlbusch, "Freiheit," *EKL,* I. 1372–1379. R. Martin Pope,

"Liberty (Christian)," *HERE,* VII, 907–911. E. Fuchs, "Freiheit." *RGG* (3), II, 1101–1104. H. Schlier, *"eleutheros," TWNT,* II, 484–500.

[40]E.g., *Church Dogmatics,* I/1 and I/2, discusses extensively the freedom of God in revelation. The intensive treatment of God's freedom is found in II/1. Section 28, Paragraph 3, "The Being of God in Freedom." When Barth discusses this in detail (in contrast to General Ethics of II/2) in connection with creation, he develops the entire theme around the concept of freedom as the gift of the Creator to the creature (III/4).

[41]*Ibid.,* II/1, p. 301.

[42]*Ibid.*

[43]Cf. E. Fahlbusch, *op. cit.,* p. 1374. *TWNT,* II, 492.

[44]*TWNT,* II, 495.

[45]*Op. cit..* p. 87. "Throughout the New Testament liberty (*eleutheria*) and its even more confident form (*exousia*) runs as a golden thread, distinguishing the New Dispensation from the Old." E. Daplyn, "Liberty," *Dictionary of Christ and the Gospels,* II, 29.

[46]Bultmann lists freedom as one of the four major characteristics of the man under faith. *Theology of the New Testament,* I, Chapter V.

[47]According to the same passage (Rom. 8:3) this present freeing power of the Spirit grows out of the work of Christ on the cross and in his resurrection. Cf. Schlier, *op. cit.,* II, 495. Otto Weber, *Grundlagen der Dogmatik,* II, 288ff.

[48]Bultmann says that by the Spirit Paul does not mean mysticism or ecstasy. "Rather, everything indicates that by the term 'Spirit' [Paul] means the eschatological existence into which the believer is placed by having appropriated the salvation deed that occurred in Christ." *Op. cit.,* I. 335. "The primary idea [of Spirit] is that of the miraculous power of God, then, since it has the effect of emancipating from the power of sin and death—i.e., grants freedom of action and opens up the possibility of reaping eternal life—it is also the norm for 'walking.' " *Ibid.,* I, 336.

[49]*Ibid.,* I, 332. Fahlbusch, *op. cit.,* i, 1374.

[50]*Op. cit.,* I, 334.

[51]Schlier, *TWNT,* II, 493.

[52]*Ibid.,* II, 494.

[53]*Ibid.,* II, 493.

[54]Fahlbusch, *op. cit.,* I, 374.

[55]H. Kittel, *Die Herrlichkeit Gottes,* p. 195.

[56]*"Klēros," TWNT,* III, 757–786. C. E. B. Cranfield, "Inherit, etc.," *Theological Word Book of the Bible,* pp. 112–114. B. S. Easton, "Heir." *ISBE.* 1369. A. J. Mclean, "Heir, etc.." *Dictionary of the Apostolic Church,* I, 534–544. *EGT,* III, 262–264. Paul Feine, *Theologie des Neuen Testaments* (8th edition), p. 228.

[57]"In the biblical language *klēronomia* is seen less as the acquisition of a property after the death of the first owner and more as the successor taking possession, and the word is thus employed more often for acquisition pure and simple, of the accession to lordship." C. Spicq, *op. cit.,* II, 5.

[58]Even here the bequeathal of the lot of Israel to his heirs is not purely legal but based upon the fidelity and promise of the Lord. *TWNT*, III. 774. Cranfield notes that the Old Testament never connects Israel's lot (*nachalah*) with the father-son metaphor. *Op. cit.*, p. 113.

[59]*TWNT*, III, 771.

[60]F. Delitzsch, *A Commentary on the Book of Psalms*, I, 283.

[61]*TWNT*, III, 781.

[62]Foerster, *op. cit.*

[63]The heir of all things means that Christ is the recipient of all things. B. S. Easton, *op. cit.*, p. 1369.

[64]*Op. cit.*, II, 5.

[65]*TWNT*, III, 782.

[66]Cf. p. 41, "Ostern ist Auferweckung Jesu zum Kyrios."

[67]*TWNT*, III, 784f.

[68]*Ibid.*, pp. 784–785.

[69]Spicq says that the concept of inheritance is a good messianic-eschatological one. *Op. cit.*, II, 5.

[70]*TWNT*, III, 779.

[71]*TWNT*, III, 782. Foerster interprets Matt. 5:5 as meaning the receiving of the riches of the lordship of God. It is not a piece of earth or a piece of heaven that is inherited but the fullness of life under the divine lordship. Sasse points out the messianic-eschatological meaning of "inheriting the earth." *TWNT*, I, 676.

[72]*TWNT*, III, 783.

[73]"In the New Testament [inheritance] gets the higher sense of the blessedness of the Messianic kingdom, the Christian's destined possession in the consummation of the kingdom of God." Salmond, *EGT*, III, 263.

[74]Even this adoption is eschatological, as the adoption of the body corresponds with the end-time glorification of the believer (Rom. 8:23).

[75]*TWNT*, III, 763 says this could mean the lots (i.e., congregations) assigned the bishops.

[76]*EGT*, III, 263.

[77]The future of inheriting is suggested in Col. 3:24, where it is associated with rewards; in Heb. 9:15, where our inheritance is called eternal; in Eph. 1:14, where we are sealed with the Spirit as an earnest until we shall receive our inheritance.

[78]Cf. "*prototokos*," *TWNT*, VI, 878.

[79]Sanday and Headlam, *op. cit.*, take *prototokos* to mean eldest born.

15

Thomas Summers

The Dogma
of Inamissible Grace Refuted

The Thesis to Be Defended

[We will show that the] saints may and do fall from grace: some partly but not totally or finally; some totally, but not finally; and others both totally and finally. And this will be shown by every kind of proof by which divine truth is set forth in the Holy Scriptures, as will appear by the following digest, or grammar, of some of the salient passages bearing on this subject.

Amissibility Set Forth in Scripture Didactically

The amissibility of grace is set forth by plain, positive didactic statement. Thus David tells Solomon: "If thou seek him, he will be found of thee; but if thou forsake him, he will cast thee off forever" (I Chron. 28:9). Thus Azariah told Asa: "The Lord is with you, while ye be with him; and if ye seek him, he will be found of you; but if ye forsake him, he will forsake you" (II Chron. 15:2). This principle of the divine government is articulately and emphatically laid down by God in the prophecy of Ezekiel:

From *Systematic Theology* (Nashville: Methodist Church Division of Higher Education, 1888), Vol. II, pp. 77–99.

"When the righteous turneth away from his righteousness, and committeth iniquity, and doeth according to all the abominations that the wicked man doeth, shall he live? All his righteousness that he hath done shall not be mentioned; in his trespass that he hath trespassed, and in his sin that he hath sinned, in them shall he die. Yet ye say, the way of the Lord is not equal. Hear now, O house of Israel, Is not my way equal? are not your ways unequal? When a righteous man turneth away from his righteousness, and committeth iniquity, and dieth in them; for his iniquity that he hath done shall he die. Again, when the wicked man turneth away from his wickedness that he hath committed, and doeth that which is lawful and right, he shall save his soul alive" (Ezek. 18:24–27). . . . We hazard nothing in saying that but for the powerful bias of a theological system, which has for one of its essential elements the inamissibility of grace, not a man upon earth would have ever dreamed of putting any other interpretation on these texts than that which lies on their very surface. They are also totally insusceptible of any other meaning. They relate facts as well known, that wicked men sometimes turn from their wickedness, and righteous men sometimes turn from their righteousness. The one case is no more hypothetical than the other; neither would have been stated with so much solemnity, and so often repeated, if the parties respectively could not possibly change their positions and characters. To say that those called righteous were not really righteous, and that their righteousness was self-righteousness, or some other factitious thing that was not good, is as absurd as it would be to say that those called wicked were not really wicked, and that their wickedness was not real, but factitious wickedness. If the wickedness of the latter was not real they ought not to turn from it; and if the righteousness of the former was not real righteousness they ought to turn from it; they will die if they do not. But the reward in the one case is life, and the penalty in the other case is death, whether temporal or eternal belongs not to this argument: only Universalists hold that those who die in their sins, as is said of these apostates, are nevertheless saved in the life eternal. But our Lord told the Jews that if they rejected him they should die in their sins, and he adds: "Whither I go ye cannot come" (John 8:21–24).

The principle in question is laid down explicitly by the apostle (II Peter 2:20–22): "For if after they have escaped the pollutions of the world through the knowledge of the Lord and Saviour Jesus Christ, they are again entangled therein, and overcome, the latter end is worse with them than the beginning. For it had been better for them not to have known the way of righteousness, than, after they have known it, to turn from the holy commandment delivered unto them. But it is happened unto them according to the true proverb, The dog is turned to his own vomit again; and the sow that has washed to her wallowing in the mire."

It speaks but little for the exegetical skill of those who say the knowledge of those apostates was "merely speculative, not experimental." If this be merely speculative knowledge, we wish there were more of it among men, as through it they would escape the pollutions of the world. Nay, this knowledge is eminently experimental and practical; it is the very same as that of which our Lords speaks in John 17:3, and the apostles in Ephesians 4; Philippians 3; I John 2:4; 3:6. And it speaks as little for the candor or common sense of those who say that these apostates were dogs and swine, and that notwithstanding their vomiting and washing their nature was never changed. This is to make, as Goodwin says, "parables or similitudes run on all fours." The only points of resemblance here are the vomiting and the cleaning, as Calvin clearly saw. "Suppose," says Goodwin, "a dog should, by casting up his vomit, be turned into a sheep, and afterward should, by a contrary means—viz., by resuming it—become a dog again; might it not truly and properly enough be said that this dog, though lately a sheep, is now become a dog again?" But it is humiliating to notice such pitiful subterfuges.

This passage agrees precisely with our Lord's declaration: "Ye are the salt of the earth; but if the salt have lost his savor, wherewith shall it be salted? it is thenceforth good for nothing, but to be cast out, and to be trodden under foot of men" (Matt. 5:13). At first view this passage seems to favor Novatianism, but it does not. It affirms that Christians may fall from grace, but it does not say that they cannot be reclaimed. The peculiar virtue of salt when once lost (as it may be) cannot be restored by any known process; it is worthless. If Christians whose business it is to purify the world fail to do so, and are corrupted by it, there is nothing in the world which can restore to them their purifying virtue; they become worthless as the world itself. He who first made the mineral can, indeed, impart to it afresh its saline property; so apostates can be restored by his grace, if they will avail themselves of it. But as the loss is total, so it may be, and frequently is, final.

> Ah, Lord, with trembling I confess
> A gracious soul may fall from grace;
> The salt may lose its seasoning power
> And never, never find it more.

Amissibility Implied in Positive Divine Injunctions

The amissibility of grace is implied in positive divine injunctions. By injunctions we mean commands, enjoining final perseverance, and interdicts of apostasy, with proper legislative sanctions. This is fully set forth in Hebrews 3, where the apostle is addressing "holy brethren, partakers of the heavenly calling" in Christ Jesus, "whose house are we, if we hold fast the confidence and the rejoicing of the hope firm unto the end." The injunctions given to these "holy brethren, partakers of the heavenly calling, the house of Christ," are of this tenor: "Wherefore as the Holy Ghost saith, To-day if ye will hear his voice, harden not your hearts, as in the provocation, in the day of temptation in the wilderness. . . . Take heed, brethren, lest there be in any of you an evil heart of unbelief, in departing from the living God. But exhort one another daily, while it is called To-day; lest any of you be hardened through the deceitfulness of sin. For we are made partakers of Christ, if we hold the beginning of our confidence steadfast unto the end; while it is said, To-day if ye will hear his voice, harden not your hearts, as in the provocation. . . . And to whom sware he that they should not enter into his rest, but to them that believed not? So we see that they could not enter in because of unbelief. Let us therefore fear, lest, a promise being left us of entering into his rest, any of you should seem to come short of it. . . . Let us labor therefore to enter into that rest, lest any man fall after the same example of unbelief. . . . Seeing then that we have a great High-priest, that is passed into the heavens, Jesus the Son of God, let us hold fast our profession'' (Heb. 3–4).

Here is the key-note of the Epistle to the Hebrews. All the exhortations, warnings, expostulations, and promises contained in the epistle are based upon this divine legislation. God commands us to persevere in faith and holiness; he forbids any dereliction under pain of exclusion from the heavenly rest. The plain English of it is simply this: Continue to the end of your lives in faith and obedience, and you will be saved; otherwise you will be lost forever. It is pitiful to see the torturing methods adopted to evade the force of this plain injunction. Apostates, say some, only *seem* to come short of entering heaven—though they really do enter, as none can finally fall from grace. But the apostle tells us what this seeming to come short means; it is obviously failing to enter heaven, just as those whose carcasses fell in the wilderness failed to enter Canaan. MacKnight, though a professed Calvinist, renders ''should actually fall short of it.'' He refers to his note on I Corinthians 7:40b, where he says:

> ''And I am certain that even I have the Spirit of God.'' The word δοκέω in this, as in many other passages, does not express *doubting,* but *certainty.* Thus 1 Cor. iv. 9: ''I am certain God hath.'' 1 Cor. viii. 2: ''If therefore any one is confident of knowing.'' Heb. iv. 1: ''Any of you should actually fall short.'' Mark x. 42: ''They who exercise rule.'' Luke viii. 18: ''What he really hath.'' 1 Cor. xi. 16: ''If any one resolves to be contentious.'' 1 Cor. xiv. 37: ''If any one really is a prophet.'' To show that the Greeks themselves used the word to denote *certainty* and *reality,* Dr. Pearce quotes Ulpian, in Demosth. Olynth. i., who says: ''Δοκεῖν is used by the ancients, not always to express what is doubtful, but likewise to express what is certain.'' From these examples it is evident that the word δυκέω in this verse does not imply that the apostle was in any doubt whether he was inspired in giving this judgment: it is only a soft way of expressing his certain knowledge of his own inspiration, and may have been used in irony of the false teacher, who called his inspiration in question.

Dr. Moses Stuart, of the same school, in his note on Hebrews 4:1, says:

> Lest any of you may fail of obtaining it. By sacred and classical usage δοκέω is frequently joined with other verbs, without making any *essential* addition to the sense of them. It is said, therefore, to be used *pleonastically;* by which, however, can be meant only that it is incapable of being precisely rendered into our own language, and *apparently* adds

nothing essential to the sense of a phrase. But even this is not exactly true of δοκέω. In many cases it is plainly designed to soften the expression to which it is attached—*e.g.*, 1 Cor. vii. 40, Paul says: "I seem to myself to possess the Spirit of God"—a modest way of asserting the fact, instead of speaking categorically. In a similar way δοκέω in 1 Cor. xiv. 37; x. 12: "He who seems to himself to stand"; iii. 18; iv. 9. In a few cases it is difficult to distinguish what addition is made to the phrase by the use of δοκέω—*e.g.*, Luke xxii. 24—δοκεῖ εἶναι=εἴη. So Luke viii. 18; ὁ δοκεῖ ἔχειν is expressed in Luke xix. 26 by ὁ ἔχει; 1 Cor. xi. 16. There can scarcely be a doubt, however, that in all cases the Greeks designed to give some coloring to a sentence by employing it. It would often seem to be something near to our *may, might, can, could,* etc., when used to soften forms of expression that might have been categorical. So Theophylact understood it in our phrase; he thus explains: "lest he may come short, and fail to enter into the promised rest." The writer uses a *mild and gentle address,* not saying μὴ ὑστερήσῃ, but μὴ δοκῇ ὑστερηκέναι. This, I apprehended, is hitting the exact force of the phrase here, an imperfect view of which is given in the lexicons.

If in these cases δοχέω be not absolutely expletive, it must be confessed as Stewart says, it is difficult to render it in English. If it does not strengthen the term, it surely does not weaken it.

Bloomfield renders: "Let us then be afraid lest, though there be a promise left us of entering into his rest, any of you should be found (lit. 'be deemed') to have fallen short of it." He says:

> I find this view of the sense confirmed by the Peschito Syriac, Vulgate, and Arabic versions and the best modern expositors; and it also seems required by the context, and the *usus linguae* as to καταλείπω, which, as it is used by Polybius, often of a *hope,* by others of an inheritance, so may it of a *promise;* especially, since the promise here has reference to the heavenly inheritance. Besides the sense, "a promise being still *left,*" is far more agreeable to the context, implying that the promised rest had not yet been enjoyed, but was *left* for others to enter upon. The above reading of δοκῆ is confirmed by the Peschito Syriac version, and by an able paraphrase. However, the full sense is, "should be *deemed by the event*"—a mild expression, intended to soften the harshness of the term ὑστερηκέναι, implying utter failure, usually by neglect.

If δοκῇ be not merely expletive, or used *urbanely,* it means to *appear, to be obvious,* which is what Bloomfield means by "deemed by the event." Apostates not only fail, but obviously fail to enter into the heavenly rest.

An apology is perhaps due for dwelling so long upon so clear a case, but it is found in the fact that it absolutely settles this question. God commands us to persevere, and threatens us that if we do not persevere, upon his oath, we shall not enter into his rest. Well may we have the *fear* which begets caution and diligent effort, as this serious warning is no empty threat. "Vengeance is mine: I will repay, saith the Lord; and again, The Lord will judge his people"—"will condemn and punish his apostatizing people," as Bloomfield and others interpret Hebrews 10:30.

This gives force to the injunction of the apostle, addressed to "all the saints in Christ Jesus, at Philippi, with the bishops and deacons": "Wherefore, my beloved, as ye have always obeyed, not as in my presence only, but now much more in my absence, work out your own salvation with fear and trembling: for it is God which worketh in you both to will and to do of his good pleasure. . . . holding forth the word of life; that I may rejoice in the day of Christ, that I have not run in vain, neither labored in vain" (Phil. 2:12-16). He gives this injunction to "saints," who could work out their own salvation, because God worked in them, and who for that very reason were bound to do so—and that with fear and trembling, lest they might prove delinquent, and so the apostle's labor, so far as they were concerned, should be lost; whereas if they complied with the injunction he should have the great privilege of rejoicing over their salvation in the day of Christ, that is, the day of final retribution. Can anything be more explicit than this?

Then look at the "commandment" to fidelity, so often repeated in "the final document of the New Testament"—The First Epistle of John—*e.g.*: "My little children, these things write I unto you, that ye sin not. . . . I have not written unto you because ye know not the truth, but because ye know it. . . . Let that therefore abide in you, which ye have heard from the beginning. If that which ye have heard from the beginning shall remain in you, ye also shall continue in the Son, and in the Father. And this is the promise that he hath promised us, even eternal life. These things have I written unto you concerning them that seduce you. . . . And now little children, abide in him; that, when he shall appear, we may have confidence, and not be ashamed before him at his coming" (I John 2).

The beloved disciple must indeed have been in his dotage—inspiration being out of the question—if he took so much pains to command his spiritual children to do what they could not help doing, and not to do what they could not help avoiding, and that under the peril of losing what was inamissibly secured to them. But we should have to transcribe a large portion of the Scriptures if we were to adduce all the passages which enjoin perseverance in piety as the condition of ultimate salvation.

Amissibility Implied in Exhortations to Perseverance

The amissibility of grace is implied in the exhortations to perseverance, with which the Scriptures abound. These exhortations are so numerous that one knows not where to begin or end in citing them. They are coupled, too, with dehortations from apostasy, of the most pointed character. Thus our Lord says repeatedly to his disciples: "Take ye heed, watch and pray. . . . Watch ye therefore; for ye know not when the master of the house cometh . . . lest coming suddenly he find you sleeping. And what I say unto you I say unto all, Watch. . . . Watch ye and pray, that ye enter not into temptation" (Mark 13-14). "Exhorting them to continue in the faith" (Acts 14:22). "Take heed therefore unto yourselves, and to all the flock, over the which the Holy Ghost hath made you overseers, to feed the church of God, which he hath purchased with his own blood. For I know this, that after my departing shall grievous wolves enter in among you, not sparing the flock. Also of your own selves shall men arise, speaking perverse things, to draw away disciples after them. Therefore watch, and remember, that by the space of three years I ceased not to warn every one night and day with tears" (Acts 20:28–31). Yet there was no possibility of their seduction to error and sin and final ruin! Paul might have spared his exhortations, and also his toils and tears!

"Be not overcome of evil, but overcome evil with good" (Rom 12:21). "It is high time to wake out of sleep: for now is our salvation nearer than when we believed. . . . Let us therefore cast off the works of darkness, and let us put on the armor of light. . . . But put ye on the Lord Jesus Christ, and make not provision for the flesh to fulfill the lusts thereof" (Rom. 13:11–14). What impertinent, supererogatory counsels are these, if *believers*, as those were whom Paul addressed, cannot fall into the scandalous sins against which they are here admonished. Truly those who do not cast off these works of darkness will be cast into outer darkness, which will be felt to be the more horrible because they once walked in the light.

"Know ye not that they which run in a race run all, but one receiveth the prize? So run, that ye may obtain. And every man that striveth for the mastery is temperate in all things. Now they do it to obtain a corruptible crown; but we an incorruptible. I therefore so run, not as uncertainly; so fight I, not as one that beateth the air: but I keep under my body, and bring it into subjection; lest that by any means, when I have preached to others, I myself should be a castaway" (I Cor. 9:24–27). Why should Paul urge the Corinthian believers to run that race and gain the crown if they could not help running, or whether they ran or not could not fail to get the crown? And why should he set himself before them as an example—exercising himself with the greatest diligence and godly fear, lest after being a herald to other athletes, he himself should be hurled from the stadium as vanquished in the contest, if there were no possibility of failure? "Therefore, my beloved brethren, be ye steadfast, unmovable, always abounding in the work of the Lord, forasmuch as ye know that your labor is not in vain in the Lord" (I Cor. 15:58). Why exhort his "beloved brethren" thus to perseverance in their "labor," if there was no danger of their ceasing to labor and losing their reward?

"We then, as workers together with him, beseech you also that ye receive not the grace of God in vain" (II Cor. 6:1). Why this exhortation, if grace be inamissible? How can it be received in vain, if it infallibly secures our salvation? "And let us not be weary in well-doing: for in due season we shall reap, if we faint not" (Gal. 6:9). Why this exhortation, if we cannot faint? or whether we faint or not, we shall be sure to reap?

After exhorting the Ephesians to abstain from the gross vices of the heathen around them, the apostle says: "Let no man deceive you with vain words; for because of these things cometh the wrath of God upon the children of disobedience. Be not ye therefore partakers with them. For ye were sometimes darkness, but now are ye light in the Lord: walk as children of the light. . . . See then that ye walk circumspectly: not as fools, but as wise. . . . Finally, my brethren, be strong in the Lord, and in the power of his might. Put on the whole armor of God, that ye may be able to stand against the wiles of the devil'' (Eph. 5-6). Why all these exhortations, if the Ephesians could not be overcome by the world, the flesh, and the devil? if there was no possibility of their being partakers with the wicked in their sins and punishment?

"Ye know how we exhorted and comforted and charged every one of you, as a father doth his children, that ye would walk worthy of God, who hath called you unto his kingdom and glory'' (I Thess. 2:11, 12). Why all this exhorting, comforting, and charging, if they could not help so walking, and if they could not fail of "his kingdom and glory"? Then see how the apostle exhorts the Thessalonian brethren in the close of this Epistle— precisely as if he knew they were both to fall into the sins which are there specified, and to neglect the duties which are there prescribed: would there be any sense or consistency in his doing so, if such had not been the case?

After calling attention to the worthies who had successfully run their race, the apostle thus exhorts the Hebrew Christians: "Wherefore, seeing we also are compassed about with so great a cloud of witnesses, let us lay aside every weight, and the sin which doth so easily beset us, and let us run with patience [perseverance] the race that is set before us, looking unto Jesus the author and finisher of our faith . . . lest ye be wearied and faint in your minds. Ye have not yet resisted unto blood, striving against sin. And ye have forgotten the exhortation which speaketh unto you as unto children. My son, despise not thou the chastening of the Lord, nor faint when thou art rebuked of him. . . . Wherefore lift up the hands which hang down, and the feeble knees; and make straight paths for your feet, lest that which is lame be turned out of the way; but let it rather be healed. Follow peace with all men, and holiness, without which no man shall see the Lord: looking diligently lest any man fail of the grace of God. . . . Wherefore we receiving a kingdom which cannot be moved, let us have grace, whereby we may serve God acceptably with reverence and godly fear: for our God is a consuming fire'' (Heb. 12). What sense or pertinency is there in these exhortations, if the readers' perseverance in the Christian race was certain, absolute, inevitable—if they could not fail of the grace of God, fall behind in the race, and so lose the prize? (Cf. Rom 3:23; Heb. 4:1).

"Wherefore, beloved, seeing ye look for such things, be diligent that ye may be found of him in peace, without spot and blameless. . . . Ye therefore, beloved, seeing ye know these things before, beware lest ye also, being led away with the error of the wicked, fall from your own steadfastness. But grow in grace, and in the knowledge of our Lord and Savior Jesus Christ'' (II Peter 3:14–18). Why should the condition of future retribution move them to diligence? Why should they beware of seduction and apostasy? Why should they be so concerned to grow in grace, if they could not lose it, and fail of their reward? Peter evidently agreed with his "beloved brother Paul,'' and the beloved disciple John, who exhorts his converts:

"Look to yourselves, that we lose not those things which we have wrought, but that we receive a full reward" (II John 8). Why should they beware of losing what cannot be lost? No matter which reading is adopted—*we* or *ye*—it is clear that the apostle considered that the reward might be lost. By saying a full reward, Bloomfield suggests that "πλήρη hints at *some* reward that the teacher would receive in the other case; which, indeed, were but just, since disciples may apostatize and bring discredit on the master, without his being to blame."

Amissibility Implied in the Expostulations Concerning Apostasy

The amissibility of grace is implied in the expostulations in regard to apostasy, with which the Scriptures abound. How pathetic are these expostulations in Ezekiel 3, 18, and 33. "Why will ye die, O house of Israel? The righteousness of the righteous shall not deliver him in the day of his transgression. . . . When I shall say to the righteous, that he shall surely live: if he trust to his own righteousness, and commit iniquity, all his righteousness shall not be remembered; but for his iniquity that he hath committed, he shall die for it." How often is this repeated by God in this prophecy, ending thus: "Yet ye say, The way of the Lord is not equal. O ye house of Israel, I will judge you every one after his ways." We have already noticed the principle of the divine government here recognized; the point now to be regarded is the great stress which is here laid upon it. It would seem that the Holy Spirit foresaw the error in question, and took this method to refute it. How strange that it should be revived and perpetuated in these last days!

How did our Lord expostulate with his disciples in regard to apostasy, of which many are guilty: "Will ye also go away?" (John 6:66, 67). He knew that there was one of the twelve that would apostatize, and this gave force to his expostulation.

The apostle, writing to the Corinthians, says: "Through thy knowledge shall the weak brother perish, for whom Christ died? But when ye sin so against the brethren, and wound their weak conscience, ye sin against Christ. Wherefore, if meat make my brother to offend, I will eat no meat while the world standeth" (I Cor. 8:11–13). Only one sense can be attached to these words. The apostle expostulates with the Corinthians on behalf of the weak brethren, that they should be exceedingly careful not to cause them to stumble, and thus those for whom Christ died should be caused to *perish*. (Cf. Rom. 14:21).

Hear how the apostle expostulates with the Galatians: "I marvel that ye are so soon removed from him that called you into the grace of Christ unto another gospel, which is not another" (Gal. 1:6, 7). "O foolish Galatians, who hath bewitched you, that ye should not obey the truth, before whose eyes Jesus Christ hath been evidently set forth, crucified among you? This only would I learn of you, Received ye the Spirit by the works of the law, or by the hearing of faith? Are ye so foolish? having begun in the Spirit, are ye now made perfect by the flesh?" (Gal. 3:1–3). "Stand fast therefore in the liberty wherewith Christ hath made us free, and be not entangled again with the yoke of bondage. Behold, I Paul say unto you, that if ye be circumcised, Christ shall profit you nothing. . . . Christ is become of no effect unto you, whosoever of you are justified by the law; ye are fallen from grace. . . . Ye did run well; who did hinder you that ye should not obey the truth? . . . Be not deceived; God is not mocked: for whatsoever a man soweth, that shall he also reap. For he that soweth to the flesh shall of the flesh reap corruption; but he that soweth to the Spirit shall of the Spirit reap life everlasting. And let us not be weary in well-doing: for in due season we shall reap if we faint not'' (Gal. 5–6). But the whole Epistle is a continued expostulation with the Galatians in regard to apostasy, into which many of them had fallen and of which the rest were in imminent danger. They did run well, but were hindered; they had sown to the Spirit, but were now sowing to the flesh, and the apostle expostulates with them on their sad defection, urging them to start afresh in the divine life, as it was necessary for them to be born again, so completely had they—at least many of them—gone back to their unregenerate state. How touchingly he addresses them: ''Where is then the blessedness ye spoke of? for I bear you record, that, if it had been possible, ye would have plucked out your own eyes, and have given them to me. . . . My little children, of whom I travail in birth again until Christ be formed in you, I desire to be present with you now, and to change my voice; for I stand in doubt of you'' (Gal. 4). Why doubt if they could not fall from grace (which he says was the case with them). or, having fallen, could not possibly fail to rise again, no matter how deep they sunk into sin, or how long they wallowed in it! The expostulations of this Epistle call to mind those of the Prophet Hosea. How tenderly, pathetically, powerfully does God address himself to his backsliding people: ''Ephraim is joined to idols; let him alone'' (Hos. 4:17). This is addressed to Judah, to keep him from going into the worship of false gods, as Ephraim had done. ''O Ephraim, what shall I do unto thee? O Judah, what shall I do unto thee? for your goodness is as a morning cloud, and as the early dew it goeth away. . . . How shall I give thee up, Ephraim? . . . O Israel, return unto the Lord thy God, for thou hast fallen by thine iniquity'' (Hos. 6, 14). And so from the beginning to the end.

All these expostulations—for what? If they could not fall, then they were not fallen. If fallen and yet could not be lost, then they must rise, and would rise without all this ado.

Amissibility Implied in the Warnings Against Apostasy

The amissibility of grace is implied in the warnings against apostasy, with which the Scriptures abound. Many of these warnings have been already noticed under the preceding heads. How pregnantly does Christ repeat the warning concerning the salt losing its savor: ''Salt is good: but if the salt have lost his savor, wherewith shall it be seasoned? It is neither fit for the land, nor for the dunghill; but men cast it out. He that hath ears to hear, let him hear'' (Luke 14: 34, 35; cf. Matt. 5:13; Mark 9:50).

See how the apostle warns the Gentiles, who, like wild olive-branches, had been grafted into the good olive tree, in place of the Jews, the natural branches: "Because of unbelief they were broken off, and thou standest by faith. Be not highminded, but fear: for if God spared not the natural branches, take heed lest he also spare not thee. Behold therefore the goodness and severity of God: on them which fell, severity; but toward thee, goodness, if thou continue in his goodness: otherwise thou also shalt be cut off" (Rom. 11:20–23). Does that mean nothing? Is that a warning against an impossibility?

Read I Corinthians 10:1–12. Here the apostle speaks of the "fathers" as baptized into the covenant of Moses, and sharing in all its blessings. "But with many of them God was not well pleased; for they were overthrown in the wilderness. Now these things were our examples, to the intent we should not lust after evil things, as they also lusted. Neither be ye idolaters... neither let us commit fornication... neither let us tempt Christ ... neither murmur ye, as some of them also murmured, and were destroyed of the destroyer. Now all these things happened unto them for ensamples; and they are written for our admonition, upon whom the ends of the world are come. Wherefore, let him that thinketh he standeth take heed lest he fall." Why this admonition? why adduce all these "examples" (τύποι). types, if there was no danger of our imitating them? Why admonish us to stand, and to take heed lest we fall, if we cannot help standing, if we cannot fall? And why warn us against falling after the example of those who fall to rise no more, if there were no danger, no possibility of our so doing?

In his Epistle to the Hebrews. as we have seen, the apostle reverts to the same melancholy examples of final apostasy, and warns the Christians against their imitation. These warnings are repeated in that Epistle with the utmost earnestness and vehemence. "Cast not away therefore your confidence," says he, "which hath great recompense of reward. For ye have need of patience, that after ye have done the will of God, ye might receive the promise.... Now the just shall live by faith; but if any man draw back, my soul shall have no pleasure in him. But we are not of them who draw back unto perdition; but of them that believe to the saving of the soul" (Heb. 10:35–39). The thirty-eighth verse ought to have been simply rendered: "But if he shall draw back," namely, the just man who lives by faith. We are disinclined to charge the translators with Calvinistic leanings in their translation, though it is difficult to free them from that charge in this place and in Hebrews 6:6: "If they shall fall away" for "And fall away." The passage shows clearly that the just man who then lived by his faith might cast away his shield and draw back from the field; and the apostle speaks of some who did thus draw back even to perdition, though he hoped that those whom he addressed would not prove to be of that number, but of those who continue to believe to the saving of the soul. His reason for that hope is given in the sixth chapter: no fancied decrees of predestination, no dream about the inamissibility of grace; but their continued obedience, which he desired that they should show "with diligence to the full assurance of hope unto the end: that ye be not slothful, but followers of them who through faith and patience inherit the promises.'' Can language be more explicit? Can warnings be more earnest or indicate more danger?

Then listen to the warnings given by Christ from the throne of his glory to the Seven Apocalyptic Churches. He says all the good he can of them, but hear him to the Church of Ephesus: ''Nevertheless, I have somewhat against thee, because thou hast left thy first love. Remember therefore from whence thou art fallen, and repent, and do the first works; or else I will come unto thee quickly, and will remove thy candlestick out of his place, except thou repent.'' So he had a few things against the Church in Pergamos, and warns them accordingly: ''Repent, or else I will come unto thee quickly, and I will fight against them with the sword of my mouth.'' So to the Church at Sardis and at Laodicea, whom he threatened with vengeance if they did not repent, and to spew them out of his mouth, if they continued in their lukewarm or backslidden state. What was the design of these warnings? To excite them to fear where no fear was? to operate irresistibly to secure the end desired? We defy any man to show where this was ever God's design in warning men from apostasy and ruin; and whether or not it was so in this case let the result show. That these things, too, were written for our admonition there can be no doubt, for every Epistle closes with this solemn *finale*: ''He that hath ears to hear, let him hear what the Spirit saith unto the Churches'' (Rev. 2-3).

See how earnestly Paul warns the Corinthians: ''Would to God ye would bear with me a little in my folly: and indeed bear with me. For I am jealous over you with a godly jealousy. . . . But I fear, lest by any means, as the serpent beguiled Eve through his subtlety, so your minds should be corrupted from the simplicity that is in Christ'' (II Cor. 11:1-3). We know how Eve was deceived; we know how through her Adam fell, and so, says the apostle, I warn you not to be so ensnared by Satan's devices. (Cf. II Cor. 12:19-21).

So Peter warns us against the enemy when he comes in another manner: ''Be sober, be vigilant; because your adversary the devil, as a roaring lion, walketh about, seeking whom he may devour: whom resist steadfast in the faith'' (I Peter 5:8. 9).

But enough, though there is no end to such warnings—while every one of them, even the least, would be an impertinence if the grace of God were inamissible.

Amissibility Implied in the Rewards Promised to Perseverance

The inamissibility of grace is implied in the promises of reward if we persevere to the end. This is the tenor of them all: ''He that shall endure unto the end, the same shall be saved'' (Matt. 24:13). ''Then said Jesus to those Jews which believed on him, If ye continue in my word, then are ye my disciples indeed; and ye shall know the truth, and the truth shall make you free'' (John 8:31, 32). ''Brethren, if any of you do err from the truth, and one convert him; let him know, that he which converteth the sinner from the error of his way shall save a soul from death, and shall hide a multitude of sins" (James 5:19, 20). "Be thou faithful unto death, and I will give thee a crown of life" (Rev. 2:10). "Whereby are given unto us exceeding great and precious promises, that by these ye might be partakers of the divine nature, having escaped the corruption that is in the world through lust. And beside this, giving all diligence, add to your faith virtue; and to virture, knowledge; and to knowledge, temperance; and to temperance, patience; and to patience, godliness; and to godliness, brotherly kindness; and to brotherly kindness, charity. For if these things be in you, and abound, they make you that ye shall neither be barren nor unfruitful in the knowledge of our Lord Jesus Christ. But he that lacketh these things is blind, and cannot see afar off, and hath forgotten that he was purged from his old sins. Wherefore the rather, brethren, give diligence to make your calling and election sure; for if ye do these things ye shall never fall: for so an entrance shall be ministered unto you abundantly into the everlasting kingdom of our Lord and Savior Jesus Christ" (II Peter 1:4–11). If there were not another syllable on the subject in holy writ, this pregnant passage would settle the question. There is no torturing it into anything else. It makes no sense at all, if grace be inamissible. Here are some, with whom the faithful are contrasted, who had forgotten that they were purged from their old sins, that is, they had so far relapsed into their state before conversion that their Christian state was passed over as a parenthesis scarcely to be noticed. But the "brethren"—the only place in the Epistle where they are so addressed—are encouraged to hold on to their religion and be faithful to the end, by the promise of a glorious triumph—which is the meaning of the entrance ministered abundantly into the everlasting kingdom: like conquerers they should drive in state through the gates, enlarged for the occasion, into the city. (Cf. Rev. 22:14). If they *add* (that is, *supply,* ἐπιχορηγήσατε) what is necessary to constitute a fully developed Christian character, God will *minister* (that is, *supply,* the same word, ἐπιχορηγηοήσεται) what is necessary for their triumph. These promises were given to stimulate them to final perseverance, to make their calling and election sure. What sense would there be to encourage them to do so by these promises, if they could not possibly fail? There are no *ifs* and *buts* about it, no room for promissory incentives to perseverance any more than for warnings from defection. If grace be inamissible the whole is a grand impertinence.

Amissibility Implied in the Prayers for Perseverance

The amissibility of grace is implied in the prayers for perseverance, with which the Scriptures abound. These prayers are deprecatory, looking to apostasy as not only possible, but certain, unless great assistance be afforded to prevent it; supplicatory, earnestly imploring persevering grace; and intercessory, offered for the perseverance of others. We can give only a few specimens. David prays, when penitent for his apostasy: "Create in me a clean heart, O God; and renew a right spirit within me. Cast me not away from thy presence; and take not thy Holy Spirit from me. Restore unto me the joy of thy salvation; and uphold me with thy free Spirit" (Ps. 51:10-12). "Uphold me according unto thy word, that I may live; and let me not be ashamed of my hope. Hold thou me up, and I shall be safe: and I will have respect unto thy statutes continually" (Ps. 119:116, 117). "Wherefore also we pray always for you, that our God would count you worthy of this calling, and fulfill all the good pleasure of his goodness, and the work of faith with power: that the name of our Lord Jesus Christ may be glorified in you, and ye in him, according to the grace of our God and the Lord Jesus Christ" (II Thess. 1:11, 12). "And the Lord said, Simon, Simon, behold, Satan hath desired to have you, that he may sift you as wheat: but I have prayed for thee, that thy faith fail not: and when thou art converted, strengthen thy brethren" (Luke 22:31, 32). "Holy Father, keep through thine own name those whom thou hast given me, that they may be one, as we are. . . . I pray not that thou shouldst take them out of the world, but that thou shouldst keep them from the evil" (John 17:11-15).

We need hardly say that neither our own prayers for ourselves, nor the intercessory prayers of others for us, including those of our great Advocate and High-priest, will keep us from falling, and secure our final persever-ance, without our voluntary concurrence with the gracious influence brought to bear upon us in answer to prayer. If this principle be not admitted, then no sinner could ever continue a moment in sin, and no saint could ever fall. In default of this, many prayers return to the bosom of those who offer them; they are not offered in vain, though they fail to effect the result intended. But it would be preposterous to pray for a thing in itself impossible, or for a thing absolutely inevitable.

Amissibility Demonstrated by Scriptural Examples of Apostasy

The amissibility of grace is demonstrated by the examples of apostasy recorded in the Scriptures, to say nothing of those that come under our personal observation. Saul, the king of Israel, was undoubtedly a good man, and was specially favored by heaven. Thus Samuel said to him: "The Spirit of the Lord will come upon thee, and thou shalt prophesy with them, and shalt be turned into another man. And let it be, when these signs are come unto thee, that thou do as occasion serve thee; for God is with thee" (I Sam. 10:6, 7).

But Saul fell from grace. "And when Saul inquired of the Lord, the Lord answered him not." And Samuel told him: "The Lord is departed from thee, and is become thine enemy," as he was before with him and was his friend. The result is known. He was overcome by his enemies. "Therefore Saul took a sword and fell upon it. . . . So Saul died" (I Sam. 28, 31). Comment is unnecessary. His fall was final.

David was an eminent saint. Yet David fell into adultery, lying, hypoc-risy, and murder, of the foulest kind. His apostasy was total. He seemed to be in a state of utter hardness and impenitency for a twelvemonth, when he was aroused to a sense of his dreadful condition, and the fifty-first Psalm is a record of his bitter repentance: "Make me to hear joy and gladness; that the bones which thou hast broken may rejoice. Hide thy face from my sins, and blot out all my iniquities. Create in me a clean heart, O God; and renew a right spirit within me." If he had died during that appalling period of his history he would have been damned like any other adulterer and murderer, and would have had his portion with hypocrites and liars: we know what that is.

Then there was his son Solomon, named also Jedidiah, that is, "Beloved of the Lord" (II Sam. 12:24, 25). "And Solomon loved the Lord, walking in the statutes of David his father" (I Kings 3:3). It is needless to descant upon his excellent piety, his superlative wisdom, his divine inspiration. He was high in the favor of God. But see how he fell. Look at him with his thousand idolatrous wives and concubines, building altars for their outlandish gods, and bowing down and worshiping them; oppressing his subjects, and bringing down upon his hoary head the curses of God and man. His fall was total; whether it was final no man can tell. We know what he himself said: "He, that being often reproved hardeneth his neck, shall suddenly be destroyed, and that without remedy" (Prov. 29:1). "The backslider in heart shall be filled with his own ways" (Prov. 14:14).

Judas was once a good man: as far as appears from the history, on a par with the other apostles. He was called by Christ to the apostolate; he was endowed with miraculous powers; he was admitted into the society of Christ and his chosen disciples, and shared his most intimate friendship. Yet Judas proved a traitor. Satan entered into him, and for thirty pieces of silver he betrayed his Lord. The Savior speaks of him as lost: "Those that thou gavest me I have kept, and none of them is lost, but the son of perdition" (John 17:12). What a loss! What a fall! Thus Peter and the other apostles and disciples speak of him as falling from this ministry and apostleship by transgression, that he might go—or so that he went—to his own place (Acts 1:25). How sad is the record of his apostasy, which was both total and final: "Then Judas, which had betrayed him, when he saw that he was condemned, repented himself, and brought again the thirty pieces of silver to the chief priests and elders, saying, I have sinned in that I have betrayed the innocent blood. And they said, What is that to us? see thou to that. And he cast down the pieces of silver in the temple, and departed, and went and hanged himself" (Matt. 27:3–5).

Then there was Peter. Surely he was an apostate; for he denied his Lord with bitter imprecations. Whether, as casuists dispute, his sin was one of infirmity or of presumption, all admit it was not a sin of ignorance. Peter sinned against the clearest light, the richest love, the highest professions, and the most timely warnings. The turpitude of his sin is seen in the intensity of his repentance: Peter wept bitterly. His triple denial calls for a triple attestation of his love when "restored by reconciling grace." His fall, if total, was not final, as he soon repented of his foul revolt.

From his bitter experience Peter was prepared to warn Christians against apostasy. He speaks of some who had known the way of righteousness, and turned from it: whose latter end was worse than the beginning, so they had returned to their vomit and to their wallowing in the mire of their unregenerate state; so that it would have been better for them not to have known the way of righteousness. If this is not a total and a final revolt we know not what can be.

Paul says explicitly of the Galatians that they had "fallen from grace." We have no assurance that they were recovered from their fall; but if they were, it was by the same repentance, faith, and regeneration by which they were first put into a state of grace.

The immoral Corinthian whom the apostle excluded from the Church because of his vile conduct, would have been lost forever if he had not bitterly repented of his sin and been restored by renewing grace.

In I Timothy 1:19, 20 Paul speaks of Hymeneus and Alexander, who concerning faith had made shipwreck (and everybody knows what shipwreck means), and had put away both faith and a good conscience. Surely it will not be disputed that they had fallen from grace totally. Whether their fall was final we cannot tell. Paul says he "delivered [them] unto Satan, that they [might] learn not to blaspheme," that is, he cast them out of the Church, that by this censure they might learn the enormity of their offense and be brought to repentance. Whether they repented we cannot tell. In the Second Epistle to Timothy (2:17, 18) Paul says that Hymeneus and Philetus erred concerning the truth by saying that the resurrection is past already and thus overthrowing the faith of some. "Alexander the coppersmith did me much evil: the Lord reward him according to his works: of whom be thou ware also; for he hath greatly withstood our words" (II Tim. 4:14, 15). Surely this was a shipwreck of the faith, total and, we should think, final also.

We need scarcely revert to the Hebrew apostates spoken of in Hebrews 6:4–6. Paul says expressly that men who were saints of no ordinary attainments "fell away"—which is the literal rendering of the aorist, which our translators unfortunately render "if they shall fall away." This rendering is deeply to be regretted, as it is very difficult to conceive how it could be made without a dogmatic bias. Macknight, who was a professed Calvinist, says:

> The verbs φωτισθέντας, γευσαμένους, and γενηθέντας, being aorists, are rightly rendered by our translators in the past time—*who were enlightened, have tasted, were made partakers.* Wherefore παραπεσόντας, being an aorist, ought likewise to have been translated in the past time, *have fallen away.* Nevertheless our translators, following Beza, who without any authority from ancient MSS. hath inserted in his version the word, *Si, If,* have rendered this clause, *If they fell away,* that this text might not appear to contradict the doctrine of the perseverance of the saints. But as no translator should take upon him to add to, or alter the Scriptures, for the sake of any favorite doctrine, I have translated παραπεσόντας in the past tense, *have fallen away,* according to the true import of the word as standing in connection with the aorists in the preceding verses. Further, as παραπεσόντας is put in opposition to what

goes before in the fourth and fifth verses, the conjunction καί, with which it is introduced, must have here its adversative signification—*and yet have fallen away.*

Wall, in his note on this verse, says:

I know of none but Beza whom the English translators could follow. The Vulgate hath, *et prolapsi sunt*; the Syriac, *qui rursum peccaverunt*; Castalio, *et tamen relabuntur*. The word παραπεσόντας, literally signifies *have fallen down.* But is is rightly translated *have fallen away,* because the apostle is speaking not of any common lapse, but of apostasy from the Christian faith. See Heb. x. 29, where a further display of the evil of apostasy is made.

This is judicious. It might be better, perhaps, to render the aorist as Rotherham renders it, "and who fell away," which makes it more distinctively refer to actual apostasy. The persons in question were well known as apostates from the faith and are spoken of accordingly. Their fall was total and it would seem final also, as was that of some of the other apostates named.

Amissibility Inculcated in Parables of Our Lord

The amissibility of grace is inculcated in several of our Lord's parables. In the parable of the sower this doctrine is clearly exhibited. There are four descriptions of ground cultivated. The sower is the same; the seed is the same in all cases. The intention of the husbandman is the same: he sows in order to get a crop. In one case the seed takes no root; in another case, it brings forth a harvest; but in two intermediate cases it takes root and grows, but fails to come to perfection; and in both these cases the fault is entirely in the soil. Thorns and stones occasion the failure.

Now, we must not make the parable run on all fours. It was not within its province to set forth the operation of prevenient grace, necessary in every case to prepare the soil for the reception and development of the seed. The wayside hearer might have improved that grace so as to have profited by the word. The stony-ground and thorny-ground hearers might have so improved that grace as to bring forth fruit to perfection, as did those who are represented by the good ground—made good by that same grace duly improved. They began well, but fell from grace, and proved as fruitless in the end as those who never used the grace at all.

The parable of the vine and its branches teaches the same lesson: "I am the true vine, and my Father is the husbandman. Every branch in me that beareth not fruit he taketh away. . . . If a man abide not in me, he is cast forth as a branch, and is withered; and men gather them, and cast them into the fire, and they are burned. If ye abide in me, and my words abide in you, ye shall ask what ye will, and it shall be done unto you. Herein is my Father glorified, that ye bear much fruit; so shall ye be my disciples. As the Father hath loved me, so have I loved you: continue ye in my love" (John

15:1-9). As no torturing can set aside this testimony, so no comment is needed to explain it. All the branches were in the vine; they belonged to it. Some ceased to imbibe the sap from the trunk, ceased to be fruitful, ceased to live; they are cut off from the vine; they are burned in the fire. If this is not total and final apostasy, what is it? and what is total and final apostasy? And if this is not the teaching of the parable, what does it teach? If the disciples to whom the parable was addressed were not liable to become barren and unfruitful, why address the parable to them? If they could not fail to continue in the Savior's love, why set forth this parable to show the fearful consequences of a failure so to do? Why tell them, "If ye keep my commandments, ye shall abide in my love"? They would abide in his love in any case, they could not get out of it, if grace be inamissible. Once in the vine, never out of it; once in grace, always in grace!

But if there were nothing else in the Scriptures touching this subject but the parable of the unmerciful servant, that would settle the question beyond controversy. A servant owed his lord ten thousand talents; he could not pay the debt; he asked to have it remitted, and it was forgiven. His fellow-servant owed him a hundred pence. He inexorably demanded payment; whereupon his lord said to him: "O thou wicked servant, I forgave thee all that debt, because thou desiredst me: shouldst not thou also have had compassion on thy fellow-servant, even as I had pity on thee? And his lord was wroth, and delivered him to the tormentors, till he should pay all that was due unto him." Suppose the moral of this parable had not been given by the Savior, could any man have been at a loss for the application? We hazard nothing in saying that no man could miss the meaning and design of the parable, unless warped by dogmatic prejudice. But our Lord gives us the moral; he delivers the lesson: "So likewise shall my heavenly Father do also unto you, if ye from your hearts forgive not every one his brother their trespasses" (Matt. 18:23-25). Do what? to whom? The answers to these questions settle the controversy.

16

G. C. Berkouwer

The Reality of Perseverance

[Some people may have the impression that it is possible to distinguish the idea and the reality of perseverance. We hasten to say that this is impossible.] The correlation between faith and the salvation of the Lord is precisely of such a nature that it is impossible to speak separately of faith and then only afterward to proceed to reality. The Reformation affirmation of *sola fide* might seem, to someone who does not accept it, as merely a narrow fideism or solipsism, with no relation to reality. But faith is concerned with nothing else than reality. Perhaps it does not deal with what some miss in the Reformation, namely, a mystical-ontical reality, a supernatural reality that invades our ordinary reality; but that does not eliminate the fact that it does not refer merely to some "idea" or unreality. It has to do with *reality*.

Nevertheless, it will be profitable for us to give separate treatment to the questions which bear on this "reality," namely, the reality of perseverance. For in the conflict about perseverance there has been much discussion about the *nature* of this reality.

For instance, the question has been asked again and again what perse-

From *Faith and Perseverance* (Grand Rapids: Wm. B. Eerdmans Pub. Co., 1958), pp. 219–239. Used by permission.

verance can mean concretely for ordinary human life, since even the lives of believers give such an impression of instability and impermanency. Are we talking about a continuity that can be pointed out and explained? And one single central problem has arisen again and again. To clarify this, we can best start with the doctrine of the *faithfulness* of God's grace, which is certainly of most decisive importance for the doctrine of the perseverance of the saints.

In this doctrine, there is great emphasis on the immutability of God's counsel in Jesus Christ. God's grace is affirmed as the *reality* of preservation. It would not be incorrect to say that faith affirms perseverance, the constancy of God's grace, the permanency of His faithfulness and of His eternal love.

The question now arises, however, whether we should speak of the *preservation* of the saints instead of the perseverance of the saints, in order to give due weight to the grace of God, to Him who does not let go the work of His hands. The question is especially important in connection with what might be called the "ontic" problem of perseverance. This refers to the nature of the "being" of the believers in the world. In connection with this "being," the question arises as to the meaning of that "change," which in the grace of God has a profound influence on human life. When we speak about this "change," we do not mean to say that God's grace and faithfulness are inadequate and that there would have to be, therefore, an *additional* change in the being of man. In that case we would have a divine preservation to which an active human persevering, a constancy in man's being, would have to be added in order to make it complete.

Such a position would do serious injustice to the sovereignty and adequacy of divine preservation. When the Church, then, speaks in its doctrine not only of God's mighty preservation but also of the perseverance of the saints, it cannot mean that there is a convergence of two concurring factors—preservation and perseverance. This would be equivalent to calling justification an act of God and sanctification an act of man. In this way the consolation of perseverance would most certainly be lost, because the final outcome would be put again in the hands of persevering man. If we affirm perseverance in this way, preservation is scarcely necessary.

The doctrine of the perseverance of the saints indeed expresses the constant interrelatedness of preservation and perseverance. They are certainly not two mutually limiting or even competing factors. It is precisely by way of the affirmation of perseverance that God's preservation is lauded. This affirmation depends on God's preservation. This interrelatedness, between preservation and perseverance finds its only explanation in the *sola fide,* which is also the living center of the doctrine of perseverance. This is already affirmed in the section on perseverance in the *Canons of Dort:* "But God is faithful, who, having conferred grace, mercifully confirms and powerfully preserves them therein, even to the end" (V, iii).

Thus when the perseverance of the saints is mentioned, it is not mentioned as something novel, in addition to preservation. It has to do with the *nature* of this divine preservation. And this is the real criterion as to whether we have a correct view of perseverance. That is already clear from the way in which Rome speaks of perseverance. We have already seen that Rome rejects perseverance as a doctrine and also rejects the sister doctrine of the assurance of salvation. That does not exclude the fact that Rome allows the possibility of persevering to the end. This admission is related, however, to Rome's view of the alienability of grace. Perseverance is only a possibility. There are those who obtain grace enough to persevere, but who do not actually persevere.[1] Grace is so closely related to free will that a tension between preservation and perseverance must arise. For this reason, the Council of Trent rejected the doctrines of perseverance and of the assurance of salvation.

Perseverance, then, cannot be thought of as a supplement to preservation but, instead, it points to God's preservation. But now arises the much disputed question as to what sort of constancy is intended in the doctrine of perseverance. How is it possible to speak of the faithfulness of God in His mighty preservation of our lives, and then go on to deal with the perseverance of the saints?

First of all, we must remember that the faithfulness of God does not spring up from our constancy and perseverance. In other words, the faithfulness of God is not "ontically" anchored in man. Justification is not an act of God performed because of something in man; it is a divine acquittal which is of grace. His faithfulness does not depend on our faithfulness, nor on anything that is or will be present in us. There is, rather, a "nevertheless," an "in spite of." Viewed from our side it is unmotivated and incomprehensible. This faithfulness is revealed in the cross of Christ, where He died while we were yet sinners. This light is given to *godless* men, men like the thief on the cross, who heard of the paradise awaiting him. It is the faithfulness which extends over the entire life of Christ's people, and which is manifest in His watchful eye, His beating heart, and His preservation.

It is clear that one need add nothing to this faithfulness and constancy. The greatness of God's faithfulness and preservation, indeed, was a temptation to many to speak no longer of perseverance but only of preservation. They wished to avoid anchoring anything *ontically,* making the real source of stability reside in the being of man, as if the favor of God could be adequate and could not be our only security.

We think here of the Biblical portrayal of Joshua, the high priest, who stands in foul clothing before the angel of the Lord. On his right hand, Satan speaks forth his condemnation. But suddenly there is another sound: "And the Lord said unto Satan. The Lord rebuke thee, O Satan; even the Lord that hath chosen Jerusalem rebuke thee: is not this a brand plucked out of the fire?" (Zech. 3:2).

This was the divine decision, not on any ontic basis, but simply as the favor of God, acquittal in Jesus Christ, without the works of the law. Is not this declaration enough? Is not all the constancy that we could ever desire concentrated in this divine acquittal? Do we require more than the continuity of forgiveness and reconciliation? Does not every other aspect of continuity pale in this marvellous light, that sends out its rays over all of temporal life? Is not the constancy of God's faithfulness in stark contrast to our guilt, and does it not remain unmotivated save by the love of God Himself? We hear the divine judgment on Israel: "But thou hast not called upon me, O Jacob; but thou hast been weary of me, O Israel. Thou hast not brought me the small cattle of thy burnt offerings; neither hast thou honored me with thy sacrifices... but... thou hast wearied me with thine iniquities" (Isa. 43:22–24). But then we hear, "I, even I, am he that blotteth out thy transgressions for mine own sake, and will not remember thy sins" (Isa. 43:25).

Should we desire more, indeed, could we desire more than this faithfulness and this divine pardon? Does Micah mean more, indeed, could he mean more, when he cries out in astonishment, "Who is a God like unto thee, that pardoneth iniquity, and passeth by the transgression of the remnant of his heritage?... he will subdue our iniquities; and thou wilt cast all their sins into the depths of the sea" (Mic. 7:18, 19)? And is it not the faithfulness of God in His forgiveness that Micah has in mind at the end of his prophecy: "Thou wilt perform the truth to Jacob, and the mercy to Abraham, which thou hast sworn unto our fathers from the days of old" (Mic. 7:20)?

All these Scriptural testimonies are so clear and forceful that to slight them in any respect would be to violate the entire Scriptural witness. Faith can have reference to nothing else than this constancy. But—and that is the singular thing—this faithfulness and preservation, this constancy and acquittal, are not just an idea, an empty scheme, an external word, a judgment that is foreign to reality. They are a divine act, which is just as much concrete reality as anyone can imagine reality to be. This faithfulness is the preservation of our lives in the love of God. And this preservation is not something which is tacked on to the divine forgiveness; it is included in this forgiveness. It is the preservation of our life in this world; we are not taken *out* of this world (John 17:15).

It is obvious, therefore, that the doctrine of God's preservation deals with our human existence, and that we cannot avoid what has been called the "ontic" problem. In recent theological discussions, there has been much use of this term, which is contrasted with "noetic." The latter term refers to the relation to our knowledge, while "ontic" refers to our "being." It is understandable that many feel great caution necessary in connection with this term. Do not we soon arrive, without our realizing it, at an "ontology" of grace, which we can see so clearly expressed in the Catholic idea of a grace which can be crushed and even lost, or in the numerous "graces" of Catholic teaching? Will we not soon be tangled in a view of grace as a mystical and optical supernatural reality, in which human perseverance is only a *possibility?* And then, in view of the changeability of our human character, can we ever transcend our uncertainties and arrive at the assurance of salvation?

Remembering the history of the Church and of theology, then, we must always be on our guard against any ontology of grace, which seeks a basis in ontic, human reality as well as in divine preservation. But though we must warn against an ontology of grace, which implicates divine preservation in the problematic of our own changeableness, we may not slight in any way the concrete reality of preservation. This reality can be seen in a truly Scriptural way only when it is viewed as a preservation in faith. Only in the *sola fide,* that is, in the recognition of God's grace, can we understand preservation concretely and existentially and still avoid slighting the fact that the doctrine of perseverance has to do with divine preservation, with our being preserved for our inheritance.

It is for this reason that the Scriptures can speak so emphatically about persevering and abiding in faith. That is not because they view faith as human addition to the part that God contributes to the constancy of our lives; it is because faith looks for everything to God's grace, to His favor and preservation. Here one cannot speak of an ontology of grace, but only of preservation and faith. In the doctrine of perseverance in faith, there is only that constancy which faith finds in Him, who remains eternally true and does not let go the work of His hands.

Hence Psalm 138 can speak the apparently contradictory but essentially harmonious words: "The Lord will perfect that which concerneth me: thy mercy, O Lord, endureth for ever: forsake not the works of thine own hands" (Ps. 138:8). This synthesis of prayer on the one hand, and confident assurance on the other, is not one of human logic, but of faith. The perseverance of the saints is nothing else, and it can be nothing else, than this abiding in this faith, this persisting in the love of God (Jude 21).

Some have always charged the doctrine of perseverance, however, with being in direct conflict with the realities of life. Life, they say, is more changeable than stable. We can most sharply formulate this problem as follows: Is it either psychologically or religiously responsible to speak of the perseverance of the saints, when we fully realize that in our lives and in those of others we seem to find only a sharply changing and intermittent existence? When we think of the examples from the *Canons,* David and Peter, can we square the affirmativeness of the doctrine of perseverance with the radicalness of their confessions of guilt after they became aware of their heinous sins? Can we describe their lives other than as miracles of God's grace and faithfulness? Is it not more in accord with such evidence if we go no further than David, who prays for a new heart?

We can indeed be grateful that the much disputed *Canons* have spoken about perseverance against the somber background of the mortal guilt in the lives of these two children of God. The illustrations of David and Peter are living warnings against any speculative ontology of perseverance. That the danger of such speculation is always present may never be lost to sight. Such speculation occurs, to be specific, where an interpretation of perseverance is given that to all intents and purposes is a casual view about an ontic work of God that, because it once is, will always continue to be. Such a view makes perseverance an abstract thing, isolated from the full reality of God's work of preservation in its manifold connections. It sometimes occurs in the Church in the following popular reasoning: What is once present in human life never disappears; the leopard does not change his spots.

Taking things for granted can spoil our amazement and profound thankfulness for being preserved in spite of our stubborn backsliding. It is one of my most striking pastoral experiences that after a long and very serious alienation of a baptized member, the pastoral admonition to the parents to be thankful stranded at this very point. They had deduced what would happen from what was supposed to be already present. They had taken the eventual restoration for granted. Here there is a radical departure from the statement of the *Canons,* "once given unto them." For in the *Canons,* preservation stands in juxtaposition not only with the power but also with the compassion of God (V, iii). If we make perseverance the object of thought in the form of causal reasoning, we are doomed to corrupt it. Once this has been done, we can no longer comfort others with the doctrine of perseverance, or be comforted by it.

Such an ontic view of continuity may seem to be a true replica of the doctrine of perseverance; but upon closer scrutiny, we can see that it is nothing more than a caricature. For it is built on a causal theory which works merely with concepts and which is supposed to have validity in itself, apart from faith. No troubled heart can be brought to rest in this way, and it is not apparent how such a causal logic leaves any room for prayer and intercession or admonition and consolation. Nor may such a logic, divorced from the life of faith, interpret this dogmatic insight as a new gnosis, as a new piece of knowledge which is self-validating. For the doctrine of perseverance is something quite different from a logical theory dealing with "being" and "abiding" as general terms. If we merely use rational techniques and try to satisfy ourselves with the abstract view of continuity we thus obtain, we will be suddenly shocked by something like the message Baruch, the son of Neriah, once had to give: "The Lord saith thus, Behold, that which I have built will I break down, and that which I have planted will I pluck up, even in this whole land" (Jer. 45:4). This passage is not cited, of course, to cast doubt on the changelessness of God's counsel and the certainty of His election in Christ, but rather to warn against making "logical conclusions" from *being* to *abiding,* conclusions in which the *nature* of this being and abiding is practically ignored.

If we use such an approach in our pastoral work, we will unavoidably be faced again and again with the distressing problem of determining whether this ontic beginning, this beginning of "being," was ever *actually* present. This would have to be asked particularly of those who, as the *Canons* say, have in their mortal sin lost the sense of grace and interrupted the practicing of faith.

But the doctrine of perseverance does not really deal with a continuity of actions and effects in the horizontal plane of logical cause and effect; it deals, rather. with the relation of our entire life to the faithfulness of God's grace.

In considering the history of this doctrine, we often run across statements which give the impression that logicistic reasoning has not entirely been eliminated. We should be very careful in our judgment, however, because in this doctrine—in preservation—we have to do with *being* and *abiding*.

Thus, in the fifth article of the *Canons* there are many items which if viewed in themselves could give the impression of being simplistic conclusions. But, if we have once grasped the fundamental thrust of this article, we will be able to understand the relation between being and abiding in the light of the doctrine as a whole. For it intends nothing more than the praise of God's grace. It is God's grace which preserves us. This comes clearly to expression in the *Bremen Confession* (IX, 3), to cite one reference out of many, in which perseverance is brought into relation with four unshakable pillars on which faith rests: "(1) The first is the effect and attribution of Christ Jesus' most holy sacrifice. (2) The second is the ever-enduring power of Jesus Christ's intercession for all believers. (3) The third is the almighty power and government of Christ Jesus at the right hand of God's majesty, by which he rules mightily over sin, death, the devil and hell and suffers not his sheep to be snatched from his hands. (4) The fourth is God's eternal love and gracious choice, whereby he has loved and elected us in Christ, before the foundation of the world was laid, and never changes this love and gracious choice of his in eternity."[2]

This religious view of the perseverance of the saints is found time and time again in Reformed symbols and dogmatic works. These command a view of the future, and it is for this reason that this doctrine is so unbreakably tied up with the assurance of salvation. "The other side of this perseverance of believers is the 'certainty (assurance) of salvation' on the believer's part."[3] There is nothing that can be taken for granted. There is only a confession of faith, which always rests anew on God's faithfulness and preservation. Preservation is indeed seen as the fruit of God's activity; but it is well to observe that it is a work of the Father, who has loved us and chosen us from eternity.[4] There is always a strong reminder of the *donum perseverantiae*, the *gift* of perseverance. This completely excludes a biologic, abstract, ontical view.

When Schneckenburger interpreted the Reformed doctrine of perseverance in an ontological and causal fashion, and thereby failed to grasp the significance of the intercession of Christ in connection with this supposed causality, he once described the Reformed position in this way: "In contrast, the Reformed thinker, since he views this new life as a stepwise, organic development, as the gradual growth and strengthening of a new personality from spiritual childhood to spiritual maturity, cannot view a deep fall as a total interruption of life. . . . "[5]

Here there is a misconception of the way in which the Reformed doctrine views the reality of perseverance. For there can scarcely be room for such an idea of organic development where, as in the *Canons,* there is so much emphasis on the interruption of the exercise of faith. It is only apparently that the sins and the lapses of believers are not taken completely seriously, and that those who reject perseverance understand them more deeply.

This impression arose because a distinction was made between different kinds of sins. To be specific, the statement that the sins of the regenerate spring out of weakness seemed to do injustice to the gravity of sin. So, for instance, the *Bremen Confession* (IX, 5) says: "Although even believers sin at times, there is still a great difference between the sins of the elect and those of the wicked.—The former sin from weakness and return to conversion; the latter from the whole of their character, and they remain without conversion."[6] The sin of believers is compared with the sins of children against their parents. They do not sin as enemies but as children. This has been interpreted, especially by the Lutherans, to be a weakening of the guilt attaching to sin.

That is not, however, what was intended by this distinction. The *Canons* themselves speak very emphatically about the sins of believers. They do not affirm perseverance because of a weakened view of sin; rather, in making this distinction they want to honor God's grace and preservation. They see in the shortcomings and sins even of the most holy people a continual reason for humility, for taking refuge in the crucified Christ, and for a yearning for the realization of perfection (V, ii). It is acknowledged that believers, by reason of their own fault, can defect from the leading of faith and be tempted by the lusts of the flesh (V, iv). Therefore they must continually watch and pray not to be led into temptation. "When these [watching and praying] are neglected, they are not only liable to be drawn into great and heinous sins by Satan, the world, and the flesh, but sometimes, by the righteous permission of God, actually fall into these evils. This the lamentable fall of David, Peter, and other saints described in Holy Scriptures, demonstrates" (V, iv).

These are crass sins, by which believers anger God and grieve the Holy Spirit. They wound their consciences, and they see God's countenance again only by way of repentance. In these reflections on the sins of believers the Scriptures are always the guide. There is never the least suggestion that the Scriptures diminish the guilt of sin because of election and communion with God. We remember the words of Amos, "You have I known of all the families of the earth: therefore will I punish you for all your iniquities" (Amos 3:2). There is also the message of Zephaniah. "And it shall come to pass at that time, that I will search Jerusalem with candles. . . ." (Zeph. 1:12). When the standards speak so seriously about believers' sins, about deadly guilt, they are completely in line with the Scriptural confession of guilt by believers themselves, after they are aware that they have been redeemed from their fall.

We think of David's confession of guilt in Psalm 51: "Have mercy upon me, O God, according to thy lovingkindness; according unto the multitude of thy tender mercies, blot out my transgressions. . . . For I acknowledge my transgressions: and my sin is ever before me. Against thee, thee only, have I sinned, and done this evil in thy sight: that thou mightest be justified when thou speakest, and be clear when thou judgest" (Ps. 51:1, 3, 4). In fact, David views his sin in connection with his conception and birth in iniquity. There is no security taken for granted in the relation between David and the Lord: "Hide thy face from my sins and blot out all mine iniquities" (Ps. 51:9). "Cast me not away from thy presence" (Ps. 51:11). He begs to receive again the joy of God's salvation (v. 12), and he asks for deliverance from bloodguiltiness (v. 14). His spirit is broken and his heart contrite. Any easy and presumptuous continuity is destroyed. There is no trace of boasting in an ontic continuity: "Create in me a clean heart, O God; and renew a right spirit within me" (Ps. 51:10). In his confession of guilt, David reviews his own life and his sin. The vision culminates when rejection is escaped through prayer. David's sin is no less serious, but is, indeed, even more serious, because he is the man after God's own heart.

Similarly, the distinction of the *Canons* between enemies and children does not weaken guilt but rather accents it. It is true that the *Canons* indicate a limit, but this limit does not mean an excuse for sin. It is a limit that is drawn by God's preservation. Therefore, the continuity which the *Canons* treat is a unique one. It is understandable only if we see its connection with the believers' deep confession of guilt, when they have been redeemed from their fall.

The examples of David and Peter, however, have been used as evidence to support the view that continuity lies altogether in God's hand and that the only constancy is that of God's favor. According to this view, if there is any constancy in the believer's life, it is only in humility and prayer, which can never be the basis for a confession of the perseverance of the saints. Furthermore, does not constancy reside in God alone, whose wonderful graciousness is manifest in that it is present in spite of all the radical interruptions and discontinuities in our lives? Are we not forced to admit the possibility of falling totally from grace, though not finally, because a final fall is excluded by God's grace? Is not the believer's life an intermittent one? Is not the greatness of God's grace this, that it forgives many times, even seventy times seven, and that it always makes a fresh start, as with the creating of the new heart for which David prays? Is it necessary to accept a continuity anthropologically and ontically, as if the constancy of God's forgiveness were not sufficient? Is there reason to object to repeated regeneration? And does not total falling from grace agree with the impression given by believers' lives? Is there reason to believe that in the life of the believer there is a real connection between the various acts of faith? Are not all of these acts separate and discrete, like the dots and dashes of a message in Morse code, not bound together in a solid line?

These questions are very important. For it has often been said that the doctrine of perseverance wants to say more than the believer himself, who is not absorbed with his own continuity but is oriented to the constancy of

God's grace. And can one interpret the deadly guilt of which the *Canons* speak as being anything else than a total falling away from grace?

Nevertheless, it is clear that the Reformed doctrine intends to point out a constancy in the actual life of the believer himself. When it speaks so emphatically about perseverance as a gift, about the gracious character of God's covenant in its manifold riches, and about the power of Christ's intercession, these are indissolubly connected with a constancy in the lives of the believers themselves. As we see it, it is an indication of the deeply religious attitude of the Reformed doctrine that it has not seen the constancy of God's faithfulness and the perseverance of the saints dualistically, as two separate, or at best two complementary things, but that it has seen them in a unique correlation. This bond has been viewed correctly because the actual life of the believer in the grace of God was considered. When we formulate this connection thus, we are not involved in simply making causal deductions. On the contrary, this connection has been accepted on the basis of the Holy Scriptures, precisely because grace has not been viewed primarily as something infused, but as forgiveness, as mercy.

Total falling, therefore, has had to be rejected time and time again. This rejection had a very definite origin. It did not originate in an underestimation of the believer's sins, as if these sins were so insignificant that they would not disrupt the believer's life. Had this been the origin of the doctrine of perseverance, the Lutherans undoubtedly would have been correct in their controversy with the Reformed. But the origin was a different one. It was the insight into God's eternal love, of that love which prevened ours, of an election which did not depend on our morality and our faith but which preceded every attitude or response of man. For this reason, faith always spoke of the constancy in the life of the believer in terms of the power of God's grace. This did not concern a logicistic *plus*, a new "Extra-Calvinisticum,"[7] that arose more out of a desire for system than out of faith.

It was the Scriptures themselves, rather, that presented the Reformed theologians with this grace and preservation. Thus they arrived at the affirmation of constancy in the believer's life.

This is the most critical point in the struggle concerning perseverance. For there was the danger that conclusions would be drawn from this constancy which were divorced from living faith. Tension and strife, temptation and admonition, and even the intercession of Christ thereby would lose their real worth, because it would be inferred that perseverance to the end would follow from the beginning in faith. As a consequence, sin would also be made relative. Everything else would pale before the light of this constancy.

We are very gratified, however, that there was no such thing in the Reformed doctrine of perseverance. It has been seen too clearly that perseverance is realized in the frail and threatened lives of believers only through prayer and exhortation, through preaching and the sacraments. In the *Canons*, therefore, the affirmation of perseverance is made only in intimate connection with these means. The doctrine was thus spared the fate of becoming a kind of exclusive theological gnosis, of which simple faith would know nothing and with which no one could be comforted.

This truth is so clear in the Scriptures that it can scarcely fail to be noticed. In David, there was no continuity that was explainable in terms of his own life. But in his prayer and confession of guilt, we can discern the presence of the love of God. Because of that love, after he stumbled he was restored, and after he was estranged, he remembered the message of grace. Therefore the *Canons* spoke in his case of the interruption of the *sense* of grace. It would be a bad mistake to infer therefrom, however, that this was only a human misunderstanding, as Ritschl supposed when he taught that the wrath of God was only a misunderstanding on the part of the religious subject, the believer.

God's grace is not in conflict with His wrath, even when it is directed against His children's sins, about which the Scriptures speak so emphatically. The interruption of the *sense* of grace does not mean that there is a misconception on the part of the believers; it means that their deep falls are being judged. David does not exaggerate when he implores God not to cast him out from His presence. But in his restoration, God's grace is again manifest. David does not first reform morally and then receive the grace of God. God's grace is shown in the broken and contrite heart, which He does not despise. Here we see again the picture of the man after God's own heart. That is the wonder of our constancy, that it is effected by the constancy of God's faithfulness.

We are confronted with the most remarkable fact, that the affirmation of perseverance is not made by those who withdraw themselves from the leading of grace (V, iv). The interruption of the sense of grace allows no room for a real affirmation of perseverance in faith.

The remarkable thing about the affirmation of perseverance is that it is possible and meaningful only in faith, in being oriented to God's grace. Apart from this faith, perseverance can be nothing more than a caricature. That is expressed very clearly in the *Canons of Dort*. It is true that they deal with "being" and "abiding" in terms of the prevenience and sovereignty of electing grace, but this occurs against the background of the grace of the Holy Spirit.

Because of this insight into the grace of God, the implanting in Christ was also spoken of through faith. Since the correlation between faith and God's salvation does not involve the merit of our faith, we can read the scriptures only in terms of *this* preservation, God's preservation, through which human life was taken from death and placed in life, and in which man's lot was decided.

This priority of God's grace is the basic meaning of *sola fide*. And the doctrine of perseverance can be maintained only in this light. For the promise of salvation includes preservation and the gift of the Spirit through the preaching of the Gospel. Hence we can no longer view the life of the believer as a collection of fragments, of separate moments; it is that life which participates in the communion of the Spirit, of the Spirit who is the earnest of our salvation.

And hence we must view the signs of perseverance in the believer's life not as completed moments with respect to God's faithfulness, but rather as a continual return to faith, which finds its rest in God's grace.

Note the striking passage in Nehemiah about Abraham: "Thou art the Lord the God, who didst choose Abram, and broughtest him forth from Ur of the Chaldees, and gavest him the name of Abraham; and foundest his heart faithful before thee . . ." (Neh. 9:7, 8a).

This does not speak of the steadfastness of Abraham's heart as the source of the constancy of Abraham's life; on the contrary, there is an intimate relation between this steadfastness and the faithfulness of God, that which was the exclusive object of Abraham's faith. His faithful heart is not something unconnected with God's acts of grace and faithfulness; it is not a second moment alongside God's faithfulness and the veracity of His promises, but rather finds its essence in the recognition of that faithfulness. So we can also speak of faithfulness and constancy in the lives of believers. Here we are confronted with the marvellous and gracious work of the Holy Spirit. Because of the correlation between faith and grace, the perseverance of the saints can be affirmed without giving honor to anything but the faithfulness of grace.

And therefore the believers are called to preserve *themselves* in the love of God.

This perseverance warns us against frivolously speaking of constancy without standing in faith. To separate the doctrine of perseverance from its living and existential relationship to the Gospel, to Word and sacrament, to promise and demand, petrifies it into a mere play of concepts drained of all life. The Church can make its affirmation here only in a living faith which knows that it has come into contact with a mystery that can never be understood in terms of our own lives. Therefore the doctrine of the perseverance of the saints must always include a profound wonder at the preservation of our lives and at the consolation of the Spirit, who will eternally abide with us.

This wonder will always remain an indispensable part of this doctrine, because preservation is realized amidst the changeableness, amidst the faults and sins, amidst the frailties of our lives.

The question has been asked whether the perseverance of the saints should not be called a mystery. If by this is meant that perseverance cannot be deduced from the empirical course of life, this designation is certainly apt. We cannot demonstrate this constancy as an irrefutable certainty, either in the lives of others or in our own lives.

How could David have seen God's preservation other than as God's grace, in and in spite of His apparent withholding of it? How could he forget those many months when he would not repent? He does not forget disturbing sins, even though God "remembers" them no more. But in repentance and the return to faith, he sees the vista of his entire life in some unfathomable way standing in God's care. In repentance and in the forgiveness granted him, God becomes a hiding place (Ps. 32:7), in which he is compassed about with mercy (Ps. 32:10). In penitence, David's lips are again opened and he desires to show forth the praise of the Lord (Ps. 51:15).

So, then, faith knows the prevenience of God's grace and the gift of perseverance, which is identical with the act of God's preservation, because through grace the transition from death unto life is irreversible.

The controversy about perseverance is closely related to the unfathomable mystery of the ingrafting into Christ through faith. To make deductions from this implanting apart from humble faith and prayer for the Holy Spirit is to destroy immediately its gloriousness. But if we understand how much the faith that is not of ourselves but of the Holy Spirit rests in Christ alone, we will allow the teaching of God's preservation to have a great place in our own lives and in the lives of others. When the Reformed fathers spoke about the consolation of perseverance, they had God's grace in mind. Hence, the doctrine of perseverance, as long as it recognizes its dependence on grace, can never be a mere abstraction which makes an eventless continuity of life. That is because here the Word of the Gospel is preached, here the sacraments are administered, here the Word is proclaimed to the Church in promise and admonition, and here faith receives the message of consolation, that no one will snatch the sheep out of Christ's hand. And if we wish to stress that these are the sheep given Him by the *Father* (John 10:29), we must also stress that these sheep hear *His* voice and follow *Him*. So, in his fellowship they will be able to bear their weakness and inconsistency, and they will not be lost for eternity.

Thus all self-assurance and frivolity are removed from the doctrine of perseverance. For this doctrine concerns itself with the profoundest depths of our experience. Because we affirm the Holy Ghost, who remains with us as our Comforter (*Heidelberg Catechism,* 20), we are forced by this affirmation to a life of watching and praying.

"If thou, Lord, shouldest mark iniquities, O Lord, who shall stand? But there is forgiveness with thee, that thou mayest be feared. I wait for the Lord, my soul doth wait, and in his word do I hope. My soul waiteth for the Lord more than they that watch for the morning: I say, more than they that watch for the morning. Let Israel hope in the Lord: for with the Lord there is mercy, and with him is plenteous redemption. And he shall redeem Israel from all his iniquities" (Ps. 139:3–8).

This is the psalm of continuity. It shows the unity of preservation and perseverance. If we do not divorce perseverance from preservation, we will not see it as something dogmatic and merely objective, which is divorced from the life of the Church; we will see it rather as a subject for preaching.

For this preaching, the proclamation of the Gospel, is a great and moving experience for the believer, one which constrains him to marvel about the constancy which is his in Christ. This marvelling will always be the deepest foundation for the thankfulness which fills the believer's life as he goes to meet the future.

"I will pay my vows unto the Lord now in the presence of all his people. In the courts of the Lord's house, in the midst of thee, O Jerusalem. Praise ye the Lord" (Ps. 116:18, 19).

Notes

[1]Cf. Thomas Aquinas, *Summa Theologica*, I-II, Q. 109, Art. 10: "For grace is given to many to whom perseverance in grace is not given." According to Thomas, the one who is in the state of grace does not require an additional sanctifying grace, but he needs the assistance of God, who leads him and protects him from the attacks of temptation. Concerning final perseverance see also Thomas, *Summa Theol.*, I-II, Q. 114, Art. 9.

[2]H. Heppe, *Reformed Dogmatics*, p. 583.

[3]*Ibid.*, p. 585.

[4]*Ibid.*, pp. 584f.

[5]Schneckenburger, *op. cit.*, I, 250.

[6]Heppe, *op. cit*, p. 582.

[7]The term, "Extra-Calvinisticum," refers to the teaching of Q. 48 of the *Heidelberg Catechism*. Here, in conscious rejection of the Lutheran view that in the Incarnation the Godhead is enclosed in the human nature, the Calvinistic confession says that the manhood of Christ, is not wherever the Godhead is. Since the Godhead is "incomprehensible and everywhere present, it must follow that it is indeed beyond the bounds of the Manhood which it has assumed, but is yet none the less in the same also and remains personally united to it" (Schaff, *Creeds of Christendom*, III, 322).

[Dr. Berkouwer is not attacking the "Extra-Calvinisticum." The emphasis falls on the words "plus" and "extra." Logicism would introduce something "extra," something beyond what a sound understanding of Calvinism would admit. For the "Extra-Calvinisticum" see Berkouwer, *The Person of Christ* (1954), pp. 93 and 271–301. (Tr.)]

PART TWO

The New Life
in Collective Expression

Editor's Introduction

The new life in Christ of which we have been learning is not merely an individualistic matter. Time and again in Scripture the Christian is pictured as part of a body—simply one member of the whole. The members of the body are to be of mutual edification to one another and to do collectively the task of carrying on Christ's work.

We begin first with general conceptions regarding the nature and the function of the church. **Edmund Clowney** describes the church under several images found in Scripture: the people of God, the kingdom and body of Christ, and the fellowship of the Spirit. Each of these has significant implications for the task of the church. **Langdon Gilkey** develops one of these concepts more fully in a treatise on "The Church as the Body of Christ." The church, he insists, is the presence of the risen Lord in the congregation, communicating himself to us in the Word and having fellowship with us as we meet together in our common worship of him. Gilkey seeks to develop this concept in terms of our worship: it is not simply a "client-centered" experience but ought to be directed toward God. We must experience him rather than merely experience ourselves worshiping. Gilkey argues that social changes in American life have also produced important changes in the religious nature of Protestant church life. He makes some suggestions regarding how meaningfulness can be recaptured. In particular, he argues for the meaningfulness of the sacraments.

We come next to a set of articles discussing the form of organization of the church or its nature and government. It generally can be said that conceptions of the nature and essence of the church vary on a spectrum. On the one end of the spectrum are views which place a strong emphasis on the visible or organized or institutional church. On the other end are those that strongly emphasize the spiritual quality of the individuals and define the church in terms of the particular spiritual condition and convictions of the members. An extreme form of the first end of the spectrum would be the traditional Roman Catholic view of the church. According to this view, the church is constituted as the church in that it has derived its origin from God, who, through Jesus Christ, established the church and granted authority to the apostles to teach doctrine and to dispense grace. These apostles transmitted that power to their successors. On the other end is the Anabaptist view of the church—wherever there is a gathering of genuinely born-again individuals (even with a minimal form of organization), there is the church. The church generates upward from the faith and life of the individuals rather than downward from the organizational structure. Other forms fall somewhere in between these two extremes.

The episcopal form of government places the seat of authority in the bishop or *episcopos*. Such matters as significant church decisions and the placement of clergy are exercised by the bishop or the collection of bishops. This form of government is found in the Methodist Church, the Episcopal or Anglican Church, and the Roman Catholic Church; the most highly developed form of episcopal government is that of the Roman Catholic Church, which ultimately rests final authority in the bishop of Rome or the pope. Authority is delegated downward in this form of government. In the more highly developed varieties, the modern office of bishop is believed to derive from the office of the apostles, who in turn received their authority from Jesus Christ. This authority has been transmitted to the successors by ordination. The episcopal form of church government is described in the article by **Leon Morris.** One might say that this form of government is a government by aristocracy. A second form could be called a government of representative democracy. This is the presbyterial form of government. As the name would indicate, here authority is vested in presbyters or elders who have ruling authority. Within the local church these presbyters form a session. The government of the larger Church is carried on through a series of ascending ecclesiastical courts. While the local church has the authority to select its own pastor, such decisions must be confirmed by the presbytery. This form of government is followed by the Presbyterian churches and the Reformed churches and is presented in our volume here by **Lewis Berkhof.**

The final form of church government is the congregational system, or the system of pure democracy. Here there is a very strong emphasis upon the equality of individual believers and upon the equal right of each believer to participate in decisions made within the local congregation. The autonomy of local congregations is also strongly emphasized. While such congregations may voluntarily affiliate with one another for cooperative activity, this affiliation can be terminated at any time and decisions made by elected bodies such as a convention are not legally binding and enforceable upon the local congregations. Baptist groups, Congregationalist churches, and several others follow this form of government. The article by **Edward Hiscox** presents this particular approach.

Another important question for the Christian church is cooperation with other churches, including those of other denominations. The ecumenical movement has concerned itself with trying to make the idea of Christian unity a real and tangible matter. In some cases, the ecumenical movement aimed at simply a conciliar arrangement in which separately identifiable denominational groups worked cooperatively through a council of churches. At other times complete organic merger was the prospect, as in the case of the Consultation on Church Union (COCU), which later changed its name to the Church of Christ Uniting. In a pair of articles **Carl Henry** discusses the dangers of extreme independency on the one hand and of extreme ecumenicity on the other hand. The impact of the two articles is to suggest that an intermediate or balanced position would be most desirable.

Another set of issues concerns the ordinances or sacraments as they are variously known in different Christian churches. We look first at the matter of baptism. Two distinct but related issues are the questions of the proper subjects of baptism and what is accomplished by baptism. On the one hand are those who believe that baptism of infants should be practiced. Some, such as the Roman Catholics and Lutherans, believe that regeneration or the forgiveness of original sin is actually accomplished by baptism. Others, such as the Reformed and Presbyterians, do not believe that baptism effects regeneration but that it is a sign of the covenant and as such has value only where the child baptized is the child of believing parents (i.e., members of the covenant). Still others, such as the Baptists, believe that baptism is a form of testimony, an outward expression of faith already present and of regeneration already experienced. Consequently, they hold that only those who are of such age and capability of making a conscious decision should be baptized. Another major issue connected with baptism is the question of the mode. Baptists, generally speaking, insist that baptism must be by immersion into water. They argue this on the grounds that this was the mode of Jesus' baptism, practiced by John the Baptist and by the early church, and consequently should be retained. They also hold that the Greek word *baptizo* conveys this meaning. Further they suggest that the symbolism of baptism as burial and resurrection in Romans 6 is retained only with this mode of baptism. Others, especially those who practice baptism of infants, hold that the particular form of baptism is not crucial, so that baptism can be carried out either by pouring or by sprinkling, as well as by immersion. In this anthology, the Baptist view is presented by **Paul Jewett** and the Reformed view by **Y. Feenstra.**

We come finally to the question of the Lord's Supper (or communion or the Eucharist, as it is variously known). Here again a variety of views can be found. These vary in terms of the question of the real presence of the flesh and blood of Christ and the efficacy of the rite. At one extreme is the classical Roman Catholic position, which is set forth in this volume by **Joseph Pohle.** According to this view, during the mass, the substance of the bread and wine is actually transformed into the substance of Christ's flesh and blood. This is known as transubstantiation. The accidents (i.e., appearance, taste, etc.) remain unchanged. The Lutheran view also sees Christ as being bodily present but not in terms of the elements ceasing to be material. Both of these views tend to be sacramental in nature, attributing an inherent value to the taking of the elements as affecting the spiritual condition of the recipient. Calvin's view, which is generally followed by the Reformed churches, is that Christ is spiritually present. While there is no actual physical presence within the elements, Christ is present in a very special way in the taking of the elements. After examining these views, **William Stevens** explains why he accepts the view of Zwingli and the Anabaptists: the bread and wine are of a merely symbolic significance; Christ is no more fully present in the elements of the Lord's Supper than anywhere else. Here the value is simply in terms of the memorial effect reminding us of Christ's death.

The Identity and Role of the Church

Edmund Clowney

Toward a Biblical Doctrine of the Church

The People of God

"But ye are an elect race, a royal priesthood, a holy nation, a people for God's own possession, that ye may show forth the excellencies of him who called you out of darkness into his marvellous light: who in time past were no people, but now are the people of God: who had not obtained mercy, but now have obtained mercy" (I Peter 2:9, 10). In this passage Peter weaves together a number of Old Testament passages (Exod. 19:6; Isa. 43:20, 21; Hos. 1:6, 9; 2:1). The relationship between God and his people was disrupted by sin. Israel was made *Lo-ammi,* not my people. But the promise of the prophets has been fulfilled. By God's grace, those who were no people, whether covenant-breaking Jews or Gentiles outside the covenant, are made the people of God and receive mercy. Out of the restored relationship of God and his people there comes praise. The phrase "show forth the excellencies" has for its background Isaiah 43:21, "the people which I formed for myself, that they might set forth my praise." In this passage of Isaiah as in the Psalms, the praises of God are declared by a redeemed people.

From *Westminster Theological Journal,* November 1968, pp. 32–81. Used by permission.

The people of God are a treasure-people, a people for God's own possession. The relationship that defines the church is this relationship of possession by God.

There is indeed an activism in the Scriptural conception of the people of God. The church is the assembly of God, those who are called to God. The Greek term ἐϰϰλησία (*ecclesia*) is used in the Septuagint to translate the Hebrew term קָהָל (*qahal*). Of the two words commonly used for the congregation of God's people in the Old Testament, *qahal* views the congregation as actually assemblied while עֵדָה (*edhah*) refers to the congregation whether assembled or not. It is natural, therefore, to speak of "the assembly [*qahal*] of the congregation [*ĕdhah*, Num. 14:5]." The Greek word *ecclesia* appropriately translates *qahal* because it, too, describes an assembly which is actually gathered. Some scholars have concluded that the term *ecclesia* came to be applied to the church because of the actual assembling of the local congregation. Paul, for example, speaks in very active terms of the *ecclesia* in I Corinthians 14:19, 28, 34. Other scholars have insisted that the term *ecclesia* has no theological significance whatever, but is simply used to describe a gathering like the "assembly" at Ephesus (Acts 19:41).

Such a conclusion, however, does not do justice to the Old Testament background for the New Testament use of the term. The fact that *qahal* and *ecclesia* are active terms does not mean that they lack theological content. To the contrary. The great and definitive assembly of Israel was the assembly at Sinai. It was the actual gathering together of Israel "in the day of the assembly" (Deut. 4:10, LXX; 9:10; 10:4; 18:16) that marked the climax of God's redemption and constituted the people as the people of God. God commanded Moses, "Gather the people to me" (Deut. 4:10). This assembly at Sinai was the immediate objective of the exodus (Exod. 5:1). The sound of the trumpet from the top of Sinai was the signal for a solemn assembly of the people before God. Numbers 10:1–10 provides for the blowing of the two silver trumpets by the priests as a signal for later assemblies of the congregation at the door of the tent of meeting.

The assemblies of Israel for worship, for war, or for the triumphant march through the desert all had a sacral character. All were solemn assemblies for worship. Later renewals of the covenant were made by an assembled Israel. The people were directed to assemble three times a year for the feasts of the sacred calendar (see Lev. 23).

Among the great assemblies of the Old Testament are: the assembly convoked by David to secure the succession for Solomon (I Chron. 28, 29); the assembly for the dedication of Solomon's temple (II Chron. 5:2); Jehoshaphat's assembly (II Chron. 20:5, 14); the assembly at the crowning of Joash (II Chron. 23:3); and the assembly of Nehemiah after the exile (Neh. 5). When the restoration of the people of God is promised by the prophet Joel, the image of the assembly is used again (Joel 2:15–17). The prophets tell of the ingathering of the Gentiles to the great festival assembly of God (Isa. 2:2–4; 56:6–8; Ps. 87). The sacred assembly includes heaven as well as earth. God was present on Mount Sinai in the midst of the heavenly assembly of his holy ones and with the earthly assembly at his feet (Deut. 33). Those who stand in God's assembly are "all his holy saints" (Deut. 33:3).

The festival assemblies on Mount Zion are used by the author of Hebrews in the twelfth chapter to describe the New Testament church. We are assembled not to the fire and smoke of Mount Sinai, fire and smoke that could be touched, but rather to God who is a consuming fire and to the festival assembly of the saints and the angels in the heavenly Zion. To this heavenly assembly we come, for here is Christ, the Mediator of the New Covenant. Indeed, the Christian church consists of this assembly. The active sense of the people of God assembled in the heavenlies with Christ dominates the New Testament conception of the church. The outpouring of the Spirit on the festival of Pentecost manifests the continuity of the church with the prophetic promises for the renewed and reformed people of God.

It is the heavenly reality which gives such significance to the earthly gathering of even two or three in Christ's name. Even when Paul speaks of the Corinthian Christians coming together in assembly (I Cor. 11:18; 14:26, 28), the phrase has theological significance. The *ecclesia* of God is that assembly before the Lord of which Sinai was the great pattern, which is realized in Corinth by those holy ones upon whom the ends of the ages are come, as they await the final gathering together in the assembly of the *parousia* (II Thess. 2:1). The holy ones stand before the Lord to bless his name with the tongues of men and angels (I Cor. 13:1; 14:16). A synonymous expression for a church in a particular locality is "those who call upon the name of our Lord Jesus Christ in that place" (*Cf.* I Cor. 1:2), where public worship is in view.

The assembly of God exists wherever God is in the midst of his people. At Corinth, as the people of God meet together and the gift of prophecy makes evident his presence, the unbeliever "will fall down on his face and worship God, declaring that God is among you indeed" (I Cor. 14:25). The hearing of the Word, the singing of psalms, the uttering of prophecy, all that occurred in the great assemblies of old finds realization in the New Testament church, but above all, the Gentiles fall down and confess the presence of God (Isa. 45:14). It is hard for us to think theologically enough to appreciate the New Testament force of the concept of the church. Our tensions between the church as universal and local, informal and institutional, do not exist for the New Testament writers. The church they know exists before the face of the Lord, in the heavenly Jerusalem and therefore at Corinth. Both the catholicity and the localization of the church are manifested in the power and presence of the Spirit. Where the Lord is, among the holy angels, there his people come; where two or three of his people gather in his name, there the Lord is in the midst.

Closely connected with the Scriptural concept of assembly is that of the house of dwelling. The concept of assembly stresses the *immediacy* of God's presence among the gathered people. The concept of the house of dwelling stresses the *permanence* of God's presence. God does not only meet with his people as they are summoned to appear before him, he also dwells with them. If Sinai in the desert was the place of meeting between God and his people, then Zion in the promised land is the place of dwelling. Psalm 68:5 blesses God in his holy habitation of heaven (see verses 33, 35), but also says of the "mountain which God hath desired for his abode" that "Jehovah will dwell in it forever" (verse 16). The tabernacle or temple symbolized the dwelling of God among his people: "And I will set my tabernacle among you: and my soul shall not abhor you. And I will walk among you, and will be your God, and ye shall be my people" (Lev. 26:11, 12).

The dwelling of God in the midst of his people creates an immediate threat. The fire of God's holiness consumes sinners. The place of God's dwelling is therefore the place of sacrifice where atonement is made for sin. The plan of the tabernacle and the temple presents a way of approach to God through the shedding of blood. Because God dwells in the midst of his people they are a kingdom of priests, a holy nation (Exod. 19:6). It is God's presence in the midst which separates his people from all the people on the face of the earth (Exod. 33:16).

In the New Testament the figure of the temple is applied both to Christ and his church. In Christ "the Word became flesh and tabernacled among us, and we beheld his glory" (John 1:14). The church itself is the temple, the house of God, sanctified by the presence of the Spirit (I Cor. 3:16). Because the temple is holy, God will destroy anyone who defiles it (verse 17). The sanctions which protected the temple are divinely directed to guard the church. The holiness of the church demands separation on the part of believers. This distinction is ethical, religious, and social (II Cor. 6:14–16). God dwells among his people (verse 16), and the church is thereby called out to holiness (verses 17, 18; chapter 7:1). Christians must go outside the gate of Jerusalem (Heb. 13:13) and Babylon (Rev. 18:4), having no fellowship with sin. Such separation shares the reproach of Christ, but also shares his holiness, for he is the stone rejected of the builders who is made the chief cornerstone of the true temple. The rejected stone is the elect stone (Isa. 28:16; I Peter 2:6), chosen of God and precious. Coming to this living stone, Christians are built spiritually into one living temple, a house not made with hands.

The spiritual edifice is the place of spiritual service: the holy priesthood of the new Israel, sanctified not in flesh and garments but in spirit, offers spiritual sacrifices of praise and benevolence acceptable to God through Christ (I Peter 2:5; Phil. 3:3; Heb. 13:15; Rom. 12:1).

The assembly and dwelling figures are intensely theological, for they show God as present in the midst of his people. The people of God are not an already existing nation brought into relationship with him. They are constituted by God's assembling and God's dwelling. Nationalism became a sin to the theocratic people; the theocracy was not founded in nationalism. God's people are united to each other only because they are united to God. God's word gives Abraham his beloved son Isaac; God's word constitutes Israel as his son in the desert. God's covenant with his people is neither individualistic nor ethnic in the modern sense. God's mercies are promised to a thousand generations of them that fear him; the circumcision of all the male children signified the sanctification of every generation to the Lord. Yet, strangers and sojourners may be admitted to the assembly and people of God, and gain an inheritance in Israel (Exod. 12:47–49; 23:9). On the other hand, rejection of the covenant merits death (*e.g.,* Lev. 24:16); a father must denounce his own son if he blasphemes (Deut. 13:6–11).

The sin of Israel brings down the curses of the covenant. So great is the resulting destruction that the restoration from exile is likened by the prophets to a resurrection (Ezek. 37:1–10). The people of God must be *made* the people of God by a new miracle of redemption.

Paul recognizes this principle in claiming for the church of the Gentiles the status and blessing of the people of God. The church is the λαός (*laos,* II Cor. 6:16), the true Israel as over against Israel of the flesh (Rom. 9:6, 7, 24–26; *cf.* I Cor. 10:18; 12:2); the people of the new covenant (II Cor. 3:3–18); the sons of Abraham (Gal. 3:7); the circumcision (Phil. 3:3); the children of the heavenly Jerusalem (Gal. 4:21–31); no longer strangers or aliens but fellow citizens with the saints and of the household of God (Eph. 2:12, 19).

The way in which the people of God are joined together by his assembling and presence produces their distinctive fellowship. The people of God are not to be numbered among the nations (Num. 23:9). James reflects this consciousness when, in the council at Jerusalem, he speaks of the calling of the Gentiles in these words: "Simeon hath rehearsed how first God visited the Gentiles [ἔυνη *ethne*] to take out of them a people [*laos*] for his name" (Acts 15:14). G. Ernest Wright has shown the balance between individual and community consciousness in the covenant people.[2] He points out, for example, the alternation between "you" and "ye" in the divine commands. Because of the theocentric character of the community the individual is neither submerged and absorbed, nor isolated and estranged. The sharing of the people of God in the inheritance given by God and in God himself as the inheritance of his people beautifully manifests the brotherhood and fellowship that is constituted by the bond of covenant redemption.

Because God is King in the covenant assembly at Sinai (Deut. 33:5), his people are made a kingdom: "and ye shall be unto me a kingdom of priests and a holy nation" (Exod. 19:6). Particularly in the praise of God in the Psalms his kingly rule over his people is celebrated, and this rule is seen to have universal scope. God's rule does not end with Israel; it extends to the ends of the earth and endures forever. Yet, the extension of God's power over all the nations does not imply that the nations are made recipients of Israel's blessing. Rather, the Gentiles are summoned to fear the Lord, and the rebellious kings are warned of the wrath of Jehovah. God's kingdom is now over every kingdom (Dan. 2:37ff.), but it will also come in power to destroy all earthly kingdoms and remain forever (Dan. 2:44). This eternal kingdom is given to the one like unto a son of man and to the saints of the Most High (Dan. 7:14, 18, 27). Only as the nations are drawn in to be numbered with the people of God can they share in the relationship of blessing.

The relation of the people of God to the nations comes to expression particularly in connection with the choosing of the people of God. Election expresses God's sovereignty in dealing with his people. They have not chosen him, he has chosen them. God chooses Abraham and calls him. Goe chooses Isaac and not Ishmael, for "in Isaac shall thy seed be called" (Gen. 21:12). God chooses Jacob rather than Esau. Paul stresses this in Romans 9:11-13, referring to Malachi 1:2, 3. The election of the nation is in fulfillment of the promise to the patriarchs (Deut. 4:37).

The free choice of God in the election of Israel is underscored by the assertion that there is no ground for election in those who are chosen. Only the undeserved love of God can account for the choosing of Israel (Deut. 7:7, 8; 10:14-17).

Yet God's sovereign choice has a ground in God himself. It is free, but not arbitrary or purposeless. God's "good pleasure" is not determined by anything outside himself, but it is his own will and is therefore determined by his own nature and purposes. The twofold purpose of election is stated in the Old Testament. It is related to God himself and to his service in the world. Recent theology has stressed election for service. It is true that the choosing and calling of Abraham has for its background the purpose of God that in Abraham all the nations of the earth should be blessed. God does bless Israel, that his way might be made known upon the earth and his salvation among all nations (Ps. 67:2).

Yet the great ground and purpose of God's election is in God himself. God does not first choose Israel that he might use Israel. God does not choose the spiritually fit. The only fitness God requires is weakness, folly, nothingness, that no flesh should glory before him (I Cor. 1:26-31). Love seeks not ours but us. God chose his people because he loved them. His greatest purpose was not to use them but to own them. That is why the elect people are a "people of possession." All the earth is the Lord's, but Israel is God's possession from the peoples (Exod. 19:5; see also Ps. 135:4; Mal. 3:17; Eph. 1:14; Titus 2:14; I Peter 2:9). The purpose of God to possess his people with jealous love and to put his name upon them in blessing does not conflict with the demands which God makes upon them. To be and to remain the people of God's possession they must keep his covenant, as these same passages show. They must manifest the holiness of the separated people.

Yet, in the Old Testament as in the New, nothing can be set above the love of God for his people. The praise and glory of God which springs from it (Isa. 43:21). only reflects the mysterious wonder of the absoluteness of that love. The two primary figures used to express God's jealous, electing love are a father's love for his firstborn son and a husband's love for his wife (Exod. 4:22, 23; Deut. 32:6; Hos. 1:10; Ezek. 16:6ff.; Zeph. 3:17).

God elects his people to a position as well as a ministry, to status as well as to service. God's love chooses his son, his bride, not merely his servant. God's love is active, but that which it creates is an assured relationship.

On the one hand, God's choosing does not create an elite people or a master race. Abuse of God's calling results in singular judgment: "You only have I known of the families of the earth; therefore I will visit upon you all your iniquities" (Amos 3:2. but see 9:9).

On the other hand, God's choosing does create his people. The people are acquired (Exod. 15:16), redeemed (Exod. 15:13). They are the Lord's portion, the lot of his inheritance (Deut. 32:9). Israel, as the Lord's inheritance, is that which he has received, as it were, by lot. God's portion may be described as his vineyard, his "pleasant portion," his house (Jer. 12:7–10). The people of God are the "apple of his eye" (Deut. 32:10). God's delight is in them (Num. 14:8). In the final realization of the covenant mercies, Zion will be named Hephzibah, "my delight is in her" (Isa. 62:4).

A host of other terms describe the position of the people of God. They are people near to him, borne on his shoulders, kept in his arms, held in his hand, lifted up by his right hand, seated at his feet, gathered before his face, engraved on the palms of his hands. In the symbol of the graven stones of the high priest's breastplate, the people of God are set on his shoulder and worn on his heart.

The extravagance of the language of love can say no more than God says to his people. All these precious promises may become a hideous caricature when they are seized in self-righteousness. Yet this sinful distortion should not blind us to the wonder of God's electing love.

When the people of God do profane the intimate relation which God has appointed for them, the "vengeance of the covenant" (Lev. 26:25) is poured out. For the adulterous wife there is stoning (Ezek. 16:40). The rebellious son may be cast out (Hos. 11:1, 8; 12:1, 14). The pleasant vineyard can be laid waste (Isa. 5:5, 6) and the planted vine uprooted and burned (Ps. 80:12–16; Ezek. 19:10–14).

The Old Testament is full of the realization of these dread prospects. A generation perishes in the wilderness, disaster fills the land of promise, destruction comes upon the city of God, and God's people are swallowed up in captivity among the nations. As the book of Deuteronomy predicts, the blessing and the curse are not only possibilities; they will be realized (Deut. 30:1).

Is God's choosing then in vain? Do his purposes come to nothing? This problem arises in the crisis of judgment; it becomes overwhelming in view of the exile. The emphasis of the Old Testament on the freedom and sovereignty of God seems to intensify the difficulty. Since God is free to choose, he is free to reject also. The potter who made a vessel is free to smash it (Isa. 30:14). None can stay his hand or question his authority (Isa. 29:16; 45:9; 64:8).

But what then of God's word of promise, spoken to his people? Will it return void? Is God's good pleasure to be frustrated? The two related answers to these questions which appear in the Old Testament are summarized by Paul in Romans 9–11. Distinctions are made in two areas: first, between the true and false people of God; second, between the present and future people of God. The first is the motif of the *remnant,* the second of the *renewal.* God's election of his people does not fail, for its operation is effective among the true people of God. "They are not all Israel that are of Israel." Election does not fail, either, for its full realization is final: "all Israel will be saved."

These distinctions acknowledge the sovereignty of God's choosing and differentiate between an outward calling, which may be made void, and effective calling of God's creative word, which creates what it names (Isa. 46:10f.; 55:11; Jer. 33:2). God's word may tarry, but it is sure. At last it must perform what the Lord has spoken.

The doctrine of the remnant presents first of all a surviving remnant. A remnant in this sense is described in Isaiah 1:9; Amos 3:12; 4:11. The surviving remnant, however, is also a purified remnant, a righteous remnant. Through chastening, those who remain confess their iniquities and return to the Lord (Lev. 26:40; Jer. 3:12, 14; Hos. 5:15–6:3). The preexilic prophets stressed the smallness of the remnant: one burning coal plucked from the conflagration (Amos 4:11); a pole on the hilltop (Isa. 30:17); two legs or a piece of an ear from the mouth of a lion (Amos 3:12); the stump of a felled tree (Isa. 6:13); the gleanings of the field or a few olives left at the top of the tree (Isa. 17:6). Yet, in spite of the smallness of the remnant, there will be restoration. The scattered remnant will be regathered (Ezek. 11:17). Their recovery will be like the resurrection of a valley of dry bones (Ezek. 37:12). God will give them his spirit, hearts of flesh for hearts of stone (Ezek. 11:19; 36:26, 27), and make his covenant with them. The good grain will not fall to the ground (Amos 9:9). Those written in the Book of Life will remain, quickened from the grave (Isa. 4:3). All things will be restored for the remnant people, and the Lord will be their crown of glory (Isa. 28:5).

These great promises are repeated to the feeble remnant that does return from captivity. They are declared to be the heirs of the blessing upon the remnant (Zech. 8:11–15). Yet the postexilic prophets show that the fullness of the restoration remains in the future. The glory of God's promises far exceeds the immediate realization on the return from the exile, and the rebuilding of the temple and the walls of Jerusalem.

This is true because in the prophetic teaching concerning the remnant both the spiritualizing and the universalizing aspects have been intensified. To the question "Has God cast off his elect people?" the first answer was "No, for he preserves a remnant." The second was, "No, for there is a renewal to come." The first answer carries into the second, and both answers are intensified in the idea of the remnant. The thought of a preserved remnant leads to a more individual and spiritual emphasis. Like the communities gathered about the prophets in days of apostasy, the remnant will appear as a band of disciples maintaining the truth of God (Isa. 8:16–18).

But the remnant is individualized in a much more significant way in the Messianic promises. The servant songs of Isaiah 42–53 address the remnant as God's servant: "But thou, Israel, my servant, Jacob whom I have chosen, the seed of Abraham my friend, thou whom I have taken hold of from the ends of the earth, and called from the corners thereof, and said unto thee, Thou art my servant, I have chosen thee and not cast thee away . . . '' (Isa. 41:8, 9; *cf.* 42:18–43:13; 44:1–5).

Against this background of the remnant as God's servant, two individual figures are shown: Cyrus, the Gentile king, declared to be anointed as the Lord's servant for bringing back God's people; and the mysterious individual servant who is distinguished from the people as sharply as Cyrus is (*cf.* Isa. 49:5, 6 with 45:4). One servant, above the remnant, above the anointed Gentile, Cyrus, will be used to redeem and restore the people of God. As the elect servant-son, called from the womb (Isa. 49:1, 5), named by Jehovah (49:1), and kept in his hand (49:2). he will realize all the promises of God.

In the individual servant the narrowing down of the remnant reaches its end at last. There is One who is the elect, called, Beloved Son.

This individualizing focus in the remnant-servant has a surprising reverse movement bound up in it. The purified remnant are not only possessed of God; they are also used. Or, to put it another way, in the remnant God possesses *all* his people. Through the final remnant, and to the final remnant, even the Gentiles are gathered in. As Manson has observed, ''the brand plucked from the burning is to become a light to lighten the Gentiles.''

God's free election of the remnant and his deliverance of them are described as creating astonishment among the nations (Ps. 40:3; Jer. 33:9; Ezek. 36:20–25; Mic. 7:15–20). They come to desire the blessings now manifest (Zech. 8:22, 23). Not only do they come in order to worship at Zion (Isa. 2:2–4; 56:3–8; 60:3; Zeph. 3:9, 10; Zech. 14:16), bringing their treasure and gifts (Isa. 60:5; 61:6), but they even bring with them the scattered remnant of Israel (Isa. 49:22; 60:4). Thus there is a remnant of the nations (Isa. 45:20; Jer. 48:47; Zech. 9:7), joined with the remnant of Israel (Isa. 19:24, 25; 66:18–23). The same sovereign election which preserves a remnant in Israel calls from the Gentiles a people for God's name. The preserved remnant becomes the restored people of God, the ''many'' gathered by the final suffering of the Lord's servant, the *fullness* of him that filleth all in all. Preservation has become renewal. Christ speaks to his disciples as the remnant in the election of grace: ''Fear not, little flock; for it is your Father's good pleasure to give you the kingdom'' (Luke 12:32).

The remnant doctrine implies discrimination. With election there is rejection. The kingdom is taken away from those who kill the Son and given to others. Many are called but few chosen (Matt. 22:14). Even Judas goes to his own place, as it is written of him (Acts 1:16, 25). Peter sets against the ''elect race'' the disobedient who stumble over God's chosen stone, ''whereunto also they were appointed'' (I Peter 2:8, 9).

With the appearance of the Great Shepherd of the sheep, those who are his own are made manifest. They hear his voice and follow him (John 10:3–5), and he pronounces upon them the blessing of peace (John 14:27). Election is made evident in faith. Because the gospel operated among them in power, the Thessalonians know their election (I Thess. 1:4). God's choosing operates effectually in "sanctification of the spirit and belief of the truth" (II Thess. 2:13, 14).

This specification of election, which views the church as the company of the elect (I Peter 1:1), expresses the inheritance and calling of the saints. Should a member of the church deny Christ, however, he would show that he is not among the number of the elect. The Apostle Paul counts not himself to have apprehended, though he does not doubt that Christ has apprehended him (Phil. 3:12, 13), and Peter urges the elect to make their calling and election sure by perseverance in the life of faith (II Peter 1:10). God's choosing of his own is fixed, nonetheless, and if Hymenaeus and Philetus apostatize, "the firm foundation of God standeth sure, having this seal. The Lord knoweth them that are his . . ." (II Tim. 2:19).

Election does not set the individual against the corporate whole in the doctrine of the church. The remnant is the elect nation, the assembly of the saints, the fullness of the new humanity in Christ. Individual sonship is not in contrast to the family of God. It might be noted that Karl Barth makes an untenable distinction when he holds that for Israel there was rejection as well as election but that in the church there cannot be elect and non-elect individuals.[3] Barth correctly emphasizes the reference of election to an elect people, the company of the saints. But the principle which operated in the Old Testament operates also in the New: not all are Israel which are of Israel. The application of the term "elect" to the people of God does not furnish the definition of election but of the people. A process of proving at once begins. There are those who go out "from us . . . that they may be manifest that they are not all of us" (I John 2:19). Therefore warnings about the rejection of Israel are appropriate to the church (*e.g.*, I Cor. 10:1–12.

The description of the people of God in the Bible is as far from the contemporary descriptions of the "New Theology" as heaven is high above the earth. The central concepts of God's action, his election of a treasure-people, are lost from view in the contemporary consensus. God's calling of his people to himself cannot be subordinated to the mission to the world, for God's ultimate plan is the renewal of the world through the new humanity that is chosen in Christ. We cannot escape the dreadful mystery of God's sovereignty by which he has chosen to redeem a remnant in Christ; but if we are to understand God's mission in the world, we must receive his revelation of it.

The Kingdom and Body of Christ

The Old Testament revelation of the people of God points forward to the renewal of that people with the coming of the Messiah. The history of the covenant in the Old Testament issues in the eschatology of the covenant people. Israel's history was a history of failure. The distinctiveness and mission which were the requirement of the covenant were abandoned and rejected. The basic covenantal principle was that there should be a people of God's own possession among whom God dwelt as Lord, a holy nation, "a people that dwelleth alone, and shall not be reckoned among the nations" (Num. 23:9). God's covenant law required religious distinctiveness (the first table of the law): Israel must worship the true God exclusively (the first commandment), and spiritually (the second commandment). The law also required ethical distinctiveness (the second table of the law). The separation of Israel to the holy God was the ground for ceremonial separation, the principle of cleanness. It was also expressed in geographical separation centered around the place which God had chosen and where he put his name (Deut. 11:31; 12:5).

As we have seen, the distinctiveness of Israel as a covenant people marked God's calling of Israel to himself but also had its purpose in covenant service, the service of sons. Israel must worship God directly, but Israel was also called to exalt the name of the Lord among the nations so that all the earth might see the salvation of God.

Yet Israel after the flesh failed completely in maintaining the covenant distinctiveness and in rendering covenant service. The failure was both repeated and progressive. From the murmuring in the wilderness to the climactic apostasy in the land, the history of Israel was a history of repeated and increasing failure. Israel forsook the covenant, stoned the prophets, and delivered up the Son of God to the cross.

The sin of Israel was judged increasingly, and in the prophets this judgment is carried to an apocalyptic climax. The curses recited on Mount Ebal as the sanctions of the covenant will indeed be poured out. Israel will be driven from the land. Having served the heathen gods in the Lord's land the apostate people will be made to serve the heathen gods in their lands (Deut. 4:28). The infliction of this judgment employs the heathen nations as instruments. The temple of God is defiled and destroyed. The totality of this judgment is declared by Christ: "The kingdom of God shall be taken away from you, and shall be given to a nation bringing forth the fruits thereof" (Matt. 21:43).

God's judgment will not stop with Israel. The heathen, in destroying Israel, do not act in submission to God, but in blasphemous pride. They, too, must be judged (Isa. 10:5-19; Jer. 25:29; Obad. 15).

But God's purposes do not end in the obliteration of his people and his promises in the wrath of judgment. Instead of the dreadful renunciation of the covenant: "Call his name Lo-ammi; for ye are not my people, and I will not be your God" (Hos. 1:9); there shall be heard the covenant blessing: "Ye are the sons of the living God" (Hos. 1:10). After the blessing and the curse have been poured out (Deut. 30:1), God will restore his people from captivity and circumcise their hearts (Deut. 30:6). The glorious triumph of God's grace will be realized in the latter days. In the ceremonial law the ultimate restoration of all things is symbolized by the year of Jubilee, the crown of the sabbatical system (Lev. 25).

Israel's judgment brought blessing to the nations, for example, in the ministry of Elijah and Elisha. But if Israel's judgment brought blessing, much more must the blessing of Israel be shared by the nations. The glory of God's blessing is that a new Israel is to be raised up under the seal of a new covenant of peace (Isa. 41:8; 54:8), an everlasting covenant (Ezek. 16:60). The new Israel is raised up not only from the death of captivity but from the death of sin (Ezek. 37:14). The new covenant is spiritual, bringing the covenant principle to final realization (Jer. 31:31–37; Ezek. 36:24–28). Through the rich outpouring of the Holy Spirit, all the blessings of the covenant are sealed in the name of God (Isa. 44:1–5) and through the Word of God (Isa. 59:21).

Often the fullness of the promised blessing is expressed in terms of restorative completeness: the temple will be reestablished (Isa. 2:2–4; Ezek. 40:2), sacrifices will again be offered (Isa. 56:7; Jer. 17:26; 31:14; 33:18; Ezek. 43), the priests and Levites will be restored (Ezek. 44:9–31), the mediatorial position of Israel among the nations will be re-established (Isa. 45:14; 66:23; Mic. 4:1–3; Zech. 14:16–19). However, the very fullness of the blessing transcends the form of the covenant which is restored, so that the realities which are symbolized in ceremonial types are actualized. That which is restored is the covenant relation in its religious heart. Therefore the restoration is more than restoration; it is renewal. The old covenant in its final restoration becomes a new covenant.

Thus it is not only a reunited remnant of both Israel and Judah that is redeemed (Isa. 11:13; Ezek. 37:15–22; Hos. 1:11; 3:5). The Gentiles are also included (Isa. 2:2–4; Mic. 4:1–3). The outcasts of other nations are brought in with Israel's captivity (Isa. 56:6–8), and their sacrifices will be acceptable on God's altar (Zech. 14:16–19). So unthinkably great will be God's sanctifying blessing that God will be worshiped by sacrifice at an altar in Egypt, and Assyrians will pilgrimage there to worship, as well as Egyptians to Assyria, so that Israel's position as the covenant people will be shared by Egypt and Assyria, the former enemies (Isa. 19:19–25)! As otherwise expressed, the heathen will be born in Zion and inscribed on the rolls of Zion's citizens (Ps. 87). The barrier between Jew and Gentile is broken down because God in mercy calls those his people who were not his people; both the Jews and the Gentiles are shut up in sin as no people in order that God might have mercy upon both. For this reason even where Hosea has been speaking of Israel and Judah (Hos. 1:11) when he enunciates this principle (Hos. 2:23), Paul rightly finds a reference to the Gentiles (Rom. 9:25, 26; see also Ps. 47:9; Isa. 25:6–8; Zeph. 3:9; Zech. 2:11).

The outward symbols of the old covenant are so intensified with the fullness of the glory of the new covenant that they are transfigured and transformed. The symbol of both the city and the temple is heightened to an apocalyptic degree (Jer. 31:38f.; Zech. 14:20). Ezekiel's vision of the new temple includes a new land. So glorious will be the dwelling of God with all the remnant of the redeemed that the ark of the covenant will not be missed (Jer. 3:16, 17)! In the eschatological newness of the worship of "that day," the ceremonial is sublimated in absolute glory. It is not a restoration of Solomon's temple but of the Garden of Eden where the river of life flows beside trees whose leaves are for the healing of the nations. The new Israel is a new humanity; the restoration of the covenant brings a new heaven and earth (Isa. 65:17; 66:22). Peace will prevail (Isa. 9:4–7; Hos. 2:18; Mic. 4:3, 4). The animals are included (Isa. 11:6–9; 35:9); heavenly bodies have their light increased (Isa. 30:26); there is no longer day and night (Isa. 60:20), for the sun and moon are replaced by God's glory.

Such eschatological blessing could not be given without the renewed manifestation of God's own covenant presence. God's presence with his people is the heart of the covenant, and any covenant renewal must be brought about through a new manifestation of his presence.

The Lord appears, amidst the rejoicing of his creation, to set up his kingdom on earth (Ps. 46:5–10; 98:7–9). In a second exodus, he leads forth his sheep as their Redeemer-Shepherd-King (Isa. 10:26; 35:1–10; 40:3, 10; 52:12; Ezek. 34:11–16). God comes to dwell himself on Zion, and this is the source of the glory (Isa. 60:20) as he rules over all nations (Zech. 14:16), fills the new temple with his glory (Ezek. 43:2, 7), shines as the light over the city of God (Ezek. 5:5), and is as a fiery wall about it (Zech. 2:5).

The mount of the temple will rise above all mountains and hills (Isa. 2:2). God's truth will appear as a light to the nations (Isa. 51:4; 60:3). God calls the nations (Ps. 50:1; Isa. 45:20–22) and spreads a feast for them in his holy mountain (Isa. 25:6–8).

The coming of God promised in the prophets is identified with the coming of the Messiah. In Isaiah 40 it is God himself who comes as the Shepherd of his people; in Isaiah 42 it is the Servant of the Lord who, in God's spirit, sets justice in the earth. In Ezekiel 34:11 God himself is Shepherd; in verse 23 "My servant David" is the Shepherd. The Messianic Davidic king of Psalms 2, 45, 72, and 110 exercises a divine rule. The root of Jesse stands as an ensign to the peoples and his resting place shall be glory (Isa. 11:10). The assembly of the Lord restores the preserved of Israel and is a light to the Gentiles (Isa. 49:6). It is the Messiah who exercises God's rule over all the nations (Isa. 9:4–7; 11:1–6; Dan. 7:14; Zech. 9:10).

Yet the Messiah who comes to manifest God's Lordship also comes to fulfill Israel's sonship. The Messiah is the seed of the promise. He is the seed of David (Ps. 89:35, 36) and of Israel, the seed of Abraham (Gen. 13:15; 17:8; Gal. 3:16) and of the woman (Gen. 3:15). He is the true Israel (Isa. 49:3–7), the Son of God (Ps. 2:7), and the Servant of God (Isa. 52:13), the true man—the second Adam.

Christ therefore fulfills the role of Israel. He manifests the true distinctiveness of the holy Son of God (Isa. 11:3–5). In him the covenant principle is realized: God with us—Immanuel! (Isa. 7:14). He is anointed with the Holy Spirit without measure (Isa. 11:2; 61:1–3), as the Prophet (Deut. 18:15), Priest (Ps. 110:4), and King (Ps. 2; Isa. 9:6, 7), the mediating Representative of all the people of God. He not only actively fulfills the role of the Son of the covenant but as the righteous Sufferer he also endures and makes atonement for the sins of the many (Ps. 22; 69; Isa. 53). He suffers as the righteous King, Prophet, and Priest.

The Old Testament promises are realized in the advent of the Messiah and the gathering of Messiah's people, the true Israel of God. Christ comes as Immanuel, the Lord of the covenant and the Son of the covenant. He thus completes both the promised work of God and the required response of his people. As true God he is the Lord who has come; as true man, he is the head of the covenant, the new and true Adam, Israel, Moses, and David. All promises are complete in him (II Cor. 1:20), for in him dwells the fullness of the Godhead in bodily form (Col. 2:9). He is the Amen (Rev. 3:14), the Alpha and the Omega (Rev. 22:13).

The New Testament presents Christ as the Lord of the covenant. It is impossible here even to outline the richness of the New Testament witness on this point. Christ is revealed in the miracle of the incarnation as the Savior Lord (Luke 2:11) who shall save his people from sins (Matt. 1:21). His authority in redemption is shown in his mighty words and deeds. In the synagogue of Nazareth he proclaims the fulfillment of the prophetic year of Jubilee. His miracles reveal not only the cleansing power of the kingdom but his own Lordship as the one having authority over sickness, death, and Satan. He is the king of the wind and the waves; his authority is seen in public actions: the cleansing of the temple at the beginning of his ministry and again at its close; the triumphal entry; his adjuration before Jewish and Gentile courts. To his disciples Jesus revealed his Lordship in word and deed. His authority was sealed in the triumph of his death and resurrection and in his exaltation to God's right hand. Christ's glory will again be manifest in his coming as King and Judge.

The Christ who is thus revealed as Lord acted as Lord to assemble to himself his people. He chose disciples, calling them to "follow me." This choosing created a division among men. It began a "gathering" and "scattering." The disciples themselves were called to share in the gathering process as laborers in the harvest field and as fishers of men. He chose twelve disciples with evident reference to the twelve tribes of Israel. As he was rejected by an unbelieving Israel, he declared the rejection of those who refused to be gathered to him. The parable of the vineyard provides a stern warning: "The kingdom of God shall be taken away from you, and shall be given to a nation bringing forth the fruits thereof" (Matt. 21:43). The stone rejected of the builders is the cornerstone of the new temple and the stone of the kingdom. Only those who receive Christ are the true flock receiving the kingdom (Luke 12:32; *cf.* Mark 14:27).

Christ then proceeded to constitute the new Israel. The confession which he elicited from Simon Peter was distinctive and apostolic. Peter confessed the work of Jesus as Messiah in spite of Christ's refusal to fill a political role. Further, in contrast to the unbelief of the multitudes, Peter also confessed Christ's deity as the Son of the living God. This confession was supernatural in origin. Only the Father can so reveal the Son. Upon this confessing apostle the church was to be built. The foundation of the church is not Peter's confession in the abstract apart from the confessing Peter; the church is built on the foundation of the apostles and prophets (Eph. 2:20; Rev. 21:14). But neither is Peter the foundation apart from his confession, for in relation to a far different utterance that followed he is called Satan

(Matt. 16:23). Nor is Peter to be separated from the eleven, for the power of the keys which is addressed to Peter in Matthew 16:19 is addressed to all the apostles in Matthew 18:18. It is only Peter as confessing, in his distinctive apostolic work, who is the rock. Peter is the rock in terms of a figure in which Christ is seen as the builder.

The new assembly of the people of God is built by Christ confessed as the Messiah. Christ will perform this work through his death and resurrection and in the sovereignty of his rule at the Father's right hand. This work is God's great work of the latter days (Amos 9:11; *cf.* Acts 15:16–18; Zech. 6:12). The church is Christ's; God's people are the Messiah's people, for the Messiah is God the Son, the Lord. The church shares Christ's resurrection victory; the gates of death cannot prevail against the people of the Lord of life.

Further, Christ orders his kingdom in his Messianic authority. The keys of the kingdom are his to give. The church is organized by Christ as the company of his disciples. Where two or three are gathered together in his name there Christ is present. Binding and loosing through the ministration of his word has heavenly validity, for the authority is his. There is an instituted government of the church to which an offended "little one" of the flock may appeal (Matt. 18:17). This government may pronounce spiritual censure, but is not given the power of the sword (John 18:36). Its declaratory authority is ministerial but real (Matt. 10:12–15, 40; Luke 9:5; 10:5–16; John 20:21–23; Acts 13:51). Along with the Lord's Supper, signifying and sealing the blessings of the new covenant (Matt. 28:19; 26:26–29). Christ exercises his lordship in the church through his Word and Spirit. The sovereignty of Christ is divine and absolute. The choosing, calling, charging, and cherishing of the people of God ascribed to the Lord of the covenant in the Old Testament are ascribed to Christ the Lord in the New Testament. The revealed word of Christ is the law of the church. His revelation is climactic and final (Heb. 1:1, 2). Not even an angel from heaven can alter it (Gal. 1:8). His Word, the "all things" which he commanded (Matt. 28:20), is confirmed to the church by those that heard (Heb. 2:3, 4)—the Spirit bringing all things to their remembrance (John 14:26) and revealing the fullness of truth in him (John 16:13, 14) so that the apostolic witness is complete (I Cor. 14:37; *cf.* Rev. 22:18, 19). The "outline of sound words" is committed by the apostles to faithful men who shall be able to teach others also (I Tim. 6:20; II Tim. 1:13, 14; 2:2). The Old Testament no less than the New witnesses to Christ (Luke 24:27. 45–47), for the testimony of Jesus is the spirit of prophecy (Rev. 19:10).

The Spirit of Christ is the life of the church. Through his Spirit sent from heaven Christ inspires the written Word and by that same Spirit he illumines men's minds to understand and proclaim the Word. In the Spirit Christ is present with his church and through the Spirit the offices instituted by Christ in his Word are equipped and called (Rom. 12:6–8; I Cor. 12:28; Eph. 4:7–12). By the Spirit union with Christ is effected, and by that union Christians are also united to one another and know the freedom of the Spirit.

In the church the kingdom of Christ is a present reality. The people of the Lord are the kingdom of God and of the Son of his love (Col. 1:13). The kingdom title of the Old Testament is pronounced upon the church: "and he made us a kingdom, priests to God and his Father" (Rev. 1:6). In this sense kingdom is synonymous with "people," "nation," "house," or "temple" as the realm of God's saving Lordship. Those who are formed together into the holy temple are fellow citizens with the saints; they are the household, the inheritance of God, the heavenly commonwealth of the new Israel (Eph. 1:11; 2:12, 19, 21; Phil. 1:27; 3:20; Heb. 11:14–16; 13:14).

Yet the Bible rarely uses the word "kingdom" in this sense of "realm." More often it means "dominion." Even when it denotes a sphere, a "domain,", the sphere is one of active power. The kingdom, therefore, is sought, given, possessed, received. Further, the full manifestation of Christ's power awaits his coming in glory. Because of this future reference, the people of God are said to inherit the kingdom rather than to compose it (Matt. 25:34).

Since "kingdom" is used in an active sense, there is a simple clue to its rich variety: to understand the kingdom consider the King. God's universal sovereignty marks the scope of his kingdom; his final judgment will establish its triumph. But God is the King of salvation who manifests his kingly power to redeem his people. Therefore the prophets promise the kingdom to come. John the Baptist could not understand how Jesus could work the signs of kingdom blessing without first using the axe of kingdom judgment.

Jesus came to bear the judgment, not to inflict it. Therefore the kingdom comes in two stages. With the Lord came Lordship; with the King came "kingdominion." In Christ the temporary and typical are surpassed and the glory of the heavenly kingdom is present. The church he builds is the final form of the people of God, the gathering of the last days in which the kingdom is actualized. Christ does baptize with fire and build with the Spirit. Christ is heir of all the promises; the kingdom realization he brings is the concrete fulfillment of the Word of God.

Yet Christ the King must first suffer and then enter into his glory. By refusing to summon legions of angels as well as by coming on the clouds with the holy angels, Christ reveals the power of his kingdom. God's kingdom of salvation cannot be revealed by force alone, for then it would be known only in wrath and judgment. The power of God to salvation is revealed on the cross. In Christ's death the righteousness of God triumphs through bearing the curse.

The program of Christ's own ministry determines the program he has appointed for the ministry of the church. The church now shares the sufferings of Christ's kingdom and will share the glory of his kingdom.

Christ himself has entered into his glory. He has ascended into heaven, received all authority in heaven and in earth, and does now smite his enemies with the breath of his lips (Acts 12:23; 13:11; Rev. 1:16; 2:12, 13). His rule over his church includes physical chastisement as well as deliverances from danger and death (Acts 5:1–11; I Cor. 11:30; Rev. 2:23; Acts 12:7). Yet Christ's judgments accomplish the purposes of his kingdom in this time of his longsuffering restraint. They are not total judgments; the great day of the wrath of the Lamb (Rev. 6:16, 17), has not yet come. Christ's judgments summon men to repentance, and they discipline and defend the church.

When the Son of Man is revealed in the glory of his *parousia,* then the apostles will sit on twelve thrones (Matt. 19:28) and the least of the saints will judge angels (I Cor. 6:3). Until then the sword of judgment is not given to the church. Christ's servants may not fight to establish his kingdom, for it will not be brought in by human power. It is not like the political states, the kingdoms of this world. Peter had to put up his sword when his King was seized; no Christian may take the sword again to prepare for the return of the King.

If the power of Christ's resurrection now carried the church to the throne rather than to the cross, all the world powers could not overcome a single Christian soldier. But Christ does not call his church to battle before he comes to judge. This is not so much a limitation of the church as a sign of its glory. The Old Testament people of God were charged with stoning the blasphemers and exterminating the Canaanites. Such theocratic actions were typical of the final judgment, but they were not part of the consummation victory. It is because the church has an eschatological form that it no longer executes typical judgments. It must wait in hope for that new order for which it is formed. Precisely because the church brings the kingdom to realization it must suffer now, not seek to implement Christ's coming judgment.

Further, the state, which is ordained of God and which wields the sword as a minister of God (Rom. 13:1–7), is not the realization of the kingdom. God's rule over the nations is given to the ascended Christ, but this providential rule must still be distinguished from the saving rule of God over his people. Christ's authority over the "powers that be," whether over the defeated demonic hosts or over earthly kings and kingdoms, is exercised on behalf of the people of God and for the coming of the kingdom of glory. But this sovereignty is not the direct exercise of his saving rule. The people of God may not use a sword in the name of the kingdom which is denied to them as a church.

Disciples may claim the protection of magistrates, and indeed carry swords for defense (Luke 22:35–38); but they may not use the sword in an effort to bring the kingdom in, for using the sword would deny the nature of the kingdom.

It is clear, then, that the terms "church" and "kingdom" must be kept distinct. "Kingdom" describes salvation from the God-ward side; to adopt it for institutional use is to risk thinking that salvation is of the church rather than of the Lord.

Further, it is clear that the stages of the kingdom, marked by Christ's work, must not be confused. It is quite evident, for example, that a patient waiting for Christ's consummation judgment will be condemned by a man who does not believe in the Second Coming of Christ.

Again, because the kingdom is the Lord's, his *present* rule of power is not committed to the church, nor to the state. Christ now exercises universal dominion; but this dominion is his own immediate sovereignty directed to the purpose for which he delays his return, namely, the ingathering of his people. Christ does not now execute full judgment either upon or through the governments of this world. He commissions no servant, king, or apostle to fight in his name, for his kingdom.

Finally, the church alone is constituted by Christ to be an embodiment of the kingdom where his rule is confessed and his presence acknowledged. The state or other social organizations may manifest the kingdom in the sense that Christ's control over them is exhibited, or in the sense that these organizations may reflect the life of the church; but no organization other than the church may be identified as Christ's kingdom.

The Lord of the covenant assembles and rules his people. He also exercises universal Lordship on behalf of his church. Jesus Christ, seated at the right hand of his Father, is Lord of the universe as well as of the church. The Prince and Savior, who gives repentance to his people, has all authority in heaven and earth (Matt. 28:18; Acts 5:31). The one Lord has one victory. His triumph is over Satan and the powers of darkness; his exaltation is by and to the right hand of God, the universal King. There can be no exception to the subjection of all things to him, no unsubdued power. Only God himself is excepted, who put all things under the feet of the God-man (I Cor. 15:27; Eph. 1:21, 22).

Yet this absolute authority of Christ, sealed at his ascension, is exercised in an invisible rule of grace before it is manifested in a visible *parousia* of glory. We do not yet see all things made subject to him (Heb. 2:8), even though all power is given to him in heaven and earth.

Both the universal, absolute character of Christ's rule and its present hidden form are required by the purpose of his Messianic dominion. This purpose is the total realization and consummation of the kingdom of God. His power must be total, for he must rule until he has removed the curse from creation, a work which requires the re-creation of heaven and earth (Rom. 8:20, 21, 38, 39; I Cor. 15:25, 26).

Christ's total power, however, must be wielded over history before it is manifested in final judgment. The building of the church requires the delay of the *parousia* while the Gentiles are gathered in. "All things are ready," but the feast cannot begin until the King's house is full (Luke 14:17, 23).

The Great Commission founds the sending of the church upon the universal dominion of Christ: "All authority hath been given unto me in heaven and on earth. Go ye therefore . . ." (Matt. 28:18f.). It is clear that Christ's Lordship over the universe is an indispensable condition for the ingathering of the church. Christ's power is not merely an auxiliary support. Christ is more than a heavenly Constantine or Charlemagne, ready to lend imperial support and protection to missionaries. Rather, the rule of Christ opens the door to the nations. The bondage of the peoples under the powers of darkness has been broken, and for this reason mission is possible. The Son is seated on the throne until the fullness of the peoples is given him of the Father (Ps. 2; 72:11; 110). The image of the miraculous catch of fish symbolizes the great ingathering under the sovereignty of the Lord of wind and wave (Luke 5:10). Christ has overcome the power of the curse: no serpent can hurt his ambassadors; the very demons must be subject to them in his name (Luke 10:19). That same sovereignty keeps the sheep of the flock: no one can snatch them from the hand of the Good Shepherd, for none can move the hand of the Father at whose right hand the Son sits (John 20:27–29). Because the rule of Christ is world-wide, his apostles may make disciples of all nations. The mission of the church to the ends of the earth and the end of the age is within the sphere of Christ's rule of the earth and the age.

Another question must be asked. If Christ's Lordship is universal, is it enough to say that his universal power is exercised on behalf of the church? Must we not rather say that Christ rules the church for the sake of the world? We have seen that contemporary theology stresses the servant role of the church in a world that is redeemed; Christ is Lord of the church only because he is Lord of the world. The church is distinguished only by its recognition of Christ's Lordship.

This contemporary universalism must circumvent the Biblical teaching of the exercise of Christ's Lordship in judgment. All things will be subjected to Christ, including the new heavens and the new earth. But his authority over the nations will culminate in the last judgment (Matt. 25:31–46; II Thess. 1:7–10; II Peter 3:8–13). The judgment of the Messianic Son according to the Bible is not dialectical but teleological (Ps. 2; 110). The judgment of the wicked is part of the deliverance of the people of God. The coming of Christ in judgment continues to be the hope of the persecuted church (II Thess. 1:5–10; Rev. 6:10). The resurrection of Christ is a call to repentance, for God has "appointed a day in which he will judge the world in righteousness by the man whom he hath ordained; whereof he hath given assurance unto all men, in that he hath raised him from the dead" (Acts 17:31).

The ultimate issues of this judgment are never left in doubt in the Bible. To share the abominations of the nations is to expose oneself to the wrath to come upon the nations (Col. 3:5–11; I Peter 4:3–5; Rev. 18:4, 5). All men are children of wrath (Eph. 2:3), and "he that obeyeth not the Son shall not see life, but the wrath of God abideth on him" (John 3:36).

The fullness of a new mankind will be restored in Christ (Rom. 11:12, 25). but the fullness is not the totality. The principle of the remnant continues to operate.

The consummation awaits the completion of the church as the "fullness," the gathering and the manifesting of the sons of God (Rom. 8:19; Col. 3:4). Christ's reigning authority over all powers assures the men called according to his purpose that no power in creation can separate them from his love (Rom. 8:28, 35–39). With Christ's victory all things are given to his people (Rom. 8:32). "All things are yours" (I Cor. 3:21). The world, the powers, the ages, all are given to the church, even as the church is Christ's and Christ is God's. The church is for the world in the sense that it has a mission to the world, but that mission makes it a savor of life unto life and death unto death. The church is not subordinated to the world in the purpose of God. Rather the world is given to the church. The church now shares Christ's suffering in the world. When he appears, the church will share his work of judging the nations. The church will constitute the new humanity and will receive the dominion of man, restored in the image of God, over a renewed universe.

One aspect of the present rule of Christ is his subjugation of the principalities and powers. This also has been viewed as a redemptive universalism. On the basis of Colossians 1:20 it has been urged that Christ has reconciled all the cosmic powers as well as all men.[4] But Paul knows of holy angels who do not need such reconciliation, the angels of power with whom Christ will appear from heaven to judge men (II Thess. 1:7). On the other hand, the evil principalities and powers are defeated and exposed by the cross of Christ rather than redeemed by it (Col. 2:15). These evil principalities are to be identified with "the power of darkness" (Col. 1:13) from which the saints are translated into the Kingdom of the Son.[5] Satan may be transformed into an angel of light (II Cor. 11:14), but neither he nor his hosts are converted by such tactics.

Paul's references to the "principalities and powers" are not explicit descriptions but assume a general understanding concerning them.[6] Included in this assumed viewpoint is a distinction between the elect angels associated with the throne of God (I Tim. 5:21) and the evil beings serving the prince of the power of the air (Eph. 2:2). The Qumran literature offers evidence of the vigor with which this distinction was made in Essenic Judaism.[7]

We must not therefore assume that "the principalities and powers in the heavenly places" to whom the wisdom of God is revealed through the church are evil (Eph. 3:10). The holy angels are to the fore in Ephesians 1:20, 21, where Christ is described as seated at God's right hand *in the heavenly places* above all principalities and powers. In Ephesians 6:12 it is surely not the phrase "in the heavenly places" which indicates the evil nature of the principalities, but the terms "darkness" and "wickedness."

Christ's victory, against the background of Psalm 110 in its New Testament interpretation, is either through subjugation or through salvation. His total Lordship, when asserted in its widest scope, includes both of these forms of victory. Philippians 2:9, 10 should be understood in this way, against the background of Isaiah 45.

In view of the distinction between the "powers" of light and darkness we ought not to press the universal language of Colossians 1:20. The "all things" which are reconciled would appear to include created *things* as well as persons: the "all things" in heaven include the "thrones, dominions, principalities, powers" of verse 16; but these are viewed in the aspect of their grandeur (angels which the Colossians might be tempted to worship). The passage describes the centrality of Christ's atonement for the eschatological reconciliation. The heavenly powers are brought to God in the renewed fellowship of a redeemed universe. The ascended Christ is the sovereign over the great "fatherdom" (Eph. 3:15) in which angels are joined with men. The making of peace benefits sinners and the heavenly angels in different ways, but the whole new order is one of reconciliation.[8]

So full is the relation of the church to the Lordship of Christ that we might think it exhaustive. But the covenant between God and his people must be restored from both sides. As Lord, God comes in Christ to gather his people. But Christ comes as Servant as well as Lord. He comes to fulfill the covenant from man's side, to be the true Son and Servant. The Messiah is the head of a redeemed humanity; his headship binds him to the church as the representative and vital head of the covenant.

His representative role and function is grounded in the Old Testament concept of covenant headship. Sin and death entered the world through Adam (Rom. 5:12; I Cor. 15:21f.). On the other hand, in Abraham, the servant of the Lord, all the families of the earth are blessed (Gen. 12:3; 18:18). In the promises of this covenant, children are chosen and blessed in their fathers (Gen. 17:7, 19). The Messianic Servant figure in the Old Testament unites all these aspects of covenant representation. As Prophet, Priest, and King he is the mediatorial head of the people of God (Deut. 18:18; Ps.2:6, 7; 110:2-4). He is the eldest Son, Seed, Servant in whom the elect people are chosen (Ps. 2:6-12; Isa. 42:1; *cf.* Gal. 3:16). He is the Called, in whom they are called and brought to God, and through whom their calling is fulfilled (Isa. 42:1; Eph. 1:3; I Peter 2:4-8). He is the true Israel, the chosen Jeshurun, the Elect and Beloved in whom the redeemed inherit the name of God and of his people (Gen. 22:2; Exod. 4:22; Deut. 33:5; Isa. 42:1; 44:2-5; Matt. 3:17; 17:5; Rom. 9:13, 25; Eph. 1:6 *cf.* Ps. 60:5; 127:2; Col. 1:13).

The figure of the body of Christ stands against this background of covenantal headship. It expresses the unity of the individual Messianic Servant with "the many" as the servant people. The one new man in Christ is not the "cosmic man" in the pattern of Hellenistic thought, but the "covenant man," the servant of the Lord.[9] According to Ephesians 2:11ff., the Gentiles were "separate from Christ, alienated from the commonwealth of Israel, and strangers from the covenants of the promise." The parallelism is revealing: Christ, commonwealth, covenants. The blood of Christ in which those who were afar off are made nigh (verse 13) is the blood of the new covenant. The new covenant is made in the Messiah, the Servant of the Lord. "Through him we both have our access in one Spirit unto the Father. So then ye are no more strangers and sojourners, but ye are fellow-citizens with the saints, and of the household of God" (verses 18, 19). Jews and Gentiles are reconciled "in one body unto God through the cross" (verse 16). The expression "in one body" is parallel to the phrases "in his flesh" and "in the blood of Christ." The body in which our reconciliation is accomplished is the crucified body of Christ. The enmity is slain in him (ἐν αὐτῷ, *en autō*), and we both have our access to the Father through him (δι'αὐτοῦ, *di' autou*). Christ represented the church in his death and resurrection. The union between Christ and his people is grounded in redemptive history.

"In Christ" we secure the blessings that are through Christ (*cf.* Eph.

1:3–5). Those who are blessed in the heavenly places *in* Christ are those who were raised together *with* him (Eph. 1:3; *cf.* 2:6, 7; Col. 3:1, 2). Christ enters heaven as the representative head of his people, as the exalted Servant-Son. He receives the inheritance promised in the covenant: the throne promised to the seed of David, the blessing promised to the seed of Abraham, the dominion promised to Adam.

He *is* the promised Seed and receives the inheritance as the Firstborn (Eph. 1:10, 11; Col. 1:18). Enthroned at the right hand of the Father, he awaits the day of judgment and consummation victory (Acts 2:34–36; I Cor. 15:25; Eph. 1:20). What is given him is also given to them who are his. They are adopted as sons through Christ (Eph. 1:5) and have received God's grace in the beloved Son (Eph. 1:6).

To be "in Christ" means first to be represented by Christ in his great work of redemption. Being "in Christ" may therefore be compared to being "in Adam" (Rom. 5:12–21; I Cor. 15:22). The basic category is not one of subjective mystical experience but of objective redemptive history. To be sure, the man in Christ enjoys a religious fellowship with the living Lord, but he enjoys this because he is in Christ as the representative covenant head. He desires to know Christ, but his hope lies in being known by Christ, being "found in him" (Phil. 3:9, 10).

Covenant representation offers the key for understanding the body of Christ figure. Since the one physical body of Christ dies and is raised on behalf of the saints, they are united representatively in that body. From this conception a figurative extension is a small step. If the many are all reconciled in Christ's body, then the unity of their new position may be pictured as a body. They are one in Christ's body; they are one body in Christ (Rom. 12:5); they are a body of Christ (without the article, I Cor. 12:27); they are the body of Christ (Eph. 4:12).

If we understand the grounding of the body figure in Christ's giving of his own body as covenantal representative, we will escape many misconceptions. We will not identify the church with the resurrection body of Christ. Christ has a literal resurrection body. He is not seeking embodiment. The reality of our access to God is sealed in the representative entrance of Christ's risen body into glory.

Further, an understanding of covenant representation will clarify our grasp of Christ's body presented in the Lord's Supper. The new covenant in Christ's blood is established representatively; therefore we may not remove the symbolism to assert a magical reality of either substance or action.

Covenantal representation accounts for the parallel development of the Christian and the church in the use of the body figure. On the one hand, Paul's teaching cannot be explained in categories of mystical or moralistic individualism. The foundation of covenantal representation requires a personal distinction as well as representative status and function. Paul uses "in Christ" and "the body of Christ" to describe this representative relation.

On the other hand, neither can Paul's figure be explained in categories of institutional or sacramental collectivism. The individual Christian is in Christ; his body is a member of Christ, a temple of the Spirit of Christ; he has put on Christ; the life of Jesus is manifest in his body (II Cor. 4:10). The free use of the body figure with the individual in mind shows the direct relation of Christians to Christ. Paul does not have to proceed from Christ to the church as his body and thence to Christians as members of the church.[10] Christians are members of Christ. Their bodies must be offered in the gratitude of devotion in analogy to the offering of his body for them in atonement. Paul argues for the unity of the collective body as an existing fact which must not be denied in schism. But he also assumes the existing fact of the believer's portion in Christ. Only one body of Christ is primary, the body of his flesh. It is in representative relation to this body that the individual believer and the group of believers have a part in ''the body of Christ.''

Further, covenant representation accounts for much of the variety in the use of the body figure. Because Christ's own body is central, all that Christ is and does in his body has meaning for the church.

Because Christ's body was the temple of the Holy Spirit, Christians are temples, and the church is a temple (John 1:14; 2:21; I Cor. 6:19; II Cor. 6:16). Christ was ''endued'' of the Spirit for his work; Christians also, as they put on Christ, are endued with his spirit (John 1:32–34; Gal. 3:26–4:6). Christ's body was offered for sin; our bodies, and the church as his body, are offered in the thankoffering of grateful praise (Rom. 12:1; 15:16). His body was raised from the dead; he is the new Adam, heading the new creation and destined to receive the absolute subjection of all things (I Cor. 15:20–28, 45). Christians are members of Christ, redeemed for new life, and even now the life of Jesus is manifest in their bodies (Rom. 8:10ff.). The church is one new man in Christ (Gal. 3:27), the second Eve, presented as a pure virgin to Christ (II Cor. 11:2, 3), the fullness of him who fills all in all.

The church as the figurative body of Christ does not repeat or continue the incarnational presence of God with man; it is not filled with the Spirit without measure; it is not offered as a sin offering; it is not the new Adam, the heavenly Bridegroom or the reigning Lord. Bold language joins the church with Christ, as his body, in all these respects. Yet the foundation of the figure guards against this deification of the church. The church is the body of Christ only because Christ ''bore our sins in his own body on the tree.''

Cerfaux rightly observes that the shift in the conception of the church as the body of Christ between the earlier epistles of Paul and Colossians and Ephesians is based on a shift in the prevailing reference to the physical body of Christ.[11] In the former epistles, it is the crucified body of Christ that is in view; in the latter it is the risen and glorified body. This distinction is by no means absolute, as Ephesians 2:13ff. makes clear; but it is marked.

Understood in this perspective, the image of the church as the body of Christ in Colossians and Ephesians adds richness to the teaching of Paul without overthrowing or replacing the concepts of the Corinthian epistles and Romans. The distinctive imagery of Colossians and Ephesians puts the church in a cosmic setting because Christ is seen in this setting as the triumphant Lord. No doubt the occasion of this emphasis was the false teaching in Asia Minor. Against the speculations which unduly exalted principalities and powers in the heavenly hierarchy, Paul asserts that Christ is over all things now and forever, just as he was before all things and is appointed as heir of all things in the good pleasure of God (Col. 1:15–17; Eph. 1:10, 20–22).

The theme of covenant representation is not here discarded but elaborated. The triumph of Christ is the culmination of the history of redemption (Eph. 1:20–22). Christ's heavenly rule is the issue of his resurrection and ascension. Christians are made a heritage in Christ (Eph. 1:11); they are chosen in him before the foundation of the world (Eph. 1:4), and are seated with him in heaven (Eph. 1:3). His exaltation is theirs, for he represents them.[12]

The structure of redemptive history brings a double authority of Christ into view. He is the Sovereign of the universe, but in a special sense he is the Lord of the church. This distinction is expressed in Ephesians 1; Christ's inheritance in the saints as God's own possession (verse 14) is different from the "all things" that are in subjection under his feet (verse 22). This picture is familiar from the Old Testament. Messiah rules the nations with a rod of iron and brings deliverance to those who put their trust in him (Ps. 2, 110). Just as God is King in two senses—as the Sovereign of the nations and the Lord of his covenant people—so the Christ has all authority in heaven and in earth, but as the beloved Son brings the redeemed into his own kingdom (Col. 1:13).

Paul uses the word "head" (κεφαλή, *kephalē*) to describe the supremacy of Christ over all things and all ages (Eph. 1:22; Col. 2:10). His usage is shaped by the Greek Old Testament, where *kephalē* is associated with ἀρχή (*archē*) in translating the Hebrew ראשׁ (*rōsh*). Primacy, origination, honor, authority, and summation are assigned to the "head" in Old Testament usage.[13] Christ is exalted to headship in all these senses. Just as all things were created in him, through him, and unto him (Col. 1:16), so all things are "headed up" by him (Eph. 1:10). The terms "firstborn" (πρωτότοκος, *prōtotokos*) and "beginning" (*archē*) describe this primacy rather than merely priority (Col. 1:15, 17, 18). This Christ who is the head of all powers in heaven and earth, every angelic power or Satanic dominion, is also the head of the church (Col. 2:10; 1:18).

It will be observed that the figure of headship is an independent metaphor and does not originate in the body figure.[14] Even when the two figures are intimately related, as when Christ is said to be the head of the body, the church (Col. 1:18), the independent force continues. When Paul writes that man is the head of the woman (I Cor. 11:3), he does not have in view the model of a single body of which the man is the head and the woman is the trunk. Paul goes on to say that Christ is the head of the man and that God is the "head" of Christ. When Paul asserts that the body grows up into the head and is nourished from the head (Eph. 4:15, 16), we are not to seek for some physiological model relating the head to the rest of the body. Rather, Christ the head nourishes his body as a man nourishes and cherishes his wife, in a position of authority and primacy.

The head figure therefore does not demand a body figure for its completion. It is mistaken to say that the head is incomplete without the body.

Christ's headship over all things does not mean that the cosmos is his body. To the contrary, this is precisely the exalted privilege of the church: the church is the body of him who is head over all. Indeed Paul writes of Christ's cosmic headship with a view to assuring the church of its privilege.[15] In his exaltation Christ fills all things (Eph. 1:23; 4:10). As God fills heaven and earth (Jer. 23:24) in the sense that his omnipresent power controls all things, so also the exalted Christ exercises as Messiah divine dominion. The church is also his fullness, for he fills the church with his dominion (Eph. 1:23; Col. 2:10). As Christ dwells in the church, he fills it with all the fullness of the divine presence and power (Eph. 3:18). Yet Christ's filling of the church is not simply the overwhelming presence of his power. He fills the church with the power of his grace, with the rich gifts which build the church up to the measure of the stature of the fullness of Christ (Eph. 4:13). Because the Christ who is head of the church is the head of the universe, the church need not fear any other power, even though the evil day comes when the people of God must do battle against the principalities and powers. Because Christ is head of all, the church now expresses the goal of his Lordship. But neither Paul's figures nor his teaching ever passes over into a merging of the church and the powers. This fundamental confusion in contemporary ecclesiology runs counter to the whole teaching of the apostle.

Union with Christ, as it is described in the New Testament, and particularly as expressed in the body figure, is not merely representational or legal, but vital, spiritual, and personal. Christ is not only the representative head but also the vital head of the covenant.

This appears from Paul's use of the phrase ἐν Χριστῷ) *en Christō*). As we have seen, this phrase often expresses the representative identification of Christians with Christ. When Paul writes, "There is therefore now no condemnation to them that are in Christ Jesus" (Rom. 8:1), this representative relation is clearly in view. This is also the case in many passages which speak of God's saving action or gift to us in Christ (*e.g.*, Rom. 6:23; II Cor. 5:19, 21; Gal. 3:14; Eph. 1:3, 6, 11; 2:13, 14; 4:32), and in passages which use the phrase to designate believers as those who sustain a saving relation to Christ (*e.g.*, Rom. 16:7; I Cor. 1:30; Phil. 1:14; 3:9; 4:21).

However, the phrase bears a fuller meaning in other passages. Paul's first letter begins, "Paul, and Silvanus, and Timothy, unto the church of the Thessalonians in God the Father and the Lord Jesus Christ . . ." (I Thess. 1:1; *cf.* II Thess. 1:1). Unless the phrase conveyed more than representation, the Father could not be joined with Christ as its object. Other passages which show a broader scope describe the life or action of the Christian "in Christ." Paul declares. "I can do all things in him that strengtheneth me" (Phil. 4:13). He charges the Colossians: "As therefore ye received Christ Jesus the Lord, so walk in him, rooted and builded up in him, and established in your faith, even as ye were taught . . ." (Col. 2:6, 7).

Just as Romans 6:1–11 emphasizes the representative side of our union with Christ, so Romans 8 emphasizes the vital side. The presence of Christ in the believer through the Spirit provides a vital relation which defines what it means to live and walk "in Christ."

When Paul writes of growing up into Christ the head through the use of the gifts which Christ provides (Eph. 4:12–16), he is stating with vigor a reality of spiritual life "in Christ."

This vital union with Christ expressed in the phrase *en Christō* appears also in the body of Christ figure. Paul's initial use of the metaphor of the many members in the one body (I Cor. 12:12–31; Rom. 12:4–8) does not stress the vital union, but it presupposes it. The organic figure and the whole idea of the gifts of the Spirit alike make it clear that every member of the body shares in the new life of Christ (*cf.* I Cor. 12:13).

When the body is viewed as a temple, its "indwelling" by God must be understood in terms of intimate personal union (I Cor. 6:19). What is true of the individual is true of the whole people of God. Vital union is again central in the marriage figure. This application of the body metaphor is particularly illuminating, for it portrays a union of Christ with the church in strongly personal terms (Eph. 5:23–30).

In Ephesians and Colossians the organic figure is approached differently, and with greater emphasis on the union of life between Christ and the church. In I Corinthians the unity of the church in the exercise of spiritual gifts was the urgent problem. In Ephesians and Colossians the position of Christ is the issue. There must be harmonious function in the body; but above all, the link of life with Christ, who is the head, must be preserved (Col. 2:19). The glory of Christ means glory for the church (Eph. 1:23), as the power, life, and fullness of Christ are communicated to the church. As we have seen, headship is ascribed to Christ apart from the body figure. On the other hand, the body figure is developed by a greater emphasis on growth. This is related both to the emphasis on edification in these epistles and to their orientation toward the consummation, the summing up of all things in Christ. Those who have been representatively raised with Christ (Col. 3:1) have also been united to Christ as their life (Col. 3:4). Those who are in Christ must grow up into Christ (Eph. 4:15). To gain Christ is not only to be found in him but to know him (Phil. 3:9, 10).

Other figures besides that of the body express the vital relation of the church with Christ. Two of these have the closest association with the body figure: the union of the temple with its foundation or cornerstone (Eph. 2:20–22; Col. 2:7; I Peter 2:4, 5; *cf.* Ps. 118:22; Isa. 28:16), and the union of the husband with his wife (Rom. 7:4; II Cor. 11:2; Eph. 5:31, 32; Rev. 19:7; *cf.* Isa. 54:5; Jer. 3:20; Hos. 2:2–5).[16] The union of the vine and its branches (John 15:1–10) offers another illustration, almost identical with that of the body. It is the more striking because the vine is the symbol of Israel (Ps. 80:8; Isa. 5:1–7; Jer. 2:21). Christ is both the realization and the life of the true people of God. When Christians are called sons of God, union with the Son of God is implied. This sonship is realized and sealed by the Spirit of Christ dwelling in believers (Rom. 8:9–17). Descriptions of the work of the Holy Spirit assert in direct terms the truth of the rich figures: Christ's spiritual union with his people (Rom. 8:9, 10; Eph. 3:16, 17; Col. 1:27).

Representative covenant union with Christ determines the status and position of the church; vital union with Christ is the source of the life of the church. Union with Christ is therefore the specific determinant of the whole doctrine of the church.

Let us note some of the consequences for ecclesiology of vital union with Christ in particular.

First, the organic figure of the body is used to relate the individual Christian to the whole church. Neither the individual nor the group is primary in the church, because Christ is primary. The church is his body. Because each member is united to him, is a member of Christ, there is no mediating institution through which the Christian is related to the Savior. The saints are those who have been chosen and called of God. They have been saved through faith. They have believed the word of the cross; their faith stands in the power of God (I Cor. 2:5). Further, each man has his own gift of God, "one after this manner, and another after that" (I Cor. 7:7). Each man must run with patience the race set before him, not counting himself to have laid hold but pressing on toward the goal (Phil. 3:13; I Cor. 9:24). In I Corinthians 10 Paul sets himself against any sacramentalist view of salvation. Those who have been baptized into Christ outwardly and come confidently to the Lord's table should remember the rejection of Israel in the wilderness. Paul did not emphasize baptism but the preaching of the gospel (I Cor. 1:17). Salvation is an individual experience: "If any man loveth God, the same is known by him" (I Cor. 8:3). "The head of every man is Christ" (I Cor. 11:3). Every Christian is a temple of the Holy Spirit (I Cor. 6:13–20).

On the other hand, just as there is no salvation apart from Christ, so there is no salvation without union in the body of Christ. The sanctified in Christ Jesus at Corinth make up the church of God at Corinth (I Cor. 1:2). Divisions among those who call upon God's name in any place would imply that Christ could be divided (I Cor. 1:13). The one crucified body of Christ in which the church is representatively included, and the one functioning body composed of "members" of Christ alike require the unity of the church. Human leaders must not be made occasions for division; they are neither Christ nor the church. There is one Christ; apostles and teachers are his servants, called by him and endued with the gifts of his Spirit (I Cor. 3:5). There is one church—Christ's; apostles and teachers are given to the church as stewards (I Cor. 3:21—4:1).

Neither may the variety of gifts of the Spirit become occasions for division. The organic figure of the body shows that diversity need not mean division. Not only do the gifts proceed from one giver, they are also interdependent in their function. A man who is "all ears" cannot in and of himself even hear successfully. The gift of speaking in tongues loses all public significance unless it is complemented by the gift of interpreting, and for its proper regulation it requires others with the gift of rule and discernment (I Cor. 12:10, 28; 14:28). So far from producing separation, the variety of the gifts of Christ requires unity. The life of Christ is manifested in his body "corporately," and division destroys this manifestation. Were all the gifts of Christ identical, the very uniformity produced would lessen the requirement of unity. As it is, the mutual sharing of the gifts of Christ is indispensable.

From this there develops a second consideration affecting the nature of the church. If the church as well as the individual is the temple and body of Christ, then communion, fellowship with Christians as well as with Christ, must determine the existence of the church. Christian life, to be in Christ, must be in the church as the body of Christ. To deny to one's brethren the ministry of the grace given to one is to be an unfaithful steward of the manifold mercies of God (I Peter 4:10). Even a cup of cold water refused to one of the least of Christ's brethren is refused to Christ. On the other hand, to refuse the ministry of grace from another, to despise the prophesying of another, is to quench the Spirit (I Thess. 5:17–22).

The growth of the body is therefore a collective process. Again, this is not to set the church above the Christian: individuals do grow in wisdom and stature, and in favor with God and man; individuals may be edified I Cor. 14:4). But edification is usually attributed to the church (I Cor. 14:4, 5, 12). The body grows in the image of Christ the head through the proper functioning of each part (Eph. 4:11–16). If a member of the body ceases to function, the health of the whole is affected. As the church is grounded in the truth through the teaching of Christ's ministers, it grows into unity of faith and knowledge of the Son of God. This edification in faith and love is in unity and unto unity, a unity of life in Christ as members of his body and a unity of function in that body, "till we all attain . . . unto a fullgrown man."

So also the sufferings of the church are borne in fellowship with Christ and with Christians. Paul's apostolic sufferings traced a conformity to Christ's death in experience to reflect his representative union with Christ's death (Phil. 3:10). Further, Paul suffered on behalf of the church in fellowship with Christ (Col. 1:24; *cf.* I Peter 4:13). The fellowship extends to all Christians: "whether one member suffereth, all the members suffer with it" (I Cor. 12:26).

Such mutual concern requires solicitude for the welfare of the other members of Christ's body. Bearing one another's burdens in the Spirit includes the gentle restoration of those overtaken in sin (Gal. 6:1, 2) as well as the exclusion of those who defile the fellowship (Matt. 18:8, 17–20; Rom. 16:17; I Cor. 5:12, 13). Each of the figures used for the union of the church with Christ has a negative side to describe the separation of those who are guilty of apostasy in faith or life. The lifeless branches of the vine are cut off and burned (John 15:1, 6); him who defiles the holy temple of God's dwelling God will destroy (I Cor. 3:17); to the disobedient Christ becomes not the foundation stone but the stone of stumbling and rock of offense (I Peter 2:8); spiritual adultery Christ will judge, for his bride must be pure and spotless (II Cor. 11:2; *cf.* 6:15; Rev. 2:22; 21:2; 22:15); even members of the body may be cut off (Matt. 18:8).

Union with Christ determines the life of the church in κοινωνία (*koinōnia*). "Fellowship" is too weak a translation for this word, although it is the best term available to render one aspect of *koinōnia*.[17] The root *koin* means "common" and the noun *koinōnia* designates a having in common. "But the primary idea expressed by *koinōnos* and its cognates is not that of association with another person or persons, but that of participation in something in which others also participate."[18] Often the verb *koinōnein* is used as a synonym for μετέχειν (*metechein*), to partake of, *share in,* with the emphasis on the partaking rather than the association.

This point needs to be made so that the "fellowship" of the church will not be regarded as the camaraderie of a religious club. The core of *koinōnia* is not social or associative, but theological and constitutive. Paul writes, "God is faithful, through whom ye were called into the fellowship of his Son Jesus Christ our Lord" (I Cor. 1:9). This does not mean that we are called into an association established by Christ, nor that we are called into association with Christ, but that we are called to participate together in Christ. The same thought is expressed in Hebrews 3:14: "for we are become partakers [μέτοχοι, *metochoi*] of Christ, if we hold fast the beginning of our confidence firm unto the end." (*Cf.* Heb. 6:4, 5, "those who were . . . made partakers of the Holy Spirit, and tasted the good word of God. . . .") In the salutation of I Corinthians, Paul addresses the church as those called to be saints, and thanks God for "the grace of God which was given you in Christ Jesus; that in everything ye were enriched in him . . . so that ye come behind in no gift . . ." (verses 4–7).

The participation in Christ to which the Corinthians were called is that very blessing of receiving of the grace of God given in Christ of which Paul had been speaking.

This is not to deny that the church is a fellowship, nor that we have fellowship with Christ as well as with each other. The same book of Hebrews which speaks of partaking of Christ and of the Spirit also emphasizes the fact that Christ is made like unto his brethren and calls them brethren (Heb. 2:11, 12, 17; *cf.* 1:9). In I John 1:3–7 the fellowship aspect of *koinōnia* is stressed; fellowship with the Father, the Son, and with one another is described.

Yet all such fellowship rests upon a vital relation to Christ which is more than associative. Paul emphasizes this core of *koinōnia* as he discusses the eating of meat offered to idols (I Cor. 10). The Christian participates in the body and blood of Christ in the sacramental feast and therefore cannot partake of the table of demons. That which is symbolized in the Lord's Supper is the spiritual experience of Christians. They are united to Christ as intimately as though they were to partake of his flesh and blood.

Perhaps a caution is needed against an opposite extreme. If *koinōnia* is more than mere association, it is less than sheer identity. Neither the term nor the teaching is clarified by lumping together all uses of *koinōnia* and *metechein*. It is true that Christ has shared in flesh and blood (Heb. 2:14) and that we are made partakers of the divine nature (II Peter 1:4). Yet the two participations differ in character. We may not say that God took man's nature that man might take God's nature. The unity that we have with God through Christ rests upon the work of the God-man, but it does not constitute God-men.

It is true, nevertheless, that our participation in Christ, our union with Christ, is a relationship that is possible only between God and man and, indeed, only through the God-man.

Such *koinōnia,* such union with Christ, stamps every aspect of the life of the church. The suffering that the church endures is a sharing in his sufferings, not in the sense that the church continues his redemptive work but in the sense that the church, redeemed by his sufferings, suffers for his name in union with him. The worship of the church is transformed by this presence of Christ not only in the midst of his people but in their hearts. In the midst of the church Christ sings his Father's praise (Ps. 22:22; Heb. 2:12). The witness of the church is sustained by this same abiding union with Christ. Paul proclaimed "the riches of the glory of this mystery among the Gentiles, which is Christ in you, the hope of glory" (Col. 1:27). Through the indwelling presence of Christ the church manifests a new order: two or three gathered in his name must acknowledge him in the midst (Matt. 18:20). Even the ministry of mercy is shaped by this fellowship. The "sharing" with impoverished saints becomes a spiritual sacrifice (II Cor. 8, 9; Heb. 13:16), a communion with Christ as well as with the least of his brethren. All ministry in the church is determined by the gift of the Christ in the midst and ministers union with him (Eph. 4:11–16). Since it is in the Spirit that Christ is present with his people and they are united to him, we must turn to the final aspect of the Biblical doctrine of the church: the church is the fellowship of the Holy Spirit.

The Fellowship of the Spirit

By the coming of Christ the people of God are gathered and renewed. As Lord, Christ claims his people for God; as Servant, Christ claims God for his people. The same covenant relation illumines the work of the Holy Spirit. The Spirit of the Living God, proceeding from the throne of Christ, actualizes and seals the new covenant. As the Spirit of God he possesses the people of God and is possessed by them. In both of these senses he seals the possession of the Father and the Son (II Cor. 1:21, 22; Eph. 1:13; 4:30).

This double relation of Giver and Gift does not betray any confusion as to the personality of the Holy Spirit. It is a mistake to think of the Giver as a divine Person and the Gift as an impersonal power. To be sure, there are gifts of the Spirit, enduements of grace resulting from his presence; but underlying these is the Gift of the Spirit himself, present as the living Seal of the bond between God and his people. To deny the deity of the Spirit or the personality of the Spirit is to rob the gospel of its crown, the realization of the covenant in the new presence of God among his people.

Those who were chosen in Christ before the foundation of the world are sealed as God's heritage by the Spirit (Eph. 1:11). By the same Spirit God is sealed to them as their inheritance. "In whom, having also believed, ye were sealed with the Holy Spirit of promise, which is an earnest of our inheritance, unto the redemption of God's own possession, unto the praise of his glory" (Eph. 1:13b, 14).

We may therefore reflect first on the Spirit as possessing the church and then on the Spirit as possessed by the church.

The Spirit's possession of the people of God comes with the climax of redemptive history. God's possession of his Old Testament people came by his epiphany on Sinai; the great renewal of the covenant came by God's epiphany in the Incarnation. We look back to Sinai from the Mount of Transfiguration. But the triumph of the ascended Christ was received by his people with the epiphany of the Spirit at Pentecost. The mighty wind and the tongues of flame recall the whirlwind, fire and earthquake of the Old Testament epiphanies (Acts 2:1–3; *cf.* 4:31; Exod. 19:18; 20:18; I Kings 19:11, 12). The coming of the Spirit is the coming of the Lord.

Lordship as sovereign power is central to the meaning of "Spirit of God" in the Old Testament. Whether in the thunder of God's wrath or in the still small voice of his counsel, the Spirit of God is supreme: "Not by might, nor by power, but by my Spirit, saith the Lord of hosts" (Zech. 4:6). The great future work of God promised in the prophets must therefore come to pass by the Spirit of the Lord. The Spirit will restore and quicken the people of God (Ezek. 37). Moses' prayer that the Lord would put his Spirit on all his people (Num. 11:29) will be fulfilled in the last days (Joel 2:28f.). The Spirit will come especially upon the Messiah (Isa. 11:2; 42:1; 61:1).

In the epiphany of Pentecost, the Spirit of God comes as the Spirit of the Father and of Christ. In his ministry Christ was anointed with the Spirit and labored in the fullness of the Spirit (Mark 1:10; Luke 4:1, 18). John promised that Jesus would baptize with the Spirit (Matt. 3:11; Mark 1:8; John 1:33; Acts 1:5). At Pentecost Christ sends the Spirit from his throne (Acts 1:4, 5; 2:33; 10:44, 45). The Spirit does not supplant the Son, but is sent in Christ's name (John 14:26) to reveal the things of Christ (John 16:13–15). In the Spirit Christ is present (John 14:18, 22; Rom. 8:9, 10. The presence of the Spirit is not a poor substitute for the presence of the risen Christ but a full and glorious form of his presence. The disciples were taught by Christ to desire his going away so that the Spirit might come (John 16:7).

So close is the abiding Spirit that he becomes not only the Spirit of Christ's Sonship but of our sonship. Christ our Advocate prays for us at God's right hand in his resurrection body. He also prays for and in us here on earth in his Holy Spirit, who is the other Advocate come in his name.

The Spirit who bears witness with our spirit that we are children of God is the Spirit of adoption whereby we cry, "Abba, Father" (Rom. 8:15, 16).

The Spirit takes possession of the house of God, and dwells among the people of God, the living temple of his presence. The Spirit is an "earnest" of the age to come, of the consummation glory to come. His presence is therefore promise as well as realization. But the promise, the pledge, lies in this, that in the Spirit the coming glory is already present. The "taste" of the Spirit it not a symbol but reality, the living presence of God.

We can only survey in barest outline the work of the Spirit in the church. As the Spirit of Life (Rom. 8:2) he created the church; as the Spirit of Truth (John 14:17; 15:26; I John 4:6; 5:7) he guides the church. The Spirit applies both the redemption and the revelation of Christ to the church.

The Spirit is the author of life in the new birth (John 3:3–8). This new life includes radical cleansing as well as renewal. As we have seen, this new life is in Christ, for vital union with Christ is the work of the Spirit (Rom. 8:12–30; Gal. 4:6). It is a heavenly life, for holiness characterizes the life of the Spirit (Rom. 8:1–13; Gal. 5:22; Eph. 5:18). Triumphant, abundant, rich with the fruits of the age to come, the life of the Spirit fills believers, saturates them, overwhelms them. The whole structure of the life of the church is a rigid shell apart from the fullness of the living Spirit.

Finally this is a *common* life in Christ. The richness of the work of the Spirit is both individual and corporate. The Spirit's "dividing" (διαίρεσις, *diairesis*) of gifts to each member is the opposite of fleshly "divisions" (αἵρεσις, *hairesis*), for it produces harmony (*cf.* I Cor. 12:4, 11 with I Cor. 11:19). There is one Spirit as there is one Lord (Eph. 4:4, 5). The unity of the church lies in the fellowship of the Spirit. Just here we must avoid "spiritualizing" the Holy Spirit! His immediate presence is real, and so is the unity his presence forges among believers. The unity of the Spirit can be as tangible as a handclasp or a cup of water.

The Spirit of Life is also the Spirit of Truth. The Word of God, living and active, is the Sword of the Spirit (Eph. 6:17; Heb. 4:12). The gulf that the modern mind puts between the Word of power and the written Word does not exist in Scripture itself. As the Spirit of Christ inspired the Old Testament prophets and the apostles and prophetic authors of the New Testament, he forged the bond of truth in which the church is built up. The true apostolicity of the church consists in its fidelity to the apostolic foundation laid by inspiration of the Spirit. Continuance in the apostolic teaching requires discipline in the truth. Submitting to the voice of the Holy Spirit speaking in Scripture, the true church finds in the rule of Christ's Word freedom from bondage to men and the unity of the Spirit in the bond of peace.

The Spirit works out his purpose for the church. In worship the Spirit is in the midst of the church and directs that response, that return of praise that is worship in Spirit and in truth. Edification is the Spirit's purpose too, in sanctification through the Word, in growth in grace by which the church grows together in the image of Christ. The mission of the church is also the result of the Spirit's work both in the witness of life and of word. Each of these areas defines an aspect of the church's ministry: to God directly in worship; to the saints in edification; to the world in witness. In each area the ministry is empowered and ordered by the Spirit.

To accomplish his saving purposes, the Spirit of God is present as Gift to the people of God. The personal presence of the Spirit overcomes the divisions that would otherwise exist between calling and gifts, communion and community, institute and organism. As Newbigin remarks, the Spirit is the Author of both order and ardor. The tensions that we create between structural forms and dynamic functions are dissolved when the Spirit operates in power, for his gifts fulfill the structure of the people of God. Paul's apostolic office, for example, is described by the phrase, "the grace given me" (Rom. 15:15). The church recognizes gifts of the Spirit that require public recognition for their proper exercise.

Every gift of the Spirit creates a stewardship, for every gift includes a calling for its exercise. The gifts of the Spirit therefore require both mission to the world and the communion of saints. For to whom will the Christian minister his gift? "Who is my neighbor?" Dare anyone limit ministry of Christ's gifts to some arbitrary classification of men?

Or, turn the question around. "Who is neighbor to me? Whose ministry do I need?" Shall a Christian select a group of like-minded friends and say, "These are my brethren. I will heed their admonitions, submit to these brethren in the Lord and rejoice with them"?

No, the man who claims the gifts of the Spirit in his own name rather than in Christ's name forgets that he has nothing that he has not received. All the gifts of the Spirit are for the glory of Christ. The very gifts in which we are most tempted to take pride are those that are given for ministry, given for the building up of the body of Christ. Consider that Christians do not differ in the *fruits* of the Spirit, except in degree. Love, joy, peace, hope—in receiving these gifts we are made like one another and like Christ. Hard hearts may manage a pharisaical prayer thanking God for extraordinary achievements in showing such fruit. But more often we boast in peculiar gifts, those graces by which we differ from others. But why does God make Christians to differ? So that they might serve in the body of Christ. Paul writes, "Now there are diversities of gifts, but the same Spirit. And there are diversities of ministrations, and the same Lord. And there are diversities of workings, but the same God, who worketh all things in all. But to each one is given the manifestation of the Spirit to profit withal" (I Cor. 12:4–7).

Differing gifts are callings to ministries. If the body were indeed "all ears" there would be no seeing, no smelling, not to speak of the lack of talking for the ears to hear. No, God has set each organ of ministry in the body as it has pleased him. What God has joined together let not man put asunder! Neither pride nor envy may disrupt the unity of the body. The proud head cannot say to the lowly feet, "I don't need you." Neither can the foot say in envy, "I am not the hand. I don't seem to count in the body. I resign."

Quite to the contrary, the members of the body suffer or rejoice together. The parts that are least necessary receive extraordinary attention—witness the coiffures of Paul's time and ours!

The apostle wrote in this way to rebuke an incipient party spirit at Corinth, a spirit that has borne such sad fruit through the ages. It is Christ's command that we keep the unity of the Spirit in sharing the Spirit's gifts. The church must receive those endued with gifts of Christ as Christ himself, and every Christian must minister his spiritual gifts as he has opportunity for the whole body of Christ.

That same concreteness of obedience that unites the church in the Spirit as Possessor unites it also in the Spirit as Possessed. The stewardship of the gifts of the Spirit is a most visible activity. It includes both the ministry of the general office of believers and the service of the special offices in the church. Paul manifests the unity of the Spirit not only in his own apostolic labors but in his concern that the Gentile churches should unite in carrying their gifts to Jerusalem, and in his warm eagerness to see that those who have labored with special gifts in one area of the church should be received and acknowledged in another.

The ministry of the Spirit orders the kingdom of Christ. The exercise of the gifts of the Spirit apart from the order of the Spirit threatened chaos at Corinth. To correct this Paul linked order and government with edification. The fellowship of the Spirit binds Christians together in spiritual discipline. If Christians do not admonish one another and even, on occasion, rebuke one another, they ignore the Spirit's own work as Lord and Sanctifier.

The refusal of discipline undermines any movement toward church unity. It is the constitutive principle of the World Council of Churches that each member church is free to interpret the basis of the organization as it sees fit. This organization, which is bold to speak in the name of the Spirit, has set aside a fundamental requirement of the ministry of the Spirit of Truth: that the church pronounce anathema in the name of the Lord the lies of antichrist. Separation is the other side of fellowship. The unity of the Spirit can be maintained only in separation from Hymenaeus and Philetus and their modern counterparts.

The ecumenical movement seeks unity but refuses to exclude those who deny apostolic doctrine. Evangelicals cling to New Testament doctrine but often ignore its requirements for the purity and unity of the church. The Apostle Paul shows a more excellent way, the way of the Spirit who both binds the church in one and purifies it as the spotless bride of Christ.

Christ calls his scattered sheep to the unity of his Spirit. We must heed his voice and buy up the opportunity. Spiritual revival for the church is revival by the Spirit of him of whom it was said, "The zeal of thine house hath eaten me up" (John 2:17). To order the fellowship of the saints by the Word of Christ is to build the holy temple of the Lord and to edify the body of Christ. The riches of Biblical revelation concerning the church come from the Lord who "loved the church, and gave himself for it; that he might sanctify and cleanse it by the washing of water by the word, that he might present it to himself a glorious church, not having spot, or wrinkle, or any such thing; but that it should be holy and without blemish" (Eph. 5:25-27).

It is time for the true bride to hear the voice of the bridegroom. The path where he calls may seem impassable, blocked by the rubble of tradition and the walls of rebellion; but Christ calls his church. He will be answered, not in the weary tones of political opportunism, but in ardor of jealous love.

Notes

[1]J. Y. Campbell, "The Origin and Meaning of the Christian Use of the Word ΕΚΚΛΗΣΙΑ," *The Journal of Theological Studies*, 49 (1948), 130-142. James Barr, *The Semantics of Biblical Language* (London: Oxford University Press, 1961), pp. 119-129.

[2]G. Ernest Wright, *The Biblical Doctrine of Man in Society* (London: SCM Press, 1954), pp. 78, 79.

[3]Karl Barth, *Church Dogmatics* (trans. G. W. Bromiley. et al., Edinburgh: T. and T. Clark), II:2. 414-430.

[4]So Alan Richardson, *An Introduction to the Theology of the New Testament* (London: SCM Press, 1958), p. 216. Oscar Cullmann's explanation of primitive Christian universalism likewise contains this view. See *Christ and Time* (Philadelphia: Westminster Press, 1950), p. 186.

[5]This is pointed out by Ernest Best, *Our Body in Christ* (London: SPCK, 1955), p. 124.

[6]Clinton D. Morrison, *The Powers That Be* (Naperville, Ill.: Alec R. Allenson, 1960), stresses this common understanding, which he would extend in large measure to Hellenistic culture as well as Judaism.

[7]Menahem Mansoor, *The Thanksgiving Hymns* (Grand Rapids: Eerdmans, 1961), p. 79, "Angels are classed in two main groups—good and evil—whose respective functions are strongly linked with the fundamental dualistic teachings of the Sect." The Scrolls are much more full in speaking of the holy angels who surround the Almighty. The final eschatological combat is described in 1QH 3:32-36.

[8]L. Cerfaux writes: "Thus Paul is aware of two different reconciliations: the reconciliation of the Jews and gentiles in the church (Eph. 2:14-16), and the reconciliation which brings about the subjection of the powers to Christ through the victory of the cross (Col. 2:14 et seq.). The two just cannot be compared. The powers and the Law are defeated in the drama of the passion, while mankind is saved, not overcome. The church is made up of the saved." L. Cerfaux, *The Church in the Theology of St. Paul* (trans. Geoffrey Webb and Adrian Walker, New York: Herder and Herder, 1959), p. 339. The main distinction here is well taken.

[9]Among the surveys of the possible origins of the body figure in Paul the following are concise: Markus Barth, "A Chapter on the Church—The Body of Christ," *Interpretation*, XII (1958), 131-156, esp. pp. 136-141. J. J. Meuzelaar, *Der Leib des Messias* (Assen: Van Gorcum, 1961), pp. 1-19. Ernest Best, *One Body in Christ* (London: SPCK, 1955), pp. 83-93.

¹⁰George Johnston puts this well: "As He is the life of each, so is He the life of the whole; and the compelling link of the Christian society is the abiding of each one in union with the life-giving Saviour." George Johnston, *The Doctrine of the Church in the New Testament* (Cambridge: Cambridge University Press, 1943), p. 93.

¹¹Cerfaux, *op. cit.*, p. 326.

¹²Cerfaux shows that the introduction of the body figure for the church in the captivity epistles does not set aside the concept of the church as the people of God (L. Cerfaux, *op. cit.*, pp. 373ff.).

¹³*Cf.* Koehler-Baumgartner, *Lexicon,* pp. 865f.; for LXX translations see Schlier, art. κεφαλή, *TDNT,* III. 675. In secular Greek *kephalē* was much more limited. It was used metaphorically for completion or total (sums were added upward) but not as a synonym for *archē. Cf.* Liddell and Scott, *Greek-English Lexicon,* under κεφαλή. On the connection in Hebrew thought of the head, the beginning, and the firstborn, see J. J. Meuzelaar, *op. cit.*, pp. 117ff.

¹⁴See Cerfaux, *op. cit.*, p. 370; Pierre Benoit, "Corps, tête et plérôme dans les Épîtres de la Captivité." *Revue biblique,* 63 (1956), 26; Stephen Bedale, "The Meaning of κεφαλή in the Pauline Epistles," *Journal of Theological Studies,* N.S. 5 (1954), 211–215.

¹⁵Herman Ridderbos, *Paulus* (Kampen: J. H. Kok, 1966), pp. 432f.

¹⁶These passages are cited by A. H. Strong, *Systematic Theology* (Philadelphia: Griffith and Rowland, 1909), III, 795f.

¹⁷On this term see D. F. Hauck, art. "κοινωνία" in Kittel, *TDNT*, III, 789–809; L. S. Thornton, *The Common Life in the Body of Christ* (London: Dacre Press, 3rd ed., 1950); J. G. Davies, *Members One of Another, Aspects of Koinonia* (London: A. R. Mowbray, 1958); J. Y. Campbell, "KOINΩNIA and Its Cognates in the N.T.," *Journal of Biblical Literature,* 51 (1932), 352–380.

¹⁸J. Y. Campbell, "KOINΩNIA," p. 353.

18

Langdon Gilkey

The Church
as the Body of Christ

[The church is the communion of the faithful who have fellowship with their Lord. It is] the body of Christ in which the living Spirit of the risen Lord dwells.[1]

We Protestants use often and warmly the word "fellowship." Usually we mean our fellowship one with another, which often refers only to friendliness, but may mean . . . a deeper unity in the Spirit of mutual love, forbearance, and trust. And we also speak of individual fellowship with God, the communion in devotion and in prayer of the individual soul with God in Christ; our hymns are filled with powerful references to this individual relationship with Christ. The early church, however, was very conscious of a third kind of fellowship which it felt to be the basis of the other two: the fellowship of the congregation of the church, with the risen Lord in worship: "For where two or three are gathered together in my name, there am I in the midst of them."[2] And for Paul to be "in Christ" meant to be in the worshiping community or congregation where the Spirit of Christ dwells; that is, to be in His Body, the church.[3] Thus for the apostles it was because the risen Lord was in the midst of His community

From pp. 104–127 in *How the Church Can Minister to the World Without Losing Itself* by Langdon Gilkey. Copyright 1964 by Langdon B. Gilkey.

as a living Spirit that the other two types of fellowship were possible, namely, that we could each as individuals have fellowship with Him, and that we could have human fellowship in the spirit of love one to another.

[The church is more than the individuals who make it up:] it is the presence of the risen Lord in the congregation, communicating Himself to us in the World and having fellowship with us as we meet together in our common worship of Him. The church, then, is not formed merely by the mutual agreement to come together of repentant and regenerate people. It is formed fundamentally by the calling of each one of us by Jesus Christ through His Word, and by His presence in grace and power in the midst of the faithful congregation. The church is the Body of Christ where His Spirit dwells.[4]

Now for the early church, the way in which the congregation together had fellowship with the risen Lord, the way in which His presence in their midst was realized and inwardly appropriated, was in or through the worship of the community, and especially through its sacraments.[5] In their regular gatherings, centered as they were around both baptism and the Lord's Supper, each individual was brought into immediate communion with Christ, and the vital center of the community was thereby renewed and its common life empowered and sanctified.

In these common acts of worship, then, the earliest congregations continued their fellowship with Christ, and through these acts the Spirit of Christ flowed into the community which was His Body.[6] And yet, as we all know, there is no point where present Protestant life exhibits a greater poverty than in worship and in the sacraments. We perform each of the "ordinances" solemnly, and we speak often of "worshipful experiences." When, however, we ask our laymen why, aside from the pressure of tradition and custom, we perform the sacraments, or what good they are to man or God, few answers are forthcoming; and when we inquire into what the worshipful experiences are, we find little sense of the divine presence, but rather only a kind of contented mood engendered by familiar hymns and procedures.[7] As countless seminary students witness, the deepest reason for the contemporary movement of clergy from the free into the liturgical churches lies in the barrenness of worship in the former and the religious emptiness of their sacramental life. My purpose in this chapter, therefore, is to try to explore how our present serious difficulties with worship and the sacraments have arisen; and, seeing in what ways they were vital and powerful in the New Testament church, to discover if possible how to strengthen them today.

For worship is central to the Christian religious life, as essential as prayer. It is the corporate relationship to God, the community coming consciously into the presence of God together. This is the most direct touch with the holy that humans can have, and thus the heart of religion and of the religious quality of the church. A church may be filled with creative ideas and overflowing with good works, but unless there be a sense of the presence of the holy there, of the presence of God—unless there be a capacity for worship—it is doubtful whether what is there is religion. Worship is not centrally an experience of *ours;* it is meaningless to speak of a "worshipful experience" as if the holy were compounded of a clever arrangement of various kinds of lighting, sober music, proper tones of voice, and the softness or hardness of the pews, all so manipulated as to create a certain experience in us. Such "client-centered" worship does not extend beyond the ceiling of the sanctuary, for here by finite media we seek to take the place of the holy, to create it synthetically. To these efforts to create a worshipful mood the usual congregational response is appropriate: "Preacher, I enjoyed it!" But our manipulation and their enjoyment are not categories appropriate to worship. For God, not our own consciousness is the object of worship; we experience *Him,* not ourselves worshiping. Worship is a response to the presence of God, our reaction to the appearance of the holy. And the point is not that we *feel* something then, though surely reverence, awe, and wonder are normal; but that we relate ourselves creatively to Him, that we respond to His presence in adoration and praise, in confession of sin and thanksgiving for mercies known and received. It is the relation to God, the felt relation to the holy—to the tremendous, majestic, awesome power and goodness of God—that is the core of worship. Thus we bow, thus we adore, thus we surrender ourselves—thus we experience *God.*

When we seek to make intelligible our present situation of dried-up, empty secularity in our worship, one principle is essential for understanding: the holy always appears through definite media or symbols. These media change widely in church history, it is true, and different forms of the church have emphasized different media. But wherever religion is vital, and wherever worship has therefore some reality and meaning, there some definite medium of the holy is to be found around which the church is built, be it the holy sacraments of Catholicism, the sacred Word in the Reformation churches, or the emotional experience of personal salvation in the evangelical churches. One might add that meaningful church architecture is likewise constructed around the central principle of worship, i.e., around the fundamental mediating locus or instrument of the holy—for example, either the altar in Catholicism or the high pulpit in the Reformed churches.[8]

... The sectarian and evangelical Christianity from which our modern denominations have largely sprung dispensed with the centrality of outward, objective symbols of the holy in order to free the inward media. Sacramental and liturgical symbols (such as candles, pictures, altars, statues, the cross, and of course the reserved host on the altar) were taken from the churches, the holiness of objective dogma was rejected, and even the Calvinist sense of the sanctity of holy preaching of the Word from a massive pulpit was compromised. In their place was put the inner experience of the Spirit, or of the Inner Light as with the Quakers, illumining a close fellowship gathered in a bare, conventional room; or, in the nineteenth century, the ecstatic experience of conversion in response to an evangelical witness delivered from a platform in a theaterlike auditorium. Such nonliturgical, nonsacramental, nondoctrinal churches, stripped of all objective, visible symbols, were however in the sects and in their evangelical descendants not at all vacant of experience of the holy, the sense of the presence of the divine. Far from it. In an old Quaker meeting or in a Methodist revival, the holy was present and worship had tremendous power. But the media, though definite and understood, were inward and subjective rather than outward and objective. That is to say, the holy was experienced inwardly, in the inner consciousness—as the Inner Light in Quakerism or the moving of the Spirit in Methodism—not through objective media such as a sacramental element, an icon, a cross, or even a doctrine or sermon. Because these sectarian congregations lived in continual contact with the divine will, through daily Scripture reading, family prayer, and the separated habits of their lives, even in the simplest, barest rooms their own inner spirits could become, and often were, genuine channels for a sense of the holy.[9]

Our problem is that the social changes in the life of denominational groups have brought about changes as well in the effectiveness and meaningfulness of these subjective forms of worship. Let me give an example: the Quakers have had, as we all know, as vivid and effective a mode of worship as church history has produced, quite without objective symbols, liturgy, reading of the Holy Word, sacraments, preaching, orders of service, or any other observable media. The medium of the holy for them was the Inner Light, the voice of the divine conscience and the divine reason that speaks, as they affirm, in the heart of each believing man. The Quakers thus pushed the sectarian principle of subjectivity, inherited by most of our denominational traditions, to its limit. Some of their current problems may, therefore, illumine to us our own.

When the writer lived in Poughkeepsie, he was often invited (if the "minister" was out of town) to come and address the local Quaker meeting—requested, that is, to prepare a "sermon" and deliver it at a definite point in the "service."[10] When the layman who extended this invitation was asked why they had so radically changed the form of Quaker worship as to have a paid minister, hymns, order of service, and sermon, he answered: "I was raised a Quaker in a Quaker family, and grew up surrounded by a Quaker community—and the Inner Light spoke to all of us at the meetings we had together. But when we moved here to Poughkeepsie, and I began to sell stocks and bonds, all I could think of in that silence was the Dow-Jones stock averages—and so we wanted to have people who didn't think only of the market all week long to talk to us about religion." One could put his—and our—problem this way: when the whole of a man's life is suffused with contact with the divine, in daily Bible reading, the requirements of a strict communal ethic, and constant habits of prayer, then through the total character of his life his subjectivity is saturated with the dimension of the holy, and he can go into a bare room, sit in silence, and religious and ethical wisdom wells up inside him. But the man whose daily life is immersed in secular, cultural, and business affairs, who seldom reads the Bible, and whose life of personal prayer is at best feeble, erratic, and unsure—when *he* goes to that bare room, divested of all religious symbols and all objective media for the holy, there is no holy *anywhere* for him to experience, and his mind is filled, and naturally so, with the stuff of his life, the Dow-Jones stock averages.

Here, in a nutshell, is the present Protestant problem of worship. The social conditions for the removal of objective symbols or media of the holy are now gone. The divine qualifies neither the communal nor the family life of our people during the week. The Bible has become a strange and little-used book; the family religion of Scripture readings and prayers has abdicated in favor of what the church can provide on Sunday; and the standards, values, and concepts of ordinary lay life are completely derived from secular society. Thus the average churchgoer comes into church out of a life, not saturated with the holy, but quite devoid of all but secular content in ideas, experiences, and values. Consequently his inner consciousness is worldly in the extreme; the true world to him is the human world around him, in which the dimension of the holy is unknown. How can he, out of this secular inwardness, have an experience of God, of worship, from his own subjectivity, from himself alone—how can he worship unless there are objective media for the holy? The sectarian layman is *in* the world now; and, as in each facet of the church's life, this new social situation makes a vast difference. It means that in our day worship can occur only where some powerful symbolic mediation of the holy takes place.[11]

As we have noted further, those media which did communicate the holy in traditional American Protestant church life have been weakened. The older Calvinist sense that the Bible, in a place of honor on the high pulpit, read and expounded, was the vehicle of the holy in worship—and that we could thus allow all other symbols to vanish from the church—is not available to us. For most of us the Bible is as much a human and fallible document as it is the oracle of God; and anyway, whatever the laity's theology of Scripture, the familiarity with its message is far less than it was a hundred years ago.

More characteristic probably as the vehicle of the holy in the Protestant churches of America was a vivid emotional experience, in response to someone's witness to the working of the Holy Spirit. In most of the evangelical churches of nineteenth-century America the sermon was less a declaration of the Word of God than a witness to the Spirit's work in one's own life and a call to similar holy experiences in the congregation. But this form of worship has also been weakened by social change. The people who could experience such emotional upheavals and revivals were on the whole themselves rural and small-town folk whose habits of life were generally so little formalized that strong and sudden expressions of emotion not only came easily to them, but also provided their most vivid contact with reality. Just as they could snap their suspenders at town meeting. hit the cuspidor in the kitchen at fifteen paces, put their feet on the stove in the country store, and take off their collars except when they went to church or the city, so could they with appropriateness be violently moved by religion, experience a sudden change of life, and unashamedly shout "Amen!" in church. To

such rural people a formalized, esthetically elegant liturgical religious service was as unnatural as it was unconnected with their own tastes; in no
sense could it be for them a vehicle of the holy—mostly because nothing in
their lives had this sort of formal character.

Between their rural folk existence and that of their present-day descendants, however, a great gulf is fixed, dug out by the social changes in these
groups. For their grandchildren have now moved to the suburbs, been
educated at college, and listen to Bach (or at least Lombardo) instead of to
country music. They sit as politely and quietly in church as in their favorite
restaurants or at a symphony, and an "Amen, Brother!" from the next pew
would make them as uncomfortable and nervous as a spittoon in their living
room. Most of our urban and suburban people, in moving upward in
culture, have become more formalized in their esthetic and religious tastes.
The formality that would have seemed a hypocritical sham to their rural
grandfathers is to them the "nice" way to do things. And the kind of
service in which for their elders there would have been real—because
emotional—religion has become hopelessly countrified and primitive to
them. Countless students returning to their home-town churches after a
year of college or seminary, in which their esthetic tastes and modes of life
have become more formalized and structured, are surprised and deeply
offended at how rustic and "corny" the services they used to love have
suddenly become. Ironically, a vivid emotional experience of conversion is
as unavailable to the modern well-to-do suburban Methodist as it was to the
aristocratic Church of Englander in the eighteenth century, who looked
down on "those emotional people called Methodists."

Thus have the objective media of the infallible Bible and a vivid emotional experience lost their symbolic power to modern educated suburban
congregations. In some of them the folksiness remains as a pathetic nostalgia for bygone days of conversions and revivals—pathetic because no such
emotional revelations of the holy now course through the pews, however
informal the hymn-singing and the lingo may be. In most denominations,
however, rural informality has given way to an educated middle-class
formality, without any corresponding vehicle of the holy to give substance
to worship. Thus in place of the evangelical experience have appeared
prayers as essays in introspection, the pulpit as a lecture platform, sacred
music as a kind of amateur concert, the communion table as an attractive
stand for flowers and candles and a handly place for the offertory plates;
while in the pews are people listening to an inspirational address that calls
them to renewed activity and revitalized giving in the church—people
waiting for the fellowship coffee hour when they will see their friends. This
sounds grim, but empirical studies show over and over that these are in fact
the elements remembered and meaningful in the present-day religious pattern.

The results of this change are everywhere evident. Revivals are held in
all the free churches of the South and into the rural Midwest, but usually
only the most faithful members attend, and no vivid experiences occur or
are expected. The old gospel hymns are sung, but the experiences they

relate—experiences of being "sunk in sin" and "rescued by Jesus"—are not known to the smooth suburban layman with his executive's self-control. As orthodox dogmas have become signs of church loyalty and not symbols of the truth, so the experiences related in the gospel hymns are for most laymen nostalgic recollections of their parents' religion, not their own. And this nostalgia is poignantly expressed in the remark repeatedly heard in our churches: "That was *real* religion"—real, but at present not experienced by those who try to profess it.[12]

Because the effectiveness of the two traditional evangelical media of the holy, the sacred biblical Word and the presence of the Spirit, is rapidly disappearing, little sense of it remains in our worship. Moral and social respectability and the personal fellowship of the church have become the important things. Over and over one hears in the South, "Come to our church—it is friendly and we have wonderful fellowship," or "We have such a fine and growing Sunday school." But *not,* "You will hear there the Word of God, or meet the Spirit." And if a controversial sermon is preached, folks are polite, but amazed and bewildered. The presence of the holy, and so all real transcendence, has gone, and with it, in the now familiar pattern, has gone also all relevance.

My central thesis has been that social change in the lives of Protestant people has brought about important changes in the religious quality of Protestant church life. The elements of the holy in historic Protestantism have by these changes been shorn of their holiness; the ethical life of Protestantism has become acclimatized to the standards of town and suburb; the ideas and beliefs of our churches are confused, dim, and empty, leaving a residue of vagueness that spells conformity to culture; and now, as we have seen, the earlier emphasis of denominational worship on inner experience has meant, in a secularly conditioned congregation, that the holy has quite vanished from our sanctuaries. In each case I have suggested that the task of contemporary Protestantism, after it has taken a realistic look at this situation, is to rediscover the separated elements that can mediate the holy to the life of man, and I have suggested doing this through a re-examination of the classic symbols of the church's life. In the area of worship this means that Word and Sacrament, as the objective means of grace given to the church, must replace our current weak concentration on subjective experiences of worship if the holy is again to appear in our churches. . . .

Let us begin with some thoughts on the sacraments as a whole, and then illustrate them specifically in terms of the Lord's Supper, which has always been a central part of the worship of the Christian church. In the sacraments we find ourselves in the world of symbols: that is, media through which Christ comes to us in faith. Now some of us tend to think of a symbol as if it were merely a sign: a somewhat casually chosen substitute that stands for something else and so reminds us of it when we see it. Thus it is typically felt that the wine (or grape juice) and the bread are reminders of Jesus, and so, in the Lord's Supper, we are merely to think again and anew of Him and what He taught. Symbols, however, are more powerful than this: the power and meaning of what they stand for, the reality they are to remind us of, are not so far away—as if Calvary were still on a hill long ago. Rather, that power and meaning and reality seem to dwell within the symbols, so that they become for us media for communicating, for presenting, making really present here and now the reality they symbolize.

In our secular experience we are familiar with many symbols of this sort: conceptual ones that create, maintain, and thus make immediately present the spirit or ideology of the community in which we live. Examples in a democratic community are "equal justice," "freedom," "liberty," "the equality of men," "natural rights," and so on. Such symbolic words or phrases have no definite, objective referent that anyone can point to, as does a sign. Their relation to their referents is at once more immediate and more mysterious. For out of these word-symbols arises in a real sense our American community, in so far as they express and present, recreate and make real, the ethos that makes us a democratic community.[13] Symbols are, therefore, foundation stones for the spiritual reality of a community, communicating to every part of it, in space and through time, the spiritual life that creates and recreates it. The great theological symbols that make up what the Reformers called "the Word of God" functioned in much the same way in the community of the church—symbols about God and what He has done: creation, incarnation, atonement, and resurrection. These are not doctrines so much as conceptual symbols around which doctrines cluster, symbols whose meaning for each generation doctrines seek to express. Much as a democratic or Communist philosophy is *about* the symbols of a democratic or a Communist community, so a Christian theology is *about* the symbols of the Christian community. And correspondingly the preaching of the Word—the other central element of Protestant worship—is the communication of the relevance and meaning of these verbal symbols to the everyday life and actual existence of the congregation.

Now, strange as it is to our rational and modern ears, words are not the only symbolic media of spiritual reality or communication. Words can express friendship and love, but (though intellectuals hesitate to believe it) a handclasp or an embrace communicates and expresses, and therefore makes real, that friendship or that love far more deeply.[14] If this were not so, we could communicate satisfactorily with our wives and sweethearts over the phone; and everyone knows how untrue that is! Thus in all communities and all human relations there are material as well as verbal symbols: physical acts and objects, ceremonies and sacraments, that communicate, express, and make real the common life. In much the same way an academic community is preserved and strengthened not only by such verbal symbols as "academic freedom," "scientific honesty," and "scholarly objectivity," but also by its liturgical ceremonies of oral examination, graduation, and convocation, and its symbolic paraphernalia of degrees, diplomas, gowns, hats, and seals.

Material symbols worry us, despite our continual repudiation of the "shallowness of rationalism." We tend to think either that what we expect them to communicate is also material (in which case we now call such thinking "magical") or that, if it is spiritual, then words can do it better. Thus material symbols are apt to seem to us either superstitious or silly; in neither case are they the centers of Christian worship and life that they have always been. Let us recall, however, what both the great Reformers said about the sacraments. Baptism in water and the Eucharist with its bread and wine are sacraments which communicate to faith the same word of promise and of love as do Scripture and preaching.[15] Receiving them in faith, we receive the same gospel of Jesus Christ as is preached and heard from the pulpit. Thus, as supplementary media of the gospel, they are aids and fortifiers of our faith—confirmations and seals of it—for they make present and real what is talked about in the sermon. The writer will never forget a remark of Reinbold Niebuhr shortly after his stroke. He said that at Easter, when we all ask the anxious questions about eternal life, he would rather receive the gospel of God's eternal love through the Eucharist than hear some theologian or preacher like himself theorize about it. There is, said he, a directness and a reality in the sacramental symbols of the Word that our own spoken words do not have.

The sacraments, therefore, and especially the Lord's Supper, communicate to us the same Word and gospel as do our reading and speaking. They are, so to speak, the enacted gospel. The reality that is communicated is not a physical reality—a "medicine of immortality" or divine power.[16] What is communicated and so made real is the Word of God; the Sacrament is, as Calvin puts it, "a fleshly mirror of spiritual blessings."[17] What it symbolizes and so makes present is the judgment and the loving mercy of God, and when these come to each one of us as we partake of the Supper in faith, Christ is really present to us, and present in the most direct and real manner possible. When, therefore, these symbols are received in faith—when, that is, the judgment and love of Christ are received through them in real inner repentance and trust, they are neither mere material objects communicating a material medicine, nor merely signs for intellectual reminder. Rather, they present Jesus Christ to our faith, who is to us the Word of God's judgment on our sins and of God's mercy and love that will accept us, being sinful, and refashion us, here and in eternity. And when that Word is received inwardly, then the judgment and love of God are immediately present, unqualifiedly real, and effectively active. Instead of implying the unreality or absence of that to which it refers, a symbol *communicates* the reality it symbolizes, when in a community it is received and inwardly participated in. And so it is that through these symbols of Word and Sacrament our Lord is really present in His church.

All well and good, we may say. We need enacted, material symbols in our religious life as well as conceptual ones—granted. But why these particular ones? Can we not fashion others that communicate the gospel to us more clearly—possibly a churchly pageant or some symbolic clerical rite? Why these elements; why washing in water, and why a meal? Why eating? These are more than esoteric questions; they are questions that lie hidden in the minds of us all, lay and clerical, as we approach the Lord's Supper. Isn't it, after all, a bit foolish or "tribal" to eat a dab of bread and drink a few drops of liquid in order to make contact with God in the Christian church? We may note that though as theologically minded Christians we speak often of our distaste for a dualism of mind and body, and of our devotion to historical particularity and uniqueness, yet when we confront these particular symbols and take part in this particular rite, with its physical media and radically historical and so very particular origin, we feel foolish—and know ourselves to be "Greeks" at heart.

The early Fathers were much interested in this question, and wrote often on the symbolic power of bread and wine. Bread and wine (but hardly grape juice, we might ruefully note!) are, they said, the staff of life, the realities by which we exist, which therefore express our absolute dependence on God's power and goodness, and in turn become in us by the divine miracle of life itself, our own body and blood. As the bread and wine in our ordinary meals nourish our bodies to earthly life, so through them in the heavenly Supper God nourishes our souls and our being to eternal life.[18] Consequently, Christ is our heavenly bread, and His shed blood our heavenly, or eschatological, wine. In Him and so through His body and blood, we live eternally as in nature we now live temporally, these two gifts of natural and then eternal life being the two great miracles of God's goodness to us. In this sense bread and wine are numinous entities themselves—sources, and so symbols, of the deep and even irrational mystery of natural life itself—as are our own bodies and our blood. Their symbolic power for the divine gift of eternal life is therefore immense.

As both the early Fathers and the Reformers realized, however, the historical symbolism of the Eucharist is far more powerful than the natural.[19] For, as our Lord Himself said, the bread and the wine refer to the great historical events among which the first supper was itself enacted.[20] They are symbols primarily for those acts in which Jesus accomplished our salvation—that is, for His death and resurrection, in which He became (to revert to the patristic phrase) our heavenly bread and the wine of eternal life. Thus in our religion do historical symbols give meaning to the natural. For in the breaking of the bread (His body) and the pouring forth of the wine (His blood), we re-enact His death for us on the cross. Through that death He brought to us at once the judgment and the loving mercy of God. In that judgment and mercy we are saved and made whole; for we are given faith in God's mercy now, and in prospect we are given the hope of love for Him and for each other. In that faithful relation to the eternal God we are also given hope for eternal life with Him. Faith, hope, and love are thus the vast gifts of Jesus Christ in His life, death, and resurrection for us—the gifts of His broken and now healed body, and of His shed and now living blood, whose symbols for us *now* are the bread and the wine. Thus the Lord's Supper means centrally for our faith not only His fellowship with the disciples in a meal long ago, but the deeper, eternal fellowship in which He takes upon Himself our sin, our death, and even the judgment of God on us. By that fellowship He establishes us in the relation to God which He has Himself, in which we were created, and in which alone we are saved.[21] To receive this message in faith through the bread and the wine is to receive the gospel and to be really present with Christ.

Church tradition has always added that we take this one loaf *together,* and that therefore the Supper symbolizes the unity of the fellowship of the church, our common bonds of love and brotherhood one to another in the worship of Christ.[22] This, one might remark, is the *optimistic* interpretation of this reference to the congregation. A broken body and shed blood point, unfortunately, not only to the Lord's act on Calvary. They point also to us, to our own broken life and fellowship in the church which is His body. There is a terrible irony in our symbolic breaking of this body and pouring out of this wine week after week in the church—symbols as they are of our terrible and costly divisions in the Body of Christ: of churches, races, and nations—and of the blood, fleshly and spiritual, that we shed moment by moment in history in our communities. Here in our continual breaking of His body, the church, and in our shedding of His blood, is the real repetition of the sacrifice of Christ—here is the Mass! Thus these symbols of broken bread and poured wine point not only to man's general need and to Christ's death. They point as well to *our* very present sin and very immediate need. When in faith we know this here and now, we know here and now the judgment of God *on us*—and the Risen One has entered His church and become its Lord in truth. Here He stands among *us*. When we know this judgment on ourselves and our life, we can know His real presence as healing grace as well. For as He came to His broken and fleeing band of disciples after His death and resurrection, so He comes to us now who, too, have broken His body, bringing us the new life of God's love and forgiveness, and at the end the new life of eternity.

The presence of the Lord in His congregation, as judgment on our sin and as healing love for our wounds, is then the sole source of the power and the reality of these symbols, the sole ground of their value and their permanence among us. Without Him, they, as we, are nothing. Without His immediate judgment—now—on our life, and His wondrous grace, they have only an old historical episode to remind us of, and the mysterious powers of nature to represent to us. It is cheering, when He is so necessary for their efficacy, to remember that we did not choose these symbols. He chose them, and used them, in the best-attested records of the gospel stories. And in using them with His disciples He promised that this bread was to be His body, and this wine the new covenant in His blood. They are not our signs of Him. They are His chosen symbols of His own promise to be in our midst when we take them in repentance, in faith, and in love.

And so we discover again the common answer to our problem in each of its facets. There *is* a transcendent element in the church, namely, the means of grace which God has given in Word and Sacrament, and around these alone can the church be built. The rediscovery of this has been the central motif of the new theology in relation to the church, and the search for this transcendent holy is the central characteristic of each serious seminary student's personal quest. Often he looks at his liberal social-gospel predecessors with disdain as "secular" or, even worse, "immanent." But let us recall that orthodoxy can lose the transcendent as quickly as can liberalism, and that without relevance to our total secular life, both personal and social, the transcendent Lord and the holy Sacrament hang there as Sunday appendages of little use to God or man. Only when they are relevant to our own life, its sins, and its needs do Word and Sacrament themselves become media of the holy, and only then is the church a holy people.

When the Word is heard in the congregation in real repentance and in faith—when the sacraments become the medium of the presence of that Word of Christ to each of us in his own immediate situation—then the church can be the new People of God, related to Him in confession and trust, and so related to one another and to their social environment in love and service. Only thus, through the presence of the transcendent, holy God in His congregation and not through any efforts of our own to enlarge our plants, attract more members, or gain more influence, can the church perform its task. For only God is holy, and only He can work wonders through His instrument, the church.

Notes

[1] Rom. 12:4, 5; I Cor. 12:12–31; Eph. 1:22, 23; 5:22, 33; Col. 1:14–18, 24. Cf. the article by F. J. Taylor in A. Richardson, ed., *A Theological Word Book of the Bible* (London: SCM Press, 1950), pp. 35–36.

[2] Matt. 18:20; 28:20.

[3] Cf. the excellent articles by A. Nygren, A. Fredrichsen, and H. Odeberg in A. Nygren, ed., *This Is the Church* (Philadelphia: Muhlenberg, 1952), esp. pp. 9–12 and 67–72.

[4] "It is in the risen Lord and his Spirit that it [the church] is possessed of its existence. The New Testament view of the Church is marked above all by the vivid experience of the activity of the Lord and his Spirit in the congregation, an activity which is prerequisite for the performance of its religious function, for all Christian activity." Fredrichsen, *op. cit.*, p. 16. Or as Nygren puts this in even stronger language: "Christ's body is Christ himself. The Church is Christ, by reason of the fact that since His resurrection He is present with us and meets with us on earth." *Op. cit.*, p. 10.... And finally F. H. Taylor: "In the earlier epistles, and in Romans and I Corinthians, Christ is conceived as the whole body of which Christians are members in particular; in Ephesians and Colossians the Church is the body and Christ is the head.... thus suggesting the absolute dependence of the Church upon Christ for its very existence, its growth and strength. The fulness which is in the head flows into the body and maintains the order of the body." In A. Richardson, *op. cit.*, p. 35.

[5] As Cyril Richardson puts this: "Furthermore, the Christians were not just a body; they were one body in *Christ*. The word has an upward reference of supreme importance.... The metaphor is further developed by Paul when he speaks of Christ as the Head of the Church. The underlying concept is the complete dependence of the Christian community upon Christ, who guides, rules and directs it, and to whose control the Church is ever submissive.... Just as the rite of baptism initiated men into the Christian community, so the sacrament of the Lord's Supper was the continuation of the life of Christ in the Church." C. C. Richardson, *The Church Through the Centuries* (New York: Scribner's Sons, 1950), p. 23. "But for the understanding of the cultus in early Christianity, one aspect of the life of the

disciples with him is of great importance: the communion between the disciples and Jesus. . . . It was just this fellowship that later became central in the early Christian worship. Its inner characteristic was that they knew themselves to be in real fellowship with the risen and present Christ . . . that fellowship with Christ was experienced not merely as something conceived or believed, but as real. Christ was *actually* present when they assembled in his name. . . . Their meetings became services of worship, cultic gatherings, because of the presence of the Risen One in the Word, in their prayers offered in his name, and above all in the high point of their coming together, the common meal, and the breaking of bread." Erik Sjöberg, "Church and Cultus in the New Testament," in Nygren, *op. cit.*, pp. 79–81. Let us note how, as these words imply, each of the three major biblical symbols of the church's existence—the People of God in love, the Word of God, and the Body of Christ—points to the presence and activity of Christ in the community. They thus all symbolize His lordship or headship and the community's dependence on that presence for its life.

[6] "This fellowship with Christ is the nerve of the whole practice of worship in early Christianity. For that reason it has its center in the sacrament, where that fellowship is experienced with particular definiteness. . . . The most notable characteristic of his [Paul's] concept of baptism is his development of the thought about the fellowship with Christ which is established by baptism. . . . In baptism the recipient is incorporated with Christ, so that he first dies with him and then arises with him . . . one is in a new creation, because he is in Christ. . . . The fellowship with Christ, which began in baptism, one subsequently experienced in the cultus. The thought of the presence of Christ was, as we saw, the most vital fact. And the cultus comes to its high point in the Lord's Supper." *Ibid.*, pp. 85–90.

[7] Cf. the discovery in his survey of the almost complete absence on the part of laymen of concern for or thought about the worship and sacramental life of the church, in Victor Obenhaus, *The Church and Faith in Mid-America* (Philadelphia: Westminster Press, 1963). pp. 136, 158f.

[8] There are, of course, several sorts of criteria, esthetic as well as religious, relevant to church architecture. The central *religious* criterion, however, springs from the mode of mediation of the holy in the form of the religion in question. That is, the architecture should express and emphasize that medium within or through which the holy communicates itself to the congregation in worship—e.g., the altar in Catholicism, the high pulpit in Calvinism, or the commonality and equality of worshipers touched by the Spirit in sectarian groups. It is "good" architecture religiously when in this way the form of the building fits—i.e., expresses—the form of worship or of the holy. It is bad architecture when, however "beautiful" or "worshipful" or "like a church" it may be or seem, the form of the building has little relation to the form of worship taking place inside it—as, e.g., when a Methodist, Baptist, or Disciples church has a split chancel which architecturally points to the altar in the middle—without a "reserved host" to put on it, all that can be set on this table in a focal position is a vase of cut flowers or the morning's collection!

[9] There seems to be little doubt that subjective emotionalism, as a medium for the holy, flourishes most easily among the less-privileged, where "breeding" and "education" and their resultant "manners" have not yet cramped the dynamic of life's emotions with the straightjacket of formalism. Most examples of corporate emotional religion (Montanism, die Schwärmerei, the Methodists in eighteenth-

century England, and the revival churches in our rural districts, white and Negro alike) have occurred among lower-class groups; and further, when they shed their lower-class status the *same* groups quickly shed their emotionalism as well. It is not accurate, however, to associate *subjective* media of the holy with lower-class status, for subjective, or inward, mediation of the holy can take other forms than those of emotional outbursts: for example, contemplative, mystical, or even rational experience of the presence and/or guidance of God. The best illustration of this is, of course, the Quakers, who were by no means solely lower-class at any point in their history, but whose view of the holy, albeit rational and mystical in character, was certainly inward or subjective. Our suggestion here is, then, not so much that the class status of these groups is of sole importance, as that their sociological situation as either a "separated" or a "culturated" group is important in providing the necessary framework for such inward experience of the holy.

¹⁰It should be said plainly that I do not mean by this example to imply that the situation of this Quaker group, which I recall with great appreciation, is typical of all Quaker meetings or even a majority, though it becomes more typical as one moves westward away from the East. I know that many meetings have been able to withstand the pressures of culture against inward religion and maintain their tradition intact even in the modern world. This case merely served to illumine in an amazingly clear way the dynamic factors at work in *all* sectarian groups when they have joined the culture and have subsequently experienced an impoverishment of their peculiarly subjective forms of worship.

¹¹While the renewed interest in the Episcopal Church has many causes, and is of course more a clerical than a lay phenomenon, nevertheless when the non-Episcopalian, lay or cleric, is asked the reasons for this interest, the answer is almost invariably something like this: "They seem to have more of a real sense of worship," "There seems to be more real *religion* in their services," "I feel the presence of God when I go to church there"; and so on. These replies clearly indicate that at present the worshiper has more of an *experience* of the holy in churches which have objective media of the holy—i.e., liturgical forms and symbols, and above all, meaningful sacraments—than in those which, having forsaken objective media in order to emphasize inner experience, now find themselves devoid of the very experiences they once fostered. Another irony in this connection appeared to the author when a ministerial student, explaining why he was changing to the Episcopalian clergy from the Methodist, said: "I want my ministry to be a religious and not a secular vocation. And I mean by that, one connected with inwardness, the holy, and the things of God, and not merely with the various activities, functions, and programs of the visible church." The irony is that very much the same reasons would have been put forward by a serious young eighteenth-century minister to explain why he was leaving the Church of England to join those who called themselves Methodists.

¹²Nostalgia is, I believe, the most dangerous cancer in the life of present Southern religion. By nostalgia I mean the effort to hold on to an older, parental (and even grandparental) form of religion, not because it has direct and relevant meaning to present existence, but because it symbolizes a way of life and of viewing life which, looked back on, seems serene, secure, meaningful, and good. It is the memory of mother singing those gospel hymns, *not* the message of the hymn as heard now. It is the conviction that there was "real religion" in those days—and that modern worshipers have somehow lost it—that drives them to assert these forms of strict biblical belief and folksy patterns of worship, though all are modern men in everything else they believe and not at all "folksy" in their other social

activities and relations in suburbia. I have called such religion nostalgic because the tie that binds the worshiper to it is not his own personal belief and commitment to a present God, but a sentimental yearning for the yesteryear which this religion symbolizes. The particular message about God, sin, and salvation for which this form of religion stands is neither experienced nor really believed in at all, for it seems to modern industrial and suburban men and women quite unreal. On the contrary, the emotional tone that characterizes such religion is one of longing and not belief; and what is longed for is not so much a contemporary walk with Jesus as to recapture aspects of the old life of which the religion reminds us.

Certainly many aspects of that now departed style of life represented by "old-time religion" may well be acutely missed in our anxious, impersonal, urban age. For that older style of life incorporated all the values of homey small-town America, with its close personal relations, its secure moral standards, and its ultimate certainties about the nature of things. This entire complex of relationships, standards, and certainties has been rudely shattered by the modern technological and commercial era, with its personal uprootedness and loneliness, its doubt about the reality of all religious affirmations, its new anxieties about the future, and its less restricted but potentially meaningless life of the suburbs. But the wealthy Baptist businessman, comfortable in his Hart, Shaffner and Marx suit and his new Lincoln, who expresses his longing for the small-town past through gospel hymns, revivals, fundamentalist slogans, and folksy worship services, does not really wish or intend to *live* in that rural, bygone age. It does not represent *his* religion, his ultimate commitment, for he is far too attached to the modern world in which he lives and works—to its opportunities, its freedoms, its gadgets, and its values—to relinquish it for the small town he left behind years ago. He misses only certain "spiritual" things about that past life which his present commercial existence seems to lack, and that emptiness of values and beliefs is partially filled by this occasional backward journey in time through his Sunday church life. Since this religion symbolizes for him only a vanished past when other people (not he) believed in God, it is really not his religion but theirs. What is communicated to him by it is only the memory of their religion, not the presence of God. It has, therefore, neither judging nor saving power for him. Further, it will itself die out when he passes on and the memory of that past generation dies. The small-town folksy religion will in a few years not even be an object of nostalgia. The current crop of young people have been brought up in the modern suburbs, in the atmosphere of high-school science, country club social life, and fraternity moral codes, and know nothing at first hand of "old-time religion." Such children of the suburbs will not be able to recall in their adult years, as their parents now do, that "Daddy had this kind of religion"—for our modern suburban daddies do not. All they will be able to say is that "Daddy used to like to sing those old songs," and at that point the accidental connection of gospel religion with a natural nostalgia for remembered childhood scenes will have vanished. Because of the present widespread character of this longing for the bygone small-town South, "old-time religion" is at present very popular among the newly mobile and rootless middle classes; correspondingly, the churches (especially the Baptist) that regard it as their mission to guard it continue to grow in numbers. One cannot but suspect, however, that this rate of growth will soon slacken and ultimately die off unless the religion of these churches is made relevant to the thought, the behavior, the emotions, and the social habits of the present-day world.

[13]The elusiveness of the referent for the democratic-political symbol "the equality of man" is well known. To what does this symbol refer? To a physical or anthropological equality, to an equality of mental powers, an equality of some sort

of "value," or equality in the sight of God? Probably other possibilities equally elusive could be mentioned. Many positivistically inclined friends have pointed out to the writer the impossibility of locating by research or by expedition the referents of such political symbols—but the same friends are more often than not to be found standing up for the rights of minority groups at great personal cost, and appealing in such existential situations, when they forget themselves, to symbols as indefinite as "the rights of men," "the equality of the races," "academic freedom," and so on. This author believes that ultimately an ontological referent for those symbols can be found, a referent that can be expressed most fully in terms of the Christian doctrine of man as the creature and the adopted son of God. But as the history of democracy and the ranks of liberalism show, the symbolic power of these phrases has been much wider than has belief in this theological-philosophical interpretation of their actual referent. For many men who knew nothing of an ultimate equality before God have risked their substance for these symbols. Thus the power of such a symbol is not dependent upon a clear understanding of its referent; rather its power lies in the fact that it expresses and communicates the intangible reality of a democratic spirit, a spirit that lives (if it lives at all) in the convictions and so in the behavior patterns of the members of any community that can be called democratic. Symbols thus point to, express, communicate, and so ultimately realize what they symbolize: the spiritual reality of the community to which they provide form and direction.

[14]Calvin gives this same example in explaining the relation of spiritual word to material symbol, be the latter a thing or an act: "What is the contact of one man's right hand with that of another, since hands are not infrequently joined in hostility? But when words of friendship and compact have preceded, the obligations of covenants are confirmed by such signs, notwithstanding they have been previously conceived, proposed and determined in words. Sacraments, therefore, are exercises, which increase and strengthen our faith in the Word of God; and because we are corporeal, they are exhibited under corporeal symbols, to instruct us according to our dull capacities, and to lead us by the hand as so many young children." John Calvin, *Institutes of the Christian Religion,* trans. J. Allen, Bk. IV, Chap. XIV, sec. VI (Philadelphia: Presbyterian Board of Christian Education, 1936), Vol. II, p. 559.

[15]"For God does not deal, nor has He ever dealt, with man otherwise than through a word of promise . . . again, we cannot deal with God otherwise than through faith in the word of His promise. . . . But while the mass is the word of Christ, it is also true that God is wont to add to wellnigh every promise of His a certain sign as a mark or memorial of His promise, so that we may thereby the more faithfully hold to His promise and be the more forcibly admonished by it. . . . We learn from this that in every promise of God two things are presented to us—the word and the sign—so that we are to understand the word to be the testament, but the sign to be the sacrament. Thus in the mass the word of Christ is the testament, and the bread and wine are the sacrament." Martin Luther, "The Babylonian Captivity of the Church," *Works of Martin Luther,* Vol II (Philadelphia: Muhlenberg, 1943), pp. 201-203. For further discussions of the promise, i.e., the word of the gospel contained in each sacrament, see *ibid.,* pp. 220-221, for baptism, and for the Eucharist, pp. 197-199, 203-204.

And this from Calvin: ". . . we see that there is never any sacrament without an antecedent promise of God, to which it is subjoined as an appendix, in order to confirm and seal the promise itself, and to certify and ratify it to us; which means God foresees to be necessary, in the first place on account of our ignorance and dullness, and in the next place on account of our weakness; and yet, strictly speaking, not so much for the confirmation of his sacred word, as for our establishment in the faith of it.'' *Op. cit.,* Bk. IV, Chap. XIV, sec. III, Vol. II, p. 556. And again: ''For seeing we are so foolish, that we cannot receive him with true confidence of heart, when he is presented by simple teaching and preaching, the Father, of his mercy, not at all disdaining to condescend in this matter to our infirmity, has desired to attach to his word a visible sign, by which he represents the substance of his promises, to confirm and fortify us, and to deliver us from all doubt and uncertainty.'' ''Treatise on the Lord's Supper,'' I, found in *Calvin: Theological Treatises,* J. K. S. Reid, ed., Library of Christian Classics, Vol. XXII (Philadelphia: Westminster Press, 1954), p. 144.

[16]An expressive but unfortunately materialistic phrase of Ignatius of Antioch (d. 117) in his letter to the Ephesians: ''At these meetings you should heed the bishop and presbytery attentively, and break one loaf, which is the medicine of immortality, and the antidote which wards off death but yields continuous life in union with Jesus Christ.'' ''Letter . . . to the Ephesians,'' sec. 20, *Early Christian Fathers,* C. C. Richardson, ed., Library of Christian Classics, Vol. I (Philadelphia: Westminster Press, 1953), p. 93.

[17]Calvin *Institutes,* Bk. IV, Chap. XIV, sec. III, Vol. II, p. 557, and the following: ''Now our heavenly Father . . . gives us the Supper as a mirror in which we contemplate our Lord Jesus Christ crucified to abolish our faults and offenses, and raised to deliver us from corruption and death, and restoring us to a heavenly immortality.'' ''Treatise on the Lord's Supper,'' II, *Calvin: Theological Treatises,* p. 145.

[18]''And just as a cutting from the vine planted in the ground fructifies in its season, or as a corn of wheat falling into the earth and becoming decomposed, rises with manifold increase by the Spirit of God, who contains all things, and then, through the wisdom of God, serves for the use of man, and having received the word of God, becomes the Eucharist, which is the body and blood of Christ; so also our bodies, being nourished by it, and deposited in the earth, and suffering decomposition there, shall rise at their appointed time, the Word of God granting their resurrection to the glory of God, even the Father, who freely gives to this mortal immortality, and to this corruptible incorruption . . .'' Irenaeus, *Against Heresies,* Bk. V, Chap. II, sec. 3, *The Ante-Nicene Fathers,* Vol. I (Grand Rapids: Eerdmans, 1950), p. 528.

[19]The close relation of the Lord's Supper to the passion, death, and resurrection of Jesus has of course always been central to its meaning and power, as not only the New Testament itself, but the following from church history make clear: ''They hold aloof from the Eucharist and from services of prayer, because they refuse to admit that the Eucharist is the flesh of our Savior Jesus Christ, which suffered for our sins and which, in His goodness, the Father raised [from the dead].'' Ignatius, ''To the Smyrnaeans,'' C. C. Richardson, *op. cit.,* p. 115. In letter 62, Cyprian continually refers to the identity of the sacrifice of Christ on Calvary and the present action of the Eucharist by and for the people; e.g., ''. . . because just as the drinking of wine cannot be attained unless the bunch of grapes be first trodden and pressed, so neither could we drink the blood of Christ unless Christ had first been trampled upon and pressed, and had first drunk the cup of which He should also give believers to drink.'' Cyprian, ''Epistle 62,'' sec. 7, *The Ante-Nicene Fathers,* Vol. V, p. 360. And even more clearly: ''For if Jesus Christ, our Lord and God, is Himself the chief priest of God the Father, and has first offered Himself a sacrifice

to the Father, and has commanded this to be done in commemoration of Himself . . . he [the priest] then offers a true and full sacrifice in the Church to God the Father, when he proceeds to offer it according to what he sees Christ Himself to have offered." *Ibid.,* sec. 14, p. 362.

The relation, however, is even more direct in Luther, not here so much as a *repetition* of the sacrifice of Christ, but as a *sign of the promise* involved in the sacrifice in Christ: "The mass, according to its substance, is, therefore, nothing else than the aforesaid words of Christ—'Take and eat'; as if He said: 'Behold, O sinful man and condemned, out of pure and unmerited love wherewith I love thee, and by the will of the Father of all mercies, I promise thee in these words . . . the forgiveness of all thy sins and life everlasting. And, that thou mayest be most certainly assured of this my irrevocable promise, I give my body and shed my blood, thus by my very death confirming this promise, and leaving thee my body and blood as a sign and memorial of this same promise.' " "The Babylonian Captivity of the Church," *Works* (Muhlenberg ed.), Vol. II, p. 199.

[20]Matt. 26:26–29; Mark 14:22–25; Luke 22:14–20; I Cor. 11:23–26.

[21]This deepest fellowship with Jesus through His death, a fellowship of sonship and communion with God, is perhaps most clearly expressed in Heb. 10:12–22. It is, however, also perhaps the central theme of all of Paul's words on salvation (cf. Rom. 5 and 8). This identification with Christ, moreover, in and through His atonement, in which He takes our place in sin and we His in righteousness, is the basic motif of Reformation views of the meaning of the atonement. For it is through this identification with us, this transference of what is ours to Him and what is His to us, that Jesus becomes the *Christus pro nobis.* the saving Christ for us, by whom we are justified despite our sin and so through whom we are received into sonship before God. Cf. Luther "Commentary on Galatians," esp. Gal. 3:13 and 4:4 ff. (in the Revell 1953 edition, pp. 268–82, 353–59), and Calvin, *Institutes,* Bk. II, Chaps. XV and XVI.

[22]Cf. the following from Cyprian: "For when the Lord calls bread, which is combined by the union of many grains, His body, He indicates our people whom He bore as being united; and when He calls the wine, which is pressed from many grapes and clusters and collected together, His blood, He also signifies our flock linked together by the mingling of a united multitude." Cyprian, "Epistle 75," sec. 6, *The Ante-Nicene Fathers,* Vol. V, p. 398. This has, incidentally, also been a main theme of the sectarian movement: breaking the bread *together* and taking the cup *together* symbolize the unity in love of the brethren in the church community; cf. B. Hübmaier, "A Form for the Celebration of the Lord's Supper." in H. E. Fosdick, *Great Voices of the Reformation* (New York: Random House, 1952), pp. 311–15.

The Nature of the Church

19

Leon Morris

Nature and Government of the Church
(Episcopalian View)

The term "episcopalian" is applied to that system of church government which sees the bishop (Gr., ἐπίσκοπος) as the principal officer. The "historic episcopate" is distinguished from modern church orders which have adopted the name "bishop" for their principal ministers (e.g., the Methodist Episcopal churches) as that episcopate which is connected with the primitive church in an unbroken line of succession by ordination. The modern groups do not have the same ideas about episcopacy, nor do they retain the other orders of ministry, the priests and deacons. The are properly to be discussed as Methodists, etc. In this article we confine ourselves to those churches which retain the historic episcopate.

Even this, however, does not give us a uniform system, for there are marked divergences among the denominations concerned. Common to all, however, is the thought that there are certain functions which belong to the bishop alone. He is a "father in God" to his people, and he has a particular responsibility to provide for their spiritual welfare. In view of the fact that through the centuries the bishops have varied a good deal in their social

From *The Encyclopedia of Christianity* (Marshallton, Delaware: The National Foundation for Christian Education, 1968), Vol. II, pp. 482–486.

(and other) status and have performed a wide variety of functions, this point is worth emphasizing. Bishops have been "princes of the church," with wide responsibilities for temporal affairs. They have been counselors of kings, to all intents and purposes ministers of state. And, in a particular form of Irish monasticism, they have been lowly brethren, subject to the abbot of their order. These things may vary and have varied. But the thing that remains constant is the pastoral responsibility. This involves care for the preservation of the catholic faith in its purity, and the performance of rites like confirmation and ordination. Indeed, the bishop may be thought of as the ordaining officer. No valid ordination is conducted without him. Presbyters join with him in the ordination of presbyters, but they may not ordain without him, as he may without them, e.g., when he ordains deacons.

The bishop has authority in government and is supreme in his diocese. He is not, however, an autocrat ruling with unlimited sway. The other orders have due authority of their own, and the bishop has no right to disregard them. He may have assistant bishops (called suffragans or coadjutors), but the bishop is the one to whom the ultimate responsibility is entrusted. He must safeguard right doctrine, see that discipline is carried out where necessary, and in general order the affairs of the diocese for the general good. Associated with him are the orders of priests and deacons. These three orders are accepted throughout the churches which retain episcopal government, though the Roman church has introduced a variant of its own. It regards the bishop as essentially of the same order as the priest, and (since 1207 A.D.) it elevates the order of subdeacons to the rank of a major order, thus making up the three major orders. The Orthodox churches retain the subdiaconate as a minor order, but in Anglicanism it has disappeared along with the other minor orders. Minor orders are retained by the Roman and the Orthodox churches, but with differences. Since 1207 A.D. the Roman church sees them as the orders of acolyte, exorcist, and doorkeeper. The Orthodox have merged the acolyte, exorcist, and doorkeeper with the subdiaconate, but readers and cantors are distinct. The minor orders have lost a good deal of their significance, and to all intents and purposes are now a stage to be taken on the way to the major orders. The threefold ministry accordingly is the one that all these churches regard as the really significant ministry.

Most, though not all, episcopalians regard this ministry as having come down in an unbroken line from the apostles, and they think of this "apostolic succession" as being of the very essence of the ministry. There have been many who have not scrupled to say that all who lack this ministry are outside the true church. The idea behind it stems from the thought, held generally by Christians at large, that Christ intended to found a church. Episcopalians often reject the idea of the "invisible church" and put their emphasis on the visible body of Christ's followers. This is the only church the NT knows, they say, and therefore we need take into consideration nothing else. (It should be added that evangelical Anglicans recognize the place and importance of the church invisible and would not agree with the reasoning of other episcopalians at this point.) Now it is impossible to think that Jesus intended His followers to be grouped in a church and to leave it without a ministry of any kind. A society must have its officers. If it was Jesus' purpose to found a church, it is surely reasonable, to put it at the lowest, that He likewise purposed that there should be officers, a ministry in His church. And when we ask who these ministers were, there can be no dispute. He appointed the twelve Apostles and there is no evidence that He ever appointed anyone else. Thus the only ministry that can be said to go back to the intention of the Founder is the apostolic ministry. The apostles in due course ordained others, and these in turn others, and so the chain continues. Any other form of ministry, it is pointed out, must have come from some human device, by men setting themselves up as officers in a society which had already been given officers by divine appointment. Sometimes appeal is made to Luke 12:42f., which is said to imply that the ministry (and thus the apostolic ministry) should continue until the second advent.

The argument is continued by pointing out that in the NT the apostles and the apostles alone exercised oversight (ἐπισκοπή). In course of time they delegated some of their functions to others. We see the process beginning in the cases of Timothy and Titus. In the NT we never hear of the church or of elders ordaining. Always it is the apostles or those commissioned by the apostles. The conclusion is drawn that the only valid ordination is that which stems ultimately from the apostles. Sometimes there is a contrast made between a ministry "from above" (i.e., from Christ, descending through His chosen channel), and one "from below" (i.e., from the church, with men elevating other men to special office). Appeal is made to statements in early writers, notably Clement of Rome and Ignatius, to show that the only ministry accepted was one which came from the apostles. Irenaeus has many statements on the subject, and he is regarded as a particularly important witness. The case is strengthened by pointing to the fact that, whatever be the truth about origins, it is unquestionable that, from the first times of which we have certain knowledge, the form of ministry prevalent everywhere in the ancient church was the familiar one of bishops, priests, and deacons. It is difficult to think that the widespread appearance of this one particular form of ministry is due to chance, or to the victory of one form of church government over another or others. In the latter case there would surely be traces of the conflict, but history knows nothing of a struggle between upholders of competing systems of church government. The conclusion that is drawn in that there was one divinely ordained form of ministry, and that the divine origin is the reason for its universal acceptance.

For reasons such as these most episcopalians have felt that this is not simply one form of church government, but that it is the only permissible form of church government. All others are of human invention, and *ipso facto* invalid, or at the least highly irregular. But this view is not universal. Evangelical Anglicans, for example, usually hold that other ministries may well be valid. They point to the difficulty of squaring a view of ministry as mechanical as this with the NT emphasis on spiritual attitudes, where even apostolic authority is conditioned upon faithfulness to the gospel (2 Cor. 11:13; Gal. 1:8f.). There is also the fact that the theory is weakest at what ought to be its strongest point, namely, the connection between the apostles and their successors. We do not lack apostolic directions to the churches, and it is surely significant that there is nothing that could be construed as a command to preserve or perpetuate any particular form of ministry. In particular, there is no record of an apostle ever conveying the power to ordain. Moreover, the theory seems to overlook the fact that the indwelling Christ is the Lord of the church (the Head over His Body). He is not bound to act through any particular channels. He did raise up the Apostle Paul without the intervention of any other apostle, and the question arises, "If He did this once, why not again?" Again, the references in early writers are called in question. Clement of Rome is ambiguous. Ignatius, though he exalts the office of bishop to the skies, never uses the one argument that would be conclusive—he never says that the episcopate was ordained by Christ or His apostles. Irenaeus, who did not flourish until towards the end of the second century, witnesses not to a succession by ordination, but to open and public succession to office without saying how the office-bearers were appointed. In fact, there seems to be no real evidence for the view of succession *by ordination* until the time of Augustine. It is countered that in the early days the church acted without conscious theory, carrying on the threefold ministry, and that when men began to ask what its significance was the answer came in terms of apostolic succession. But this will not do. If apostolic succession is the explanation, if ordination outside the succession is invalid, then it is imperative that the succession be conserved. Men must be warned of the consequences of losing the succession, either by deliberately abandoning it or by exercising insufficient care. It cannot be seriously maintained that a matter of such importance should be left to chance. If the apostles have left no record of such a command emanating from Christ, nor given one of their own, nor even hinted that ordination in the succession is desirable, then we cannot hold that this form of ordination is a *sine qua non*.

We are on safer grounds if we point to the undeniable facts that the Lord promised that His Holy Spirit would guide His followers and that the threefold ministry emerged universally. While it is impossible to prove on the available evidence that apostolic succession was divinely enjoined, it is quite possible to maintain that the threefold ministry emerged worldwide at a very early time, and that in the providence of God this indicates that this ministry is of value to the church and is not lightly to be discarded. But we must leave open the possibility that in other days God may raise up other ministries as seem good to Him. We ought not to hold that the ministry is constitutive of the church.

The episcopal churches in general pay a good deal of attention to the four "notes" of the church as given in the ancient creeds, namely, that the church is one, holy, catholic, and apostolic. For our present purpose the first note is particularly important. All agree that there is but one church, but just what constitutes unity? The Roman church tends to answer in terms of submission to the pope, whatever else may be included. That is to say, a Roman Catholic definition of the church, or of the oneness of the church, will probably include a reference to the faith and to the sacraments, but it will also mention subjection to the Roman pontiff. Other churches may agree with Rome on catholic teaching and on the sacraments, but because they do not submit to the pope they are not regarded as part of the true church. It is held that Christ established His church on Peter, the rock. There is but one church, and therefore it must be that built on Peter. Those who do not own allegiance to Peter, as embodied in the papacy, by that fact put themselves outside the church. The Orthodox Church also puts a very great emphasis on the unity of the church (though it is doubtful that it has given official definition of what this unity entails). It maintains that Christ founded one church, and that the unity of the church is inherent in this divine foundation. In the course of time the Westerners separated themselves from the true church, but this does not divide the church. The church is indivisible. By definition it must be one. The schism means that, on account of their innovations, the Romans have put themselves outside the church. And, of course, the Orthodox hold that in later times the Protestants missed the opportunity of returning to the church and perpetuated their separation from it. By virtue of their historical continuity with the church of NT times the Orthodox think that their claim to be the one church is demonstrated. Among Anglicans the "branch theory" is put forward. This sees one church, united by possessing the apostolic succession, but divided into three branches, the Orthodox, the Roman, and the Anglican. As, however, none of these three is in communion with either of the others it is not a very impressive kind of unity. It is much better to see the essence of the unity as spiritual and inward, and to regard this note as incompletely fulfilled. This, as a matter of fact, is the case with all the notes. The church is holy, but few would claim that this is perfectly the case here and now. Similarly, the church is catholic only in ideal and in approximation. And while the note of apostolicity is there, we cannot think that all the apostolic teaching has been fully preserved. The four notes are useful, but they remind us that the ideals for the church are but partially reached here on earth.

Finally, we must notice the place ascribed to the tradition of the church. Most episcopalians recognize that their system is not to be found in the NT, and they make their appeal to the early church. This is often taken so far as to make tradition equally authoritative with Scripture. There are difficulties in this. In the first place, tradition is hard to define. Nobody knows exactly where the limits are to be set. Then, churches which appeal to tradition come up with very different answers to many questions. And it should not be overlooked that the most ancient tradition is unanimous in appealing to the Bible as the supreme authority.

Louis Berkhof

The Government
of the Church

A. Different Theories Respecting the Government of the Church

1. The View of Quakers and Darbyites

It is a matter of principle with the Quakers and Darbyites to reject all Church Government. According to them every external Church formation necessarily degenerates and leads to results that are contrary to the spirit of Christianity. It exalts the human element at the expense of the divine. It neglects the divinely given charisms and substitutes for them offices instituted by man, and consequently offers the Church the husk of human knowledge rather than the vital communications of the Holy Spirit. Therefore they regard it as not only unnecessary but decidedly sinful to organize the visible Church. Thus the offices fall by the way, and in public worship each simply follows the promptings of the Spirit. The tendency that becomes apparent in these sects, which gives clear evidence of the leaven of Mysticism, must be regarded as a reaction against the hierarchical organization and the formalism of the Established Church of England. In our

From *Systematic Theology* (Grand Rapids: Wm. B. Eerdmans Pub. Co., 1941), pp. 579–592. Used by permission.

country some of the Quakers have regularly ordained ministers and conduct their worship very much as other Churches do.

2. The Erastian System, Named After Erastus, 1524–1583

Erastians regard the Church as a society which owes its existence and form to regulations enacted by the State. The officers of the Church are merely instructors or preachers of the Word, without any right or power to rule, except that which they derive from the civil magistrates. It is the function of the State to govern the Church, to exercise discipline and to excommunicate. Church censures are civil punishments, though their application may be entrusted to the legal officers of the Church. This system has been variously applied in England, Scotland, and Germany (Lutheran Churches). It conflicts with the fundamental principle of the Headship of Jesus Christ, and does not recognize the fact that Church and State are distinct and independent in their origin, in their primary objects, in the power they exercise, and in the administration of that power.

3. The Episcopalian System

The Episcopalians hold that Christ, as the Head of the Church, has entrusted the government of the Church directly and exclusively to an order of prelates or bishops, as the successors of the apostles: and that He has constituted these bishops a separate, independent, and self-perpetuating order. In this system the *coetus fidelium* or community of believers has absolutely no share in the government of the Church. In the early centuries this was the system of the Roman Catholic Church. In England it is combined with the Erastian system. But the Bible does not warrant the existence of such a separate class of superior officers, who have the inherent right of ordination and jurisdiction, and therefore do not represent the people nor, in any sense of the word, derive their office from them. Scripture clearly shows that the apostolic office was not of a permanent nature. The apostles did form a clearly distinct and independent class, but it was not their special task to rule and administer the affairs of the churches. It was their duty to carry the gospel to unevangelized districts, to found churches, and then to appoint others from among the people for the task of ruling these churches. Before the end of the first century the Apostolate had disappeared entirely.

4. The Roman Catholic System

This is the Episcopal system carried to its logical conclusion. The Roman Catholic system pretends to comprise, not only successors of the apostles, but also a successor to Peter, who is said to have had the primacy among the apostles, and whose successor is now recognized as the special representative of Christ. The Church of Rome is of the nature of an absolute monarchy, under the control of an infallible Pope, who has the right to determine and regulate the doctrine, worship, and government of the Church. Under him there are inferior classes and orders, to whom special grace is given, and whose duty it is to govern the Church in strict accountability to their superiors and to the supreme Pontiff. The people have absolutely no voice in the government of the Church. This system also conflicts with Scripture, which recognizes no such primacy of Peter as that on which the system is built, and distinctly recognizes the voice of the people in ecclesiastical affairs. Moreover, the claim of the Roman Catholic Church, that there has been an unbroken line of succession from the time of Peter down to the present day, is contradicted by history. The papal system is, both exegetically and historically, untenable.

5. The Congregational System

This is also called the system of independency. According to it each church or congregation is a complete church, independent of every other. In such a church the governing power rests exclusively with the members of the church, who are entitled to regulate their own affairs. Officers are simply functionaries of the local church, appointed to teach and to administer the affairs of the church, and have no governing power beyond that which they possess as members of the church. If it is considered expedient that the various churches should exercise communion with one another, as is sometimes the case, this fellowship finds expression in ecclesiastical councils and in local or provincial conferences, for the consideration of their common interests. But the actions of such associated bodies are held to be strictly advisory or declarative, and are not binding on any particular church. This theory of popular government, making the office of the ministry altogether dependent on the action of the people, is certainly not in harmony with what we learn from the Word of God. Moreover, the theory that each church is independent of every other church fails to express the unity of the Church of Christ, has a disintegrating effect, and opens the door for all kinds of arbitrariness in church government. There is no appeal beyond any of the decisions of the local church.

6. The National-Church System

This system, also called the Collegial system (which supplanted the Territorial system), was developed in Germany especially by C. M. Pfaff (1686–1780), and was later on introduced into the Netherlands. It proceeds on the assumption that the Church is a voluntary association, equal to the State. The separate churches or congregations are merely subdivisions of the one national Church. The original power resides in a national organization, and this organization has jurisdiction over the local churches. This is just the reverse of the Presbyterian system, according to which the original power has its seat in the consistory. The Territorial system recognized the *inherent* right of the State to reform public worship, to decide disputes respecting doctrine and conduct, and to convene synods, while the Collegial system ascribes to the State only the right of supervision as an *inherent right,* and regards all other rights, which the State might exercise in Church matters, as rights which the Church by a tacit understanding or by a formal pact conferred upon the State. This system disregards altogether the autonomy of the local churches, ignores the principles of self-government and of direct responsibility to Christ, engenders formalism, and binds a professedly spiritual Church by formal and geographical lines. Such a system as this, which is akin to the Erastian system, naturally fits in best with the present-day idea of the totalitarian State.

B. The Fundamental Principles of the Reformed or Presbyterian System

Reformed Churches do not claim that their system of Church government is determined in every detail by the Word of God, but do assert that its fundamental principles are directly derived from Scripture. They do not claim a *jus divinum* for the details, but only for the general fundamental principles of the system, and are quite ready to admit that many of its particulars are determined by expediency and human wisdom. From this it follows that, while the general structure must be rigidly maintained, some of the details may be changed in the proper ecclesiastical manner for prudential reasons, such as the general profit of the churches. The following are its most fundamental principles.

1. Christ Is the Head of the Church and the Source of All Its Authority

The Church of Rome considers it of the greatest importance to maintain the headship of the Pope over the Church. The Reformers maintained and defended the position, in opposition to the claims of the Papacy, that Christ is the only Head of the Church. They did not entirely avoid the danger, however, of recognizing . . . the supremacy of the State over the Church. Consequently the Presbyterian and Reformed Churches had to fight another battle later on, the battle for the Headship of Jesus Christ in opposition to the unwarranted encroachments of the State. This battle was fought first of all in Scotland, and later on also in The Netherlands. The very fact that it was fought against such external powers as the Papacy and the State or the King, both of whom claimed to be the head of the visible Church, clearly implies that they who were engaged in this battle were particularly interested in establishing and maintaining the position that Christ is the only lawful Head of the *visible* Church, and is therefore the only supreme Lawgiver and King of the Church. Naturally, they also recognized Christ as the *organic* Head of the *invisible* Church. They realized that the two could not be separated, but, since the Pope and the King could hardly claim to be the organic head of the invisible Church, this was not really the point in question. Respecting the Scottish teachers Walker says: "They meant that Christ is the real King and Head of the Church, as a visible organisation, ruling it by His statues, and ordinances, and officers, and forces, as truly and literally as David or Solomon ruled the covenant people of old."[1]

The Bible teaches us that Christ is Head over all things: He is the Lord of the universe, not merely as the second person of the Trinity, but in His mediatorial capacity (Matt. 28:18; Eph. 1:20–22; Phil. 2:10, 11; Rev. 17:14; 19:16). In a very special sense, however, He is the Head of the

Church, which is His body. He stands in a vital and organic relation to it, fills it with His life, and controls it spiritually (John 15:1–8; Eph. 1:10, 22, 23; 2:20–22; 4:15; 5:30; Col. 1:18; 2:19; 3:11). Premillenarians claim that this is the only sense in which Christ is the Head of the Church, for they deny the very point for which our Reformed Fathers contended, namely, that Christ is the Head of the Church, not only in virtue of His vital relationship to it, but also as its Legislator and King. In the organic and vital sense He is the Head primarily, though not exclusively, of the invisible Church, which constitutes His spiritual body. But He is also the Head of the visible Church, not only in the organic sense, but also in the sense that He has authority and rule over it (Matt. 16:18, 19; 23:8, 10; John 13:13, I Cor. 12:5; Eph. 1:20–23; 4:4, 5, 11, 12;5:23, 24). This Headship of Christ over the visible Church is the principal part of the dominion bestowed upon Him as the result of His sufferings. His authority is manifested in the following points: (a) He instituted the Church of the New Testament (Matt. 16:18) so that it is not, as many regard it in our day, a mere voluntary society, which has its only warrant in the consent of its members. (b) He instituted the means of grace which the Church must administer, namely, the Word and the sacraments (Matt. 28:19, 20; Mark 16:15, 16; Luke 22:17–20) I Cor. 11:23–29). In these matters no one else has the right to legislate. (c) He gave to the Church its constitution and officers, and clothed them with divine authority, so that they can speak and act in His name (Matt. 10:1; 16:19; John 20:21–23; Eph. 4:11, 12). (d) He is ever present in the Church when it meets for worship, and speaks and acts through its officers. It is Christ as King that warrants their speaking and acting with authority (Matt. 10:40; II Cor. 13:3).

2. Christ Exercises His Authority by Means of His Royal Word

The reign of Christ is not in all respects similar to that of earthly kings. He does not rule the Church by force, but *subjectively* by His Spirit, which is operative in the Church, and *objectively* by the Word of God as the standard of authority. All believers are unconditionally bound to obey the Word of the King. As Christ is the only sovereign Ruler of the Church, His Word is the only word that is law in the absolute sense. Consequently, all despotic power is contraband in the Church. There is no ruling power independent of Christ. The Pope of Rome stands condemned in that he, while professing to be Christ's vicar on earth, virtually supplants Christ and supersedes His Word by human innovations. He not only places tradition on an equal footing with Scripture, but also claims to be the infallible interpreter of both when speaking *ex cathedra* in matters of faith and morals. Scripture and tradition may be the mediate or remote rules of faith; the immediate rule is the teaching of the Church, which has its guarantee in papal infallibility.[2] The word of the Pope is the word of God. But while it is true that Christ exercises His authority in the Church through the officers, this is not to be understood in the sense that He *transfers* His authority to His servants. He Himself rules the Church through all the ages, but in doing this, He uses the officers of the Church as His organs. They have no absolute or independent, but only a derived and ministerial power.

3. Christ as King Has Endowed the Church with Power

A rather delicate question arises at this point, namely, Who are the first and proper subjects of Church power? To whom has Christ committed this power in the first instance? Roman Catholics and Episcopalians answer: to the officers as a separate class, in contradistinction from the ordinary members of the Church. This view has also been held by some eminent Presbyterian divines, such as Rutherford and Baillie. Diametrically opposed to this is the theory of the Independents, that this power is vested in the Church at large, and that the officers are merely the organs of the body as a whole. The great Puritan divine, Owen, adopts this view with some modifications. In recent years some Reformed theologians apparently favored this view, though without subscribing to the separatism of the Independents. There is another view, however, representing a mean between these two extremes, which would seem to deserve preference. According to it ecclesiastical power is committed by Christ to the Church as a whole, that is, to the ordinary members and the officers alike; but in addition to that the officers receive such an additional measure of power as is required for the performance of their respective duties in the Church of Christ. They share in the original power bestowed upon the Church, and receive their authority and power as officers directly from Christ. They are representatives, but not mere deputies or delegates of the people. Older theologians often say: "All Church power, in *actu primo,* or fundamentally, is in the Church itself; in *actu secundo,* or its exercise, in them that are specially called thereto." This is substantially the view held by Voetius, Gillespie (in his work on Ceremonies), Bannerman, Porteous, Bavinck, and Vos.

4. Christ Provided for the Specific Exercise of This Power by Representative Organs

While Christ committed power to the Church as a whole, He also provided for it that this power should be exercised ordinarily and specifically by representative organs, set aside for the maintenance of doctrine, worship, and discipline. The officers of the Church are the representatives of the people chosen by popular vote. This does not mean, however, that they receive their authority from the people, for the call of the people is but the confirmation of the inner call by the Lord Himself; and it is from Him that they receive their authority and to Him that they are responsible. When they are called representatives, this is merely an indication of the fact that they were chosen to their office by the people, and does not imply that they derive their authority from them. Hence they are no deputies or tools that merely serve to carry out the wishes of the people, but rulers whose duty it is to apprehend and apply intelligently the laws of Christ. At the same time they are in duty bound to recognize the power vested in the Church as a whole by seeking its assent or consent in important matters.

5. The Power of the Church Resides Primarily in the Governing Body of the Local Church

It is one of the fundamental principles of Reformed or Presbyterian government, that the power or authority of the Church does not reside first of all in the most general assembly of any Church, and is vested in the governing body of the local church; but that it has its original seat in the consistory or session of the local church, and is by this transferred to the major assemblies, such as classes (presbyteries) and synods or general assemblies. Thus the Reformed system honors the autonomy of the local church, though it always regards this as subject to the limitations that may be put upon it as the result of its association with other churches in one denomination, and assures it the fullest right to govern its own internal affairs by means of its officers. At the same time it also maintains the right and duty of the local church to unite with other similar churches on a common confessional basis, and form a wider organization for doctrinal, judicial, and administrative purposes, with proper stipulations of mutual obligations and rights. Such a wider organization undoubtedly imposes certain limitations on the autonomy of the local churches, but also promotes the growth and welfare of the churches, guarantees the rights of the members of the church, and serves to give fuller expression to the unity of the Church.

C. The Officers of the Church

Different kinds of officers may be distinguished in the Church. A very general distinction is that between extraordinary and ordinary officers.

1. Extraordinary Officers

a. *Apostles.* Strictly speaking, this name is applicable only to the Twelve chosen by Jesus and to Paul; but it is also applied to certain apostolic men who assisted Paul in his work, and who were endowed with apostolic gifts and graces (Acts 14:4, 14; I Cor. 9:5, 6; II Cor. 8:23; Gal. 1:19 [?]). The apostles had the special task of laying the foundation for the Church of all ages. It is only through their word that believers of all following ages have communion with Jesus Christ. Hence they are the apostles of the Church in the present day as well as they were the apostles of the primitive Church. They had certain special qualifications. They (1) received their commission directly from God or from Jesus Christ (Mark 3:14; Luke 6:13; Gal. 1:1); (2) were witnesses of the life of Christ and especially of His resurrection (John 15:27; Acts 1:21, 22; I Cor. 9:1); (3) were conscious of being inspired by the Spirit of God in all their teaching, both oral and written (Acts 15:28; I Cor. 2:13; I Thess. 4:8; I John 5:9–12); (4) had the power to perform miracles and used this on several occasions to ratify their message (II Cor. 12:12; Heb. 2:4); and (5) were richly blessed in their work as a sign of the divine approval of their labors (I Cor. 9:1, 2; II Cor. 3:2, 3; Gal. 2:8).

b. *Prophets*. The New Testament also speaks of prophets (Acts 11:28; 13:1, 2; 15:32; I Cor. 12:10; 13:2; 14:3; Eph. 2:20; 3:5; 4:11; I Tim. 1:18; 4:14; Rev. 11:6). Evidently the gift of speaking for the edification of the Church was highly developed in these prophets, and they were occasionally instrumental in revealing mysteries and predicting future events. The first part of this gift is permanent in the Christian Church, and was distinctly recognized by the Reformed Churches (prophesyings), but the last part of it was of a charismatic and temporary character. They differed from ordinary ministers in that they spoke under special inspiration.

c. *Evangelists*. In addition to apostles and prophets, evangelists are mentioned in the Bible (Acts 21:8; Eph. 4:11; II Tim. 4:5). Philip, Mark, Timothy, and Titus belonged to this class. Little is known about these evangelists. They accompanied and assisted the apostles, and were sometimes sent out by these on special missions. Their work was to preach and baptize, but also to ordain elders (I Tim. 5:22; Titus 1:5) and to exercise discipline (Titus 3:10). Their authority seems to have been more general and somewhat superior to that of the regular ministers.

2. Ordinary Officers

a. *Elders*. Among the common officers of the Church the *presbuteroi* or *episkopoi* are first in order of importance. The former name simply means "elders," that is, older ones, and the latter, "overseers." The term *presbuteroi* is used in Scripture to denote old men, and to designate a class of officers somewhat similar to those who functioned in the synagogue. As a designation of office the name was gradually eclipsed and even superseded by the name *episkopoi*. The two terms are often used interchangeably (Acts 20:17, 28; I Tim. 3:1; 4:14; 5:17, 19; Titus 1:5, 7; I Peter 5:1, 2. *Presbuteroi* are first mentioned in Acts 11:30, but the office was evidently well known already when Paul and Barnabas went to Jerusalem, and may have been in existence even before the institution of the diaconate. At least the term *hoi neoteroi* in Acts 5 seems to point to a distinction between these and the *presbuteroi*. Frequent mention is made of them in the book of Acts (14:23; 15:6, 22; 16:4; 20:17, 28; 21:18). Probably the presbyterial or episcopal office was first instituted in the churches of the Jews (Heb. 13:7, 17; James 5:14), and then, shortly after, also in those of the Gentiles. Several other names are applied to these officers, namely, *proistamenoi* (Rom. 12:8; I Thess. 5:12); *kuberneseis* (I Cor. 12:28); *hegoumenoi* (Heb. 13:7, 17, 24); and *poimenes* (Eph. 4:11). These officers clearly had the oversight of the flock that was entrusted to their care. They had to provide for it, govern it, and protect it, as the very household of God.

b. *Teachers*. It is clear that the elders were not originally teachers. There was no need of separate teachers at first, since there were apostles, prophets, and evangelists. Gradually, however, the *didaskalia* was connected more closely with the episcopal office; but even then the teachers did not at once constitute a separate class of officers. Paul's statement in Ephesians 4:11, that the ascended Christ also gave "pastors and teachers," mentioned as a single class, to the Church, clearly shows that these two did not constitute two different classes of officers, but one class having two related functions. I Timothy 5:17 speaks of elders who labor in the Word and in teaching, and according to Hebrews 13:7 the *hegoumenoi* were also teachers. Moreover, in II Timothy 2:2 Paul urges upon Timothy the necessity of appointing to office faithful men who shall also be able to teach others. In course of time two circumstances led to a distinction between the elders or overseers that were entrusted only with the government of the church, and those that were also called upon to teach: (1) when the apostles died and heresies arose and increased, the task of those who were called upon to teach became more exacting and demanded special preparation (II Tim. 2:2; Titus 1:9); and (2) in view of the fact that the laborer is worthy of his hire, those who were engaged in the ministry of the Word, a comprehensive task requiring all their time, were set free from other work, in order that they might devote themselves more exclusively to the work of teaching. In all probability the *aggeloi* who were addressed in the letters to the seven churches of Asia Minor were the teachers or ministers of those churches (Rev. 2:1, 8, 12, 18; 3:1, 7, 14). In Reformed circles the ministers now rule the churches together with the elders, but in addition to that administer the Word and the sacraments. Together they make the necessary regulations for the government of the Church.

c. *Deacons.* Besides the *presbuteroi* the *diakonoi* are mentioned in the New Testament (Phil. 1:1; I Tim. 3:8, 10, 12). According to the prevailing opinion Acts 6:1-6 contains the record of the institution of the diaconate. Some modern scholars doubt this, however, and regard the office mentioned in Acts 6, either as a general office in which the functions of elders and deacons were combined, or as a merely temporal office serving a special purpose. They call attention to the fact that some of the seven chosen, as Philip and Stephen, were evidently engaged in teaching; and that the money collected at Antioch for the poor in Judea was delivered into the hands of the *elders*. No mention is made of deacons whatsoever in Acts 11:30, though these, if they had existed as a separate class, would have been the natural recipients of that money. And yet in all probability Acts 6 does refer to the institution of the diaconate, for: (1) the name *diakonoi,* which was, previous to the event narrated in Acts 6, always used in the general sense of servant, subsequently began to be employed, and in course of time served exclusively, to designate those who were engaged in works of mercy and charity. The only reason that can be assigned for this is found in Acts 6. (2) The seven men mentioned there were charged with the task of distributing properly the gifts that were brought for the *agapae,* a ministry that is elsewhere more particularly described by the word *diakonia* (Acts 11:29; Rom. 12:7; II Cor. 8:4; 9:1, 12, 13; Rev. 2:19). (3) The requirements for the office, as mentioned in Acts 6, are rather exacting, and in that respect agree with the demands mentioned in I Timothy 3:8-10, 12. (4) Very little can be said in favor of the pet idea of some critics that the diaconate was not developed until later, about the time when the episcopal office made its appearance.

3. The Calling of the Officers and Their Induction into Office

A distinction should be made between the calling of the extraordinary officers, such as apostles, and that of the ordinary officers. The former were called in an extraordinary way with an immediate calling from God, and the latter, in the ordinary manner and through the agency of the Church. We are concerned more particularly with the calling of the ordinary officers.

a. *The calling of the ordinary officers.* This is twofold:

(1) *Internal calling.* It is sometimes thought that the internal calling to an office in the Church consists in some extraordinary indication of God to the effect that one is called—a sort of special revelation. But this is not correct. It consists rather in certain ordinary providential indications given by God, and includes especially three things: (a) the consciousness of being impelled to some special task in the Kingdom of God, by love to God and His cause; (b) the conviction that one is at least in a measure intellectually and spiritually qualified for the office sought; and (c) the experience that God is clearly paving the way to the goal.

(2) *External calling.* This is the call that comes to one through the instrumentality of the Church. It is not issued by the Pope (Roman Catholic), nor by a bishop or a college of bishops (Episcopalian), but by the local church. Both the officers and the ordinary members of the church have a part in it. That the officers have a guiding hand in it, but not to the exclusion of the people, is evident from such passages as Acts 1:15–26; 6:2–6; 14:23. The people were recognized even in the choice of an apostle, according to Acts 1:15–26. It would seem that in the apostolic age the officers guided the choice of the people by calling attention to the necessary qualifications that were required for the office, but allowed the people to take part in the choosing (Acts 1:15–26; 6:1–6; I Tim. 3:2–13). Of course, in the case of Matthias God Himself made the final choice.

b. *The officers' induction into office.* There are especially two rites connected with this:

(1) *Ordination.* This presupposes the calling and examination of the candidate for office. It is an act of the classis or the presbytery (I Tim. 4:14). Says Dr. Hodge: "Ordination is the solemn expression of the judgment of the Church, by those appointed to deliver such judgment, that the candidate is truly called of God to take part in this ministry, thereby authenticating to the people the divine call."[3] This authentication is, under all ordinary circumstances, the necessary condition for the exercise of the ministerial office. It may briefly be called a public acknowledgement and confirmation of the candidate's calling to this office.

(2) *Laying on of hands.* Ordination is accompanied with the laying on of hands. Clearly, the two went hand in hand in apostolic times (Acts 6:6; 13:3; I Tim. 4:14; 5:22). In those early days the laying on of hands evidently implied two things: it signified that a person was set aside for a certain office, and that some special spiritual gift was conferred upon him. The Church of Rome is of the opinion that these two elements are still

included in the laying on of hands, that it actually confers some spiritual grace upon the recipient, and therefore ascribes to it sacramental significance. Protestants maintain, however, that it is merely a symbolical indication of the fact that one is set aside for the ministerial office in the Church. While they regard it as a Scriptural rite and as one that is entirely appropriate, they do not regard it as absolutely essential. The Presbyterian Church makes it optional.

D. The Ecclesiastical Assemblies

1. The Governing Bodies (Church Courts) in the Reformed System

Reformed Church government is characterized by a system of ecclesiastical assemblies in an ascending or a descending scale, according to the point of view from which they are considered. These are the consistory (session), the classis (presbytery), the synod(s), and (in some cases) the general assembly. The consistory consists of the minister (or, ministers) and the elders of the local church. The classis is composed of one minister and one elder of each local church within a certain district. This is somewhat different in the Presbyterian Church, however, where the presbytery includes all the ministers within its boundaries, and one elder from each of its congregations. The synod, again, consists of an equal number of ministers and elders from each classis or presbytery. And, finally, the general assembly is (in the case of the Presbyterians) composed of an equal delegation of ministers and elders from each of the presbyteries, and not, as might be expected, from each of the particular synods.

2. The Representative Government of the Local Church and Its Relative Autonomy

a. *The representative government of the local church.* Reformed churches differ, on the one hand, from all those churches in which the government is in the hands of a single prelate or presiding elder, and on the other hand, from those in which it rests with the people in general. They do not believe in any one-man rule, be he an elder, a pastor, or a bishop; neither do they believe in popular government. They choose ruling elders as their representatives, and these, together with the minister(s), form a council or consistory for the government of the local church. Very likely the apostles were guided by the venerated custom of having elders in the synagogue rather than by any direct commandment, when they ordained elders in the various churches founded by them. The Jerusalem church had elders (Acts 11:30). Paul and Barnabas ordained them in the churches which they organized on the first missionary journey (Acts 14:23). Elders were evidently functioning at Ephesus (Acts 20:17) and at Philippi (Phil. 1:1). The Pastoral Epistles repeatedly make mention of them (I Tim. 3:1, 2; Titus 1:5, 7). It deserves attention that they are always spoken of in the plural (I Cor. 12:28; I Tim. 5:17; Heb. 13:7, 17, 24; I Peter 5:1). The elders are chosen by the people as men who are specially qualified to rule the church. Scripture evidently intends that the people shall have a voice in the matter of their selection, though this was not the case in the Jewish synagogue (Acts 1:21-26; 6:1-6; 14:23). In the last passage, however, the word *cheirotoneo* may have lost its original meaning of *appointing by stretching out the hand,* and may simply mean *to appoint.* At the same time it is perfectly evident that the Lord Himself places these rulers over the people and clothes them with the necessary authority (Matt. 16:19; John 20:22, 23; Acts 1:24, 26; 20:28; I Cor. 12:28; Eph. 4:11, 12; Heb. 13:17). The election by the people is merely an external confirmation of the inner calling by the Lord Himself. Moreover, the elders, though representatives of the people, do not derive their authority from the people, but from the Lord of the Church. They exercise rule over the house of God in the name of the King, and are responsible only to Him.

b. *The relative autonomy of the local church.* Reformed Church government recognizes the autonomy of the local church. This means:

(1) That every local church is a complete church of Christ, fully equipped with everything that is required for its government. There is absolutely no need that any government should be imposed upon it from without. And not only that, but such an imposition would be absolutely contrary to its nature.

(2) That, though there can be a proper affiliation or consolidation of contiguous churches, there may be no union which destroys the autonomy of the local church. Hence it is better not to speak of classes and synods as higher, but to describe them as major or more general assemblies. They do not represent a higher, but the very same, power that inheres in the consistory, though exercising this on a broader scale. McGill speaks of them as *higher* and *remoter* tribunals.[4]

(3) That the authority and prerogatives of the major assemblies are not unlimited, but have their limitation in the rights of the sessions or consistories. They are not permitted to lord it over a local church or its members, irrespective of the constitutional rights of the consistory, nor to meddle with the internal affairs of a local church under any and all circumstances. When churches affiliate, their mutual rights and duties are circumscribed in a Church Order or Form of Government. This stipulates the rights and duties of the major assemblies, but also guarantees the rights of the local church. The idea that a classis (presbytery) or synod can simply impose whatever it pleases on a particular church is essentially Roman Catholic.

(4) That the autonomy of the local church has its limitations in the relation in which it stands to the churches with which it is affiliated, and in the general interests of the affiliated churches. The Church Order is a sort of Constitution, solemnly subscribed to by every local church, as represented by its consistory. This on the one hand guards the rights and interests of the local church, but on the other hand also, the collective rights and interests of the affiliated churches. And no single church has the right to disregard matters of mutual agreement and of common interest. The local group may be even called upon occasionally to deny itself for the far greater good of the Church in general.

3. The Major Assemblies

a. *Scripture warrant for major assemblies.* Scripture does not contain an explicit command to the effect that the local churches of a district must form an organic union. Neither does it furnish us with an example of such a union. In fact, it represents the local churches as individual entities without any external bond of union. At the same time the essential nature of the Church, as described in Scripture, would seem to call for such a union. The Church is described as a spiritual organism, in which all the constituent parts are vitally related to one another. It is the spiritual body of Jesus Christ, of which He is the exalted Head. And it is but natural that this inner unity should express itself in some visible manner, and should even, as much as possible in this imperfect and sinful world, seek expression in some corresponding external organization. The Bible speaks of the Church not only as a spiritual body, but also as a tangible body, as a temple of the Holy Spirit, as a priesthood, and as a holy nation. Every one of these terms points to a visible unity. Congregationalists or Independents and Undenominationalists lose sight of this important fact. The existing divisions in the visible Church at the present time should not cause us to lose sight of the fact that there are certain passages of Scripture which seem to indicate rather clearly that, not only the invisible Church, but also the visible Church is a unity. The word *ekklesia* is used in the singular as an indication of the visible Church in a wider sense than that of the purely local church (Acts 9:31 [according to the now accepted reading], I Cor. 12:28, and probably also I Cor. 10:32). In the descriptions of the Church in I Corinthians 12:12–31 and Ephesians 4:4–16 the apostle also has its visible unity in mind. Moreover, there are reasons for thinking that the Church at Jerusalem and at Antioch consisted of several separate groups, which together formed a sort of unity. And, finally, Acts 15 acquaints us with the example of the council of Jerusalem. This council was composed of apostles and elders, and therefore did not constitute a proper example and pattern of a classis or synod in the modern sense of the word. At the same time it was an example of a major assembly, and of one that spoke with authority and not merely in an advisory capacity.

b. *The representative character of the major assemblies.* In the abstract it may be said that the major assemblies might have been composed of *all* the representatives of all the local churches under their jurisdiction; but, on account of the number of the churches represented, such a body would in most cases prove unwieldy and inefficient. In order to keep the number of representatives down to reasonable proportions, the principle of representation is carried through also in connection with the major assemblies. Not the local churches, but the classes or presbyteries, send their representatives to synods. This affords the gradual contraction that is necessary for a well-compacted system. The immediate representatives of the people who form the consistories or sessions are themselves represented in classes or presbyteries, and these in turn are represented in synods or general assemblies. The more general the assembly, the more remote it is from the people; yet none of them is too remote for the expression of the unity of the Church, for the maintenance of good order, and for the general effectiveness of its work.

c. *The matters that fall under their jurisdiction.* The ecclesiastical character of these assemblies should always be borne in mind. It is because they are Church assemblies, that purely scientific, social, industrial, or political matters do not, as such, fall under their jurisdiction. Only ecclesiastical matters belong to their province, such as matters of doctrine or morals, of church government and discipline, and whatever pertains to the preservation of unity and good order in the Church of Jesus Christ. More particularly, they deal with (1) matters which, as to their nature, belong to the province of a minor assembly, but for some reason or other cannot be settled there; and (2) matters which, as to their nature, belong to the province of a major assembly, since they pertain to the churches in general, such as matters touching the Confession, the Church Order, or the liturgy of the Church.

d. *The power and authority of these assemblies.* The major assemblies do not represent a higher kind of power than is vested in the consistory or session. The Reformed churches know of no higher kind of ecclesiastical power than that which resides in the consistory. At the same time the authority of the major assemblies is greater in degree and wider in extent than that of the consistory. Church power is represented in greater measure in the major assemblies than in the consistory, just as apostolic power was represented in greater measure in the Twelve than in a single apostle. Ten churches certainly have more authority than a single church; there is an accumulation of power. Moreover, the authority of the major assemblies does not apply to a single church only, but extends to all the affiliated churches. Consequently, the decisions of a major assembly carry great weight and can never be set aside at will. The assertion sometimes made that they are only of an advisory character and therefore need not be carried out, is a manifestation of the leaven of Independency. These decisions are authoritative, except in cases where they are explicitly declared to be merely advisory. They are binding on the churches as the sound interpretation and application of the law—the law of Christ, the King of the Church. They cease to be binding only when they are shown to be contrary to the Word of God.

Notes

[1] *Scottish Theology and Theologians,* p. 130.

[2] *Cf.* Wilmers, *Handbook of the Christian Religion,* p. 134.

[3] *Church Polity,* p. 349.

[4] *Church Government,* p. 457.

Edward Hiscox

Church Government

Is there any particular form of Church government revealed in the New Testament? And if so, what is it?

These questions will be variously answered by Christian scholars and Bible students. Some hold that no specific form can be deduced from the sacred records, and that no one form is best suited for all people and for all places; and that it was purposely left for Christian wisdom and prudence, guided by experience, to decide that question. But the greater part believe that a specific form is at least outlined in the New Testament; and, naturally enough, each one believes the form with which he is identified is that divinely given form. It may be safely allowed that no one class or company of Christians has attained to all the truth, leaving all others exclusively in error; and it is a comfort to know that, however believers may differ in opinion as to any matter of doctrine or of duty, if with loving hearts they sincerely desire to know the right and do it, they are blessed of God. As Peter said at the house of Cornelius, we may say, "Of a truth I perceive that God is no respecter of persons: but in every nation he that feareth Him, and worketh righteousness, is accepted with Him" (Acts 10:34, 35).

From *The New Directory for Baptist Churches* (Valley Forge, Pennsylvania: The Judson Press, 1894), pp. 142–159.

If, however, there be any definite plan plainly taught or clearly deducible from the words of Christ or His inspired Apostles, we should, if possible, ascertain that fact and be guided accordingly. Or if—what would be equivalent—we can ascertain how the Apostles, under the guidance of the Spirit, organized and ordered the churches they founded, with what regulations they were instituted, and what polity was impressed upon them, our questions will be substantially, and, it should seem, satisfactorily answered. Indeed, there appears to be light on the subject in this direction; for though no formal plan of government is detailed, yet there are numerous incidental references in the Epistles which clearly disclose formative and conclusive facts in the case.

I. Three Principal Forms

Three different forms of Church government are in current use among the denominations:

1. *The Prelatical*—the governing power is in the hands of prelates or bishops, and the clergy generally, as in the Roman, Greek, English, and most of the Oriental communions.

2. *The Presbyterian*—the governing power resides in Assemblies, Synods, Presbyteries, and Sessions, as in the Scottish Kirk, the Lutheran, and the various Presbyterian bodies.

3. *The Independent*—the governing power rests entirely with the people, *i.e.,* the body of the members of each local Church, each being entirely separate from and independent of all others, so far as authority and control are concerned, as among Baptists, Congregationalists, Independents, and some others.

Now, is any of these forms taught in the New Testament? And if so, which? And which best accords with the genius of the gospel, and with what we know of the constitution and government of the apostolic churches?

Baptists claim that a Christian Church is a congregation of baptized believers associated by mutual covenant, self-governing, and independent of all others; having no ecclesiastical connection with any other, though maintaining friendly and associational intercourse with all of like faith and order. It has no power to enact laws, but only to administer those which Christ has given.

The government is administered by the body acting together, where no one possesses a preeminence, but all enjoy an equality of rights; and in deciding matters of opinion, the majority bears rule. The pastor exercises only such control over the body as his official and personal influence may allow, as their teacher and leader and the expounder of the great Lawgiver's enactments. His influence is paramount, but not his authority. In the decision of questions he has but his single vote. His *rule* is in the moral force of his counsels, his instruction and guidance in matters of truth and duty, and also is wisely directing the assemblies whether for worship or business. Much less have the deacons any authoritative or dictatorial control over Church affairs. Matters of administration are submitted to the *body* and by them decided.

II. Church Independency

As has been said, each particular and individual Church is actually and absolutely independent in the exercise of all its churchly rights, privileges, and prerogatives; independent of all other churches, individuals, and bodies of men whatever, and is under law to Christ alone. The will and law of the great Lawgiver are to be found in the New Testament, which is the only authoritative statute book for His people.

This statement is broad and comprehensive, and needs not defence, but explanation only. That Independency is the true form of Church government, as opposed to Prelacy and Presbyterianism, will not now be argued, but is assumed, as accepted by all Baptists, taught in the New Testament, verified by history, and justified by the genius of the gospel itself. But all human liberty is under limitations; strictly speaking it is not absolute.

How Is Church Independence Limited?

1. The liberty which the independence of churches exercises is limited by the laws of Christ as expressed or clearly implied in the Scriptures. A Church is not a legislative body, but administrative only. It cannot make laws, but it is the interpreter of the laws of Christ—the interpreter for itself, not for others. Nor can others interpret laws for it. The opinions of the wise and good have their weight, but no man or body of men external to itself has the right to become authoritative interpreters of the word of God to a Church (or indeed to an individual, even), and compel submission to their *dicta*.

Churches may perform many unwise and unjustifiable acts. They may misapply or misinterpret, or openly do violence to both the letter and spirit of law. But there is no human tribunal to which they can be brought for trial and punishment, except that of public opinion. Others, in the exercise of their personal or Church liberty, may condemn their acts and disclaim all responsibility in connection with them; they may withdraw all fellowship and intercourse from them. But farther than this they cannot go, except by the moral force of their dissent and condemnation. And it is fortunate that such is the case, since to crush liberty and destroy independence in the churches of Christ would be a greater calamity than to bear all the evils which may spring from a misunderstanding [or misuse of the law].

2. The independence of the churches is limited, so far as corporate acts are concerned, or any matters of personal rights or legal equity may be in question, by the laws of the State in which they are located. This, however, has reference only to the temporalities of Church life, and cannot touch any question of doctrine, worship, or Christian duty. Most churches, by an organized "society," or in some other way, hold relations to civil law, in order to enjoy its protection in rights of property. To this extent they are subject to civil authority, and both as bodies and as individuals they should

be law-keepers and not law-breakers. But as to all matters of spiritual concern in questions of religious faith and practice, the State and civil law have no rights of control over, or interference with, the churches in any manner whatever, except to protect them in the enjoyment of all their lawful privileges.

It may also happen that in the exercise of its ecclesiastical functions in acts of discipline or exclusion, a Church or even a Council may be charged with decisions which are defamatory in their nature, calculated to injure the reputation or interfere with the secular interests of the individual, and he may seek redress at the civil courts. Such occurrences have sometimes transpired, and, under stress of circumstances, are liable to take place. Civil courts usually observe this rule when appealed to in ecclesiastical matters, viz., that the established usages of any body of Christians have a right to be followed, and if these have been carefully observed and not transcended, the courts will not interfere. But if from passion, prejudice, or ignorance, these have been disregarded, and the precedents and customs of the denomination have been violated, the court may interfere to give relief, only so far, however, as to require that the case have a new trial, in which their own established rules and precedents shall be strictly observed.

3. By some it has been held, that, while each Church is independent in theory, its liberty is somewhat abridged by its relations to other churches, and because of that fellowship and comity which exists between them. By such it is claimed that the relation of each Church to the great body of churches is similar to the relation of each member of a Church to the body of members which constitute that Church; and, therefore, as each member relinquishes something of his personal liberty on becoming a member, and consents to be subject to the authority of the body, so the individual Church does on becoming one of the general fellowship of churches. Or, they argue, to take another figure: as each particular State, though in a sense sovereign and independent, yet has its independency limited by being a member of the federation of States, and submits in certain matters to be subject to the general government, while represented in it, so is it with a single Church in the federation of churches.

This condition of affairs has sometimes been called the *interdependence* of churches. Precisely what that term means is not easily explained. But it is safe to pronounce it a fiction. There is no such thing as interdependence in the sense of a limitation of the self-governing right and authority of a Church. And that is the sense in which interdependence is asserted. One Church may be poor and need help from one that is rich; or it may be in perplexity and need advice from one supposed to be more experienced—as the Church at Antioch sought counsel of the older and more experienced Church at Jerusalem, or as the churches in Macedonia and Achaia contributed to the poor saints in Judea. But these facts do not touch the question of polity or government: relations of churches to each other in these respects remain the same. Fellowship and fraternal concord may be strengthened; the helpfulness of the one and the gratitude of the other may be increased, but the one is none the more independent, nor the other any the less so, because of these friendly interchanges.

But this whole course of argument alluded to is fallacious and misleading, and the illustrations used are unauthorized, inapplicable, and contrary to the facts. There is no such relation subsisting between the various churches constituting a general fellowship as exists between the individual members of a single Church. No hint or intimation of any such similarity is found in the New Testament, where the constitution and polity of a Church is taught. There is no other and larger organization provided for, with officers, orders, and regulations, including many smaller ones, called churches, as its units. If this similarity of relation be insisted on, then we shall have this comprehensive confederacy of churches claiming authority over the individual churches, receiving, disciplining, and excluding them, and otherwise exercising powers similar to those exercised by the individual Church over its members. Admit so much, and we have prelacy or papacy at once, in spirit and in fact.

Nor is there any relation subsisting between the separate churches, which can be fitly compared to the union of States in a federal government. If it were so we should have a *de facto* Presbyterianism. This whole course of reasoning, if carried out to its logical results, would not leave a vestige of Church independency. The only limitation, the only check upon the exercise of Christian liberty required by the gospel, is loyalty to Christ as King in Zion, fidelity to His truth, and a constant exercise of that kindly courtesy which is innate in the gospel and essential to the true Christian life, whether individual or organic, whether personal, social, or official. This spirit dominant will give all the fellowship which churches need or can demand—and all which a Scriptural polity can render or allow.

4. It is sometimes objected that Baptists are too independent, and that their liberty degenerates into license. Now, on calm reflection, all this must be denied. They cannot, as churches, be too independent, using that word in a true Christian sense. Nor can liberty become license.

Ignorant and foolish men may be charged with many wrong acts They may practise injustice and oppression in the name of liberty, and under pretence of independence. But liberty and independence are, at the very most, only the occasion, and are in no sense to be made responsible for the evils which perverse and wrong-headed persons perpetrate under the shelter of their name. Church independency has its peculiar liability to misuse and abuse, but it cannot be shown that its difficulties are any more numerous, or any more serious than those to which other forms of Church government are liable. Indeed, if this be the true, the divine plan, then it is the best plan, with the fewest evils and the most advantages. The defects lie not in the plan, but in those who administer the government; and, as a matter of fact, it can be shown that churches acting under the independent polity, actually suffer from fewer and less serious difficulties than those subject to stronger and more centralized governments.

5. The independence of a Church is limited by the personal rights of its

individual members. That is to say, the liberty of the body to act cannot lawfully be used to infringe the lawful liberty of its members. A Church, as a body, has no right to violate the rights of its members in the exercise of its authority. These rights need to be clearly defined and well understood on both sides. If the morals of the member do not coincide with the morals of the gospel, the Church has the right to put him away from itself, if he cannot be reclaimed. But the body cannot properly interfere with the rights of faith, or conscience, on the part of the individual. If his faith be judged heretical, and an element of discord, they can withdraw fellowship from him; but they can neither compel uniformity nor punish dissent—except by separation.

6. And still further, the liberty of a Church is limited by the terms of the great Commission, and by its divine institution, to the pursuits and the purposes contemplated in the gospel. Whatever its members may do in their individual capacity as citizens and members of society, the Church as such must confine itself to the mission for which it was founded—the spread of the gospel, and the advancement of the Kingdom of God in the world. It cannot become a corporation for mercantile or manufacturing pursuits; it cannot become a political organization; it cannot become a scientific or literary association. On all moral questions, however the Church as a body, as well as its individual members, should be plainly pronounced and clearly understood as standing for the defence of virtue, purity and good order, since these are essential elements of Christianity. Also it should have an unmistakable record as an abettor and helper of good works, charitable and benevolent endeavors, since these are inherent in, and grow out of, the gospel. The Church cannot dictate what a member shall eat or drink or wear; what shall be his business or his pleasure. But if, in any of these matters, questions of morals and religion come to be involved to the reproach of truth and the Christian profession, then the Church has the right to interpose.

III. Evidence of It

Wherein lies the proof that the primitive Church government was an *independency?*

In Matthew, chap. 18:15–17, where our Saviour for the first time, and, with one exception, the only time, in His personal conversation, speaks of the *Church* distinctively, His recognition of it as the only source of ecclesiastical authority is positive and complete. In giving directions for the adjustment of difficulties among brethren and the pacification of their social disturbances. He first expounds their personal duties; but when He speaks of authoritative action, *that* belongs to the Church. And the Church's action is *final*. That action admits of no reversal and of no review. There was to be no court beyond or above the single Church. He recognized no hierarchy, no presbytery, no synod, no assembly, no council; but "tell it to the Church." That ends the matter of appeal. "If he neglect to hear the Church, let him be unto thee as a heathen man and a publican."

The course pursued by the Church at Antioch in Syria is suggestive. When a difficulty arose pertaining to the engrafting of Jewish customs upon a Christian polity, respecting which they were in doubt, they sent a delegation to the Church at Jerusalem, as being not only at the seat of the Jewish *cultus,* but of the earliest Christian knowledge as well, besides having in their fellowship the apostles. From this source, therefore, they would obtain authoritative instruction (Acts 15). This deputation, including Paul and Barnabas, on their arrival did not appeal to any select company of officials, not even to the inspired Apostles; but to the *whole Church,* inclusive of these. "And when they came to Jerusalem they were received of the Church, and of the Apostles and elders" (v. 4). After a full statement and discussion of the case, and an expressed opinion by James, the pastor of the Church, they agreed on what reply to make to the Church at Antioch. "Then pleased it the Apostles, and elders, with the whole Church, to send chosen men of their own company to Antioch, with Paul and Barnabas" (v. 22). In addition to this delegation they sent letters also conveying their judgment in the case. And these letters recognized the Church in its three estates. "The Apostles and elders and brethren send greeting unto the brethren which are of the Gentiles in Antioch" (v. 23). And they added: "It seemed good unto us, being assembled with one accord." And "it seemed good to the Holy Ghost, and to us" (vv. 25, 28).

One independent Church, wishing advice, sought counsel of another independent Church, in whose experience and wisdom they had more confidence than in their own. And the Church appealed to, in the exercise of their independence, gave the advice sought. Nor did the Apostles, though inspired, assume to dictate in this matter, or to act without the cooperation of the elders and brethren. Nor yet did the Apostles and elders assume to act alone; "all the multitude," and "the whole Church," were present to hear and act with their leaders.

The Apostles regarded and treated the churches as independent bodies, having the rights of self-government, without subjection to any other authority. They reported their own doings to the churches, and addressed their Epistles to them, as to independent bodies, and not to a confederacy including many distinct congregations, nor yet to any official representatives of these congregations. In communicating with them the Apostles recognized their right to choose their own officers, to admit, discipline, and exclude members—primary and fundamental rights, which, being conceded, imply all other rights necessary to a self-governing community acting under divinely enacted laws. The Apostles also enjoined upon them, as the responsible and authoritative executives of this power, the exercise of these functions, especially in the discipline and exclusion of unworthy members.

And nothing could more distinctly or more emphatically declare what is here claimed, than the fact that the Lord, in the Apocalyptic Epistles, addressed specifically the individual churches of Asia, through the angels, or pastors of these churches. The counsels, warnings, reproofs and commendations are in each case for the particular Church addressed, as responsible, censurable, or commendable. They were not addressed as a combination, or system of churches, either hierarchical or synodical; not as "the Church of Asia," but the *churches,* individual and separate.

Mosheim, the Church historian, says of the first century:

> In those primitive times each Christian Church was composed of the *people,* the presiding *officers,* and the *assistants* or deacons. These must be the component parts of every society. The principal voice was that of the people, or the whole body of Christians. . . . The assembled people therefore elected their own rulers and teachers. [Of the second century, he adds:] One president or bishop presided over each Church. He was created by the common suffrages of the whole people. . . . During a great part of this century all the churches continued to be, as at first, *independent* of each other. Each Church was a kind of small independent republic, governing itself by its own laws, enacted or at least sanctioned by the people. (*Eccl. Hist. Cent. I. part I. Ch. II, secs. 5, 6; Cent. II. Ch. II secs. 1, 2*)

Gieseler, in his Church history, speaking of the changes which occurred in ecclesiastical order during the second century, says:

> Country churches, which had grown up around some city, seem, with their bishops, to have been unusually, in a certain degree, under the authority of the mother Church. With this exception, all the churches were alike independent, though some were especially held in honor, on such ground as their Apostolic origin, or the importance of the city in which they were situated. (*Ch. Hist. Period I. Div. I. Ch. 3. sec. 52*)

Schaff, in his history, says:

> Thus the Apostolic Church appears as a free, independent, and complete organization; a system of supernatural divine life, in a human body. It contains in itself all the offices and energies required for its purpose. It produces the supply of its outward wants from its own free spirit. Instead of receiving protection and support from the secular power, it suffers deadly hatred and persecution. It manages its own internal affairs with equal independence. Of union with the State, either in the way of hierarchical supremacy or of Erastian subordination, the first three centuries afford no trace. (*Ch. Hist. Vol. I. sec. 45, p. 138*)

Waddington, on this subject, says:

> It is also true that in the earliest government of the first Christian society, that of Jerusalem, not the elders only, but the whole Church, were associated with the apostles. And it is even certain that the terms *bishop* and *elder* or presbyter, were in the first instance, and for a short period, sometimes used synonymously. (*Hist. of the Ch., p. 41*)

Archbishop Whately says of the primitive churches:

> Though there was one Lord, one Faith, and one Baptism for all of these, yet they were each a distinct independent community on earth, united by the common principles on which they were founded, by their mutual agreement, affection and respect. (*Kingdom of Christ, pp. 101-156*)

Dr. Burton says:

> Every Church had its own spiritual head, or bishop, and was independent of every other Church, with respect to its own internal regulations and laws. (*Cited by Coleman, Primitive Christianity, p. 50*).

Dr. Barrow says:

> At first every Church was settled apart under its bishops and presbyters, so as independently and separately to manage its own affairs. Each was governed by its own head, and had its own laws. (*Treatise on the Pope's Suprem. Works, Vol. 1. p. 662—Col. Prim. Christ.*)

Dr. Coleman says:

> These churches, wherever formed, became separate and independent bodies, competent to appoint their officers and administer their own government without reference or subordination to any central authority or foreign power. No fact connected with the history of the primitive churches is more fully established or more generally conceded. (*Prim. Christ. Exemp. Ch. 4. sec. 4, p. 95*)

Dr. Francis Wayland says:

> The Baptists have ever believed in the entire and absolute independence of the churches. By this we mean that every Church of Christ—that is, every company of believers united together according to the laws of Christ—is wholly independent of every other. That every Church is capable of self-government; and that therefore no one acknowledges any higher authority under Christ, than itself; that with the Church all ecclesiastical action commences, and with it all terminates. . . . The more steadfastly we hold to the independency of the churches and abjure everything in the form of a denominational corporation, the more truly shall we be united, and the greater will be our prosperity. (*Princ's and Prac's of Bap. Chs., pp. 178, 190*)

Dr. David Benedict, the Baptist historian says:

> The doctrine of absolute Church independence has always been a favorite one with people. Under it they have greatly flourished, and very few have complained of its operation. (*Fifty Years Among the Baptists, p. 399*)

That the apostolical churches, therefore, were independent in their form of government seems to be clearly proven. Many prelatists, as well as others besides those here cited, concede this point. In this respect, therefore, and so far as their independency is concerned, Baptists are manifestly founded on the New Testament order of Church building and Church life; and, so far, are true successors of the Apostles. Nor does it avail to urge objections to this independency, or magnify the difficulties to which it is liable. It can be shown that other forms have inherent in them even greater liabilities to misuse; while this, if it were established by divine wisdom, must be the best fitted to its purpose, and is the one to be used and preserved.

Church Cooperation

Carl Henry

The Perils of Independency

The contemporary American church scene discloses significant spiritual trends. Tendencies originating obscurely in the past have now assumed forms quite obvious to the students of religious life.

American Christianity is dynamic, not static. It exists in a shifting historical situation, not in a vacuum. The visible Church cannot fully escape this fact of historical change as the climate of the day. From day to day, reactions to it may appear quite imperceptible; in the span of a generation they will become quite apparent, and may even be cataclysmic.

The Protestant Reformation in the sixteenth century represented a break with both the doctrines and the hierarchy of Romanism. Justification by faith alone was not the only cardinal theological tenet of the Reformers. Intrinsic in the movement of reform was a desire to break with the suzerainty of Rome. Against the papal claim of ultimate authority in the Church and thus in the pope of Rome, the Reformers re-elevated to authority the written Word of God as the sole regulator and restrainer of conscience.

Protestant churches became independent and autonomous bodies, although often within the framework of national states. Yet in many instances independency, or existence outside these bodies, was not tolerated.

From *Christianity Today*, 12 November 1956, pp. 20–23. Used by permission.

The nonconformists in England were viciously persecuted. In Lutheran countries, Baptists and others eked out an uncomfortable survival. Even in early America, often pictured as the land of religious freedom, the same situation prevailed. In New England, for example, dissenters from the Puritan hope were exposed to the wrath of persecutors. Roger Williams, Henry Dunster and Anne Hutchinson shared in it personally.

More recently, certain trends in the United States have brought into sharp focus at least two virtually contradictory forces operating in community religious life. These forces are diametrically opposed, representing ultimates or extremes. Beyond them, it is impossible to move much to the right or to the left. These forces have not reached their limits in either case, but are headed in the direction of ultimates. But these two movements do not hold the field alone, for between these antitheses, other groups stand uncomfortably exposed to the pressures of history, keenly conscious that the immoderate forces of extremity bode ill for Protestantism.

The two clashing movements of which we speak are Independency and Organic Church Union, embodied in agencies familiar to all. Their conflicting tendencies are visible in the big cities and the tiny hamlets of the nation. The Independents could be illustrated by many diverse groupings, but the extreme right wing is the American Council of Christian Churches, which finds its larger orientation in the International Council of Christian Churches. Organic Church Union could be represented in its most intense form by the National Council of Churches of Christ in the U.S.A., which is integrated within the framework of the World Council of Churches.

Each has its own tensions and perils. Independency tends to be intolerant, Church Unionism to be tolerant. The former moves in the direction of exclusivism, the latter toward inclusivism. One holds a low view of the Church in its visible and historical aspects, and the other a high view. The one glorifies separateness, while the other reaches out toward ecclesiasticism. Independency remains highly creedal in minute detail, while Church Unionism becomes vague and ill-defined in theological basis. One can easily become Pharisaic, the other Sadducean.

Some may object to any implication that Church Unionism is well-nigh creedless, pointing to the Thirty-Nine Articles of Anglicanism, the Westminster Confession of Presbyterianism and the Canons of the Synod of Dort of the Reformed churches. But Church Unionism relegates creeds to a peripheral position. With the statement that Jesus Christ is Lord and Savior, the forces of Organic Union halt, and even this affirmation they leave to whatever interpretation a particular group within the Council may wish to put upon it.

By contrast, Independency has become more and more creedal. And, with its dissociation from organized Christianity. this movement has frequently incorporated secondary doctrines into its creeds with an absoluteness that is incredible. A particular brand of millennialism or an insistence on a dispensational pretribulation rapture of the Church is a case in point. . . . Western Baptist Theological Seminary in Portland, Oregon, was divided and its faculty scattered over just such concerns. Its creedal statement. which could not be changed legally, was interpreted to require a pretribulation rapture, so that the creedal statement itself was supplemented by the interpretation, and institutional rupture was the result.

Between Independency and Church Unionism stand the middle parties. Many of them have a mutual ground in the National Association of Evangelicals. Consciously or unconsciously this group is opposed in temper to both the American Council and the National Council. But its position is not so easily defined, since the lines are not so sharply drawn. It subscribes to some concepts of each of the extremist groups, but opposes others, finding its rationale in a mediating view, or perhaps better described as a perspective above the extremes. Extreme positions are easier to perceive and less difficult to defend to the popular mind. Whether they are truer is a matter for debate.

We do not purpose on this occasion to discuss the problems of Organic Church Union, but to speak rather of the perils of Independency. What we say should not, therefore, be construed as a blanket condemnation of Independency. We merely point out dangers inherent in Independency in the movement of contemporary Church history, and indicate some factors with which its adherents must reckon.

One major truth about the foundations of Independency must first be stated. This movement is grounded in a desire to defend the orthodox faith by exalting the Word of God and glorifying the Christ of the Scriptures. Whatever disagreements and errors exist within the extremes of the movement, those who honor fidelity to doctrine cannot but endorse the concern for theological soundness. Such a high goal, however, gives its adherents no automatic guarantee against a blundering course, nor does it, by itself, safeguard the movement of Independency from shipwreck. Indeed, failure to avoid the pitfalls peculiar to Independency can bring about the deterioration and destruction of the movement in a single generation. Independency is as answerable to the verdict of history and as susceptible to the judgments of God as any other movement.

Independency tends to produce a divisive spirit. It refuses to cooperate even with those with whom it is in essential theological agreement. Its concept of separation forbids fellowship with men sound in the faith but associated with objectionable movements. It indicts others for allegiances they have held for years, and often promotes a divisiveness that is disruptive.

Independency usually begins, as we have noted, as a movement against heresy or apostasy. Where this is true it cannot be accurately labeled as divisive. No one can justify inveigh against that form of Independency which comes out of apostasy and holds to a positive doctrinal witness.

But in many instances the apostasy condemned by Independency is not as clearly discernible as is assumed. The movement sometimes arrogates to itself judgment belonging to God. Even though concern for doctrine is necessary, a spirit of divisiveness may be stimulated so that a good end is subordinated and the danger of an evil one looms large. The form of separation with which a movement originates often tends to deteriorate, and internal divisiveness may even raise doubts over the justification of the original separation. Recent history eloquently confirms this danger, and indeed supplies new evidence that the danger stage has passed into ugly historical fact.

Years ago the Presbyterian Church in the U.S.A. witnessed a movement of separation marked by the formation of the Independent Board for Presbyterian Foreign Missions. Led by men like J. Gresham Machen, this movement resulted in the formation of the Orthodox Presbyterian Church. While this denomination was committed to carry out Presbyterian principles of government, the independent spirit within the new group occasioned further fragmentation as evidenced by the establishment of the Bible Presbyterian Church and Faith Theological Seminary. More recently, further division has taken place, caused by a clash of personalities rather than differences of doctrine. Faith Theological Seminary has been rent asunder and a new college and seminary, Covenant, has been formed in St. Louis, Missouri.

Two educational institutions have been involved in [more] recent schisms. Highland College of Los Angeles, a strict separationist institution, lost its president and members of the faculty to the new Covenant College, after an internal upheaval among men of like faith. A similar situation existed at Shelton College. Originally located in New York City under the name of the National Bible Institute, it was wooed into the framework of the American Council of Christian Churches. Then its properties were disposed of, a new location in New Jersey found, and the name changed to Shelton College. J. Oliver Buswell, Jr., who was among the early separationists from the Presbyterian Church in the U.S.A. and who had separated from the Westminster-Machen forces, was now caught in the toils of a new schism. Deposed from the presidency of Shelton College, deprived of his chair at Faith Theological Seminary, he joined in the establishment of Covenant College in St. Louis.

The charge of apostasy or Modernism has occasioned none of these divisions since the original departure from the Presbyterian Church in the U.S.A. The divisive spirit that led to new splits was in no sense related to the heart of theological orthodoxy. Independency, clearly, is involved not only in tension with theological infidelity outside, but with the divisive temper inside.

The divisiveness of Independency becomes so highly exclusive that it excludes true believers from its fellowship. Herein lies one of the great misfortunes of extremism on the right. Because Independency by definition is dogmatic and because extreme dogmatism is often conducive to a condemnatory spirit, the unity of the Spirit is easily quenched. True believers are separated one from another. Afraid for the safety and purity of its movement. Independency erects thicker and higher hedges for self-protection. As it moves in the direction of Phariseeism, man-made appendages to the Gospel become all-important, constituting a test for fellowship. Not one's belief in Christ as God and Savior but whether one sits in the right millennial pew, and properly dots every "i" and crosses every "t" according to the approved subsidiary requirements, is determinative. Ultimately, this chokes orthodoxy in the maze of the peripheral; it majors in minors, departing from the heart of the true faith while protesting that it alone possesses the "real" truth.

Another peril of Independency lies in its refusal to communicate with those with whom it is in disagreement. This results often in shocking rudeness and incivility. It refuses to reckon with the possibility that other camps may hold sincere and earnest seekers after truth. Independency sometimes labors under the suspicion that whoever is unaffiliated with it, if not a rascal, is at least an ecclesiastical enemy. Whether this suspicion arises from a deep-seated inferiority or from the misunderstanding of "compromise" is hard to judge. But woe betide the orthodox brother caught in conversation with the "opposition." The scourge of the brethren, or a high-level brain washing, is his ministerial prospect. The ideal of separation from "the apostasy" is stretched to exclude traffic with the persons who corverse with those infected with the disease.

Independency is tempted easily to use a vocabulary of stigma and reproach. It draws a razor-thin dividing line and everyone is judged by its cut. Deviationism leads swiftly to vicious name calling. Two words common to the vocabulary of Independency are "compromise" and "modernist." Whoever does not conform closely to the "line" is likely to be accused either of compromise or of Modernism. Differences over minor points of eschatology have resulted in charges of latent Modernism, or of compromise of the historic faith, leveled against some of the most competent defenders of the evangelical position. It is true enough that Modernism has its own vocabulary, and can use it for sharp ends, but this does not excuse Independency for the same vice. "Scapegoating" in its ecclesiastical form has done much to harm the reputation of men true to the Word of God, and to destroy the confidence in them of other true believers, especially among weaker brethren anxious to believe any charge uttered by the tribal council.

But the most serious deficiency of Independency is its departure from the New Testament theology of the Church. If any teaching is clear in the New Testament, it is the teaching of the unity of the true body of Christ. A transcendental outlook detaches Independency from the present historical scene in relation to the heavenly and otherworldly side of life. This detachment produces more and more fragmentation, and encourages militant opposition to efforts looking toward an undivided Church. While concentrating on the heavenly body, or the invisible Church, Independency often loses sight of the empirical Church in history, and fails to realize its own continuity with this historical phenomenon. "Not of this world" is unfortunately and erroneously taken to be the virtual equivalent of "not in this world.'' But Christianity teaches an ambivalence the Church cannot escape: it is both "not of this world" and "in this world" at the same time.

If Independency is not to disintegrate in riot, it must reconstruct its theology of the Church in the light of biblical teaching. The solution of its related problems does not lie in easy acquiescence to a completely separationist and divisive philosophy. There is a biblically defined unity of the body, even in diversity. The witness of believers can never be wholly transcendental. The Church has empirical as well as transcendental aspects, and neither can be overlooked without impairing the biblical view.

Perhaps among the very grave problems of Independency is the lurking assumption that true Independency implies individualism. What frequently has been identified with Independency is individualism of an unrestrained and frightening sort. This individualism stresses the autonomy of the human spirit while professing to be shackled to divine revelation and repudiating dependency upon other human beings in this relationship to God. True biblical Independency is essentially a group enterprise, banding together men of like mind and spirit for the preservation of what they believe to be true. Only where two or three are gathered together with Christ in their midst is there a true church. Refusing subjection to superior ecclesiastical powers and authorities, Independency has in it the seeds of individualism. When Independency allows these seeds to germinate, the fruit ripens into the man who becomes a law unto himself, even though he may attempt to validate his proclamations and deeds on the assumption that they are performed for the glory of Christ. The biblical Christian knows nothing of such individualism. No man is a law unto himself; each is to be subject to the brethren, and no one person can make himself the arbiter and judge of others.

Independency run riot produces individualism in the end, as depicted in the Old Testament where we are told that in some areas every man did what was right in his own eyes. Independency may be the spawning ground of spirits not truly in the tradition of Independency, but in the tradition of individualism. The end of individualism is a "church" in which each man is his own ministry and congregation, ruler and subject, making and judging his own laws. In such an assembly there is little regard for Jesus Christ, the Head of the Church, or for fellow believers who make up the visible body of Christ on earth.

One dare not charge that all who are identified with Independency have succumbed to these tensions and dangers. Nor can it be fairly alleged that the whole movement has succumbed to them. But the dangers have been actualized sufficiently to indicate the historical direction if the movement continues on its present path. Undoubtedly many adherents within the camp of Independency are not victims of the defects we have outlined, and their catholicity of spirit and irenic pursuit of the truth are exemplary. They embrace the doctrine of Christ in the spirit of Christ. While subject to the temptations and tensions common to Independency, they have not yielded to them. They are the hope of their movement, and the guidance they give or fail to give may be the decisive factor that will avert or lead to a complete disintegration.

Independency will collapse if it surrenders to its peculiar temptations. Contrariwise, it can help to purify the Christian Church. To purify without destroying, and without being destroyed, is its critical challenge in the movement of Church history.

23

Carl Henry

The Perils of Ecumenicity

The discussion of "The Perils of Independency" in the last [chapter] was not based upon a predisposition to condemn Independency, but rather was intended to examine its foundations and to assess its weaknesses. It is time now to reflect on its antithesis, ecumenicity. In this issue we propose to speak of its perils.

Independency is often motivated, we conceded, by a commendable desire to glorify Christ and to exalt the Word of God. The ecumenical movement likewise gains its appeal from a worthy biblical concept. That concept is the unity of the body of Christ. While it has been elaborated from time to time since the Reformation, not until lately have multitudes in the churches regarded it with great seriousness.

The Christian leader can point to much in the Bible which speaks of Christian unity. We do not say there is never a biblical basis for division. Apart from the issue of apostasy, so much invoked by the separatists, there exists another biblical basis for separation about which little is said today in any Christian circle. There is clear biblical precedent for the discipline of true believers who, falling into gross sin, thereby invite excommunication.

From *Christianity Today,* 26 November 1956, pp. 20–22. Used by permission.

Such an act of discipline, which purposes the exclusion of the impenitent lest he contaminate other believers, is exercised not with a penal objective in view but aims to reclaim the offending person through refusing him fellowship in the ordinances or sacraments. But except for these reasons, divisions in the body of Christians originating in the pride of men are sinful.

The unity of the body, virtually all would stress, is a clear teaching and requirement of the Word of God. Nor should we minimize the fact that much of the current literature devoted to the study of church unity is biblically oriented. Thus John Bennett could assert (as one example): "The new emphasis upon the Church has been accompanied by a return to the Bible as the medium of revelation" (*Toward World-Wide Christianity* [edited by O. Frederick Nolde] [italics supplied], Harper, 1946). Men look to the Scriptures as to a polished mirror which reflects the true unity of the body. This biblical appeal is significant. It acknowledges, consciously or unconsciously, a formal principle which Independency has always stressed, and represents in reality a dynamic change from that attitude and spirit of Liberalism long rampant in America.

Unfortunately, for the ecumenist, two main problems follow when he resorts to the Bible either as a temporary authority or witness. These problems jeopardize the major logic of the ecumenical movement because of the impasse to which they lead.

In the first place, proponents of organic church union who appeal to the Scriptures as a basis for the movement seldom choose to go much beyond this preliminary dependency on the Bible. But the Bible witnesses, in fact, to far more than the unity of believers. The question may rightly be asked: "Since the ecumenist lays stress on the biblically-taught unity of the body, why stop there? Why not accept the other teachings of the Scriptures, truths on which the Bible lays emphasis no less vigorously than on the truth of the unity of the body?" Many proponents of the ecumenical movement clearly resist such a step. They proclaim unity from the housetops, but they shy away from the virgin birth, the bodily resurrection of the dead, the substitutionary atonement of Jesus Christ, as well as from the historical trinitarianism of the Church and other clear implications of Scripture. By what logic and authority, then, is there any justification for the isolation of one strand of the biblical teaching from all else, elevating it to a position of supreme importance and degrading the other teachings to positions of relative inconsequence? For such doctrines are as much a part of biblical theology as is the unity of the body.

The ecumenical movement in general elevates the doctrine of the unity of the body above every other doctrine. There is a driving emphasis on this unity accompanied by a rather pale and anemic concern for basic Christian doctrine. This trend is regarded by those who cannot support ecumenicity as a key reason for their fears. Doctrinal laxity to many is vitally related to participation in a movement, and unless the great fundamentals of the faith have been spelled out intelligibly they cannot warm up to the concept of unity without dogma.

This theological vagueness which has been characteristic of ecumenicity makes it vulnerable to the charge of doctrinal inclusivism. Whereas Independency errs on the side of exclusivism, tending to spell out its position so minutely that it separates itself readily from true believers as well as from unbelievers, the ecumenical adherents tend to be so inclusive that they regard outsiders as members of the body. One group excludes some persons who really ought to be included; the other includes some whose lack of adequate credentials ought to exclude them from an apostolic fellowship.

A second problem which faces the ecumenical movement, if it professes to find its rationale in the Word of God, has to do with the nature of unity. No one can disagree with the emphasis that the Bible has a specific view of the nature of Christian unity. And, if there is to be unity, there must first be some agreement upon the nature of that unity. Precisely what is it? Here again the vessel of ecumenicity floats in waters filled with perilous shoals.

It would be unfair to ascribe to the ecumenical movement one definitive and authoritative voice touching the nature of the unity it seeks. There are divergent opinions on this subject. The question is being debated vigorously. These considerations suggest an adventurous search for a goal which is itself uncertain. Ecumenicity is "going someplace," but it has not officially defined just where it is going. Passionately it believes *in* unity, but *which* unity it cannot, or does not tell. Therefore those alert to the perils of ecumenicity must forge their criticisms with a view to what the advocates of union say.

Sincere, devoted men in the ecumenical grouping assert that the ultimate goal of the movement is organic union of the churches. This is not to say that all of them believe in it but a substantial number do and they are vocal and active in their desires to make this union a reality. Bishop G. Bromley Oxnam in a 1948 episcopal address in Boston before the Bishops of his church disclosed the concept of unity cherished by him. He plainly advocated the ultimate union of all Protestant churches, looking forward to a future merger of the two remaining churches—Protestant and Roman Catholic—into one holy catholic Church. Prior to the remarks of Bishop Oxnam, Harper and Brothers published the Interseminary Series. This series contained material written by leading ecumenists, and at least one volume of that series bulwarks Bishop Oxnam's expressions.

John C. Bennett quotes Henry Pitt Van Dusen (and he agrees with Mr. Van Dusen): "Henry Pitt Van Dusen rightly says that 'Christian Unity which does not imply and make possible whatever degree of Church Union may be held to be the ultimate desideratum is something less than genuine and true Christian Unity.'" John A. Mackay of Princeton Theological Seminary is a fervent believer in union. He has declared that a world Church will make the greatest contribution to world community. Thus, in 1946, he said: "While it is true that nothing will make a greater contribution to world community than a world Church, the possibility must also be contemplated that a world Church, a Church united in Jesus Christ with a membership in every part of the inhabited globe, might find itself in a very hostile world.'' In a further word he says: ''It would be much better that *union be postponed until* their differences have been frankly faced.'' Henry Smith Leiper and Abdel R. Wentz have stated: ''. . . a basic, if not the most important aspect of the ecumenical movement is its vision of a universal Church.''

H. Paul Douglass reflected the feeling of the Madras Conference of 1938 which foretold the same story. ''It was especially emphasized by the Madras Conference of 1938 that there 'has come in many fields a deep and growing conviction that the Spirit of God is guiding the various branches of His church to seek for a realization of a visible and organic union.' ''

Such statements of sentiment can be expanded by quotations from men in the ''Who's Who of Ecumenicity'' (O. Frederick Nolde, ed., Interseminary Series, Harper and Brothers, 1946, pp. 42, 44, 61, 66, 80, 197).

Still other perils, however, lurk in the background of the movement. Ecclesiasticism bedevils all movements which seek union. One need not go beyond the Roman Church to discover how true this is. Therein the right of private opinion and of private interpretation of the Scripture is denied. The concentration of power in the hands of the few is a corrupting device. The experiences of secular and religious history demonstrate that power corrupts and that complete power corrupts completely. When men are dependent upon their superiors for position and preference, they easily lose their freedom to speak the truth in charity without suffering ecclesiastical censure and loss of preferment. The seeds of this evil already exist in some of the denominations. More men would testify to these evils if they did not fear official reprisal.

Another certainty is that ecumenicity can never achieve the absolute visible organic union of Christ's body in history. Assuming for the moment that the ultimate goal is the reunion of Christendom, then the ecumenical movement itself contains seeds of divisiveness as does Independency. There will always be those who will insist that unity is spiritual, and not visible nor organizational, and that true unity has in it a transcendental element in view of the communion of saints. Never will it be possible to bring together all these diverse elements which make up the true body of Christ. As long as so much as one segment of the body is excluded, absolute unity does not exist. It has never fully existed in history, although the Roman and Greek Churches before the Great Schism provide the fullest approximation in history. Any goal of absolute unity is ephemeral and chimerical; at best, visible unity can never be more than partial.

Ecumenicity tends to be just as intolerant as Independency, although this intolerance is expressed in a somewhat different fashion. Whereas Independency draws narrow lines, defining beliefs in such a detailed and technical fashion that it rules out many, ecumenicity also draws lines which are narrow and intolerant. It has little use or respect for those with whom it differs, easily regarding as fanatical and divisive those who refuse to cooperate within its orbit of inclusivism. It will tolerate and welcome those who will submit to its inclusivistic theology, but will try ruthlessly to crush and eliminate the opposition by ecclesiastical devices.

One of the tragic weaknesses of Independency is that it majors on minors. And ecumenicity does not entirely escape this same peril. It reverses the process, however. It minors on majors, exalting to a place of primacy what is not important, relegating to a secondary position that which is basic and necessary to a full-orbed Gospel. Both attitudes are essentially heretical. While they are opposite in polarity, they both rise from a departure from the apostolic base. One narrowly excludes divergence of opinion, so that it becomes difficult for some undoubted Christians to find standing room. The other is so broad and so indefinite that one cannot be sure on what ground he stands. Neither one is truly biblical nor finally acceptable. The narrow obscurantism of Independency is more widely known and challenged. The broad vistas of ecumenicity, indefinite and elusive, are less generally recognized as participating in the same spirit which characterizes those who major on minors. But the one is no less a peril than the other.

The discussion here does not concern the question of "elements of good" in ecumenicity or in Independency. Rather, the purpose is to speak about the perils which beset both. This much is clear: neither movement is entirely in error. But neither possesses the sum total of truth. Neither movement possesses the ingredients of a permanent and suitable solution to the problems which vex the Church of Christ in history. The end of one is an unrestrained individualism: every man his own master, priest and congregation. The end of the other makes one man the master of all; its ultimate form is the pope of Rome, or another pope like him. The fact that these movements head in these directions does not mean that the end is inevitable. But it does suggest that, unless substantial changes are made to redirect the movements, this sad outcome remains a live possibility.

These observations are made neither in a spirit of criticism nor of condemnation. They follow rather from an earnest attempt to see the patterns in history, and from them to anticipate, however dimly, the shape of things to come. Silence has little influence; a word in season, spoken in an irenic spirit, may give pause for reflection and revision.

The Special Rites
of the Church

Paul Jewett

Baptism
(Baptist View)

In OT times various ceremonial ablutions and washings incident to the Mosaic law were prescribed for God's people as signifying spiritual cleansing by the symbolic act of washing or dipping in water. Not only parts of the body, but also physical objects with which the worshipper came in contact were thus cleansed. The Greek words βάπτω and βαπτίζω, with their cognates, are used in the LXX and the NT to describe many of these rites, translating from the Hebrew טָבַל.

Definition

Subsequent to OT times, the Jews came to adopt the practice of plunging proselytes in water as symbolical of their cleansing from their former heathen way of life and civil regeneration to membership in the commonwealth of Israel. There is no conclusive evidence for this practice in pre-Christian times, though in the thinking of many scholars it may have been the source of John the Baptist's baptism. Evidence from the Dead Sea Scrolls would indicate baptismal rites among certain Jewish sects which

From *The Encyclopedia of Christianity* (Marshallton, Delaware: The National Foundation for Christian Education, 1964), Vol. I, pp. 517–525.

may have been known to John during his wilderness sojourn. More significant than the historical derivation, however, is the radically new meaning which John gave the rite as the baptism of repentance unto the remission of sins preparatory to Messiah's appearance (Mt. 3:1–2; Luke 3:3). Whether or not John's baptism was Christian baptism, it should be noted that as it was received by our Lord and His disciples, who in turn baptized others (John 4:1–2), it must be regarded as the precursor of Christian baptism. For the purpose of this article we shall define Christian baptism as that initiatory washing with water into the Name of the sacred Trinity, which the risen Lord commissioned His apostles to administer to all His followers as a mark of their discipleship. "Go ye therefore, and teach all nations, baptizing them into the name of the Father, and of the Son, and of the Holy Ghost: teaching them to observe all things whatsoever I have commanded you" (Mt. 28:19–20).

First of all, then, baptism is an ordinance which rests upon a positive divine enactment. It is because Christ, the Lord of the church and gospel institutions, appointed baptism, that it is to be observed. Baptists, therefore, in common with all Protestants, reject the five falsely so-called sacraments of the RC Church, as well as all ceremonies and forms in the rite of baptism, like exorcism of the water, fasting, chrism, partaking of milk and honey, and signing the cross, as resting upon the tradition of men, and therefore of no authority in the Christian church and of no material part of true baptism.

Inasmuch also as our Lord did not prescribe it, Baptists have never contended for a precise rubric of administration with reference to external circumstances. It is immaterial whether the candidate be baptized immediately upon conversion or after a period of instruction; whether baptism take place in a river or in a baptistry made for the purpose; whether it be administered on some festival day, as Easter or Pentecost, or on any day; and whether the administrator be duly ordained or a layman. Of course all worship is to be decent and in order, and therefore baptism may not be privately administered at the whim of any individual, but only in the presence of the assembled church and by someone duly appointed thereunto.

Baptists agree with most evangelical Protestants that the efficacy of baptism is not so tied to the water that the act of baptism itself, when duly administered, shall convey the grace of the new birth. The doctrine of baptismal regeneration is repudiated as a medieval superstition and magic. It is admitted, however, that the meaning of the symbol and the symbol itself have become so intimately associated in the NT that the symbol may be used upon occasion for the thing symbolized, as when Paul is commanded to be baptized and wash away his sins (Acts 22:16). Actually, baptism is not itself a cleansing and renewal, but rather a proclamation on God's part, signified by the outward sign to those who believe the gospel, that their sins are cleansed by the blood of Christ and that they are engrafted into Him by His Holy Spirit to partake of all His benefits. It is on man's part a confession of sin and sign of his giving up himself to Christ to walk in newness of life and blamelessly to keep the ordinances of divine worship in the Christian church, which is the body of Christ (Acts 2:41; Rom. 6:3; I Cor. 12:13; Gal. 3:27).

Not only is baptism a washing with water, but also one is baptized into the Name of the Father, the Son, and the Holy Spirit, according to the commission of Christ. This involves not only the subjective recognition on the part of the candidate that the God he confesses is triune in His being, but also that he is now admitted into the covenant of grace which this God has made with His people and of which baptism is a sign. Peter's command at Pentecost that his hearers should be baptized "in the name of Jesus Christ" (Acts 2:38) need not be taken as a contradiction of the ordinary Trinitarian formula of baptism, inasmuch as the Godhead is uniquely revealed in the Savior and, under the circumstances, it was especially appropriate that they who had been privy to Jesus' crucifixion a few days previously should now express their repentance by calling upon His name in baptism.

The Baptists differ from the main stream of Protestant theory and practice in their view that the washing with water in baptism should be by immersion as a part of the right administration of the ordinance of baptism and in their conviction that only believers should receive this ordinance.

Mode

As for the question of the proper mode, it is too much to say, as is often done, that the Greek NT word βαπτίζω can mean *nothing* else but immersion. Nor can it be established that the essential theological significance of baptism is entirely lost if some mode other than immersion is used. On the other hand, a Baptist can only express wonder at the cavalier way in which many Protestants, from Reformation times to the present, while admitting immersion to be the original practice of the church, can yet declare that the mode is entirely indifferent. Says Calvin: "But whether the person baptized be wholly immersed, and whether thrice or once, or whether water be only poured or sprinkled upon him, is of no importance; churches ought to be left at liberty, in this respect, to act according to the differences of countries. The very word *baptize,* however, signifies to immerse; and it is certain that immersion was the practice of the ancient church" (*Institutes,* IV, xv, 19).

Let us address ourselves to two questions: First, can it be established that immersion was the original practice? And secondly, if so, what difference does it make? As for the former question, happily the day is passed when immersion is ridiculed for its eccentricity and scorned for its indecency. Lexicographers universally agree that the primary meaning of βαπτίζω is "to dip" or "to immerse." Virtually all scholars agree that John's baptism was by immersion, and while it cannot be proved to a mathematical demonstration, NT baptisms seem to be by immersion in those instances where the mode is reflected upon. Why, for example, should John baptize in Aenon, near to Salim? The answer is: because there was much water there (John 3:23). To argue this was drinking water for animals and the large crowd is to inject a foreign element into the universe of discourse. Why should the Ethiopian eunuch think of baptism when he saw a natural body of water along the way (Acts 8:36–38)? Surely in a caravan traveling such a distance, water sufficient for effusion (pouring) or aspersion (sprinkling) was readily available. It is, further, to be noted that in the *Didache* 7 (A.D. 100–106), the oldest baptismal manual in existence, immersion (triple in form) is assumed, and pouring is allowed, if there is a shortage of water. (The word used for pouring is ἐκχέω, not βαπτίζω.) Sprinkling seems to have developed even later as an abbreviated form of pouring, and was connected with so-called clinical baptism, that is, baptism of those too infirm to leave their beds. Eusebius, the church historian, preserves a letter written by Cornelius of Rome (A.D. 251) stating that some had opposed the ordination of Novatian on the ground that no one should be admitted to the clergy who "had been baptized in his bed in a time of sickness." As late as the 13th century immersion was still the common practice throughout Christendom, though in France from about A.D. 500 pouring began to be used in baptizing those of sound health, whence it came gradually to prevail in the West. Immersion, in its triple form, even for infants, has been retained to the present day by the Eastern Church. Says Wall, an advocate of pedobaptism:

> The general and ordinary way was to baptize by immersion. . . . This is so plain and clear by an infinite number of passages that as one cannot but pity the weak endeavors of such Paedobaptists as would maintain the negative of it; so also we ought to disown and show a dislike of the profane scoffs which some people give to the English antipaedobaptists merely for their use of dipping. It is one thing to maintain that circumstance is not absolutely necessary to the essence of baptism, and another, to go about to represent it as ridiculous and foolish, as shameful and indecent, when it was in all probability the way by which our blessed Saviour, and for certain was the most usual and ordinary way by which the ancient Christians did receive their baptism. . . . It is a great want of prudence, as well as of honesty, to refuse to grant to an adversary what is certainly true, and may be proved so. It creates a jealousy of all the rest that one says (Wall, *The History of Infant Baptism*, Oxford, 1862, I, 570–571).

As for the question, what difference does it make whether we baptize by one mode or another, the Baptist would answer that while he has no zeal for triple or single immersion, nor is the position assumed by the candidate when he is immersed of any consequence, yet the fact that immersion was practiced from the beginning ought to be enough to lend plausibility to the thesis that this is the proper mode of administration. While Pedobaptists admit immersion as legitimate in their creeds, they never practice it (except when the applicant specifically requests to be immersed). Furthermore, can it be doubted that union with Christ in His death and resurrection, which is centrally signified in baptism, is more adequately symbolized in the act of sinking below the water and rising again above the water, than in sprinkling or pouring? As Paul says, "Therefore we are buried with him by baptism into death, that like as Christ was raised up from the dead by the glory of the Father, even so we also should walk in newness of life" (Rom. 6:4; Col. 2:11-12). It might be replied that in Rom. 6:6 Paul also says, "We have been crucified with Christ," and since this figure of being hung on a cross with Jesus does not lend itself well to immersion, we should not conclude that his reference to burial and resurrection was intended to reflect on the mode of baptism either. But it is not argued that immersion satisfies all the language of Scripture regarding our union with Christ. Besides, the figure of burial and resurrection is brought into closer conjunction with baptism in Romans 6 than is the figure of crucifixion. After all, Paul does say we are buried with Him by baptism, but he does not say we are crucified with Him by baptism. Though this latter would be theologically true, the way in which Paul expresses himself implies the mode of immersion. There surely would seem to be no better explanation of his manner of expression.

Subjects of Baptism

The hallmark of the Baptist position, however, contrary to much popular opinion, is not the question of mode but that of the proper subjects of baptism. The early Swiss and Dutch Anabaptists, for the most part, used pouring, and it was not till *c.* A.D. 1640 in England that Jessey promulgated the view that immersion was essential to baptism, a view which rapidly gained the ascendancy among English Baptists, though the Mennonites and other descendants of the original Anabaptists still practice believers' baptism by pouring. We shall therefore give over the remainder of our discussion to a defense of believers'—not necessarily adult—baptism, and a refutation of the error of infant baptism.

It is beyond all cavil that in the NT faith is the threshold over which the individual must step into the Christian life, a step which is symbolically taken in the initiatory rite of baptism. Baptism, like preaching (kerygma), involves the act of confession, whereby it seals to the one baptized participation in the saving event of Christ's death and resurrection. Johannes Schneider is well taken in his observation:

> The apostolic history shows, beyond all peradventure, the place which baptism assumed in the order of salvation. At the beginning of the book of Acts, in Ch. 2, we have in this regard a typical report. First comes the Spirit-filled preaching of Peter. The *Heilsbotschaft,* the message of salvation, is heard. It pricks the heart and leads to the interrogation, "What shall we do?" The answer is "Turn about and get yourselves baptized." To those who shall be baptized the Holy Ghost is promised. The order of sequence is thus: preaching—believing acceptance of the message—baptism—reception of the Holy Spirit (*Die Taufe im Neuen Testament,* Stuttgart, 1951, pp. 33 f.).

This radical structuring of the NT data proves the appeal to Jewish proselyte baptism (according to which infants were baptized) as the model of Christian baptism too facile, too superficial. Even if the chronological problem be overlooked, the formal similarities between Christian and proselyte baptism are more than offset by the central place given to personal faith in the former, which makes for an inner essential difference. The emphasis on repentance in Acts indicates that the primitive church in its practice of baptism was oriented in terms of John's baptism, not proselyte baptism. Repentance followed by baptism "unto the remission of sins" is the NT pattern, and it is only when one denies this pattern that he can justify infant baptism. This, in brief, is why Baptists believe that a credible—not necessarily infallible—confession of faith should be required of all those who receive baptism.

As Kierkegaard once remarked,

> The truth is, one cannot become a Christian as a child. . . . Becoming a Christian presupposes (according to the NT) being fully a man. . . . Becoming a Christian presupposes (according to the NT) a personal consciousness of sin and of oneself as a sinner. So one readily sees that this whole thing about becoming a Christian as a child, yea, about childhood being above all other ages the season for becoming a Christian, is neither more nor less than puerility . . ." ("The Formula of Christendom, The Instant, No. 7," *Attack Upon Christendom,* Princeton, 1946, p. 213).

Evaluation of Pedobaptist View

From the earliest moments of the Reformation, Pedobaptists have wrestled with this problem. Though it cannot be denied that many Anabaptists showed a streak of radicalness and intransigence which so alienated the Reformers that they were driven to a churchly defense of the *status quo* out of fear of anarchy, yet much of their polemic against the Anabaptists must be classed as rant. The crux of the problem, theologically, was (and still is): What is the saving answer to the medieval doctrine of *ex opere operato,* according to which the grace of cleansing and renewal is effectually bound to the water of the sacrament? It can be nothing else than *nullum sacramentum sine fide* (where there is no faith, there is no sacrament).

In the sacramental system of Rome the defense of infant baptism is easy. The infant is born a sinner; ergo, he must be baptized and have his sin washed away or his soul will be in danger of the unquenchable flame. Both the Lutheran and Anglican doctrine of infant baptism is still oriented quite largely in terms of this sacramental doctrine, though it is more mildly framed and the possibility of evangelicalism is an open possibility. In the Reformed tradition, by contrast, there has been an emphatic repudiation of the Roman *opus operatum* and a sincere and challenging effort to be forthrightly evangelical as to the efficacy of baptism, but at the same time the usage of infant baptism as found in the RC Church has been retained.

But the uneasy conscience of Pedobaptists is nowhere more clearly seen than in the asymmetry between their definitions of baptism and the practice of infant baptism. Faithfulness to the NT and to the pillar and ground of all evangelicalism, that without faith there can be no sacrament, has compelled them to write faith into the very definition and meaning of the ordinance of baptism. Let anyone take Schaff's *Creeds of Christendom* and run through the classic Protestant creeds and he will discover a study in paradox at this point. According to these statements, Pedobaptists declare that they confess their faith in baptism, and yet they give it to infants without their confessing anything; they engage in baptism to be the Lord's, and yet they give it to infants who engage nothing; they confess baptism to be a sacrament of faith and penitence, and yet they grant it to those who have neither the one nor the other; they call baptism a sign of profession, and yet they give it to those who make no profession. And this bale of contradictions is bound together by a hoop of "buts," "neverthelesses," "althoughs" and "not onlys."

The oldest and most widely held solution to this riddle is *fides vicaria,* faith by proxy. Antedating the Reformation by centuries, the usage of sponsors (god-parents) was simply taken over by the Pedobaptists, especially the Lutherans and Anglicans, while the early Puritans in England contended that sponsorship should be at least limited to the parents. (Luther espoused infant faith and Calvin held the seed of faith was in the covenant infant by virtue of the promise.) Officially, Presbyterian and Reformed baptismal liturgies feature no other sponsors than the parents of the child, who confess no other faith than their own, promising for the child that they will so instruct him that hopefully he will confess Christ for himself when he shall come to years of discretion. But whether the child baptized confess his faith in the person of his sponsors (Anglican and Lutheran usage) or whether he is baptized looking to a future personal confession (Reformed and Presbyterian usage), the sacrament of infant baptism is incomplete and must be consummated by some sort of confirmation.

It is for this reason that confirmation, in one form or other, survived the besom of the Reformation in some of the Protestant communions. Infant baptism lifted up its voice for completion. Calvin's pen scorched the page as he denounced Roman Confirmation ("Sacrilegious mouth, dost thou dare to place an unction which is only defiled by thy fetid breath and enchanted by the muttering of a few words on a level with the sacrament of Christ, and to compare it with water sanctified by the word of God?" *Institutes,* IV, xix, 10). Yet at the same time, he pleads:

> It was an ancient custom in the church for the children of Christians, after they were come to years of discretion, to be presented to the bishop in order to fulfill that duty which was required of adults who offered themselves to baptism. . . . Therefore those who had been baptized in their infancy, because they had not then made a confession of faith before the church, at the close of childhood or the commencement of adolescence, were again presented by their parents and were examined by the bishops according to the form of the catechism then in common use. . . . Thus the youth, after having given satisfaction respecting his faith, was dismissed with a solemn benediction . . . (*Institutes,* IV, xix, 4).

Calvin then expresses a wish that this primitive usage might be restored, free from papal corruption. Here is one of the few paragraphs in the *Institutes* devoid of all reference to Scripture. The best Calvin can do is call it an "ancient custom," which should be restored. But he does not give any relevant evidence, even from the Fathers. The quotations from Leo and Jerome—omitted here because we study brevity—have to do with the reception of baptized heretics back into the church. The truth is, the "ancient custom" to which Calvin refers is non-extant. Impregnated by a theological necessity, his own fancy brought forth this child named confirmation.

> Pedobaptists are here between Scylla and Charybdis. If they stress confirmation they are threatened with a third sacrament, but without it the evangelical principle of faith as necessary to the sacraments is jeopardized. A. A. Hodge once observed, "As far as we misunderstand or ignore this beautiful ordinance of confirmation, we abandon to the mercies of our Baptist brethren the whole rational ground of infant baptism" (*Popular Lectures on Theological Themes,* 1887, p. 389). Reformed and Presbyterian orders of worship, however, have generally eschewed the word "confirmation." But the idea is retained in such liturgical services as *Form for the Public Profession of Faith,* in which baptized children openly accept God's covenant promise sealed to them in baptism. Sometimes instead of the word "accept" the word "ratify" is used. Upon occasion the very word "confirm" appears, as in the question, "Do you confirm [italics ours] the vows taken for you in baptism?" (*Constitution of the United Presbyterian Church in the U.S.A., Directory for Worship;* Chapter IX, *Of the Admission to Full Communion of Baptized Persons*). But where does Scripture speak of confirming baptismal vows taken by proxy?

Pedobaptists have bent every effort to discover evidence corroborating their practice of infant baptism in the NT and in the practice of the ancient church. As for the latter, they have from time immemorial claimed the *consensus patrum,* declaring that infant baptism was the unchallenged practice of the Christian church from the very beginning, the Latin schismatic Tertullian (*c.* A.D. 200) being the first and only troubler in Israel. But as one goes back up the stream of evidence from church history, it dwindles to a feeble trickle and disappears altogether with Irenaeus in Gaul about A.D. 180. Clement of Rome, Ignatius, Barnabas, Hermas, Papias, Diognetus, Justin Martyr, Tatian, and the lesser apologists have several references to baptism, but nothing that implies infant baptism. Especially significant is the case of Justin, who devotes a whole chapter (LXI) of his *Apology* to baptism, yet says nothing about infant baptism, but much about believers' baptism. Pedobaptists seize upon his reference (I, 156) to many who were "disciples from youth," which they commonly translate "from infancy," as evidence for infant baptism. (The word is παῖς not βρέφος.) Likewise the *Didache* (A.D. 100–160), the most ancient document, outside the NT, extant on baptism, is silent. It contains over 70 rules for the baptism of believers, including all the circumstances of the water, yet never a word about infants. Can we imagine such a lacuna occurring under Anglican, Lutheran, Presbyterian, or Reformed auspices? In some modern Pedobaptist handbooks, the liturgy of infant baptism is longer than the service of believers' baptism. Also it is striking that several prominent Christians like Gregory Nazianzen, Basil the Great, Chrysostom, and Augustine, though all born of at least one Christian parent, were not baptized in childhood. If infant baptism was not regarded as obligatory in such families as these, how can it have come down from the apostles and been maintained in the church *semper ubique et ab omnibus?*

The question is sometimes put: If infant baptism was not apostolic, how can we account for such an innovation in the church? We might better ask, If it *was* apostolic, how can we account for the silence in the early record? If church history teaches anything, it teaches that in matters of ritual it is much simpler for something to be added than for it to be taken away. It is quite as easy to suppose that infant baptism would gradually commend itself in post-apostolic times, as it is difficult to suppose that it fell into disrepute in many places after it had been established by apostolic authority.

As for the corroborative evidence from the NT for infant baptism, the Pedobaptist position is fraught with ambivalence. On the one hand, it is freely admitted that this evidence is insufficient, apart from the implications of covenant theology (which we shall consider presently). On the other, this casual indifference to the lack of express evidence for infant baptism in the NT is denied by the intense exegesis to which all possible Scriptures are submitted, some of which speak of baptism but not of infants, others of infants but not of baptism, and some of neither infants nor baptism. A few are worthy of mention.

First of all there are the household baptisms (Acts 10:47–48; Acts 16:15; Acts 16:29–34; I Cor. 1:16; 16:15). For the Baptists to deny the possibility, even the probability, of infants in these homes, and for Pedobaptists to insist that if there were such they must have been baptized, is much theological ado about nothing. These passages and many more are concerned with the illustrious displays of grace which marked the way along which Christianity marched in triumph over paganism. Here we have a picture not of parents converted and whole families baptized, but of whole families converted and then baptized. When there is household salvation, there is household baptism under Baptist as well as Pedobaptist auspices.

Even more prominent in Pedobaptist apology is the appeal to Jesus' blessing of children (Mt. 19:13–14; Mark 10:14–16; Luke 18:15–17). It is hardly tenable to argue, as some Baptists do, that these Scriptures pertain only to those who are childlike in spirit, or to children old enough to come to Christ of their own volition. (Luke uses βρέφη, infants.) But there is no need for such evasion. Baptists have no objection to dedicating children to the Lord and invoking His blessing upon them. This they have done for centuries. Only they do not make such a service a substitute for baptism. Why, then, must it be supposed, because Jesus was displeased with His disciples for keeping children from coming to *Him,* He is therefore displeased with Baptists for keeping them from the *font?* Is not this a leap of logic? As Charles Spurgeon once said: "See that you read the word as it is written and you will find no water in it, but Jesus only. Are the water and Christ the same thing? Nay, here is a wide difference, as wide as between Rome and Jerusalem . . . between false doctrine and the gospel of our Lord Jesus Christ" (*Children Brought to Christ Not to the Font,* a sermon delivered July 24, 1864).

The lodestar of Reformed and Presbyterian reasoning, by which an effort is made to lilliputianize the above difficulties, is the argument from the covenant, as it is called. We must conclude our discussion with a brief look at this. The pith of the argument is that the NT age is the fulfillment of the covenant made with Abraham, as signed and sealed by circumcision. Since there is a fundamental continuity between the Abrahamic covenant and the blessings of the church age, therefore baptism may fairly be said to take the place of circumcision, as the Apostle Paul says in Col. 2:11, 12, "In whom you were also circumcised with a circumcision not made with hands, in the putting off of the body of the flesh, in the circumcision of Christ; having been buried with him in baptism, wherein you were also raised with him through faith in the working of God, who raised him from the dead" (cf. also Rom. 4:11; Eph. 2:11–12). Once it is fairly admitted that baptism takes the place of circumcision, it may be inferred—the Pedobaptists plead—that infants of believing parents are to receive the covenant sign now, as they did circumcision in the OT. Calvin calls this the "whole of the subject" (*Institutes,* IV, xvi, 24).

The theological conception, sometimes called "covenant theology," which undergirds the Pedobaptist argument at this point, is too grand, too challenging, too persistent to be ignored with impunity. The dogmatician who slights it despises his own reputation. This is perhaps to concede that the Baptists as a whole have not been outstanding theologians. The stream of their rebuttal has run so thin at this juncture that only the hollow eyes of predisposition could fail to see its inadequacy and adjudge the counter arguments superior. We do not deny the essential correctness of this approach. Though most Baptists do not believe it, it is indeed true that the NT fulfills the Old and that even the analogy between circumcision and baptism is beyond cavil. The basic weakness in the Pedobaptist argument is that it falls short of what is meant and implied in saying revelation is historical. (This movement in redemptive history has been called—to use traditional theological terminology—a diversity of covenantal administration.) Admitting that the New Covenant in Christ's blood is the unfolding and fruition of the covenant made with Abraham, so that baptism in the new economy corresponds to circumcision in the old, yet this emphasis on the *affinity* of the old to the new must always be counterpoised by a proper emphasis on the *diversity* between the two. And what is the diversity? Well, obviously in the OT dispensation, though the promise of salvation, then as now, had its foundation in Christ, yet to encourage the OT saints to hope in the celestial inheritance, God condescended to their weakness by exhibiting the promise of eternal life for their partial contemplation and enjoyment under the figure of temporal and terrestrial blessing. This temporal and terrestrial aspect of the covenant blessing has now passed away; it has dropped from the great house of salvation like scaffolding from a finished edifice.

But when the Pedobaptist begins to argue for infant baptism from infant circumcision, he conveniently forgets this significant fact. In wielding his great sword of circumcision, he should keep this historical development in better focus. Proceeding from the postulate that baptism stands in the place of circumcision, he has urged this to a distortion. He has so far pressed the unity of the covenant as to suppress the diversity of its administration. He has atrophied the movement of history; he has, to be specific, judaized the New Covenant. For this reason he reads the OT concept of a literal seed into the NT and argues that his children are Christians and members of the church by birth, with a right to baptism, just as in the OT a man was born a Jew with the right to circumcision as a citizen of the OT Jewish theocracy. Whereas the NT teaches that we become children of Abraham and of the covenant by *faith,* the Pedobaptist speaks of his children as children of the covenant by *birth* with a *hereditary* right to its blessing. This led to the Halfway Covenant error in New England and is the reason why many Pedobaptists interpret I Cor. 7:14, which refers to the children of mixed marriages as "holy" (ἅγιος), as meaning "in covenant." All the theological formulations which Pedobaptists use to expound the sense of this passage with reference to the children drop from sight when they speak of the unbeliever who is "sanctified." The "collective holiness" which gathers in the child yet leaves the unbelieving (but "sanctified") parent uncollected. Though he was in the family before the child, yet he has no part or lot in the "baptismal solidarity" of that family.

But such whimsies are mild compared to the contradictions into which Pedobaptists are plunged when they seek to defend believers' communion. Here the parallelism (which they so much love between circumcision and baptism) is even more apparent, for the Eucharist was established on the very night Christ celebrated His final Passover. Why then should "covenant children" not come to the Lord's table without faith? Pedobaptists argue vehemently that there is a great difference between the two types of ordinances, one is passive (baptism), the other active (Eucharist); one is initiatory, the other not. But all these matters are quite irrelevant, as is the fact that sucklings cannot eat solid food. Nor is it correct to say children did not eat the Passover. They did, and in the ancient church they also partook of Holy Communion, and still do in the Eastern Church. On most of these matters Pedobaptists are silent, *et pour cause.* These problems evaporate, however, when we recognize that even as in the age of type and figure all the literal seed, being delivered from Egypt, had a right to the OT Passover, so in the age of fulfillment all the spiritual seed, delivered from the bondage of sin, have a right to the Christian Passover, which is the Eucharist. And this corresponds to the Pedobaptist practice of believers' communion. Why then may we not reason the same with baptism? As in the old economy circumcision belonged to all the natural seed of Abraham, so in the new, believers who are the spiritual seed of Abraham, typified by the literal seed, are to be baptized. "They which are the children of the flesh, these *are* not the children of God, but the children of the promise are counted for the seed" (Rom. 9:8). The Baptists, therefore, have not only the advantage of better evidence for their practice, but that practice is also compatible with covenant theology and consistent within itself.

Y. Feenstra

Baptism
(Reformed View)

The Institution of Baptism

A. The Background

1. *Proselyte Baptism.* Baptism, as a sacrament of the Christian church, had an antecedent not only in the baptism of John but also in Jewish proselyte baptism, the ceremonial bath of people who entered Jewish life from paganism. Although many scholars think that this Jewish baptism dates from a much later time and is itself an imitation of the Christian practice, the priority of Jewish proselyte baptism is to be maintained. First of all, when we consider the Jewish attitude against the early church, it is not very likely that they would imitate Christian baptism. Secondly, the Jewish writings from which we have our information, although their present form is of a later date, refer to disputes concerning proselyte baptism between such schools as that of Shammai and Hillel in the first century A.D.

2. *The Baptism of John.* The similarity between the baptism of John and that of Jewish proselytes consists in the fact that in both of them there

From *The Encyclopedia of Christianity* (Marshallton, Delaware: The National Foundation for Christian Education, 1964), Vol. I, pp. 526–537.

is an act of lustration, performed once for all and associated with the transition from one state of life to another. A startling innovation, however, was that the baptism of John was administered to those who were already Jews. Moreover, it did not have a ritualistic but a purely moral character. It was a "baptism of repentance for the remission of sins" (Mark 1:4). Furthermore, it was not only thoroughly moral, but also thoroughly eschatological. There is the closest connection between John's baptism and his proclamation of the kingdom of God. Both drew together a circle of people who were ready to hear the words of Jesus and to follow Him as His disciples.

B. Christian Baptism

1. *Jesus and His Disciples.* It is most remarkable that Jesus Himself accepted baptism at the hands of John. When John protested, He replied: "Suffer it to be so now; for thus it becomes us to fulfil all righteousness" (Mt. 3:15). This was the inauguration of His ministry, in which He took upon Himself the sins of His people. According to the Johannine tradition, Jesus Himself also baptized (John 3:26), although the same evangelist records that "Jesus himself baptized not, but his disciples" (John 4:2). Probably we are to understand that the disciples baptized, rather than Jesus Himself, but that they did so under His authority.

2. *The Baptismal Command.* As a sacrament of the NT church, baptism was instituted by Christ Himself. The missionary command which He gave His disciples is also a baptismal command. And it is of the greatest importance for the correct interpretation of baptism that He charged them to baptize all nations "into the name of the Father, and of the Son, and of the Holy Ghost" (Mt. 28:19). The meaning of these words has been disputed down to our time. They do not mean that one is dipped into the Father, the Son, and the Holy Ghost. Nor are we to think of baptizing "on account" of God or Christ, as has been recently suggested. To baptize into the name of someone most probably means to baptize in relation to, or with regard to, some one (cf. John Murray, *Christian Baptism*). Jesus commands that all nations be put into communion with the Holy Trinity, and this is symbolized by baptism. The threefold name that is used denotes complete salvation: the adoption by the Father in virtue of the reconciling work of the Son, resulting in the gift of the Holy Spirit. The difference between this baptism and that of John is due to the changed dispensation. The extension of baptism to all nations has its basis in the great change announced by John's preaching: the coming of the kingdom of God.

3. *Baptism in the Apostolic Church.* In conformity with the command of Christ, baptism has been practiced as a rite of entry into the new community from the earliest days of the primitive church. Wherever the preaching of the apostles was believed, it was followed by baptism to testify that the new believer shared in the fruit of the work of Christ, performed in His death and resurrection. Thus it is clear that baptism has an

outward and an inward aspect. A distinction may be made between the outward rite and the spiritual reality which that rite embodies. But the distinction may not result in a separation of the two, for both aspects formed an indivisible unity for the early Christians.

Baptism as a Means of Grace

A. According to the New Testament

It is suggested by many that according to the NT the act of baptizing as such is the cause of the spiritual reality. They refer to the strong expressions used by the apostles. The baptized community is "washed" (I Cor. 6:11; cf. Eph. 5:26). Baptism is called a "washing of regeneration" (Titus 3:5). Paul is summoned, "Arise, and be baptized, and wash away thy sins" (Acts 22:16). In one and the same breath the apostle says, "having our hearts sprinkled from an evil conscience, and our bodies washed with pure water" (Heb. 10:22). Nevertheless this causal view is not tenable, as is shown by a closer investigation. Baptism is not the *sine qua non* of Christianity, but rather faith in Jesus Christ is. We do not participate in the grace of God by baptism, but baptism itself points to the death and resurrection of Christ. It accomplishes in its own way what in another way is already in force, namely, that we are included in Christ, that we were dead and also are raised "with him" (Rom. 6:8, 9; cf. II Cor. 5:14). It is an act of incorporation in so far as it applies, expresses, and confirms this inclusion in Christ. Though baptism is administered by men, God in Christ is acting in it. If we keep this in mind, we will exclude on the one hand every magical view and, on the other, every reduction to a mere symbol.

B. In Church History

1. *The First Centuries.* The thesis that even in early times baptism was viewed as a magic act results from a misunderstanding of the development of Christian thought. We may not ascribe to the terms then used the same dogmatic weight which these same terms have in our ears. This must be maintained even in respect to Tertullian, whose doctrine of baptism we know from his treatise *De Baptismo.* When he speaks of the sanctification of the water when the Holy Spirit comes into it, one can scarcely decide whether the words are meant in a realistic or symbolic sense, because such questions were not asked then. Neither can we find a fixed definition with respect to the benefits of baptism. One statement, however, may be made: among the benefits, remission of sins had a first place—remission, that is, of sins committed before the moment of baptism. New sins caused the loss of grace, and that loss was seen as irreparable. This led to the practice of delaying baptism even until the death-bed, especially in the E church of the fourth century, until it met with a strong resistance from the Cappadocian fathers and finally was surmounted. But unfortunately this was attended by a shift from the emphasis on remission as the most central gift of baptism.

In this E theology, first place was given to purification and sanctification through the Holy Spirit and the renewal of man unto immortality.

Great importance should be given to the teaching of Augustine. In his attempt to come to an exact formulation, he made a distinction between the *sacramentum* as the outward sign and the *virtus sacramenti* as the spiritual substance of the sacrament. The sacrament is a visible word, a visible form of the invisible grace. The act of baptizing, in itself, is a mere symbol. It comes to its purpose only by the divine action that is connected with it. Only the Lord baptizes inwardly. At first, Augustine taught that grace could be received in some cases without receiving baptism. Later, in the conflict with the Donatists, he taught that baptism is necessary for salvation, since it incorporates the penitent into the church, outside of which the Holy Spirit will not save him. In this respect Augustine prepared the position of the church of the Middle Ages, when the communication of divine grace was tied more and more to the administration of the sacraments.

2. *The Reformation.* The antithesis of the Reformers was twofold. They opposed the RC Church on the one hand and the Anabaptists and Spiritualists on the other. To the Roman Church, baptism had become the first of seven sacraments. It communicates divine grace and makes man acceptable to God by restoring the original righteousness which enables him to perform meritorious works. At the Council of Trent the "anathema" was pronounced against all those who deny the necessity of baptism for salvation. Justification is not obtainable without "the washing of regeneration" or without at least the desire for it. Baptism provides the basis for all the other sacraments. Baptismal grace, however, is lost by mortal sin and can be restored only by the sacrament of penance.

In the early teaching of Luther we encounter a return to the thoughts of Augustine, for he, too, calls the sacrament a visible form of invisible grace. This standpoint, however, though never explicitly renounced, was abandoned more and more by the Reformer. Then the baptismal water was taken to be charged with grace as iron is penetrated by fire.

The cause of this change in Luther's thinking is to be found partly in his reaction to the opinions of Zwingli and the Spiritualists. Although Zwingli shared the general opposition to the Roman Catholics and stood in the Reformed tradition, he failed to work out his doctrine of the sacraments according to the Holy Scriptures. With him the sacrament is not above all things an action of God, but only of man. Baptism is a sign by which believers confess their faith and accept the obligation to newness of life. Faith comes forth not from outward things, but from God only, and Zwingli apparently could not imagine that God would avail Himself in a sovereign way of these visible signs to seal unto us His divine grace.

Nor could this view of the sacraments as a means of grace find acceptance in the circles of the Anabaptists. Here, also, baptism is a sign by which we testify that through Christ we have peace with God and have been regenerated by the Holy Spirit. If baptism testifies anything to us from

God's side, it is at most that we are received into the community of the holy people.

As for the Spiritualists of those days, some of them viewed the sacraments as an invention of the Antichrist (Sebastian Franck), while others, though acknowledging the institution of baptism by Christ, denied its significance as a means of grace by maintaining that the communion with Christ through the Holy Spirit is a direct one (Schwenckfeld).

Calvin also recognized that there is in the sacraments, in baptism as well as in the Lord's Supper, an element of confessing of faith. But it is of much more importance to him that we receive baptism from the hand of God as a means of nourishing and strengthening our faith. In this way we are to understand his speaking of the sacraments as signs *and* seals added to the Word of God. He defined them as outward signs, by which the Lord in our conscience seals the promises of His good will toward us to strengthen our weak faith; and by which we on our part testify our piety toward Him in His presence and that of angels, as well as before men. Following Augustine, Calvin emphasizes the figurative character of the sacrament, so that the sacrament is a picture or a mirror to show to us the grace of God in Christ. But he goes further. The sacraments not only place a picture before our eyes, but they are also organs of the Holy Spirit by which grace is conferred upon us. He who receives baptism also receives the remission of sins, although they may not always be simultaneous. Because God is true, the conjunction of sign and the thing signified must be maintained. However, it must be remembered that the grace of the sacrament is received by faith only and Calvin stresses their mutual relation. When faith is lacking, the sacrament becomes an empty and idle sign. This emptiness comes not because of God, however, but only because of man's unbelief. Thus the sign and the thing signified are in conjunction in virtue of the relation between sacrament and faith, as is taught by the Bible.

Describing what is given to us in baptism, Calvin places the remission of sins first. He rejects the age-old error that baptism should only concern the sins committed in the past. We have been washed and cleansed once and for all, and whenever we are distressed because of our sins, we may think of our baptism. In this way, though denying the absolute necessity of baptism, he maintains its relative necessity. Contempt of the sacrament is trampling on the blood of Christ. What is given to us as a means of grace ought not to be neglected but thankfully used.

C. The Reformed Confessions

The Confessions are further evidence of the fact that the Reformed doctrine of the sacraments is not sufficiently characterized when we call them symbolical. In all of the confessions it is obvious that the sacraments are added to the Word and have their significance only in this connection. Both Word and sacraments have the same contents. "For the Holy Spirit teaches us in the gospel and assures us by the sacraments that the whole of our salvation stands in the one sacrifice of Christ made for us on the cross" (Heidelberg Catechism, Answer 67). Other confessions indicate that the covenant of grace is the content of the sacraments (Westminster Confession, XXVII, 1). And it is clear that the benefits of that covenant are meant to apply without any restriction: our ingrafting in Christ, our regeneration, the remission of our sins (Westminster Confession, XXVIII, 1). However, the sacraments are always spoken of as both signs and seals. The element of symbolism, to be sure, is present. But never are they represented as bare signs. According to the Belgic Confession (Article XXXIII) we are to view them as "visible signs and seals of an inward and invisible thing, by means whereof God works in us by the power of the Holy Spirit." Concerning the moment of that working nothing is determined. As the Westminster Confession expresses it: "The efficacy of baptism is not tied to that moment of time wherein it is administered" (XXVIII, 6). But that does not mean that once again everything is unsettled, for "yet, notwithstanding, by the right use of this ordinance the grace promised is not only offered, but really exhibited and conferred by the Holy Ghost, to such (whether of age or infants) as that grace belongeth unto, according to the counsel of God's own will, in His appointed time" (*ibid.*). It is stated repeatedly that the sacraments have been instituted by the Lord because of our infirmity. In these sacraments He shows us His mercy and good-will, His divine condescension, that make these earthly elements the instruments of His grace.

Infant Baptism

A. Scriptural Grounds for Infant Baptism

The Biblical basis for the practice of baptizing infants of believers is seen in the following propositions:

1. *God established a covenant of grace with Abraham.* The heart of it was that Jehovah would "be a God" to Abraham (Gen. 17:7). This signified salvation in its highest reaches.

2. *This covenant included children.* Infants were considered as an integral part of Israel, as the people of God. Jehovah said that He would be a God not only to Abraham but also to his seed after him (Gen. 17:7). Therefore, a sign of this covenant was to be placed on all the children, even on the infants who were not old enough to have a saving faith in the coming Messiah (Gen. 17:11, 12). This was the standard practice in the OT, in accord with which Jesus and Paul were circumcised the eighth day. God dealt with Israel organically and not simply atomistically as individuals separated from one another.

3. *The covenant in operation in the OT is essentially the same as the covenant in the NT.* There are two different dispensations, different administrations, different sacraments, and different emphases. But there is only one basic, underlying covenant in all ages. In both the OT and the NT the covenant had only one Mediator, namely Jesus Christ; there was only one condition for salvation, namely faith (Gen. 15:6; Rom. 4:3); one blessing, namely, justification, regeneration, eternal life, and heaven. God promised that it would be an "*everlasting* covenant" (Gen. 17:7). The blessings of Abraham came upon the Gentiles through Christ (Gal. 3:13, 14). Anyone

who is in Christ is a seed of Abraham (Gal. 3:29). The OT church was similar to a child under a tutor; and the NT church is similar to a child without a tutor, but it is the same child (Gal. 3:23–4:7). Rom. 11:16–21 teaches that the church is not two separate organisms (an OT one and a NT one), growing out of two different roots or stocks. Rather, it teaches that the church is one tree. It has many branches, but they grow from one root and form one organic life. Or, to use another Pauline illustration (Eph. 2:11–22), the Gentiles who were once separated from Israel by a wall are now incorporated into the "commonwealth of Israel." Christ broke down the middle wall of partition and united the Jew and Gentile in Himself.

4. *Circumcision and baptism, though differing in form, have the same fundamental import.* Both are initiatory rites. Both symbolize salvation in its deepest and fullest reaches. The NT blessings can hardly be more richly described than in the words of the OT covenant: "I will be your God and ye shall be my people." And circumcision was a sign of this blessing (Gen. 17). Circumcision was a sign of the cutting away of sin, of repentance from sin, of a change of heart, of obedient listening to God, of spiritual cleansing, of being enabled "to love Jehovah thy God with all thy heart, and with all thy soul" (Deut. 10:16; 30:6; Jer. 4:4; 6:10; 9:25, 26). Paul calls circumcision "a seal of the righteousness of faith," i.e., a seal of the justification that comes by faith (Rom. 4:11). "Neither," says Paul, "is that circumcision which is outward in the flesh, but . . . circumcision is that of the heart, in the spirit not in the letter . . ." (Rom. 2:28, 29). The true circumcision, he writes the Philippians, are those who "worship by the Spirit of God, and glory in Christ Jesus, and have no confidence in the flesh" (Phil. 3:3).

In a similar fashion, the Bible indicates that baptism also refers to the washing away of sin (Acts 2:38; Titus 3:5; I Peter 3:21) and to spiritual renewal (Rom. 6:4; Col. 2:11, 12). Especially Col. 2:11, 12 show the identity of the fundamental import of circumcision and baptism. This pericope teaches that true spiritual circumcision (which was represented by fleshly circumcision) is fulfilled by spiritual baptism (which is represented by fleshly baptism). Thus both the OT and NT teach that circumcision and baptism are basically the same in that both signify the highest blessings that man can attain in relation to his God.

5. *Since God has established only one spiritual covenant in all ages, since the children (even those who could not have knowledge and conscious faith) were included in that covenant, and since God commanded that an external sign of that covenant be put not only upon the believing adults but also upon their infants, it is incumbent upon all God's people to continue to put a sign of the covenant upon themselves and their children until God says otherwise.* Since, however, circumcision is a bloody rite which found its fulfillment and end in Christ; and since baptism is identical in meaning with circumcision, it must be concluded that baptism should be used instead of circumcision, just as the bloody Passover lamb was replaced by the Lord's Supper. The mode of the sign of the covenant is typical, national, and incidental; but the command that there be a sign on

all in the covenant (which includes children) is permanent and has not been abrogated.

In this light, the fact that the NT repeatedly speaks of the baptism of whole families (I Cor. 1:16 [Stephanas]; Acts 16:15 [Lydia]; 16:33 [the Philippian jailor]; and 18:8 [Crispus]) is very significant. It is true that the Bible never expressly says that there were children in these families. But the emphasis with which Acts 16:33 speaks of "and all his" and 18:8 of "all" his house (cf. also Acts 11:14) clearly shows that no one who belonged to these "households" was excluded from baptism. Considering the social status of the church members, it is very doubtful that in all of the cases mentioned above there was a large number of servants. Therefore, it would seem highly probable that we must think first of all of children as being present in these families.

The use of the word οἶκος (house) in similar cases in the OT points in the same direction (e.g., I Sam. 22:16 and 19; Gen. 45:18 compared with v. 19 and 46:7; I Sam. 1:21 compared with v. 22; and finally Gen. 17:23 compared with v. 12). From these examples it is apparent that in the idiom of the Bible, someone's "house" does not refer incidentally to the children, but *primarily* to the children. It is also very probable that the NT term οἶκος is borrowed from the OT term and has the same connotations as the OT term in similar cases. Naturally, that does not mean that in each of the above-mentioned NT examples young children were actually present. But it is certainly true that Paul and Luke would hardly have used this term if they had meant that only adult believers were baptized.

Finally, we must remember that the concept that the whole family was included in the father and that his decision was determinative for his family was taken much more for granted in the days of the early Christian church than in our day of strongly individualistic thinking. We need think only of the fact that, according to available data, whenever anyone received the proselyte baptism, this same baptism was also administered to his children.

B. Refutation of the Objections Against Infant Baptism

1. Foremost, naturally, is the old objection that nowhere does the NT tell us that the children of believers must be baptized nor does it record anywhere the baptism of a child.

Naturally, all objections which can be marshalled against an "argumentum e silentio" (argumentation based on the fact of silence) are in force here. It should be noted, too, that this objection is based on a hermeneutical rule to which the Baptists themselves do not always adhere, as, for example, when they teach that women should partake of the Lord's Supper. For the Bible is silent on this practice. In the case of infant baptism, the silence of the NT may mean just the opposite of the Baptistic conclusion that no children were baptized. Many see the NT silence as a thunderous affirmation that infant baptism was so taken for granted that no explicit mention of it was necessary. Furthermore, if God promised Abraham an *eternal* covenant, if He commanded him to put a sign of the covenant on his children, and if this commandment was practiced for 2,000 years, then the very silence, the very omission of a command to counteract the first one, would indicate that the practice should continue.

Furthermore, if it really were true that in the first centuries the children of believers were not baptized, then there must have grown up in the church a great number of children and young people who had not yet been incorporated into it through baptism. But it is significant that we do not read of such a situation anywhere, that there is not one place where mention is made of such young people being baptized, and that nowhere are they exhorted to seek baptism.

2. A second Baptistic objection is that faith must precede baptism. Jesus said: "He that believeth and is baptized shall be saved; but he that believeth not shall be damned" (Mark 16:16). Acts 10:44 ff. (Cornelius), 16:14 ff. (Lydia), and 31 ff. (Philippian jailor) give examples of instruction and faith preceding baptism. Well then, reason the opponents of infant baptism, if baptism can be administered only upon apparent faith and if a newborn baby cannot have faith, then it is clear that the baptism of children is out of the question.

But notice that Jesus is speaking of baptism in a particular situation. He commands His apostles to go into the whole world to preach the gospel and the reference is to those who hear the preaching of the gospel and to their decision respecting that gospel. He who believes and is baptized shall be saved. He who does not believe shall be damned. Naturally, then, we may correctly deduce from this that when dealing with adults the church can administer this sacrament only to those who, through their confession and life, actually give evidence of their uniting with Christ and His people. Concerning this point there is scarcely any difference of opinion. The difference however, concerns the children of believers, those who are born within the church. But it is precisely here that Mark 16:16 says nothing, and therefore no conclusions may be drawn from this text regarding the baptism of infants. Likewise, the instruction to the Philippian jailor first to believe and then be baptized has absolutely nothing to say about the propriety of baptizing infants. Paul was talking about what the jailor, *an adult,* should do.

3. Another objection of Baptists is this: Can we speak of a strengthening of faith in those who have not yet come to a faith, or in any case not to a conscious faith? This objection is particularly convincing for those who have come to view baptism as a means of grace, instituted by God specifically for the strengthening of one's faith.

First of all, we must bear in mind that it is impossible for us to determine what means the Holy Spirit uses to work in the hearts of the youngest children as well as of adults. Whoever gives heed to what the Holy Spirit says about Jeremiah (1:5) and John the Baptist (Luke 1:41 and 44) will be cautious at this point. Otherwise, he may be compelled to exclude from salvation children who die in infancy. The Reformers, and especially Calvin, allowed fully for the possibility of the regenerating work of the Holy Spirit in the hearts of children. Likewise, Calvin was just as firm in rejecting any attempt to fix that work of the Spirit in a particular moment of time, as if the possibility and validity of baptism were dependent upon such a fixed moment. It is advisable for us to be just as cautious. We do not know at what moment the Holy Spirit performs His regenerating work, whether it is before, during, shortly after, or much later than baptism. And we do not need to know. For baptism administered to the children of believers is not based on any assumption regarding whether or not this work of the Spirit has already been accomplished, but it is based on the command and promise of God. Our minds turn to the classic manner in which the Heidelberg Catechism (Question 74) confesses that they (i.e., the young children of believers) "as well as adults, are included in the covenant and Church of God, and since both redemption from sin and the Holy Spirit, the Author of faith, are through the blood of Christ promised to them no less than to adults, they must also by baptism, as a sign of the covenant, be ingrafted into the Christian Church, and distinguished from the children of unbelievers." Here the matter is stated in a scriptural way. The Holy Spirit, who causes faith, is promised to children no less than to adults. And, with regard to their belonging to the covenant of God, that is decisive. Thus it follows that the sign of that covenant must be granted to them. But then that sign of baptism accompanies them all along life's way and is not confined to a particular moment, i.e., when baptism is received. It acts as a continuous attestation to and sealing of the grace of the triune God. And during all their life they may derive strength and comfort from this sign.

There is, of course, a necessary connection between baptism and faith. But that does not mean that faith must precede baptism in time. It does mean that baptized children must be brought up in accord with their baptism, that they must learn to understand their baptism, and they must be active in it through faith. But all of this must be done in order that thereby that baptism may, in their lives, increasingly prove to be the rich assurance of all the benefits which God, in His covenant, grants to His people.

4. Against such reasoning, the objection is often raised that the baptism of children is then something entirely different from the baptism administered to an adult on the ground of profession of his faith. But such an objection is closely bound up with one's view regarding the baptism received by an adult believer. The difficulty in the discussion is precisely that those who reject infant baptism all too often view baptism, not as a means of grace given by God, but as an act on our part, as a confession of our faith and our union with Christ, of our conversion and the change which has been wrought in our life. Whenever it is thus expressed, so that the act of profession by man is the dominating factor, then infant baptism must indeed be viewed as an entirely different matter. In that case, it is understandable that the baptism of a small child, at best, would be considered a "half-baptism," which soon would have to be supplemented by a "third sacrament," confirmation, and which only then would become a real sacrament. This way of thinking, however, arises from a failure to see baptism as a means of grace, that is, a means, not used by us to strengthen ourselves in our faith, but used by God, who grants us this strengthening on His part.

Wherever there is a baptism, He is the person who really acts. It is His testifying and sealing work. That is the very meaning of baptism, and therefore His sealing work is completely independent of whether a child or an adult is being baptized. It does not make any real difference if this benefit of God is consciously appreciated at the moment or if this appreciation begins at some later time.

Even in the baptism of an adult, regardless of what his baptism means to him at the moment he receives it, it is nevertheless significant to him for the rest of his life. Those who say that baptism in the case of children does not become complete until supplemented by the "new" sacrament, confirmation, are clearly basing their argument on a misunderstanding. Baptism received by a child does indeed demand a believing acceptance. However, this acceptance does not make it a sacrament, but is only a thankful recognition of what God in His grace has already granted. Nor does the fact that a great number of baptized children later manifest themselves as unbelievers mean that there is a real difference between infant and adult baptism. In any case, we may not say that the baptism which they received appears to have been worthless. From God's side, this baptism, administered according to His Word, was earnestly meant as a sealing of His grace. And it renders even more grave the guilt of those who reject such great grace in indifference. We are, without a doubt, confronted here by a fearful possibility. There is here also a warning for the church not to render this sacrament hollow by baptizing everyone who is presented for baptism, even when guarantees for Christian upbringing are altogether lacking. But the same difficulty arises whenever someone who once professed his faith and was baptized on that profession later falls away. In both cases, the judgment of the church regarding who may be baptized is a "judgment of love": in the case of the baptism of an adult, a judgment based on his own testimony of faith; in the case of the baptism of a child, it is based on the testimony of God's covenant promise. And it is really a serious thing to attach so much more value to the former than to the latter. The decisive question is then, in our opinion, whether we see the wealth of God's covenant and the joy of His promise for the believers and their seed. That promise does not automatically insure that everything will turn out all right for the children of believers. The promise must be accepted and experienced in faith. But the church has no other alternative than, holding fast to God's promise in faith, to view and deal with these children as heirs of the covenant until such a time in their lives as the opposite should become apparent.

5. Finally, the objection is raised that infant baptism supposedly was unknown during the first centuries of the history of the church, and that it arose only later.

It has now been admitted, even by scholars who reject infant baptism, that toward the end of the second century infant baptism appears to have been a commonly accepted custom. Tertullian (c. 160-c. 220), who rejected infant baptism during a certain period of his life, never used the argument that it was an innovation. Nor was it ever labeled as a fad of a particular group in the church. When Cyprian (d. 258) wrote a letter to Bishop Fidus, the question was not whether or not children should be baptized, but whether they should be baptized immediately after birth or not until the eighth day, as was prescribed for circumcision. Nor was the practice of infant baptism ever contested by Hippolytus (c. 170-c. 236). The epitaphs in the catacombs, dating from the beginning of the third century, present the same evidence. A child who died at the age of one year is called a servant of God. Children twelve years old are described as "believers from their birth," which can mean only that they were baptized as infants. A child who died at the age of nine is said to have died "in peace." It is repeatedly apparent from these data that baptism was also administered to the very youngest children. And the fact that no mention is made anywhere of an official ecclesiastical pronouncement prescribing infant baptism can mean only that the commencement of this practice goes back to the earliest times.

At the same time, it must be stated that there is not a comparable unanimity regarding the significance which is attached to infant baptism. Origen (c. 185-c. 254), with his Platonic manner of approaching things, sees in birth a certain defilement which must be taken away by baptism. He also believes in the purification from sins committed in a previous existence. When Cyprian insists that baptism must be administered on the second or third day after birth, he derives his reason for doing so from the fact that children are subject to original sin from their birth. As is commonly known, this standpoint was brought to the fore with great emphasis by Augustine in his struggle against Pelagianism, which also accepted infant baptism but naturally had to attach a totally different meaning to it. Hence, the very lack of unanimity with regard to the theological basis for infant baptism makes the general acceptance of it, mentioned above, all the more surprising. First came the practice, and then followed the deliberations regarding the significance of it. And it is exactly this fact which clearly shows that infant baptism was not invented for the sake of some doctrine, for example, the doctrine of original sin, nor even less for the support of the so-called "corpus christianum-thought" or something like it. Rather, the early church accepted it as "a tradition of the apostles," as Origen calls it, which had authority independent of the meaning which was believed to be expressed by it.

The Administration of Baptism

A. The Administrators

Because the Word and sacraments are inseparably connected, baptism should be administered only by those who have been ordained as ministers of the Word. This is also confirmed by the NT examples and by Pauline instruction. Any form of private baptism with one's own hands must be absolutely excluded. Neither should physicians or nurses baptize, as is practiced in the RC Church and to a certain extent in the Lutheran churches in cases of need. The supposed doctrinal basis for this practice, the necessity of baptism for salvation, almost loses sight of the connection between Word and sacrament.

B. *The Mode of Administration*

There is a rather searching difference about the mode of administration, which often coincides with the difference concerning infant baptism. Surely both questions do not have the same weight. Yet the matter is important. The question is this: Is baptism by immersion or submersion the original and proper mode according to the NT?

In the LXX the word Βαπτίζειν appears only twice, once in a clearly metaphorical sense (Isa. 21:4), and the second time in such a way that it can mean "immersion," but not necessarily so (Naaman, II Kings 5:14). The word Βάπτειν is used more often and in one case it must refer to immersion (Lev. 11:32). But alongside of this one place there are a number of places where it could mean "immersion" but does not necessarily or even probably mean it. Furthermore, there are also places where it cannot possibly be rendered as "immersion." For example, in Lev. 14:6, 51 the command is given to dip a live bird in the blood of another bird. Now certainly Βάπτειν here cannot be translated "immerse," for one bird does not provide enough blood that another bird may be immersed in it. In the same way Lev. 14:16 speaks of the priest dipping (Βάπτειν) his finger into the oil in the palm of his hand. Again, the amount of oil contained in the palm of the hand is not sufficient for immersing a finger. The NT yields the same evidence. The word Βαπτίζειν can in several places mean "immersion," but it can in these same places also be used for "affusion" or "pouring." In fact, Luke 11:38, which uses Βαπτίζειν, can mean only "dip," since the ceremonial bathing was done with a cupped hand (Mark 7:3). Consequently, the word itself can give no support to the argument for the necessity of baptism by immersion.

After having been baptized, Jesus went up "straightway from the water" (Mt. 3:16). But do we know exactly what happened in the water? As to the baptism of the Ethiopian eunuch (Acts 8:26–40), some reason that the eunuch must have been immersed because Luke says that he "went down into the water" and "came up out of the water." But if these phrases indicate that the eunuch was immersed, then they indicate the same thing of Philip, since Luke employs both phrases of the baptizer as well as of the baptized! And the question asked by Peter in the house of Cornelius (Acts 10:47) suggests that water was to be brought.

There is not much certainty in all this and it points more to Christian liberty than to Jewish legalism, which demands fixed rules. We encounter the same free approach in the *Didache*. Instruction is given there to baptize in living (running) water. Afterwards, however, we read: "But if you have not living water, then baptize in other water; and if you are not able in cold, then in warm. But if you have neither, then pour water on the head thrice, in the name of the Father, and of the Son, and of the Holy Spirit." Early pictures show a nude, youthful figure standing in the water, with the hand of an older man held above his head. Does this point to a certain mode of immersion or to a practice of affusion?

But is not the question already decided by the words of Paul (Rom. 6:4 ff.)? It has been stated with much emphasis that the description of immersion as the scriptural mode of baptizing is generally accepted by scholars of all denominations and needs no argument. The idea is that the immersion into the water of baptism represents the entering into the death of Christ. Immersion, then, is seen as a sort of burial in the water, and emergence from it as a sort of resurrection.

But Paul's purpose here is not to tell the Romans the proper mode of baptism, but rather to oppose antinomianism. He does this by reasoning from the believer's union with Christ, and he clarifies this union and freedom from dominating sin by the illustration of the burial and resurrection of Christ. He also uses the parallel illustrations of being "crucified together" with Christ and "planted together" with Christ. It is purely arbitrary to make one analogy to the exclusion of others, without an explicit indication from Paul, determinative of the mode of baptism.

Similarly, notice the close parallel between Gal. 3:27 and Rom. 6:3. In Rom. 6:3 Paul writes, "So many of us as were baptized into Jesus Christ were baptized into his death"; and in Gal. 3:27 he says, "For as many of you as have been baptized into Christ have put on Christ." Again, it is completely indefensible exegetically to take one analogy, and not the other, as the norm for deciding the mode of baptism. The same can be said of I Cor. 12:13, which compares baptism to the union with an organism.

C. *Place and Time*

The place of administering baptism should be in the midst of the congregation, in public worship. The church as an organization was intrusted by Christ with its two sacraments, baptism and the Lord's Supper; and it is un-Biblical for individuals to usurp the prerogatives that belong to the church alone.

As to the time of administration, we can say only that it is to be sought for as soon as possible. When one's eyes are opened to the wonderful grace of God, testified to by baptism, he will avoid any delay in receiving it for himself or for his children. The custom in vogue in some churches of holding special baptism services at certain times, during which a greater number of children are baptized at the same time, may have the appearance of lending increased splendor to the administration of the sacrament. Actually, however, this practice stands in the way of a thankful appreciation of baptism. Therefore, since the days of the Reformation, many Reformed churches have warned against such customs, as well as against the needless waiting until certain persons—relatives or sponsors—can be present. (The presence of sponsors is necessary only when neither of the parents is competent to accept the responsibility of the baptismal vows.)

D. *Validity*

Finally, the question arises whether baptism administered in the midst of heretics or schismatic groups is to be recognized as a valid Christian baptism. In this connection it is important to distinguish between different kinds of heresies and schisms. The early church rightly differentiated between those heretics who denied the Trinity and those who did not. It was generally considered that a baptism administered by one who denied the Trinity should not be considered valid. Thus a Socinian or Unitarian baptism should not be recognized.

Another question is this: Does the validity of baptism depend upon the spiritual condition of the person who administers it? Augustine, in his struggle against the Donatists, felt that the answer should be decidedly negative. Otherwise, the church would fall into an unallowable subjectivism. This judgment of the early church is generally accepted today.

After much uncertainty in the first centuries, the view became increasingly accepted that whenever baptism was administered in a circle of Christian believers, at the hands of a Christian minister qualified to perform the baptismal act, and in the name of the Father and of the Son and of the Holy Ghost, it should be recognized as valid. It is this standpoint that is shared by far the greater part of Christian churches, Roman Catholics included. In the case of transfer to the RC church, however, baptism often is repeated. The reason is that Rome considers a certain way of baptism to be essential, and since the church cannot be absolutely sure of the correctness of the mode, it is safer to rebaptize. Rome, however, does not abandon the principle of the recognition of baptism administered by other churches.

26

Joseph Pohle

Eucharist

The Church honours the Eucharist as one of her most exalted mysteries, since for sublimity and incomprehensibility it yields in nothing to the allied mysteries of the Trinity and Incarnation. These three mysteries constitute a wonderful triad, which causes the essential characteristic of Christianity, as a religion of mysteries far transcending the capabilities of reason, to shine forth in all its brilliance and splendour, and elevates Catholicism, the most faithful guardian and keeper of our Christian heritage, far above all pagan and non-Christian religions. The organic connexion of this mysterious triad is clearly discerned, if we consider Divine grace under the aspect of a personal communication of God. Thus in the bosom of the Blessed Trinity, God the Father, by virtue of the eternal generation, communicates His Divine Nature to God the Son, "the only begotten Son who is in the bosom of the Father" (John, i, 18), while the Son of God, by virtue of the hypostatic union, communicates in turn the Divine Nature received from His Father to His human nature formed in the womb of the Virgin Mary (John, i, 14), in order that thus as God-man, hidden under the Eucharistic Species, He might deliver Himself to His Church, who, as a tender mother,

From *The Catholic Encyclopedia* (New York: Encyclopedia Press, Inc., 1913), Vol. V, pp. 573-576, 584-588.

mystically cares for and nurtures in her own bosom this, her greatest treasure, and daily places it before her children as the spiritual food of their souls. Thus the Trinity, Incarnation, and Eucharist are really welded together like a precious chain, which in a wonderful manner links heaven with earth, God with man, uniting them most intimately and keeping them thus united. By the very fact that the Eucharistic mystery does transcend reason, no rationalistic explanation of it, based on a merely natural hypothesis and seeking to comprehend one of the sublimest truths of the Christian religion as the spontaneous conclusion of logical processes, may be attempted by a Catholic theologian.

The modern science of comparative religion is striving, wherever it can, to discover in pagan religions "religio-historical parallels," corresponding to the theoretical and practical elements of Christianity, and thus by means of the former to give a natural explanation of the latter. Even were an analogy discernible between the Eucharistic repast and the ambrosia and nectar of the ancient Greek gods, or the haoma of the Iranians, or the soma of the ancient Hindus, we should nevertheless be very cautious not to stretch a mere analogy to a parallelism strictly so called, since the Christian Eucharist has nothing at all in common with these pagan foods, whose origin is to be found in the crassest idol—and nature—worship. What we do particularly discover is a new proof of the reasonableness of the Catholic religion, from the circumstance that Jesus Christ in a wonderfully condescending manner responds to the natural craving of the human heart after a food which nourishes unto immortality, a craving expressed in many pagan religions, by dispensing to mankind His own Flesh and Blood. All that is beautiful, all that is true in the religions of nature, Christianity has appropriated to itself, and like a concave mirror has collected the dispersed and not unfrequently distorted rays of truth into their common focus and again sent them forth resplendently in perfect beams of light.

It is the Church alone, "the pillar and ground of truth," imbued with and directed by the Holy Spirit, that guarantees to her children through her infallible teaching the full and unadulterated revelation of God. Consequently, it is the first duty of Catholics to adhere to what the Church proposes as the "proximate norm of faith" *(regula fidei proxima)*, which, in reference to the Eucharist, is set forth in a particularly clear and detailed manner in Sessions XIII, XXI, and XXII of the Council of Trent. The quintessence of these doctrinal decisions consists in this, that in the Eucharist the Body and Blood of the God-man are truly, really, and substantially present for the nourishment of our souls, by reason of the transubstantiation of the bread and wine into the Body and Blood of Christ, and that in this change of substances the unbloody Sacrifice of the New Testament is also contained. . . .

I. The Real Presence of Christ in the Eucharist

[That the Real Presence of Christ in the bread and wine is a fact can be proved from Scripture.]

This may be adduced both from the words of promise (John, vi, 26 sqq.) and, especially, from the words of Institution as recorded in the Synoptics and St. Paul (I Cor., xi, 23 sqq.). By the miracles of the loaves and fishes and the walking upon the waters, on the previous day, Christ not only prepared His hearers for the sublime discourse containing the promise of the Eucharist, but also proved to them that He possessed, as Almighty God-man, a power superior to and independent of the laws of nature, and could, therefore, provide such a supernatural food, none other, in fact, than His own Flesh and Blood. This discourse was delivered at Capharnaum (John, vi, 26–72), and is divided into two distinct parts, about the relation of which Catholic exegetes vary in opinion. Nothing hinders our interpreting the first part [John, vi, 26–48(51)] metaphorically and understanding by "bread of heaven" Christ Himself as the object of faith, to be received in a figurative sense as a spiritual food by the mouth of faith. Such a figurative explanation of the second part of the discourse (John, vi, 52–72), however, is not only unusual but absolutely impossible, as even Protestant exegetes (Delitzsch, Köstlin, Keil, Kahnis, and others) readily concede. First of all the whole structure of the discourse of promise demands a literal interpretation of the words: "eat the flesh of the Son of man, and drink his blood." For Christ mentions a threefold food in His address, the manna of the past (John, vi, 31, 32, 49, 59), the heavenly bread of the present (John, vi, 32 sq.), and the Bread of Life of the future (John, vi, 27, 52). Corresponding to the three kinds of food and the three periods, there are as many dispensers—Moses dispensing the manna, the Father nourishing man's faith in the Son of God made flesh, finally Christ giving His own Flesh and Blood. Although the manna, a type of the Eucharist, was indeed eaten with the mouth, it could not, being a transitory food, ward off death. The second food, that offered by the Heavenly Father, is the bread of heaven, which He dispenses *hic et nunc* to the Jews for their spiritual nourishment, inasmuch as by reason of the Incarnation He holds up His Son to them as the object of their faith. If, however, the third kind of food, which Christ Himself promises to give only at a future time, is a new refection, differing from the last-named food of faith, it can be none other than His true Flesh and Blood, to be really eaten and drunk in Holy Communion. This is why Christ was so ready to use the realistic expression "to chew" (John, vi, 54, 56, 58: τρώγειν) when speaking of this, His Bread of Life, in addition to the phrase, "to eat" (John, vi, 51, 53: φαγεῖν). Cardinal Bellarmine (De Euchar., I, 3), moreover, calls attention to the fact, and rightly so, that if in Christ's mind the manna was a figure of the Eucharist, the latter must have been something more than merely blessed bread, as otherwise the prototype would not substantially excel the type. The same holds true of the other figures of the Eucharist, as the bread and wine offered by Melchisedech, the loaves of proposition *(panes propositionis),* the paschal lamb. The impossibility of a figurative interpretation is brought home more forcibly by an analysis of the following text: "Except you eat the flesh of the Son of man, and drink his blood, you shall not have life in you. He that eateth my flesh and drinketh my blood, hath everlasting life: and I will raise him up in the last day. For my flesh is meat indeed: and my blood is drink indeed'' (John, vi, 54–56). It is true that even among the Semites, and in Scripture itself, the phrase, ''to eat some one's flesh,'' has a figurative meaning, namely, ''to persecute, to bitterly hate some one.'' If, then, the words of Jesus are to be taken figuratively, it would appear that Christ had promised to His enemies eternal life and a glorious resurrection in recompense for the injuries and persecutions directed against Him. The other phrase, ''to drink some one's blood,'' in Scripture, especially, has no other figurative meaning than that of dire chastisement (cf. Is., xlix, 26; Apoc., xvi, 6); but, in the present text, this interpretation is just as impossible here as in the phrase, ''to eat some one's flesh.'' Consequently, eating and drinking are to be understood of the actual partaking of Christ in person, hence literally.

This interpretation agrees perfectly with the conduct of the hearers and the attitude of Christ regarding their doubts and objections. Again, the murmuring of the Jews is the clearest evidence that they had understood the preceding words of Jesus literally (John, vi, 53). Yet far from repudiating this construction as a gross misunderstanding, Christ repeated them in a most solemn manner, in the text quoted above (John, vi, 54 sqq.). In consequence, many of His Disciples were scandalized and said: ''This saying is hard, and who can hear it?'' (John, vi, 61); but instead of retracting what He had said, Christ rather reproached them for their want of faith, by alluding to His sublimer origin and His future Ascension into heaven. And without further ado He allowed these Disciples to go their way (John, vi, 62 sqq.). Finally He turned to His twelve Apostles with the question: ''Will you also go away?'' Then Peter stepped forth and with humble faith replied: ''Lord, to whom shall we go? thou hast the words of eternal life. And we have believed and have known, that thou art the Christ, the Son of God'' (John, vi, 68 sqq.). The entire scene of the discourse and murmurings against it proves that the Zwinglian and Anglican interpretation of the passage, ''It is the spirit that quickeneth,'' etc., in the sense of a glossing over or retractation, is wholly inadmissible. For in spite of these words the Disciples severed their connexion with Jesus, while the Twelve accepted with simple faith a mystery which as yet they did not understand. Nor did Christ say: ''My flesh is spirit,'' i.e., to be understood in a figurative sense, but: ''My words are spirit and life.'' There are two views regarding the sense in which this text is to be interpreted. Many of the Fathers declare that the true Flesh of Jesus (σάρξ) is not to be understood as separated from His Divinity *(spiritus),* and hence not in a cannibalistic sense, but as belonging entirely to the supernatural economy. The second and more scientific explanation asserts that in the Scriptural opposition of ''flesh and blood'' to ''spirit,'' the former always signifies carnal-mindedness, the latter mental perception illumined by faith, so that it was the intention of Jesus in this passage to give prominence to the fact that the sublime mystery of the Eucharist can be grasped in the light of supernatural faith alone, whereas it cannot be understood by the carnal-minded, who are weighed down under the burden of sin. Under such circumstances it is not to be wondered at that the Fathers and several ecumenical councils (Ephesus, 431; Nicæa, 787) adopted the literal sense of the words, though it was not dogmatically defined (cf. Council of Trent, Sess. XXI, c.i). If it be true that a few Catholic theologians (as Cajetan, Ruardus Tapper, Johann Hessel, and the elder Jansenius) preferred the figurative interpretation, it was merely for controversial reasons, because in their perplexity they imagined that otherwise the claims of the Hussite and Protestant Utraquists for the partaking of the Chalice by the laity could not be answered by argument from Scripture. (Cf. Patrizi, "De Christo pane vitæ," Rome, 1851; Schmitt, "Die Verheissung der Eucharistie bei den Vätern," 2 vols., Würzburg, 1900–03.)

The Church's Magna Charta, however, is the words of Institution, "This is my body—this is my blood," whose literal meaning she has uninterruptedly adhered to from the earliest times. The Real Presence is evinced, positively, by showing the necessity of the literal sense of these words, and negatively, by refuting the figurative interpretations. As regards the first, the very existence of four distinct narratives of the Last Supper, divided usually into the Petrine (Matt., xxvi, 26 sqq.; Mark, xiv, 22 sqq.) and the double Pauline accounts (Luke, xxii, 19 sq.; I Cor., xi, 24 sqq.), favours the literal interpretation. In spite of their striking unanimity as regards essentials, the Petrine account is simpler and clearer, whereas the Pauline is richer in additional details and more involved in its citation of the words that refer to the Chalice. It is but natural and justifiable to expect that, when four different narrators in different countries and at different times relate the words of Institution to different circles of readers, the occurrence of an unusual figure of speech, as, for instance, that bread is a sign of Christ's Body, would, somewhere or other, betray itself, either in the difference of word-setting, or in the unequivocal expression of the meaning really intended, or at least in the addition of some such remark as: "He spoke, however, of the sign of His Body." But nowhere do we discover the slightest ground for a figurative interpretation. If, then, the natural, literal interpretation were false, the Scriptural record alone would have to be considered as the cause of a pernicious error in faith and of the grievous crime of rendering Divine homage to bread *(artolatria)*—a supposition little in harmony with the character of the four Sacred Writers or with the inspiration of the Sacred Text. Moreover, we must not omit the very important circumstance, that one of the four narrators has interpreted his own account literally. This is St. Paul (I Cor., xi, 27 sq.), who, in the most vigorous language, brands the unworthy recipient as "guilty of the body and of the blood of the Lord." There can be no question of a grievous offence against Christ Himself, unless we suppose that the true Body and the true Blood of Christ are really present in the Eucharist. Further, if we attend only to the words themselves, their natural sense is so forceful and clear that even Luther wrote to the Christians of Strasburg in 1524: "I am caught, I cannot escape, the text is too forcible" (De Wette, II, 577). The necessity of the natural sense is not based upon the absurd assumption that Christ could not in general have resorted to the use of figures, but upon the evident requirements of the case, which demand that He did not, in a matter of such paramount importance, have recourse to meaningless and deceptive metaphors. For figures enhance the clearness of speech only when the figurative meaning is obvious, either from the nature of the case (e.g., from a reference to a statue of Lincoln, by saying: "This is Lincoln") or from the usages of common parlance (e.g., in the case of this synecdoche: "This glass is wine"). Now, neither from the nature of the case nor in common parlance is bread an apt or possible symbol of the human body. Were one to say of a piece of bread: "This is Napoleon," he would not be using a figure, but uttering nonsense. There is but one means of rendering a symbol improperly so called clear and intelligible, namely, by conventionally settling beforehand what it is to signify, as, for instance, if one were to say: "Let us imagine these two pieces of bread before us to be Socrates and Plato." Christ, however, instead of informing His Apostles that He intended to use such a figure, told them rather the contrary in the discourse containing the promise: "the bread that I will give, is my flesh, for the life of the world" (John, vi, 52). Such language, of course, could be used only by a God-man; so that belief in the Real Presence necessarily presupposes belief in the true Divinity of Christ. The foregoing rules would of themselves establish the natural meaning with certainty, even if the words of Institution, "This is my body—this is my blood," stood alone. But in the original text *corpus* (body) and *sanguis* (blood) are followed by *significant* appositional additions, the Body being designated as "given for you" and the Blood as "shed for you [many]"; hence the Body given to the Apostles was the selfsame Body that was crucified on Good Friday, and the Chalice drunk by them, the selfsame Blood that was shed on the Cross for our sins. Therefore the above-mentioned appositional phrases directly exclude every possibility of a figurative interpretation.

We reach the same conclusion from a consideration of the concomitant circumstances, taking into account both the hearers and the Institutor. Those who heard the words of Institution were not learned Rationalists, possessed of the critical equipment that would enable them, as philologists and logicians, to analyse an obscure and mysterious phraseology; they were simple, uneducated fishermen, from the ordinary ranks of the people, who with childlike *naïveté* hung upon the words of their Master and with deep faith accepted whatever He proposed to them. This childlike disposition had to be reckoned with by Christ, particularly on the eve of His Passion and Death, when He made His last will and testament and spoke as a dying father to His deeply afflicted children. In such a moment of awful solemnity, the only appropriate mode of speech would be one which, stripped of unintelligible figures, made use of words corresponding exactly to the meaning to be conveyed. It must be remembered, also, that Christ as omniscient God-man must have foreseen the shameful error into which He would have led His Apostles and His Church by adopting an unheard-of metaphor; for the Church down to the present day appeals to the words of Christ in her teaching and practice. If then she practises idolatry by the adoration of mere bread and wine, this crime must be laid to the charge of the God-man Himself. Besides this, Christ intended to institute the Eucharist as a most holy sacrament, to be solemnly celebrated in the Church even to the end of time. But the content and the constituent parts of a sacrament had to be stated with such clearness of terminology as to exclude categorically every error in liturgy and worship. As may be gathered from the words of consecration of the Chalice, Christ established the New Testament in His Blood, just as the Old Testament had been established in the typical blood of animals (cf. Ex., xxiv, 8; Heb., ix, 11 sqq.). With the true instinct of justice, jurists prescribe that in all debatable points the words of a will must be taken in their natural, literal sense; for they are led by the correct conviction, that every testator of sound mind, in drawing up his last will and testament, is deeply concerned to have it done in language at once clear and unencumbered by meaningless metaphors. Now, Christ, according to the literal purport of His testament, has left us as a precious legacy, nor mere bread and wine, but His Body and Blood. Are we justified, then, in contradicting Him to His face and exclaiming: ''No, this is not your Body, but mere bread, the sign of your Body!''

The refutation of the so-called Sacramentarians, a name given by Luther to those who opposed the Real Presence, evinces as clearly the impossibility of a figurative meaning. Once the manifest literal sense is abandoned, occasion is given to interminable controversies about the meaning of an enigma which Christ supposedly offered His followers for solution. There were no limits to the dispute in the sixteenth century, for at that time Christopher Rasperger wrote a whole book on some 200 different interpretations: ''Ducentæ verborum, 'Hoc est corpus meum' interpretationes'' (Ingolstadt, 1577). In this connexion we must restrict ourselves to an examination of the most current and widely known distortions of the literal sense, which were the butt of Luther's bitter ridicule even as early as 1527. The first group of interpreters, with Zwingli, discovers a figure in the copula *est* and renders it: ''This signifies [*est* = *significat*] my Body.'' In proof of this interpretation, examples are quoted from Scripture, as: ''The seven kine are seven years'' (Gen., xli, 26) or: ''Sara and Agar are the two covenants'' (Gal., iv, 24). Waiving the question whether the verb ''to be'' (*esse,* εἶναι) of itself can ever be used as the ''copula in a figurative relation'' (Weiss) or express the ''relation of identity in a metaphorical connexion'' (Heinrici), which most logicians deny, the fundamental principles of logic firmly establish this truth, that all propositions may be divided into two great categories, of which the first and most comprehensive denominates a thing as it is in itself (e.g., ''Man is a rational being''), whereas the second designates a thing according as it is used as a sign of something else (e.g., ''This picture is my father''). To determine whether a speaker intends the second manner of expression, there are four criteria, whose joint concurrence alone will allow the verb ''to be'' to have the meaning of ''signify.'' Abstracting from the three criteria, mentioned above, which have reference either to the nature of the case, or to the usages of common parlance, or to some convention previously agreed upon, there remains a fourth and last of decisive significance, namely:

when a complete substance is predicated of another complete substance, there can exist no logical relation of identity between them, but only the relation of similarity, inasmuch as the first is an image, sign, symbol, of the other. Now this last-named criterion is inapplicable to the Scriptural examples brought forward by the Zwinglians, and especially so in regard to their interpretation of the words of Institution; for the words are not: "This bread is my Body," but indefinitely: "This is my Body." In the history of the Zwinglian conception of the Lord's Supper, certain "sacramental expressions" *(locutiones sacramentales)* of the Sacred Text, regarded as parallelisms of the words of Institution, have attracted considerable attention. The first is to be found in I Cor., x, 4: "And the rock was [signified] Christ." Yet it is evident that, if the subject *rock* is taken in its material sense, the metaphor, according to the fourth criterion just mentioned, is as apparent as in the analogous phrase: "Christ is the vine." If, however, the word *rock* in this passage is stripped of all that is material, it may be understood in a spiritual sense, because the Apostle himself is speaking of that "spiritual rock" *(petra spiritalis),* which in the Person of the Word in an invisible manner ever accompanied the Israelites in their journeyings and supplied them with a spiritual fountain of waters. According to this explanation the copula would here retain its meaning "to be." A nearer approach to a parallel with the words of Institution is found apparently in the so-called "sacramental expressions": "Hoc est pactum meum" (Gen., xvii, 10), and "est enim Phase Domini" (Ex., xii, 11). It is well known how Zwingli by a clever manipulation of the latter phrase succeeded in one day in winning over to his interpretation the entire Catholic population of Zurich. And yet it is clear that no parallelism can be discerned between the aforesaid expressions and the words of Institution—no real parallelism, because there is question of entirely different matters. Not even a verbal parallelism can be pointed out, since in both texts of the Old Testament the subject is a ceremony (circumcision in the first case, and the rite of the paschal lamb in the second), while the predicate involves a mere abstraction (covenant, Passover of the Lord). A more weighty consideration is this, that on closer investigation the copula *est* will be found to retain its proper meaning of "is" rather than "signifies." For just as the circumcision not only signified the nature or object of the Divine covenant, but really was such, so the rite of the paschal lamb was really the Passover *(Phase)* of Pasch, instead of its mere representation. It is true that in certain Anglican circles it was formerly the custom to appeal to the supposed poverty of the Aramaic tongue, which was spoken by Christ in the company of His Apostles; for it was maintained that no word could be found in this language corresponding to the concept "to signify." Yet, even prescinding from the fact that in the Aramaic tongue the copula *est* is usually omitted and that such an omission rather makes for its strict meaning of "to be," Cardinal Wiseman (Horæ Syriacæ, Rome, 1828, pp. 3–73) succeeded in producing no less than forty Syriac expressions conveying the meaning of "to signify" and thus effectually exploded the myth of the Semitic tongue's limited vocabulary.

A second group of Sacramentarians, with (Ecolampadius, shifted the diligently sought-for metaphor to the concept contained in the predicate *corpus,* giving to the latter the sense of "signum corporis," so that the words of Institution were to be rendered: "This is a sign [symbol, image, type] of my Body." Essentially tallying with the Zwinglian interpretation, this new meaning is equally untenable. In all the languages of the world the expression "my body" designates a person's natural body, not the mere sign or symbol of that body. True it is that the Scriptural words "Body of Christ" not unfrequently have the meaning of "Church," which is called the mystical Body of Christ, a figure easily and always discernible as such from the text or context (cf. Col., i, 24). This mystical sense, however, is impossible in the words of Institution, for the simple reason that Christ did not give the Apostles His Church to eat, but His Body, and that "body and blood," by reason of their real and logical association, cannot be separated from one another, and hence are all the less susceptible of a figurative use. The case would be different if the reading were: "This is the bread of my Body, the wine of my Blood." In order to prove at least this much, that the contents of the Chalice are merely wine and, consequently, a mere sign of the Blood, Protestants have recourse to the text of St. Matthew, who relates that Christ, after the completion of the Last Supper, declared: "I will not drink henceforth of this fruit of the vine [*genimen vitis*]" (Matt., xxvi, 29). It is to be noted that St. Luke (xxii, 18 sqq.), who is chronologically more exact, places these words of Christ before his account of the Institution, and that the true Blood of Christ may with right still be called (consecrated) wine, on the one hand, because the Blood was partaken of after the manner in which wine is drunk, and, on the other hand, because the Blood continues to exist under the outward appearances of the wine. In its multifarious wanderings from the old beaten path, being consistently forced with the denial of Christ's Divinity to abandon faith in the Real Presence also, modern criticism seeks to account for the text along other lines. With utter arbitrariness, doubting whether the words of Institution originated from the mouth of Christ, it traces them to St. Paul as their author, in whose ardent soul something original supposedly mingled with his subjective reflections on the value attached to "Body" and on the "repetition of the Eucharistic banquet." From this troubled fountain-head the words of Institution first found their way into the Gospel of St. Luke and then, by way of addition, were woven into the texts of St. Matthew and St. Mark. It stands to reason that the latter assertion is nothing more than a wholly unwarrantable conjecture, which may be passed over as gratuitously as it was advanced. It is, moreover, essentially untrue that the value attached to the Sacrifice and the repetition of the Lord's Supper are mere reflections of St. Paul, since Christ attached a sacrificial value to His Death (cf. Mark, x, 45) and celebrated His Eucharistic Supper in connexion with the Jewish Passover, which itself had to be repeated every year. As regards the interpretation of the words of Institution, there are at present three modern explanations contending for supremacy—the symbolical, the parabolical, and the eschatological. According to the symbolical interpretation, *corpus* is supposed to designate the Church as the mystical Body and *sanguis* the New Testament. We have already rejected this last meaning as impossible. For is it the Church that is eaten and the New Testament that is drunk? Did St. Paul brand the partaking of the Church and of the New Testament as a heinous offence committed against the Body and Blood of Christ? The case is not much better in regard to the parabolical interpretation, which would discern in the pouring out of the wine a mere parable of the shedding of the Blood on the Cross. This again is a purely arbitrary explanation, an invention, unsupported by any objective foundation. Then, too, it would follow from analogy, that the breaking of the bread was a parable of the slaying of Christ's Body, a meaning utterly inconceivable. Rising as it were out of a dense fog and labouring to take on a definite form, the incomplete eschatological explanation would make the Eucharist a mere anticipation of the future heavenly banquet. Supposing the truth of the Real Presence, this consideration might be open to discussion, inasmuch as the partaking of the Bread of Angels is really the foretaste of eternal beatitude and the anticipated transformation of earth into heaven. But as implying a mere symbolical anticipation of heaven and a meaningless manipulation of unconsecrated bread and wine, the eschatological interpretation is diametrically opposed to the text and finds not the slightest support in the life and character of Christ. . . .

II. The Blessed Eucharist as a Sacrament

Since Christ is present under the appearances of bread and wine in a sacramental way, the Blessed Eucharist is unquestionably a sacrament of the Church. Indeed, in the Eucharist the definition of a Christian sacrament as "an outward sign of an inward grace instituted by Christ" is verified. The investigation into the precise nature of the Blessed Sacrament of the Altar, whose existence Protestants do not deny, is beset with a number of difficulties. Its essence certainly does not consist in the Consecration or the Communion, the former being merely the sacrificial action, the latter the reception of the sacrament, and not the sacrament itself. The question may eventually be reduced to this, whether or not the sacramentality is to be sought for in the Eucharistic Species or in the Body and Blood of Christ hidden beneath them. The majority of theologians rightly respond to the query by saying that neither the species themselves nor the Body and Blood of Christ by themselves, but the union of both factors constitute the moral whole of the Sacrament of the Altar. The species undoubtedly belong to the essence of the sacrament, since it is by means of them, and not by means of the invisible Body of Christ, that the Eucharist possesses the outward sign of the sacrament. Equally certain is it, that the Body and the Blood of Christ belong to the concept of the essence, because it is not the mere unsubstantial appearances which are given for the food of our souls, but Christ concealed beneath the appearances. The twofold number of the Eucharistic elements of bread and wine does not interfere with the unity of the sacrament; for the idea of refection embraces both eating and drinking, nor do our meals in consequence double their number. In the doctrine of the Holy Sacrifice of the Mass, there is a question of even a higher relation, in that the separated species of bread and wine also represent the mystical separation of Christ's Body and Blood or the unbloody Sacrifice of the Eucharistic Lamb. The Sacrament of the Altar may be regarded, under the same aspects as the other sacraments, provided only it be ever kept in view that the Eucharist is a permanent sacrament. . . . Every sacrament may be considered either in itself or with reference to the persons whom it concerns. Passing over the Institution, which was discussed above in connexion with the words of Institution, the only essentially important points remaining are the outward sign (matter and form) and inward grace (effects of Communion), to which may be added the necessity of Communion for salvation. In regard to the persons concerned, we distinguish between the minister of the Eucharist and its recipient or subject.

(1) The Matter or Eucharistic Elements

There are two Eucharistic elements, bread and wine, which constitute the remote matter of the Sacrament of the Altar, while the proximate matter can be none other than the Eucharistic appearances under which the Body and Blood of Christ are truly present.

(a) The first element is wheaten bread *(panis triticeus)*, without which the "confection of the Sacrament does not take place" (Missale Romanum: De defectibus, §3). Being true bread, the Host must be baked, since mere flour is not bread. Since, moreover, the bread required is that formed of wheaten flour, not every kind of flour is allowed for validity, such, e.g., as is ground from rye, oats, barley, Indian corn or maize, though these are all botanically classified as grain *(frumentum)*. On the other hand, the different varieties of wheat (as spelt, amel-corn, etc.) are valid, inasmuch as they can be proved botanically to be genuine wheat. The necessity of wheaten bread is deduced immediately from the words of Institution: "The Lord took bread" (τὸν ἄρτον), in connexion with which it may be remarked, that in Scripture *bread* (ἄρτος), without any qualifying addition, always signifies wheaten bread. No doubt, too, Christ adhered unconditionally to the Jewish custom of using only wheaten bread in the Passover Supper, and by the words, "Do this for a commemoration of me," commanded its use for all succeeding times. In addition to this, uninterrupted tradition, whether it be the testimony of the Fathers or the practice of the Church, shows wheaten bread to have played such an essential part, that even Protestants would be loath to regard rye bread or barley bread as a proper element for the celebration of the Lord's Supper.

The Church maintains an easier position in the controversy respecting the use of fermented or unfermented bread. By leavened bread *(fermentum, ζῦμος)* is meant such wheaten bread as requires leaven or yeast in its preparation and baking, while unleavened bread *(azyma, ἄζυμον)* is formed from a mixture of wheaten flour and water, which has been kneaded to dough and then baked. After the Greek Patriarch Michael Cærularius of Constantinople had sought in 1053 to palliate the renewed rupture with Rome by means of the controversy concerning unleavened bread, the two Churches, in the Decree of Union at Florence, in 1439, came to the unanimous dogmatic decision, that the distinction between leavened and unleavened bread did not interfere with the confection of the sacrament, though for just reasons based upon the Church's discipline and practice, the Latins were obliged to retain unleavened bread, while the Greeks still held on to the use of leavened (cf. Denzinger, Enchirid., Freiburg, 1908, no. 692). Since the Schismatics had before the Council of Florence entertained doubts as to the validity of the Latin custom, a brief defence of the use of unleavened bread will not be out of place here. Pope Leo IX had as early as 1054 issued a protest against Michael Cærularius (cf. Migne, P. L., CXLIII, 775), in which he referred to the Scriptural fact, that according to the three Synoptics the Last Supper was celebrated "on the first day of the azymes" and so the custom of the Western Church received its solemn sanction from the example of Christ Himself. The Jews, moreover, were accustomed even the day before the fourteenth of Nisan to get rid of all the leaven which chanced to be in their dwellings, that so they might from that time on partake exclusively of the so-called *mazzoth* as bread. As regards tradition, it is not for us to settle the dispute of learned authorities, as to whether or not in the first six or eight centuries the Latins also celebrated Mass with leavened bread (Sirmond, Döllinger, Kraus) or have observed the present custom ever since the time of the Apostles (Mabillon, Probst). Against the Greeks it suffices to call attention to the historical fact that in the Orient the Maronites and Armenians have used unleavened bread from time immemorial, and that according to Origen (In Matt., XII, n. 6) the people of the East "sometimes," therefore not as a rule, made use of leavened bread in their Liturgy. Besides, there is considerable force in the theological argument that the fermenting process with yeast and other leaven, does not affect the substance of the bread, but merely its quality. The reasons of congruity advanced by the Greeks in behalf of leavened bread, which would have us consider it as a beautiful symbol of the hypostatic union, as well as an attractive representation of the savour of this heavenly Food, will be most willingly accepted, provided only that due consideration be given to the grounds of propriety set forth by the Latins with St. Thomas Aquinas (III, Q. lxxiv, a. 4), namely, the example of Christ, the aptitude of unleavened bread to be regarded as a symbol of the purity of His Sacred Body, free from all corruption of sin, and finally the instruction of St. Paul (I Cor., v, 8) to keep the Pasch "not with the leaven of malice and wickedness, but with the unleavened bread of sincerity and truth."

(b) The second Eucharistic element required is wine of the grape (*vinum de vite*). Hence are excluded as invalid, not only the juices extracted and prepared from other fruits (as cider and perry), but also the so-called artificial wines, even if their chemical constitution is identical with the genuine juice of the grape. The necessity of wine of the grape is not so much the result of the authoritative decision of the Church, as it is presupposed by her (Council of Trent, Sess. XIII, cap. iv), and is based upon the example and command of Christ, who at the Last Supper certainly converted the natural wine of grapes into His Blood. This is deduced partly from the rite of the Passover, which required the head of the family to pass around the "cup of benediction" *(calix benedictionis)* containing the wine of grapes, partly, and especially, from the express declaration of Christ, that henceforth He would not drink of the "fruit of the vine" *(genimen vitis)*. The Catholic Church is aware of no other tradition and in this respect she has ever been one with the Greeks. The ancient Hydroparastæ, or Aquarians, who used water instead of wine, were heretics in her eyes. The counter-argument of Ad. Harnack ["Texte und Untersuchungen," new series, VII, 2 (1891), 115 sqq.], that the most ancient of Churches was indifferent as to the use of wine, and more concerned with the action of eating and drinking than with the elements of bread and wine, loses all its force in view not only of the earliest literature on the subject (the Didache, Ignatius, Justin, Irenæus, Clement of Alexandria, Origen, Hippolytus, Tertullian, and Cyprian), but also of non-Catholic and apocryphal writings, which bear testimony to the use of bread and wine as the only and necessary elements of the Blessed Sacrament. On the other hand, a very ancient law of the Church which, however, has nothing to do with the validity of the sacrament, prescribes that a little water be added to the wine before the Consecration (Decr. pro Armenis: *aqua modicissima*), a practice whose legitimacy the Council of Trent (Sess. XXII, can. ix) established under pain of anathema. The rigour of this law of the Church may be traced to the ancient custom of the Romans and Jews, who mixed water with the strong southern wines (see Prov., ix, 2), to the expression of *calix mixtus* found in Justin (Apol., I, lxv), Irenæus (Adv. hær., V, ii, 3), and Cyprian (Ep. lxiii, ad Cæcil., n. 13 sq.), and especially to the deep symbolical meaning contained in the mingling, inasmuch as thereby are represented the flowing of blood and water from the side of the Crucified Saviour and the intimate union of the faithful with Christ (ef. Council of Trent, Sess. XXII, cap. vii). . . .

(2) The Sacramental Form or the Words of Consecration

In proceeding to verify the form, which is always made up of words, we may start from the indubitable fact that Christ did not consecrate by the mere fiat of His omnipotence, which found no expression in articulate utterance, but by pronouncing the words of Institution: "This is my body-. . . this is my blood," and that by the addition: "Do this for a commemoration of me," He commanded the Apostles to follow His example. Were the words of Institution a mere declarative utterance of the conversion, which might have taken place in the "benediction" unannounced and articulately unexpressed, the Apostles and their successors would, according to Christ's example and mandate, have been obliged to consecrate in this mute manner also, a consequence which is altogether at variance with the deposit of faith. It is true that Pope Innocent III (De Sacro altaris myst., IV, vi) before his elevation to the pontificate did hold the opinion, which later theologians branded as "temerarious," that Christ consecrated without words by means of the mere "benediction." Not many theologians, however, followed him in this regard, among the few being Ambrose Catharinus, Cheffontaines, and Hoppe, by far the greater number preferring to stand by the unanimous testimony of the Fathers. Meanwhile, Innocent III also insisted most urgently that at least in the case of the celebrating priest, the words of Institution were prescribed as the sacramental form. It was, moreover, not until its comparatively recent adherence in the seventeenth century to the famous "Confessio fidei orthodoxa" of Peter Mogilas (cf. Kimmel, "Monum. fidei eccl. orient.," Jena, 1850, I, p. 180), that the Schismatical Greek Church adopted the view, according to which the priest does not at all consecrate by virtue of the words of Institution, but only by means of the Epiklesis occurring shortly after them and expressing in the Oriental Liturgies a petition to the Holy Spirit, "that the bread and wine may be converted into the Body and Blood of Christ." Were the Greeks justified in maintaining this position, the immediate result would be that the Latins, who have no such thing as the Epiklesis in their present Liturgy, would possess neither the true Sacrifice of the Mass nor the Holy Eucharist. Fortunately, however, the Greeks can be shown the error of their ways from their own writings, since it can be proved that they themselves formerly placed the form of Transubstantiation in the words of Institution. Not only did such renowned Fathers as Justin (Apol., I, lxvi), Irenæus (Adv. hær., V, ii, 3), Gregory of Nyssa (Or. catech., xxxvii), Chrysostom (Hom. i, de prod. Judæ, n. 6), and John Damascene (De fid. orth., IV, xiii) hold this view, but the ancient Greek Liturgies bear testimony to it, so that Cardinal Bessarion in 1439 at Florence called the attention of his fellow-countrymen to the fact that as soon as the words of Institution have been pronounced, supreme homage and adoration are due to the Holy Eucharist, even though the famous Epiklesis follows some time after.

The objection that the mere historical recitation of the words of Institution taken from the narrative of the Last Supper possesses no intrinsic consecratory force would be well founded, did the priest of the Latin Church merely intend by means of them to narrate some historical event rather than pronounce them with the practical purpose of effecting the conversion, or if he pronounced them in his own name and person instead of the Person of Christ, whose minister and instrumental cause he is. Neither of the two suppositions holds in the case of a priest who really intends to celebrate Mass. Hence, though the Greeks may in the best of faith go on erroneously maintaining that they consecrate exclusively in their Epiklesis, they do, nevertheless, as in the case of the Latins, actually consecrate by means of the words of Institution contained in their Liturgies, if Christ has instituted these words as the words of Consecration and the form of the sacrament. We may in fact go a step farther and assert that the words of Institution constitute the only and wholly adequate form of the Eucharist and that, consequently, the words of the Epiklesis possess no inherent consecratory value. The contention that the words of the Epiklesis have a joint essential value and constitute the partial form of the sacrament was indeed supported by individual Latin theologians, as Toutée, Re-

naudot, and Lebrun. Though this opinion cannot be condemned as erroneous in faith, since it allows to the words of Institution their essential,
though partial, consecratory value, it appears nevertheless to be intrinsically repugnant. For, since the act of Consecration cannot remain, as it
were, in a state of suspense, but is completed in an instant of time, there
arises the dilemma: Either the words of Institution alone and, therefore, not
the Epiklesis, are productive of the conversion, or the words of the Epiklesis alone have such power and not the words of Institution. Of more
considerable importance is the circumstance that the whole question came
up for discussion in the council for union held at Florence in 1439. Pope
Eugene IV urged the Greeks to come to a unanimous agreement with the
Roman faith and subscribe to the words of Institution as alone constituting
the sacramental form, and to drop the contention that the words of the
Epiklesis also possessed a partial consecratory force. But when the Greeks,
not without foundation, pleaded that a dogmatic decision would reflect
with shame upon their whole ecclesiastical past, the ecumenical synod was
satisfied with the oral declaration of Cardinal Blessarion recorded in the
minutes of the council for 5 July, 1439 (P. G., CLXI, 491), namely, that
the Greeks follow the universal teaching of the Fathers, especially of
"blessed John Chrysostom, familiarly known to us," according to whom
the "Divine words of Our Redeemer contain the full and entire force of
Transubstantiation."

The venerable antiquity of the Oriental Epiklesis, its peculiar position in
the Canon of the Mass, and its interior spiritual unction, oblige the theologian to determine its dogmatic value and to account for its use. Take, for
instance, the Epiklesis of the Ethiopian Liturgy: "We implore and beseech
Thee, O Lord, to send forth the Holy Spirit and His Power upon this Bread
and Chalice and convert them into the Body and Blood of Our Lord Jesus
Christ." Since this prayer always follows after the words of Institution
have been pronounced, the theological question arises as to how it may be
made to harmonize with the words of Christ, which alone possess the
consecratory power. Two explanations have been suggested, which, however, can be merged in one. The first view considers the Epiklesis to be a
mere declaration of the fact that the conversion has already taken place,
and that in the conversion just as essential a part is to be attributed to the
Holy Spirit as Co-Consecrator as in the allied mystery of the Incarnation.
Since, however, because of the brevity of the actual instant of conversion,
the part taken by the Holy Spirit could not be expressed, the Epiklesis takes
us back in imagination to the precious moment and regards the Consecration as just about to occur. A similar purely psychological retrospective
transfer is met with in other portions of the Liturgy, as in the Mass for the
Dead, wherein the Church prays for the departed as if they were still upon
their bed of agony and could still be rescued from the gates of hell. Thus
considered, the Epiklesis refers us back to the Consecration as the centre
about which all the significance contained in its words revolves. A second
explanation is based, not upon the enacted Consecration, but upon the
approaching Communion, inasmuch as the latter, being the effective means

of uniting us more closely in the organized body of the Church, brings forth in our hearts the mystical Christ, as is read in the Roman Canon of the Mass: "Ut *nobis* corpus et sanguis fiat," i.e., that it may be made *for us* the body and blood. It was in this purely mystical manner that the Greeks themselves explained the meaning of the Epiklesis at the Council of Florence (Mansi, Collect. Concil., XXXI, 106). Yet since much more is contained in the plain words than this true and deep mysticism, it is desirable to combine both explanations into one, and so we may regard the Epiklesis, both in point of liturgy and of time, as the significant connecting link, placed midway between the Consecration and the Communion in order to emphasize the part taken by the Holy Spirit in the Consecration of bread and wine, and, on the other hand, with the help of the same Holy Spirit to obtain the realization of the true Presence of the Body and Blood of Christ by their fruitful effects on both priest and people. . . .

(3) The Effects of the Holy Eucharist

The doctrine of the Church regarding the effects or the fruits of Holy Communion centres around two ideas: (a) the union with Christ by love and (b) the spiritual repast of the soul. Both ideas are often verified in one and the same effect of Holy Communion.

(a) The first and principal effect of the Holy Eucharist is union with Christ by love (Decr. pro Armenis: *adunatio ad Christum*), which union as such does not consist in the sacramental reception of the Host, but in the spiritual and mystical union with Jesus by the theological virtue of love. Christ Himself designated the idea of Communion as a union by love: "He that eateth my flesh, and drinketh my blood, abideth in me, and I in him" (John, vi, 57). St. Cyril of Alexandria (Hom. in Joan., IV, xvii) beautifully represents this mystical union as the fusion of our being into that of the God-man, as "when melted wax is fused with other wax." Since the Sacrament of Love is not satisfied with an increase of habitual love only, but tends especially to fan the flame of actual love to an intense ardour, the Holy Eucharist is specifically distinguished from the other sacraments, and hence it is precisely in this latter effect that Suarez recognizes the so-called "grace of the sacrament," which otherwise is so hard to discern. It stands to reason that the essence of this union by love consists neither in a natural union with Jesus analogous to that between soul and body, nor in a hypostatic union of the soul with the Person of the Word, nor finally in a pantheistical deification of the communicant, but simply in a moral but wonderful union with Christ by the bond of the most ardent charity. Hence the chief effect of a worthy Communion is to a certain extent a foretaste of heaven, in fact the anticipation and pledge of our future union with God by love in the Beatific Vision. He alone can properly estimate the precious boon which Catholics possess in the Holy Eucharist, who knows how to ponder these ideas of Holy Communion to their utmost depth. The immediate result of this union with Christ by love is the bond of charity existing between the faithful themselves, as St. Paul says: "For we, being many, are one bread, one body, all that partake of one bread" (I Cor., x, 17). And so the Communion of Saints is not merely an ideal union by faith and grace, but an eminently real union, mysteriously constituted, maintained, and guaranteed by partaking in common of one and the same Christ.

(b) A second fruit of this union with Christ by love is an increase of sanctifying grace in the soul of the worthy communicant. Here let it be remarked at the outset, that the Holy Eucharist does not *per se* constitute a person in the state of grace as do the sacraments of the dead (baptism and penance), but presupposes such a state. It is, therefore, one of the sacraments of the living. It is as impossible for the soul in the state of mortal sin to receive this Heavenly Bread with profit, as it is for a corpse to assimilate food and drink. Hence the Council of Trent (Sess. XIII, can. v), in opposition to Luther and Calvin, purposely defined that the "chief fruit of the Eucharist does not consist in the forgiveness of sins." For though Christ said of the Chalice: "This is my blood of the new testament, which shall be shed for many unto remission of sins" (Matt., xxvi, 28), He had in view an effect of the sacrifice, not of the sacrament; for He did not say that His Blood would be drunk unto remission of sins, but shed for that purpose. It is for this very reason that St. Paul (I Cor., xi, 28) demands that rigorous "self-examination," in order to avoid the heinous offence of being guilty of the Body and the Blood of the Lord by "eating and drinking unworthily," and that the Fathers insist upon nothing so energetically as upon a pure and innocent conscience. In spite of the principles just laid down, the question might be asked, if the Blessed Sacrament could not at times *per accidens* free the communicant from mortal sin, if he approached the Table of the Lord unconscious of the sinful state of his soul. Presupposing what is self-evident, that there is question neither of a conscious sacrilegious Communion nor a lack of imperfect contrition *(attritio),* which would altogether hinder the justifying effect of the sacrament, theologians incline to the opinion that in such exceptional cases the Eucharist can restore the soul to the state of grace, but all without exception deny the possibility of the reviviscence of a sacrilegious or unfruitful Communion after the restoration of the soul's proper moral condition has been effected, the Eucharist being different in this respect from the sacraments which imprint a character upon the soul (baptism, confirmation, and Holy orders). Together with the increase of sanctifying grace there is associated another effect, namely, a certain spiritual relish or delight of soul *(delectatio spiritualis).* Just as food and drink delight and refresh the heart of man, so does this "Heavenly Bread containing within itself all sweetness" produce in the soul of the devout communicant ineffable bliss, which, however, is not to be confounded with an emotional joy of the soul or with sensible sweetness. Although both may occur as the result of a special grace, its true nature is manifested in a certain cheerful and willing fervour in all that regards Christ and His Church, and in the conscious fulfillment of the duties of one's state of life, a disposition of soul which is perfectly compatible with interior desolation and spiritual dryness. A good Communion is recognized less in the transitory sweetness of the emotions than in its lasting practical effects on the conduct of our daily lives.

(c) Though Holy Communion does not *per se* remit mortal sin, it has nevertheless the third effect of "blotting our venial sin and preserving the soul from mortal sin" (Council of Trent, Sess. XIII, cap. ii). The Holy Eucharist is not merely a food, but a medicine as well. The destruction of venial sin, and of all affection to it, is readily understood on the basis of the two central ideas mentioned above. Just as material food banishes minor bodily weaknesses and preserves man's physical strength from being impaired, so does this food of our souls remove our lesser spiritual ailments and preserve us from spiritual death. As a union based upon love, the Holy Eucharist cleanses with its purifying flame the smallest stains which adhere to the soul, and at the same time serves as an effective prophylactic against grievous sin. It remains for us to ascertain with clearness only the manner in which this preservative influence against relapse into mortal sin is exerted. According to the teaching of the Roman Catechism, it is effected by the allaying of concupiscence, which is the chief source of deadly sin, particularly of impurity. Therefore it is that spiritual writers recommend frequent Communion as the most effective remedy against impurity, since its powerful influence is felt even after other means have proved unavailing (cf. St. Thomas, III, Q. lxxix, a. 6). Whether or not the Holy Eucharist is directly conducive to the remission of the temporal punishment due to sin, is disputed by St. Thomas (ibid., a. 5), since the Blessed Sacrament of the Altar was not instituted as a means of satisfaction; it does, however, produce an indirect effect in this regard, which is proportioned to the communicant's love and devotion. The case is different as regards the effects of grace in behalf of a third party. The pious custom of the faithful of "offering their Communion" for relations, friends, and the souls departed, is to be considered as possessing unquestionable value, in the first place, because an earnest prayer of petition in the presence of the Spouse of our souls will readily find a hearing, and then, because the fruits of Communion as a means of satisfaction for sin may be applied to a third person, and especially *per modum suffragii* to the souls in purgatory.

(d) As a last effect we may mention that the Eucharist is the "pledge of our glorious resurrection and eternal happiness" (Council of Trent, Sess. XIII, cap. ii), according to the promise of Christ: "He that eateth my flesh and drinketh my blood, hath everlasting life: and I will raise him up on the last day." Hence the chief reason why the ancient Fathers, as Ignatius (Ephes., 20), Irenæus (Adv. haer., IV, xviii, 4), and Tertullian (De resurr. carn., viii), as well as later patristic writers, insisted so strongly upon our future resurrection, was the circumstance that it is the door by which we enter upon unending happiness. There can be nothing incongruous or improper in the fact that the body also shares in this effect of Communion, since by its physical contact with the Eucharistic Species, and hence (indirectly) with the living Flesh of Christ, it acquires a moral right to its future resurrection, even as the Blessed Mother of God, inasmuch as she was the former abode of the Word made flesh, acquired a moral claim to her own bodily assumption into heaven. The further discussion as to whether some "physical quality" (Contenson) or a "sort of germ of immortality" (Heimbucher) is implanted in the body of the communicant, has no sufficient foundation in the teaching of the Fathers and may, therefore, be dismissed without any injury to dogma. . . .

(4) The Necessity of the Holy Eucharist for Salvation

We distinguish two kinds of necessity, (1) the necessity of means *(necessitas medii)* and (2) the necessity of precept *(necessitas praecepti)*. In the first sense a thing or action is necessary because without it a given end cannot be attained; the eye, e.g., is necessary for vision. The second sort of necessity is that which is imposed by the free will of a superior, e.g., the necessity of fasting. As regards Communion a further distinction must be made between infants and adults. It is easy to prove that in the case of infants Holy Communion is not necessary to salvation, either as a means or as a precept. Since they have not as yet attained to the use of reason, they are free from the obligation of positive laws; consequently, the only question is whether Communion is, like Baptism, necessary for them as a means of salvation. Now the Council of Trent, under pain of anathema, solemnly rejects such a necessity (Sess. XXI, can. iv) and declares that the custom of the primitive Church of giving Holy Communion to children was not based upon the erroneous belief of its necessity to salvation, but upon the circumstances of the times (Sess. XXI, cap. iv). Since according to St. Paul's teaching (Rom., viii, 1) there is "no condemnation" for those who have been baptized, every child that dies in its baptismal innocence, even without Communion, must go straight to heaven. This latter position was that usually taken by the Fathers, with the exception of St. Augustine, who from the universal custom of the Communion of children drew the conclusion of its necessity for salvation. On the other hand, Communion is prescribed for adults, not only by the law of the Church, but also by a Divine command (John, vi, 50 sqq.), though for its absolute necessity as a means to salvation there is no more evidence than in the case of infants. For such a necessity could be established only on the supposition that Communion *per se* constituted a person in the state of grace or that this state could not be preserved without Communion. Neither supposition is correct. Not the first, for the simple reason that the Blessed Eucharist, being a sacrament of the living, presupposes the state of sanctifying grace; not the second, because in case of necessity, such as might arise, e.g., in a long sea-voyage, the Eucharistic graces may be supplied by actual graces. It is only when viewed in this light that we can understand how the primitive Church, without going counter to the Divine command, withheld the Eucharist from certain sinners even on their deathbeds. There is, however, a moral necessity on the part of adults to receive Holy Communion, as a means, for instance, of overcoming violent temptation, or as a viaticum for persons in danger of death. Eminent divines, like Suarez, claim that the Eucharist, if not absolutely necessary, is at least a relatively and morally necessary means to salvation, in the sense that no adult can long sustain his spiritual, supernatural life who neglects on principle to approach Holy Communion. This view is supported, not only by the solemn and earnest words of Christ, when He promised the Eucharist, and by the very nature of the sacrament as the spiritual food and medicine of our souls, but also by the fact of the helplessness and perversity of human nature and by the daily experience of confessors and directors of souls.

Since Christ has left us no definite precept as to the frequency with which He desired us to receive Him in Holy Communion, it belongs to the Church to determine the Divine command more accurately and prescribe what the limits of time shall be for the reception of the sacrament. In the course of centuries the Church's discipline in this respect has undergone considerable change. Whereas the early Christians were accustomed to receive at every celebration of the Liturgy, which probably was not celebrated daily in all places, or were in the habit of Communicating privately in their own homes every day of the week, a falling-off in the frequency of Communion is noticeable since the fourth century. Even in his time Pope Fabian (236–250) made it obligatory to approach the Holy Table three times a year, viz. at Christmas, Easter, and Pentecost, and this custom was still prevalent in the sixth century [cf. Synod of Agde (506), e. xviii]. Although St. Augustine left daily Communion to the free choice of the individual, his admonition, in force even at the present day, was: *Sic vive, ut quotidie possis sumere* (De dono persev., c. xiv), i.e. "So live, that you may receive every day." From the tenth to the thirteenth century, the practice of going to Communion more frequently during the year was rather rare among the laity and obtained only in cloistered communities. St. Bonaventure reluctantly allowed the lay brothers of his monastery to approach the Holy Table weekly, whereas the rule of the Canons of Chrodegang prescribed this practice. When the Fourth Council of Lateran (1215), held under Innocent III, mitigated the former severity of the Church's law to the extent that all Catholics of both sexes were to communicate at least once a year, and this during the paschal season, St. Thomas (III, Q. lxxx, a. 10) ascribed this ordinance chiefly to the "reign of impiety and the growing cold of charity." The precept of the yearly paschal Communion was solemnly reiterated by the Council of Trent (Sess. XIII, can. ix). The mystical theologians of the later Middle Ages, as Eckhart, Tauler, St. Vincent Ferrer, Savonarola, and later on St. Philip Neri, the Jesuit Order, St. Francis de Sales, and St. Alphonsus Liguori were zealous champions of frequent Communion; whereas the Jansenists, under the leadership of Antoine Arnauld (De la fréquente communion, Paris, 1643), strenuously opposed them and demanded as a condition for every Communion the "most perfect penitential dispositions and the purest love of God." This rigorism was condemned by Pope Alexander VIII (7 Dec., 1690); the Council of Trent (Sess. XIII, cap. viii; Sess. XXII, cap. vi) and Innocent XI (12 Feb., 1679) had already emphasized the permissibility of even daily Communion. To root out the last vestiges of Jansenistic rigorism, Pius X issued a decree (24 Dec., 1905) wherein he allows and recommends daily Communion to the entire laity and requires but two conditions for its permissibility, namely, the state of grace and a right and pious intention.

27

William Stevens

The Lord's Supper

The Lord's Supper is an ordinance instituted by our Lord while here on earth. Sometimes the ordinance is called communion; but such is not an adequate name, for it applies to only one aspect of the rite. It is found in I Corinthians 10:16: "The bread which we break, is it not a communion of the body of Christ?" The Greek word translated "communion" is better translated "participation," for the ordinance concerns not so much communion one with another (or fellowship) as communion with the Lord.

Another name sometimes used for this rite is Eucharist, which is derived from the Greek word *eucharistēsas,* translated "give thanks," in Jesus' words concerning the cup in Matthew 26:27. Later in Christian history the two elements came to be regarded as thank-offerings, thereby making the term *Eucharist* even more appropriate. However, this concept is purely unscriptural, so this term is undersirable also.

The Roman Catholic term *Mass,* their term for the Lord's Supper and one of their seven sacraments, is unscriptural and unwarranted. It is a contraction of the Latin *missa est,* a phrase equivalent to "it is over" and used as a dismissal formula. The term *sacrament* should not be used for the

From *Doctrines of the Christian Religion* (Grand Rapids: Wm. B. Eerdmans Pub. Co., 1967), pp. 341–350. Used by permission.

Lord's Supper any more than it should for baptism, although many denominations use this term instead of "ordinance." The Bible refers to the Lord's Supper as "the breaking of bread" (Acts 2:42 and Acts 20:7). This is a good scriptural term which, for some reason or other, has not caught on. The term *Lord's Supper* is still the best available for this rite.

1. Scriptural Teaching

(1) Instituted by Jesus

The following scriptural passages depict the institution of the Lord's Supper: Matthew 26:26-29; Mark 14:22-25; Luke 22:17-20; and I Corinthians 11:23-26. The Matthew passage and Mark passage are similar to each other; the Luke passage and the First Corinthians passage are similar one to the other. The Matthew passage is as follows: "And as they were eating, Jesus took bread, and blessed, and brake it; and he gave to the disciples, and said, Take, eat; this is my body. And he took a cup, and gave thanks, and gave to them, saying, Drink ye all of it; for this is my blood of the covenant, which is poured out for many unto remission of sins. But I say unto you, I shall not drink henceforth of this fruit of the vine, until that day when I drink it new with you in my Father's kingdom." The bread represents his body and the wine his blood, a symbolical representation; Jesus definitely does not speak literally.

Paul's account, which is very similar to that of Luke, is as follows: "For I received of the Lord that which also I delivered unto you, that the Lord Jesus in the night in which he was betrayed took bread; and when he had given thanks, he brake it, and said, This is my body, which is for you: this do in remembrance of me. In like manner also the cup, after supper, saying, This cup is the new covenant in my blood: this do, as often as ye drink it, in remembrance of me. For as often as ye eat this bread, and drink the cup, ye proclaim the Lord's death till he come.

From these passages we see that Jesus instituted and gave the Lord's Supper to his apostles and through them to all of his disciples through the ages. It is truly the Lord's Supper. Just how or where Paul "received of the Lord" is hard to determine, but it must have been through some special revelation. Paul also quotes Jesus as using the phrase "as often as ye drink it," thereby revealing his desire that we should perpetuate the rite.

Therefore Jesus instituted the rite and meant for it to be observed until his second coming. In fact, only after his death could its purpose as a commemorative feast be meaningful. The uniform practice, as seen in the New Testament and early churches, in keeping this important rite shows that the disciples so understood Jesus' remarks relative to the Supper. "And they continued stedfastly in the apostles' teaching and fellowship, in the breaking of bread and the prayers" (Acts 2:42).

(2) Analogous to Passover Meal

It was during the passover, or paschal, meal that Jesus delivered to the apostles the Lord's Supper. He instructed two of his apostles to prepare for the passover in an upper room. On the appointed evening, the fifteenth day of the Jewish month Nisan, Jesus met with the twelve to partake of the paschal lamb, the unleavened bread, the wine, and the bitter herbs. Toward the end of the meal ("and as they were eating") he instituted the Lord's Supper; this was probably after Judas had left the company for the purpose of betraying him.

What the passover was to the Jew the Lord's Supper is to the Christian, and more! The passover was a memorial feast, a yearly reminder that God had delivered them out of bondage in Egypt. God did not want them to forget for a moment that he had passed over their houses in Egypt, the houses with the blood of the lamb on the doorposts and the lintel, and had not killed their firstborn, but had killed the firstborn in every Egyptian house. The Lord's Supper is a memorial feast also, a memorial of the fact that Jesus has redeemed us out of the bondage of sin into the glorious light of his eternal love. In regard to eating the bread Jesus says, "This do in remembrance of me" (I Cor. 11:24); in regard to drinking the cup he says, "This do, as often as ye drink it, in remembrance of me" (I Cor. 11:25). The whole rite is a memorial of Calvary and its redeeming power. In addition, Paul remarks, "For our passover also hath been sacrificed, even Christ" (I Cor. 5:7). He is our Paschal Lamb, and the Lord's Supper is our paschal meal. It is our redemption feast. Paul's use of the word *our* shows that the Lord's Supper is the New Testament antitype of the Old Testament prototype, the passover. According to John's Gospel Jesus was crucified on the day the paschal lamb was slain, the fourteenth day of Nisan, the day of preparation. Paul's naming Jesus our passover correlates with the Johannine view.

Yet there is another way that the Lord's Supper is correlative to the Jewish passover. The passover not only looked back to the great deliverance from Egypt; it also looked forward to a new deliverance by the Messiah for whom the Jews looked in anticipation. There was an eschatological aspect to the paschal meal. Likewise with the Lord's Supper, for in the observance of it the participants do "proclaim the Lord's death till he come" (I Cor. 11:26)—preach Calvary till the second advent. This also has an eschatological aspect.

2. Mode

(1) The Elements

The followers of Christ are to partake of both the bread and the cup. The bread used by Jesus was doubtless the unleavened bread of the passover meal, as the wine he used was doubtless the fermented juice of the grape. But this does not mean that we must of necessity use unleavened bread, nor does it mean that we cannot use the unfermented juice of the grape. Unleavened bread is what Jesus had at hand, and his phrase "fruit of the vine" in Matthew 26:29 would include unfermented juice as well. The bread and the cup are symbolical only. To insist on literalism would be tantamount to legalism.

(2) Both Elements Essential

Christ says, in speaking of the cup, "Drink ye all of it" (Matt. 26:27). Yet the Roman Catholic Church withholds the cup from the laity; only the priest partakes of it. This has been the case since the Council of Constance in 1415. The communicant receives only the bread, which Catholics term the "host," or "wafer consecrated in the Eucharist." The Roman Church withholds the cup in spite of the fact that it believes the bread and wine actually become the body and blood of Christ respectively. This withholding is directly a disobedience of the command of Christ when he says, "Drink ye all of it." Mark tells us that "they all drank of it" (Mark 14:23). Such withholding would imply that the communicant receives only a portion of the benefits of the death of Christ. The Greek Orthodox Church does not withhold the cup from the laity as the Roman Church does; the bread and wine are mixed and given by means of a spoon.

(3) Function of Assembled Church

The Lord's Supper was never intended to be administered as an individual act. Rather, it was intended as something for the church assembled. Luke says in the "we" section of Acts, "And upon the first day of the week, when we were gathered together to break bread, Paul discoursed with them" (20:7). The same idea is found in the longer passage, I Corinthians 11:17–34. This would indicate that the Lord's Supper is not intended as a solitary observance for individuals. Nowhere in the New Testament do we find the Lord's Supper celebrated in each family by itself. No individual has a right to partake of it alone, nor does a minister have the similar right to administer it at the sickbed. When Paul gives his instructions in I Corinthians 11 he is talking to "the church of God which is at Corinth" (I Cor. 1:2).

(4) Frequency of Observance

Since the New Testament gives no specific direction as to how often the Lord's Supper should be observed, each local church should decide the issue. We have biblical examples of what appear to be daily and weekly observances. "And day by day, continuing stedfastly with one accord in the temple, and breaking bread . . ." (Acts 2:46). "And upon the first day of the week, when we were gathered together to break bread . . ." (Acts 20:7). Jesus' phrase, "as often as ye drink it" (I Cor. 11:25), is the nearest approach to any instruction relative to frequency, and this statement is certainly not definite. Some churches observe the rite on every Lord's day; some observe it every three months; some observe it every six months; and some go for longer periods yet.

3. Meaning

There are four main views that have been attached to the Lord's Supper through the centuries. Every present-day denomination holds to one of these four views, with modifications here or there.

(1) Roman Catholic

The Roman Catholic view, commonly called transubstantiation, is that the substance of the bread and the wine is actually changed into the body and blood of Christ. This was formally enunciated in 1551 in the Decrees and Canons of the Council of Trent, at which time all other views were condemned. The decree concerning this "sacrament" is long, but a significant statement is as follows:

> And because that Christ our Redeemer declared that which he offered under the species of bread to be truly his own body, therefore, has it ever been the firm belief in the Church of God, and this holy Synod doth now declare it anew, that by the consecration of the bread and of the wine a conversion is made of the whole substance of the bread into the body of Christ our Lord, and of the whole substance of the wine into the substance of his blood; which conversion is by the Holy Catholic Church suitably and properly called transubstantiation.

This is the belief that the bread and wine are changed by sacerdotal consecration into the very body and blood of Christ, thus reenacting Christ's atoning sacrifice. The partaking of these elements mediates saving grace from God to the communicant.

Our reply is that this view constitutes a false interpretation of Scripture, for it rests upon a literal interpretation of the figurative language in our Lord's institution of this important rite. When Jesus said, "This is my body," he meant, "This is a symbol of my body." Transubstantiation is as preposterous today as it was absurd for the initial event that first evening. It is absurd that a priest should change a small wafer and a small bit of wine into the real body and blood of Christ, and it is even more absurd to think that an unfit priest could work a divine miracle such as this.

> There is no word of a sacramental magic happening, of a "miracle" either in the account of the first Lord's Supper or in Paul—who is indeed the only person who gives instruction about the Lord's Supper (I Cor. 10:16, 17). How could there be the thought of any such thing, seeing that in the first celebration of the Supper the broken body and the shed blood were still present, unbroken and unshed in the bodily presence of Jesus?[1]

Besides, such a view changes that which was meant for a symbolism into an object of worship, not to mention the fact that it contradicts the evidence of our senses. If we cannot trust our senses here, how can we trust them anywhere? It denies the "once and for all" view of Christ's sacrifice, implying the necessity for a priestly repetition of this atoning act, or implying that further sacrificial acts are necessary in a supplemental sense. This view of what the Catholics call the Mass, or Eucharist, must of necessity be dismissed.

(2) Lutheran

The Lutheran view, commonly called consubstantiation, is that the body and blood of Christ are truly present in the elements of bread and wine and are therefore taken by the communicant. The communicant eats the true body and drinks the true blood of Christ in the bread and wine; yet these elements, in contrast to the view of transubstantiation, do not cease to be material. This is clearly stated in the Augsburg Confession, Article X: "Of the Supper of the Lord they teach that the body and blood of Christ are truly present and are there communicated to those that eat in the Lord's Supper." The later German edition adds after the words, "are truly present," the words, "under the form of bread and wine." Later statements yet attempt to elaborate the view and to contrast it with opposing doctrines (Roman Catholic and Reformed). This view also led to further argumentation as to the mode of the Lord's presence in the elements. It is held by the Lutherans and High Church Episcopalians.

Our reply to this view is that it is as unscriptural as the Roman view and leads to psychological questionings and unnecessary mysteries. Explanations are of necessity highly involved and unsatisfactory. This belief cannot be separated from the sacramental system of which it is a part; for it makes materialistic elements the means and condition for receiving Christ, thus violating the simple doctrine of justification by faith alone. The rite becomes a means of salvation, a means of grace. This view, like that of transubstantiation, requires a priestly, or sacerdotal, order to consecrate the elements. The miracle demanded is practically the same as in the Roman view. The whole theory tends toward ritualism.

(3) Calvinistic

The Calvinistic view is that the body and blood of Christ are dynamically present in the elements of bread and wine. This view mediates between that held by Luther and that held by Zwingli and was the view of the Reformed Churches as distinguished from the Lutheran Church in the Reformation. It is held by some Presbyterians and some Episcopalians. A good statement of this view is as follows:

> While Calvin denied the real presence of the body and blood of Christ in the eucharist, in the sense in which that presence was asserted by Romanists and Lutherans; yet he affirmed that they were dynamically present. The sun is in the heaven, but from that glorified body there radiates an influence other than the influence of the Spirit (although through his agency) of which believers, in the Lord's Supper, are the recipients. In this way they receive the body and blood of Christ, or their substance or life-giving power.[2]

Therefore it is plainly discerned that this view argues for the miraculous even in this "dynamic presence" of the body and blood of Christ.

Our reply is that this view is too vacillating, too wavering. Its lack of definiteness necessitates its nonacceptance. We turn now to the simplest view of all.

(4) Zwinglian

This view, that the two elements are symbolical of the body and blood of Christ offered up as a sacrifice for our sins, is the view held by most evangelical Christians and is the one that most nearly fits all the conditions surrounding this important rite. Zwingli, a contemporary of Martin Luther, opposed Luther hotly on his view of the Lord's Supper.

This view is [that the Lord's Supper is] commemorative, since it looks back to his death. "This do in remembrance of me" (Luke 22:19). As the passover was commemorative of a great deliverance for Israel, so the Lord's Supper is commemorative of a great deliverance for the Christian, a spiritual deliverance from sin by the death of the Son of God. It is related to the present, since it is a proclamation of Christ's death till he comes. "For as often as ye eat this bread, and drink the cup, ye proclaim the Lord's death till he come" (I Cor. 11:26). It is a public proclaiming, a means of confessing Christ and of witnessing to our faith in the saving power of his death. It is anticipatory, since it looks forward to the coming perfection of life in the kingdom of God. It looks toward future glory, the great festival, "the marriage supper of the Lamb" (Rev. 19:9). "But I say unto you, I shall not drink henceforth of this fruit of the vine, until that day when I drink it new with you in my Father's kingdom" (Matt. 26:29).

The Lord's Supper has no regenerative power, it possesses no sanctifying grace. There is nothing magical or mystical about its nature. It is a symbol of the relation of the believer to Christ, who alone does the sanctifying. The outward tokens devised by Christ himself are the symbols of the atoning power and forgiving love of his great sacrifice, which was once and for all efficacious. The sacrifice cannot be, and does not have to be, reenacted by priests down through the centuries. This view is made explicit in the Heidelberg Catechism and is held by Baptists, by some Presbyterians, and generally by Methodists.

The Lord's Supper seems to convey a threefold symbolism.

a. *Symbol of Death of Christ for Our Sins.* Concerning the bread Jesus says, "This is my body, which is given for you," and concerning the cup, "This cup is the new covenant in my blood, even that which is poured out for you" (Luke 22:19, 20). Paul says, "For as often as ye eat this bread, and drink the cup, ye proclaim the Lord's death till he come" (I Cor. 11:26). His blood seals the new covenant between God and man, the covenant upon which our salvation depends. It is the blood of the atoning death of our Lord, poured forth that we might live. His death constitutes the giving of his life "a ransom for many" (Matt. 20:28), of which the Lord's Supper is an eternal and proclaiming witness. "Body and blood, then, represent and fitly symbolize two different aspects of sacrifice—namely the dedicated victim and the sacrificed life."[3] Therefore we see that Jesus himself regarded his death as the climax of his great redemptive act and the crowning glory of his atoning work. It is the supreme sacrifice eternally remitting sin. The Lord's Supper attests to this central place of his death in the mind of Jesus.

b. *Symbol of Appropriation of Benefits of That Death for Believer.* Jesus says, "This is my body, which is for you" (I Cor. 11:24). Paul says, of Jesus, "For our passover also hath been sacrificed, even Christ" (I Cor.

5:7). Just as the paschal lamb symbolized for the Israelites deliverance from the bondage of Egypt, so the Lord's Supper symbolizes for the Christian deliverance from the bondage of sin, which is the appropriation of the benefits of his death.

c. *Symbol of Means of That Appropriation: Union with Christ.* Through union with Christ one appropriates the saving benefits of his death; this also is symbolized in the Lord's Supper. Paul states, "The cup of blessing which we bless, is it not a communion of the blood of Christ? The bread which we break, is it not a communion of the body of Christ?" (I Cor. 10:16). The word translated "communion" is *koinōnia,* which is usually translated "fellowship" in the New Testament. Here it can easily be translated "participation," as it is in the marginal reading of the American Standard Version. So what Paul is virtually saying is: "Does it not symbolize the participation in . . . ?" This union with Christ is also signified in the statement: "Verily, verily, I say unto you, Except ye eat the flesh of the Son of man and drink his blood, ye have not life in yourselves" (John 6:53). This spiritual union with Christ is symbolized in the Lord's Supper.

4. Administrator

All the decisions relative to the administration of the Lord's Supper should rest with the church, including who should lead in the service as well as who should assist. Normally it is understood that the pastor assumes the leadership in observance and is aided by the deacons. However, in case there is temporarily no pastor, the church can appoint one of its members to direct the observance. As in baptism, merely the laying on of hands in ordination to the ministry does not invest with authority to administer the Lord's Supper. . . . The church must decide in all cases relative to administration.

5. Prerequisites to Participation

Jesus did not give the Supper to the world at large, but only to his disciples. Then what are the requirements for its celebration?

(1) Regeneration

The Lord's Supper is symbolical of spiritual life in the believer, the one partaking. Therefore, [for the Lord's Supper] to be partaken of by one who is spiritually dead, one who is "dead through . . . trespasses and sins," would be a desecration of that which is holy. As the physically dead do not need physical food, the spiritually dead do not need the food symbolical of the sacrificial and atoning death of our Lord. There is no evidence in the New Testament of the Supper being administered to unbelievers. "Wherefore whosoever shall eat the bread or drink the cup of the Lord in an unworthy manner, shall be guilty of the body and the blood of the Lord. But let a man prove himself, and so let him eat of the bread, and drink of the cup. For he that eateth and drinketh, eateth and drinketh judgment unto himself, if he discern not the body" (I Cor. 11:27–29). How could one not a Christian "discern the body"? This would necessitate saving faith, which he does not possess.

(2) Baptism

It appears from various New Testament readings that the apostles celebrating the Lord's Supper had been baptized. Peter, in speaking to the one hundred and twenty soon after Jesus' ascension, says, "Of the men therefore that have companied with us all the time that the Lord Jesus went in and went out among us, beginning from the baptism of John, unto the day that he was received up from us, of these must one become a witness with us of his resurrection" (Acts 1:21, 22). Then they select one to take Judas' place. The phrase "from the baptism of John" is very significant. Christ is baptized by John, and it is very probable that he selects for his apostles only those who likewise have submitted to John's baptism. And he definitely recognizes John's baptism as being ordained of God (Matt. 21:25).

Besides this fact, Jesus places baptism as first in prominence after profession of faith. "Go ye therefore, and make disciples of all the nations, baptizing them into the name of the Father and of the Son and of the Holy Spirit: teaching them to observe all things whatsoever I commanded you" (Matt. 28:19, 20). Make disciples, then baptize—this is the order in the command of Christ. If it is argued that there is no formal command in the Bible to admit to the Lord's Supper only those who have been baptized, it can also be stated that there is no formal command that only the regenerate may be baptized. In both cases we must judge from the practice of the apostles as that practice is discerned in the New Testament. Statements such as the following show this: "They then that received his word were baptized. . . . And day by day, continuing stedfastly with one accord in the temple, and breaking bread . . ." (Acts 2:41, 46).

(3) Church Membership

The Lord's Supper is a church rite, to be observed by the assembled church. Therefore does it not follow that church membership is a prerequisite to participation? Luke speaks of "the first day of the week, when we were gathered together to break bread" (Acts 20:7). Paul's admonition to the Corinthians in regard to the Lord's Supper is directed to the whole church (I Cor. 11). The Lord's Supper is a symbol of fellowship, fellowship with the Lord and with one another. "We, who are many, are one bread, one body: for we all partake of the one bread" (I Cor. 10:17).

Notes

[1]Emil Brunner, *The Christian Doctrine of the Church, Faith, and the Consummation*, III, 61, 62.

[2]Charles Hodge, *Systematic Theology*, III. 611ff.

[3]L. S. Thornton, *The Common Life in the Body of Christ*, p. 331.

PART THREE

The New Life in Future Extension

Editor's Introduction

We come now to the doctrine of the last things or eschatology as it is known technically in theology. Our day has seen a great revival of interest in the future. This shows itself in the interest in death and in life after death. It is also manifested in the interest in attempted contacts with people from the other world and also in the revival of doctrinal speculation regarding the future. The Christian faith has a great deal to say about the future. Indeed, a rather major portion of Scripture points ahead to what is yet to happen.

We begin with basic conceptions of the nature of eschatology. The traditional view is represented by **James O. Buswell,** taking eschatology in a rather literal sense of the word. Here eschatology deals with the events and conditions of the future, the last things temporally. **C. H. Dodd,** on the other hand, presents the view of "realized eschatology"—that the "last things" have already taken place. Thus, the Day of the Lord spoken of by the Old Testament prophets was fulfilled in the life and person of Jesus. The new age has already come to pass—it is not something toward which we should still be looking forward. **Rudolf Bultmann,** however, detemporalizes eschatology. It is not something future, or past either, for that matter. It is true of every moment of existence. This is an existential form of eschatology.

Here arises the question of the intermediate state, that is, the issue of the condition of persons between death and resurrection. A number of answers have been given to this question. The traditional Roman Catholic view conceives of a number of states or even "compartments" of the afterlife. Some, totally outside the faith, go directly to hell. Some believers are so perfectly penitent and sanctified at the moment of death that they go immediately to heaven. Most Christians, however, must enter purgatory, a place of expiation and spiritual perfecting. When this process is complete, they may enter heaven. Some, such as Seventh Day Adventists, Jehovah's Witnesses, and a few recent theologians, have held that the soul reposes in a state of unconsciousness, a sort of dreamless sleep, from death to resurrection.

The customary Protestant view is that between death and resurrection the person exists in an incomplete state, similar to the permanent final state, but less intense. In older forms of this view, such as that presented here by **William G. T. Shedd,** the soul survives separate from the body, in a disembodied condition. More recent forms of the Protestant view, recognizing that energy and matter are interconvertible, speak in terms of materialized and immaterialized states of being. Yet another recent view, presented here by **W. D. Davies,** is that a person immediately upon death receives a new body. This of course eliminates any need for a future resurrection.

The traditional understanding of the events surrounding the second coming of Christ has been that Christ will return in a bodily, literal, personal fashion, in much the same manner as his disciples saw him departing (Acts 1:11). At the time of his return there will be a resurrection of those who are dead and then a time of judgment in which there will be a separation of the righteous from the unrighteous. While the details of the order of these events and what other events may intervene differ in the understanding of various conservative Christians, there nonetheless is basic consensus on this fact, that at a definite point in history the Lord will return, the resurrection will take place, and there will be judgment. This view is expounded by **E. Y. Mullins** in the selection that we have here. A quite different approach is that of **Harry Emerson Fosdick.** Fosdick was one of those known as modernists, who attempt to update the Christian faith by retaining what they consider the historic essentials of the faith and placing them in categories that make sense to modern man. They believe that the biblical way of stating these truths is now outmoded. In his book, *The Modern Use of the Bible,* Fosdick says we must attempt to determine the unchanging experiences which are the substance of biblical faith, and then, rather than continue to state them in the outmoded form of expression found in Scripture, restate them, using categories drawn from modern man's experience. Thus he asks what the doctrine of the second coming represents. The traditional view, of course, is that Christ is actually to return bodily. Fosdick believes this to be untenable. The real essence or the substance of that teaching, says Fosdick, is belief in the ultimate triumph of the power of God. Is there, he asks, a way in which this can be stated for our time? He believes he finds this in the category of progress (not necessarily inevitable progress). Thus he believes we must lay aside the old form of understanding and cling closely to the new form because it expresses the real meaning of the biblical teaching.

The Bible also has a great deal to say about the future state which will follow the second coming, the resurrection, and the judgment. The traditional belief holds that there will be an actual, conscious, personal existence of all individuals. Those who have been righteous will exist in a state of blessedness in the presence of the Holy God. Those who are found not to be righteous will be separated from God in a place of intense anguish. Sometimes this is seen as actual physical flame, sometimes as mere psychological anguish, but in any event, as a real and excruciating experience. In the view of **L. Harold DeWolf** the aim of the traditional teaching is to affect human behavior. The teaching that there will be a place of endless and intense eternal reward for the righteous and a time and place of great suffering and punishment for unbelievers is intended to motivate people to repent and accept Jesus Christ. DeWolf points out that in actuality these teachings have the exact opposite effect. They are contrary to the Christian conception of God. God is a loving God, not a vindictive God. The attempt to describe him in such contrasting or alternating ways produces only moral confusion; there needs to be a proper reformulation of the Christian doctrine of judgment and future punishment. In so doing not only New Testament studies but related fields such as ethics, criminology, and law should be utilized.

To be sure, the doctrines of heaven and hell have sometimes been stated in rather crude and even gross fashion. **C. S. Lewis** recognizes this in his chapters on heaven and hell in *The Problem of Pain*. He emphasizes that these are not so much the reward or punishment administered by God, but rather the actual result of the choices made by men. Thus God should not be seen as vindictively sending unbelievers to hell in order to punish them; rather it is that a person chooses hell and after a lifetime of telling God to go away and leave him alone, God actually does that. Hell thus is man's own self-chosen separation from God.

There has also been a great deal of discussion in recent years about the temporal relationship of certain events connected with the end. Two of these events are the millennium and the tribulation. In Revelation 20 there is reference to a one-thousand-year period. One of the questions of eschatology concerns the status of this thousand-year period and its relationship temporally to the second coming of Christ. In our final group of selections we have four differing viewpoints presented. It is logically possible to think of the millennial views as three. One is the view which says that the millennium will be an actual period of time of Christ's earthly reign, probably one thousand years in length, but not necessarily literally and exactly so. This period of time will precede Christ's return. It will come to pass through the successful preaching of the gospel so that as more and more persons are converted to faith in Christ, God actually takes up reign in their heart and thus it can be said that the kingdom of God is present, even if the Lord himself is not personally and bodily present. According to this scheme, at the end of the thousand years Christ will return bodily; and the resurrection and judgment will take place at that point. This view, known as postmillennialism, was very popular in evangelical Christian circles in the latter part of the nineteenth and the early twentieth century, but has now declined considerably in popularity. It is presented here by **Loraine Boettner.**

The second view, often referred to as amillennialism and presented here by **W. J. Grier,** insists that the thousand years of Revelation 20 are to be understood symbolically or figuratively rather than literally. In other words, there will be no substantial period of earthly reign of Christ either before or after his second coming. While there are varieties of interpretations of the amillennial position, the most popular understanding of Revelation 20 is that the period of one thousand years is symbolic either of the completeness of Christ's reign when he does return or of the church in its present intermediate state. The two resurrections of Revelation 20 are to be understood differently. Usually it is argued that the first resurrection is a spiritual resurrection or regeneration, whereas the second resurrection is a literal or bodily resurrection.

Premillennialism is the view that Christ will return bodily and then will establish a thousand-year period of reign on earth. Prior to his return, things may become very bad and the gospel of the kingdom may not be very widely received. With Christ present, however, every knee will bow and he will be totally, sovereignly, in control of the world. At the end of the one thousand years there will be a small flare-up of satanic activity before the final banishment of evil. The thousand-year period is taken literally though not all of the exponents of this view regard it as exactly one thousand years. Both resurrections are seen as bodily resurrections. Thus, the first resurrection is the resurrection of the righteous or believers. The second resurrection, also a bodily resurrection, is of the unrighteous or unbelievers. The premillennial position is represented by the articles of **George Eldon Ladd** and **John F. Walvoord.**

There is a further distinction that can be made, however, among premillennialists. The Bible speaks of a period of great and intensive tribulation and suffering that is to come immediately prior to the return of Christ. Some premillennialists believe that Christ will come secretly before the tribulation and remove his church or rapture them so that they will not go through this time of intense anguish. These premillennialists are known as pretribulationists. The references to the elect during the seven-year period based upon the seventieth week of Daniel are to elect Jews. The church will be absent and will have already been judged. At the end of that period

Christ will return to the earth, bringing these believers with him. Thus, the second coming is divided into two phases, a coming for the church and a coming with the church. Walvoord argues for this particular position. Ladd, on the other hand, represents the posttribulational view. According to this, the church will be present during the tribulation. The grace of God will shield the church from the most severe aspects of this great anguish, but the church will nonetheless be here to experience it. The second coming is a unitary event—there are no separate coming for and coming with the saints. The church will be caught up to meet Christ at his coming, and will then return with him to the earth to reign with him.

The General Nature
of Eschatology

James O. Buswell

What Is Eschatology?

I. Definition

Eschatology is the systematic study of eventualities. The word is derived from the Greek adjective *eschatos* which means "the last," and is quite equivalent to the English word "last." *Eschatos* may be used with reference to the last item in any series, but the implication of the word "eschatology" is not the limited use of the word, but cosmic eventuality or finality. The writers of the Bible frequently refer to an eschatological complex of events as the climax of world history, the resolution and the consummation of God's cosmic program.

II. New Testament Examples

The word *eschatos* has reference to cosmic finality in the following New Testament passages:

From *A Systematic Theology of the Christian Religion,* Vol. II, by James Oliver Buswell, Jr., pp. 295–303. Copyright Zondervan Publishing House. Used by permission.

A. John's Gospel

In the discourses of Jesus recorded in John's gospel, the phrase, "the last day," occurs six times. In chapter 6:39, 40 it is said to be the will of the Father "that with reference to everything which He has given to me I should lose nothing from it, but should raise it up in the last day. This indeed is the will of my Father, that everyone who beholds the Son and believes in Him, should have eternal life, and I should raise him up in the last day." Again in verse 44 Jesus says, "No one is able to come to me unless the Father who sent me draws him, and I will raise him up in the last day." The same thought is emphasized in verse 54 in a sharper metaphor, "He who eats my flesh and drinks my blood has eternal life, and I will raise him up in the last day." In John 11:24, after Jesus' words, "Your brother will arise again," Martha replies, "I know that he will arise in the resurrection in the last day." Finally in chapter 12:48 Jesus says, "He who disregards me and does not receive my words has one who judges him. The word which I have spoken, that will judge him in the last day."

B. Other New Testament Usage

Paul uses a similar expression in II Timothy 3:1, "You must know this, that in the last days dangerous times will occur." James clearly has cosmic eventualities in mind when he refers to the hoardings of selfish men as bearing witness against them "in the last days" (James 5:3). Peter refers to those who "in the last days" will mock at the promise of the coming of Christ (II Peter 3:3), and Jude (Jude 18) also refers to mockers "in the last time," though Jude does not here mention the Second Coming of Christ as the object of their mockery.

The reader will be conscious at this point that much of the literature of contemporary existential and neo-orthodox theology denies or ignores the New Testament concept of a future eschatological complex of events. However, in all these references just cited, it is clear that the New Testament writers believed, specifically in a future complex of events which would constitute a climax and which would give finality to the history of the human race in this world. From the point of view of their current affairs, the eschatological complex was future. The time to elapse before "the last day" was not known, and was not to be known among men, but the futurity of the events is clear.

C. Double Lens Perspective

Nevertheless, the New Testament writers were quite capable of adjusting the perspective of their view of prophecy. They recognized that from a broader cosmic point of view they were already in the eschatological complex. The end time of human history on earth had already begun. Nowhere is this double lens perspective more clear than in I John 2:18, "Children, it is the last hour; and just as you have heard that Antichrist is coming, even now many antichrists have come into being, wherefore we know that it is the last hour." John does not blur, but rather sharply distinguishes the present from the future. Just as there are now antichrists, so there will be that particular Antichrist of the future.

Probably to be classified with these words of John are I Peter 1:20 and Hebrews 1:2. Peter refers to Christ as the sacrificial lamb "foreknown before the foundation of the world, but made known through us at the end of the times." The author of the epistle to the Hebrews writes in a similar vein. God, having spoken to the fathers by the prophets, "at the end of these days has spoken to us in the Son." Both of these passages reveal the fact that an age of history had closed, or was in the process of closing, and a new age had opened up. As Paul says (I Cor. 10:11), we, the heirs of the past, are those "for whom the final things of the ages have arrived."

True, the last three references might be interpreted as signifying simply the end of one age and the beginning of another, but they harmonize with the thought that the New Testament events were, from the broad cosmic point of view, within the eschatological complex; and I think these three references belong in such a context.

In his great address on the day of Pentecost, Peter (Acts 2:16, 17) said, "This is that which was spoken of by the prophet Joel, And it shall be in the last days. . . ." It should be perfectly clear that Peter does not declare that everything predicted in Joel 2:28–32, the verses which he quotes, took place on the day of Pentecost. On the contrary, he indicates (v. 21) that Joel's prophecy, the fulfillment of which was *initiated* on the day of Pentecost, contemplates an extended period of time during which men may "call upon the name of the Lord" and be saved.

Still more clear are the words of Christ in the discussion found in the fifth chapter of John beginning with verse 17. I refer to the words, "the hour cometh and now is," in verse 25.

In the context Jesus had just healed a sick man at the pool of Bethesda on the Sabbath day. In the discussion which followed, Jesus called God His own Father, "Making Himself out to be equal with God" (v. 18). Jesus further insisted, "Just as the Father raises the dead, and makes them alive, so also the Son makes alive those whom He will" (v. 21). Jesus states His claim to absolute deity in the strongest terms, "That all should honor the Son even as they also honor the Father" (v. 23). He claims that the Father had delivered all judgment into the hands of the Son, and He announces that those who hear His words and believe in Him who sent Him will not come into judgment but have already passed from death into life (v. 24). It is as a climax to these claims that Jesus announces, "Truly, truly I tell you that the hour is coming and now is when the dead shall hear the voice of the Son of God, and those who hear will live" (v. 25).

Opinion is divided as to whether these last quoted words refer to spiritual life or bodily resurrection. In favor of the spiritual interpretation, John 8:51 is cited, "Truly, truly I say to you, if anyone cherishes my word, he will never, never see death." Compare also John 6:50, "This is the bread which comes down from heaven, so that one may eat of it and not die."

Note, too, the words of Jesus to Martha, "He who believes in me though he die, he will live; and everyone who lives and believes in me will never die" (John 11: 25, 26).

The first clause of the last reference, however, clearly speaks of physical death and resurrection, and in my opinion the phrase, "everyone who lives," introducing the second clause means "everyone who experiences the resurrection." Certainly we cannot close the door to a spiritual interpretation of John 5:25, but it is equally certain that we cannot close the door to a literal interpretation. The words, "and now is," would naturally be taken as referring forward to the resurrection of Lazarus, which proves that Jesus at that time had power to raise the dead.

But whether or not John 5:25 refers to literal resurrection, there can be no possible doubt in regard to verses 28 and 29. Verse 27 makes it plain that because Christ has the office of the Son of Man, the power of judgment has been delivered over to Him. With this introduction Jesus continues, "Do not be astonished at this, because the hour is coming in which all those who are in the grave will hear His voice and will come forth, those who have done the good things unto the resurrection of life, those who have done the evil things unto the resurrection of judgment."

It is the use of the word "hour" in John 5:25–29 to which I am now calling attention in discussing the meaning of eschatology. It has been necessary to go into the exegesis and the background in some detail in order to bring out the meaning of Jesus' use of "hour" in this context. Note, then, that in verse 25 He uses the expression with reference to the dead coming to life, "The hour cometh *and now is.*" But in verse 28 where the reference is only to events yet future, He simply says, "The hour cometh." This illustrates what I have called "double lens perspective."

This seems to me exactly the same usage which we find in I John 2:18, "It is the last hour." In both of these passages, then, John shows the double lens perspective of New Testament eschatology. From the overall cosmic point of view, eschatology began with the earthly life of Jesus. In John's time, although he clearly recognized the futurity of the "resurrection of life" and of the "resurrection of judgment," yet Jesus had, and exercised, His power to raise the dead. In John's time, although the spirit of Antichrist was already manifested and there were many antichrists in the world, John clearly recognized the future coming of a particular Antichrist as the Scriptures predicted.

Gerhardus Vos in his *Pauline Eschatology* points out that from the Old Testament point of view, history was divided into "this age" and "the age to come," and that the New Testament writers "had to recognize the eschatological process as in principle already begun."[1] Vos continues, ". . . nevertheless the scheme of successiveness was not . . . discarded . . . the Messianic appearance . . . had unfolded itself into two successive periods, so that even after the first appearance, and after making full allowance for its stupendous effect, the second epoch had, after the fashion of cell separation, begun to form a new complex of hope moving forward into the future. . . . The age to come was perceived to bear in its womb another age to come. . . ."

It should not seem strange that the "end" or the resolution of world history, so far as man is concerned, should turn out to be an extended process. Man has been on the earth for a long, long time. Eschatology began with the Incarnation and the unrepeatable events connected therewith, the active obedience of Christ during His earthly life, His suffering on the cross, His death and His resurrection, all these are events in cosmic eschatology. We are not given any idea of the time which may elapse before the Second Coming of Christ, but however long it may be, it will be short relative to the total span of man's life on the earth. From the cosmic point of view, "It is the last hour."

And yet this viewpoint is not in the least inconsistent with the fact that the New Testament writers definitely looked forward to the still future eschatological complex of events connected with the Second Coming of Christ.

III. Old Testament Examples

A. Acharith Hayyamim

The Old Testament presents a variety of expressions designating cosmic eschatology. In each case, as in the New Testament usage of the word *eschatos,* it is not the words or phrases alone which point to cosmic eschatology. Each of these phrases might be used to indicate the conclusion of a very limited program or series of events. It is the words plus the context which must be examined. It is not my purpose to examine them all, but to give enough examples to indicate the Old Testament concept of finality in the future of world history.

Corresponding to the New Testament phrase, "the last days," the contemporary prophets Isaiah and Micah use the word from which the New Testament expression doubtless came. Isaiah predicts, "And it shall come to pass in the last days that the mountain of the Lord's house shall be established in the top of [or, as the chief of] the mountains, and shall be exalted above the hills; and all nations shall flow into it" (Isa. 2:2). Micah (4:1) may be quoting Isaiah, for he uses almost exactly the same words in giving the same prediction. It can scarcely be doubted that in these words of prophecy there is definite intention to indicate a future cosmic climax or consummation of God's redemptive program.

The words of Joel quoted by Peter on the day of Pentecost (Acts 2:17–21; Joel 2:28–32) contain a similar expression. Joel says *acharey-chen,* and Peter translates, "in the last days."

In Genesis 49:1, in Jacob's final blessing to his sons under the general heading of "that which shall befall you in the last days," Jacob includes the Messianic prediction, "The scepter shall not depart from Judah, nor a law giver from between his feet, until Shiloh come; and unto Him shall the gathering of the people be" (v. 10). Other noteworthy usages of *acharith hayyamim* are Jeremiah 48:47; 49:39; Daniel 2:28 (the Aramaic form of the same words); Daniel 10:14. It is not held that this formula of words is always eschatological, but that it is so in these instances.

B. The Day of the Lord, Yom Jahweh

An important and frequently occurring designation of the eschatological complex is "the day of Jahweh," yet this phrase, like the others under discussion, does not always designate eschatological events. It literally refers to any time in which Jahweh takes conspicuous and decisive action. Such passages as Isaiah 2:12; 13:6 seem clearly eschatological. See also Amos 5:18; Malachi 4:5, etc. The New Testament writers adopt the phrase in its specifically eschatological significance. See I Corinthians 5:5; II Corinthians 1:14; I Thessalonians 5:2; II Peter 3:10.

C. That Day, Yom Hahou

Sometimes the antecedent of the demonstrative pronoun is not explicitly given in the context, but must be understood from the general subject matter. See such passages as Isaiah 29:18; Hosea 2:18, and Paul's similar usage, II Timothy 1:12, 18; 4:8. Lack of expressed antecedent generally characterizes the use of the phrase, "that day."

IV. Terms Not Technical

There are students of prophecy who have endeavored to distinguish among the various words and phrases referring to the eschatological complex, and to make out that some of these terms designate particular phases of that complex. The reader can prove for himself that such an effort is futile. I repeat, any word or phrase referring to the eschatological complex may designate any particular part or phrase of that complex. Furthermore, there is no technical word or phrase which is always eschatological, or which may not refer to some event or activity in a non-eschatological context. It is always the context which must determine what events are referred to. These facts will become more and more apparent as the study progresses.

V. Denial of Futurity

I believe enough Scripture has been presented above to indicate that the writers of the Old Testament as well as the New Testament believed and taught a definite specific future climax of events in which God's cosmic redemptive program will come to a consummation and resolution. I have already suggested that, as over against this clear biblical teaching, philosophical theology has sometimes been beclouded by obscure notions as to the nature of time itself, and the meaning of futurity. In general it may be said that the denial of specific futurity for biblical eschatology always involves philosophical confusion in the definition of time. May I suggest a review of the category of time as discussed in *Being and Knowing,* chapter on the categories, pages 37–48.

The obscurity is greater at the present time, I believe, than ever before. Professor John Sanderson in an article in *His* for March, 1962, has briefly summarized the problem. Barth, in his *Dogmatics in Outline*, p. 133, says, "Christ's coming again . . . has all taken place. . . . He has already accomplished it. . . ." Professor Oscar Cullmann of Basel and of the Sorbonne presents much more of a common-sense view, and objects[2] to Karl Barth's view that "with Christ calendar time is abolished." Cullmann recognizes that Jesus expected a literal interval of time to pass between His death and His Second Coming,[3] but Cullmann still leaves no room for genuine eschatology.

VI. The Main Points in Evangelical Eschatology

Now that we have made clear the definition of biblical eschatology in its minimum connotation, it will be profitable to ask ourselves: What are the main points which form the content of eschatology in the minds of evangelical Christians? I refer to those who have not made a special study of prophecy. but who do have faith in Christ as their personal Saviour and faith in the Bible as the revealed Word of God. In enumerating the following points, I am seeking to pursue the order of psychology which I believe corresponds to the concept in the minds of ordinary Christians. . . .

A. Personal Immortality

In the common, worldly sense of the word, immortality is, I believe, a prominent element in the minds of all evangelical people when they think of the future. The non-material being of man continues after death. We must note that the word "immortality" as it occurs in the English Bible does not have the same meaning as the word has in secular philosophy or in popular speech. "Immortality" in the New Testament translates *aphtharsia,* which literally means "incorruption," and which the biblical writers used to designate the future state of the redeemed only.[4] Some Bible students have urged that Christians should not use the word "immortality" except in its biblical sense. I should change this recommendation and suggest that while we use the language of our day with its words in the usage which is current, we must always keep in mind such difference in biblical usage as may be clearly demonstrated. I believe it is correct, therefore, to say in modern English that evangelical Christians believe that all men are personally immortal.

B. The "Great Gulf" Between Heaven and Hell

Although the thought of many devout evangelicals may be very confused as to the details, it is reasonable to say that evangelical Christians believe not only in what the Deists used to call "future rewards and punishments," but evangelicals believe in a future heaven of bliss for those who are saved through Jesus Christ, and a future hell of torment for those who have rejected the grace of God in Christ. Probably the content of information about heaven, in the minds of those who have not carefully studied the matter, is confined to what is taught in the first few verses of the fourteenth chapter of John. "In my Father's house are many mansions. If it were not so I should have told you. I go to prepare a place for you; and if I go to prepare a place for you, I will come again and receive you unto myself, that where I am there ye may be also.''

I suppose the ordinary content of thought in regard to the future status of those who have rejected Christ is confined to the substance of Jesus' remarks about *gehenna,* plus the references to the lake of fire in the closing chapters of the Revelation.[5]

C. The Second Coming of Christ

I suppose that many evangelical Christians have a vague notion of the meaning of the return of Christ. Probably many of them think only of going to be with the Lord at death. Rather generally, however, even the non-instructed evangelicals have the idea that at some future remote time Christ will return and institute judgment which will declare the eternal status of the saved and the lost. Not so many are clear as to Christ's millennial kingdom.

D. The Intermediate State and the Resurrection

Although there is great confusion and very little clarity in the minds of devout Christians who have not studied the matter, I believe most evangelical Christians understand that there is a distinction between the status of the blessed dead now in heaven, and their status when Christ comes to raise the dead. Similarly, it is vaguely understood that although the lost are now in Hades they will reach their final and eternal state only after the future resurrection and judgment.

E. Summary

My purpose in enumerating the four points given above has been to bring our minds to a focus on the great essentials. These elements—(1) personal immortality, (2) the great gulf between heaven and hell in the future state, (3) the personal return of Christ, (4) the distinction between the intermediate state and the final state following the future resurrection—are, I believe, common to all Bible-believing Christians throughout all the centuries of church history.[6] This, I believe, is the consensus of devout Christian minds, and these points, taken together, constitute the bare minimum of biblical eschatology.

Notes

[1]Gerhardus Vos, *Pauline Eschatology,* published by the author, 1930. Reprint by Eerdmans, 1952, pp. 36ff.

[2]*Christ and Time,* trans. Filson, p. 92.

[3]Ibid., pp. 149f.

[4]The word will be found in Romans 2:7; I Corinthians 15:42, 50, 53, 54; Ephesians 6:24; II Timothy 1:10. And the corresponding adjective will be found in Romans 1:23; I Corinthians 9:25; 15:52; I Timothy 1:17; I Peter 1:4, 23; 3:4.

⁵Jesus used the word *gehenna* in the following passages: Matthew 5:22, 29, 30; 10:28 (parallel to Luke 12:5); Matthew 18:9; 23:15, 33; Mark 9:43, 45, 47. James uses the word figuratively in 3:6. The lake of fire is referred to in Revelation 19:20; 20:10, 14, 15; 21:8.

⁶I do not deny that there have been individuals and even minor movements within the visible church which have denied some of these essentials.

C. H. Dodd

Eschatology and History

Those writings of the Old Testament which we are accustomed to call the historical books are in the Jewish canon reckoned among the prophets—and rightly so. One of the direct results of the work of the prophets of the eighth and seventh centuries B.C. was an outburst of historical composition. Other Oriental peoples had for a long time produced chronicles—which have a high value as a record of events. But the corpus of historical writings which runs from the Book of Joshua to the second Book of Kings, and indeed includes also the narrative parts of the Pentateuch, is something different from a chronicle of events. It exhibits history as a unity, with a meaning which makes sense of all its parts. As Dr. Clement Webb has recently put it, "The 'historical element' in the Old Testament is already, in intention and profession, not a mere collection of stories, but a history of the world, although no doubt a history of the world told from a special point of view and with a practical intent."[1]

The principle which gives unity and meaning to the whole is the idea of the moral government of the world by a divine providence which manifests itself in divers parts and divers manners in the successive episodes of the

From *The Apostolic Preaching and Its Developments* (Kent, England: Hodder and Stoughton, 1939), pp. 79–86. Used by permission.

experience of the people of God, and is working toward the fulfillment of a divine purpose.

But while recorded history is the field within which the divine purpose is being worked out, it can never be said, in the prophetic view, that recorded history fully reveals the purpose of God. This revelation will not be given until the last term in the historical series has come into view—the day of the Lord. It is only prophetic foresight of the day of the Lord that makes it possible to see the whole of history as divinely governed. It seems probable that the idea of the day of the Lord is a part of primitive Hebrew mythology. Certainly it is older than the earliest of the prophets whose works we possess. But if so, we must suppose that in popular mythology the idea stood for an unconditioned and unrelated catastrophe, supervening incalculably upon the course of history. The prophets strenuously endeavored to give to the idea an ethical and rational meaning by relating it to the course of events in the past and to the tendencies of the present. It was thus not simply one more detached event, though of a different order, but the consummation of the whole series of events.

To prophecy succeeded apocalypse. It works with the prophetic scheme of history, but with certain differences. In particular, it virtually gives up the attempt to recognize divine meaning in the present. The mighty hand of the Lord is to be seen in events of the remote past, and will again be seen in the future, but in the present the power of evil obscures it. This does not mean that events have escaped the divine control. "The Most High ruleth in the kingdom of men," but his rule is hidden. This change of perspective, which can be sufficiently accounted for by the prolonged subjection and sufferings of the faithful, serves to give greater emphasis to the belief, which, as we have seen, was also the belief of the prophets, that only in the day of the Lord will the divine meaning and purpose of history come to light.

At the same time, the radical contrast of "this age" and "the age to come," which now begins to be expressed, serves to bring out the suprahistorical character of the day of the Lord. If on one side it is an event— the last term in the series of events—on the other side it is not an event in history at all, for it is described in terms which remove it from the conditions of time and space. In one sense this is no doubt a reversion to the pre-prophetic mythology; but again it brings into bold relief an essential character of the idea, which it bears even in the prophets. The *eschaton*, even though it may be conceived in terms of the devastation of Israel by Assyria, or, again, of a glorious return of Judah from Babylonian exile, is never simply one event following upon another, as the giving of the Law followed upon the exodus, or the return upon the Babylonian captivity, only with the difference that no further event will follow upon it in turn. It is such that no other event either could follow or need follow upon it, because in it the whole purpose of God is revealed and fulfilled.

In prophecy and apocalypse alike, the divine event, the *eschaton*, is always "round the corner." The prophet never conceives himself as standing midway in the course of history, surveying the past through its centuries of change, and foreseeing the future in terms of a similar series of changes. It is not true that either prophets or apocalyptists write, in this sense, "reversed history," or an imaginary narrative of a future course of events, like Mr. Shaw or Mr. Wells.

The idea that they do so is an illusion based upon two facts. First, later exegesis found the "fulfillment" of prophecy in a series of events, often covering a long span of time. Although we have disavowed such exegesis, its ghost may still haunt us. Second, the apocalypses are frequently attributed to personages who lived long before the actual composition of the books, and who are represented as surveying the *actual* course of history through centuries, in the guise of predictions. Although we recognize the fiction for what it is, it is not easy wholly to escape its effects on the mind.

Actually the prophet foresees one thing only, the day of the Lord, the *eschaton*. This statement needs to be qualified only so far: that some prophets or apocalyptists emphasize the nearness in time of the *eschaton* by giving a turn to contemporary events, such that they melt, after a brief development, into the mythical or supernatural traits of the day of the Lord. In the *eschaton* is concentrated the whole meaning which, *if* history were to go on, might be diffused throughout a long process. In this sense the prophetic view may be said to "foreshorten" history; for so it appears to us, who know that many centuries elapsed after the debacle of Judah in 586 B.C., or the Seleucid persecution of 168 B.C., which were the immediate prelude to the End for Jeremiah and for the author of Daniel respectively.

In reality time measurement is irrelevant here. An absolute end to history, whether it be conceived as coming soon or late, is no more than a fiction designed to express the reality of teleology within history. If the maxim, *Die Weltgeschichte ist das Weltgericht,* is to be maintained in its fullest sense, then there must somehow be in history an element of finality. If, as Solon said, a man may not be pronounced happy until he is dead, or as Aristotle put it, happiness can be predicated only of a "complete life," then similarly the significance of history can be estimated only when history is over and can be looked at as a closed whole. It is this that is symbolized in the myth of the last judgment, the end of the world. Since no man has ever experienced the end of history, it can be expressed only in the form of fantasy.

When our modern apocalyptists set forth the shape of things to come, their imaginative skill is used to produce a fictitious narrative which *looks* so like history as we know it that we almost forget that it has no closer relation to actuality than the vision of Jewish apocalyptists. The form of forecasting a process rather than a single event laden with meaning does not alter the fact that we are dealing with symbol and not with actuality in the one case as in the other. The time scale is irrelevant to that which has never received embodiment in the forms of time and space and therefore has no existence in the temporal order. Where the prophets chiefly differ from our modern writers about the future is not so much in predicting an *early* end of the world, but in clothing the coming event in forms which do not properly belong to time at all, but to eternity. They thereby imply that the teleology of history is not purely immanent, but is determined by the purpose of a God who transcends the temporal order.

We may now consider more closely the character attributed to the day of the Lord.

It is in the first place supernatural. Not, indeed, that the supernatural factor is absent from any part of history, for in the prophetic view all history is the field of divine action. But the *eschaton* is manifestly supernatural. The hidden rule of God in history is revealed. "Then his kingdom shall *appear* throughout all his creation" (Assumption of Moses, x. 1). After long centuries of waiting, mankind shall *see* the glory of the Lord.

Second, since the will of God is absolute right, the day of the Lord will be marked by the overthrow of the powers of evil, and judgment upon the sins of men.

Third, since the will of God for man is perfection of life in his image and in fellowship with him, the day of the Lord will bring to those in whom his will is fulfilled a new life which is both glorious and endless.

In all these respects, the day of the Lord is the "fulfillment" of history. While it belongs, in the last resort, to the realm of the "wholly other," it is nevertheless not something alien and unrelated to the recorded course of events. For history depends for its meaning and reality upon that which is other than history. The real, inward, and eternal meaning, striving for expression in the course of history, is completely expressed in the *eschaton,* which is therefore organically related to history. Nevertheless, it is unique and unlike any other event, because it is final. It is not as though the Creator had arbitrarily fixed a certain date as the "zero hour" of his world, so that events which might conceivably have followed it are not permitted to happen. It is such that nothing more *could* happen in history, because the eternal meaning which gives reality to history is now exhausted. To conceive any further event on the plane of history would be like drawing a check on a closed account.

At the same time the day of the Lord is not the end of things in the sense that it negates the values inherent in history, so that it might be conceived as a kind of nirvana or holy nothingness in which the illusions of the time process are finally laid to rest. On the contrary, the values implicit in history are here fully affirmed. They are not destroyed but sublimated. The day of the Lord brings with it new heavens and a new earth, and transforms human nature into the likeness of "the angels of God." Thus the *eschaton,* or ultimate, is also a beginning. It is the end of history, but the beginning of the "age to come," which is not history but the pure realization of those values which our empirical life in time partly affirms and partly seems to deny. Inevitably, the only way in which this can be described is in imagery of a sensuous type, which often gives the appearance of being a crude materialism. For example, one of the most common images is that of the heavenly banquet. But some at least of the apocalyptists surely knew that the kingdom of God is not eating and drinking, but righteousness, peace, and joy; that is, it is the pure reality which we partly apprehend in the most exalted moments of our human experience in time.

In the New Testament the apocalyptic symbolism of the Old recurs freely, but with a profound difference. The divine event is declared to have happened. Consider the following propositions, taken from all parts of the New Testament:

"The kingdom of God has come upon you" (Matt. 12:28).

"This is that which was spoken by the prophet" (Acts 2:16).

"We are being transfigured from glory to glory" (II Cor. 3:18).

"If any man is in Christ, there is a new creation" (II Cor. 5:17).

"He has rescued us out of the dominion of darkness and transferred us into the kingdom of the Son of his Love" (Col. 1:13).

"He has saved us by the washing of rebirth and the renewal of the Holy Spirit" (Titus 3:5).

"Having tasted the powers of the age to come" (Heb. 6:5).

"Born again, not of corruptible seed, but of incorruptible" (I Peter 1:23).

"The darkness is passing, and the real light is already shining . . . it is the last hour" (I John 2:8, 18).

From these and many similar passages it is surely clear that, for the New Testament writers in general, the *eschaton* has entered history; the hidden rule of God has been revealed; the age to come has come. The gospel of primitive Christianity is a gospel of realized eschatology.

In other words, a particular historical crisis, constituted by the ministry, the death, and the resurrection of Jesus Christ, is interpreted in terms of a mythological concept, which had been made by the prophets into a sublime symbol for the divine meaning and purpose of history in its fullness. The characteristics of the day of the Lord as described in prophecy and apocalypse are boldly transferred to the historical crisis.

First, it is fulfillment. "The time is fulfilled" is the declaration which Mark inscribes over the whole gospel record. Similarly, Paul declares, "When the fullness of time had come, God sent forth his Son." The frequent appeals to the fulfillment of prophecy, which the modern reader is likely to find tedious and unconvincing, are a piecemeal assertion of the one great fact that the meaning of history is now summed up. We mistake them if we suppose that the writers would have been equally interested in *any* prediction of *any* casual event which happened to be fulfilled. That which the prophets foresaw was the day of the Lord, and that alone. The fulfillment of prophecy means that the day has dawned.

Second, the supernatural has manifestly entered history. The arm of the Lord is made bare. "The blind see, the lame walk, lepers are cleansed and the deaf hear, the dead are raised, and to the poor good tidings are proclaimed." The miracle stories of the Gospels correspond closely with the symbols which the prophets had used to depict the supernatural character of the age to come. They may be regarded, once again, as a piecemeal assertion of the one great fact that with the appearance of Christ the age of miracle arrived.[2] The story of his ministry is told as a realized apocalypse.

Third, this open manifestation of the power of God is the overthrow of the powers of evil. "If I by the finger of God cast out demons, then the kingdom of God has come upon you," says Jesus in the Synoptic Gospels. The Christ of the Fourth Gospel, on the eve of his death, declares, "Now is the prince of this world cast out." Paul says that in the cross God triumphed over principalities and powers. The theme recurs in other parts of the New Testament.

Fourth, this is the judgment of the world. In the death of Christ, says Paul, God manifested his righteousness and condemned sin in the flesh. "This [according to the Fourth Gospel] is the judgment, that the Light has come into the world [with the incarnation of the Word], and men loved darkness rather than light."

Finally, eternal life, the "life of the age to come," is now realized in experience. Christ is risen from the dead, the first fruits of them that sleep, and we are raised with him in newness of life. He who believes *has* life eternal.

Notes

[1]*The Historical Element in Religion* (London, Allen & Unwin, 1935), pp. 39–40.

[2]See my article, "Miracles in the Gospels," *Expository Times,* Vol. XLIV, no. II, pp. 504ff.

30

Rudolf Bultmann

The Interpretation
of Mythological Eschatology

I

In the language of traditional theology eschatology is the doctrine of the
last things, and "last" means last in the course of time, that is, the end of
the world which is imminent as the future is to our present. But in the
actual preaching of the prophets and of Jesus this "last" has a further
meaning. As in the conception of heaven the transcendence of God is
imagined by means of the category of space, so in the conception of the end
of the world, the idea of the transcendence of God is imagined by means of
the category of time. However, it is not simply the idea of transcendence as
such, but of the importance of the transcendence of God, of God who is
never present as a familiar phenomenon but who is always the coming
God, who is veiled by the unknown future. Eschatological preaching views
the present time in the light of the future and it says to men that this present
world, the world of nature and history, the world in which we live our lives

Reprinted by permission of Charles Scribner's Sons from pp. 22–34 of *Jesus Christ
and Mythology*, by Rudolf Bultmann. Copyright 1958 by Rudolf Bultmann.

and make our plans, is not the only world; that this world is temporal and transitory, yes, ultimately empty and unreal in the face of eternity.

This understanding is not peculiar to mythical eschatology. It is the knowledge to which Shakespeare gives grand expression:

> The cloud-capp'd towers, the gorgeous palaces,
> The solemn temples, the great globe itself,
> Yea, all which it inherit, shall dissolve,
> And like this insubstantial pageant faded,
> Leave not a rack behind. We are such stuff
> As dreams are made on; and our little life
> Is rounded with a sleep. . . .
>
> *Tempest IV, 1*

It is the same understanding which was current among the Greeks who did not share the eschatology which was common to the prophets and to Jesus. Permit me to quote from a hymn of Pindar:

> Creatures of a day, what is anyone? what is he not?
> Man is but a dream of a shadow.
>
> *Pythian Odes 8, 95–96*

and from Sophocles:

> Alas! we living mortals, what are we
> But phantoms all or unsubstantial shades?
>
> *Ajax 125–126*

The perception of the boundary of human life warns men against "presumption" (ὕβρις) and calls to "thoughtfulness" and "awe" (σωφροσύνη and αἰδώς). "Nothing too much" (μηδὲν ἄγαν) and "of strength do not boast" (ἐπὶ ῥώμῃ μὴ καυχῶ) are sayings of Greek wisdom. Greek tragedy shows the truth of such proverbs in its representations of human destiny. From the soldiers slain in the Battle of Plataea we should learn, as Aeschylus says, that

> Mortal man needs must not vaunt him overmuch. . . .
> Zeus, of a truth, is a chastiser of overweening pride
> And corrects with heavy hand.
>
> *Persians 820–828*

And again in the *Ajax* of Sophocles Athene says of the mad Ajax,

> Warned by these sights, Odysseus, see that thou
> Utter no boastful word against the gods,
> Nor swell with pride if haply might of arm
> Exalt thee o'er thy fellows, or vast wealth.
> A day can prostrate and a day upraise
> All that is mortal; but the gods approve
> Sobriety and frowardness abhor.
>
> *127–133*

II

If it is true that the general human understanding of the insecurity of the present in the face of the future has found expression in eschatological thought, then we must ask, *what is the difference between the Greek and the Biblical understanding?* The Greeks found the immanent power of the beyond, of the gods compared with whom all human affairs are empty, in "destiny." They do not share the mythological conception of eschatology as a cosmic event at the end of time; and it may well be said that Greek thought is more similar to that of modern man than to the Biblical conception, since for modern man mythological eschatology has passed away. It is possible that the Biblical eschatology may rise again. It will not rise in its old mythological form but from the terrifying vision that modern technology, especially atomic science, may bring about the destruction of our earth through the abuse of human science and technology. When we ponder this possibility, we can feel the terror and the anxiety which were evoked by the eschatological preaching of the imminent end of the world. To be sure, that preaching was developed in conceptions which are no longer intelligible today, but they do express the knowledge of the finiteness of the world, and of the end which is imminent to us all because we all are beings of this finite world. This is the insight to which as a rule we turn a blind eye, but which may be brought to light by modern technology. It is precisely the intensity of this insight which explains why Jesus, like the Old Testament prophets, expected the end of the world to occur in the immediate future. The majesty of God and the inescapability of His judgment, and over against these the emptiness of the world and of men were felt with such an intensity that it seemed that the world was at an end, and that the hour of crisis was present. Jesus proclaims the will of God and the responsibility of man, pointing towards the eschatological events, but it is not because he is an eschatologist that he proclaims the will of God. On the contrary, he is an eschatologist because he proclaims the will of God.

The difference between the Biblical and the Greek understanding of the human situation regarding the unknown future can now be seen in a clearer light. It consists in the fact that in the thinking of the prophets and of Jesus the nature of God involves more than simply His omnipotence and His judgment touches not only the man who offends Him by presumption and boasting. For the prophets and for Jesus God is the Holy One, who demands right and righteousness, who demands love of neighbour and who therefore is the judge of all human thoughts and actions. The world is empty not only because it is transitory, but because men have turned it into a place in which evil spreads and sin rules. The end of the world, therefore, is the judgment of God; that is, the eschatological preaching not only brings to consciousness the emptiness of the human situation and calls men, as was the case among the Greeks, to moderation, humility and resignation; it calls men first and foremost to responsibility toward God and to repentance. It calls them to perform the will of God. Thus, the characteristic difference between the eschatological preaching of Jesus and that of the Jewish apocalypses becomes evident. All the pictures of future happiness in which apocalypticism excels are lacking in the preaching of Jesus.

Though in this connection we do not examine other differences between Biblical and Greek thought, as, for instance, the personality of the one holy God, the personal relationship between God and man, and the Biblical belief that God is the creator of the world, we must consider one more important point. The eschatological preaching proclaims the imminent end of the world, not only as the final judgment, but also as the beginning of the time of salvation and of eternal bliss. The end of the world has not only a negative but also a positive meaning. To use nonmythological terms, the finiteness of the world has not only a negative but also a positive meaning. To use nonmythological terms, the finiteness of the world and of man over against the transcendent power of God contains not only warning, but also consolation. Let us ask whether the ancient Greeks also speak in this way about the emptiness of the world and of this-worldly affairs. I think that we can hear such a voice in Euripides' question,

> Who knows if to live is really to die,
> and if to die is to live?
>
> *Frg. 638 (ed. Nauck)*

At the end of his speech to his judges, Socrates says,

> But now the time has come to go away. I go to die and you to live; but which of us goes to the better lot, is known to none but God.
>
> *Apol. 42a*

In a similar vein the Platonic Socrates says,

> If the soul is immortal, we must care for it, not only in respect to this time, which we call life, but in respect to all time.
>
> *Phaedo 107c*

Above all, we should think of this famous saying,

> practice dying
> *Phaedo 67e*

This, according to Plato, is the characteristic feature of the life of the philosopher. Death is the separation of the soul from the body. As long as man lives, the soul is bound to the body and to its needs. The philosopher lives his life detaching his soul as much as possible from communion with the body, for the body disturbs the soul and hinders it from attaining the truth. The philosopher looks for cleansing, that is, for release from the body, and so he "gives heed to dying."

If we may call the Platonic hope in life after death an eschatology, then the Christian eschatology agrees with the Platonic eschatology in so far as each expects bliss after death and also in so far as bliss may be called *freedom*. This freedom is for Plato the freedom of the spirit from the body, the freedom of the spirit which can perceive the truth which is the very reality of being; and for Greek thinking, of course, the realm of reality is also the realm of beauty. According to Plato, this transcendent bliss can be described not only in negative and abstract, but also in positive terms. Since the transcendent realm is the realm of truth and truth is to be found in discussion, that is, in dialogue, Plato can picture the transcendent realm positively as a sphere of dialogue. Socrates says that it would be best if he could spend his life in the beyond in examining and exploring as he did on this side. "To converse and associate with them and examine them would be immeasurable happiness" (*Apol.* 41c).

In Christian thinking freedom is not the freedom of a spirit who is satisfied with perceiving the truth; it is the freedom of man to be himself. Freedom is freedom from sin, from wickedness, or as St. Paul says, from the flesh, from the old self, because God is holy. Thus, obtaining bliss means obtaining grace and righteousness by God's judgment. Moreover, it is impossible to depict the ineffable blessedness of those who are justified, save in symbolic pictures such as a splendid banquet, or in such pictures as the Revelation of John paints. According to Paul, "the kingdom of God does not mean food and drink but righteousness, and peace, and joy in the Holy Spirit" (Rom. 14:17). And Jesus said, "When they rise from the dead, they neither marry nor are given in marriage, but are like angels in heaven" (Mark 12:25). The physical body is replaced by the spiritual body. To be sure, our imperfect knowledge will then become perfect, and then we shall see face to face, as Paul says (I Cor. 13:9–12). But that is by no means knowledge of truth in the Greek sense, but an untroubled relationship with God, as Jesus promised that the pure in heart shall see God (Matt. 5:8).

If we can say anything more, it is that the action of God reaches its fulfilment in the glory of God. Thus the Church of God in the present has no other purpose than to praise and glorify God by its conduct (Phil. 1:11) and by its thanksgiving (Rom. 15:6f.; II Cor. 1:20; 4:15). Therefore, the future Church in the state of perfection cannot be thought of otherwise than as a worshiping community which sings hymns of praise and thanksgiving. We can see examples of this in the Revelation of John.

Surely both conceptions of transcendent bliss are mythological, the Platonic conception of bliss as philosophical dialogue as well as the Christian conception of blessedness as worship. Each conception intends to speak about the transcendent world as a world where man reaches the perfection of his true, real essence. This essence can be realized only imperfectly in this world, but nevertheless it determines life in this world as a life of seeking, and longing, and yearning.

The difference between the two conceptions is due to different theories of human nature. Plato conceives the realm of spirit as a realm without time and without history because he conceives human nature as not subject to time and history. The Christian conception of the human being is that man is essentially a temporal being, which means that he is an historical being who has a past which shapes his character and who has a future which always brings forth new encounters. Therefore the future after death and beyond this world is a future of the totally new. This is the *totaliter aliter*. Then there will be "a new heaven and a new earth" (Rev. 21:1; II Peter 3:13). The seer of the future Jerusalem hears a voice, "Behold, I make all things new" (Rev. 21:5). Paul and John anticipate this newness. Paul says, "If any one is in Christ, he is a new creation; the old has passed away, behold, the new has come" (II Cor. 5:17); and John says, "I am writing you a new commandment, which is true in him and in you, because the darkness is passing away and the true light is already shining" (I John 2:8). But that newness is not a visible one, for our new life "is hid with Christ in God" (Col. 3:3) and "it does not yet appear what we shall be" (I John 3:2). In a certain manner this unknown future is present in the holiness and love which characterize the believers, . . . and in the worship of the Church. It cannot be described except in symbolic pictures: "For in this hope we were saved. Now hope that is seen is not hope. For who hopes for what he sees? But if we hope for what we do not see, we wait for it with patience" (Rom. 8:24, 25). Therefore, this hope or this faith may be called readiness for the unknown future that God will give. In brief, it means to be open to God's future in the face of death and darkness.

This, then, is the deeper meaning of the mythological preaching of Jesus—to be open to God's future which is really imminent for every one of us; to be prepared for this future which can come as a thief in the night when we do not expect it; to be prepared, because this future will be a judgment on all men who have bound themselves to this world and are not free, not open to God's future.

III

The eschatological preaching of Jesus was retained and continued in its mythological form by the early Christian community. But very soon the process of demythologizing began, partially with Paul, and radically with John. The decisive step was taken when Paul declared that the turning point from the old world to the new was not a matter of the future but did take place in the coming of Jesus Christ. "But when the time had fully come, God sent forth his Son" (Gal. 4:4). To be sure, Paul still expected the end of the world as a cosmic drama, the *parousia* of Christ on the clouds of heaven, the resurrection from the dead, the final judgment, but with the resurrection of Christ the decisive event has already happened. The Church is the eschatological community of the elect, of the saints who are already justified and are alive because they are in Christ, in Christ who as the second Adam abolished death and brought life and immortality to light through the gospel (Rom. 5:12–14; II Tim. 1:10). "Death is swallowed up in victory" (I Cor. 15:54). Therefore, Paul can say that the expectations and promises of the ancient prophets are fulfilled when the gospel is proclaimed: "Behold, now is the acceptable time [about which Isaiah spoke]; behold, now is the day of salvation" (II Cor. 6:2). The Holy Spirit who was expected as the gift of the time of blessedness has already been given. In this manner the future is anticipated.

This demythologizing may be observed in a particular instance. In the Jewish apocalyptic expectations, the expectation of the Messianic kingdom played a role. The Messianic kingdom is, so to speak, an *interregnum* between the old world time (οὗτος ὁ αἰών) and the new age (ὁ μέλλων αἰών). Paul explains this apocalyptic, mythological idea of the Messianic *interregnum,* at the end of which Christ will deliver the Kingdom to God the Father, as the present time between the resurrection of Christ and his coming *parousia* (I Cor. 15:24); that means, the present time of preaching the gospel is really the formerly expected time of the Kingdom of the Messiah. Jesus is now the Messiah, the Lord.

After Paul, John demythologized the eschatology in a radical manner. For John the coming and departing of Jesus is the eschatological event. "And this is the judgment, that the light has come into the world, and men loved darkness rather than light, because their deeds were evil" (John 3:19). "Now is the judgment of this world, now shall the ruler of this world be cast out" (12:31). For John the resurrection of Jesus, Pentecost and the *parousia* of Jesus are one and the same event, and those who believe have already eternal life. "He who believes in him is not condemned; he who does not believe is condemned already" (3:18). "He who believes in the Son has eternal life; he who does not obey the Son shall not see life, but the wrath of God rests upon him" (3:36). "Truly, truly, I say to you, the hour is coming, and now is, when the dead will hear the voice of the Son of God, and those who hear will live" (5:25). "I am the resurrection and the life; he who believes in me, though he die, yet shall he live; and whoever lives and believes in me shall never die" (11:25f).

As in Paul, so in John demythologizing may be further observed in a particular instance. In Jewish eschatological expectations we find that the figure of the anti-Christ is a thoroughly mythological figure as it is described, for example, in II Thessalonians (2:7–12). In John false teachers play the role of this mythological figure. Mythology has been transposed into history. These examples show, it seems to me, that demythologizing has its beginning in the New Testament itself, and therefore our task of demythologizing today is justified.

The Intermediate State

31

William G. T. Shedd

Intermediate State

The Early-Patristic and Reformed view of the Intermediate State agrees with the Scriptures, as the following particulars prove.

1. Both the Old and New Testaments represent the intermediate state of the soul to be a disembodied state. Genesis 49:33, "Jacob . . . yielded up the ghost, and was gathered unto his people." Job 10:18, "Oh that I had given up the ghost." Job 11:20; 14:20. Ecclesiastes 8:8, "There is no man that hath power over the spirit to retain the spirit; neither hath he power in the day of death." Ecclesastes 12:7, "Then shall the dust return to the earth as it was; and the spirit shall return to God who gave it." Jeremiah 15:9, "She hath given up the ghost." Matthew 27:50, "Jesus, when be had cried again with a loud voice, yielded up the ghost." Luke 23:46, "When Jesus had cried with a loud voice, he said, Father, into thy hands I commend my spirit; and having said this, he gave up the ghost." Acts 7:59, "Stephen called upon God, saying, Lord Jesus, receive my spirit." II Corinthians 5:2, 3, "We groan, earnestly desiring to be clothed upon with our house which is from heaven: if so be that being clothed we shall not be found naked." II Corinthians 5:8, "We are . . . willing rather to be

From *Dogmatic Theology* (Grand Rapids: Zondervan Publishing House, 1888), pp. 610–640.

absent from the body, and to be present with the Lord." II Corinthians 12:2, "I knew a man in Christ about four years ago, whether in the body or out of the body, I cannot tell." II Peter 1:14, "Knowing that shortly I must put off this my tabernacle, even as our Lord Jesus Christ hath showed me." Revelation 6:9, "I saw under the altar the souls of them that were slain for the word of God." Revelation 20:4, "I saw the souls of them that were beheaded for the witness of Jesus." In accordance with this, the prayer for the burial of the dead in the Episcopal Order begins as follows: "Forasmuch as it hath pleased Almighty God, in his wise providence, to take out of this world the soul of our deceased brother, we therefore commit his body to the ground." And God is addressed as the One "with whom do live the spirits of those who depart hence in the Lord; and with whom the souls of the faithful, after they are delivered from the burden of the flesh, are in joy and felicity."

Belief in the immortality of the soul, and its separate existence from the body after death, was characteristic of the Old economy, as well as the New. It was also a pagan belief. Plato elaborately argues for the difference, as to substance, between the body and the soul, and asserts the independent existence of the latter. He knows nothing of the resurrection of the body, and says that when men are judged, in the next life, "they shall be entirely stripped before they are judged, for they shall be judged when they are dead; and the judge too shall be naked, that is to say, dead; he with his naked soul shall pierce into the other naked soul, as soon as each man dies" ("Gorgias," 523).

That the independent and separate existence of the soul after death was a belief of the Hebrews, is proved by the prohibition of necromancy in Deuteronomy 18:10–12. The "gathering" of the patriarchs "to their fathers" implies the belief. Death did not bring them into association with nonentities. Jehovah calls himself "the God of Abraham, Isaac, and Jacob," and this supposes the immortality and continued existence of their spirits; for, as Christ (Luke 20:38) argues in reference to this very point, "God is not the God of the dead, but of the living—not of the unconscious, but the conscious. Our Lord affirms that the future existence of the soul is so clearly taught by "Moses and the prophets," that if a man is not convinced by them, neither would he be "though one should rise from the dead" (Luke 16:31).

Some, like Warburton, have denied that the immortality of the soul is taught in the Old Testament, because there is no direct proposition to this effect, and no proof of the doctrine offered. But this doctrine, like that of the Divine existence, is nowhere formally demonstrated, because it is everywhere assumed. Upon the supposition that the soul dies with the body, and that the sacred writers knew nothing of a future life, most of the Old Testament would be nonsense. For illustration, David says, "My soul panteth after thee." He could not possibly have uttered these words, if he had expected death to be the extinction of his consciousness. The human soul cannot long for a spiritual communion with God that is to last only seventy years, and then cease forever. Every spiritual desire and aspiration has in it the element of infinity and endlessness. No human being can say to God, "Thou art my God, the strength of my heart, and my portion, for threescore years and ten, and then my God and portion no more forever." When God promised Abraham that in him should "all the families of the earth be blessed" (Gen. 12:3), and Abraham "believed in the Lord; and he counted it to him for righteousness" (Gen. 15:6), this promise of a Redeemer, and this faith in it, both alike involve a future existence beyond this transitory one. God never would have made such a promise to a creature who was to die with the body, and such a creature could not have trusted in it. In like manner, Adam could not have believed the protevangelium, knowing that death was to be the extinction of his being. All the Messianic matter of the Old Testament is absurd, on the supposition that the soul is mortal. To redeem from sin a being whose consciousness expires at death, is superfluous. David prays to God, "Take not the word of truth out of my mouth; ... so shall I keep thy law continually *forever and ever*" (Ps. 119:43, 44). Every prayer to God in the Old Testament implies the immortality of the person praying. "My flesh ... faileth, but God is the strength of my heart ... *forever*" (Ps. 73:26). "Trust ye in the Lord *forever*, for in the Lord Jehovah is everlasting strength" (Isa. 26:4). The nothingness of this life leads the Psalmist to confide all the more in God, and to expect the next life. "Behold, thou hast made my days as an handbreadth; and mine age is as nothing before thee: verily, every man at his best state is altogether vanity.... And now, Lord, what wait I for? my hope is in thee" (Ps. 39:5, 7). As Sir John Davies says of the soul, in his poem on Immortality:

> Water in conduit pipes can rise no higher
> Than the well-head from whence it first doth spring:
> Then since to eternal God she doth aspire,
> She cannot be but an eternal thing.

That large class of texts which speak of a "covenant" which God has made with his people, and of a "salvation" which he has provided for them, have no consistency on the supposition that the Old Testament writers had no knowledge and expectation of a future blessed life. The following are examples. Genesis 17:7, "I will establish my covenant between me and thee, and thy seed after thee, in their generations, for an everlasting covenant, to be a God unto thee, and to thy seed after thee." Genesis 49:18, "I have waited for thy salvation, O Lord." Exodus 6:7, "I will take you to me for a people, and I will be to you a God." Deuteronomy 33:3, 29, "Yea, he loved the people; all his saints are in thy hand.... Happy art thou, O Israel: who is like unto thee, O people saved by the Lord." Job 13:15, "Though he slay me, yet will I trust in him." Psalm 31:5, "Into thine hand I commit my spirit; thou hast redeemed me, O Lord God of truth." Isaiah 33: 22, "For the Lord is our judge, the Lord is our lawgiver, the Lord is our king; he will save us." Habakkuk 1:12, "Art thou not from everlasting, O Lord my God, mine Holy One? we shall not die."

It is impossible to confine this "covenant" of God, this "love" of God, this "salvation" of God, this "trust" in God, and this "redemption" of God, to this short life of threescore years and ten. Such a limitation empties them of their meaning, and makes them worthless. The words of St. Paul apply in this case: "If in *this* life only we have hope in Christ, we are of all men most miserable" (I Cor. 15:19). Calvin (*Inst.*, II.x.8) remarks that "these expressions, according to the common explanation of the prophets, comprehend life, and salvation, and consummate felicity. For it is not without reason that David frequently pronounces how 'blessed is the nation whose God is the Lord, and the people whom he hath chosen for his own inheritance'; and that, not on account of any *earthly* felicity, but because he delivers from death, perpetually preserves, and attends with everlasting mercy, those whom he hath taken for his people." In the same vein, Augustine (*Confessions*, VI.xi.19) says: "Never would such and so great things be wrought for us by God, if with the death of the body the life of the soul came to an end." When God said to Abraham, "Thou shalt go to thy fathers in peace" (Gen. 15:15), he meant spiritual and everlasting peace. It was infinitely more than a promise of an easy and quiet physical death. When Jacob, on his death-bed said: "I have waited for thy salvation, O Lord" (Gen. 49:18), he was not thinking of deliverance from physical and temporal evil. What does a man in his dying hour care for this?

The religious experience delineated in the Old Testament cannot be constructed or made intelligible upon the theory that the doctrine of immortality was unknown, or disbelieved. The absolute trust in God, the unquestioning confidence in his goodness and truth, the implicit submission to his will, the fearless obedience of his commands whatever they might be, whether to exterminate the Canaanites or slay the beloved child, and the hopeful serenity with which they met death and the untried future, would have been impossible, had the belief of Enoch, Abraham, Moses, Samuel and the prophets, concerning a future existence, been like that of Hume, Gibbon, Voltaire, and Mirabeau.

Another reason why the Old Testament contains no formal argument in proof of immortality and a spiritual world beyond this is that the intercourse with that world on the part of the Old Testament saints and inspired prophets was so immediate and constant. God was not only present to their believing minds and hearts, in his paternal and gracious character, but, in addition to this, he was frequently manifesting himself in theophanies and visions. We should not expect that a person who was continually communing with God would construct arguments to prove his existence; or that one who was brought into contact with the unseen and spiritual world by supernatural phenomena and messages from it, would take pains to demonstrate that there is such a world. The Old Testament saints "endured as *seeing* the invisible."[1]

2. The Scriptures teach that the Intermediate State for the believer is one

of blessedness. The disembodied spirit of the penitent thief goes with the disembodied Redeemer directly into Paradise. Luke 23:43, "To-day shalt thou be with me in paradise." Paradise has the following marks: (*a*) It is the third heaven. II Corinthians 12:2, 4, "I knew a man . . . caught up to the third heaven. . . . He was caught up into paradise, and heard unspeakable words which it is not lawful for a man to utter." Revelation 2:7, "To him that overcometh will I give to eat of the tree of life, which is in the midst of the paradise of God." (*b*) It is "Abraham's bosom." Luke 16:22, "The beggar died, and was carried by the angels into Abraham's bosom." Matthew 8:11, "Many shall come from the east and west, and shall recline [ἀνακλιθήτονται] with Abraham, and Isaac, and Jacob, in the kingdom of heaven." (*c*) It is a place of reward and happiness. Luke 16:25, "Remember that thou in thy lifetime receivedst thy good things, and likewise Lazarus evil things: but now he is comforted." II Corinthians 5:8, "To be absent from the body [is] to be present with the Lord." Philippians 1:21, "For me . . . to die is gain." Philippians 1:23, "I am in a strait betwixt two, having a desire to depart, and to be with Christ; which is far better." I Thessalonians 5:10, "[Christ] died for us, that, whether we wake or sleep, we should live together with him." Acts 7:59, "They stoned Stephen, calling upon God, and saying, Lord Jesus, receive my spirit." And according to Luke 9:30, 31, Moses and Elijah coming directly from the Intermediate State "appear in glory," at the transfiguration.

The Old Testament, with less of local description, yet with great positiveness and distinctness, teaches the happiness of believers after death. Genesis 5:24, "Enoch walked with God: and he was not; for God took him." In Genesis 49:18, the dying Jacob confidently says, "I have waited for thy salvation, O Lord." Numbers 23:10, "Let me die the death of the righteous, and let my last end be like his." Psalm 16:9–11, "My flesh shall rest in hope. For thou wilt not leave my soul in hell; neither wilt thou suffer thine Holy One to see corruption. Thou wilt show me the path of life: in thy presence is fulness of joy; at thy right hand there are pleasures forevermore." Psalm 17:15, "As for me, I shall behold thy face in righteousness: I shall be satisfied, when I awake, with thy likeness." Psalm 49:15, "God will redeem my soul from the power of the grave: for he shall receive me." Psalm 73:24–26, "Thou shalt guide me with thy counsel, and afterward receive me to glory. Whom have I in heaven but thee? and there is none upon earth that I desire beside thee. My flesh and my heart faileth: but God is the strength of my heart, and my portion forever." Psalm 116:15, "Precious in the sight of the Lord is the death of his saints." Isaiah 25:8, "He will swallow up death in victory." This is quoted by St. Paul, in I Corinthians 15:54, to prove the resurrection of the body. Hosea 13:14, "I will ransom them from the power of the grave; I will redeem them from death: O death, I will be thy plagues; O grave, I will be thy destruction." This also is cited by St. Paul, in I Corinthians 15:55. Daniel 12:2, 3, "Many of them that sleep in the dust of the earth shall awake . . . to everlasting life. . . . And they that be wise shall shine as the brightness of the firmament; and they that turn many to righteousness as the stars forever and ever.'' Also note Job 19:25–27, ''I know that my Redeemer liveth, and that he shall stand at the latter day upon the earth: And though after my skin worms destroy this body, yet in my flesh shall I see God: Whom I shall see for myself, and mine eyes shall behold.''[2] St. Paul teaches that the Old Testament saints, like those of the New, trusted in the Divine promise of the resurrection. ''I stand and am judged for the hope of the promise made of God unto our fathers: unto which promise [of the resurrection] our twelve tribes, instantly serving God day and night, hope to come. For which hope's sake, king Agrippa, I am accused of the Jews. Why should it be thought a thing incredible with you, that God should raise the dead?'' (Acts 26:6–8; cf. 23:6). ''These all died in faith, not having received the promises, but having seen them afar off, and were persuaded of them, and embraced them, and confessed that they were strangers and pilgrims on the earth. For they that say such things declare plainly that they seek a country. And truly, if they had been mindful of that country from whence they came out, they might have had opportunity to have returned. But now they desire a better country, that is, an heavenly'' (Heb. 11:13–16). These bright and hopeful anticipations of the Old Testament saints have nothing in common with the pagan world of shades, the gloomy Orcus, where all departed souls are congregated.

3. The Scriptures teach that the Intermediate State for the impenitent is one of misery. The disembodied spirit of Dives goes to Hades, which has the following marks: (*a*) Hades is the place of retribution and woe. Luke 16: 23, 25, ''In Hades he lifted his eyes, being in torments. . . . And Abraham said, Son, remember that thou in thy lifetime receivedst thy good things, . . . and now thou art tormented.'' Christ describes Dives as suffering a righteous punishment for his hardhearted, luxurious, and impenitent life. He had no pity for the suffering poor, and squandered all the ''good things'' received from his Maker, in a life of sensual enjoyment. The Redeemer of mankind also represents Hades to be inexorably retributive. Dives asks for a slight mitigation of penal suffering, ''a drop of water.'' He is reminded that he is suffering what he justly deserves, and is told that there is a ''fixed gulf'' between Hades and Paradise. He then knows that his destiny is decided, and his case hopeless, and requests that his brethren may be warned by his example. After such a description of it as this, it is passing strange that Hades should ever have been called an abode of the good.[3]

(*b*) Hades is the contrary of heaven, and the contrary of heaven is Hell. Matthew 11:23, ''Thou Capernaum, which art exalted unto heaven, shalt be brought down to Hades.'' This is explained by our Lord's accompanying remark, that it shall be more tolerable in the day of judgment for the land of Sodom than for Capernaum. To be brought down to Hades, then, is the same as to be sentenced to Hell.

(*c*) Hades is Satan's kingdom, antagonistic to that of Christ. Matthew 16:18, ''The gates of Hades shall not prevail against [my church].'' An underworld, containing both the good and the evil, would not be the kingdom of Satan. Satan's kingdom is not so comprehensive as this. Nor would an underworld, including Paradise and its inhabitants, be the contrary of the church.

(*d*) Hades is the prison of Satan and the wicked. Christ said to St. John, "I have the keys of Hades and of death" (Rev. 1:18), and describes himself as "he that openeth, and no man shutteth; and shutteth, and no man openeth" (Rev. 3:7). As the supreme judge, Jesus Christ opens and shuts the place of future punishment upon those whom he sentences. "I saw an angel come down from heaven, having the key of the bottomless pit and a great chain in his hand. And he laid hold on the dragon, that old serpent, which is the Devil, and Satan, and bound him a thousand years. And cast him into the bottomless pit, and shut him up" (Rev. 20:1-3). All modifications of the imprisonment and suffering in Hades are determined by Christ. "I saw the dead, small and great, stand before God; and the books were opened . . . and the dead were judged out of those things which were written in those books; . . . and death and Hades gave up the dead which were in them; and they were judged every man according to their works. And death and Hades were cast into the lake of fire" (Rev. 20:12-14). This indicates the difference between the intermediate and the final state, for the wicked. On the day of judgment, at the command of incarnate God, Hades, the intermediate state for the wicked, surrenders its inhabitants that they may be re-embodied and receive the final sentence, and then becomes Gehenna, the final state for them. Hell without the body becomes hell with the body.[4]

(*e*) Hades is inseparably connected with spiritual and eternal death. "I have the keys of Hades and of death" (Rev. 1:18). "I saw a pale horse; and his name that sat upon him was Death, and Hades followed him" (Rev. 6:8). "Death and Hades gave up the dead which were in them" (Rev. 20:13). Hades here stands for its inhabitants, who are under the power of ("follow") the "second death" spoken of in Revelation 2:11; 20:6, 14; 21:8. This is spiritual and eternal death, and must not be confounded with the *first* death, which is that of the body only. This latter, St. Paul (I Cor. 15:26) says was "destroyed" by the blessed resurrection of the body, in the case of the saints but not of the wicked. (See p. 458). The "second death" is defined as the "being cast into the lake of fire" (Rev. 20:14). This "death" is never "destroyed," because those who are "cast into the lake of fire and brimstone [—with the devil that deceived them—] shall be tormented day and night forever and ever" (Rev. 20:10).

(*f*) Hades is not a state of probation. Dives asks for an alleviation of penal suffering, and is solemnly refused by the Eternal Arbiter. And the reason assigned for the refusal is that his suffering is required by justice. But a state of existence in which there is not the slightest abatement of punishment cannot be a state of probation. Our Lord, in this parable, represents Hades to be as immutably retributive as the modern Hell. There is no relaxation of penalty in the former, any more than in the latter. Abraham informs Dives that it is absolutely impossible to get from Hades to Paradise. "Between us and you there is a great gulf fixed, so that they which would pass from hence to you cannot; neither can they pass to us that would come from thence'' (Luke 16:26). After this distinct statement of Abraham, Dives knows that the case of a man is hopeless, when he reaches Hades. "Then, said he, I pray thee, therefore, father, that thou wouldst send [Lazarus] to my father's house: for I have five brethren; that he may testify unto them, lest they also come to this place of torment'' (Luke 16:27, 28). The implication is that if they do come to it, there is no salvation possible for them. Abraham corroborates this by affirming that he who is not converted upon earth will not be converted in Hades. "If they hear not Moses and the prophets, neither will they be persuaded, though one rose from the dead'' (Luke 16:31).

In the nine places from the New Testament which have been cited in this discussion, the connection shows that Hades denotes the place of retribution and misery. There are three other instances in the received text (two in the uncials) in which the word is employed, and denotes the *grave:* namely, Acts 2:27, 31; I Corinthians 15:55. In I Corinthians 15:55, ℵ, A, B, C, D, (Lachmann, Tischendorf, Hort, and the Revised Version read θάνατε.

In Acts 2:27, it is said: "Thou wilt not leave my soul in Hades, neither wilt thou suffer thine Holy One to see corruption." The soul, here, is put for the body, as when we say, "The ship sank with a hundred souls." The same metonymy is found frequently in the Old Testament. Leviticus 19:28, "Ye shall not make any cuttings in your flesh for the dead'' (Heb., "for a soul"). Leviticus 21:1, "There shall none be defiled for a dead body" (Heb., "for a soul"). Numbers 6:6, "He shall come at no dead body" (Heb., "dead soul"). Compare Leviticus 5:2; 22:4; Numbers 18:11, 13; Haggai 2:13. (See p. 461, note 9, for Pearson's proof of this metonymy.)

That soul is put metonymically for body, and that Hades means the grave, in Psalm 16:10, is proved by the following considerations: (*a*) St. Peter says that "David . . . being a prophet . . . spake of the *resurrection* of Christ, that his soul was not left in Hades, neither did his flesh see corruption" (Acts 2:29–31). But there is no resurrection of the *soul*, in the ordinary literal use of the word. The use here, therefore, must be metonymical. Soul, as in the Old Testament passages cited above, must therefore stand for body. (*b*) Christ's resurrection could not be a deliverance of *both* soul and body from Hades, because both of them together could not be in Hades. Whichever signification of Hades be adopted, only one of the two could be in Hades, and consequently only one of the two could be delivered from Hades. If Hades be the underworld, then only Christ's soul was in Hades, not his body. If Hades be the grave, then only Christ's body was in Hades, not his soul. Accordingly, if Hades be the underworld, then "not to leave Christ's soul in Hades" was to take his soul out of the underworld. But to call this a resurrection of his body, as St. Peter does in Acts 2:31, is absurd. If Hades be the grave, then "not to leave Christ's soul in Hades" was to take his body out of the grave. To call this a resurrection of his body is rational. The choice must be made between the two explanations, because to take both the soul and body of Christ out of Hades is an impossibility. (*c*) The connection shows that "to leave Christ's soul in Hades" is the

same thing as "to suffer the Holy One to see corruption." David's reasoning, as stated by St. Peter, in Acts 2:25–27, implies this. David "foresaw
the Lord," that is, the Messiah. Respecting this Messiah, David argues
that "his flesh shall rest in hope," *because* his "soul shall not be left in
Hades, nor he be suffered to see corruption." Now, unless "soul" is here
put for "flesh" and Hades means the grave, there is a non sequitur in
David's reasoning. That Christ's soul was not left in an underworld would
be no reason why his body should rest in hope and not see corruption.

Again, St. Peter's own reasoning (Acts 2:22–27) proves the same thing.
After saying that God had raised up Jesus of Nazareth, "having loosed the
pangs of death," he shows that this event of Christ's resurrection was
promised, by quoting the words of David, "Thou wilt not leave my soul in
Hades, neither wilt thou suffer thine Holy One to see corruption." That is
to say, the promise "not to leave Christ's soul in Hades" was fulfilled by
raising up Jesus of Nazareth, and loosing the pains of death. And yet again,
St. Paul's quotation, in Acts 13:35, of this passage from David, shows that
he understood soul to be put for body, and Hades to mean the grave. For he
entirely *omits* the clause, "Thou wilt not leave my soul in Hades," evidently regarding the clause, "Thou wilt not suffer thine Holy One to see
corruption," as stating the whole fact in the case: namely, the resurrection
of Christ's body from the grave. In Acts 2:31, the uncials, Lachmann,
Tischendorf, Hort, and the Revised Version omit ἡ ψυχή αὐτοῦ.

The Old Testament term for the future abode of the wicked, and the
place of future punishment, is Sheol (שְׁאוֹל). This word, which is translated by Hades (ᾅδης) in the Septuagint, has two significations: (*a*) The
place of future retribution; (*b*) the grave.

Before presenting the proof of this position, we call attention to the fact
that it agrees with the explanation of Sheol and Hades common in the
Early-Patristic and Reformation churches, and disagrees with that of the
Later-Patristic, the Mediaeval, and a part of the Modern Protestant church.
It agrees also with the interpretation generally given to these words in the
versions of the Scriptures made since the Reformation, in the various
languages of the world.[5]

1. That Sheol in the Old Testament signifies the place of future punishment is proved by the following considerations:

(*a*) Sheol is pronounced against sin and sinners, and not against the
righteous. It is a place to which the *wicked* are sent, in distinction from the
good. "A fire is kindled in my anger, and it shall burn to the lowest Sheol"
(Deut. 32:22). "The wicked in a moment go down to Sheol" (Job 21:13).
"The wicked shall be turned into Sheol, and all the nations that forget
God" (Ps. 9:17). "If I ascend up into heaven, thou art there; if I make my
bed in Sheol [the contrary of heaven], behold thou art there" (Ps. 139:8).
"Her steps take hold on Sheol" (Prov. 5:5). "Her house is the way to
Sheol, going down to the chambers of death" (Prov. 7:27); "Her guests
are in the depths of Sheol" (Prov. 9:18). "The way of life is above to the
wise, that he may depart from Sheol beneath" (Prov. 15:24). "Thou shalt
beat [thy child] with a rod, and shalt deliver his soul from Sheol" (Prov.

23:14). "Sheol is naked before him, and destruction [Abaddon, R.V.] hath no covering" (Job 26:6). "Sheol and destruction [Abaddon, R.V.] are before the Lord" (Prov. 15:11). "Sheol and destruction [Abaddon, R.V.] are never satisfied" (Prov. 27:20). If in these last three passages the revised rendering be adopted, it is still more evident that Sheol denotes Hell; for Abaddon is the Hebrew for Apollyon, who is said to be "the angel [and king] of the bottomless pit" (Rev. 9:11).

There can be no rational doubt that in this class of Old Testament texts the wicked and sensual are warned of a future *evil* and *danger*. The danger is that they shall be sent to Sheol. The connection of thought requires, therefore, that Sheol in such passages have the same meaning as the modern Hell, and like this have an *exclusive* reference to the wicked. Otherwise, it is not a warning. To give it a meaning that makes it the common residence of the good and evil is to destroy its force as a Divine menace. If Sheol be merely a promiscuous underworld for all souls, then to be "turned into Sheol" is no more a menace for the sinner than for the saint, and consequently a menace for neither. In order to be of the nature of an alarm for the wicked, Sheol must be something that pertains to them alone. If it is shared with the good, its power to terrify is gone. If the good man goes to Sheol, the wicked man will not be afraid to go with him. It is no answer to say that Sheol contains two divisions, Hades and Paradise, and that the wicked go to the former. This is not in the Biblical text, or in its connection. The sensual and wicked who are threatened with Sheol, as the punishment of their wickedness, are not threatened with a part of Sheol, but with the *whole* of it. Sheol is one, undivided, and homogeneous in the inspired representation. The subdivision of it into heterogeneous compartments is a conception imported into the Bible from the Greek and Roman classics. The Old Testament knows nothing of a Sheol that is partly an evil, and partly a good. The Biblical Sheol is always an evil, and nothing but an evil. When the human body goes down to Sheol in the sense of the "grave," this is an evil. And when the human soul goes down to Sheol in the sense of "hell and retribution," this is an evil. Both are threatened, as the penalty of sin, to the wicked, but never to the righteous.

Consequently, in the class of passages of which we are speaking, "going down to Sheol" denotes something more dreadful than going down to the grave, or than entering the so-called underworld of departed spirits. To say that "the wicked shall be turned into Sheol," implies that the righteous shall *not* be; just as to say that "they who obey not the gospel of our Lord Jesus Christ . . . shall be punished with everlasting destruction" (II Thess. 1:8, 9), implies that those who do obey it shall *not* be. To say that the "steps" of the prostitute "take hold on Sheol," is the same as to say that "whoremongers . . . shall have their part in the lake which burneth with fire and brimstone" (Rev. 21:8). To "deliver the soul of a child from Sheol" by parental discipline, is not to deliver him either from the grave, or from a spirit-world, but from the future misery that awaits the morally undisciplined and rebellious. In mentioning Sheol in such a connection, the inspired writer is not mentioning a region that is common alike to the righteous and the wicked. This would defeat his purpose to warn the latter.[6] Sheol, when pronounced against the wicked, must be as peculiar to them, and as much confined to them, as when "the lake of fire and brimstone" is pronounced against them. All such Old Testament passages teach that those who go to Sheol suffer from the wrath of God, as the eternal Judge who punishes iniquity. The words, "The wicked is snared in the work of his own hands. . . . The wicked shall be turned into Sheol, and all the nations that forget God" (Ps. 9:16, 17), are as much of the nature of a Divine menace against sin, as the words, "In the day thou eatest thereof, thou shalt surely die" (Gen. 2:17). And the interpretation which eliminates the idea of endless punishment from the former, to be consistent, should eliminate it from the latter.

Accordingly, these texts must be read in connection with, and be explained by, that large class of texts in the Old Testament which represent God as a *judge,* and assert a *future judgment,* and even a future resurrection for this purpose. "Shall not the Judge of all the earth do right?" (Gen. 18:25). "To me belongeth vengeance, and recompense; their feet shall slide in due time" (Deut. 32:35). "The wicked is reserved to the day of destruction; they shall be brought forth to the day of wrath" (Job 21:30). "The ungodly shall not stand in the judgment . . . the way of the ungodly shall perish" (Ps. 1:5, 6). "Verily he is a God that judgeth in the earth" (Ps. 58:11). "Who knoweth the power of thine anger? even according to thy fear, so is thy wrath" (Ps. 90:11). "O Lord God, to whom vengeance belongeth, shew thyself. Lift up thyself, thou judge of the earth: render a reward to the proud" (Ps. 94:1, 2). "There is a way that seemeth right unto a man, but the end thereof are the ways of death" (Prov. 16:25). "God shall judge the righteous and the wicked: for there is a time for every purpose, and every work" (Eccl. 3:17). "Walk in the ways of thine heart, and in the sight of thine eyes; but know thou, that for all these things God will bring thee into judgment" (Eccl. 11:9). "God shall bring every work into judgment, with every secret thing, whether it be good, or whether it be evil" (Eccl. 12:14). "The sinners in Zion are afraid; fearfulness hath surprised the hypocrites. Who among us shall dwell with devouring fire: who among us shall dwell with everlasting burnings? (Isa. 33:14). Of "the men that have transgressed against God," it is said that their "worm shall not die, neither shall their fire be quenched" (Isa. 66:24). "I beheld till the thrones were cast down, and the Ancient of days did sit. . . . His throne was like the fiery flame, and his wheels like burning fire . . . thousand thousands ministered unto him, and ten thousand times ten thousand stood before him; the judgment was set, and the books were opened" (Dan. 7:9, 10). "Many of them that sleep in the dust of the earth shall awake, some to everlasting life, and some to shame and everlasting contempt" (Dan. 12:2). "The Lord hath sworn by the excellency of Jacob, Surely I never will forget any of their works" (Amos 8:7). "They shall be mine, saith the Lord of hosts, in that day when I make up my jewels" (Mal. 3:17).

A final judgment, unquestionably, supposes a *place* where the sentence is executed. If there is a day of doom, there is a world of doom. Consequently, these Old Testament passages respecting the final judgment throw a strong light upon the meaning of Sheol, and make it certain, in the highest degree, that it denotes the world where the penalty resulting from the verdict of the Supreme Judge is to be experienced by the transgressor. The "wicked," when sentenced at the last judgment, are "turned into Sheol," as "idolaters and all liars," when sentenced, "have their part in the lake which burneth with fire and brimstone" (Rev. 21:8).

(*b*) A second proof that in the Old Testament Sheol signifies the place of future punishment is the fact that there is no other proper name for it in the whole volume; for Tophet is metaphorical, and rarely employed. If Sheol is not the place where the wrath of God falls upon the transgressor, there is no place mentioned where it does. But it is utterly improbable that a final sentence would be announced so clearly as it is under the Old dispensation, and yet the place of its execution be undesignated. In modern theology, Judgment and Hell are correlates—each implying the other, each standing or falling with the other. In the Old Testament theology, Judgment and Sheol sustain the same relations. The proof that Sheol does not signify Hell would, virtually, be the proof that the doctrine of Hell is not contained in the Old Testament; and this would imperil the doctrine of the final judgment. Universalism receives very strong support from all versions and commentaries which take the idea of retribution out of the term "Sheol," because no texts that contain the word can be cited to prove either a future sentence, or a future suffering. They prove only that there is a world of disembodied spirits, whose moral character and condition cannot be inferred from anything in the signification of Sheol; for the good are in Sheol, and the wicked are in Sheol. When it is said of a deceased person merely that he is in the world of spirits, it is impossible to decide whether he is holy or sinful, happy or miserable.

(*c*) A third proof that Sheol, in these passages, denotes the dark abode of the wicked, and the state of future suffering, is found in those Old Testament texts which speak of the contrary bright abode of the righteous, and of their state of blessedness. According to the view we are combating, Paradise is in Sheol, and constitutes a part of it. But there is too great a contrast between the two abodes of the good and evil to allow of their being brought under one and the same gloomy and terrifying term "Sheol." When "the Lord put a word in Balaam's mouth," Balaam said, "Let me die the death of the righteous, and let my last end be like his" (Num. 23:5, 10). The Psalmist describes this "last end of the righteous" in the following terms: "My flesh shall rest in hope. . . . Thou wilt show me the path of life; in thy presence is fulness of joy; at thy right hand, there are pleasures for evermore" (Ps. 16:9, 11). "As for me, I will behold thy face in righteousness; I shall be satisfied, when I awake, with thy likeness" (Ps. 17:15). "God will redeem my soul from the power of Sheol; for he shall receive me" (Ps. 49:15). "Thou shalt guide me with thy counsel, and afterward receive me to glory. Whom have I in heaven but thee?" (Ps. 73:24, 25). In like manner, Isaiah (25:8) says respecting the righteous, that the Lord God "will swallow up death in victory; and . . . will wipe away tears from all faces''; and Solomon asserts that ''the righteous hath hope in his death'' (Prov. 14:32). These descriptions of the blessedness of the righteous when they die have nothing in common with the Old Testament conception of Sheol, and cannot possibly be made to agree with it. The ''anger'' of God ''burns to the lowest Sheol.'' This implies that it burns through the whole of Sheol, from top to bottom. The wicked are ''turned'' into Sheol, and ''in a moment go down'' to Sheol; but the good are not ''turned'' into ''glory,'' nor do they ''in a moment go down'' to ''the right hand of God.'' The ''presence'' of God, the ''right hand'' of God, the ''glory'' into which the Psalmist is to be received, and the ''heaven'' which he longs for, are certainly not in the dreadful Sheol. They do not constitute one of its compartments. If between death and the resurrection the disembodied spirit of the Psalmist is in ''heaven,'' at the ''right hand'' of God, in his ''presence,'' and beholding his ''glory,'' it is not in a dismal underworld. There is not a passage in the Old Testament that asserts, or in any way suggests, that the light of the Divine countenance, and the blessedness of communion with God, are enjoyed in Sheol. Sheol, in the Old Testament, is gloom, and only gloom, and gloomy continually. Will any one seriously contend that in the passage, ''Enoch walked with God: and he was not; for God took him,'' it would harmonize with the idea of ''walking with God,'' and with the Old Testament conception of Sheol, to supply the ellipsis by saying that ''God took him to Sheol''? Was Sheol that ''better country, that is, an *heavenly,* '' which the Old Testament saints ''desired,'' and to attain which they ''were tortured, not accepting deliverance'' (Heb. 11:16, 35)?

(*d*) A fourth proof that Sheol is the place of future retribution is its inseparable connection with spiritual and eternal death. The Old Testament, like the New, designates the punishment of the wicked by the term ''death.'' And spiritual death is implied, as well as physical. Such is the meaning in Genesis 2:17. The death there threatened is the very same θάνατος to which St. Paul refers in Romans 5:12, and which ''passed upon all men'' by reason of the transgression in Eden. Spiritual death is clearly taught in Deuteronomy 30:15, ''I have set before thee this day life and good, and death and evil''; in Proverbs 8:36, ''All they that hate me love death''; in Jeremiah 21:8, ''I set before you the way of life, and the way of death''; in Ezekiel 33:11, ''I have no pleasure in the death of the wicked; but that the wicked turn from his way and live.'' Spiritual death is also taught, by implication, in those Old Testament passages which speak of spiritual life as its contrary. ''Thou wilt show me the path of life'' (Ps. 16:11). ''With thee is the fountain of life'' (Ps. 36:9). ''There the Lord commanded the blessing, even life for evermore'' (Ps. 133:3). ''As righteousness tendeth to life, so he that pursueth evil pursueth it to his own death'' (Prov. 11:19). ''Whoso findeth me findeth life'' (Prov. 8:35). ''He is in the way of life that keepeth instruction'' (Prov. 10:17).

Sheol is as inseparably associated with spiritual death and perdition, in the Old Testament, as Hades is in the New Testament, and as Hell is in the common phraseology of the Christian church. ''Sheol is naked before him, and destruction hath no covering" (Job 26:6). "Her house inclineth unto death, and her paths unto the dead" (Prov. 2:18). "Her feet go down to death; her steps take hold on Sheol" (Prov. 5:5). "Sheol and destruction are before the Lord" (Prov. 15:11). "Sheol and destruction are never full" (Prov. 27:20). "Her house is the way to Sheol, going down to the chambers of death" (Prov. 7:27). The sense of these passages is not exhausted by saying that licentiousness leads to physical disease and death. The "death" here threatened is the same that St. Paul speaks of when he says that "they which commit such things are worthy of death" (Rom. 1:32), and that "the end of those things is death" (Rom. 6:21). Eternal death and Sheol are as inseparably joined in Proverbs 5:5, as eternal death and Hades are in Revelation 20:14. But if Sheol be taken in the mythological sense of an underworld, or spirit-world, there is no inseparable connection between it and "death," either physical or spiritual. Physical death has no power in the spirit-world over a disembodied spirit. And spiritual death is separable from Sheol, in the case of the good. If the good go down to Sheol, they do not go down to eternal death.

2. That Sheol, in one class of Old Testament passages, denotes the grave, to which all men, the good and evil alike, go down, is clear from the following citations. Before proceeding, however, it is to be remarked that this double signification of Hell and the grave is explained by the connection between physical death and eternal retribution. The death of the body is one of the consequences of sin, and an integral part of the total penalty. To go down to the grave is to pay the first installment of the transgressor's debt to justice. It is, therefore, the metonymy of a part for the whole, when the grave is denominated Sheol. As in English, "death" may mean either physical or spiritual death, so in Hebrew, Sheol may mean either the grave or hell.

When Sheol signifies the "grave," it is only the *body* that goes down to Sheol. But as the body is naturally put for the whole person, the *man* is said to go down to the grave, when his body alone is laid in it. Christ "called Lazarus out of his grave" (John 12:17). This does not mean that the soul of Lazarus was in that grave. When a sick person says, "I am going down to the grave," no one understands him to mean that his spirit is descending into a place under the earth. And when the aged Jacob says, "I will go down into Sheol, unto my [dead] son mourning" (Gen. 37:35), no one should understand him to teach the descent of his disembodied spirit into a subterranean world. "The spirit of man . . . goeth upward, and the spirit of the beast . . . goeth downward" (Eccl. 3:21). The soul of the animal dies with the body; that of the man does not. The statement that "the Son of man shall be three days and three nights in the heart of the earth" (Matt. 12:40) refers to the burial of his body, not to the residence of his soul.[7] When Christ said to the penitent thief, "To-day shalt thou be with me in Paradise," he did not mean that his human soul and that of the penitent should be in "the heart of the earth," but in the heavenly Paradise. Christ is represented as dwelling in heaven between his ascension and his second advent. "Him must the heavens receive, till the time of the restitution of all things" (Acts 3:21). "Our conversation is in heaven, from which we look for our Saviour the Lord Jesus" (Phil. 3:20). "The Lord shall descend from heaven with a shout, with the voice of the archangel, and with the trump of God" (I Thess. 4:16). But the souls of the redeemed, during this same intermediate period, are represented as being with Christ. "Father, I will that they whom thou hast given me be with me where I am, that they may behold my glory which thou hast given me" (John 17:24). "We desire rather to be absent from the body, and to be present with the Lord" (II Cor. 5:8). When, therefore, the human body goes down to Sheol, it goes down to the grave, and is unaccompanied by the soul.

The following are a few out of many examples of this signification of Sheol. "Thy servants shall bring down the gray hairs of thy servant our father with sorrow to Sheol" (Gen. 44:31).[8] Korah and his company "went down alive into Sheol . . . and they perished from the congregation" (Num. 16:33). "The Lord killeth, and maketh alive: he bringeth down to Sheol, and bringeth up" (I Sam. 2:6). "O that thou wouldest hide me in Sheol" (Job 14:13). "Sheol is my house. . . . I have said to corruption, Thou art my father: to the worm, Thou art my mother, and my sister" (Job 17:13, 14). "In Sheol, who shall give thee thanks?" (Ps. 6:5). "My life draweth nigh unto Sheol" (Ps. 88:3). "What man is he that liveth, and shall not see death? shall he deliver his soul from the hand of Sheol?" (Ps. 89:48). "Our bones are scattered at the mouth of Sheol" (Ps. 141:7). "There is no . . . wisdom in Sheol, whither thou goest" (Eccl. 9:10). "I will ransom thee from the power of Sheol . . . O Sheol, I will be thy destruction" (Hos. 13:14). "The English version," says Stuart, "renders Sheol by grave in thirty instances out of sixty-four, and might have so rendered it in more."

Sheol in the sense of the grave is invested with gloomy associations for the good, as well as the wicked; and this under the Christian dispensation, as well as under the Jewish. The Old economy and the New are much alike in this respect. The modern Christian believer shrinks from the grave, like the ancient Jewish believer. He needs as much grace in order to die tranquilly as did Moses and David. It is true that "Christ has brought immortality to light in the gospel," has poured upon the grave the bright light of his own resurrection, a far brighter light than the Patriarchal and Jewish church enjoyed; yet man's *faith* is as weak and wavering as ever, and requires the support of God.

Accordingly, Sheol in the sense of the grave is represented as something out of which the righteous are to be delivered by a resurrection of the body to glory, but the bodies of the wicked are to be left under its power. "Like sheep, [the wicked] are laid in Sheol; death shall feed on them. . . . But God will redeem my soul [me = my body] from the power of Sheol" (Ps. 49:14, 15). "Thou wilt not leave my soul [me = my body] in Sheol; neither wilt thou suffer thine Holy One to see corruption" (Ps. 16:10).[9] This passage, while Messianic, has also its reference to David and all believers. "I will ransom them from the power of Sheol. . . . O death, I will be thy plagues; O Sheol, I will be thy destruction" (Hos. 13:14). St. Paul quotes this (I Cor. 15:55) in proof of the blessed resurrection of the bodies of believers—showing that "Sheol" here is the "grave," where the body is laid, and from which it is raised.

The bodies of the wicked, on the contrary, are not delivered from the power of Sheol, or the grave, by a blessed and glorious resurrection, but are still kept under its dominion by a resurrection "to shame and everlasting contempt" (Dan. 12:2). Though the wicked are raised from the dead, yet this is no triumph for them over death and the grave. Their resurrection bodies are not "celestial" and "glorified," like those of the redeemed, but are suited to the nature of their evil and malignant souls. "Like sheep they are laid in Sheol; death shall feed upon them" (Ps. 49:14). Respecting sinful Judah and the enemies of Jehovah, the prophet says, "Sheol hath enlarged herself, and opened her mouth without measure, and their glory . . . shall descend unto it" (Isa. 5:14). Of the fallen Babylonian monarch, it is said, "Sheol from beneath is moved for thee to meet thee at thy coming. . . . Thy pomp is brought down to Sheol: the worm is spread under thee, and the worms cover thee" (Isa. 14:9, 11). To convert this bold personification of the "grave," and the "worm," which devour the bodies of God's adversaries, into an actual underworld where the spirits of all the dead, the friends as well as the enemies of God, are gathered, is not only to convert rhetoric into logic, but to substitute the mythological for the Biblical view of the future life. "Some interpreters," says Alexander, on Isaiah 14:9, "proceed upon the supposition, that in this passage we have before us not a mere prosopopoeia or poetical creation of the highest order, but a chapter from the popular belief of the Jews, as to the locality, contents, and transactions of the unseen world. Thus Gesenius, in his Lexicon and Commentary, gives a minute topographical description of Sheol as the Hebrews believed it to exist. With equal truth a diligent compiler might construct a map of hell, as conceived by the English Puritans, from the descriptive portions of the Paradise Lost." The clear perception and sound sense of Calvin penetrate more unerringly into the purpose of the sacred writer. "The prophet," he says (on Isa. 14:9), "makes a fictitious representation, that when this tyrant shall die and go down to the grave, the dead will go forth to meet him and honor him." Theodoret explains the verse in the same way. He remarks on the words, "Hell from beneath is moved for thee, to meet thee," etc., that, "it is the custom of Scripture sometimes to employ a figure, in order to state a thing more clearly. In this place the prophet introduces death as endowed with mind and reason, and expostulating with the king of Babylon."

From this examination of texts, it appears that Sheol, in the Old Testament, has the same two significations that Hades has in the New. The only difference is, that in the Old Testament, Sheol less often, in proportion to the whole number of instances, denotes "Hell," and more often the "grave," than Hades does in the New Testament. And this, for the reason that the doctrine of future retribution was more fully revealed and developed by Christ and his apostles, than it was by Moses and the prophets.

If after this study of the Biblical data, there still be doubt whether Sheol and Hades denote sometimes the place of retribution for the wicked, and sometimes the grave, and not an underworld, or spirit-world, common to both the good and evil, let the reader substitute either spirit-world or underworld in the following passages, and say if the connection of thought, or even common sense, is preserved: "The wicked in a moment go down to the spirit-world." "The wicked shall be turned into the spirit-world, and all the nations that forget God." "Her steps take hold on the spirit-world." "Her guests are in the depths of the spirit-world." "Thou shalt beat thy child with a rod, and shalt deliver his soul from the spirit-world." "The way of life is above to the wise, that he may depart from the spirit-world beneath." "In the spirit-world, who shall give thee thanks?" "There is no wisdom in the spirit-world, whither thou goest." "I will ransom them from the power of the spirit-world; O spirit-world, I will be thy destruction." "Like sheep the wicked are laid in the spirit-world; death shall feed upon them. But God will redeem my soul from the power of the spirit-world." "The gates of the spirit-world shall not prevail against the church." "Thou, Capernaum, which art exalted unto heaven shalt be brought down to the spirit-world." "Death and the spirit-world were cast into the lake of fire." "I saw a pale horse, and his name that sat upon him was Death, and the spirit-world followed him."

Notes

[1]Compare Mozley, "Essay on Job."

[2]The common opinion of the church, ancient, mediaeval, and modern, is that this passage teaches both immortality and the resurrection. De Wette, Ewald, and even Renan find the doctrine of immortality in it. See Perowne, *On Immortality*. Note III.

[3]Müller regards it as so unquestionable, from the description in the parable of Dives and Lazarus, that Hades is not a place for repentance and salvation, that he places future redemption after the day of judgment. He asserts that "those theories of ἀποκατάστασις which represent it as taking place in the interval between death and the general resurrection directly violate the New Testament eschatology. If, therefore, the idea of an ἀποκατάστασις πάντων is to be maintained, it must be referred to a period lying beyond the general resurrection." *Sin,* II. 426.

[4]If Hades in this passage means an underworld, it would include Paradise, and thus Paradise would be cast into the lake of fire.

[5]In committing themselves, as the translators of the Revised Version of the English Bible do in their Preface to the Old Testament, to the position that Sheol and Hades, in the Scriptures, "signify the abode of departed spirits, and correspond to the Greek Hades or the underworld," and that neither term denotes either the place of punishment, or the grave, they have placed themselves in doctrinal opposition, on a very important subject, to James's translators, to Luther and the translators of the principal European versions, and to the missionary translators generally. In all these versions, Sheol and Hades are understood to mean either hell, or the grave, and never an underworld containing all spirits good and bad. The view of the Reformers, upon this point, is stated in the following extract from the *Schaff-*

Herzog Encyclopedia (Article "Hades"): "The Protestant churches rejected, with purgatory and its abuses, the whole idea of a middle state, and taught simply two states and places—heaven for believers, and hell for unbelievers. Hades was identified with Gehenna, and hence both terms were translated alike in the Protestant versions. The English (as also Luther's German) version of the New Testament translates Hades and Gehenna by the same word 'hell,' and thus obliterates the important distinction between the realm of the dead (or nether-world, spirit-world), and the place of torment or eternal punishment; but in the Revision of 1881 the distinction is restored, and the term Hades introduced."

[6]"The meaning of the Hebrew word Sheol is doubtful, but I have not hesitated to translate it hell. I do not find fault with those who translate it grave, but it is certain that the prophet means something more than common death; otherwise he would say nothing else concerning the wicked, than what would also happen to all the faithful in common with them." Calvin, "On Psalm 9:17."

[7]That "the heart of the earth" means the grave, Witsius (Apostles' Creed, Dissertation XVII) argues in the following manner: "Jonah says, that while he was in the bowels of the fish, he was 'in the belly of hell,' or of the grave, and 'in the midst (Heb., heart) of the sea': and in this respect he was a figure of Christ placed in the heart of the earth. This does not mean the hell of the damned, which, as Jerome says, is commonly said to be 'in the midst of the earth'; but an earthen receptacle, which has earth above, below, and on every side; or more briefly, which is within the earth. As the Scripture places Tyre 'in the heart of the sea,' that is, surrounded by the sea; as 'the way of a ship is in the heart of the sea,' when it is surrounded on all sides by the sea; as Absalom was 'alive in the heart of the oak,' that is, in the oak, within its branches—so the grave is 'the heart of the earth.' Chrysostom remarks that 'the sacred writer doth not say in the earth, but in the heart of the earth, that the expression might clearly denote the grave, and that no one might suspect a mere appearance [of death].'"

[8]This text, and Gen. 42:38, are parallel to Gen. 37:35, and explain Jacob's words, "I will go down mourning into Sheol, unto my son." "Gray hairs" are matter, and cannot go into a world of spirits.

It is objected that Sheol does not mean the "grave," because there is a word (קֶבֶר) for grave. A grave is bought and sold, and the plural is used; but Sheol is never bought and sold, or used in the plural. The reply is that "grave" has an abstract and general sense, denoted by שְׁאֹל, and a concrete and particular, denoted by קֶבֶר. All men go to *the* grave, but not all men have *a* grave. When our Lord says that "all that are in their graves [μνημείοις] . . . shall come forth" (John 5:28, 29), he does not mean that only those shall be raised who have been laid in a particular grave with funeral obsequies. A man is "in the grave," in the general sense, when his soul is separated from his body and his body has "returned to the dust" (Gen. 3:19). To be "in the grave," in the abstract sense, is to have the elements of the body mingled with those of the earth from which it was taken (Eccl. 12:7). The particular spot where the mingling occurs is unessential. Moses is in the grave, but "no man knoweth of his sepulchre unto this day." We say of one drowned in the ocean that he found a watery grave. These remarks apply also to the use of ἅδης and μνημεῖον. According to Pearson (Creed, Art. V), the Jerusalem Targum, with that of Jonathan, and the Persian Targum, explain שְׁאֹל, in Gen. 37:35; 42:38, by קֶבֶר. To the objection that Jacob knew, or supposed, that his son had been devoured by wild beasts, and consequently had no grave, and, therefore, meant to say that he should go down to the world of spirits to meet him, Rivetus (Exercitatio CLI, in Gen.) replies as follows: "Per *sepulchrum* non intelligimus stricte, id de quo apud jurisconsultos disputatur, cum agunt de sepulchro violato, sed id referimus ad rationem humationis in genere, quandocumque modo terra reddatur terrae, juxta sententiam divinam, 'Pulvis es, et in pulverem reverteris.' Sepeliri enim dicuntur quicunque terrae redduntur. etiam qui sepeliuntur 'sepultura asini,' quod de Joachimo pronuntiavit Jeremias (22:19). Igitur verba Jacobi 'Descendam ad filium meum lugens iu in infernum,' id est, in sepulchrum, non possumus melius explicare quam verbis Albini, qui sic ingemiscentis patris exponit querelam: 'In luctu permanebo, donec me terra suscipiat, ut filium meum sepulchrum jam suscepit.' Id ipse Jacobus etiam intellexit, qui per vocem sheol locum denotat 'quo senum *cani* cum dolore deducuntur.' ''

[9]In support of this interpretation of these words, we avail ourselves of the unquestioned learning and accuracy of Bishop Pearson. After remarking that the explanation which makes the clause, "He descended into hell," to mean "that Christ in his body was laid in the grave," is "ordinarily rejected by denying that 'soul' is ever taken for 'body,' or 'hell' for the 'grave,' '' he proceeds to say that "This denial is in vain: for it must be acknowledged, that sometimes the Scriptures are rightly so, and cannot otherwise be, understood. First, the same word in the Hebrew, which the psalmist used, and in the Greek, which the apostle used, and we translate 'the soul,' is elsewhere used for the body of a dead man, and rendered so in the English version. Both נֶפֶשׁ and ψυχή are used for the body of a dead man in the Hebrew, and Septuagint of Num. 6:6; 'He shall come at no dead body' (מֵת נֶפֶשׁ). The same usage is found in Lev. 5:2; 19:28; 21:1, 11; 22:4; Num. 18:11, 13; Haggai 2:13. Thus, several times, נֶפֶשׁ and ψυχή are taken for the body of a dead man; that body which polluted a man under the Law, by the touch thereof. And Maimonides hath observed, that there is no pollution from the body till the soul be departed. Therefore נֶפֶשׁ and ψυχή did signify the body after the separation of the soul. And it was anciently observed by St. Augustine, that the soul may be taken for the body only: 'Animae nomine corpus solum posse significari, modo quodam locutionis ostenditur, quo significatur per id quod continetur illud quod continet.' Epist. 157, al. 190, ad Optatum; De animarum origine, c. 5, § 19. Secondly, the Hebrew word שְׁאֹרֵב, which the psalmist used, and the Greek word ἅδης, which the apostle employed, and is translated 'hell' in the English version, doth certainly in some other places signify no more than the 'grave,' and is translated so. As when Mr. Ainsworth followeth the word, 'For I will go down unto my son, mourning, to hell'; our translation, arriving at the sense, rendereth it, 'For I will go down into the grave, unto my son, mourning,' Gen. 37:35. So again he renders, 'Ye shall bring down my gray hairs with sorrow unto hell,' that is 'to the grave,' Gen. 42:38. And in this sense we say, 'The Lord killeth and maketh alive: he bringeth down to the grave, and bringeth up,' 1 Sam. 2:6. It is observed by Jewish commentators that those Christians are mistaken who interpret those words spoken by Jacob, 'I will go down into sheol,' of hell [in the sense of underworld]; declaring that Sheol there is nothing but the grave,'' Pearson, *On the Creed,* Article V. The position that נֶפֶשׁ is sometimes put for a dead body, and that Sheol in such a connection denotes the grave, was also taken by Usher (as it had been by Beza, on Acts 2:27, before him), and is supported with his remarkable philological and patristic learning. See his discussion of the Limbus Patrum and Christ's Descent into Hell, in his "Answer to a Challenge of a Jesuit in Ireland." *Works,* Vol. III.

This metonymy of "soul" for "body" is as natural an idiom in English, as it is in Hebrew and Greek. It is more easy for one to say that "the ship sank with a hundred souls," than to say that it "sank with a hundred bodies." And yet the latter is the real fact in the case.

32

W. D. Davies

The Old and the New Hope: Resurrection

[In reference to Paul's analogy (in I Corinthians 15:35ff.) of the seed and the glorious new body we will receive, we cannot assume] that because the essential ego is to persist there is, therefore, to be a continuity between the old and the new form which this ego assumes.[1] It is at least equally agreeable that such is the difference between the σῶμα ψυχικόν and the σῶμα πνευματικόν that no continuity need exist between them, and that therefore the interval during the "sleep" of death, which intervened before the formation of the new body, would make no difference. It would be hazardous therefore to follow [those who think] that II Corinthians 5 makes explicit what was implicit in I Corinthians 15 or that it is the logical development from the latter.

Next we have to refer to the view of those scholars who have claimed that there is no change in Paul's thought in II Corinthians 5:1f. Kennedy,[2] for example, has sharply criticized the theory that there is a change, as literalistic and pedantic. Emphasizing that Paul is not presenting a systematic theology in his Epistles. he claims in connection with II Corinthians 5:1 that "there is no reference here to the detail of time. He does not yet

---

From *Paul and Rabbinic Judaism* (London: The Society for Promoting Christian Knowledge, 1955), pp. 310–318. Used by permission.

specify a period. The ἔχομεν ('we have') is simply equivalent to 'there awaits us as a sure possession.'"[3] The Apostle's assertion is merely a repetition in another form of the statement in I Corinthians 15:38: "God giveth it a body." Kennedy goes on to suggest that "these words give a hint of Paul's earnest desire and hope of surviving to the Parousia, and so escaping the terrifying experience of death."[4] It is difficult, however, to accept this view. There is nothing in the text to suggest Paul's hope of surviving to the Parousia.[5] Far more likely is it that two factors had constrained Paul to give more thought than he had previously done to what happens to the Christian at death; he himself had been at the gates of death[6] and the problem of Christians who died was becoming a pressing one; and Paul was thus led to state the fact that the Christian at death is not left naked but receives a heavenly body.[7]

What we find in I Corinthians 15 and II Corinthians 5, then, is the juxtaposition of two different views, first, that the Christian waits for the new body till the Parousia and, secondly, that immediately at death he acquires the heavenly body. How are we to explain this juxtaposition? It will be well first to expound the view of those who have found here at least a partial Hellenization of Paul's thought. Schweitzer has examined the views of Pfleiderer, Teichmann and Holtzmann in this connection and we may refer to his treatment in his book, *Paul and His Interpreters*.[8] The most convenient discussion of the subject for our purpose is that of Knox.[9] The argument of the latter scholar runs somewhat as follows. His experience at Athens had convinced Paul that the eschatological presentation of the Gospel would not avail with a Gentile world, and "from this point forward his Epistles show a progressive adaptation of the Christian message to the general mental outlook of the Hellenistic world."[10] Part of this process is visible in I Corinthians 15, where we find a "spiritualization of the doctrine of the resurrection." This, however, did not go far enough. Knox writes: "It appears that Paul's admission of the immaterial nature of the risen body and his suggestion of some kind of reabsorption of all things unto God were not enough to satisfy the difficulties of the Corinthians. The Second Epistle is largely devoted to a complete revision of Pauline eschatology in a Hellenistic sense."[11] In support of this thesis Knox shows how the ideology of II Corinthians 5:1f. can be paralleled in Hellenistic sources. To summarize briefly, he suggests that in this passage: (*a*) Paul regards the body as a burden from which he longs to be delivered, although his intense Jewishness forbids his contemplating a bodiless existence in the hereafter and retains for him the conception that "the soul did not simply lay aside the body, but put on a new and glorious one."[12] The parallels drawn from Hellenistic literature to Paul's language in II Corinthians 5:1f. are many. The most striking is the reference to the earthly body as σκῆνος in Wisdom 9:15: φθαρτὸν γὰρ σῶμα βαρύνει ψυχήν, καὶ βρίθει τὸ γεῶδες σκῆνος νοῦν πολυφροντίδα (σκῆνος was a Pythagorean term).[13] (*b*) The conception of the spirit as being a present possession Knox explains in terms of the divine afflatus of Hellenistic belief.[14] (*c*) The idea that the Christian life in this world is an exile is essentially

Hellenistic—"the only real reason why the soul was in exile in this life was that it, or the highest part of it, was of divine origin, and although a celestial being, imprisoned in the material world."[15] (*d*) The one element in the passage that is not Hellenistic is the idea of judgement. At this point we may be permitted a lengthy quotation.[16] Paul

> was ready to abandon the apocalyptic tradition in favour of the ascent of the soul or spirit of man to the firmament which was the abode of God, and its transmutation into a radiant state of glory by the work of the Spirit; he was not prepared to abandon the eternal responsibility of man for his deeds. His discussion of the destiny of the soul of man ended with the statement that all must stand before the judgement seat of Christ (5:10), a phrase borrowed from the traditional picture of the final judgement of mankind. This judgement, as in the book of Wisdom, retained a formal position in the scheme of things, though it had ceased to possess any real significance when the thought of the gradual transformation of the soul from the material to the spiritual during life, and the completion of the process at death, had been substituted for the final assize at the end of the world-process.

What shall we say to all this? Knox allows that there are two elements in II Corinthians 5:1f. that are essentially Jewish, namely, the horror of "nakedness"[17] at death, which is implied, and the retention of the judgement. It is in (*a*), (*b*) and (*c*) above that Knox finds Hellenistic influences. Let us take these in inverse order. The idea of this present life being an exile is surely so commonplace that we need not postulate any specifically Hellenistic influence to account for it. [Moreover, Paul's conception of the spirit] is very far removed from Hellenistic ideas. It is the language of II Corinthians 5 that seems to suggest Hellenistic influences most strongly. Let us look, however, at the passage again. In II Corinthians 4:7 Paul has compared himself to an earthen vessel, a figure which may have often been used. Thus a Rabbi living in the period A.D. 140–65 uses the figure:

> There was a man in Sepphoris whose son had died. A heretic sat by his side. R. Jose b. Halafta came to visit him. The heretic saw that he was smiling. He said unto him, "Rabbi, why do you smile?" He replied, "I trust in the Lord of Heaven that the man will see his son again in the world to come." Then that heretic said, "Is not his sorrow enough for the man that you should come and sadden him yet more? Can broken sherds be made to cleave again together? Is it not written, 'Thou shalt break them in pieces like a potter's vessel'?" [Ps. 2:9]. Then R. Jose said, "Earthen vessels are made by water and perfected by fire; vessels of glass are both made by fire and perfected by fire; the former, if broken, cannot be repaired: the latter, if broken, can be repaired." The heretic said, "Why?" He replied, "Because they are made by blowing. If the glass vessel which is made by the blowing of a mortal man can be repaired how much more the being who is made by the blowing of God."[18]

Later on, in II Corinthians 5:1, Paul calls the earthly body a σκῆνος and although there are abundant parallels to this, as we saw, in Hellenistic literature, the term would also be quite natural to a Rabbi. We accept the suggestion made by T. W. Manson[19] . . . that Paul's thought is here influenced by the Feast of Tabernacles. The term σκῆνος is used in the LXX to translate the Hebrew *sukkâh*. Thus the LXX renders Leviticus 23:42, thus: 'Εν σκηναῖς κατοικήσετε ἑπτὰ ἡμέρας, πᾶς ὁ αὐτόχθων ἐν 'Ισραὴλ κατοιχήσει ἐν σκηναῖς, ὅπως ἴδωσιν αἱ γενεαὶ ὑμῶν ὅτι ἐν σκηναῖς κατῴκισα τοὺς υἱοὺς 'Ισραήλ, ἐν τῷ ἐξαγαγεῖν ηε αὐτοὺς ἐκ γῆς Αἰγύπτου. [Since in II Corinthians 3 Paul has been] thinking of the Christian dispensation as a new Exodus and since in chapter 4 he has been dealing with the frailty and transitory nature of his life in the body of flesh, he would naturally be led to think of the latter in terms of the *sukkâh* which was essentially a temporary dwelling in which the Jew dwelt for seven days at the Feast of Tabernacles, a dwelling designed to recall "the time which our forefathers spent in the wilderness and . . . the life they led in tents and booths.''[20] The Christian, so it might have occurred to Paul, would have to live in a booth before reaching the Promised Land. If, as Manson suggests, the Epistle was written near the time of the Feast, this interpretation of σκῆνος carries added conviction.[21] Throughout the passage under consideration, therefore, the language of Paul can be explained without recourse to Hellenistic sources. Finally, according to Knox, the Hellenization of Paul's presentation of the hereafter arose out of a crisis of thought; it was the result of a need felt to restate the Gospel in terms understood by the Hellenistic world. We cannot elaborate our position at this point, but we [do question] both Knox's assumption that Paul's experience at Athens was of such profound significance for his thought, as he suggests, and his view that I Corinthians implies the "dematerializing'' of the Resurrection. In view of all this we cannot accept the interpretation of II Corinthians 5 as the Hellenization of Paul's thought.

How then are we to account for the difference that we have found between I Corinthians 15 and II Corinthians 5? The solution to this question we believe lies in [Paul's] conception of the Age to Come as having already dawned. . . . We shall now examine the relevance of this for the understanding of our problem.

We begin with the teaching of Judaism on the nature of the Age to Come. Frey[22] has quoted with approval the saying that "le trait le plus caractéristique du système théologique juif, c'est de n'avoir pas de système.'' This is especially true with reference to the conception of the *'ôlâm ha-bâ'*. "There is in this sphere,'' writes Moore,[23] "not merely an indefiniteness of terminology, but an indistinctness of conception . . . there was not only no orthodoxy, but no attempt to secure uniformity in such matters.'' The general distinction between this age and the Age to Come has often been described and here we need only refer to the treatment of the subject in Strack-Billerbeck,[24] Bonsirven[25] and Moore, and remark only that this distinction was as familiar to the Rabbis as to the apocalyptists. For our immediate purpose the complexity arises when we ask when the

Age to Come was to be experienced. There are two possible answers to this question which are to be very carefully noted.

On the one hand, there are passages which clearly imply that the Age to Come always exists "in heaven" or "in the unseen." Thus in a passage in the Book of Enoch, which Charles, although he regards it as an interpolation, nevertheless dates in the pre-Christian period,[26] we read:

> And he said unto me,
> He proclaims unto thee peace in the name of the world to come.
> *For from hence has proceeded peace since the creation of the world.*
> And so shall it be for ever and for ever and ever.[27]

Further, there have always existed dwelling-places of the righteous:

> And there I saw another vision, the dwelling places of the holy,
> And the resting places of the righteous.
> Here mine eyes saw their dwelling places with his righteous angels,
> And their resting places with the holy.[28]

There is no need to find here with Charles that "the unities of time and place are curiously neglected";[29] there is here merely the recognition of a realm that always IS. Into this Age to Come that always IS the souls of the righteous enter at death. Thus this world is the vestibule of the Age to Come, i.e., it immediately precedes the latter.

R. Jacob (A.D. 140–65) said: "This world is like a vestibule before the world to come; prepare thyself in the vestibule that thou mayest enter into the banqueting hall."[30]

At death then the soul comes to experience *'ha ôlâm ha-bâ'*, and the initial experience in that sphere is judgement. This comes out clearly in a passage concerning R. Johanan b. Zakkai:[31]

> When R. Johanan b. Zakkai was ill, his disciples went in to visit him. On beholding them, he began to weep. His disciples said to him, "O lamp of Israel, right hand pillar [I Kings 7:21], mighty hammer, wherefore dost thou weep?" He replied to them, "If I was being led into the presence of a human king, who to-day is here and to-morrow in the grave, whose anger, if he were wrathful against us, would not be eternal, whose imprisonment, if he imprisoned me, would not be everlasting, whose death sentence, if he condemned me to death, would not be for ever, and whom I could appease with words and bribe with money—even then I would weep; but now, when I am being led into the presence of the king of kings, the Holy One, blessed be He, who lives and endures for all eternity, whose anger, if He be wrathful against me, is eternal, whose imprisonment, if He imprisoned me, would be everlasting, whose sentence, if He condemned me to death, would be for ever, and whom I cannot appease with words or bribe with money—nay, more, when before me lie two ways, one towards the Garden of Eden and the other towards Gehinnom, and I know not towards which I am to be led—shall I

not weep?'' They said to him, ''Our master, bless us!'' He said to them, ''May it be His will that the fear of heaven be upon you [as great] as the fear of flesh and blood.'' His disciples exclaimed, ''Only as great!'' He replied, ''Would that it be [as great]; for know, that when a man intends to commit a transgression, he says, 'I hope nobody will see me.' ''

Into the details of the way in which the soul was led to judgement we need not here enter. God Himself was most often the judge and His decisions were given according to works. Following the judgement, which was definitive in the sense that it pronounced God's final valuation of the soul's merits and demerits, the soul proceeded to Sheol. In the latter, however, the just and the unjust were not treated alike. According to the Book of Enoch there were four different compartments into which the souls were severally placed, two blessed compartments for the righteous and two designed for punishment. In other books Sheol was exclusively reserved for the wicked and became identified with Gehenna.

While the souls of the wicked were punished, those of the righteous received the reward of blessedness. The geography of this blessed state varied considerably from author to author. For our purpose the significant fact is that, as Strack-Billerbeck, Bonsirven and Moore point out, the *'ôlâm ha-bâ'* was conceived of as eternally existent; it always IS in the heavens and we awake to it at death.[32]

On the other hand, however, the *'ôlâm ha-bâ'* is said to come into being *after* the Messianic Age and the general resurrection; the Age to Come *follows* these latter events. The examples of this usage are legion and need not be given again at this point.

Obviously then there are two phases to the *'ôlâm ha-bâ'*—it both IS and COMES, and in those passages where there is mentioned resurrection, the *'ôlâm ha-bâ'* which we enter at death finds its consummation in that *'ôlâm ha-bâ'* which follows the resurrection. The case has been well put by Strack-Billerbeck. They write:

> . . . Yet the striking phenomenon that the Rabbinic teachers have used the expression *hâ-'ôlâm ha-bâ'* to designate both the heavenly world of the souls and also the future Age of Consummation would have made it clear to us, as it were, that the heavenly Aeon of the Souls and the future Aeon of consummation on earth were regarded as one and the same great *'ôlâm ha-bâ'*. This great *'ôlâm ha-bâ'* at present had its place in heaven (I Enoch 71.14ff.) . . . into it the souls of the righteous entered at the hour of death for a preliminary blessedness. That is their first phase in which it serves as the world of the souls until it enters through the resurrection of the dead into its second phase in order now to become the earthly sphere of the Aeon of full blessedness.[33]

This two fold conception of the *'ôlâm ha-bâ'* which we have traced would be familiar to Paul. We do not mean by this that he consciously and precisely distinguished between the two phases of the *'ôlâm ha-bâ'* referred to, as we have done, but that the conceptions outlined would be entertained by him without any sense of a possible contradiction. In his pre-Christian days, Paul, like other Rabbis, would have thought of the Age to Come as awaiting him at death and at the same time he could and did conceive of it as a final consummation of all created being. This unconscious ambiguity of his thought will help us to understand the difference between I Corinthians 15 and II Corinthians 5. In the former Paul is concerned with the impending advent of the Lord when the general resurrection already in process would be consummated. His mind is centred on the '*ôlâm ha-bâ*' as the End of all history, and he can argue eloquently, but nevertheless dispassionately, about the nature of the resurrection body. In II Corinthians 5:1f., on the other hand, it is not resurrection as characteristic of "the End" that concerns him. His experience in Asia had made him recognize the possibility that he himself might die before the Parousia as had many Christians around him; in chapter 4 he has been thinking of the strain and stress of his ministry; his outward man is perishing and thoughts of death crowd upon him; and the Apostle is led naturally to think of what lies immediately beyond death.

We have seen what Paul the Pharisee would see beyond death. Death would be for him the advent of the judgement, and then, as he would have hoped, the entry into Paradise—he would be in the Age to Come. But he would be in the Age to Come only in its first phase, so to speak; he would still be disembodied until the resurrection, although participating in blessedness.

For Paul the Christian, however, things were different. Not only would Paul believe that it was Christ and not Torah[34] that availed him in death, but he would also have to consider another new factor. . . . He now believed that the Age to Come eternally existent in the Heavens had already appeared in its initial stages in the Resurrection of Jesus. Already the resurrection body, the body of the final Age to Come, was being formed. Paul had died and risen with Christ and was already being transformed. At death, therefore, despite the decay of his outward body, Paul would already be possessed of another "body." The heavenly body was already his.[35] Because the Age to Come had dawned in its second phase, both on this side of the grave and on the other Paul would be embodied. The final Act of God had transformed both this world and the world beyond death for Paul. To be "in Christ" in this world and to be "with Christ"[36] in the sphere beyond death was the final blessedness, the Age to Come in its second and last phase.

We have now seen that in II Corinthians 5:1f. Paul expresses the view that the dead in Christ would not be disembodied at death, the fate which awaited the righteous according to Rabbinic Judaism—and then undergo an intermediate period of waiting till the general resurrection. They would, on the contrary, be embodied; there is no room in Paul's theology for an intermediate state of the dead.[37] It agrees with this that Paul in the later passages of his Epistles speaks not of the resurrection of Christians but of their revelation. In Romans 8:19 we read: "The earnest longing of the creation waiteth for the revelation of the sons of God"; and in Colossians

3:4, we read: "When Christ who is our life shall be revealed then shall ye also be revealed with him in glory." There is no need to resurrect those who have already died and risen with Christ and received their heavenly body, but they may be revealed.[38] The final consummation would merely be the manifestation of that which is already existent but "hidden" in the eternal order. All this is related, it will be recognized, with what has been called Paul's "Christ-mysticism." The unity of Christians with Christ their Lord is such for Paul that just as Christ Himself had already passed into the eternal order so had Christians also, although they still lived in the flesh. Thus the Colossians[39] had already risen with Christ and although still living in the flesh yet they are "dead" and their "life is hid with Christ in God." In the words of Dr. Dodd:[40] "The personality of Christ," which we note is now in the eternal world, "receives, so to speak, extension in the life of His Body on earth. Those 'saving facts,' the death and resurrection of Christ, are not merely particular facts of past history, however decisive in their effect; they are re-enacted in the experience of the Church. If Christ died to this world, so have the members of His Body; if He has risen into newness of life, so have they;[41] if He being risen from the dead dieth no more, neither do they;[42] if God has glorified Him, He has also glorified them.[43] They are righteous, holy, glorious, immortal, according to the prophecies, with the righteousness, holiness, glory and immortality which are His in full reality, and are theirs in the communion of His Body—'in Christ.'" This means that Christians are already partakers in the Age to Come "in Christ" and that future events can only make this fact explicit.

If the above interpretation be correct, it will be seen that we need not go outside Rabbinic Judaism to account for Paul's thought in II Corinthians 5:1f. This fact is, indeed, recognized by Knox despite his insistence on the Hellenization of Paul's thought. He writes on this passage: "It seems probable that Paul was employing a traditional argument, which would be recognized as entirely orthodox from the point of view of rabbinical learning, in which he had a solid advantage over his Jewish Christian opponents."[44] It was not a crisis of thought in II Corinthians 5, as Knox suggests; rather it was a crisis in experience, the necessity to reconcile himself to death as a physical event. It is part of a process not of Hellenization but of what Dr. Dodd has called "reconciliation to experience."[45]

Notes

[1]For a discussion of this, see H. A. A. Kennedy, *St. Paul's Conceptions of the Last Things,* p. 242. He writes: "How would St. Paul in his thought connect the γυμνὸς κόκκος with its future σῶμα? What for him is the organic link between them? His answer is extraordinarily typical. It is the only one we can expect him to give, and it is given in the clause immediately following: 'The sovereign power of God.' 'He giveth it a body according as He willed (ἠθέλησε); the aorist denotes the final act of God's will determining the constitution of nature'—so Edwards, ad loc. admirably." Also J. Moffatt, *First Corinthians (M.N.T.C.),* p. 261: "[Paul] repudiates any notion of a material identity between the present and future body."

[2]Op. cit., p. 263.

[3]Kennedy, op. cit., p. 265. The same position is maintained by L. S. Thornton, *The Common Life in the Body of Christ*, p. 284, additional note A.; A. Plummer, *Second Corinthians (I.C.C.)*, p. 161; J. Denney, *Second Corinthians (Expositor's Bible)*, ad loc.

[4]Kennedy, op. cit., p. 256; cf. A. Schweitzer, *Paul and His Interpreters*, p. 69.

[5]Cf. S. Cave, *The Gospel of St. Paul*, p. 255, n. 1.

[6]II Cor. 1:8, 9.

[7]Cf. S. Cave, op. cit., p. 254; C. H. Dodd, *Ryl. Bull.* (Jan. 1934), vol. XVIII, no. 1, pp. 28f.

[8]Pp. 69ff.

[9]*St. Paul and the Church of the Gentiles*, pp. 128f.

[10]Ibid., p. 26.

[11]Ibid., p. 128.

[12]Ibid., p. 137.

[13]Ibid., p. 136, n. 8, for parallels and see especially H. Windisch, in Meyer, *Kommentar zum Neuen Testament, Der Zweite Korintherbrief*, p. 158; H. St. J. Thackeray, *The Relation of St. Paul to Contemporary Jewish Thought*, pp. 131f. Referring to Paul's connection with the Book of Wisdom, Thackeray writes: "The occurrence of the same expressions (γεῶδες, σκῆνος, βαρέω, βαρύνω, ἐπίγειος) in conjunction points to a literary connection...."

[14]*St. Paul and the Church of the Gentiles*, p. 140.

[15]Ibid., p. 140.

[16]Ibid., p. 141.

[17]Cf. *M. Ber.* 3.5.

[18]*Gen. Rabba* 14.7.

[19]*J.T.S.* (Jan.–April 1945), vol. XLVI, pp. 1–10.

[20]Cf. Tabernacle Services [*The Book of Prayer or Order of Service According to the Custom of Spanish and Portuguese Jews* (1906)]. See also *Mishnah Sukkah* (Danby, pp. 172f.); *Sukkah, Mishnah and Tosefta* (A. W. Greenup).

[21]Manson also holds that "Paul's καταλυθῇ suits better the dismantling of the booth of Tabernacles than the striking of a tent." There is only doubtful support for this view in Liddell and Scott.

[22]*Biblica* (1932), vol. XIII, p. 130.

[23]Vol. II, p. 378.

[24]Str.-B., vol. IV, pp. 799f.

[25]*Le Judaïsme Palestinien*, vol. I, pp. 307f.

[26]See R. H. Charles, *The Book of Enoch* (Oxford. 1893), p. 33.

[27]I Enoch 71.15.

[28]I Enoch 39.4.

[29]*Ap. and Ps.*, vol. II, p. 120; *The Book of Enoch,* pp. 114f., n. 4.

[30]*P. Aboth* 4.16; cf. also for the same thought *Sifra Lev.* 85*d.*; *J. Yeb.* 15.14*d.*

[31]*b. Ber.* 28*b.*

[32]For all the above see especially J. B. Frey, *Biblica* (1932), vol. XIII, pp. 135f.

[33]Str.-B., vol. IV, pp. 819f. See also J. Bonsirven, *Le Judaïsme Palestinien,* vol. I, p. 313.

[34]For the efficacy of Torah at death, cf. *P. Aboth* 6.9.

[35]Cf. A. E. J. Rawlinson, *The New Testament Doctrine of the Christ,* pp. 154f.; cf. II Cor. 4:16f.; Col. 3:3; Rom. 8:11.

[36]Cf. C. H. Dodd, *Romans* (*M.N.T.C.*), p. 89.

[37]See G. B. Stevens, *The Pauline Theology,* pp. 358f.

[38]Cf. R. H. Charles, *Eschatology,* p. 402.

[39]Col. 3:1–4.

[40]*The Apostolic Preaching and Its Developments,* pp. 147f.

[41]Rom. 6:4.

[42]Rom. 6:8, 9.

[43]Rom. 8:29, 30.

[44]Cf. W. L. Knox, *St. Paul and the Church of the Gentiles,* p. 143.

[45]See C. H. Dodd, ''The Mind of Paul: Change and Development,'' in *Ryl. Bull.* (Jan. 1934), vol. XVIII, no. 1, pp. 38f., 44.

The Second Coming

33

E. Y. Mullins

Last Things

The Second Coming of Christ

1. The uniform teaching of the New Testament is that the Second Coming is to be an outward, visible, and personal return of Christ. . . . This is the clear teaching of Jesus himself. It is equally clear in the teachings of the book of Acts and in the Epistles. In Acts 1:11 we read, "This Jesus, who was received up from you into heaven, shall so come in like manner as ye beheld him going into heaven." The phrase "in like manner" (*hon tropon*) does not express the certainty of Christ's return merely, but also the manner. As he was received up visibly so will he return visibly to the earth. In I Thessalonians 4:16 Paul declares, "For the Lord himself shall descend from heaven with a shout, with the voice of the archangel, and with the trump of God." In II Peter 3:3, 4 we read, "In the last days mockers shall come . . . saying, Where is the promise of his coming?" In James 5:8 also: "Be ye also patient; establish your hearts; for the coming of the Lord is at hand." And in Revelation 22:12 the language is: "Behold, I come quickly;

From E. Y. Mullins, *The Christian Religion in Its Doctrinal Expression* (Valley Forge, Pennsylvania: The Judson Press, 1917), pp. 439–503. Used by permission of the American Baptist Board of Education and Publication.

and my reward is with me, to render to each man according as his work is.'' Those passages could be greatly multiplied if necessary. They serve to show indisputably that the expectation of a visible personal return of Christ was common to the New Testament writers.

2. The exact time of the personal return of Christ is unrevealed. Jesus declared that he himself did not know the day or the hour of his return (Matt. 24:36; Mark 13:32). In Acts 1:7 he is represented as cautioning disciples against attempting to pry into the events of the future: ''It is not for you to know times or seasons, which the Father hath set within his own authority.'' In verse 8 he adds that they should receive power after the coming of the Holy Spirit, and that they should witness for him to the ends of the earth. Evidently Jesus was concerned much more about the devotion of his people to their practical duties and tasks than that they should know the details of the future.

3. We repeat here the statement previously made that Jesus recognized subordinate comings in the events of history in addition to the Second Coming itself in its visible and personal aspect. This principle is expressed in the Gospel of John in his promise to come through the Holy Spirit and make his abode in disciples. It appears in unmistakable terms in the statement in Matthew 26:64: ''Henceforth,'' that is, ''From now,'' from the present time, ''ye shall see the Son of man . . . coming on the clouds of heaven.''

4. The attitude of the New Testament writers and the disciples generally toward the Second Coming was one of constant expectancy. There is scarcely any difference of opinion on this point among interpreters of the New Testament. To them his coming was ever imminent. It might occur at any time, even during the lives of the generation then on earth. According to some passages certain events are to precede. The ''falling away'' and the rise of Antichrist, or the man of sin, were among these as set forth by Paul in II Thessalonians 2:1–12. Some have thought that Paul's doctrine of the Second Coming underwent a change toward the latter part of his career. But there is no real contradiction between his earlier and later views. The variations in emphasis which we find in his Epistles are explained by the variations in the circumstances of his readers and the situation which he desired to meet.

The question arises: How then are we to explain this uniform expectation of the near return of Christ? Was Paul mistaken? Were the other apostles in error? This inference is often drawn. But it is an inference which overlooks certain important factors which are required by the New Testament records themselves. It overlooks, first of all, the difference between a mental and spiritual attitude and a dogmatic teaching. The disciples looked for the return at any time. But they did not expressly assert that Christ would, without fail, come during their lives. The inference that Paul and others were mistaken also overlooks the clear warnings given by Paul himself (II Thess. 2:1–12) and by Peter (II Peter 3:3–12) against the premature expectation of Christ's return. It overlooks, in the third place, the fact that this expectation of the near return was in obedience to repeated commands of

Jesus while on earth. In a number of instances he enjoined upon the disciples the duty of constant watchfulness and expectancy (Matt. 24:42; 25:13; Mark 13:35-37). When we compare the words of Jesus in these passages with what we find in the later New Testament writings, we are struck with their agreement with each other. If the apostles, after Jesus' departure, had abandoned the thought of his personal return, we should be at a loss to understand their attitude. In the above passages the very ignorance of disciples as to the time of the return and their uncertainty regarding it were made the basis of the exhortation to watch constantly.

5. There are at least two ways in which the expectation of Christ's near return served the ends of the kingdom of God among these early Christians. First, it was a moral and spiritual incentive of the highest values. The age was one of great trial and suffering. The thought of Christ's return in power was a source of great consolation, and inspired to zeal and devotion. Whenever it led to extravagant or fanatical forms of conduct, these were at once corrected by the apostles. The belief was turned to moral and spiritual account, to the uses of sobriety and of holy living. Secondly, the expectation of Christ's personal return gave unity to the faith of believers. The Christ who had already come was the Christ who would come again. If Christ had abandoned the world forever after the ascent from Olivet, a great blank would have been left in the future for his followers. What is to be the outcome of Christian effort? How is the ongoing of history to terminate? What is the dominant force in the history of the world? Questions like these would have been left without satisfactory answer apart from the doctrine of the Second Coming. His return in glory was thus a truth which held him closely bound to the fortunes of his people on earth. For them he was ever thus the Christ who stood within the shadow, "keeping watch above his own." These same principles apply to Christians of today under the changed circumstances of the world. Any age of self-indulgence needs the same stimulus to holy living. There have been vast ingenuity and arduous labor on the part of scholars in dealing with this element in the religion of Christ as set forth in the New Testament. But there has often been a notable lack of spiritual insight and of sympathy with the genius of the Christian faith. Jesus Christ as Revealer of God and Redeemer of men fills the horizon of the Christian believer, the horizon of the future as well as of the present and the past. The whole of the personal life in its relation to God and to history must be construed in terms of the personal relation to Christ himself. . . .

The Resurrection

The resurrection of the body is a leading topic in the New Testament doctrine of last things. . . . It came into clear recognition in the later stages of the Old Testament revelation. (See Isa. 26:19; Ezek. 37:1-14; Dan. 12:2.) We give now a brief presentation of New Testament passages.

The most explicit teaching of Jesus is in reply to the Sadducees who denied the resurrection of the body. This appears in all the synoptic Gospels (Matt. 22:23–33; Mark 12:18–27; Luke 20:27–40). In brief Jesus says to his questioners that "as touching the resurrection of the dead" they were in error, "not knowing the Scriptures nor the power of God." He then quotes Exodus 3:6. God says, "I am the God of Abraham, and the God of Isaac, and the God of Jacob." Then he adds, "God is not the God of the dead, but of the living." Other passages clearly imply the doctrine of the resurrection, such as Matthew 8:11; Luke 13:28, 29. In the Fourth Gospel the same teaching appears. There the spiritual resurrection is taught, along with explicit statements as to the resurrection of the body. Notable passages are John 11:23–26, where Jesus declares to Martha that he is "the resurrection and the life," and John 5:25–29, where Jesus foretells the resurrection of the righteous and the unrighteous: "All that are in the tombs shall hear his voice, and shall come forth; they that have done good, unto the resurrection of life; and they that have done evil, unto the resurrection of judgment."

In the books of Acts the resurrection of Jesus is everywhere assumed as a fundamental fact of the gospel, and along with it appears the doctrine of the resurrection of men generally (Acts 1:3; 2:30–33; 17:18; 22:7–9; 24:15). In the last passage the apostle Paul announces explicitly a resurrection of the "just and unjust." Ordinarily, in the many passages in his Epistles dealing with the resurrection, Paul has in mind believers. But there is no convincing evidence that, as some have held, he denied the resurrection of the unrighteous. All the evidence we have points the other way.

In the Epistles the resurrection bulks large in Paul's teachings. It is discussed in various aspects, and is a presupposition of all his exposition on the spiritual life in Christ. We need present only the chief points in his doctrine. The resurrection of Christ is the cornerstone of his teaching. Christ was "marked out" to be the Son of God with power "by the resurrection from the dead" (Rom. 1:4). The resurrection of Christ is the basis of the Christian hope and the guaranty of the resurrection of all those who are in Christ. The fifteenth chapter of First Corinthians is devoted to this great theme. Again, Paul declares repeatedly that all believers are now living a resurrection life in the spiritual sense of the word (Eph. 2:5, 6; Col. 2:20; 3:4). In Romans 8:11 he declares that the present indwelling of the Holy Spirit in believers is the pledge of their resurrection. The present spiritual resurrection and the future raising of the body are conceived of as one continuous process. In harmony with this he speaks of "attaining unto the resurrection from the dead" by sacrifice and spiritual struggle. In Romans 8:19–24 Paul declares that nature itself, that is, creation apart from man, will share in the resurrection glory. Nature groans and awaits the resurrection, "the redemption of our body" (Rom. 8:23). In harmony with this doctrine of the resurrection in the four Gospels, in Acts, and in the Pauline Epistles, is the teaching in the other books of the New Testament.

We may next consider two questions about the resurrection, one as to the spirit, the other as to the body. The first is this: May we not interpret the New Testament teaching as a vivid and figurative way of declaring simply the continued life of the spirit, or what we ordinarily mean by the immortality of the soul? The answer must be a decisive negative. The current beliefs of the Jews when Christ spoke forbid this. The issue between Sadducees and Pharisees was clear. One affirmed and the other denied the resurrection. Christ's assertion on the subject could not have meant merely the continued spiritual existence of the soul. Paul refutes those who asserted that "the resurrection is past already" (II Tim. 2:18), thus showing that the body and not the spirit alone was involved in the resurrection in I Corinthians 15:44. By this he can mean only a body adapted to the spirit in its perfected state, a body which would be a perfect instrument of the spirit. In general, we may add that there is no basis whatever in the New Testament for the conception of the Greek philosophy which tended to disparage the body because it is made of matter, and to insist simply upon an incorporeal life of the spirit in the future. Human nature as a whole, in both its aspects, as body and as spirit, is the biblical conception of the true life.

The second question relates to the body. How is the body raised from the dead? Through what changes does it pass? The body dies and is buried, or it is burned, or it is drowned in the sea. Its particles are dissipated in all directions. They reappear in vegetation or in other material forms. Our bodies constantly change, even before death. We are all the time shedding the old and forming new bodies by the processes of life. From these facts it is clear that the resurrection body is not identical in material particles with the present body, or the body that is laid in the grave. How, then, shall we conceive of the resurrection body? Does God create a new body entirely? Or does the spirit of man fashion for itself a spiritual body after death? Or do we possess such a body within the present body?

Here we are on speculative ground. The Scriptures exhibit a remarkable restraint and reserve in this matter. There are no assertions which are negatived by any of the difficulties suggested. There are none which dissipate all our ignorance.

A bright shaft of light penetrates the veil and we see enough to assure and comfort us, but we have no general view of the world beyond. Paul's discussion in the fifteenth chapter of First Corinthians yields the following general statements: (1) The new body will be a "spiritual body" as contrasted with the present natural and perishable body. It will be perfectly adapted to the needs of our spirit. Our spirit will be perfectly clothed. (2) This spiritual body will differ greatly from the present body. Paul contrasts the "bare grain" of wheat that is sown with the stalk of wheat that comes from it. The point of contrast is between the morality and corruption of the body as we now know it and the immortality and glory of the resurrection body. Christ's risen body, with its power of rapid movement, of vanishing and reappearing, of exemption from the ordinary laws of time and space, suggests the nature of the contrast. (3) And yet there is a connection between the old and the new body. "It" is sown, and "it" is raised. What the connection is we do not know.

Summary of the New Testament Teaching

We sum up what has been said about the resurrection in the following general statements based on a correlation and comparison of the pertinent passages in the New Testament. First, the resurrection of Christ is the controlling fact of history in all doctrinal statements about the resurrection. The Christian religion in its present form began to be a regenerative, a recreative force when Jesus arose from the dead. The first gospel related to Jesus and the resurrection.

Secondly, the resurrection of the bodies of believers became an article of faith of the early Christians for the twofold reason that Jesus had risen, and that he had made manifest his power as risen Lord in the experience of his disciples. The hope of resurrection became thus not a detachable belief. It could not be laid aside without vital injury to the whole system of facts and forces to which it belonged.

Thirdly, a present spiritual resurrection was regarded as the preliminary to the final resurrection of the body. The two were bound up in an indissoluble unity. The Holy Spirit had already made believers alive in Christ. The culmination of his divine working would be manifested in risen and glorified bodies.

Fourthly, for the apostle Paul the combination of these two thoughts, the present spiritual resurrection and that of the body hereafter, led to the thought of the resurrection of the body as an attainment. In Philippians 3:7–16 he declares that he suffers the loss of all things that he may "gain Christ," and be "found in him," "that I may know him, and the power of his resurrection," "being conformed unto his death; if by any means I may attain unto the resurrection from the dead." We are, of course, not to understand the apostle as doubting the fact of the resurrection of the body, nor as hoping to win it by merit. He is simply thinking of the resurrection of the body as the last stage in a moral and spiritual process. The mystic union with Christ, the present resurrection life, has its own proper goal, the resurrection of the body. For Paul, the power working in him must be understood as moving toward an end in harmony with itself. Thus the resurrection of the body was implicit, as it were, in the logic of the life in Christ. Experience demands the resurrection as its fruit and goal.

Fifthly, the resurrection of the body was implicit in the first creation. "If there is a natural body," says the apostle, "there is also a spiritual body. So also it is written, the first man Adam became a living soul. The last Adam became a life-giving spirit. Howbeit that is not first which is spiritual, but that which is natural; then that which is spiritual. The first man is of the earth, earthy; the second man is of heaven . . . As we have borne the image of the earthy, we shall also bear the image of the heavenly" (I Cor. 15:44–49). In this passage it seems evident that Paul thinks of the first creation as a stage in a plan which moved toward a higher goal. God's thought was not fully realized in the creation of a perishable body for an immortal being. A spiritual organism was required by a divinely endowed spirit. In Christ, the new head of the race, the new level is attained in both body and spirit. Through him man now partakes of the resurrection life in his spirit. To match this he will have in due time a body possessing the same qualities. Then the new creation in Christ will correspond in both respects with the first creation in Adam.

Sixthly, physical nature itself is related closely to the resurrection hope of Christians. The passage in Romans 8:19–25 declares that the "earnest expectation" of the creation waiteth for the revealing of the sons of God; that "the creation was subjected to vanity"; that this was "not of its own will"; that this subjection was in hope that "the creation itself shall be delivered from the bondage of corruption into the liberty of the glory of the children of God"; and also that the goal in view is "our adoption, to wit, the redemption of our body."

These words suggest that there is a maladjustment between God's children and God's world. The true end of nature is being defeated because of this want of adjustment due to sin. It is as if nature itself longs to become the complete and fit instrument for the promotion of the welfare of God's children, as if it were protesting against the present abnormal situation, as if it strained its gaze into the future in "earnest expectation" of the coming glory.

In his doctrine here the apostle transcends every form of dualism in his outlook upon the future. Nature and spirit are not irreconcilable elements in a finite world. In both shall be realized God's purpose of grace, a purpose which can be expressed in no terms lower than the "liberty of the glory of the children of God."

The Judgment

The statements of the New Testament regarding the final judgment may be grouped under the following heads: The Fact, the Judge, the Subjects, the Purpose, the Necessity of the Final Judgment.

1. The Fact. As to the fact itself little need be said, since this appears in connection with each of the other points. The principle of judgment runs through the Scriptures from beginning to end. The earliest sections of the Old Testament as well as all parts of the New show this in unmistakable terms. The great final judgment takes definite shape in the revelation in Jesus Christ. It is this we now consider.

2. The Judge. In the teaching of Christ and the apostles, God is of course the final Judge; but it is God in Christ. In Matthew 25:31–46 Jesus predicts that he, the Son of man, will come in his glory, and all the angels with him; that he shall sit upon the throne of his glory; that all nations shall be gathered before him; and that he shall separate them as the shepherd separates the sheep from the goats. Acts 17:31 declares that God has appointed a day in which he will judge the world in righteousness, by the man whom he hath ordained, "whereof he hath given assurance unto all men, in that he hath raised him from the dead."

In Romans 2:16 Paul declares that God hath appointed a day in which he will judge the secrets of men "according to my gospel, by Jesus Christ."

In II Corinthians 5:10 it is declared that we must all be made manifest before the judgment-seat of Christ. See also Matthew 19:28; Luke 22:28–30; John 5:22–27; Hebrews 9:27, 28; Revelation 3:21; 20:12.

The fitness of Christ to exercise the authority of final Judge of men grows out of his twofold relations: to God and to men. He is the revelation of God to men. God is now dealing with men in and through him. Men come unto God by him. He is the Way, the Truth, and the Life for men. What God requires of men, and what God is willing to bestow upon men, come into the clearest expression through him. The invisible and eternal God thus adopts a historical mode of manifestation of himself, his grace, his holiness, his power. It is fit therefore that the culmination of his plan should find expression in the Person of his Son.

Again, Christ is "a Son of man," as John reports him as saying. He is Judge of men for this reason (John 5:27). As man Christ knows men. He was tempted in all points as men are tempted, but without sin (Heb. 4:15). He thus possesses the knowledge and sympathy required for equitable and just decisions regarding men.

3. The Subjects. All men are to be judged. There are Scriptures which suggest also that the evil angels are to be judged. In Revelation 20:12 the dead, "small and great," are represented as standing "before God." All are judged (See also II Peter 2:4–9; Jude 6.)

4. The Purpose. The purpose of the final judgment is not the discovery of character, but its manifestation. As Paul expresses it: "We must all be made manifest before the judgment seat of Christ; that each one may receive the things done in the body, according to what he hath done, whether it be good or bad" (II Cor. 5:10). So also in Romans 2:5, 6 men are said to treasure up for themselves wrath in the day of wrath and revelation of the righteous judgment of God, who will render to every man according to his works. They are to give account of "every idle word" that they shall speak (Matt. 12:36). Again, "there is nothing covered up, that shall not be revealed; and hid, that shall not be known" (Luke 12:2).

From the preceding we may state the purpose as follows: To judge means, literally, to discriminate, and from this follows the idea of separate. In judgment God discriminates between the righteous and unrighteous and separates them from each other. But this is simply to uncover or make manifest what previously existed in principle. Deeds done in the body are taken as the criterion of judgment because deeds declare character. The inward state is of course presupposed. No secret thing is hidden from God. The union of men by faith with Christ will be a cardinal fact which will be recognized. The great "deed," the true "work of God," is that men believe on Christ (John 6:29). No other deed means so much as this. It is the mother deed, the root principle of all good deeds. All the good deeds which God approves are in principle the offspring of this. But this is not a meritorious good work which buys salvation. It is the gift of God's grace. And all the deeds which spring from it arise from the same grace. Christians, then, are not saved by works, but by grace through faith. They are rewarded according to the use they make of the grace as manifest in deeds.

5. The Necessity of the Judgment. There are those who object to the idea of a final judgment. They assume that the biblical pictures of the last day are designed merely to impress the imagination, and to set forth vividly a principle which is to be recognized in continuous operation throughout

history. "The world's history is the world's judgment," according to a saying of Schiller.

Now in reply we may say at once that the principle of judgment is in constant operation. In a real sense moral law works itself out inevitably. But its action is not after the manner of physical law. Human freedom and sin have greatly complicated the mechanism of the moral order, if such a phrase be permissible. Bodies attract each other by a fixed law. Chemical changes proceed in ways which may be expressed in exact terms. Matter, force, and motion are changeless and remorseless in their results under given conditions. If the mind of man could grasp the physical universe in all its meaning as merely physical and apart from the actions of free moral beings, and if it could perform the necessary calculations, it could also predict exact conditions a thousand years from now. This is because natural law rules in all the forms of matter. But in a realm of free moral personalities no such mechanical certitude is possible. Human wills are centers of new initiative. They originate new energies in the social order. As evil they render it liable to many complexities and forms of justice. Only another and divine will can readjust these disturbed and abnormal relations. The final judgment is the Christian expression of this fact. We may say then that judgment is the finality demanded by the kingdom of God in all its aspects. We note the following:

(1) Judgment is the finality for the conscience. The idea of a judgment-day arose in the course of history in the religious life of men as the moral sense was deepened. The conscience is the witness in man to the immanent moral law of the universe. Its verdicts in ordinary conduct imply the final verdicts of him who planted the moral nature in us. Conscience is the moral glimpse which the soul obtains of the future. Wrongdoing is accompanied by a forward look upon a fiery judgment (Heb. 10:27). The moral law written in our nature is a copy of the eternal moral law written in God's nature. This law immanent in us implies judgment. A judgment-day means only that that which is implicit shall become explicit.

(2) Judgment is the finality also for history. That which works in the individual conscience works in the corporate conscience of the race. The crimes of nations stand out as clearly in the light of conscience as do the crimes of individuals. The wrongs which the innocent suffer when power rules in the place of right fill the pages of a large part of human history. Posthumous influence is a large part of a man's moral power. His work is not done when he dies. His deeds live after him, and will live in history until the new order which follows judgment shall arise. Heredity and solidarity are forces which must be reckoned with in the final awards to individuals. So also freedom and the corporate choice of low ideals and immoral standards must be applied as principles of judgment in dealing with men in social groups. The slow progress of the moral ideal in history points to a culmination which shall crystallize the contending forces of good and evil and bring about their final separation. This is clear to ordinary human experience. It is even clearer to Christian experience. The

redeemed saints in Revelation are represented as calling for the vengeance of God upon evildoers. Perhaps this moral demand enters character in its perfected form as it does not now. We are commanded to forgive and to avenge not ourselves. There is no contradiction here. But the perfected saints share more completely the divine reaction against sin. All morally vigorous natures partake of this quality in large measure. A contemplation of history as a whole deepens it in every one. A climax which shall bring about a suitable adjustment seems most appropriate.

(3) Judgment is a finality for the theistic view of the world. If God is a Person; if he is in moral relations with men, and men are moral personalities in relations with God; if, in short, we live in a universe of freedom and obligation, God's vindication of his ways to men calls for a final judgment of affairs. He cannot consistently ignore the clamor of the human soul for some sort of understanding of the moral universe. Pantheism reduces us to the level of things. We are passing phenomena, like plants and flowers, the product of an eternal substance or force without moral dignity. But theism puts us on a higher pedestal. We reflect the eternal intelligence and moral cravings.

Now if philosophy generalizes the bare facts presented at any given moment, it gives us a dualism or pluralism of contending forces which forever struggle for the mastery. Such a generalization dethrones God. But if we recognize the purposiveness of the moral sense in us, in Christian experience and in history, and in the theistic view of the world, we look forward to a higher solution. Teleology implies judgment. We may illustrate by the principles of progress and unity in literature and art generally. The kingdom of God is like a great drama. It moves forward to a climax. All the apparently loose ends of the development are slowly combined and gathered together. The unity of the whole is seen only in the final outcome. Without the climax the drama is meaningless. It is mere motion without progress. The book of Revelation, obscure as it is in some ways, is nevertheless an expression of the dramatic principle in the moral kingdom. And it is an expression which cannot be misunderstood. Evil takes many forms. Subdued in one form, it returns in another. The beast, the false prophet, the evil woman, the wicked city, appear from stage to stage. The end is victory, the overthrow of evil, the judgment and separation of the good and the bad, the descent of the New Jerusalem, the habitation of God with men.

In conclusion we affirm, therefore, that in God's kingdom judgment operates constantly as an immanent principle in the ongoing of history. It expresses itself in a gradual process. But it also expresses itself in signal events and great climaxes. In both aspects judgment is in close agreement with the nature of man and the course of history in other respects—the slow process followed by the sudden revolution; the beginning, the ascent toward a goal, the climax, and then a new beginning, a new ascent, a new climax. These are familiar processes in history. The final judgment is the biblical expression of this principle in the moral kingdom.

34

Harry Emerson Fosdick

Abiding Experiences and Changing Categories

I

[It is our endeavor] to describe the problem presented to the modern preacher by the contrasts between Biblical thinking and our own. Our first need as preachers is . . . that scholars should make us so familiar with the contrasts that we shall take them for granted. These divergencies between the Scripture and modern thinking should become so thoroughly the commonplaces of our thought that in our preaching they will not be paraded, exploited, oracularly announced, but assumed. There doubtless was a time when a brave, progressive, young preacher, impressed by the fresh fact that the earth revolves around the sun, must have been tempted to announce it upon all occasions. He was self-conscious about the great discovery. It was a brand-new fact and had an irresistible fascination for the mind. If he preached on ''Love not the world, neither the things that are in the world,'' he almost certainly would take advantage of the text to allude to the fact that the world is not stationary; it moves. But we have long ceased that, not because we are ignorant of the fact or afraid of it, but because we are so familiar with it that we take it for granted.

So some preachers are impressed by the truth, vividly presented to us with fresh and startling illustrations, that the Bible has ways of thinking that are no longer ours. The cure of their obsession and bewilderment is not ignorance; it is familiarity.

With this conviction in mind let us consider certain typical contrasts between Biblical thinking and our own. For example, I believe in the persistence of personality through death, but I do not believe in the resurrection of the flesh. Many of our forefathers could not conceive immortality apart from a resurrected body. The resurrection of the flesh was a mental setting in which alone they supposed that faith in life everlasting ever could be found, and they believed in that setting, argued for it, and fought all doubt about it with the vehemence of those who were sure that if the setting went the jewel would be lost. With what vividness popular Christianity used to visualize judgment day and the resurrected bodies of the dead rising from the sea, restored from dust and ashes, or even reintegrated by the assembling of far-scattered members, you know well. When one goes back to early apologists like Justin Martyr, one finds immortality inextricably associated with what the Apostles' Creed calls "resurrectionem carnis." They put it boldly and unequivocally: "We expect to receive our bodies again after they are dead and laid in the ground."[1]

The basis for this physical phrasing of immortality is plainly laid in the Bible. In the first place, the earliest conception of man's nature which meets us in Scripture would logically necessitate a physical resurrection if there were to be any restored life after death at all. For, at the beginning, what we would call the physical and spiritual elements in man were not distinguished, much less regarded as separable.[2] Man was as yet an undifferentiated unity, so that the continuity of a man's spirit apart from his preserved or restored flesh was an inconceivable idea. One of those strands of development in the Bible most rewarding to the student is the gradual differentiation between the flesh and the spirit, until Paul at last can say that flesh and blood cannot inherit the kingdom of God.[3] At the beginning, however, such an idea would have been incredible. When Enoch was translated or Elijah went to heaven in a chariot of fire, the whole man went. Our rarefied conception of a soul had not yet arisen.

In the second place, the earliest idea of the abode of the dead necessitated the phrasing of immortality in terms of resurrection. For the dead went to Sheol, a definite place below the surface of the earth where, ghosts of their real selves, they yet retained material form. This empty and meaningless existence of Sheol, however, was not immortality. Sheol was a barren dread, not an eager hope. The hope which gradually arose was of restoration to the earth, and that expectation inevitably took the form of resurrection from Sheol. We never should have used the word *resurrection* in expressing hope of life eternal if such had not been its history.

The development of Israel's expectation of a resurrected life makes a fascinating narrative. The eager dream of a Messianic kingdom here on earth grew vivid among the Jews; the question arose whether any one should enjoy it save those who happened to be alive when the consummation came; the sense of justice demanded that at least the eminently righteous should be restored to share the victory;[4] and finally the scene was completed by the expectation that the eminently wicked would also be restored in order that they might be adequately punished for their sins. Only in the late book of Daniel do we find in the Old Testament this fully developed way of thinking: "Many of them that sleep in the dust of the earth shall awake, some to everlasting life, and some to shame and everlasting contempt."[5]

With such a view of man's nature and with such a picture of the estate of the dead, bodily resurrection would have been an inevitable phrasing of life after death even if Zoroastrian influence had not come in. As it was, during the Exile Zoroastrianism became the mold into which the Hebrew expectations of life beyond death were run. The result is familiar: an intermediate state between death and judgment day, then a general resurrection, a gathering of restored body-souls before the throne of God, and the pronouncement of final destinies.[6]

This mental framework in the minds of New Testament folk is revealed in passage after passage. The new and vivid hopes of life eternal which came with Christ still clothed themselves in a familiar category. In the book of Revelation the whole Zoroastrian-Jewish paraphernalia was employed with picturesque effect. To be sure, the new Christian meaning was beginning to burst through its archaic phrasing. In John's Gospel, addressed as it is to Hellenists, the old apocalyptic is largely replaced by eternal life which begins here; and Paul, while he kept the picture of the general resurrection and the judgment day, definitely altered the old tradition by insisting that the resurrection body is not the old flesh restored, but is as different from the old as new grain is from the sown seed.[7] Never in the New Testament, however, does the hope of life eternal altogether escape from the influence of the inherited framework.

This, then, is the question which the modern church must face: are we forever bound to the old category as an expression of our living faith in immortality? A great deal of water has flowed under the bridge since the days when those first disciples thought of life everlasting in Zoroastrian terms. Historically the major agency in crowding out the older ways of thinking has been the Greek philosophy. Its basic premise was the evil of the physical body and the desirability of the soul's escape from its fleshly imprisonment to the realm of eternal spirit. It did not want a bodily resurrection; it wanted to escape from the body altogether. When Origen, for example, expressed his faith in life everlasting, he frankly dematerialized it,[8] and thus became one of the first of that long succession of Christians who, believing earnestly in immortality, have not associated it with the resurrection of the flesh.

Personally, I do not pretend to know the details of the future life. I am sufficiently sense-bound so that I do not easily imagine a completely disembodied existence. I wonder just what we mean by the persistence of personality if we do not include in our thought some such idea as Paul's "not for that we would be unclothed, but that we would be clothed upon."[9] But I am sure that the old Scriptural framework with its background of a Hebrew Sheol and a Zoroastrian judgment day is not in my mind.

Today there are two parties in the churches. They are in active controversy now, and every day their consciousness of difference becomes more sharp and clear. The crux of their conflict lies at this point: one party thinks that the essence of Christianity is its original mental frameworks; the other party is convinced that the essence of Christianity is its abiding experiences. To one party a mental category once worked out and expressed in Scripture is final. Men must never carry the living water in any other receptacle than that; to do so is to forego the right to call oneself a Christian. As a recent writer put it: "The originators of the Christian movement . . . did have an inalienable right to legislate for all generations that should choose to bear the name of 'Christian.' "[10] To the other party nothing in human history seems so changeable as mental categories. They are transient phrasings of permanent convictions and experiences. They rise and fall and pass away. To bind our minds to the perpetual use of ancient matrices of thought just because they were employed in setting forth the eternal principles of the New Testament seems intellectual suicide. What is permanent in Christianity is not mental frameworks but abiding experiences that phrase and rephrase themselves in successive generations' ways of thinking and that grow in assured certainty and in richness of content.

The matter of immortality is simply one illustration of the crucial difference between these two conceptions of Christianity. If the majority of Christians in America would face the facts, they would have to confess that they do not believe in some of the mental frameworks in which Scriptural faith in immortality first arose. Yet for all that they do believe in life everlasting. The two things are separable. Many of us for years have been preaching the Christian hope of life eternal with certitude and joy. We have been comforting the bereaved, solemnizing the frivolous, rebuking the sinful, and undergirding the strong, by the message of life's abiding issues. We have helped to make youth's struggle for character and maturity's devotion to spiritual aims more worthwhile, and to render the "patient continuance" of old age more joyful by the gospel of everlasting life. We believe it with assurance; we have seen its power. But we no more believe in some of the mental categories from which that gospel first emerged like a fine flower out of a green cup, than we believe that the earth is flat.

II

Consider another illustration of this same principle. I believe in the victory of righteousness upon this earth, in the coming kingdom of God whereon Christ looking shall see of the travail of his soul and be satisfied, but I do not believe in the physical return of Jesus. Multitudes of our fathers never thought of separating the two. All history to them was a drama whose dénouement was a literal return of Jesus in the clouds of heaven.

Let us not forget the world-view which possessed the mind of the church when this phrasing of expectancy grew up. It was a world-view in which the literal second coming of our Lord was easily picturable. Cosmas, for example, in the sixth century A.D., gave a precise and detailed statement of the cosmology which with only minor alterations had held the consent of the church from its beginning. The earth, according to Cosmas, is a parallelogram; it is flat; on every side of it are seas; it is four hundred days' journey long and two hundred broad; beyond the seas are massive walls which enclose the whole structure and support the heavenly vault; above the vault are the celestial dwellings.[11] In such an easily picturable world the farewell of Jesus to the earth could be imagined literally as a physical levitation until he was received into heaven a definite distance above the ground, and his return could be literally imagined as a physical descent from the place where he had gone. The marvel is not that such a picture of the Master's going and return should arise in the setting of such a world-view; the marvel is that after that world-view has been so long outgrown, after we have known for centuries that this earth is a globe whirling through space with no ups nor downs any longer meaningful in the old sense, so that if one man ascend from Melbourne and another from London they go in opposite directions, many folk should still retain the old picture of our Lord's ascent and descent from the sky and should regard that picture as a test of a standing or falling church and an indispensable item in the evangelical faith.

The reason for the persistence of this special phrasing of Christian confidence in God's final victory lies of course in the fact that this phrasing is to be found in the Scriptures. The rise of it is not difficult to trace. Given the passionate belief of the Hebrew people that they were Jehovah's chosen race; given the high hopes associated with the Davidic kingdom and the stirring words of prophets predicting a glorious future; given the catastrophes which one by one fell upon the nation, crashing in upon its fortunes as Persia succeeded Assyria, Greece succeeded Persia, and Rome succeeded Greece; and, clearly, if the Hebrews were to cherish hope at all they would cherish it in terms of divine intervention. In some writers, although not in all, this expectation of supernatural help took Messianic form. At first the Davidic kingdom and dynasty were to be restored; then the personality of the Messiah assumed more definite and more glorious importance, until finally the Day of the Lord was to come when the Son of man should appear upon the clouds of heaven. The full flower of this hope is not found in the Old Testament. Only foreshadowings of it are there. The full development of the Messianic expectation came between the Testaments and is now laid bare to us in the apocalyptic writings. They differed in innumerable details but they were unanimous. They were utterly pessimistic about the present; there was no good in it and no hope. They were all concerned about a future which would not be an outgrowth of the present but a catastrophic upsetting of it, its final calcining and annihilation. The Day of the Lord would come suddenly with a Messianic invasion from heaven.

Such was the popular phrasing of hope in the environment where Christianity began, and the effects of that phrasing, the outlines and implications of it, are visible in passage after passage of the New Testament. It is present in some sayings attributed to our Lord, and unless one accepts Matthew Arnold's principle, "Jesus over the heads of all his reporters," at least some elements of it were in the background of his thought. A few years ago Jesus was widely interpreted by scholars as an apocalyptic thinker; today the swing of scholarly opinion is rather the other way and the Master's thought of the victorious future is seen to be rooted in the prophets and psalmists and not in the apocalyptists. Certainly, he never indulged in fanciful pictures of the established kingdom, as the Jewish apocalyptists did. He had no interest in their carnal materializations of the coming era of God's sovereignty over man; he made the kingdom thoroughly moral, a life of filial fellowship with God and fraternal relations between men. Moreover, he emphasized inward preparation for the kingdom's coming. His expectation of God's triumph was not primarily an occasion for proud joy, but for humble penitence. Purity, self-forgetting love, sincerity—such are the attributes of life in the coming kingdom, and a man should repent and seek inward cleansing and renewal when he hears that the Day of God is coming.

More important still, the Master made no such gulf between the present and the future ages as the Jewish apocalyptists did. In his thought the kingdom of God already was throwing foregleams of the new day into the life of man. There was a spiritual sense in which the kingdom was in the earth now—"The kingdom of God is within you."[12] One could feel its power when divine strength and goodness overcame evil—"If I by the finger of God cast out demons, then is the kingdom of God come upon you."[13] It was possible for a man by the quality and spirit of his life to enter the kingdom now—"Thou art not far from the kingdom of God"; "Blessed are the poor in spirit: for theirs is the kingdom of heaven"; "Suffer the little children to come unto me . . . for to such belongeth the kingdom of God."[14] The kingdom, therefore, was not merely something in the future, that is, something to be awaited. Rather it was something to be sought now in spirit like a pearl of great price or a treasure hidden in a field.[15] In this spiritual approach to the idea of God's coming sovereignty over life one loses the apocalyptic way of thinking altogether, and the kingdom, already here, like a grain of mustard seed will grow into a great tree, or like a bit of leaven will gradually transform the whole lump.[16]

Finally, the Master denationalized the kingdom. It was to be no triumph of the Jews over their enemies, but the rule of God over all mankind, and when he lifted up the eyes of his faith he saw men coming into the kingdom from east, west, north, and south.[17] Thus the Master took a current category in which all his people phrased their hope of God's victory on earth, and transformed it. In his hands its fantastic features were stripped away, its deep spiritual requirements were exalted, its present meanings were put to the front, and its narrow national boundaries were broken down.

Nevertheless, the outline of the old thought-form meets us constantly in the New Testament. John's Gospel is one notable exception. That was a brave attempt to reinterpret the Christian hope. It asserted Christ's second coming, but it spiritualized the event. John was addressing his Gospel to Hellenistic readers. They did not understand Jewish apocalyptic; they did not like it; its dramatics, its catastrophic arrival of the day of judgment, its physical resurrections were alien from Greek thought. Just as John's Gospel, therefore, presented Christ, not primarily in terms of Jewish Messiah, but of Greek Logos, so it presented the Christian hope on earth, not in terms of an apocalyptic kingdom, but of an immediately possessed eternal life. Even upon the lips of Jesus at the last supper is put the reiterated teaching that his second coming is now, in the hearts of his true disciples, and that he dwells in them.[18]

Elsewhere in the New Testament, however, the old framework is the familiar setting of hope. The book of Revelation is built upon it. When Paul lets his imagination dwell on God's coming victory he draws the familiar picture with which his Jewish training had acquainted him long before he had known Jesus: the sudden, physical coming of the Messiah upon the clouds, the ascension of the living saints to meet him in the air, the resurrection of the righteous dead, the day of judgment, and the final destinies.

Once more, then, the church faces an issue: are we bound to continue forever expressing in this ancient category our living hope of God's victory on earth? Even John reinterpreted the form of expectation that he might preach God's coming sovereignty in terms that his Hellenistic hearers could understand. Must we then retrace our steps, give up what have seemed to us the gains of centuries, go back to the ways of thinking which developed among Jewish apocalyptists between the Testaments, and become premillenarians that we may be Christians?

Many of us for years have been preaching the victory of God's purpose on earth. We have not surrendered to that superficial modernity which thinks that man, blowing upon his hands, can tackle the task of transforming human character and society and can win against the dead weight of a materialistic universe. Our hope has been in God. We believe that his purpose undergirds human life, that his providence directs it, that his victory lies ahead. The proudest title that we can think of is found in Paul's phrase, "God's fellow-workers."[19] To be ourselves of such a spirit that God can work his victory in and through us; to persuade others to be transformed by the renewing of their minds; to strive for the better organization of society that the divine purpose may be furthered, not hindered, by our economic and political life; and then to await the event in his way and time—such have been our attitude and our preaching, and they have seemed to us Christian.

Those first disciples were expressing in terms of thought familiar to their generation this fundamental hope which we are preaching still. A changed category does not mean an abandoned conviction. At any rate, an increasing number of Christian ministers will go back to the New Testament as the fountainhead of their faith in God and of their assurance that his kingdom will come and his will be done on earth, without its occurring to them to expect the physical return of Jesus on the clouds of heaven.

Notes

[1]Quoted by George Foot Moore, *History of Religions,* Vol. II, p. 162.

[2]H. Wheeler Robinson, *The Religious Ideas of the Old Testament,* p. 83.

[3]I Corinthians 15:50.

[4]Isaiah 26:10.

[5]Daniel 12:2.

[6]See George Foot Moore, *History of Religions,* Vol. II, pp. 55, 75.

[7]I Corinthians 15:35–38.

[8]Origen, *Against Celsus,* Book VI, Ch. XXIX, in *The Ante-Nicene Fathers,* Vol. IV, p. 586.

[9]II Corinthians 5:4.

[10]J. Gresham Machen, *Christianity and Liberalism,* p. 20.

[11]Andrew D. White, *A History of the Warfare of Science with Theology in Christendom,* Vol. I, p. 93.

[12]Luke 17:21.

[13]Luke 11:20.

[14]Mark 12:34; Matthew 5:3; Mark 10:14.

[15]Matthew 13:45, 46; 13:44.

[16]Luke 13:18–21.

[17]Matthew 8:11; Luke 13:20.

[18]John 14:19–23. Cf. Ernest F. Scott, *The Fourth Gospel, Its Purpose and Theology,* Ch. X, "The Return of Christ."

[19]I Corinthians 3:9.

35

L. Harold DeWolf

The Last Judgment

Present Uncertainty Concerning the Judgment

I. An Uneasy Conscience

Great numbers of Christians have developed an uneasy conscience in relation to the traditional doctrine of the last judgment, but not in the way that its proponents might have expected. For these persons are not stirred by this teaching to more serious thought about their own sinful acts or condition. Instead they are morally repelled by the notion that they should regard as supremely good a deity who would divide all human beings into two classes and then condemn all in the one class to inescapable and endless torment.

This dissatisfaction has doubtless been much affected by modern changes in ideals of penology, changes influenced, in turn, both by Christian teaching and by technical studies in criminology. It seems far less evident than it once did that every wrong deed ought to be punished by a penalty proportionate to the offense, whether that offense be measured by external effect or responsible intent. The philosophy of penal justice is in a transitional and highly uncertain state at present and this fact is reflected in thought about divine as well as human judgment upon the wrongdoer.

Does justice mean the application of a *lex talionis?* In view of Jesus' emphatic repudiation of that principle in the Sermon on the Mount, a repudiation which has persuaded increasing numbers of thoughtful men in the last generation, it is doubtful whether "an eye for an eye" can again seem right to the more sensitive Christian conscience, whether the penalty is exacted by a human or a divine judgment. Even when the retributive principle is employed in our courts the tendency is to employ it with increasing moderation and mercy. In such a time men are bound to question the justice of a sentence to everlasting torture for any offense committed in a finite time, especially in a life so obviously affected by ignorance, confusion and insecurity.

Traditional doctrines are also called into question for the absolute and indeed infinite division which they would introduce between people whose actual moral differences a careful ethical analysis shows to be far from absolute. Psychological and ethical study shows that human beings simply cannot be divided into two classes, the good and the bad. Making the infinite difference of destiny to depend on the presence or absence of a certain belief or even of a faithful commitment is not likely to allay the objection but may rather render it more acute.

Underneath these changes in penological and ethical thought is the growing influence of the Christian conviction that God is our loving Father. Jesus did not hesitate to argue that since a good human father would be prompted by love to give good gifts in response to his son's petition, God could be the more surely counted on to do likewise. This teaching has often been hidden under a mass of contrary social and theological teaching. But gradually it has gained a central place in the thought of millions concerning God. As its implications come into recognition, the question is bound to arise: will this loving Father consign some of the persons He has created to a torture which will not awaken them to righteous faith but in which they will have no other possible destiny than torment forever?

2. Resulting Denial of the Judgment

Such critical considerations as have just been suggested have led many Christians simply to reject every notion of a divine judgment. It seems to them that either the doctrine of God's love or the doctrine of judgment, with its heaven and hell, must go. Since the belief in His love seems more central in Christian teaching and more tenable in its own right, as well as more comfortable, all notion of the judgment, they think, must be discarded.

This conclusion, however, has troublesome consequences. For one thing, teaching about the judgment is so prominent in the New Testament, especially in the Gospels, that it seems hard to repudiate it without denying the whole teaching of Jesus, as well as of his disciples. It is true that in the earliest of the Gospels there is only one reference to punishment which may be interpreted as implying everlasting, retributive suffering and even there the figures of the "unquenchable fire" and the "Gehenna, where their worm does not die," are cryptic and somewhat uncertain in precise meaning.[1] But there are many references to divine judgment in other forms. In the later Gospels, especially Matthew and John, the teachings are much more explicit and numerous. Moreover, without a doctrine of divine judgment in some form, there would be no point to a belief in divine forgiveness nor repentance to God. In fact, sin in the Biblical sense would be quite impossible, for there can be no such sin without disobedience to divine command and resultant estrangement from God.

The discarding of belief in all divine judgment has further implications of immediate, far-reaching and serious consequence. If above all human preferences and moral opinions there is not a supreme and decisively normative judgment, then thought can give no coherent account of a genuine moral law. In a world not under divine judgment there could be *differences* of conduct, opinion, custom and mores, but no real good and evil, better and worse.... There is good evidence of an absolute standard, a divine point of reference for all moral opinions. But this is implicitly denied when it is denied that God speaks the decisive word concerning sin and righteousness in a judgment which is beyond all opinions. We are then left to a morally, religiously and intellectually superficial relativism which threatens our very existence through inviting men to make their own truth by willing it so and backing their wills with force capable of demolishing opposition.

3. Need for Reformulation

The situation just described calls loudly for a re-examination of the Christian teaching concerning the judgment. The doctrine must be so formulated as to concur with the evidence, including the newer evidence, and particularly with basic Christian conceptions of God. Only then can it command respect and summon the waning moral forces of the world to the commitment in which alone is personal and social salvation. A teaching which blows hot and cold, describing God as love and then as the vindictive everlasting torturer, will, once men see the contrast as so many now do, produce similarly inconsistent human lives. In their moral confusion such men will minimize the seriousness of their own sin because God is loving and can be counted on to forgive all, while they will resentfully mete out vindictive destruction upon other men in imitation of the supposed judgment of God.

This need for reformulation is recognized by many theologians and philosophers of religion. As evidence we may note the upsurge of interest in conditional immortality—the doctrine that those persons not found prepared for admission into eternal life with God will simply cease to exist at all. But this doctrine, too, would place an infinite gulf (annihilation versus infinite length and value of life) between persons of quite finite (not to say minute) difference.[2]

Another trend is toward belief that all persons are to be saved, a view not now confined to avowed liberals, but defended by such different theologians as Karl Barth and Nels Ferré. Yet none of the first-rate thinkers who hold this view would maintain that it constitutes in itself a doctrine of divine judgment. Neither Barth nor Ferré, for example, would think of saying that God simply looks on all human beings and their various modes of conduct as equally good or evil and indulgently lets them all into eternal fellowship with him.[3]

The proper reformulation of the Christian doctrine of divine judgment is a major task, and will require the efforts of many scholars in such related fields as ethics, criminology, law and New Testament studies, as well as systematic theology. The barest beginnings have been made.[4] All that can be expected here is the suggesting of some considerations, relative to the judgment, which seem true and which ought to be taken into account in a complete statement yet to be made.

Notes

[1] See Mark 9:43–49.

[2] For a brief account of this doctrine, with arguments for and against it, and bibliography, see my article, "Immortality, conditional," in V. Ferm, *An Encyclopedia of Religion.*

[3] What they do say may be found, among other places, in Barth, *Die Kirchliche Dogmatik*, II. 2, pp. 453-563; and Ferré, *The Christian Understanding of God*, Ch. 9. Concerning Barth's universalism, cf. H. Emil Brunner, "The New Barth," *Scottish Journal of Theology*, Vol. 4 (1951), p. 134.

[4] One of the more significant is in Emil Brunner, *Justice and the Social Order.* Another is Norman L. Robinson, *Christian Justice.*

36

C. S. Lewis

Hell

What is the world, O soldiers?
  It is I:
I, this incessant snow,
  This northern sky;
Soldiers, this solitude
  Through which we go
    Is I.

W. de la Mare. *Napoleon*
Richard loves Richard; that is, I am I.
Shakespeare

[We begin with certain premises: (1) the pain that alone can rouse the bad man to a knowledge that all is not well can also lead to a final and unrepented rebellion; (2) man has free will and] all gifts to him are therefore two-edged. From these premises it follows directly that the Divine labour to redeem the world cannot be certain of succeeding as regards every individual soul. Some will not be redeemed. There is no doctrine which I would more willingly remove from Christianity than this, if it lay

Reprinted with permission of Macmillan Publishing Co., Inc., from *The Problem of Pain* by C. S. Lewis. Published in the United States by Macmillan Publishing Co., Inc., 1943. Published in the United Kingdom by Collins Publishers. Used by permission of Collins Publishers.

in my power. But it has the full support of Scripture and, specially, of Our Lord's own words; it has always been held by Christendom; and it has the support of reason. If a game is played, it must be possible to lose it. If the happiness of a creature lies in self-surrender, no man can make that surrender but himself (though many can help him to make it) and he may refuse. I would pay any price to be able to say truthfully, "All will be saved." But my reason retorts, "Without their will," I at once perceive a contradiction; how can the supreme voluntary act of self-surrender be involuntary? If I say, "With their will," my reason replies, "How if they *will not* give in?"

The Dominical utterances about Hell, like all Dominical sayings, are addressed to the conscience and the will, not to our intellectual curiosity. When they have roused us into action by convincing us of a terrible possibility, they have done, probably, all they were intended to do; and if all the world were convinced Christians it would be unnecessary to say a word more on the subject. As things are, however, this doctrine is one of the chief grounds on which Christianity is attacked as barbarous, and the goodness of God impugned. We are told that it is a detestable doctrine—and indeed, I too detest it from the bottom of my heart—and are reminded of the tragedies in human life which have come from believing it. Of the other tragedies which come from not believing it we are told less. For these reasons, and these alone, it becomes necessary to discuss the matter.

The problem is not simply that of a God who consigns some of His creatures to final ruin. That would be the problem if we were Mahometans. Christianity, true, as always, to the complexity of the real, presents us with something knottier and more ambiguous—a God so full of mercy that He becomes man and dies by torture to avert that final ruin from His creatures, and who yet, where that heroic remedy fails, seems unwilling, or even unable, to arrest the ruin by an act of mere power. I said glibly a moment ago that I would pay "any price" to remove this *doctrine*. I lied. I could not pay one-thousandth part of the price that God has already paid to remove the *fact*. And here is the real problem: so much mercy, yet still there is Hell.

I am not going to try to prove the doctrine tolerable. Let us make no mistake; it is *not* tolerable. But I think the doctrine can be shown to be moral, by a critique of the objections ordinarily made, or felt, against it.

First, there is an objection, in many minds, to the idea of retributive punishment as such. . . . [We can, of course, discover a core of righteousness within the vindictive passion itself, in the demand that the evil man must not be left perfectly satisfied with his own evil, that it must be made to appear to him what it rightly appears to others—evil. Pain plants the flag of truth within a rebel fortress—pain, that is, which might still lead to repentance. But what if it does not—if no further conquest than the planting of the flag ever takes place?] Let us try to be honest with ourselves. Picture to yourself a man who has risen to wealth or power by a continued course of treachery and cruelty, by exploiting for purely selfish ends the noble motions of his victims, laughing the while at their simplicity; who, having thus attained success, uses it for the gratification of lust and hatred and finally parts with the last rag of honour among thieves by betraying his own accomplices and jeering at their last moments of bewildered disillusionment. Suppose, further, that he does all this, not (as we like to imagine) tormented by remorse or even misgiving, but eating like a schoolboy and sleeping like a healthy infant—a jolly, ruddy-cheeked man, without a care in the world, unshakably confident to the very end that he alone has found the answer to the riddle of life, that God and man are fools whom he has got the better of, that his way of life is utterly successful, satisfactory, unassailable. We must be careful at this point. The least indulgence of the passion for revenge is very deadly sin. Christian charity counsels us to make every effort for the conversion of such a man: to prefer his conversion, at the peril of our own lives, perhaps of our own souls, to his punishment—to prefer it infinitely. But that is not the question. Supposing he *will* not be converted, what destiny in the eternal world can you regard as proper for him? Can you really desire that such a man, *remaining what he is* (and he must be able to do that if he has free will), should be confirmed forever in his present happiness—should continue, for all eternity, to be perfectly convinced that the laugh is on his side? And if you cannot regard this as tolerable, is it only your wickedness—only spite—that prevents you from doing so? Or do you find that conflict between Justice and Mercy, which has sometimes seemed to you such an outmoded piece of theology, now actually at work in your own mind, and feeling very much as if it came from above, not from below? You are moved not by a desire for the wretched creature's pain as such, but by a truly ethical demand that, soon or late, the right should be asserted, the flag planted in this horribly rebellious soul, even if no fuller and better conquest is to follow. In a sense, it is better for the creature itself, even if it never becomes good, that it should know itself a failure, a mistake. Even mercy can hardly wish to such a man his eternal, contented continuance in such ghastly illusion. Thomas Aquinas said of suffering, as Aristotle had said of shame, that it was a thing not good in itself, but a thing which might have a certain goodness in particular circumstances. That is to say, if evil is present, pain at recognition of the evil, being a kind of knowledge, is relatively good; for the alternative is that the soul should be ignorant of the evil, or ignorant that the evil is contrary to its nature, "either of which," says the philosopher, "is *manifestly* bad."[1] And I think, though we tremble, we agree.

The demand that God should forgive such a man while he remains what he is, is based on a confusion between condoning and forgiving. To condone an evil is simply to ignore it, to treat it as if it were good. But forgiveness needs to be accepted as well as offered if it is to be complete—and a man who admits no guilt can accept no forgiveness.

I have begun with the conception of Hell as a positive retributive punishment inflicted by God because that is the form in which the doctrine is most repellent, and I wished to tackle the strongest objection. But, of course, though Our Lord often speaks of Hell as a sentence inflicted by a tribunal, He also says elsewhere that the judgement consists in the very fact that men prefer darkness to light, and that not He, but His "word," judges men.[2] We are therefore at liberty—since the two conceptions, in the long run, mean the same thing—to think of this bad man's perdition not as a sentence imposed on him but as the mere fact of being what he is. The characteristic of lost souls is "their rejection of everything that is not simply themselves."[3] Our imaginary egoist has tried to turn everything he meets into a province or appendage of the self. The taste for the *other,* that is, the very capacity for enjoying good, is quenched in him except in so far as his body still draws him into some rudimentary contact with an outer world. Death removes this last contact. He has his wish—to live wholly in the self and to make the best of what he finds there. And what he finds there is Hell.

Another objection turns on the apparent disproportion between eternal damnation and transitory sin. And if we think of eternity as a mere prolongation of time, it is disproportionate. But many would reject this idea of eternity. If we think of time as a line—which is a good image, because the parts of time are successive and no two of them can co-exist; *i.e.,* there is no *width* in time, only length—we probably ought to think of eternity as a plane or even a solid. Thus the whole reality of a human being would be represented by a solid figure. That solid would be mainly the work of God, acting through grace and nature, but human free will would have contributed the base line which we call earthly life; and if you draw your base line askew, the whole solid will be in the wrong place. The fact that life is short, or, in the symbol, that we contribute only one little line to the whole complex figure, might be regarded as a Divine mercy. For if even the drawing of that little line, left to our free will, is sometimes so badly done as to spoil the whole, how much worse a mess might we have made of the figure if more had been entrusted to us? A simpler form of the same objection consists in saying that death ought not to be final, that there ought to be a second chance.[4] I believe that if a million chances were likely to do good, they would be given. But a master often knows, when boys and parents do not, that it is really useless to send a boy in for a certain examination again. Finality must come some time, and it does not require a very robust faith to believe that omniscience knows when.

A third objection turns on the frightful intensity of the pains of Hell as suggested by mediæval art and, indeed, by certain passages in Scripture. Von Hügel here warns us not to confuse the doctrine itself with the *imagery* by which it may be conveyed. Our Lord speaks of Hell under three symbols: first, that of punishment ("everlasting punishment," Matt. 25:46); second, that of destruction ("fear Him who is able to destroy both body and soul in Hell," Matt. 10:28); and thirdly, that of privation, exclusion, or banishment into "the darkness outside," as in the parables of the man without a wedding garment or of the wise and foolish virgins. The prevalent image of fire is significant because it combines the ideas of torment and destruction. Now it is quite certain that all these expressions are intended to suggest something unspeakably horrible, and any interpretation which does not face that fact is, I am afraid, out of court from the beginning. But it is not necessary to concentrate on the images of torture to the exclusion of those suggesting destruction and privation. What can that be whereof all three images are equally proper symbols? Destruction, we should naturally assume, means the unmaking, or cessation, of the destroyed. And people often talk as if the "annihilation" of a soul were intrinsically possible. In all our experience, however, the destruction of one thing means the emergence of something else. Burn a log, and you have gases, heat and ash. To *have been* a log means now being those three things. If soul can be destroyed, must there not be a state of *having been* a human soul? And is not that, perhaps, the state which is equally well described as torment, destruction, and privation? You will remember that in the parable, the saved go to a place prepared for *them,* while the damned go to a place never made for men at all.[5] To enter heaven is to become more human than you ever succeeded in being in earth; to enter Hell is to be banished from humanity. What is cast (or casts itself) into Hell is not a man: it is "remains." To be a complete man means to have the passions obedient to the will and the will offered to God: to *have been* a man—to be an ex-man or "damned ghost"—would presumably mean to consist of a will utterly centred in its self and passions utterly uncontrolled by the will. It is, of course, impossible to imagine what the consciousness of such a creature—already a loose congeries of mutually antagonistic sins rather than a sinner—would be like. There may be a truth in the saying that "Hell is Hell, not from its own point of view, but from the heavenly point of view." I do not think this belies the severity of Our Lord's words. It is only to the damned that their fate could ever seem less than unendurable. And it must be admitted that as . . . we think of eternity, the categories of pain and pleasure, which have engaged us so long, begin to recede, as vaster good and evil loom in sight. Neither pain nor pleasure as such has the last word. Even if it were possible that the experience (if it can be called experience) of the lost contained no pain and much pleasure, still, that black pleasure would be such as to send any soul, not already damned, flying to its prayers in nightmare terror; even if there were pains in heaven, all who understand would desire them.

A fourth objection is that no charitable man could himself be blessed in heaven while he knew that even one human soul was still in Hell; and if so, are we more merciful than God? At the back of this objection lies a mental picture of heaven and Hell co-existing in unilinear time as the histories of England and America co-exist, so that at each moment the blessed could say, "The miseries of Hell are *now* going on." But I notice that Our Lord, while stressing the terror of Hell with unsparing severity, usually emphasises the idea not of duration but of *finality*. Consignment to the destroying fire is usually treated as the end of the story—not as the beginning of a new story. That the lost soul is eternally fixed in its diabolical attitude we cannot doubt; but whether this eternal fixity implies endless duration—or duration at all—we cannot say. Dr. Edwyn Bevan has some interesting speculations on this point.[6] We know much more about heaven than Hell, for heaven is the home of humanity and therefore contains all that is implied in a glorified human life, but Hell was not made for men. It is in no sense *parallel* to heaven; it is "the darkness outside," the outer rim where being fades away into nonenity.

Finally, it is objected that the ultimate loss of a single soul means the defeat of omnipotence. And so it does. In creating beings with free will, omnipotence from the outset submits to the possibility of such defeat. What you call defeat, I call miracle; for to make things which are not Itself, and thus to become, in a sense, capable of being resisted by its own handiwork, is the most astonishing and unimaginable of all the feats we attribute to the Deity. I willingly believe that the damned are, in one sense, successful, rebels to the end—that the doors of Hell are locked on the *inside*. I do not mean that the ghosts may not *wish* to come out of Hell, in the vague fashion wherein an envious man "wishes" to be happy; but they certainly do not will even the first preliminary stages of that self-abandonment through which alone the soul can reach any good. They enjoy forever the horrible freedom they have demanded, and are therefore self-enslaved, just as the blessed, forever submitting to obedience, become through all eternity more and more free.

In the long run the answer to all those who object to the doctrine of Hell is itself a question: "What are you asking God to do?" To wipe out the past sins of the damned and, at all costs, to give them a fresh start, smoothing every difficulty and offering every miraculous help? But He has done so, on Calvary. To forgive Him? They will not be forgiven. To leave them alone? Alas, I am afraid that is what He does.

One caution, and I have done. In order to rouse modern minds to an understanding of the issues, I ventured to introduce in this chapter a picture of the sort of bad man whom we most easily perceive to be truly bad. But when the picture has done that work, the sooner it is forgotten the better. In all discussions of Hell we should keep steadily before our eyes the possible damnation, not of our enemies nor our friends (since both these disturb the reason), but of ourselves. This chapter is not about your wife or son, nor about Nero or Judas Iscariot; it is about you and me. . . .

C. S. Lewis

Heaven

It is required
You do awake your faith. Then all stand still;
On; those that think it is unlawful business
I am about, let them depart.
                              Shakespeare. *Winter's Tale*

Plunged in thy depth of mercy let me die
The death that every soul that lives desires.
                              Cowper out of *Madame Guion*

"I reckon," said Paul, "that the sufferings of this present time are not worthy to be compared with the glory that shall be revealed in us."[7] If this is so, a book on suffering which says nothing of heaven is leaving out almost the whole of one side of the account. Scripture and tradition habitually put the joys of heaven into the scale against the sufferings of earth, and no solution of the problem of pain which does not do so can be called a Christian one. We are very shy nowadays of even mentioning heaven. We are afraid of the jeer about "pie in the sky," and of being told that we are trying to "escape" from the duty of making a happy world here and now into dreams of a happy world elsewhere. But either there is "pie in the sky" or there is not. If there is not, then Christianity is false, for this doctrine is woven into its whole fabric. If there is, then this truth, like any other, must be faced, whether it is useful at political meetings or no. Again, we are afraid that heaven is a bribe, and that if we make it our goal we shall no longer be disinterested. It is not so. Heaven offers nothing that a mercenary soul can desire. It is safe to tell the pure in heart that they shall see God, for only the pure in heart want to. There are rewards that do not sully motives. A man's love for a woman is not mercenary because he wants to marry her, nor his love for poetry mercenary because he wants to read it, nor his love of exercise less disinterested because he wants to run and leap and walk. Love, by definition, seeks to enjoy its object.

You may think that there is another reason for our silence about heaven—namely, that we do not really desire it. But that may be an illusion. What I am now going to say is merely an opinion of my own without the slightest authority, which I submit to the judgement of better Christians and better scholars than myself. There have been times when I think we do not desire heaven; but more often I find myself wondering whether, in our heart of hearts, we have ever desired anything else. You may have noticed that the books you really love are bound together by a secret thread. You know very well what is the common quality that makes you love them, though you cannot put it into words; but most of your friends do not see it at all, and often wonder why, liking this, you should also like that. Again, you have stood before some landscape, which seems to embody what you have been looking for all your life, and then turned to the friend at your side who appears to be seeing what you saw—but at the first words a gulf yawns between you, and you realise that this landscape means something totally different to him, that he is pursuing an alien vision and cares nothing for the ineffable suggestion by which you are transported. Even in your hobbies, has there not always been some secret attraction which the others are curiously ignorant of—something, not to be identified with, but always on the verge of breaking through, the smell of cut wood in the workshop or the clap-clap of water against the boat's side? Are not all lifelong friendships born at the moment when at last you meet another human being who has some inkling (but faint and uncertain even in the best) of that something which you were born desiring, and which, beneath the flux of other desires and in all the momentary silences between the louder passions, night and day, year by year, from childhood to old age, you are looking for, watching for, listening for? You have never *had* it. All the things that have ever deeply possessed your soul have been but hints of it—tantalising glimpses, promises never quite fulfilled, echoes that died away just as they caught your ear. But if it should really become manifest—if there ever came an echo that did not die away but swelled into the sound itself—you would know it. Beyond all possibility of doubt you would say, "Here at last is the thing I was made for." We cannot tell each other about it. It is the secret signature of each soul, the incommunicable and unappeasable want, the thing we desired before we met our wives or made our friends or chose our work, and which we shall still desire on our deathbeds, when the mind no longer knows wife or friend or work. While we are, this is. If we lose this, we lose all.[8]

This signature on each soul may be a product of heredity and environment, but that means only that heredity and environment are among the instruments whereby God creates a soul. I am considering not how, but why, He makes each soul unique. If He had no use for all these differences, I do not see why He should have created more souls than one. Be sure that the ins and outs of your individuality are no mystery to Him, and one day they will no longer be a mystery to you. The mould in which a key is made would be a strange thing, if you had never seen a key; and the key itself a strange thing if you had never seen a lock. Your soul has a curious shape because it is a hollow made to fit a particular swelling in the infinite contours of the divine substance, or a key to unlock one of the doors in the house with many mansions. For it is not humanity in the abstract that is to be saved, but you—you, the individual reader, John Stubbs or Janet Smith. Blessed and fortunate creature, your eyes shall behold Him and not another's. All that you are, sin apart, is destined, if you will let God have His good way, to utter satisfaction. The Brocken spectre "looked to every man like his first love," because she was a cheat. But God will look to every soul like its first love because He is its first love. Your place in heaven will seem to be made for you and you alone, because you were made for it—made for it stitch by stitch as a glove is made for a hand.

It is from this point of view that we can understand Hell in its aspect of privation. All your life an unattainable ecstasy has hovered just beyond the grasp of your consciousness. The day is coming when you will wake to find, beyond all hope, that you have attained it, or else, that it was within your reach and you have lost it forever.

This may seem a perilously private and subjective notion of the pearl of great price, but it is not. The thing I am speaking of is not an experience. You have experienced only the *want* of it. The thing itself has never actually been embodied in any thought, or image, or emotion. Always it has summoned you out of yourself. And if you will not go out of yourself to follow it, if you sit down to brood on the desire and attempt to cherish it, the desire itself will evade you. "The door into life generally opens behind us" and "the only wisdom" for one "haunted with the scent of unseen roses, is work."[9] This secret fire goes out when you use the bellows; bank it down with what seems unlikely fuel of dogma and ethics, turn your back on it and attend to your duties, and then it will blaze. The world is like a picture with a golden background, and we the figures in that picture. Until you step off the plane of the picture into the large dimensions of death you cannot see the gold. But we have reminders of it. To change our metaphor, the blackout is not quite complete. There are chinks. At times the daily scene looks big with its secret.

Such is my opinion; it may be erroneous. Perhaps this secret desire also is part of the Old Man and must be crucified before the end. But this opinion has a curious trick of evading denial. The desire—much more the satisfaction—has always refused to be fully present in any experience. Whatever you try to identify with it, turns out to be not it but something else, so that hardly any degree of crucifixion or transformation could go beyond what the desire itself leads us to anticipate. Again, if this opinion is not true, something better is. But "something better"—not this or that experience, but beyond it—is almost the definition of the thing I am trying to describe.

The thing you long for summons you away from the self. Even the desire for the thing lives only if you abandon it. This is the ultimate law—the seed dies to live, the bread must be cast upon the waters, he that loses his soul will save it. But the life of the seed, the finding of the bread, the recovery of the soul, are as real as the preliminary sacrifice. Hence it is truly said of heaven, "In heaven there is no ownership. If any there took upon him to call anything his own, he would straightway be thrust out into hell and become an evil spirit."[10] But it is also said, "To him that overcometh I will give . . . a white stone, and in the stone a new name written, which no man knoweth saying he that receiveth it."[11] What can be more a man's own than this new name which even in eternity remains a secret between God and him? And what shall we take this secrecy to mean? Surely, that each of the redeemed shall forever know and praise some one aspect of the Divine beauty better than any other creature can. Why else were individuals created, but that God, loving all infinitely, should love each differently? And this difference, so far from impairing, floods with meaning the love of all blessed creatures for one another, the communion of the saints. If all experienced God in the same way and returned Him an identical worship, the song of the Church triumphant would have no symphony; it would be like an orchestra in which all the instruments played the same note. Aristotle has told us that a city is a unity of unlikes,[12] and St. Paul that a body is a unity of different members.[13] Heaven is a city, and a Body, because the blessed remain eternally different. [It is] a society, because each has something to tell all the others—fresh and ever fresh news of the "My God" whom each finds in Him whom all praise as "Our God." For doubtless the continually successful, yet never completed, attempt by each soul to communicate its unique vision to all others (and that by means whereof earthly art and philosophy are but clumsy imitations) is also among the ends for which the individual was created.

For union exists only between distincts; and, perhaps, from this point of view, we catch a momentary glimpse of the meaning of all things. Pantheism is a creed not so much false as hopelessly behind the times. Once, before creation, it would have been true to say that everything was God. But God created; He caused things to be other than Himself that, being distinct, they might learn to love Him, and achieve union instead of mere sameness. Thus He also cast His bread upon the waters. Even within the creation we might say that inanimate matter, which has no will, is one with God in a sense in which men are not. But it is not God's purpose that we should go back into that old identity (as, perhaps, some Pagan mystics would have us do) but that we should go on to the maximum distinctness there to be reunited with Him in a higher fashion. Even within the Holy One Himself, it is not sufficient that the Word should *be* God, it must also be *with* God. The Father eternally begets the Son and the Holy Ghost proceeds; Deity introduces distinction within itself so that the union of reciprocal loves may transcend mere arithmetical unity or self-identity.

But the eternal distinctness of each soul—the secret which makes of the union between each soul and God a species in itself—will never abrogate the law that forbids ownership in heaven. As to its fellow-creatures, each soul, we suppose, will be eternally engaged in giving away to all the rest that which it receives. And as to God, we must remember that the soul is but a hollow which God fills. Its union with God is, almost by definition, a continual self-abandonment—an opening, an unveiling, a surrender, of itself. A blessed spirit is a mould ever more and more patient of the bright metal poured into it, a body ever more completely uncovered to the meridian blaze of the spiritual sun. We need not suppose that the necessity for something analogous to self-conquest will ever be ended, or that eternal life will not also be eternal dying. It is in this sense that, as there may be pleasures in Hell (God shield us from them), there may be something not all unlike pains in heaven (God grant us soon to taste them).

For in self-giving, if anywhere, we touch a rhythm not only of all creation but of all being. For the Eternal Word also gives Himself in sacrifice—and that not only on Calvary. For when He was crucified He "did that in the wild weather of His outlying provinces which He had done at home in glory and gladness."[14] From before the foundation of the world He surrenders begotten Deity back to begetting Deity in obedience. And as the Son glorifies the Father, so also the Father glorifies the Son.[15] And, with submission, as becomes a layman, I think it was truly said, "God loveth not Himself as Himself but as Goodness; and if there were aught better than God, He would love that and not Himself."[16] From the highest to the lowest, self exists to be abdicated and, by that abdication, becomes the more truly self, to be thereupon yet the more abdicated, and so forever. This is not a heavenly law which we can escape by remaining earthly, nor an earthly law which we can escape by being saved. What is outside the system of self-giving is not earth, nor nature, nor "ordinary life," but simply and solely Hell. Yet even Hell derives from this law such reality as it has. That fierce imprisonment in the self is but the obverse of the self-giving which is absolute reality; [it is] the negative shape which the outer darkness takes by surrounding and defining the shape of the real, or which the real imposes on the darkness by having a shape and positive nature of its own.

The golden apple of selfhood, thrown among the false gods, became an apple of discord because they scrambled for it. They did not know the first rule of the holy game, which is that every player must by all means touch the ball and then immediately pass it on. To be found with it in your hands is a fault; to cling to it, death. But when it flies to and fro among the players too swift for eye to follow, and the great master Himself leads the revelry, giving Himself eternally to His creatures in the generation, and back to Himself in the sacrifice, of the Word, then indeed the eternal dance "makes heaven drowsy with the harmony." All pains and pleasures we have known on earth are early initiations in the movements of that dance, but the dance itself is strictly incomparable with the sufferings of this present time. As we draw nearer to its uncreated rhythm, pain and pleasure sink almost out of sight. There is joy in the dance, but it does not exist for the sake of joy. It does not even exist for the sake of good, or of love. It is Love Himself and Good Himself, and therefore happy. It does not exist for us, but we for it. The size and emptiness of the universe . . . should awe us still, for though they may be no more than a subjective byproduct of our three-dimensional imagining, yet they symbolise great truth. As our Earth is to all the stars, so doubtless are we men and our concerns to all creation; as all the stars are to space itself, so are all creatures, all thrones and powers and mightiest of the created gods, to the abyss of the self-existing Being, who is to us Father and Redeemer and indwelling Comforter, but of whom no man nor angel can say nor conceive what He is in and for Himself, or what is the work that He "maketh from the beginning to the end." For they are all derived and unsubstantial things. Their vision fails them and they cover their eyes from the intolerable light of utter actuality, which was and is and shall be, which never could have been otherwise, which has no opposite.

Notes

[1] *Summa Theol.,* I,II[ae], Q. xxxix, Art. 1.

[2] John 3:19; 12:48.

[3] See von Hügel, *Essays and Addresses,* 1st series, *What do we mean by Heaven and Hell?*

[4] The conception of a "second chance" must not be confused either with that of Purgatory (for souls already saved) or of Limbo (for souls already lost).

[5] Matt. 25:34, 41.

[6] *Symbolism and Belief,* p. 101.

[7] Rom. 8:18.

[8] I am not, of course, suggesting that these immortal longings which we have from the Creator because we are men, should be confused with the gifts of the Holy Spirit to those who are in Christ. We must not fancy we are holy because we are human.

[9] George Macdonald, *Alec Forbes,* cap. XXXIII.

[10]*Theologia Germanica,* LI.

[11]Rev. 2:17.

[12]*Politics,* II, 2, 4.

[13]I Cor. 12:12–30.

[14]George Macdonald, *Unspoken Sermons: 3rd Series,* pp. 11, 12.

[15]John 17:1, 4, 5.

[16]*Theol. Germ.,* XXXII.

The Millennium
and the Tribulation

37

Loraine Boettner

Christian Hope
and a Millennium

When we speak of postmillennialism, we mean that view of the last things which holds that the kingdom of God is now being extended in the world through the preaching of the Gospel and the saving work of the Holy Spirit, that the world eventually is to be Christianized, and that the return of Christ will occur at the close of a long period of righteousness and peace, commonly called the millennium.

This view is to be distinguished from that optimistic, but false, view of human progress and betterment which holds that the kingdom of God on earth will be achieved through a natural, rather than a supernatural, process by which mankind will be improved and social institutions will be reformed and brought to a higher level of culture and efficiency. The latter view regards the kingdom of God as the product of natural laws in an evolutionary process and represents only a spurious or pseudo-postmillennialism.

The word *millennium,* a thousand years, is found just six times in Scripture, all in the first seven verses in the twentieth chapter of Revelation. Some Bible students take the word literally and hold that Christ will set up a kingdom on earth which will continue for precisely that length of

From *Christianity Today,* 29 September 1958, pp. 13–14. Used by permission.

time. We believe, however, that the word is to be understood figuratively, as meaning an indefinitely long period.

Outstanding theologians who have held the postmillennial position are: David Brown, whose book, *The Second Advent* (1849), was for many years the standard work on the subject, Charles Hodge, W. G. T. Shedd, Robert L. Dabney, Augustus H. Strong and Benjamin B. Warfield. James H. Snowden's book, *The Return of the Lord* (1919), is an able presentation of the postmillennial system.

This system has been much neglected during the past third of a century, but the other systems too have had their periods of neglect and decline. For nearly a thousand years between the time of Augustine and the Protestant Reformation, premillennialism was in almost total eclipse; and amillennialism as a system has received its fullest expression only in comparatively recent times.

Evangelical Agreement

The essential presuppositions of the three systems are similar, and each has been held by men of unquestioned sincerity and ability. Each holds to the full inspiration and authority of Scripture. Each holds to the same general concept of the death of Christ as a sacrifice to satisfy divine justice and as the only ground for the salvation of souls. Each holds that there will be a future, glorious, visible, personal coming of Christ. Each system is, therefore, consistently evangelical.

The differences between these systems arise not out of any conscious or intended disloyalty to Scripture, but primarily out of the distinctive method employed by each in the interpretation of Scripture; and they relate chiefly to the time and purpose of Christ's second coming and to the kind of kingdom that is being set up or will be set up at his coming. Premillennialists insist on literal interpretation as the only means by which the true meaning of Scripture can be set forth, while post- and amillennialists readily accept a figurative interpretation where that seems preferable.

Literal and Spiritual

But while, as postmillennialists, we spiritualize some prophecies or other statements of the Bible, that does not mean that we explain them away. Sometimes their true meaning is to be found only in the unseen spiritual world. We hold that to literalize and materialize those prophecies is to keep them on an earthly level and so to miss their true and deeper meaning. That was the method followed by the Jews in their interpretation of Messianic prophecy. They looked for literal fulfillments with a political ruler and an earthly kingdom, and as a result, they missed the redemptive element so completely that when the Messiah came they did not recognize him, but instead rejected and crucified him. The fearful consequences of literalistic interpretation as it related to the first coming should put us on guard against making the same mistake regarding the second.

The millennium to which the postmillennialist looks forward is a golden age of spiritual prosperity embraced in the larger Church age. We hold that the present age gradually merges into the millennial age as an increasingly larger proportion of the world's inhabitants are converted to Christianity. We do not hold that every person will be a Christian, nor that sin will be completely eliminated, but only that sin will be reduced to a minimum. Sinless perfection belongs only to the heavenly state. The earth during the present age can never become paradise regained. But a Christianized world can afford a foretaste of heaven, an earnest of the good things that God has in store for those who love him.

World Will Get Better

As the millennium becomes a reality, Christian principles of belief and conduct will be the accepted standard for nations and individuals. Figuratively, the wolf and the lamb shall dwell together when people and forces formerly antagonistic and hateful to each other are so changed that they work together in one harmonious purpose. The desert shall blossom as the rose, literally, as economic and scientific advances lead to generally prosperous conditions the world over; and figuratively, as moral and spiritual conditions are improved. Health and education will be the rule, and wealth will be vastly more abundant and more widely shared.

Life at that time will compare with life in the world today in much the same way that life in a truly Christian community compares with that in a pagan or irreligious community. The millennium embodies, therefore, not a political world-power kingdom of Jewish supremacy continuing for an exact one thousand years, but a spiritual kingdom in the hearts of men, of which the Church will continue to be then as now the outward and visible manifestation. It closes with the second coming of Christ, the general resurrection and judgment.

What the Scripture Says

But the important question is, What do the Scriptures say about a future golden age? Do they warrant such an expectation? In both the Old and New Testaments we find an abundance of evidence to that effect, although lack of space prevents us from giving more than a small portion of that evidence. Isaiah tells us that "the earth shall be full of the knowledge of Jehovah, as the waters cover the sea" (11:9). Jeremiah gives the promise that the time is coming when it no longer will be necessary for a man to teach his neighbor or his brother, saying, "Know the Lord: for they shall all know me, from the least of them unto the greatest of them" (31:34).

Speaking through the psalmist, God says, "Ask of me, and I shall give thee the heathen for thine inheritance, and the uttermost parts of the earth for thy possession" (2:8); and again, "All the ends of the world shall remember and turn unto the Lord: and all the kindreds of the nations shall worship before thee" (22:27). The last book of the Old Testament contains a promise that "from the rising of the sun even unto the going down of the same my name shall be great among the Gentiles" (Mal. 1:11). These great and precious promises are so far-reaching and expansive that they stagger the imagination.

In the New Testament we find the same clear teaching. Strong emphasis is placed on the fact that it is *the world* that is the object of Christ's redemption. "God was in Christ, reconciling the world unto himself" (II Cor. 5:19). "For God sent not the Son into the world to condemn the world; but that the world through him might be saved" (John 3:17). The parable of the leaven teaches the universal extension and triumph of the Gospel as society is transformed by the kingdom influences.

Victory Certain

The redemption of the world, then, is a long, slow process, extending through the centuries, yet surely approaching an appointed goal. We live in the day of advancing victory and see the conquest taking place. From the human viewpoint there are many apparent setbacks, and it often looks as though the forces of evil are about to gain the upper hand. But as one age succeeds another, there is progress. Looking back across the nearly 2,000 years that have elapsed since the coming of Christ, we see that there has been marvelous progress. All over the world, pagan religions have had their day and are disintegrating. None of them can stand the open competition of Christianity. They await only the *coup de grâce* of an aroused and energetic Christianity to send them into oblivion.

We have been commanded by our Lord to go and make disciples of all the nations. We are engaged in a mighty struggle that rages through the centuries; there can be no compromise. The Church *must* conquer the world, or the world will destroy the Church. Christianity is *the* system of truth, the only one that through the ages has had the blessing of God upon it. We shall not expect the final fruition within our lifetime, nor within this century. But the goal is certain and the outcome is sure. The future is as bright as the promises of God. The great requirement is faith that the Great Commission of Christ will be fulfilled through the outpouring of the Holy Spirit and preaching of the everlasting Gospel.

W. J. Grier

Christian Hope
and the Millennium

The term "amillennial," or "non-millennial," sometimes produces misunderstanding. It might lead some to suppose that those who hold this view reject what is said in Revelation 20 about "the thousand years." Of course, this is not so. That passage is very precious to amillennialists; they delight in what it has to say about "the thousand years," and they insist that the passage has been misunderstood by "pre-mils" and by some "post-mils."

It is also sometimes assumed that this view is of recent origin. Its fundamental ideas, however, are found in Augustine (A.D. 354–430). Indeed, Professor D. H. Kromminga, who was himself a "pre-mil," contended that the Epistle of Barnabas (one of the earliest Christian writings outside the Bible) shows "a very early amillennial type of eschatology" (*Millennium in the Church*, p. 40), but this conclusion is disputed. Certain it is that the "a-mil" view is quite in harmony with the statements of the Apostles' Creed, the great ecumenical creeds, and confessions of the Reformation.

From *Christianity Today*, 13 October 1958, pp. 18–19. Used by permission.

A Change of View

For some twelve years after his conversion, the present writer was inclined to the "pre-mil" view. He received a jolt, however, from an American expositor who affirmed that the early part of the Acts of the Apostles was a "national offer" to the Jews, while only in the latter part was there the gospel of the grace of God. A further jolt came when he met with the suggestion that there was a new age to come when men would be saved on some basis other than the grace of God. These statements—which are no doubt typical of only a section of "pre-mils"—led the writer to devote himself to a study of the whole subject afresh. Two sections of Scripture had inclined him to the "pre-mil" view: (1) certain Old Testament prophecies which seemed on the face of them to predict a national restoration of Israel to Palestine, and (2) Revelation 20, which seemed on the face of it to predict a literal thousand-year reign.

Old Testament Prophecy

When setting out to study the subject afresh, the writer was engaged in giving Bible class talks on the book of Ezekiel. Among commentaries consulted were those by Bishop Wordsworth and Principal P. Fairbairn. These expositors revealed a wealth of meaning in the prophecies; they were faithful to the text and brought from it a rich message. While still a "pre-mil," the present writer read—with the best will to follow and assimilate—commentaries on Joel and Zechariah by a prominent American "pre-mil," but found them remarkably barren in spiritual help. In comparison the line of thought followed by Wordsworth and Fairbairn was rich and satisfying. It seemed to open a new realm.

In the course of study, the writer noted that Old Testament prophecy at times bore on the face of it a warning against a literal interpretation. For example, Ezekiel prophesied that "my servant David shall be king over them" (37:24); yet even some of the most ardent literalists admit that the reference is not to the actual David, but to Christ.

The writer was also impressed with the difficulties confronting the uniformly literal interpretation of Old Testament prophecy, *e.g.*, the future restoration of the temple, of sin-offerings for atonement, of Israel, of the great Old Testament world powers such as the Assyrians, and of such neighboring nations as the Moabites.

Most important of all was the fact that the New Testament in its application of Old Testament passages compelled us to give an enlarged meaning and spiritual significance to prophecies which, at first sight, seemed to apply only to the Jew.

The writer also examined the teaching of the New Testament afresh, and was tremendously struck with the testimony everywhere in its pages to the general resurrection and general judgment. Everywhere the judgment of the righteous and of the wicked was spoken of as one great event. This is so in the parables of our Lord (Matt. 13:30, 41–43) and in his teaching elsewhere in the Gospels (Matt. 16:27; cf. John 6:40 with 12:48). The writings of Paul and Peter speak also of a general judgment. Not only is there no mention of a thousand-year reign on earth, there seems to be no room left for such a reign (Rom. 2:5–16; II Thess. 2; II Peter 3). Even in the book of Revelation, we seem to have pictures of a general judgment. In chapter 11 the saints are rewarded and the wicked "destroyed" at the same time. At the close of Revelation 20 "the dead, small and great, stand before God," those whose names are in the book of life apparently being present (verses 12 and 15).

The Thousand Years

Does Revelation 20:1–10 strike a different note? It is to Augustine, as Dr. H. B. Swete points out, that we owe the first serious effort to expound Revelation 20. He saw in the captivity of Satan nothing else than the binding of the strong man by the Stronger than he (of which our Lord spoke in Matthew 12:29). The thousand years he took to be the whole interval between the first advent and the second. Dr. Swete says that these ideas "find a place in most of the ancient Greek and Latin commentators, who wrote after Augustine's time" (*Apocalypse,* p. 266).

Amillennialists follow the line of teaching in which Augustine led the way. In this whole gospel age, there is a restraint put upon Satan's activities. This restraint is what may be termed the earthly aspect of the thousand years. Satan is a defeated and conquered foe, for Christ triumphed over him by his cross (John 12:31; 16:11; Col. 2:15; Heb. 2:14). Even in other portions of the Revelation (see chap. 12) it is evident that there is a restraint on Satan; he cannot work his will against Christ or Christ's people. The special restraint upon Satan in this present age which is emphasized in Revelation 20 is a restraint with regard to the nations. From verse 8 it appears that he is restrained from luring the nations on to the battle of the great day of God Almighty, that is, to the final conflict and their own ruin. Near the end of time, this restraint will be withdrawn and the last great conflict will ensue, in which he will be utterly worsted (Rev. 20:7–10).

Revelation 20 also sets forth what may be termed the heavenly aspect of the thousand years, that is, of the long period between the advents. John says: "I saw the souls. . . ." What is here set forth is the bliss of the blessed dead in the period between advents. They are "risen with Christ" (Christians are so described in Rom. 6, Eph. 2, Col. 3, etc.) and so they are "the first resurrection." Their warfare on earth is over; they are "dead" as far as the body is concerned, but in their spirits they "live and reign" with Christ in the highest heaven. In contrast with these, "the rest of the dead" are dead in every sense, bodily and spiritually, and they will come to life again, in the body, only to die the dreadful second death.

The term "1000" in the thousand-year binding of Satan indicates the completeness of Christ's victory over him, though he is permitted a period of *continuing restless activity* (to which the book of Revelation bears abundant witness). The term "1000" in the thousand-year reign of the saints signifies its heavenly completeness, security and bliss. As Dr. War-field says: "The sacred number seven in combination with the equally sacred number three, forms the number of holy perfection ten, and when this ten is cubed into a thousand, the seer has said all that he could say to convey to our minds the ideal of heavenly completeness."

This interpretation of Revelation 20:1–10 emphasizes the completeness of Christ's victory on Calvary and the thoroughness of his defeat of Satan, as well as the glory and bliss of the redeemed in heaven.

New Heavens and New Earth

The Lord's return ushers in the new heavens and new earth. The "a-mil" takes many promises thich the "pre-mil" relates to the earthly millennium as more appropriately applied to the new earth. In fact, many prophecies which are claimed for the thousand-year kingdom explicitly refer to the *eternal* kingdom (II Sam. 7:16; Isa. 9:7; Dan. 7:14; Luke 1:33). In the new earth the triumph of righteousness will be absolute and forever; no Satanic rebellion will ever mar its peace. There will then be nothing to hurt or destroy in all God's holy mountain—then and not until then.

It is sometimes said that the "a-mil" view is pessimistic. True, it does not hold forth the hope of a converted world or of a general triumph of righteousness, as "post-mils" usually do. But then the Scriptures teach that evil and good will continue side by side to the end; wheat and tares will grow together till the harvest. Is it so, however, that "a-mils" are very pessimistic? Dr. G. Vos, an outstanding "a-mil," looked for "a com-prehensive conversion of Israel" before the second advent, and while he spoke of "the forces of evil gathering strength," he also spoke of "an extension of the reign of truth" before the end.

This view bears testimony to the one great event which lies ahead, the second advent, an event to be accompanied by the resurrection of all, the judgment of all, and the end of the world. Christ will sit on his judgment-throne, and all nations of men which have lived will be gathered before him, to be consigned to their eternal destiny. As John L. Girardeau said: "Heaven will lend its glories and hell its horrors to emphasize the proceed-ings of that day." It is the day of perdition of ungodly men, but the day for which Christians earnestly look (II Peter 3:7, 12).

George Eldon Ladd

The Revelation
of Christ's Glory

Discussions of the millennium or of any theme of biblical prophecy require a humble approach. The prophetic word is a lamp shining in the darkness until the day dawns and the full light of God's accomplished purpose breaks upon us (II Peter 1:19). Prophecy is a light to keep men in the Way through the darkness of This Age until the light of Christ's coming dispels the darkness forever. This suggests that we should not look to prophecy for pre-written history or for a blueprint of the future. Prophecy's primary purpose is to *give light* for our present journey, not to satisfy our curiosity. Since we do not have the full light and our knowledge is admittedly partial (I Cor. 13:12), we may not expect complete unity of interpretation among God's servants in prophetic truth. Paul himself asserts that while there is indeed "one faith," full unity of the faith has not yet been attained (Eph. 4:4, 13). Therefore, humility and charity in such study is more important than perfect agreement. Furthermore, the existence of unsolved problems should be no embarrassment to any interpretation.

Nevertheless, God's Word does speak about the future, and we are justified, indeed, required to attempt to understand and to interpret the

From *Christianity Today,* 1 September 1958, pp. 13–14. Used by permission.

prophetic outlook of Scripture. Redemption is uniformly viewed as incomplete, and we must search Scripture to understand all about the completion of God's redemptive purpose.

The problems which cluster around the question of a millennium, so far as the New Testament is concerned, are theological, not exegetical. The millenarian who accepts Augustine's sound dictum that "the New is in the Old concealed while the Old is in the New revealed" may feel embarrassed by the paucity of New Testament teachings about this theme. Sound exegesis of Revelation 20 requires a millennial interpretation; non-millennialists usually do not appeal so much to exegesis as to theological consistency for support of their position. They interpret such passages as Revelation 20 in a non-millenarian way because they are convinced that the totality of new Testament truth has no room for an interregnum and that there is no alternative in view of the New Testament eschatology as a whole but to interpret Revelation spiritually.

However, it is this author's conviction that not only exegesis, but also New Testament theology, require a millennial interregnum; for the millennium is the era of the revelation of Christ's glory.

The Two Ages

Underlying biblical theology is the structure of the two ages: This Age and the Age to Come. Unfortunately, this fact has been obscured to three centuries of English-speaking Bible students because the Authorized Version incorrectly translates *aion* "world" instead of "age." The two ages constitute the entire course of human existence (Matt. 12:32; Eph. 1:21). The transition between the two ages is the second coming of Christ (Matt. 24:3), resurrection (Luke 20:35), and judgment (Matt. 13:40f.). So long as This Age lasts, evil—demonic, satanic evil—will plague human history. Such influence has God, the King of the Ages (I Tim. 1:17), permitted Satan to exercise in This Age that he is called the god of This Age (II Cor. 4:4). This Age is evil (Gal. 1:4), characterized by sin and death.

Only in the Age to Come will God's people enter into the full experience of what is meant by eternal life (Matt. 25:31, 46; Mark 10:30). Only in the Age to Come will the full blessing of the kingdom of God become man's possession. For the fact is that eternal life and the kingdom of God (Mark 10:24f.) both belong to the Age to Come, not to This Age.

On the basis of this so-called antithetical structure of the two ages, it can be argued that there is no room for an interregnum between This Age and the Age to Come. The New Testament, it is said, makes the second coming of Christ the dividing point between the ages. At his coming, we shall enter into the full enjoyment of the redemptive blessings of eternal life and the kingdom of God. The coming of Christ is the center of the New Testament expectation of the future. God's purposes will then be consummated; the Age to Come will then begin.

Facing the Difficulties

The difficulty with this apparently persuasive reasoning is that it proves too much; for in this same antithetical structure, both eternal life and the kingdom of God are exclusively future, not a present possession. Yet every Sunday School child knows that Jesus came to give men eternal life here and now; for he who believes on the Son *has* eternal life (John 3:36). Furthermore, the kingdom of God is something present which men enter by the new birth (John 3:3, 5); the redeemed are already in the kingdom of God's Son (Col. 1:13).

Long ago, Professor Geerhardus Vos pointed out in his *Pauline Eschatology* that the great themes of redemption—justification, the Holy Spirit, as well as eternal life and the kingdom of God—are "semi-eschatological" realities. That is, although they belong to the Age to Come, they have entered into human history through the Incarnation and redemptive work of Christ. The redeemed man experiences in This Age, evil as it is, a bit of the life of the Age to Come. There is, in other words, an overlapping of the ages. The redeemed live "between the times"—in two ages at once. We may taste of the powers of the coming age (Heb. 6:5) and thereby be delivered from this present evil age (Gal. 1:4), no longer being conformed to it even though we live in it (Rom. 12:2).

Professor Vos correctly sketches this relationship by two overlapping lines on different levels. Therefore, although the Age to Come is future and begins with the coming of Christ in glory, this new age has already begun with the Incarnation—the coming of Christ in humility. The two ages have come together. However, it is important to note that many passages of Scripture make no reference to this fact. The Age to Come is usually viewed as altogether future, even though it is "spiritually" present.

The millennium is a further stage in this overlapping of the ages. The Age to Come, which is now working secretly in This Age within the lives of God's people, will manifest itself in outward glory *before the final inauguration of the Age to Come*. The life of the Age to Come will show itself more splendidly in this world before the final judgment falls and God brings the new heavens and the new earth.

Theological Necessity

The theological necessity for such a period is seen in I Corinthians 15:23–28. In the days of his flesh, Christ emptied himself, pouring himself out in humility even to the point of death—"But made himself of no reputation, and took upon him the form of a servant, and was made in the likeness of men: And being found in fashion as a man, he humbled himself, and became obedient unto death, even the death of the cross" (Phil. 2:7, 8). He is now exalted—"Wherefore God also hath highly exalted him, and given him a name which is above every name" (Phil. 2:9)—and seated at the right hand of God; but his glory does not appear to the world. This Age is still the evil age. Christ's glory is known only to his people, but even they suffer and die. Christ's rule is hidden from the world. He is indeed now reigning in victory and enthroned with his Father (Rev. 3:21); but the world does not know it, for his reign has not been disclosed to the world. In fact, so far as the world is concerned, his reign is in a sense potential and not realized. "As it is, we do not yet see everything in subjection to him" (Heb. 2:8, RSV).

Yet, "he must reign until he has put all his enemies under his feet" (I Cor. 15:25). His reign must become public in power and glory. The "reign of grace" must become a "reign of power."

The Age to Come

However, the Age to Come is not the age of Christ's reign; it is the age of the Father's glory. First Corinthians 15:21–24 designates three stages in God's redemptive purpose. First is the resurrection of Christ, the first fruits of the resurrection (vv. 21, 23). Then will occur the resurrection of those who are Christ's at his coming. "After that [the literal meaning of the Greek particle] comes the end, when he delivers the kingdom to God the Father" (v. 24). Here is the third stage, which is the Age to Come. Then, "the Son himself will also be subjected to him who put all things under him, that God may be all in all" (v. 28).

The Age to Come after "The End" is the age of the Father's all-encompassing dominion. The Church age—the era between the Resurrection and the Parousia—is the age of the Son's hidden rule. The millennium will be the age of the manifestation of Christ's glory when the sovereignty, which he now possesses but does not manifest, and which he will give over to the Father in the Age to Come, will be manifested in glory in the world. God yet has a glorious destiny for the race which will be accomplished by the Son when he comes to reign in glory.

40

John F. Walvoord

Dispensational Premillennialism

The objective of this limited discussion is to provide a brief definitive study of dispensationalism, to analyze its interpretative principles and schools of thought, and relate it as such to premillennialism. Obviously a defense of the doctrine cannot be undertaken here.

In the last decade, dispensationalism has attracted increasing attention as a major factor in theological interpretation. Though the distinctives of its system are not new, the contemporary theological scene seems to call for discussion of them. Most of the comment has been critical. Liberals have opposed dispensationalism because it is fundamentalist in approach. Amillenarians attack it because it is premillennial. Some premillenarians, under criticism anyway, have sought to escape opposition by disavowing dispensationalism.

Dispensationalists themselves, embarrassed by extremists in their ranks, have had difficulty clarifying the situation. Unfortunately, the critical literature produced has sought in too many cases to win an argument rather than present an objective study. The result is one of the most confusing spectacles found in contemporary theology.

From *Christianity Today,* 15 September 1958, pp. 11–13. Used by permission.

Definitions

Premillennialism is generally recognized as the proper name for that system of biblical interpretation which places the second advent of Christ as preceding and introducing his future reign on earth for one thousand years. The relation of dispensationalism to premillennialism, however, is an area of some disagreement. A normative definition generally accepted by dispensationalists is that furnished by C. I. Scofield in the Scofield Reference edition of the Bible: "A dispensation is a period of time during which man is tested in respect of obedience to some *specific* revelation of the will of God" (p. 5).

As used in Scripture, the word *dispensation* is a translation of the noun *oikonomia* and is found in the following passages: Luke 16:2–4; I Corinthians 9:17; Ephesians 1:10; 3:2, 9; Colossians 1:25; and I Timothy 1:4. It is variously translated *dispensation* or *stewardship*. The verb form *oikonomeo* is found in Luke 16:2 and the noun form referring to a person, *oikonomos*, is found in Luke 12:42; 16:1, 3, 8; Romans 16:23; I Corinthians 4:1, 2; Galatians 4:2; Titus 1:7; and I Peter 4:10. In most of these instances it is translated *steward*. In its biblical usage, the concept is not explicitly a time period and for this reason the Scofield definition has been questioned.

Objections to the definition of a dispensation as a time period are based on partial truth. The time element is a consequence rather than an explicit meaning of the word. *Webster's New International Dictionary* defines *dispensation* as "a system of principles, promises, and rules ordained and administered; schemes; economy; as the patriarchal, Mosaic, and Christian dispensations." As the definition indicates, a dispensation is not a time period, but is in the nature of a stewardship; the responsibility involved has a beginning in time and an ending in time and the period between is the period of stewardship. The *Winston Dictionary* defines *dispensation* in its theological meaning as "a system of principles and rules ascribed to divine inspiration in operation during a specific period."

Though its biblical use embodies principally the idea of stewardship, theologians for generations have been using the word *dispensation* as a time period. . . . The definition of dispensation as a time period in which a specific stewardship obtains is by no means a recent development (cf. John Edwards, *A Compleat Survey of All the Dispensations*, 790 pp., published 1699). All theologians have some sort of a dispensational division if no more than to divide the Old and New Testaments. The principles involved in such divisions and their significance have caused the rise of modern dispensationalism in the post-Reformation period.

The principles involved in dispensationalism are as old as the history of biblical interpretation. Of these the most important is literal interpretation of prophecy, which is, rightly considered, the guiding principle of dispensational premillennialism. Unlike Augustine, who advocated a separate hermeneutics for prophetic interpretation, namely, the spiritual or figurative method, dispensationalists follow the more literal interpretation. The charge that dispensationalism demands that all Scripture be interpreted literally is false, however. All schools of interpretation necessarily regard some Scripture as not subject to literal interpretation. Premillennial dispensationalism, however, follows the principle that prophecy is not a special case and is to be treated like other forms of Scripture revelation, that is, that the literal interpretation should be followed unless the context indicates otherwise.

The second major principle is derived from the definition of dispensationalism itself. A dispensation is considered a divinely-given stewardship based on a particular rule of life revealed in the progressive unfolding of divine truth in Scripture. Each new major deposit of truth had its own demand for faith and obedience. Generally speaking, a dispensation is created by the revelation of a major system of truth sufficient to constitute a new rule of life and is often marked off from the preceding period by some spiritual crisis in the history of God's people. Dispensationalism does not deny that revealed truth is cumulative and that new revelation is obviously built upon the old even though to some extent it replaces a former situation.

The third principle in dispensationalism is the time element. As indicated in the definition, a dispensation is, strictly speaking, a divine deposit of truth, not an age in itself. A stewardship by its nature, however, has a beginning and ending with the idea of a dispensation as an age coming into view. Hence, most theologians refer to a dispensation as a time period, even if they do not accept some dispensational distinctions.

The fourth principle is that a dispensation is specifically a rule of life, rather than a way of salvation. The frequent charge that dispensationalists teach more than one way of salvation is not sustained by their literature and is actually foreign to the true system. Though dispensationalists find faith manifested in obedience to a particular divine revelation in every dispensation, the way of salvation is always faith, the principle of salvation is always grace, and the ground of salvation is always the death of Christ, even if imperfectly understood prior to the full revelation in the New Testament.

A wide divergence of belief is found within the general designation of dispensationalism. This has frequently tended to confuse the issue as opponents of dispensationalism have resorted to citation of the most extreme statements they could find instead of trying to discover the normative position. In general, four attitudes exist in relation to dispensationalism:

Nondispensational view. This includes all points of view which oppose dispensationalism by emphasizing a central divine plan and purpose for human history as excluding any division into dispensations. This unity of purpose is usually supplied by making the salvation of the elect the central purpose of God, and if dispensations are included at all, they are regarded as successive phases of this one plan. Nondispensationalists usually regard Israel and the Church essentially as one, and kingdom truth is considered to be soteriological, or related to salvation, rather than culminating in an earthly political kingdom such as is normal in premillennialism.

Normative dispensationalism. Within this classification, the great majority of dispensationalists are properly placed. Characteristic of this school of thought is the view as illustrated in Scofield that there are seven dispensations revealed in Scripture: innocence, conscience, human government, promise, law, grace, and millennial kingdom. Each of these dispensations constitutes a test of faith and obedience according to the rule of life provided, and under each dispensation man fails and is saved only by divine grace. This school of thought does not dispense with grace.

Major Dispensations

Some variations exist in the statement of these seven dispensations, but it is generally agreed that three major dispensations are the subject of extensive revelation in the Bible, namely, the dispensation of the law, the dispensation of grace, and the dispensation of the millennial kingdom. The law began with Moses and was the rule of life for Israel from Moses to the Church. The dispensation of grace, or the church period, was introduced by Christ, began at Pentecost, and will close with the translation of the Church. The millennium will begin with the second advent of Christ and the judgment of the world and will conclude with the creation of the eternal state. While dispensationalists regard the major dispensations as bound together by many common doctrines, such as the way of salvation, doctrine of God, and inspiration of Scripture, dispensationalism necessarily insists that as rules of life the three major dispensations differ extensively with each other and that each replaces the former dispensation.

Bullingerism. Numerically small but quite vocal are those who go beyond the Scofield system. Most extreme is the position of E. W. Bullinger who found two dispensations within the church period, the first being the period of the Jewish church extending through Acts 28 and the second being the dispensation of the Gentile church as the body of Christ beginning after Acts. He rejected both water baptism and the Lord's Supper. True followers of Bullinger, however, are almost extinct and practically all dispensationalists today deny that they are followers of his position.

Church as exclusively Pauline. Less extreme than the view of Bullinger, but considered ultradispensational by followers of Scofield, is the view of dispensationalism expressed by the Grace Gospel Fellowship and defined in the volume by Cornelius R. Stam, *The Fundamentals of Dispensationalism.* The key to their system is the belief that the truth of the Church as the body of Christ is exclusively taught in the epistles of Paul and that therefore the Church could not begin until Paul's conversion in Acts 9 or later. In contrast to Bullinger, who rejected both the ordinance of the Lord's Supper and water baptism, the more moderate position excludes only water baptism, which they regard as a Jewish rite not intended for the church today. The great majority of dispensationalists, however, consider this as an extreme view and insist that the Church as both the body and bride of Christ began with the outpouring of the Holy Spirit on the day of Pentecost when 3000 souls were saved.

Relation to Premillennialism

Contrast between Israel and the Church. As related to premillennial interpretation, normative dispensationalism tends to emphasize certain important distinctives. One of the most significant is the contrast provided between God's program for Israel and God's present program for the Church. The Church composed of Jew and Gentile is considered a separate program of God which does not advance nor fulfill any of the promises given to Israel. The present age is regarded as a period in which Israel is temporarily set aside as to its national program. When the Church is translated, however, Israel's program will then proceed to its consummation. Though dispensationalists have tended to contrast Israel and the Church, it is false that they alone make this distinction, as is frequently alleged. Postmillenarians like Charles Hodge and amillenarians like William Hendriksen, though not dispensationalists, also believe that Israel has special promises that belong only to those who are in the racial seed of Jacob, and do not equate Israel and the Church.

The offer of the kingdom at the first advent. Dispensationalists usually consider that Christ at his first coming offered himself to Israel as their Messiah and King. His subsequent crucifixion was the occasion of their rejection of him. The hypothetical question as to what would have eventuated if Israel had accepted Christ as their King has led to the charge, which is entirely unjustified, that dispensational teaching tends to minimize the cross or declare it unnecessary.

Pretribulation rapture. The tendency to contrast Israel and the Church and to interpret prophecy literally has led most dispensationalists to accept a pretribulational rapture of the Church. Their point of view is that predictions of a future time of tribulation in both the Old and New Testaments are related to the divine program for Israel and for Gentiles, but that the Church is never explicitly in view. Though this relationship of dispensationalism to pretribulationism is indirect, it is significant that posttribulationists are seldom dispensationalists.

Reign on Earth

Literal earthly millennium. Dispensational premillennialism tends to emphasize the governmental and political character of the millennium itself. Christ will reign on the throne of David on earth over restored Israel as well as the Gentile world. Spiritual qualities such as righteousness and peace, spiritual power, and the visible glory of God will be evident. The millennium will fulfill literally the glowing expectation of Old Testament prophets for a kingdom of God on earth embracing all nations. Satan will be bound and inactive. The curse upon the earth will be lifted and the desert will blossom. All will know the Lord from the least to the greatest. This final dispensation before the creation of the new heavens and new earth will in many respects be climactic in blessing and a demonstration of divine sovereignty and glory. Christ's reign on earth will gloriously fulfill Old Testament prophecy.

Agreement with Other Conservatives

On all major doctrines of Scripture, dispensationalists are in hearty agreement with other conservatives. Their distinctive doctrines result from the attempt to interpret prophecy with the same literal method as is used for other Scripture. This leads to sharper contrasts between the dispensation of law, the present dispensation of grace, and the future dispensation of the millennial kingdom following the second advent. Separate prophetic programs are traced in Scripture for Israel, for the Church, and for the Gentiles. These distinctives, however, are balanced by agreement that many unifying factors bind all dispensations together. The unity of Scripture is strongly maintained by those who hold the dispensational viewpoint.

Dispensationalists do not deny the unity of the divine plan of salvation as progressively revealed in Scripture and do not teach two ways of salvation. Every dispensation as a rule of life reveals failure on the part of man, but at the same time Scripture reaffirms unfailing faithfulness and grace on the part of God. Dispensationalism is a matter of degree. Lewis Sperry Chafer was wont to say: "Anyone is a dispensationalist who no longer offers lambs on brazen altars or who does not observe Saturday as the day of rest." Modern usage indicates a more restricted meaning, but dispensationalism deserves more objective treatment, more normative definition than has characterized most contemporary discussion.